Linking to the Past
A Brief Introduction
to Archaeology

D1009232

Linking to the Past

A Brief
Introduction
to Archaeology

Second Edition

Kenneth L. Feder
Central Connecticut State University

New York   Oxford
OXFORD UNIVERSITY PRESS
2008

Oxford University Press, Inc., publishes works that further Oxford University's
objective of excellence in research, scholarship, and education.

Oxford   New York
Auckland   Cape Town   Dar es Salaam   Hong Kong   Karachi
Kuala Lumpur   Madrid   Melbourne   Mexico City   Nairobi
New Delhi   Shanghai   Taipei   Toronto

With offices in
Argentina   Austria   Brazil   Chile   Czech Republic   France   Greece
Guatemala   Hungary   Italy   Japan   Poland   Portugal   Singapore
South Korea   Switzerland   Thailand   Turkey   Ukraine   Vietnam

Copyright © 2004, 2008 by Oxford University Press, Inc.

Published by Oxford University Press, Inc.
198 Madison Avenue, New York, New York 10016
http://www.oup.com

Oxford is a registered trademark of Oxford University Press

Library of Congress Cataloging-in-Publication Data

Feder, Kenneth L.
   Linking to the past: a brief introduction to archaeology /
Kenneth L. Feder. —2nd ed.
      p. cm.
   Includes bibliographical references and index.
   ISBN 978-0-19-533117-2 (pbk.)
   1. Archaeology.   2. Archaeology—Field work.   I. Title.
   CC75.F43 2007
   930.1—dc22   2007012557

Printing number: 9 8 7 6 5 4 3 2

Printed in the United States of America
on acid-free paper

To a house filled with life

Melissa, Josh, Jacob, Randolph, Harpo,
Busterella, Groucho, Aslan, and Commander Xander

Contents

Chapter 2. **A Biography of Archaeology** • 40

Chapter 3. **What Archaeologists Want to Know** • 73

Chapter 4. **Doing Archaeology: Practical Considerations** • 86

Chapter 5. **A Community's Shadow: The Archaeological Site** • 112

Chapter 6. **Searching for the Past: Archaeological Site Survey** • 132

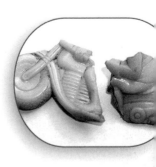

Chapter 7. **Revealing the Past: The Archaeological Excavation** • 167

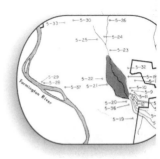

Chapter 8. **Interpreting the Past: Gauging the Age of an Archaeological Site** • **199**

Chapter 9. **Interpreting the Past: The Environmental Contexts of Antiquity** • **237**

Chapter 10. **Technology: How People Made Things** • 255

Chapter 11. **Putting Food on the Table: Reconstructing Ancient Diets** • 292

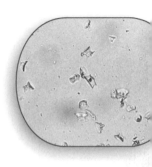

Chapter 12. **Families, Neighbors, and Strangers: Reconstructing Ancient Social Systems** • 323

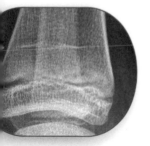

Chapter 13. **Conversing with the Dead: Bioarchaeology** • 355

Chapter 14. **Wood Lily: Archaeological Portrait of a Life** • 385

Epilogue: Can We Reconstruct the Past • 398

Preface

On the first day of each semester, I conduct an informal survey of the ninety-five or so students who register for Introduction to Archaeology. I ask those students a single, simple question: Why did you register for the course? In most years, only about five or six reveal that they are planning to or have already declared anthropology as their major and or archaeology as their minor. The other ninety or so are in it for the general education credit. Then I ask: Among all of the possible alternatives to fulfill those general education credits, how many of you are taking archaeology simply because it's an interesting topic? The overwhelming majority raise their hands.

They sign up for archaeology because they liked the Indiana Jones movies, or because they enjoy archaeology documentaries on the National Geographic, Discovery, or History channels, or because ever since they were kids they thought that digging in the dirt and finding really old stuff seemed like a cool thing for a grown person to do.

As a result, those of us who teach the introductory archaeology course are presented both with a tremendous advantage as well as a challenge. Because of students' already existing fascination with archaeology, we don't need, necessarily, to work particularly hard to generate interest in the topic, but we do need to work very hard indeed to channel that existing interest toward the scientific investigation of the past. It is my goal in *Linking to the Past* to help both student and instructor satisfactorily and scientifically navigate that investigation.

The Original Conception

The first edition of any book represents an interesting and challenging adventure. *Linking to the Past* entered a market that was, if not saturated, certainly not lacking for texts presenting differing strategies for the teaching of introductory archaeology. It would be fair, I think, to characterize my approach as unlike that of any of the existing introductory archaeology texts—otherwise, why bother? Instead of the standard, chapter-by-chapter coverage of the field, my tack was different: I chose to use the Sunday supplement–like description of an excavation I directed as the framework for asking and answering general questions about archaeological methodology. Queries the curious reader might naturally raise during the course of reading the archaeological narrative were presented and linked to their answers elsewhere in the first edition's "units."

For example, upon reading in the narrative that the site in question was 3,000 years old, one might inquire as to how archaeologists determine the age of sites; or after a discussion of the subsistence of the site's inhabitants, the question of how archaeologists can reconstruct an ancient diet would naturally arise. The narrative triggered these and many other questions; those questions became the organizational framework of the book.

Beyond this, the overall structure of *Linking* was intentionally nonlinear. In writing the book, I attempted to emulate the model of an internet website where links between topics could be easily explored in novel ways. So enamored was I of the web model, we even placed the entire text on a CD that accompanied the printed text, which allowed students to explore the book not just figuratively but literally in the manner by which they might research a topic on the internet.

 ## The Second Edition

The first edition was an interesting experiment and the substantial feedback it generated has contributed greatly to the reconfiguring of this second edition. The consensus among those who used and reviewed the book—both colleagues and students alike—was that although the free-wheeling, nonlinear nature of the text's organization accommodated exploration, a more traditional framework—a more tightly structured organization where everybody passes along the same intellectual pathway together—simply made more sense in an introductory, undergraduate course in archaeology. The second edition reflects this major reorganization. The unique elements and strategies employed in the first edition for teaching introductory archaeology yet remain: the framework of a core archaeological narrative; the raising of questions about the specific procedures used in the excavation and analysis of the site that is the focus of the narrative; the linkages between these questions to answers about how archaeologists approach those topics; and the overall conversational tone of the writing with anecdotes, amusing stories, and the connections between archaeology and our own lives. By presenting the material in the second edition of *Linking to the Past* in a simpler, more directly linear format, the organization no longer complicates the pathway students traverse on their journey toward an understanding of how archaeologists ask and answer questions about the past. This reorganization will make *Linking* a much better fit for introductory archaeology courses.

 ## Organization: The Archaeological Narrative

The archaeological narrative describing the discovery, excavation, and analysis of the 3,000-year-old Wood Lily site in Barkhamsted, Connecticut, continues to represent the core of the book. That narrative is now set out in chapter 1—a separate chapter read before the reader delves into the details of archaeological method and theory. The narrative provides the framework for explaining how archaeologists do what they do. It is a brief, informal account of an archaeological survey and excavation conducted in north-central Connecticut. Along the course of that narrative, a series of fundamental questions should be raised in the mind of the reader. Those related questions are addressed within the book's subsequent chapters. Within each chapter, those specific questions that naturally come to mind in the narrative are explicitly presented and addressed as headings. Secondary and even tertiary queries provide further framework for the discussion and appear as subheadings in each of the chapters.

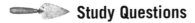 Study Questions

Along with providing a novel way of presenting archaeology, this unique format provides an advantage when it comes to studying and testing. The book provides a study guide inherent within its structure. Each chapter's title page presents the primary, secondary, and tertiary questions addressed in that chapter. Students preparing for a test need only ask themselves the questions presented in those chapters covered in an exam; if they can answer those questions/headings, they are prepared for the test. To provide even more study help, I've added a number of detailed study questions at the end of each unit in the text. Beyond this, assignments can include having students gather additional information about the practice of archaeology from the web pages linked to the text.

Topics New to the Second Edition

My intention in *Linking* was and continues to be to create a text that, in length and in depth, falls between the very short published introductions to the field and the voluminous, essentially encyclopedic treatments of archaeology that also are available. I've used both types in my own courses and have found the short ones simply do not cover enough ground, and the enormous texts are so overwhelmingly comprehensive, they simply won't be read by most students in a single-semester course. Reviewers of the first edition had very strong opinions about the topics that needed to be included in such a mid-sized book, and their wise counsel resulted in expansion of the discussion of some topics in the second edition and the inclusion of topics that were missing entirely in the first. The second edition of *Linking* is more inclusive and thorough while maintaining a manageable length and depth for the general education courses for undergraduate students for which the book is intended. In particular, the reader will encounter much improved and expanded discussions of ethics in archaeology, federal legislation protecting archaeological resources, GIS and aerial photography, environmental reconstruction (in particular, the contribution of the oxygen isotope curve in paleoenvironmental analysis), and an entirely revamped and expanded presentation on ceramics (and other nonlithic technologies). There also is a new section on the archaeology of the sacred with a focus on the Moundbuilders of the American Midwest.

Additional Features and Ancillary Materials

Key terms are highlighted throughout the text. Definitions for these key terms appear in an alphabetized, end-of-text glossary. Definitions for the more than 250 glossary terms also appear on the accompanying CD; they are searchable and accessible through a hot-linked alphabet, which makes checking glossary definitions convenient in preparing for exams.

In the margins of the text are a number of icons that direct the reader to the included CD. There you will find slide shows and interactive exercises related to the material covered in the chapter. In addition to providing readers with additional visual support for information discussed in the text, these images are freely available for instructors to use and project in class to support their own lectures.

 ## Slide Shows and Interactive Exercises Linking to Text Chapters

Chapter	Slide Show	Interactive Exercises
Chapter 1 How I Spent My Summer Vacation: Finding, Excavating, and Interpreting the Wood Lily Site in North-Central Connecticut	Excavating the 3,000-year-old Wood Lily site that is the focus of the chapter.	
Chapter 2 A Biography of Archaeology		Timeline of the history of archaeology. Students are asked to identify the timing of key event blocks in the history of archaeology.
Chapter 3 What Archaeologists Want to Know		Matching game for identifying the goals of various kinds of archaeological research projects.
Chapter 4 Doing Archaeology: Practical Considerations		Identifying the federal legislation that protects cultural resources. Matching game with federal law names, descriptions, and years voted into law.

continued

Chapter	Slide Show	Interactive Exercises
Chapter 5 A Community's Shadow: The Archaeological Site.	The broad diversity of the kinds of sites that archaeologists investigate.	
Chapter 6 Searching for the Past: Archaeological Site Survey	The search for sites in our 2005 summer field school in West Simsbury, Connecticut.	Assessing the potential of an area for human settlement. By moving the cursor over parts of a USGS topographic map, characteristics of the area that might have attracted human settlement are revealed.
Chapter 7 Revealing the Past: The Archaeological Excavation	The process of archaeological excavation in the Farmington River Archaeological Project.	
Chapter 8 Interpreting the Past: Gauging the Age of an Archaeological Site		Calibrating radiocarbon dates. A selection of radiocarbon dates derived for sites in the Farmington River Archaeological Project are provided. Students are asked to calibrate the carbon dates to determine their calendar dates (http://www .calpal-online.de/)
Chapter 9 Interpreting the Past: The Environmental Contexts of Antiquity	Views of the modern climatic analogs of the biomes that once characterized southern New England as indicated by pollen analysis.	
Chapter 10 Technology: How People Made Things	Examples of experimental archaeology focusing on student projects in an experimental	Schematic drawings of stone tool use and typical wear patterns that result from such use are provided. Using an outline that lists the most common wear

Chapter	Slide Show	Interactive Exercises
		patterns that result from specific kinds of use, students are asked to identify that tasks performed by a series of stone tools by reference to drawings of those tools edges.
Chapter 11 Putting Food on the Table: Reconstructing Ancient Diets		Determining seasonality from the ages of animals killed and eaten by an ancient people. Students are given information concerning the mating season, gestation length, and age at death of animals reflected in a faunal assemblage and asked to determine the season of a site's occupation.
Chapter 12 Families, Neighbors, and Strangers: Reconstructing Ancient Social Systems		Given a series of drawings of different edge forms, bases, shapes, students can play with artifact variability. By choosing different expressions of different morphologies of different variables, students can see for themselves the broad array of possible, functionally equivalent by stylistically different, artifact forms.
Chapter 13 Conversing with the Dead: Bioarchaeology		Students are asked to identify the ages at which human teeth erupt, long bones fuse to their end caps, and cranial sutures fuse. Given skeletal developmental data for five individuals, students are asked to determine the ages of those individuals.

continued

Chapter	Slide Show	Interactive Exercises
		Students are given a small database extracted from colonial gravestones. Students are asked to use the database to calculate the demographic characteristics of the sample and then performa seriation of gravestone design.
Chapter 14 Wood Lily: Archaeological Portrait of a Life	Photographs of the Wood Lily assemblage.	

An Instructor's Manual and Test Bank is available on CD for instructors who adopt the text. It includes a list of glossary terms, short essay questions, and multiple-choice questions for each unit. In addition, I've provided a "transition guide" that I hope will make it easier to understand how the chapters in this book correspond to the chapters in other texts.

I had great fun writing and preparing this work. It forced me to consider connections and linkages among the various introductory archaeology topics that I had not previously thought much about. It is my hope that this format causes students to consider these connections and linkages as well. If you have questions or comments, please direct them to me at feder@ccsu.edu.

Acknowledgments

Writing the acknowledgments for a book can be a daunting task. Invariably, there are more people to thank than the author even realizes, and one always manages to forget to thank individuals whose help materially contributed in ways both small and large. Nevertheless, a number of people fulfill two important criteria: (1) their help was indispensable, and (2) I remember their help.

I wish I could tell you that this book was my idea, but actually, it wasn't. Jan Beatty, executive editor at Oxford University Press suggested this book to me in the first place, and I am forever in her debt for that. Thanks, Jan!

I think that every author of every edition of every book requires more than a just little hand holding from his or her publisher and I would be remiss not to acknowledge the support of all the folks at Oxford University Press. In particular, a big "thank you" to Jan Beatty's assistant Cory Schneider whose daily contribution enabled the timely completion of this edition. Thanks as well to the senior production editor for *Linking to the Past*, Christine D'Antonio, whose work on both the first and current editions has been invaluable. Finally, I should convey my appreciation to the copyeditor for *Linking*, 2/e, Stephen

Chasteen. His suggestions were always good ones; I can't remember scrawling "STET" in the margin of a manuscript fewer times!

I was amazed at the generosity of my colleagues in my search for photographs and figures. Without exception, every email or phone call made, almost always to people who I did not know personally, resulted in my obtaining a photograph, figure, or chart for this book. Many thanks especially to Abigail Adams, Matthew Barrett, Nick Bellantoni, David Bernstein, Bruce Bradley, Lawrence Conyers, Noel Coonce, Peter Dana, Regina Dardzienski, Jeff Eighmy, Gretchen Jones, Harold Juli, Bill Keegan, Keith Kintigh, John Lynch, William McGrew, Kevin McBride, Cindy McWeeney, Michael Park, Deborah Pearsall, Warren Perry, Tara Prindle, Douglas Scott, John Seidel, Brian Tidey, and Emma Waas.

I would also like to express my appreciation to my colleagues who attended a meeting at the 2006 SAAs in Puerto Rico whose focus was the proposed second edition of *Linking*: Anita Cook, Catholic University, George (Wolf) Gumerman IV, Northern Arizona University, Brian Hoffman, Hamline, Phil Neusius, Indiana University of Pennsylvania; and Kevin Vaughn, Purdue. The sandwiches were mediocre, but the conversation, counsel, and company were all extraordinary and very much appreciated.

The thanks I convey to my extended family of people and critters is neither perfunctory nor simply obligatory. My wife is a role model for me; her energy and joy are contagious and inspire my work. My two sons, Josh and Jacob, never fail to inspire me with their intellectual curiosity. They'd better never lose that. Kitties too, those here only in spirit (Harpo and Randolph), and those currently prowling the house (Busterella, Groucho, Aslan, and now Xander), can inspire my muse as well, though Aslan's tendency to stretch out on the computer keyboard (how comfortable can that be?) can interrupt the writing process or, at least, result in some interesting keystroke combinations. Thanks to you all.

Textbooks benefit tremendously from the sage advice, thoughtful suggestions, and constructive criticisms of colleagues in the proverbial trenches–an interesting metaphor for reviewers of an archaeology text. *Linking to the Past* has benefited greatly from the assistance both of those who have used the book in their courses, as well as those who haven't. I don't know that I have thoroughly satisfied all of the reviewers of *Linking*, but they should know that every one of their suggestions was seriously considered and thoroughly appreciated. *Linking to the Past* is a much better book in its second edition because of the help of the following colleagues:

Mark Aldenderfer, University of Arizona
Timothy E. Baumaann, University of Missouri–St. Louis
Kenneth L. Brown, University of Houston
Anita G. Cook, The Catholic University of America
Debra L. Gold, St. Cloud State University
George Gumerman, Northern Arizona University
Eric Johnson, University of Massachusetts–Amherst
Heather McKillop, Louisiana State University

Ruben Mendoza, California State University–Monterey Bay
Karen Metheny, Boston University
Eric Ozolins, Mt. San Jacinto College
Trimothy Pugh, Queens College
Fred Valdez, Jr., University of Texas–Austin

Thank you all.

Prologue

THE PAST IN THE PRESENT

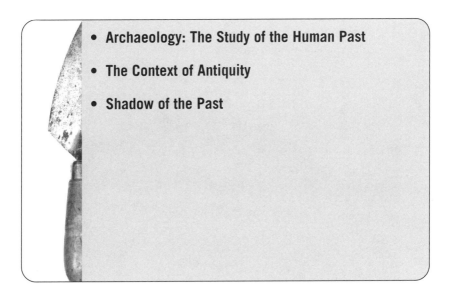

- **Archaeology: The Study of the Human Past**

- **The Context of Antiquity**

- **Shadow of the Past**

Our first house was built in 1924. It was a sweet little place, with clapboard siding, black wooden storm shutters, and, our favorite feature, a time-worn tin roof. That roof provided a charmingly rustic, antique look to the house. I tried to remember that during heavy downpours when rain falling against that roof produced a noise not unlike that of a machine gun going off directly above our heads. It was during one of those intense storms with associated high winds that one of the oak trees adjacent to the house photosynthesized its last and fell over. The fallen oak was one of several similar trees that were standing when the house was built and that, though having seen better days, was still alive when my wife and I bought the place in 1985.

In the thirteen or so years we lived there we became depressingly familiar with an affliction common to old oaks in the northeast: those industrious and aptly named "carpenter" ants who carve out extensive galleries for their nests in the trunks and limbs of these trees. The large oak near the driveway simply could not withstand the complex network of tunnels the ants had excavated through its massive trunk over the years, succumbing to the combined effects of wind, gravity, and the relentless ant species *Camponotus pennsylvanicus*.

Luckily, no one was injured—other than the tree—and after the town-contracted tree service cleared the road all that was left behind, along with enough wood to fuel our woodstove for the following heating season, was a large stump adjacent to the end of our driveway. The top of the stump was vaguely circular and about 3.5 feet in diameter. Across its surface marched the familiar parade of annual growth rings. We counted more than one hundred in all, some thick, some thin, each one demarcating a year in the life of an old tree with which we had shared our half-acre lot for more than a dozen years (Figure P.1).

FIGURE P.1 A cross-section of a downed tree, showing annual growth rings. (K. L. Feder)

Our oak had left behind a record of its life in the form of annual growth rings, loops of new wood added by trees each year they are alive. The tree had lived through more than one hundred snowy New England winters and an equal number of long, humid summers. More than one hundred times, its leaves had turned brown, withered, and fallen, and an equal number of times buds had formed on the tree's branches and leaves had unfolded to capture the warming solar energy of spring with which the tree maintained its life. The rings on the stump were each like the pages of a book, telling in their own alien language the story of the tree's life: the droughts, insect infestations, lightning strikes, and industrious ants it had encountered and ultimately surrendered to.

 ## Archaeology: The Study of the Human Past

This book is not about oak trees. It is a brief guide to the practice of **archaeology**, the science that studies the human past. By looking at the rings on the stump of our old oak, however, we were conducting a sort of archaeological review of the life of that tree—studying the past by examining the remains left behind by a once-living thing. There is even a method of analysis used in archaeology called **dendrochronology** that does precisely this, reconstructing ancient environments by examining tree rings. We'll look at how this form of analysis works later in the book.

Though they don't leave a year-by-year record of their passing, animals, like trees, also leave a trail of their existence, as bones within ordered layers of rock and soil. Their biographies are written on those bones just as surely as our oak tree's biography was written in its rings, in a code that scientists attempt to translate.

Human beings are animals, and, like other such organisms, we also leave behind our bones, which can, under the right conditions, survive for long stretches of time to be examined by scientists in future generations. Like other animal bones, ours record our histories, telling stories of disease, nutrition, labor, trauma, and even family ties. Part of the job of the archaeologist is to study those bones for the stories they can tell of the times and lives that make up the human past. We'll discuss how scientists interpret human remains later in this book.

Like other life forms, we humans possess inborn, biological **adaptations** to our environments. These adaptations are physical characteristics we are born with that allow us to live. In this sense we are no different from polar bears, butterflies, or, for that matter, oak trees, who, like all animal and plant species, possess physical adaptations, inborn strategies for survival. Some of these adaptations—for example, the way we walk on two feet and the ways in which we can hold and manipulate objects with our hands—are reflected by the form of our bones. Those who study the human past examine how our ancestors lived, in part, by the analysis of their skeletons.

Unlike animals or oak trees, we human beings leave behind something more than just the remnants of our physical selves because the human adaptation is not only inborn, not only passively inherited, it is also constructed, actively invented, reinvented, and revised in each generation. It can be argued, in fact, that our primary adaptation is not strictly biological but cultural. We do not adjust to our environment only through the slow-acting biological process Charles Darwin labeled "natural selection," by which individual members of a species who happen to possess advantageous characteristics are more likely to survive life's struggle's and pass those characteristics down to subsequent generations. We humans also can dynamically and nearly instantly adjust to our physical environments by using our great intelligence to figure out how to make the most out of what nature has to offer. We invent and make tools that enable us to better extract resources from our surroundings, not in generations removed but right here and right now. We construct homes from wood, stone, and earth that buffer us against the cold of winter and the heat of summer. We make and wear clothing and footwear from animal hides and plant fibers. We manufacture vessels of clay in which we cook our food and containers of bark, wood, and fiber to store our valuables. We differentiate, distinguish, and identify ourselves with items of adornment made of every imaginable raw material—bone, antler, ivory, metal, stone, wood—that communicate to others our marital status, social standing, religion, and group membership. The raw materials from which we build these structures and manufacture these objects often are more durable than the raw materials from which nature has constructed our bodies. The houses that enclose us, the tools we hold in our hands, the pots in which we cook our food, the rings we wear on our fingers, and the symbols we suspend from chains around our necks often outlast us and may serve, like the tree rings of our old oak, to convey in their own language the story of who we are and who we were. The science that attempts to read this language of objects—those things that make up our **material culture**—is archaeology, and we will spend much of the remainder of this book discussing the methods archaeologists use to find, recover, and study the material culture that was left behind by past people and that has fortuitously endured.

 ## The Context of Antiquity

Though old in comparison to a human lifespan, our fallen oak was not a particularly ancient tree. Living examples of the justifiably famous giant sequoias (*Sequioadendron giganteum*) of the American West that reach dizzyingly into the sky can be more than 3,000 years old. Dendrochronologists can extract thin slices across the radius of a tree's trunk, allowing for a ring count without causing harm. Using this method, the oldest living giant sequoia has been calculated to be 3,270 years old. That's enormously old, but even that pales in comparison to the true longevity champions among trees, the bristlecone pines (*Pinus longaeva*), also in the American West (Figure P.2). One of the oldest living bristlecones has been named "Methuselah" for the biblical patriarch who is supposed to have lived for 969 years. In fact, he would have been a real youngster compared to the tree named for him; Methuselah the bristlecone pine is a stupendous 4,793 years old. (See the website http://www.rmtrr.org/oldlist.htm for a listing of the oldest known trees for a number of species.)

It is remarkable to consider that those of us alive today share the planet with living organisms so breathtakingly ancient. The old-grove bristlecone pines, Methuselah among them, were alive in 1901, at the turn of the twentieth century. Remarkably, these very same trees were alive during the American War of Independence in 1776. It is amazing to consider that living trees you can see today were happily photosynthesizing when Columbus's ships plied the waters of the Atlantic in 1492. William the Conqueror invaded England in 1066. Blissfully unaware of this crucial historical event memorized by high school history students everywhere, bristlecones that are alive today collected solar energy with their needles and drew up moisture through their roots in that same year. The birth of the Muslim prophet Muhammad (A.D. 570) and the birth of the Christian messiah Jesus (most likely 4 B.C.) occurred during the lifetimes of bristlecone pines that continue to live in the twenty-first century. The Bible story recounted in the Old Testament of the Hebrew prophet Moses leading his people out of bondage in Egypt relates to historical events that probably occurred in the thirteenth century B.C.—sometime soon after 3,300

FIGURE P.2 The oldest living trees on our planet are bristlecone pines, some of which are nearly 5,000 years old. The growth rings on a bristlecone pine and on other trees as well present a version of their life histories. (K. L. Feder)

years ago. Living bristlecone pines that you can walk by today, the fragrance of whose needles you can smell, were already more than a thousand years old when Moses implored Pharaoh to let his people go. The Egyptian pharaoh Khufu ascended the throne in 2589 B.C. soon thereafter initiating construction of the Great Pyramid, truly one of the wonders of the ancient world and emblematic of human antiquity (Figure P.3). Today you can hike the trail to the old-grove bristlecone pines in Inyo National Forest in central California and stand in the shadows of living trees that had already been casting shadows for nearly 200 years when Khufu built his pyramid.

The Bible characterizes a reasonable human lifespan as "three-score and ten," or seventy years, not quite 1.5% of the longevity of an ancient bristlecone pine tree, and therein lies an interesting insight. Like all living things, such as our oak tree, we humans are temporary residents of this planet, and not particularly long-lived ones at that. Unlike all other living things, however, we are conscious of our transience. Among all Earth's creatures, we are probably the only ones who are aware that there is more to time than our own "now." All human beings know that we have a future in which we will succeed or fail at what we attempt—and probably do a little of both. If we're lucky we will live a happy and successful life, be surrounded by good friends, and live to a ripe old age, but lucky or not, successful or not, long-lived or not, we all eventually die.

Along with a future each one of us also is aware that we have a past, a period of personal development during which we were born and slowly matured. Beyond this we know that we have more than an immediate, personal past;

FIGURE P.3 Bristlecone pine trees still alive in California were already thriving when these icons of the ancient world were constructed by the Egyptians on the Giza plateau overlooking the Nile. (K L. Feder)

we have a family history as well. Certainly you recognize, though it may be challenging to imagine, that there was a time not so very long ago when your parents were your age, a time when they experienced some of the same pressures, confusions, frustrations, and, yes, joys that you do now. Of course, your parents had parents, too. Your grandparents were young in a time even more different and distant than your parents'. Consider, when you look at the fading, presumably ancient photographs of your grandparents taken when they were young that the seemingly enormous amount of time since your grandparents were your age is only the tiniest bit of a fraction of the time that the human lineage has walked this planet. The human family has substantial time depth, and our lives today represent only the current page of an ongoing and ancient story.

 ## Shadow of the Past

Every generation of human beings asserts sovereignty over its time on life's stage, but the members of each generation pass, succumbing to the inexorable unwinding of time. It may be a burden to know our fate, but it also provides our species with an opportunity—and a rationale—to know even more. Although the only time in which we can live is now, the past casts its shadow into the present. We can contemplate and even explore the time before our own because, in a sense, there is an element of immortality to everything that rises up for its brief stint on the center stage of existence.

Archaeology is the science that examines the shadows of the human past. This book is about how we make sense of these shadows.

It is a short book. It is not encyclopedic or all inclusive. It cannot, in its relatively few pages, tell you everything there is to know about archaeology. Reading this book will not make you an archaeologist, not even close. That was never my goal. Its entire purpose simply is to get you to think about how we study human history in its broadest sense, beginning long before our ancestors developed the capacity to actually write down that history. The subject matter of archaeology comprises a story that we cannot read directly. We can recover that history only from the "library" of objects people left behind. That library of objects is the archaeological record, and how we study that record is the focus of this book. If you are in a course for which this book is a text simply because you think archaeology is an incredibly interesting topic, you've come to the right place.

Study Questions

1. What was the point of the story of the old oak tree that crashed down on my property?
2. How can the old, dead oak tell the story of its life?

3. Trees and animals (including human animals) leave behind physical remains in the form of wood and bones that can be studied long after they are dead. What else do human beings leave behind?

4. I assert that "the past casts its shadow into the present," allowing those of us residing in the present to study the past. How does the human past cast its shadow into the present?

1 How I Spent My Summer Vacation

FINDING, EXCAVATING, AND INTERPRETING THE
WOOD LILY SITE IN NORTH-CENTRAL CONNECTICUT

June 1986 marked a starting point for two long-term undertakings with which I was intimately associated. The first of these—and the more relevant to this discussion—was a research project involving **archaeological fieldwork** in Peoples State Forest, located in the town of Barkhamsted, in north-central Connecticut (Figure 1.1). The second project of June 1986, the birth of my son Josh, initiated my wife and me into the world of parenting. The only significant and relevant connection between Josh's birth and the subject at hand had to do with timing. As the result of astonishingly bad planning, our first child was due to arrive exactly as I was to begin work as the **principal investigator** of an archaeological **survey** project. Beginning on June 1, my wife's due date, I was supposed to be deep in the woods of north-central Connecticut directing a team of archaeological fieldworkers, digging **test pits** throughout 4,000 acres of state forest land.

We were searching for remnants of earlier human settlement and activity in the wooded upland that became a Connecticut state forest in the early decades of the twentieth century. Luckily, I had a terrific crew of fieldworkers, a great **crew chief**, and an amazing **field director.** Although it was difficult to hand over a project I had designed and shepherded through an agonizing funding and planning process, at least I knew that I was leaving the day-to-day work to an exceptionally competent crew of archaeologists. Also luckily—not for my wife, but for me—Josh was born about two weeks late. My wife was comfortable with me going out into the field with the crew a few times during the twelve-day period between the beginning of our research on the first of June and Josh's delayed arrival on the twelfth, so, though admittedly more than just a

A Biography of Archaeology

(see chapter 2)

FIGURE 1.1 Overview of the Farmington River, the major watercourse in Barkhamsted, Connecticut. (K. L. Feder)

little bit distracted—OK, I was a wreck—I wasn't entirely isolated from the initial fieldwork.

What Archaeologists Want to Know

(see chapter 3)

Though I couldn't spend as much time in the field as I might have wished that summer, I nevertheless continued to play an active role in the project from my home. Often the entire crew would stop off at my house on their way out into the field in the morning (expecting doughnuts!), and we would go over the particular plan for the day, discussing the established survey lines, or **transects**, along which they would search for **sites** during the next eight hours or so (Figure 1.2).

Though we had a fairly detailed plan outlining our strategy in the search for sites, as in any scientific project we needed to be flexible, and our plans regularly changed as a result of inclement weather or impossible field conditions that were not initially recognized on our **topographic maps** (Figure 1.3).

Doing Archaeology: Practical Considerations

(see chapter 4)

Beyond this, on a good day the discovery of some interesting "stuff" that required additional work and time in an area might also cause us to alter our strategy. So, although we had a good general plan and rough

FIGURE 1.2 Setting up a test pit transect. Using a sighting compass, the crew chief (in the foreground) is shooting in a line for the crew (in the background). Test pits were excavated every 10 meters along this line. (K. L. Feder)

schedule, that plan and schedule needed to be reassessed each day and changed accordingly.

At the end of each day, my field director would stop by my house, dropping off paperwork consisting of maps, **test pit forms**, and paper bags containing any archaeological material recovered during the field day—mostly **artifacts** that, through any one of a number of **site formation processes**, had been transformed from their original functions as tools and objects people used in everyday life in the distant and not-so-distant past to their present incarnations as elements of the archaeological record.

Part of our **research strategy** that summer involved a walkover of the entire forest surface, looking for above-ground evidence of historical uses of the area. In our walkover, called a **pedestrian survey**, of Peoples, we found house foundations, the remains of old mill buildings and their associated facilities, animal pens, stone walls, historical trash dumps, and even an old burial ground (Figure 1.4). These were visible on the surface because they were large, built-up features composed of durable material and because they weren't particularly ancient, dating only to the last few hundred years. Not nearly enough time had passed to cover these sites in their particular settings, and they were visible to anyone who took the time to walk around off-trail deep into the woods.

A Community's Shadow: The Archaeological Site

(see chapter 5)

Though archaeologists can in some instances find sites, including quite ancient sites, through above-ground visual inspection, in southern New England, where our survey took place and elsewhere, a series of entirely

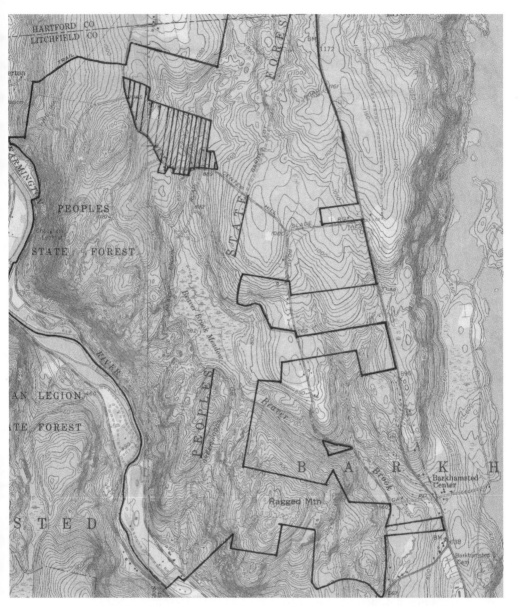

FIGURE 1.3 Topographic map of Peoples State Forest, Barkhamsted, Connecticut.

natural processes serve to cover material that reposes on the ground for very long.

Thus, except for relatively recent materials, the archaeological remains that we sought had been buried by a host of natural processes, and the only way we could find them was to peer beneath the surface. Even now, with various high-tech devices at our disposal for mapping and analysis, in most places the best way to do that—meaning the way in which most sites in an area can be found and described—is simply to dig (Figure 1.5).

FIGURE 1.4 This small cemetery, with graves indicated by simple fieldstones, is located in our pedestrian survey in Peoples State Forest. (K. L. Feder)

FIGURE 1.5 In many parts of the world, southern New England included, archaeological material is buried by a broad array of natural processes. In order to find and recover this evidence of past life, archaeologists need to dig using a series of careful and controlled procedures. (K. L. Feder)

Searching for the Past: Archaeological Site Survey

(see chapter 6)

Of course, we couldn't excavate an entire 4,000-acre forest in our search for archaeological sites. We didn't have the time, the personnel, or the money—and we certainly didn't want to destroy 4,000 acres of forest land merely to satisfy our archaeological curiosity. For much of the time my crew members spent in the field, they investigated only a **representative sample** of the subsurface soil in the forest.

We defined a representative sample in the early planning stages of the project by subdividing the forest lands into a number of zones based on the characteristics each possessed that might have been of importance for human use. Applying our modern perceptions to land patterns, we divided Peoples into the following categories: major river floodplains, small streams and their associated terraces, uplands, and bedrock exposures (Figure 1.6, left). Next, we established a series of transects through each of these zones, lines along which we planned to excavate regularly spaced **test pits.** In establishing the transects along which we planned to test the subsurface, we made sure that we covered each of these subdivisions of forest land (Figure 1.6, right). Furthermore, we sampled the forest in a manner that ensured that each of the defined zones was investigated at a level of intensity that reflected its spatial proportion in the forest.

After my son's rather eventful entry into the world on June 12—everything turned out just great in the end—we maintained our established pattern in the

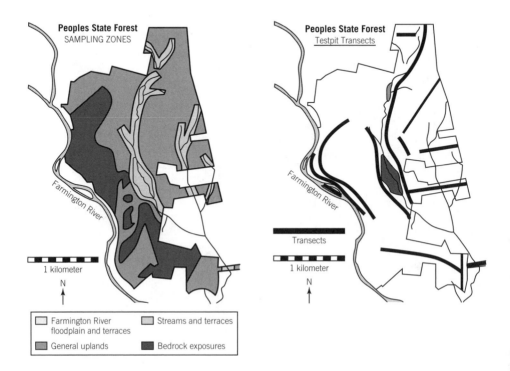

FIGURE 1.6 Divisions of Peoples State Forest. (K. L. Feder)

survey project. I continued staying home most days for my son's first few weeks of life, having a great time getting to know the new member of our family. On most mornings—we weren't getting any sleep then, anyway—the crew would drop by the house, to go over the planned work for the day and to make funny faces at the baby. In the evenings—we weren't getting any sleep then, either—the crew would drop by the house, and I went over the field forms and did a preliminary examination of whatever had been recovered in the test pits on that day before the material was transported to the archaeology laboratory at my university.

On one otherwise uneventful day, my field crew chief stopped by in the morning with map in hand to discuss the fieldwork planned for that day in a part of the forest we had not previously entered. The section in question was just to the east of a paved, public road that crosscut state forest land. Eastward, the land was quite flat, the exception rather than the rule in north-central and northwest Connecticut, and then after about 100 meters dropped off rather abruptly to another flat terrace of land, far narrower than the first. Another quick drop to the east brought the crew down to a small unnamed but permanent stream (Figure 1.7) flowing south into a larger watercourse (Beaver Brook), which, true to its name, was impounded by a textbook-perfect little beaver dam (Figure 1.8).

Beaver Brook, in turn, flowed into the Farmington River, the major watercourse in north-central Connecticut (Figure 1.9) and the environmental feature that bounded and gave a name to our Farmington River Archaeological Project (FRAP). (When we started this project, we had considered naming ourselves the Farmington Archaeological Research Team, but we suspected the acronym wouldn't work all that well on our project T-shirts.)

The positioning of our planned transect that day in early July was determined by a combination of our **research strategy** and the practical concerns of the Connecticut Historical Commission, the agency that was funding our project with monies provided by the U.S. Department of the Interior. Our funding required us to test state forest lands broadly. Although the particular plot through which the day's transect cut might otherwise have been overlooked (it was a rather narrow appendix of property surrounded to the north and the south by private holdings that abutted the public lands), it was a section we had promised to investigate in our grant proposal.

During the first two weeks of fieldwork, my crew had not found any substantial archaeological evidence of occupation of the forest. That's not terribly surprising. In some regions sites are few and far between and difficult to find. Surprising or not, after a little more than two weeks of digging test pits, the crew was getting a bit crabby over the lack of any exciting discoveries.

I certainly could empathize, but it is important to understand that archaeology is not a scavenger hunt and that "finding stuff" is not the goal. Our purpose, instead, was to "find out stuff," which may be an entirely different thing. There is a rule in archaeology that all field crews understand, at least on an intellectual level, that states that not finding any archaeological evidence in a given spot is every bit as important as finding spectacular archaeological remains. "Negative information is just as important as positive information" is

FIGURE 1.7 The unnamed brook that flows into Beaver Brook, the major drainage stream in Peoples State Forest. (K. L. Feder)

FIGURE 1.8 Beaver Brook is impounded by a textbook-perfect Beaver Dam, part of which can be seen in the center of this photograph. The beaver pond is visible behind the dam. This area has long been beaver habitat and is indicated as "Beaver Meadow" on maps going back to the mid-1800s. (K. L. Feder)

FIGURE 1.9 The Farmington River, the major watercourse that flows through north-central Connecticut and that has served as a focus for my archaeological research. (K. L. Feder)

a virtual mantra for field archaeologists intoned, albeit, with a bit of a wink and a sigh.

Certainly, in large measure the rule is true. Knowing that human groups did not inhabit a given region or microenvironment, and trying to understand why they didn't, is an important part of archaeological analysis. Emotionally, however, it must be admitted that this can be a little difficult to accept at times. Negative information may be important, but not many of us are so intellectually disciplined that we leave the field after a long day digging dry test pits enthusiastic about the contribution we have made to our understanding of the ancient past—by not finding anything. Even the most serious-minded archaeologist has to admit that finding stuff is a hell of a lot more fun than not finding stuff. This doesn't make archaeology a treasure hunt. Really. It's just that in the humid, buggy, muddy, sweaty, exhausting reality of archaeological fieldwork with mosquitoes, ticks, broken bones, poisonous snakes, poison ivy, poison sumac, food poisoning, and so on, it feels so much better if instead of negative information at the end of the day you have something tangible (ancient stone tools, potsherds, butchered animal bones, anything) to show for your literal blood, sweat, and tears.

When Marina Mozzi, the chief of my increasingly whiny crew, and I looked over the **United States Geological Survey (USGS)** topographic map of the area the crew was scheduled to test that morning, I noted the location of the east-west transect line we had drawn on the map previously, starting at the paved road, cutting across the flat, briefly ending at the steep slope, continuing again across the lower flat, and terminating at the stream. I took my pencil and marked an "X" on the lower terrace, just west of the stream (Figure 1.10), telling Marina not to despair but that at long last the field crew would find a **prehistoric** site exactly where I had marked the map. Marina smiled and nodded, saying that she was going to hold me to that "promise."

It was all done in a joking manner, of course, but I was, at least in part, quite serious. Certainly, I had no way of knowing whether an ancient site really was located where I predicted, and the location of the "X" I had scrawled on the map that morning was not all that exact anyway. Nevertheless, I believed that there was a fair probability of the crew finding evidence of past human habitation of the forest somewhere on the lower terrace adjacent to the stream.

My stock as a "psychic archaeologist" rose considerably several hours later. The entire crew made it a point to stop by my house at the end of their workday to lay themselves prostrate at the feet of their great "guru" archaeologist. Well, nobody actually did that, but they

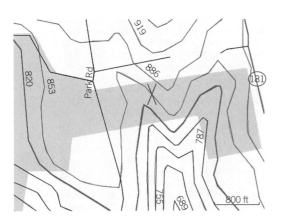

FIGURE 1.10 The section we were about to survey was located in this narrow swath of land in Peoples State Forest.

were appropriately impressed by my apparent clairvoyance. A few skeptics even accused me of having advance knowledge of the site and sending them to it to boost morale, but, in truth, I had no foreknowledge of the site and merely used standard archaeological reasoning to hypothesize where a site might be located. "X," indeed, did "mark the spot," and the crew encountered a number of 3,000-year-old artifacts almost exactly where I had marked the map that morning.

To be honest, while being spot-on in locating the Peoples State Forest site (the result of luck as well as a bit of archaeological prescience), accurately predicting the location of archaeological remains is something archaeologists do on a regular basis. There is nothing supernatural or extrasensory about it; a commonsense understanding of the **settlement patterns** of an ancient group of people is all one needs to perform this apparent act of magic.

By the time we were done with our survey of Peoples State Forest in 1986, we had excavated more than 1,000 test pits. The 3,000-year-old site we called Wood Lily (for the beautiful flowers that marked the point on Center Road where we started the test pit transect that ended up in the middle of the ancient settlement) was only the first of more than twenty prehistoric archaeological sites we discovered that summer in Peoples through the process of subsurface testing (Figure 1.11).

In a few more instances that summer, site locations were predicted with a reasonable degree of accuracy. In all of the other cases, in hindsight anyway, discovering buried sites where we did was not terribly surprising and could have been predicted. These sites were found in places in the forest where it would have made perfect sense for small groups of **foragers** to have settled for short periods of time while hunting animals, fishing, collecting seeds or nuts, or just overnighting while passing through.

In addition to locations used by ancient Native Americans, six sites were identified in our pedestrian survey of the forest associated with people of European descent who had begun moving into the area in the late eighteenth century. These sites included the remains of two separate mill buildings, with associated dams impounding flowing stream water and their "raceways" directing water to the mill wheels, as well as a couple of house foundations (Figure 1.12).

During our walkover in one section of the forest, we encountered a series of very small, irregular, and rather crudely made stone-lined foundations and cellar holes. We were disabused in a hurry of our initial reaction that we had made a spectacular discovery here when we exited the forest onto the nearby road and noticed a brass plaque memorializing the site we had just "discovered." Even if our discovery was not extraordinary—everybody in town already knew about the village remains—the story behind the place was spectacular. The foundations were the remains of houses from the Lighthouse, an eighteenth- and nineteenth-century village of people at the social and economic margins, who were a mixed group of Native, European, and African descent. We were to spend several years investigating the site (Figure 1.13; Feder 1994).

But the detailed investigation of our sites was to take place in the future. Our job in the summer of 1986 was to conduct an archaeological survey and

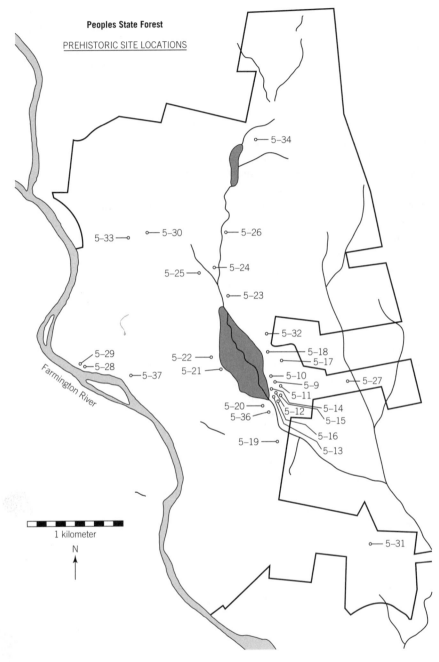

FIGURE 1.11 Outline of Peoples State Forest with sites we located in our 1986 survey. (K. L. Feder)

FIGURE 1.12 This late eighteenth-century foundation is one of several historical sites located in Peoples State Forest and identified in our pedestrian survey. (K. L. Feder)

FIGURE 1.13 One of the simple stone foundations located in the late eighteenth-century, early nineteenth-century village called the Lighthouse, in Peoples State Forest. (K. L. Feder)

FIGURE 1.14 Students excavating at the Wood Lily archaeological site in Peoples State Forest. (K. L. Feder)

produce a map identifying for the Connecticut Historical Commission the location of archaeological remains within the borders of Peoples State Forest. The thirty-three sites we identified fulfilled the goal of this element of the project. Our secondary mandate was to determine the approximate size of the sites and to provide a preliminary description, including how long ago the sites had been occupied and the activities that had been carried out by their inhabitants. Our strategy to accomplish these tasks involved excavating additional test pits in the vicinity of the original units in which archaeological materials had been recovered to get a broader perspective of the remains at each site. We did precisely this at the aforementioned 3,000-year-old occupation we called the Wood Lily site.

Chapter 1:
Slide Show

This preliminary work convinced us that the Wood Lily site possessed great potential to help illuminate the lives of the ancient people of north-central Connecticut. We returned to the site in the summers of 1987 and 1989 to conduct a more detailed investigation through **archaeological excavation.** During both summers my crew consisted of students who were pursuing training in archaeology, students who were not interested in pursuing archaeology as a career but who wanted to work on an excavation, and a number of nonstudent volunteers who simply were interested in archaeology (Figure 1.14).

Revealing the Past: The Archaeological Excavation

(see chapter 7)

In the New Testament of the Christian Bible in the Book of 1 Corinthians is a phrase that conveys the difficulty we human beings have in understanding the meaning of our own existence: "For now, we see through a glass, darkly...." In our investigations of the ancient past, archaeologists are usually faced with the same problem. Our goal is to understand ways of life that preceded our own. Often we must attempt to accomplish this goal based on the recovery and examination of a mere handful of objects made and lost long ago. We are, in fact, peering at the past "through a glass, darkly," trying to bring into focus long ago events that have projected often indistinct images into the present.

FIGURE 1.15 A quartz knife photographed in situ, in its exact place of discovery at the Wood Lily site. (K. L. Feder)

These indistinct images of past events, activities, patterns, and processes are brought into sharper focus for the archaeologist by recovery and analysis of the physical objects left behind by ancient peoples. In the process of digging the Wood Lily site, we found the remnants of objects that the people who lived there made, used, used up, broke, lost, discarded, secreted away for safekeeping, forgot about, and so on (Figure 1.15). We found and then carefully recovered those objects through the process of archaeological **excavation.**

At the same time that people were making, using, losing, and discarding objects that were becoming part of the archaeological record, nature was depositing material at the site, leaving evidence of the environment at the time the site was occupied. Some of those environmental remnants provided us with the material that allowed a determination of the age of Wood Lily; the site had been occupied approximately 3,000 years ago.

Interpreting the Past: Gauging the Age of an Archaeological Site

(see chapter 8)

Seeds from plants growing in the vicinity, snail shells, insect parts, rodent bones, and **pollen** may become incorporated into the same matrix as archaeological artifacts and "ecofacts". The vegetation that produced the seeds, the snails that left behind the shells, the insects and rodents that died, and the plants that rained their pollen down over the site all were part of and reflect the characteristics of the environment to which ancient human inhabitants adapted (Figure 1.16). The presence of this natural evidence allows us to reconstruct a past environment.

Interpreting the Past: The Environmental Contexts of Antiquity

(see chapter 9)

We worked at Wood Lily, in a sense, in the manner of detectives, collecting the physical evidence left behind by the people who lived at the site. In excavation we take enormous care in removing all

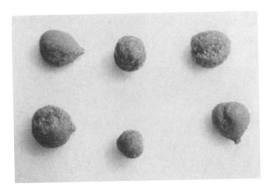

FIGURE 1.16 Charred seeds recovered in the Wood Lily excavation. (K. L. Feder)

FIGURE 1.17 Photo of a stone point, broken at the tip, located in situ at the Tulmeadow North site in West Simsbury, Connecticut. (K. L. Feder)

the material that has covered over the site.

Archaeologists excavate slowly and methodically, removing the overburden of soil that has built up on top of and around the objects that people, mostly unintentionally, left behind. Then, perhaps a bit ironically, we take the site apart bit by bit (essentially destroying it in order to remove the remains) and take our finds to a laboratory for analysis. Surely you have noticed in television police dramas how before a dead body is taken to the morgue, before blood stains are recovered for analysis, and before weapons are dropped into evidence bags, a crime scene photographer takes an abundance of photographs, essentially preserving the crime scene in the form of those two-dimensional images. Archaeologists also take lots of photographs (Figure 1.17), make lots of spatial measurements, and draw lots of maps (Figure 1.18), in an attempt to preserve the three-dimensional spatial data of an archaeological site that we need to take apart in order to study further. If we are clever enough and—it is not inaccurate to characterize it in this way—obsessive enough in our recording of a site's spatial data, we can put it back together again to examine it more closely.

Somewhere in the back of your mind, you probably have an image of the vanishing Cheshire Cat from Lewis Carroll's *Alice in Wonderland*. Perhaps you have seen Disney's animated version of the story, in which the large, disconcertingly inscrutable striped cat was played with the perfect degree of disinterest by the languid-voiced actor Sterling Holloway. One minute the cat is lounging on the branch of a tree, chatting with Alice, and then, bit by bit, piece by piece, he slowly fades into translucency and then invisibility, until all that remains is his fading smile. Finally, even the all-knowing grin vanishes without a trace. At first you can still hear Holloway's hypnotic voice, but that too fades out. Finally, nothing at all is left of the cat.

Envision that bit of animation, as the Cheshire Cat slowly fades into invisibility. Now reverse that sequence in your mind. Instead of disappearing, the

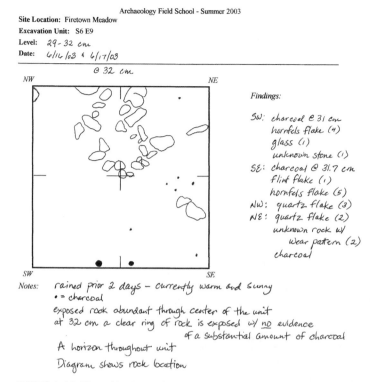

Archaeology Field School - Summer 2003

Site Location: Firetown Meadow

Excavation Unit: S6 E9

Level: 29-32 cm

Date: 6/16/03 & 6/17/03

@ 32 cm

NW   NE

SW   SE

Findings:

SW: charcoal @ 31 cm
     hornfels flake (4)
     glass (1)
     unknown stone (1)
SE: charcoal @ 31.7 cm
     flint flake (1)
     hornfels flake (5)
NW: quartz flake (3)
NE: quartz flake (2)
     unknown rock w/
          wear pattern (2)
     charcoal

Notes: rained prior 2 days — currently warm and sunny
        • = charcoal
        exposed rock abundant through center of the unit
        at 32 cm a clear ring of rock is exposed w/ no evidence
                           of a substantial amount of charcoal
        A horizon throughout unit
        Diagram shows rock location

FIGURE 1.18 Map of in situ artifacts. (Drawn by Laura Jensen)

Cheshire Cat bubbles forth into existence, manifesting itself first as just a smile and adding the face, the torso, the legs, and finally the tail. At last, as Alice might have put it, we have a complete and "proper cat." With that reverse animation in mind, you have a nice analogy for what it is like to be an archaeologist and slowly uncover a complete artifact in the process of excavation. One of my students, Carolyn White, surely experienced this as she worked in excavation unit N25W4 on a steamy July day in 1989.

We had found lots of small, discarded fragments of chipped stone at Wood Lily. These bits of debris, called **debitage**, are largely produced in **percussion flaking**, whereby a **hammerstone** or antler hammer is used to detach flakes from a **core** by striking it. Interestingly, although entire, perfect specimens of tools may be more aesthetically pleasing and end up in museum displays, often we can learn more about the process of tool making through analysis of discarded material: the rejects and mistakes. Errors may, in a sense, freeze a moment in time and preserve a step in the tool manufacturing process that might otherwise have become obscured by subsequent steps in tool making.

**Technology:
How People
Made Things**

(see chapter 10)

During a television interview a rather bored reporter offhandedly inquired on camera about the scientific validity of conclusions archaeologists might reach concerning peoples and events of long ago based simply on what amounted to their trash. At that moment I had excavated two sections of a spear point that pretty obviously had broken during the final stages of its manufacture (Figure 1.19). I suggested to the reporter that while it might be true that we would never know the name of the artisan who produced the broken weapon I held in my hand, I could fairly accurately guess what the tool maker had said upon accidentally snapping the spear point in two at the end of a laborious and exacting process of tool making. I'm not sure that's the best example of the kinds of insights we gain from the discovery of broken rather than perfect specimens, but it is, nevertheless, a good story.

Carolyn White was expecting little beyond additional debitage when she began excavating that July morning deep in the woods at the Wood Lily site. Like the reappearing Cheshire Cat who teased Alice by revealing nothing more

FIGURE 1.19 Two pieces of the same, nearly 5,000-year-old spear point found at the Alsop Meadow site in Avon, Connecticut. The point had broken, probably while it was being manufactured, and its two halves were discarded, only to be recovered within several centimeters of each other in the same stratigraphic layer of the site. (K. L. Feder)

than a toothy grin or who sometimes fully materialized in all his tubby glory, it is impossible to know, as your trowel first makes contact with an object, if the artifact will turn out to be nothing more than a tiny chip of stone no bigger than what the trowel initially exposes, which is valuable in its own right, or something quite a bit more. Exchanging her hard-edged metal trowel for a piece of soft bamboo carved into a flat blade to avoid damaging the artifact, Carolyn began the process of exposing what she presumed would be a small stone chip.

She recognized almost immediately that the piece of stone was made of flint, a favorite raw material for tool making at the Wood Lily site and virtually anywhere this rock type was available to ancient peoples. Flint flakes rather easily; more important, it flakes regularly, consistently, and predictably. Finally, flint can be flaked into relatively durable, extremely thin, almost dangerously sharp edges. Striking a piece of flint with the right kind of **percussor** at the right place and at the appropriate angle produces an edge that is perfect for tools intended for cutting and piercing soft materials such as animal hides and flesh.

The flint recovered at Wood Lily and throughout our research study area in north-central and northwest Connecticut was nonlocal; we call it an **exotic material.** In its common usage, the term *exotic* may be used to denote something out-of-the-ordinary or strange, but here we mean it to imply only that the stone came from a distant source. The geology of our area had not been conducive to the natural production of flint, and, therefore, there isn't much of it available in Connecticut. However, about 80 kilometers (50 miles) to the west in the Hudson River Valley of New York state, there were (and are) abundant sources of flint. The aboriginal people of Connecticut clearly had access to this flint and obtained it in large quantities.

Flint is a far superior raw material for making sharp-edged tools than most of the locally available rock types (like quartz and quartzite) and assorted volcanics (like basalt) available in Connecticut. When possible and increasingly after about 4,000 years ago, the native inhabitants of Connecticut either traveled to the flint source or, more likely, had established trading networks in order to obtain this prized **lithic** material. In fact, at some Connecticut sites dating to about 1,000 years ago, flint constitutes nearly 100% of the lithic assemblage. Flint made up 52.3% of the lithic debitage and about 46.3% of the finished tools found at the 3,000-year-old Wood Lily site.

When Carolyn White first encountered what she had assumed was a stone flake in the soil, she was fairly certain it was flint because of its color and reflectivity: It was black and shiny, as is the New York state flint, and unlike almost all the other rock types we might expect to find in southern New England. But remember, at this point in the excavation, all that was exposed to her was a small piece of stone, not unlike the literally thousands of pieces of debitage already encountered and recovered at the site.

As she began to slowly strip the soil from around the artifact, instead of the ends of the flake becoming exposed (as would have happened had the piece been just a small fragment of flint), it became clear that though extremely narrow, the piece of flint was substantially longer than any of the flakes we had previously found. Also, instead of a randomly shaped piece of stone struck off a stone **core** while making a tool, it was apparent that this stone had been carefully flaked into a symmetrical form. Excavation slowly revealed a long, narrow shape that must have been painstakingly chipped. It was quickly clear to

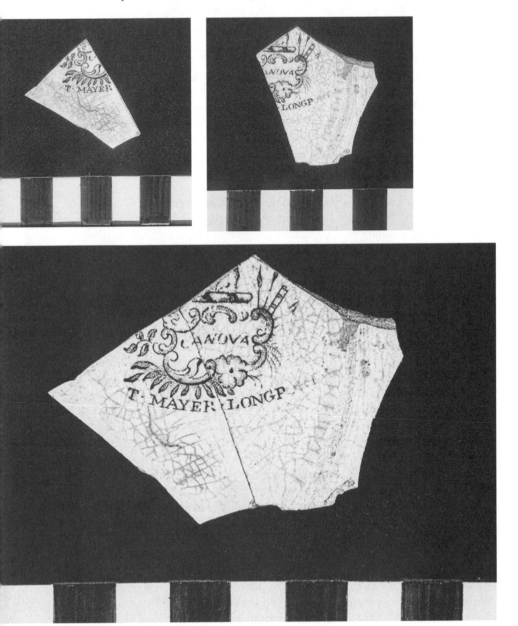

FIGURE 1.20 Conjoined fragments of an early nineteenth-century dish. Note the name T. Mayer, the potter who produced the ware, the location of his operation, Longport (in Staffordshire, England), and the name of the ware design, Canova.

Carolyn that she had found not simply a piece of debitage, but a precisely shaped, carefully flaked tool, or at least a large part of one.

The excitement of the unknown is a fascinating part of excavation. When you begin exposing an object, you really have no idea how much of it is intact. As you slowly and carefully remove the soil from above and around it, taking great care to leave it in place in order to preserve its **spatial context** and **stratigraphic** positioning, you are aware that at any point in this process the broken edge of a tool may be exposed as you scrape away the soil, and there may be nothing more.

The rest of the tool may be somewhere else in the site. If you are lucky, another digger may find it, and the two fragments will fit together, or **conjoin** (Figure 1.20). The tool may be somewhere else entirely, never to be found; perhaps the tip broke off when the spear was thrown, and only the base, still attached to the retrieved wooden handle, was returned to the village that is now the archaeological site you are excavating.

As Carolyn slowly and carefully followed the path of the stone in the soil, it became apparent that, broken or not, she had found at least a substantial part of the object. After a little more work it was clear that she had found not just most of but an entire, unbroken stone tool.

The tool she had uncovered was a complete drill (Figure 1.21). The tip and edges of the drill bit evidenced the tool's pattern of use, matching the **wear patterns** on other stone drills found by archaeologists and mirroring those seen on replica tools of a similar form used experimentally for drilling.

The bit was long and delicate, exquisite, really. The base of the drill flared out to facilitate its attachment to a handle, probably of wood, that had not been preserved in our acidic New England soil. The artisan who had produced this tool had been a master, knowing precisely where to apply pressure—almost certainly with the narrow, durable tip of a deer antler (a tine)—to the edge of the stone blade without snapping the bit in two. The tool maker obviously knew exactly how to apply pressure to remove small flakes from the bit's edge to produce a light yet strong, symmetrical, functional, and, at the same time, quite lovely piece of stonework. It is a tool that I continue

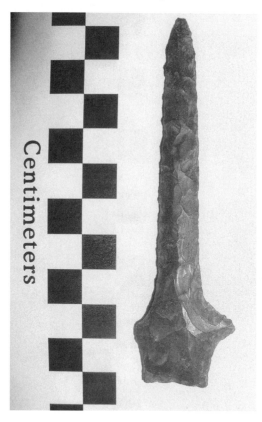

FIGURE 1.21 The beautifully crafted, complete flint drill found at the Wood Lily site in Peoples State Forest, Barkhamsted, Connecticut. (K. L. Feder)

to use 3,000 years after the lithic artist produced it, not for drilling, of course, but as a model in my **experimental archaeology** course on the craft of stone tool manufacture, or **knapping.**

The flint drill may have been the finest example of stone tool making found at the Wood Lily site, but it was far from being the only such example. In fact, in two field seasons of excavation, we recovered fifty-three complete or partial stone tools at the site. Among those were the bits or tips of four more drills (Figure 1.22).

The diversity of functional tool types found at a site is used by archaeologists as an indicator of the range of activities that were carried out there. In the logical process employed by archaeologists, it is the degree of diversity of activities carried out at a site, as exhibited by the diversity of the functions reflected by the tools recovered, that allows us to deduce the kind of community we are exploring: a village site where adult men and women as well as children lived and where a broad range of tasks were carried out with an equally broad array

FIGURE 1.22 The nearly complete Wood Lily flint drill is shown in the center of this photograph. The four additional drill fragments recovered at Wood Lily are also shown. (K. L. Feder)

of tools; or perhaps more specialized sites such as hunting or gathering camps, military encampments, quarry sites, or sacred places, all where the diversity of functional tool types would have been far more restricted, reflecting a narrower range of activities.

Based on the diversity of material we recovered at Wood Lily, we concluded that it was a small village, a habitation site. Because we found lots of debitage (the debris of the process of stone tool making), as well as the instruments by which these waste flakes were struck from cores, we knew that tool making was a significant part of the repertoire of activities carried out by the site's inhabitants.

We didn't find any artifacts directly related to cooking or eating at the site—no pots or plates—but this doesn't mean that food preparation and eating weren't important activities here as well. The age of Wood Lily (3,000 years old) places the site at the very end of the **pre-ceramic** period in southern New England. The oldest **ceramic** objects recovered by archaeologists in Connecticut are about 3,000 years old (Figure 1.23). The oldest dated ceramic objects we have found in the Farmington River Valley are about 500 years more recent than that; we have **thermoluminescence** dates from ceramics found at another site in the valley of about 2,500 years ago.

In this part of America, ceramic technology was not independently invented, but it moved into the area from the south and west. We found no

FIGURE 1.23 A fragment of pottery (called a sherd) found at an archaeological site in the Farmington Valley in Connecticut, which has been dated to about 2,500 years ago. The rough exterior surface resulted from pressing a cord-wrapped paddle onto the pot when the clay was still wet. Cord marking may have served a utilitarian function—strengthening the bonds between the clay coils used in building the pot—as well as an artistic one—creating an interestingly textured surface on the finished vessel. (K. L. Feder)

FIGURE 1.24 A soapstone quarry located in north-central Connecticut. The two vaguely circular pedestals seen here are what was left when hemispheres of soft soapstone were carved out of the bedrock (Swiss army knife added for scale). Those hemispheres of soft stone would have been hollowed out to produce bowls. (K. L. Feder)

stone bowls at Wood Lily either. **Steatite**, also called **soapstone**, is a soft rock that the native peoples of North America used, where it was available, to carve sturdy cooking vessels that, although generally quite bulky, have marvelous heat retention qualities (Figure 1.24).

However, we found no soapstone at the site. In all likelihood, the people at Wood Lily used perishable materials such as bark, wood, or reeds to make containers for storing and cooking food, and none of them have survived in the acidic soil of southern New England.

So, while we believe that Wood Lily was a habitation site, it is not surprising that we found no pottery. We did find cooking **features** at the site, however, and some evidence of food remains (Figure 1.25). Based on our analysis of these remains, it was clear that the people who lived at Wood Lily three millennia ago had eaten deer meat, acorns, and hickory nuts and also had collected and eaten the seeds of a number of different kinds of plants that grew in abundance near the stream that marked the eastern margin of their settlement (Figure 1.26).

Putting Food on the Table: Reconstructing Ancient Diets

(see chapter 11)

Evidence concerning the subsistence base of the former inhabitants at the Wood Lily site was also apparent in the stone tool **assemblage.** Among the whole or partial tools we found at the site, twenty-five were hunting weapons collectively called projectile points (Figure 1.27) and seventeen were half-moon shaped knives that would have served well in butchering the carcasses of hunted animals (Figure 1.28).

The **morphology** of projectile points indicates their function; they are bilaterally symmetrical and aerodynamic. One end—the "business end"—is sharply pointed to pierce an animal's hide, and the other often has specific features (notches, tangs, a stem) to enable hafting onto a wooden shaft (a spear, arrow, or dart shaft). The cutting tools at Wood Lily were blunt along their straight, back ends, where they would have been held in the hand or on a handle, and very thin and sharp along their curved working surfaces (Figure 1.29). A careful examination of the edges and tips of projectile

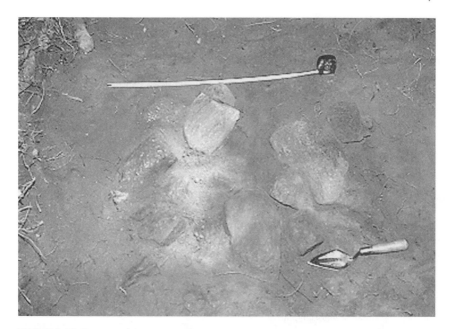

FIGURE 1.25 This cluster of stones and burned soil are the remains of a hearth at the Wood Lily site. Careful analysis of the soil matrix in and around the stones provided us with burned wood, used in radiocarbon dating the site, and bits of bone as well as seed and nut fragments used in reconstructing the diet of the site's inhabitants. (K. L. Feder)

points and the cutting edge of knives shows that careful **pressure flaking** was employed in their production.

Wood Lily was not a permanent village in which people lived year-long or for many years. The subsistence pattern of native New Englanders during the period of occupation at Wood Lily did not allow for such stability. Wood Lily was occupied long before the native peoples of New England had adopted the historically well-known diet based on maize (corn), beans, and squash. The wild ancestors of these crops were not native to the area—in fact, maize and beans are tropical plants. Native New Englanders did not initially develop these plants but instead adopted them from cultures to the south and west, and reliance on these domesticated foods developed relatively late in this area. The oldest evidence of maize in New England does not predate A.D. 1000, and it did not achieve preeminence in subsistence here until at least a couple of centuries later.

Some locations provide a rich enough bounty of wild food resources on a year-round basis for a nonagricultural people to settle permanently; unfortunately, southern New England was not one of those places. The inhabitants of Wood Lily, like their neighbors throughout New England in the period before 1,000 ago, were **foragers** or **hunter-gatherers.** Most foragers needed to be **nomadic** rather than **sedentary.** They needed to move in relation to the seasonal availability of resources necessary for their subsistence. They needed to adjust their group size as the local natural productivity of

Centimeters

FIGURE 1.26 Charred nutshell fragments like these were found in the hearths excavated at the Wood Lily site. (K. L. Feder)

specific places changed during the year. During some seasons populations might have aggregated at particularly rich spots. At other times smaller groups, perhaps individual families, needed to disperse across the landscape, spreading out when resources available during those seasons were themselves more dispersed.

Our desire was to reconstruct the **culture** of the people who lived at Wood Lily. Culture is complex, though, made up of all the behaviors and strategies a human group invents and passes down to subsequent generations. Culture, in fact, has been defined as the invented and learned (as opposed to instinctive) patterns of behavior, signifying that culture is an intellectual phenomenon, made up of a web of ideas about, among other things, how to behave toward other people, organize labor, make tools, educate the young, worship, and treat those who don't follow the rules of behavior. The archaeologist's challenge rests in the fact that these ideas about how to live are nonmaterial and leave no direct impression in the archaeological record, which is material by its very nature as well as by definition. What we had left to examine at Wood Lily, as is the case at all archaeological sites, in essence, were the physical residues of ideas: the objects that were the products of a group's strategies for hunting, storing food, protecting themselves from the elements, and even organizing their social relationships and worshipping their gods.

Families, Neighbors, and Strangers: Reconstructing Ancient Social Systems

(see chapter 12)

Sometimes these physical residues are many and straightforward, such as tools used in hunting. Other times these residues are more complex and open to interpretation: A gold ring found on the finger of a skeleton recovered at Pompeii or the crown depicted on the head of an Egyptian pharaoh in ancient carvings can be challenging to translate into their social or political meanings to the ancient people who wore them. And the residues of some elements of human societies simply are not to be found: We did not recover a single object at Wood Lily that we can confidently ascribe to a religious belief system. Yet, because anthropologists have never found a society without a belief system that we can include in the category of religion, we can be pretty confident that the inhabitants of Wood Lily possessed what we would recognize as religion.

Indeed, the archaeological record is limited to material objects, and some common human activities—storytelling and dance, for example—may involve no material objects and are, therefore, invisible to the archaeologist looking only at the material record at a site. Like all archaeologists, we are "peering through a glass, darkly" at the 3,000-year-old Wood Lily village in our direct examination of the archaeological site.

The people who lived at the Wood Lily site reflect in their material culture just what we would expect in southern New England of the Native Americans who lived here three millennia ago. However, although the tools they made, the hearth fires they warmed themselves over, and the trash they discarded are available for us to study, their actual physical remains did not survive the rigors of New England's soil. In this part of the world, high acidity; vigorous biological action on the part of small animals, burrowing worms, and insects;

FIGURE 1.27 Examples of spear points found at the Wood Lily site. (K. L. Feder)

and the voracious appetites of bacteria, along with rough mechanical weathering due at least in part to freezing and thawing, produce a depositional environment not particularly hospitable to organic based material. The act of burning tends to protect bones, seeds, and nuts from various forms of decay, but animal bodies, including those of human beings, tend to last a very short time in the soil; flesh may take only decades to disappear, and bones may last only a century or two.

In other regions human remains fare far better, and skeletons commonly last quite well for centuries and even millennia. Under certain circumstances, where the insects and bacteria that recycle our bodies cannot thrive because it is too dry, too cold, or a combination of the two or where chemicals in the ground serve as a natural preservative, not only will skeletons survive, but so will flesh.

Conversing with the Dead: Bioarchaeology

(see chapter 13)

FIGURE 1.28 Examples of sharp-edged stone cutting tools found at the Wood Lily site. (K. L. Feder)

FIGURE 1.29 Close-up (ten power) of the used edge of one of the stone cutting tools found at the Wood Lily site. The irregular nature of the edge is the result, at least in part, of damage produced simply by using the tool in the manner in which it was intended. (K. L. Feder)

FIGURE 1.30 A moment seared in time; a child living in Pompeii, killed in the eruption of Vesuvius, A.D. 79. His body was covered in ash. When the ash hardened and his body decayed, a hollow mold was all that remained. Archaeologists filled the mold with plaster of Paris, producing the eerie specter of the child. (K. L. Feder)

In Danish peat bogs, for example, the natural chemical soup in the peat acts as a natural preservative, and nearly intact bodies have been recovered. Complete faces, hands, and fingers with observable fingerprints have been preserved for more than 4,000 years after burial (or was it disposal?) in the bogs. "Otzi," also called the Ice Man, is a relatively well preserved body that froze nearly 5,300 years ago; tattoos can still be discerned on his body (Spindler 1994).

Some cultures did not rely on nature to preserve dead bodies and attempted to preserve the remains of at least some important people. The desiccated, often ghoulish, remains of Egyptian mummies testify to the only partial success they achieved in their preservation practices.

On occasion, volcanic ash has preserved, if not human bodies, impressions of those bodies. For example, the ash fall produced by the cataclysmic eruption of Mt. Vesuvius in A.D. 79 encapsulated the bodies of some of the people (and even a dog) killed in the eruption that destroyed the Roman city of Pompeii. The remains disintegrated, leaving hollows in the precise form of the bodies of the people and dog at the moment of their deaths. Upon discovery of these natural molds, researchers poured in plaster, producing eerie casts of the victims of the eruption (Figure 1.30).

Preservation as found in the Ice Man, Egyptian mummies, and the Pompeii casts are the rare exception to the norm. When human remains are preserved at all, it is usually in the form of skeletons. A human skeleton is of great interest to the archaeologist because it provides, essentially, the autobiography of an ancient person with significant events written thereupon.

Conclusion

As I write this at the beginning of 2007, my son Josh, the baby whose birth coincided with the inception of the archaeological survey in Peoples State Forest that led us to the discovery of the Wood Lily site, is a twenty-year-old college student more than half-way through his junior year. His life, just like yours, is enormously different from that of a young adult who lived in the community we call Wood Lily. Consider just the stuff he has in his room here at home—his laptop, iPod, cell phone, digital camera, television (hooked up to cable), DVD player, and all the other crap that seems ready to explode from his bookshelves and that covers every available square inch of space on his furniture and even the floor. Compare just this material culture with the stuff we recovered through our excavation of the Wood Lily site, consisting almost entirely of stone tools used by people his and your age 3,000 years ago.

Wood Lily: Archaeological Portrait of a Life

(see chapter 14)

As we will see, some of those stone tools were used to chop, cut, and carve wood. Others were used to grind seeds or nuts and to dig up and then process root crops. Some may have been used to cut bark or reeds to make baskets. Many of the stone tools we found were used as parts of weapons to kill animals and prepare their remains for use—to butcher them, process them for eating, skin them, make cloth from their hides and then make clothing from the end product. Some of the excavated tools were used to make the stone tools just enumerated. There wasn't a digital device anywhere.

Now consider the fact that if you were to look at where your stuff was manufactured, you will probably find sources worldwide; we are part of a global economic system. For example, the iPod I ordered for my wife from the on-line Apple store on November 1, 2006, was shipped directly to our house from a factory in Shanghai and arrived in time for her November 9 birthday. Amazing. Compare that to the objects we found at Wood Lily. Almost certainly those stone tools were made right there with raw materials from no more than about one hundred miles away.

You, yourself, likely travel more in a year than a resident of that community would have traveled in his or her entire life. With satellite radio, cable news, and the internet you have constant access to prodigous quantities of information from all over the world. You probably drive a car, buy your food at a grocery store, have access to sophisticated medical care, and so on.

As different as your lives may be from those lived by the residents of Wood Lily, however, you share fundamental commonalities with them as well, and one of these, I suspect, is an innate curiosity about the world. I imagine the people who lived at Wood Lily would have been eager to know what the future held in store for the human race. It is unlikely that they could have imagined what the future held, and they certainly had no way of visting that future to find out. Here we all have a distinct advantage over the people at Wood Lily. Just as they may have been curious about what was to come, we are curious about what has been, but we can visit the past, we can travel through time thanks to the vehicle of archaeology. This book is about how we do it.

2 A Biography of Archaeology

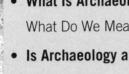

- **What Is Archaeology?**
  What Do We Mean by the Term *Culture*?

- **Is Archaeology a Science?**

- **How Did Archaeology Get Started in the First Place?**
  Why Is Archaeology in the Anthropology Department?

- **How Do You Get to Be an Archaeologist?**
  Who Owns the Past?
  What Kinds of People Go into Archaeology?

My brief introduction to the field research I directed in 1986 raises some obvious questions, not the least of which is: "What is archaeology, anyway?" There are so many misconceptions about what it is that archaeologists do and how they get to be archaeologists, this chapter provides answers to the most fundamental and obvious questions you might ask when I tell you that I am an archaeologist.

 What Is Archaeology?

A few years ago I received a phone call from a reporter who some months earlier had spent a few hours with my students and me at a 5,000-year-old archaeological site in the town of Avon, Connecticut. In preparing an article about the work I was doing in the Farmington River Valley, the reporter had asked lots of questions about what I do, and I had done my best—or so

I thought—to convey what it is that archaeologists hope to accomplish by spending their summers digging in the dirt.

We talked a lot about what archaeology is and what it isn't. "The dry, text-book definition," I told him, "usually presents archaeology as the study of the material remains of human behavior. People live and work at a place, using things that they have made. These things end up in the ground as people lose them, throw them away, or even put them away for safekeeping, and archaeologists attempt to figure out the nature of their lives by recovering and analyzing what remains of these things."

I tried to elaborate on this—let's face it—pretty boring description of the discipline to which I have devoted my life. "It's really all about passion," I told the reporter, "a passion for knowing about the past times and past lives of the human family." Where'd we come from and when? How have people survived for thousands, hundreds of thousands, and, if you include our most ancient ancestors, even millions of years? How did we, as a species, develop ways of life, a breathtaking variety of different **cultures**?

How did we, as a species, go from making tools that were little more than busted up rocks to creating things like Stonehenge and the pyramids? "Archaeology," I told the reporter, "focuses on the vast history of humanity, and it just so happens that we go about this by finding and analyzing some really cool stuff." The recognition that there actually is anything left from which to recover the ancient human story is, in itself, relatively recent, and archaeology, therefore, is really a rather young discipline, just a bit more than a century old.

As a result of this "immaturity," we don't have the answers to all the questions we might pose about the human past, and new and exciting discoveries are constantly being made. Archaeologists are always rewriting the past. That's part of what makes the discipline so exhilarating. I thought I did a good job of conveying my genuine excitement about the study of the human past, and the resulting article prepared by the reporter was well done. So, needless to say, I was more than a little perplexed when, just a few months later, this same reporter called me hoping to get a quote or two from me, as the resident expert on all things old and crumbly, for an article he was doing on a fascinating discovery that had just been made in Connecticut: dinosaur footprints behind the new mall being built just down the road from my university.

Dinosaur footprints. I don't know anything about dinosaur footprints (Figure 2.1). Dinosaurs became extinct some 65 million years ago. The earliest fossil forms of human ancestors have been dated to a little more than 4 million years old. I reminded the reporter of our lengthy discussion of just a few months before about what it is that I do, about how archaeology focuses on the *human* past. There had been nothing in our previous conversation that even hinted at a connection between archaeology and dinosaurs. "You may find it surprising to learn," I good-naturedly chided the reporter, "that *The Flintstones* is not based on a true story. Brontosauruses have never been used by people as excavating equipment at rock quarries, and nobody ever kept a dinosaur as a pet. There's a more than 60-million-year gap between the dinosaurs and what I study. It sounds like a fascinating discovery but I really can't help you on your article about the footprints."

FIGURE 2.1 Dinosaur footprints, indeed, are "really neat," but my succinct characterization to the newspaper reporter belied my general ignorance. I am, after all, an archaeologist and not a paleontologist. (K. L. Feder)

The poor reporter was crushed. He genuinely thought that, as an archaeologist, of course I would know all about dinosaur footprints and could provide him with an informative and juicy sound bite for the next day's paper. I tried to help out and gave him the name and number of a geologist who would be a far more appropriate source of information about dinosaurs and their footprints, but the reporter was not entirely satisfied. He was on a tight deadline to get the article into the next day's paper. He promised that he would try to contact the geologist but asked me for any insights that I could give him about dinosaurs. Feeling somewhat responsible for not making it clearer the last time we spoke that archaeologists are not **paleontologists** and that we don't study dinosaurs, I told the reporter, "Look. Dinosaur footprints are really neat. You can learn a lot about dinosaur behavior by looking at the prints. Now go and call a real expert, and you'll get something a lot more intelligent than that." You probably can guess the punch line for this story. The reporter was unable to contact the geologist, and, rather predictably, there I was in the paper the next day, the "expert" quoted—painfully accurately, I might add—as characterizing dinosaur footprints as "really neat." I have yet to live that one down among my colleagues in geology and paleontology.

OK, so archaeology is not paleontology. It's not geology, either. Though archaeologists need to know a fair amount about the various Earth sciences, we are not necessarily experts in any of them. People bring me rocks on a regular basis, expecting me to be able to expound on their age and origin. In one case a gentleman tracked me down because he needed an archaeologist to confirm his identification of a rock he had found as being a part of a meteorite. What possible connection this guy had made between the science that studies the human past and rocks of extraterrestrial origin that have fallen to Earth, I have no idea. I professed ignorance of meteors and sent the fellow to the meteorology professor on campus. Meteorology is, of course, the study of weather and has nothing to do with meteors, but at least *meteorology* has the word *meteor* in it.

A more common misconception about archaeology involves a narrowing of the geographic and temporal focus of the field. People are regularly surprised when they learn that I dig in Connecticut and not Egypt or Greece. My dentist confessed that he assumed that the archaeological research he knew I was conducting in Connecticut represented little more than practice, a sort of rehearsal for the really important work I might someday do in Egypt. Certainly there are archaeologists who excavate sites in Egypt and Greece, not to mention Rome and Israel. But there also are vibrant, active archaeology programs in India, China, England, Zimbabwe, Australia, Peru, Mexico, and all places in between (and, oh yeah, Connecticut, New Jersey, Arizona, Alaska, and the rest). Anywhere people lived in the past, archaeology can help us discover the nature of their lives (Figure 2.2).

Further, contrary to most people's assumption, archaeology is not restricted to any particular period of time in the past. Archaeology is not the study of people before the birth of Christ or before the Bible or before agriculture or before the development of urban life or necessarily before anything. Archaeology cannot even be defined as the study of the past before writing. The first written records of king lists, palace inventories, genealogies, tax roles, calendars, and so on do not replace the archaeological record of these ancient societies, they complement and supplement it, adding to the database of our study of the human past.

I often have a difficult time convincing people that I am not looking for jewels or treasures that will one day make me fabulously wealthy. Many people assume a stereotype of archaeology based on what they may have heard about King Tut's spectacular tomb or people who call themselves "archaeologists" and plunder old ships for profit, looking for gold coins, precious stones, and other valuable cargo. The truth is that the vast majority of what I have dug up in the nearly three decades I have been involved in archaeological fieldwork has been not treasure but trash, stuff people thought so little of they disposed of it in a garbage pit, tossed it on the disposal pile, or simply left it where it dropped, but in that trash archaeologists find a narrative written in the language of **material culture,** a text that tells the story of ancient lives and past cultures.

Finally, I suppose I will never quite understand what inspired a property owner in a nearby town to leave a frantic message on the department voicemail expressing the immediate need for an archaeologist because giant bees were burrowing a hole in her backyard. Archaeology is not about dinosaurs (or their footprints), rocks, meteors, or giant burrowing bees. It is about the study of the material record left behind by past people's in an attempt to shine a light on the human experience, a story whose origins stretch back across the millennia.

What Do We Mean by the Term *Culture*?

Archaeologists use the word *culture* a lot. It comes with the territory; we are, after all, **anthropologists,** and culture is a concept central to that field. We anthropologists argue a lot, and you probably would have a hard time getting any group of us to come up with a universally accepted or approved definition of culture. In one approach culture is defined as the extrasomatic means of adaptation. The prefix *extra* means "beyond" and the word *somatic* means "the body." A "means of adaptation" is just another way of saying "a strategy for survival." Translating our original definition, then, our characterization of the word *culture* becomes "the beyond-the-body strategy for survival," and in yet other words, those elements of human existence beyond what our body offers that enable us to live.

FIGURE 2.2 Assortment of archaeological sites: Wood Lily (Connecticut, top); Skara Brae (Scotland, center); Pueblo Bonito (New Mexico, bottom). (K. L. Feder)

That definition, however, may be a bit too restrictive, especially if you interpret it to mean that culture consists only of those practical behaviors that enable us physically to survive. Certainly culture includes the hardware—tools, clothing, housing—and practices—hunting animals, fishing, shellfish collecting, gathering wild plants, agriculture, raising livestock—that contribute to our subsistence and immediate survival, but it is much, much more. Culture is inclusive, encompassing all the stuff that human beings, with our large brains and enormous intelligence, have thought up, discovered, created, devised, learned, formulated, contrived, and conceived. Of course, culture comprises all the ways in which we manipulate the environment to suit our needs and wants, including how we fabricate our tools, make our clothing, build houses, and so on. At the same time, all customs, beliefs, ceremonies, traditions, social practices, religious behaviors, politcal systems, economic practices, and moral beliefs and how we educate our children, make social connections, marry, live our lives, and even bury our dead are all practices that represent culture. In a very real sense all such behaviors, whether directly related to survival or further removed from the day-to-day practices of putting food on the table and a roof over your head, also are part of a strategy for survival for a species that lives and works cooperatively in social groups.

Human beings are not the only organisms that have culture. A good argument can be made that chimpanzees rely to some extent on their invention of tools (which they have been seen to refine, improve, and elaborate), whose manufacture adults explicitly assist their young to master, and the styles of which vary from group to group (Figure 2.3; Mercader, Panger, and Boesch 2002).

We humans, however, are the only species for whom culture is the primary means by which it adapts to its surroundings. Human beings can live anywhere on the face of the planet and, for that matter, underwater and even in outer space, not because we have developed physical or somatic adjustments to life in these places, but because we have *invented* ways to survive. Consider the following comparison of two species of mammals that inhabit the Arctic: polar bears (*Ursus maritimus*) and people (*Homo sapiens*). Polar bears thrive in the extreme conditions that characterize the Arctic because they are supremely well adapted to life there; that is, they are somatically tailored to life under the Arctic's frigid conditions (Figure 2.4).

Perhaps most obviously, polar bears are supremely well-adapted hunters as a result of their great size, enormous strength, sharp claws, and powerful jaws. Beyond this polar bears have a thick coat of fur, and each hair is actually hollow. The air trapped inside provides an additional boost to the fur's insulative properties. Polar bears also have a thick layer of fat as much as 11.5 centimeters (4.5 inches) thick beneath their protective fur. Between the fur and the blubber polar bears suffer virtually no heat loss; apparently, the bears can scarcely be picked up by infrared tracking devices because they experience so little heat loss from their bodies. Polar bears may look white, but their fur is actually free of pigment; each strand is transparent. The hollow shaft of each strand of fur scatters visible sunlight, producing the appearance of whiteness, much in the way that snow looks white even though it is just a form of frozen water without any color. The white appearance of a polar bear is highly advantageous for

FIGURE 2.3 Wild chimp using stone hammers and stone anvils in Liberia, West Africa, to crack open nutritious nuts, the shells of which litter the ground. Chimps use tools, refine them, and teach their offspring how to use them, and chimps living in different territories have even developed their own different styles of tools. (Courtesy William C. McGrew; Alison Hannah, photographer)

FIGURE 2.4 Polar bears are supremely well adapted to life in the harsh conditions of the Arctic. Their adaptation is biological; nature has provided them with the physical characteristics necessary for their survival. (© John Conrad/ CORBIS)

a predator who needs to be able to sneak up on its prey in an environment with lots of snow-covered, white backgrounds.

Further, polar bear skin exudes a thick, waterproofing oil that serves as a protective barrier against moisture. I recently spent a cold and rainy day at a zoo where one of the resident polar bears was leisurely and quite comfortably swimming in the frigid waters of its artificial pond. When the bear came out of the water, a quick shake almost instantly removed nearly all the water from its fur.

Polar bears also have roughly circular, enormously broad feet, up to 30.5 centimeters (12 inches) in diameter. This feature allows polar bears, which can weigh nearly 700 kilograms (1,500 pounds) in the case of large adult males, to walk efficiently on top of a relatively thin skim of ice overlying a powdery snow base. Other animals—caribou, for example—will quickly exhaust their energy cracking through the ice while attempting to escape from a hungry polar bear. Furthermore, polar bear toes are webbed, making them handy and efficient paddles when the polar bear goes for a swim, which is often, seals being a favorite food.

The natives of the American Arctic, the Inuit people (more commonly called Eskimos) have none of the polar bear's somatic adaptations to life in the Arctic: no dense layer of blubber underlying their skin, no thick coat of insulative fur, no large webbed feet, and so on. However, the Inuit have something the polar bears don't: a human brain that affords them the ability to respond to the challenges of the Arctic intellectually, to invent a culture that is brilliantly well adapted to life under the same conditions in which polar bears live (Figure 2.5)

FIGURE 2.5 The Inuit people have adapted to life in Arctic not by any particular physical adaptation, but by their intelligence and ingenuity. Their strategy for survival has resulted from their ability to respond intellectually to the challenges of life in their environment. (© Galen Rowell/ CORBIS)

Inuit people may not have a thick layer of fur, but they know who does and they know how to get it from them (polar bears, among other animals) by techniques of hunting, butchering, hide preparation, and the production of clothing. Similarly, unlike the polar bear, Inuit feet aren't particularly well adapted to walking on snow, but the Inuit figured out the practical physics behind the advantages of a broad distribution of body weight for walking on top of snow and ice and applied this knowledge in their invention of snow-shoes. The parka, a knee- or thigh-length outer garment that includes a fur-lined hood, is another invention of the Inuit. The igloo (an Inuit word), which is an efficiently designed little domed domicile that retains heat and is manufactured from the most abundant raw material available in the Arctic, ice; the kayak (another Inuit word), a boat used in their tradition of hunting marine mammals; harpoons; waterproof clothing; and even eye protection against the bright Arctic Sun (not quite sunglasses, but a wrap-around piece of bone or ivory with a thin slit that lets in just enough light to see but not enough to produce snow-blindness) are all elements of Inuit inventiveness and resourcefulness. These objects and the behaviors that led to their invention, elaboration, refinement, and application are part of Inuit culture, indeed, their "extrasomatic means of adaptation."

So, when archaeologists dig up stuff, the items we painstakingly recover, return to the lab, and intensively analyze represent the material remains of a people's culture, the physical remnants of their extrasomatic means of adaptation. By studying these objects, in other words, archaeologists reveal the nature of past people's strategies for survival.

Read More

To learn more about how anthropologists think about culture—and to see how the study of chimpanzee tool-making traditions are causing us to reassess how we define what makes us uniquely human—any of the following resources offer a good start:

Haviland, W. 2001. *Cultural Anthropology*. Wadsworth, Belmont, California.

Kottak, C. 2004. *Anthropology: The Exploration of Human Diversity*. McGraw-Hill, New York.

Mercader, J., M. Panger, and C. Boesch. 2002. Excavation of a Chimpanzee Stone Tool Site in the African Rainforest. *Science* 296:1452–55.

Park, M. A. 2003. *Introducing Anthropology: An Integrated Approach*. McGraw-Hill, New York.

Schultz, E. A., and R. H. Lavenda. 2000. *Anthropology: A Perspective on the Human Condition*. McGraw-Hill, New York.

 ## Is Archaeology a Science?

Today most archaeologists would agree that archaeology is the scientific pursuit of the past. We think about the past, about how people lived at a certain place and time, how they adapted to local environmental conditions, how they responded when those conditions changed, how they got along with their neighbors (or how they didn't), how they altered their behavior when new people moved into the neighborhood, how new technologies changed their lives; in other words, archaeology is the scientific study of the cultures of past peoples. We assess these elements of the lives of those peoples by reference to the material, archaeological record, the stuff that people made, used, discarded, lost, and generally just left behind.

It is our goal to examine this evidence of past times and past lives in a way that is unbiased and objective. We have no axe to grind or point to prove— at least we shouldn't. We look for patterns or correlations in the evidence we collect and raise questions about those patterns and correlations. For example:

1. Why did the people at the Wood Lily site use flint to make their tools when other stone could have been obtained more easily?
2. Why did the people at the Netiv Hagdud site in Israel shift their subsistence focus about 11,000 years ago from wild plants and animals to domesticates?
3. What motivated people living in Europe more than 30,000 years ago to begin painting on cave walls realistic images of the animals they encountered outside the caves?
4. How can we explain the fact that beginning more than 6,000 years ago people in various places throughout the Old and New Worlds independently abandoned egalitarian social patterns in which everyone had equivalent amounts of wealth and control over their own lives and adopted stratified systems whereby the few accumulated sufficient wealth and power to mobilize—some might say "coerce"—the many to build great monuments such as pyramids and palaces?

Based on the preserved physical evidence of (1) the use of lithic raw materials at a particular site, (2) the diet of an ancient people, (3) the artwork in a particular place and time, or (4) communally constructed monuments worldwide, archaeologists suggest explanations and propose hypotheses to explain the— perceived patterns. Following the patterns noticed above

1. Perhaps flint is so superior to local materials for producing sharp-edged tools, the people at the Wood Lily site were willing to travel or trade for it.
2. Maybe climate change in the Middle East 11,000 years ago made a shift toward agriculture sensible.
3. Conceivably, the cave painters of Europe were recording successful hunts in their artwork.
4. Perhaps the need to coordinate the labor of large groups of people— for defensive walls around settlements or irrigation canals to extend agricultural fields in order to produce food for an increasing population— led to social and economic divisions within societies that resulted, ultimately, in power and wealth concentrated in the hands of a small group of people.

Next, we deduce what additional data should be found if our initial hypotheses are to be upheld. In testing each hypothesis just suggested

1. We should be able to show experimentally that flint is more efficient—it cuts more readily and maintains an edge longer—than the quartz or horn-fels available close to Wood Lily for cutting into animal flesh.
2. Paleoclimatological data should show a shift in climate—perhaps it got drier or cooler, diminishing the productivity of the wild foods upon which inhabitants in the Middle East relied immediately before the people at Netiv Hagdud shifted their food base. Others in the same region might be expected to exhibit the same process.
3. Archaeological evidence at habitation sites outside the European painted caves should reveal the bones of killed and butchered animals matching the species depicted in the cave art.
4. In Egypt, Mesopotamia, the Indus Valley, Mesoamerica, and elsewhere we would expect the archaeological record to show the presence of large, communal, utilitarian projects that benefited the great mass of people—things like canals and defensive walls—preceding the appearance of large-scale projects that would have benefited only a few wealthy and powerful people.

We go out and test our hypotheses by assessing such lists of predictions of what must have been true if the hypotheses we suggested based on patterns we initially saw in the data are to be upheld. In this way we may uphold them, refute them entirely, or propose revisions that will require further research, rethinking, and retesting. Archaeology is a social science that reveals the nature of the human past through the study of the material remnants of that past.

How Did Archaeology Get Started in the First Place?

The presumption that is at the core of archaeology—that there is a past that is not written down or spoken, but that we can nevertheless learn about, a past that can teach us things about ourselves and our species—is not exactly self-evident. After all, the present is fleeting, and it isn't all that obvious that much remains materially of the present once it becomes a part of the past. The science of archaeology, however (as well as the focus of this book), is all about retrieving and studying those material remains of the past that endure. The recognition that the past prevails into the present, at least in an attenuated form, rests at the heart of archaeology, no matter the particular agendas of those who spend their time revealing that past. If we hope to answer the question posed by the title of this section, we need to learn when people first recognized the fundamental fact of a materially enduring past upon which all archaeology ultimately is based.

It is probably fair to say that the origins of archaeology, long before it earned that name, can be traced to the recognition that some elements of the past—abandoned structures, things people lost or discarded, items left behind and simply not reclaimed—continue to survive in the present and can be recovered and studied for the insights they may provide about the lives lived before our own. Of course, it is impossible to determine exactly when this recognition was made, when a human being, perhaps walking along the eroding edge of a stream channel, first picked up a broken piece of pottery whose style and form were unrecognizable. The discoverer may have wondered about the person who made it and in so doing presaged the work of archaeology. We cannot know when someone burying the remains of a comrade first encountered the bones of an unknown individual, coincidentally interred at that same spot at some time in the past, and then wondered who this past person was and when they lived. Events like these must have occurred on countless occasions in the past, but they have left little evidence for us in the present.

Consider, for example, King Nabonidus, who ruled Babylon more than 2,500 years ago. Though not an archaeologist in a modern sense, Nabonidus was fascinated by the ruins of Larsa, one of his predecessor's cities and which, as one of his scribes noted, "had long been a desert and become ruins, beneath dust and rubble" (from the *Inscription of Larsa*, a 2,500-year-old account of Nabonidus's discovery as cited in Schnapp 1996). Nabonidus conscripted a force armed not with swords and arrows but picks and shovels, setting them to work removing that "dust and rubble" that had encased the ancient city. Nabonidus next gathered together specialists to read the ancient inscriptions and to restore the site to its original glory. Nabonidus's explicit agenda in his archaeological and restorative endeavors was to pay homage to the kings and Babylonian gods of antiquity and, in so doing, gain the favor of the gods who had ruled over the excavated city in its heyday. It wasn't archaeology in any sense we now recognize, but the actions of the Babylonian king were based on a recognition that the past endures in material ways and that, with the removal of enough "dust and rubble," it can be revealed in the present.

It is clear, at least in terms of the development of the historical sciences in Western societies, that an explicit recognition of the persistence of the past in the present, enabling "modern" people to study the past directly, became obvious and important as far back as the Renaissance. At that point scholars and researchers explicitly recognized that ancient remains represented a form of evidence about the past. These thinkers further conluded that study of these remains illuminates the lives of the people who made, used, and left them behind, much in the way that reading a historical monograph provides insights into the life and time of the person who wrote it.

The Renaissance of the 1300s though 1500s involved an explicit attempt on the part of Europeans to recapture the knowledge of the ancients, specifically the Greeks, Romans, and, before them, the Egyptians, knowledge that was supposed to have been lost and forgotten after the fall of Rome in the fifth century A.D. Though travel was difficult, with parts of the land afflicted by difficult and unstable political conditions, a small handful of Europeans were able to travel to Egypt before the end of the eighteenth century. These visitors returned with stories of the remnants of a spectacular antique civilization whose obvious great age and level of architectural achievement seemed to provide evidence for the notion of

FIGURE 2.6 Engraving depicting the great emperor of France, Napoleon, contemplating the sculpted visage of one of the great pharaohs of ancient Egypt as presented in the Great Sphinx. Napoleon's attempt at conquest in Egypt was a military and political failure, but it played an important role in encouraging the study of Europeans of that nation's ancient history. (© Bettman/ CORBIS)

FIGURE 2.7 Ancient features of the historical landscape, such as this well-preserved segment of a wall built by the Romans under their emperor Hadrian (A.D. 122–126) in England, provide physical evidence of ancient societies. (Courtesy Michael A. Park)

a past "golden age" whose study might allow for the recapture of lost knowledge and wisdom (Fagan 1994; Stiebing 1993). The trickle of European visitors to Egypt became a torrent after Napoleon Bonaparte led a military campaign there in 1798. In his ultimately failed attempt at conquest, Napoleon brought along a contingent of scholars as well as soldiers who spent their time measuring, mapping, drawing, and studying the monuments of ancient Egypt (Figure 2.6).

Closer to home, Greek temples and Roman ruins abounded, and not just in Greece and Rome. The Romans, especially, had a far-flung empire, and the aboveground ruins of Roman roads, baths, and walls are found in much of Europe. It certainly made sense for Europeans during the Renaissance to study these material remnants of the past if they wished to recover and rejuvenate the art, architecture, and science of the perceived golden age of classical civilization (Figure 2.7). An awareness of a surviving material manifestation of the past, a sort of ancient history written in crumbling walls and ruined Roman temples, alerted scholars of the time to the existence of a much broader and far more ancient language of human antiquity written not in crumbling roads and deteriorating temples but in bronze daggers, shards of pottery, and stone spearheads and axes, all things that substantially predated classical civilization.

The stone tools found in deep deposits especially perplexed and fascinated European scholars. The Old and New Testaments of the Bible represented not just blueprints for how people should live their lives but also a chronology of the history of the world beginning with its creation by God. That chronology had no opening for a period of time in human history in which tools were made primarily of stone; in fact, according to Genesis, brass metallurgy was used at least as far back as Noah's time. In 1650 James Ussher, archbishop of Ireland, had managed to cram the entire history of the world as represented in the Old and New Testaments of the Bible into a little more than 5,600 years. Ussher had determined that God began the creation week in 4004 B.C. In Ussher's calculation the entire universe that modern scientists believe to be something like 15 billion years old was actually only about 0.00004% of that age.

So, with no existing concept of a "stone age" and an incredibly compressed time scale to work with, it was not apparent to many European thinkers who examined the often quite artfully rendered stone axes found in deep deposits that these objects were the products of human craft from some ancient age. Some actually believed that the stones had resulted from the recent activities of gnomes and elves, going so far as to call the finely crafted stone axes "fairy stones." Others took a more "scientific" approach, ascribing them to natural causes, especially lightning strikes, calling the symmetrical stone axes "thunderstones." Of course, a few discoverers who found these objects in the soil and then analyzed them realized that no natural process could have crafted them, and, barring a belief in fairies, the objects had to be the work of human artisans.

A young Englishman, John Frere, found some of these objects at the bottom of a deep shaft in a quarry in the English village of Hoxne in 1797 (Figure 2.8). The tools were located at a depth of at least 12 feet and beneath three distinct layers of soil. Furthermore, the soil layer directly overlying the stone tools contained marine shells and the bones of extinct animals (Stiebing 1993). Frere reported on the appearance and context of the stone tools he had excavated to the London Society of Antiquaries, deducing that their context led to the inevitable conclusion that they dated to "a very remote period indeed; even beyond that of the present world,"

FIGURE 2.8 One of the finely crafted stone tools recovered and analyzed by John Frere deep in a clay pit in the English village of Hoxne in 1797. Objects like these caused a stir because the possibility that there had been a time in history when stone tools dominated human material culture seemed not to fit the accepted biblical chronology of the world.

and clearly indicated the existence of an ancient race of human beings who, again as Frere phrased it, "had not the use of metals" (Frere 1800:204).

Frere's report and the work of others who discovered and reported on stone tools and weapons in contexts that implied great antiquity played a significant role in opening and broadening the vista of the past. Most significant, in the context of the discussion here, whatever debates ensued about the specific meaning of the stone tools, they clearly showed that items made in what turned out to be an ancient period had survived into the present. The discovery at Hoxne and those that followed showed absolutely that ancient objects could be found in the soil where they had been left by their makers in a remote period and could be studied, analyzed, and argued about; in other words, these objects could make a contribution to our understanding of the past, and this forms the basis for the science of archaeology.

Just as in the Old World, archaeology in America began as an attempt to solve a number of historical mysteries, not the least of which concerned (as detailed in the next section of this chapter) the origin of the native peoples. At the same time, as settlers moved west from the original thirteen colonies and settled in areas that were to become the states of Ohio, Illinois, and Indiana, an enormous level of interest arose after the discovery of apparently ancient monuments of piled and shaped earth that were ubiquitous across the landscape of the American Midwest. These included thousands of conical mounds up to 24 meters (80 feet) in height that had been built as apparent burial monuments overlaying the graves of sometimes dozens of individuals, effigy mounds (essentially monumental sculptures made of earth in the shapes of bears, birds, human beings, snakes, etc.), and truly enormous flat-topped pyramids of piled-up earth that had served as the platforms for wooden temples (Figure 2.9).

Who could have produced the enormous number of monuments scattered across the landscape? Had it been Indians? Many disclaimed this idea, libeling the ability of Native Americans to have produced earthworks of a size that would have required large, coordinated workforces. Archaeologists Gordon Willey and Jeremy Sabloff (1993) reasonably characterize the first phase of American archaeology as "The Speculative Period" as artifacts were collected and analyzed in an attempt not so much to test but to bolster the speculations of those who felt that the mounds must have been built by ancient visitors from Asia, Europe, or Africa.

Many archaeologists (and you were an archaeologist if you simply called yourself one) had pet "theories" about the origins of American Indians and the builders of the midwestern mounds and, rather then testing them, went out and uncritically accepted virtually any data—some of it fabricated in the form of artifacts engraved with text written in Old World alphabets—that seemed to fit those preconceived notions. The two "Newark Holy Stones", ostensibly found in association with two Ohio mound sites, are an example. The "Keystone" and the "Decalogue" were engraved with inscriptions in two quite different versions of Hebrew; the Keystone bore four brief religious phrases, and the Decalogue presented a version of the Ten Commandments. The two artifacts were fakes intended to convince historians and archaeologists that

FIGURE 2.9 Three different kinds of earthworks built by Native Americans in the American Midwest: a 20-meter high, conical burial mound (the Miamisburg Mound, in central Ohio, top); an effigy mound (Serpent Mound, in southern Ohio, center); and a temple mound (Monks Mound, a 30-meter high truncated pyramid that served as the platform for a temple, at the Cahokia site in Collinsville, Illinois, bottom). (K. L. Feder)

ancient Jewish visitors to the American Midwest had something to do with the construction of the earthworks (Lepper and Gill 2000).

As American archaeology evolved and as speculations about America's past were tested with data, researchers recognized that an accurate chronological framework for New World prehistory was crucial. At the turn of the twentieth century, researchers began to emphasize stratigraphy, the layering apparent at many archaeological sites, and to interpret that layering in terms of regional chronological sequences. Much of the archaeology conducted in the first half of the twentieth century focused on the illumination of regional sequences, an enumeration of what happened when. When did people first arrive in the New World? What was their adaptation? What was the sequence of change in their spear point styles? When did they develop ceramics? What was the sequence of change in their pottery styles? When did they develop agriculture? How did they respond to the arrival of Europeans in the fifteenth and sixteenth centuries? In the first half of the twentieth century, archaeology was oriented toward the collection of data, its sometimes relentless description, and understanding the variable of time.

For a long time many archaeologists assumed that chronology and description were about all archaeologists could accomplish, Although there were glimmerings of the desire to do more with the archaeological record, it was not until the 1960s that a truly dramatic alteration of the focus and purpose of archaeological research—a paradigm shift—occurred. A catalyst for this revolution in thinking about the past was archaeologist Lewis Binford, who wrote a highly influential article titled "Archaeology as Anthropology."

Binford argued that archaeology could do far more than merely provide descriptive time charts about the human past. Archaeology, he argued, was in a unique position to illuminate the evolution of the human cultural adaptation. After all, archaeological evidence is uniquely deep, reflecting not just a thin slice of time in the history of a particular group or of humanity as a whole, but revealing long stretches of time. Archaeology is anthropology over the long haul, showing how human groups change, react, adapt, adjust, and respond to challenges over the entire history of a specific group or, of humanity as a whole. Even the longest-lived cultural anthropologist can investigate and experience a particular group of people over the course of only several decades. The process, nature, and meaning of culture change may be best understood over the course of many human generations, extending far beyond the lifetime of any individual scholar researching such change. The archaeologist, however, can examine the ebb and flow of a group of people over the course of several millennia, tens of millennia, and even millions of years in the case of the human species.

Read More

The following sources (including John Frere's own discussion of his discoveries and a compendium of first-hand accounts of many of the most significant archaeological discoveries in Fagan 1996) provide a wealth of information about the roots and history of archaeology.

Fagan, B. M., ed. 1996. *Eyewitness to Discovery: First-Person Accounts of More Than Fifty of the World's Greatest Archaeological Discoveries.* Oxford University Press, Oxford.

Frere, J. 1800. Account of flint weapons discovered in Hoxne in Suffolk. *Archaeologia* 13:204–05.

Stiebing Jr., W. H. 1993. *Uncovering the Past: A History of Archaeology.* Oxford University Press, New York.

Van Riper, A. B. 1993. *Men Among the Mammoths: Victorian Science and the Discovery of Human Prehistory.* University of Chicago Press, Chicago.

Willey, G. R., and J. A. Sabloff. 1993. *A History of American Archaeology.* W. H. Freeman & Co., New York.

WHY IS ARCHAEOLOGY IN THE ANTHROPOLOGY DEPARTMENT?

In all likelihood the course you are taking and for which you are reading this book is offered by the anthropology department at your college or university. You might have thought that a course about ancient history would be in the history department or, perhaps, in a department of its own, but, at least in America, that is not generally the case. The reason for this is primarily historical.

The archaeological study of ancient Greece and Rome naturally fell within the purview of European historians and history departments because those cultures possessed writing systems that, conveniently, could be read by modern Europeans. In other words, in excavating archaeological sites produced by ancient Romans and Greeks, European scholars were merely extending the focus of history from written documents to the tools, buildings, and burials left behind by the same people who had written the documents. Archaeology in Europe became history through the analysis of hardware.

Even when the writing systems found on artifacts were indecipherable to European historians in the seventeenth, eighteenth, nineteenth, and even twentieth centuries (for example, the ancient Etruscan language found in Italy), and even if there was no writing system at all (for example, in the settlements of the first farmers of Europe or among the people who built monuments like Stonehenge), archaeology conducted in Europe still was the study by European scholars of the ancient history of their own ancestors as broadly defined. As such, even the archaeology of very ancient preliterate societies in Europe was considered by most an extension of the work of historians and was conducted within history departments.

The people of ancient America, however, pretty clearly were not Europeans. They were recognized as "others," and the study of such non-European "others" was understood by European scholars as being the focus of anthropologists. As a result, the study of the ancestors of living, native peoples who clearly were not connected to European history was similarly viewed as being the purview of anthropologists, in this case a cadre of archaeologists who were not, strictly speaking, historians but anthropologists of lives past.

During the European Age of Exploration, when Europeans encountered peoples for the first time in Africa and in Asia, they interpreted their presence within a biblical framework. The Bible story of a great flood that destroyed most life on the planet, including all but a handful of human beings, was taken literally by most Europeans; in this view, all living human beings must be descendants of the few who were saved from the Flood. Tracing all of humanity back to those believed to have ridden out the universal deluge onboard Noah's ark, Europeans linked individuals in Noah's family, especially his three sons and each of their wives, to the human races as recognized by Europeans. The Bible states that Noah and his wife had three sons, Japheth, Ham, and Shem, and many European thinkers identified these men as the ancestors of, respectively, Europeans, Africans, and Asians. It was believed that once the flood waters receded, each of the sons along with their respective wives and children headed off from the ark's landing place on "the mountains of Ararat." Japheth traveled to the north and west to Europe, Ham migrated to the south and west to Africa, and Shem moved to the east to Asia.

This interpretation seemed reasonable so long as Europeans could argue that there were, indeed, three and only three separate human races. However, upon entering into the New World, Europeans encountered indigenous peoples whose existence and presence didn't quite fit into the existing paradigm. How were the Indians traceable to the three sons of Noah? Were they the descendants of Japheth, Ham, or Shem? Or were the Indians members of a different, previously unknown race of people. Did the presence of people in the New World represent, perhaps, a separate creation of human beings by God, a creation not discussed in the Bible?

European curiosity about the presence of Native Americans inspired some to study them in an effort either to connect them historically to one of the three recognized human races—and, therefore, to one of Noah's three sons—or to prove that they were the result of a separate "genesis." Missionaries and others collected information about Indian religions, traditions, and practices, searching for similarities between them and those of people in the Old World. For example, where Indians practiced circumcision, a historical connection was proposed between them and Old World Jews. The physical attributes of Indians, especially their often thick, dark hair and the appearance of their eyes, were seen by some as evidence of a link between the native population of the New World and Asia, evidence that they were descendants of Noah's son Shem.

At the same time that the physical characteristics and cultural practices of Indians were being examined in an attempt to determine their ancestry, the physical remnants of their ancient, abandoned villages and monuments were being investigated, again in an effort to find evidence linking them to specific groups in the Old World. Were the pyramids of Mesoamerica evidence of the movement of ancient Egyptians to the New World? Were the great earthen mounds of the American Midwest traceable to Asia? Were artifacts found in Ohio genuinely inscribed with ancient Hebrew characters, proving a connection between Native Americans and ancient Israelites?

The desire to solve the riddle of the origins of the native peoples of the New World required the combined use of ethnographic and archaeological evidence—the study both of living peoples and of the archaeological remains of the ancestors of those living people. This two-pronged approach to the perceived mystery of the native peoples of the New World is broadly responsible for the joining of what were, in other parts of the world, two separate disciplines: one that studied living groups of people and one that studied the ancient past.

Chapter 2: Interactive Exercise

 ## How Do You Get to Be an Archaeologist?

I call myself an archaeologist and have undergraduate and graduate training in archaeology, along with more than twenty years of experience conducting archaeological research. That makes me an archaeologist. But the fact of the matter is, there is no universally accepted, legal definition of the term *archaeologist*, no formal or binding prerequisites for calling yourself an archaeologist. In truth, anyone can have a set of business cards and some stationary printed saying that he or she is an archaeologist, and she or he can excavate sites on private property as long as permission has been obtained from the landowner (see What Laws Regulate Where Archaeologists Can Dig? in chapter 4). And, in fact, while you rarely will find neurosurgery hobbyists or avocational nuclear physicists, there are probably more amateur archaeologists than there are trained professionals.

On the other hand, the federal and most state governments, in a sense, do legally define "who is an archaeologist" through a set of regulations and guidelines determining who can conduct archaeological research, at least on federal and state property. Most governmental agencies also have policies concerning who can participate in archaeological projects, mandated by those agencies to conform to federal, state, and local laws protecting archaeological and historical sites. You may call yourself an "archaeologist," but if you don't fulfill the requirements for training and experience established by the federal or local state government, you cannot practice archaeology on public lands, although under most circumstances these restrictions do not apply on private property. For example, in the group of federal regulations labeled 43 CFR 7, Section 7.8a, a less than catchy title, I will admit (http://www.cr.nps.gov/lawlinks.htm), the federal government lists the training and experiential requirements for an applicant who proposes to excavate an archaeological site on federal property. These include, among a number of guidelines, a graduate degree in anthropology, archaeology, or equivalent training and experience; at least 16 months of experience or training in archaeological fieldwork, laboratory work, or library work; and a demonstrated ability to conduct research to its timely completion. These regulations are in place to ensure that any individual who applies for a permit to dig on public lands or any person who submits an archaeological proposal in response to a call for bids for legally required research has adequate training and enough experience to properly conduct the work.

These governmental policies concerning the qualifications of an archaeologist who wants to dig on federal land or participate in a federally funded archaeological project make a lot of sense. Archaeological sites on federal land are perceived to belong to us all and, in essence, to be held in trust by the government for the communal good, resources from which all American citizens can learn and be inspired. The government takes its responsibility seriously, and a fundamental goal of policies and regulations concerning who can excavate archaeological sites on federal property is that of protection, ensuring that if sites are excavated, they are done so proficiently and that the information they contain is shared with the public who, after all, "own" the sites and pay, through taxes, for their study.

The cardinal rule for physicians in their Hippocratic Oath applies equally well to archaeologists: "First, do no harm." Archaeological evidence is rare, precious, and of enormous scientific value. Without careful data recovery objects can be damaged or destroyed, and their **contexts** and **spatial associations** may be lost. Archaeological data can be likened to a nonrenewable, endangered resource; in fact, archaeological materials are often called **cultural resources.** No one is making any more 2,000-year-old pottery or 10,000-year-old stone tools. It would be a terrible irony if in the attempt to recover these kinds of objects they were destroyed by someone ignorant of the best ways to preserve the information they can provide.

To maintain the integrity of the information provided by the archaeological record, it certainly is best for an archaeologist to have appropriate training and experience. In the United States a trained archaeologist ordinarily will have obtained an undergraduate degree, most often in the discipline of **anthropology,** the general study of humanity, although there are archaeologists with undergraduate degrees in history, geography, geology, art history, classical studies, and even archaeology itself. A few universities in the United States offer a separate degree in archaeology, but most archaeology programs continue to be subsumed under anthropology departments. Undergraduate training ordinarily includes an extensive and diverse program of coursework in the study of **culture, prehistory,** history, genealogy, **material culture,** geology, **osteology,** ecology, statistical analysis, and archaeological theory and method. Virtually all archaeology programs require laboratory and field experience before conferral of a degree. Many universities offer field schools in archaeology—intensive projects, ordinarily offered in the summer, in which students are trained in the basic skills of archaeological **site survey, excavation,** mapping, lab work, and analysis. It is learning by doing, and it is the only way to train in archaeological fieldwork. Field school training is not a one-way street, and students make a valuable contribution to the research. My own field research has been made possible by the labor of countless students who were being trained in archaeological field methods.

Individuals with an undergraduate degree in anthropology or a related field and training in fieldwork or lab work as a part of that degree program can gain employment in archaeology or work as a volunteer on a project, usually as a digger on a field crew or as a lab assistant cleaning and cataloging artifacts and preparing samples for more detailed analysis. An individual with a great deal of field experience might serve as a field crew chief, directing those digging **test pits** or in **excavation units.**

Archaeologists do much more than dig, and some focus on the analysis of sites already excavated. In fact, my Ph.D. dissertation (Feder 1982) focused on the spatial distribution of archaeological material at a site in the Aleutian

Islands (a place called Anangula) that had already been excavated when I entered graduate school. Especially because many archaeological sites have been excavated recently as a result of federal and state historic preservation laws, there is a backlog of sites that have been excavated but not fully analyzed and published. Some archaeologists spend very little time in the field and occupy much of their time examining archaeological materials excavated by and records produced by other researchers.

Ordinarily, to progress in archaeology and to go on to conduct one's own research, eventually to be the **principal investigator** of a project or to teach at a university, a graduate degree is essential. Like all sciences, archaeology has a vast and growing database, and in general one needs an intensive exposure to what is already known about the human past and its study before one can direct a complex field project. Though some archaeologists conclude their academic training at the master's degree level, completion of a doctoral dissertation is sometimes perceived as a necessary indicator that an individual is capable of designing a research project, conducting research, and conveying the results of the work. A Ph.D. is often a requirement for employment as a professor at a university.

Finally, there is a private and voluntary listing of qualified archaeologists called the Register of Professional Archaeologists (RPA). This listing compiles the names of archaeologists who have applied to and been accepted for inclusion on the basis of their academic training in archaeology, their experience, and their conformance to basic ethical standards of archaeological research and reporting. Membership in the RPA requires a commitment to a set of rules of ethical behavior toward the archaeological record and toward the descendants of the people who left that record behind (http://www.rpanet.org).

There are valuable websites of a number of other professional archaeological organizations that also provide information concerning the goals, standards, and ethical considerations of professional archaeologists. These include the home pages for the Society for American Archaeology (http://www.saa.org), the Society for Historical Archaeology (http://www.sha.org), and the Archaeological Institute of America (http://www.archaeological.org). It is hoped that membership in each of these groups signifies that an archaeologist subscribes to the ethical tenets of the organization concerning preservation of the past, the competent and legal excavation of sites, and the timely publication of the results of archaeological research.

WHO OWNS THE PAST?

In the provocative title of one of her courses, University of Wisconsin–Milwaukee anthropology professor Bettina Arnold poses the question "Who Owns the Past?" A PBS documentary and accompanying website ask the same question regarding the archaeological record (http://www.pbs.org/wotp/). The question of who owns the past can be narrowly interpreted, focusing on ownership of the actual objects recovered by archaeologists. Phyllis Messenger (1993) calls these objects "cultural property" in the title of her book *The Ethics of Collecting Cultural Property: Whose Culture, Whose Property?*

Indeed, it can be a vexing legal, not to mention moral, question: To whom do the objects that archaeologists recover belong legally? To whom should they belong morally? Should the rule of the playground, "finders, keepers," apply, and, therefore, should "cultural property," wherever it is found, always become the property of the archaeologist or arrowhead collector who found it? Should artifacts belong to the owner of the land on which the materials were found, even though they were left there long before the current owner took title to the property? Should, instead, archaeological material belong to the state or nation in which the land is located? Should archaeological artifacts accrue to the person, organization, governmental agency, or museum that funded the project? Or how about this: Should objects found by archaeologists or artifact collectors revert to the descendants of the people who left the materials in the ground in the first place?

For much of the history of archaeology, European and American scientists excavated the pasts of places like Egypt, Mexico, Pakistan, and Peru and spirited off the prized artifacts to their home nations and institutions. It is a terrible irony, indeed, as MacIntosh, McIntosh, and Togola (2006) point out, for example, that modern Nigerians interested in the marvelously artful works in bronze produced by their ancestors have to travel to the British Museum in London to see the finest specimens. Modern Nigerians are not alone in this. Some of the most impressive artwork of the Aztecs of Mexico, Polynesians of the Pacific, Inca of South America, and ancient Egyptians are not to be found in Mexico, Polynesia, Peru, or Egypt but in museums located in western Europe and North America. Things have changed in this regard, in particular since the 1970 passage of the UNESCO Convention on the Means of Prohibiting the Illicit Import, Export, and Transfer of Ownership of Cultural Property (see http://exchanges.state.gov/culprop/unesco01.html for the complete text). Though the convention is not legally binding, most nations and museums adhere to its tenets, which maintain that "cultural property"—and this explicitly includes antiquities—(at least material excavated since the 1970 passage of the convention) should remain the cultural property of the nation where it was found unless it is transferred in such a way that adheres to the laws of the nation where the material originated.

Within the United States archaeological material found on federal land (for example, national parks, forests, and military bases) belongs to all American citizens communally, not to any one of us individually. Most archaeological material found on private property, no matter how scientifically or monetarily valuable, belongs to the owner of the property on which the material was found. Legally, the property owner can keep archaeological material found on his or her land, display it, sell it, give it away, or even destroy it.

Human remains, however, are not considered property—at least they are no longer so treated—and human skeletal remains don't belong to a landowner simply because they are located on his or her land. Certainly this makes sense. After all, how would you feel if it were your great-grandfather whose remains were being used as a conversation piece on someone's fireplace mantle, displayed to tourists at a roadside museum, or used as a Halloween decoration, all with the justification that they were found on private property and, therefore, belonged to the property owner for use as he or she saw fit?

Most people agree that human remains should not be considered property or mere specimens, but things can get pretty dicey when we move beyond human bones and consider objects that may be deemed sacred by the descendants of the people who left them behind. Instead of your great-grandfather's bones, the found objects could be the crucifix he wore around his neck when he was buried or the wedding ring he wore for more than fifty years in life and that he intended and expected to continue to circle his finger in death, expressing for eternity his bond with your great-grandmother. Would you view these things as artifacts, mere specimens for people to collect, however noble their intention?

This is not an easy issue. Fortunately, the overwhelming majority of the materials archaeologists find were disposed of as trash by ancient peoples and almost certainly were not considered sacred or meaningful by the folks who tossed them in the garbage pit or compost heap. Nevertheless, I was once told by a Native American that everything archaeologists dig up is sacred and was intended by his ancestors to remain in the ground forever (Feder 1999a). A corollary to the question "Who owns the past?" raised by this individual might then be "Who owns the right to decide what is sacred among the things found by archaeologists?" If everything left in the ground by ancient peoples is sacred, there can be no archaeology. It is a quandary, indeed, and there are no easy answers and, perhaps, not even difficult answers.

The mistrust many Native Americans feel and express about the motives behind archaeological research is understandable. The U.S. government, for example, has much to atone for in terms of its treatment of the skeletal remains of Native Americans. Curiosity about racial differences—and an indifference to the lives and belief systems of the indigenous peoples of the New World—led to a skeleton-collecting frenzy on the part of U.S. government agencies in the nineteenth century. Fresh graves were robbed and ancient graves despoiled, all in an attempt to produce a huge database of "scientific materials" that also happened to be the remains of human beings (Thomas 2001). Many of these complete and partial skeletons (in some cases only the skulls were kept) ended up at the Smithsonian Institution; others were housed at various museums and university laboratories throughout the United States. Certainly, these bones were of value for the scientific information they provided. Equally certainly, these bones were the remains of people whose loved ones were and are understandably aggrieved that they are lying in drawers in museums and laboratories.

Largely as a result of the efforts of Native Americans and sympathetic nonnative people, the **National Museum of the American Indian Act** of 1989 (http://www.nmnh.si.edu/anthro/repatriation/pdf/nmai_act.pdf) and the **Native American Graves Protection and Repatriation Act (NAGPRA)** of 1990 (http://www.cr.nps.gov/nagpra/MANDATES/25USC3001etseq.htm) were passed by the U.S. Congress to redress the nineteenth-century grave-robbing policies of the federal government. Federal laws in the United States reflect the feelings of many, probably most, people, Native American or not; the dead have a right to rest in peace, and the concerns of their families trump scientific interest in their remains. As a result of NAGPRA, the National Museum of Natural History at the Smithsonian Institution established a repatriation office in 1991, whose function continues to be the careful inventory of human remains and sacred funerary objects curated by the museum and the return of these remains and artifacts to the tribes from which they originated (http://www.nmnh.si.edu/anthro/repatriation/). Many Native American tribes have availed themselves of the opportunity to bring their ancestors and sacred objects home for reconsecration and sometimes reburial (Figure 2.10). A state-by-state and regional listing of the enormous number of individuals (to date, the bones of more than 8,000 people whose remains have been returned to their tribal groups for reconsecration; information about repatriation can be found at http://www.nmnh.si.edu/anthro/repatriation/.)

Beyond the issue of who owns the actual skeletons and artifacts, the question of "Who owns the past?" as Bettina Arnold poses it, has far broader implications. It's not just ancient things, but the interpretation of those ancient things, that also is at issue. Who owns the right to "parse" the past, to provide the definitive description and explanation for what happened in antiquity? Who has the right to be the "official" authority about a group's past, and who is the rightful mediator between the archaeological record and an interested citizenry? Is it tribal elders? Professional archaeologists? Textbook authors?

Consider a complete stranger, someone who doesn't know the language of your ancestors, has little if any shared cultural experiences with your family, and is ignorant and even dismissive of the stories told within your family of its own history. Would you be totally (or even a little) comfortable with such a person being the official chronicler and interpreter of your story, the source everyone relies on for information about your family's history? Probably not, and many Native Americans feel exactly this way about the stories white archaeologists tell of their native history (Biolsi and Zimmerman 1997). Then again, should those outside your family, who are interested in its history, accept without reservation the family's own version with its likely closeting of episodes and individuals whom the family is uncomfortable with and without sufficient objective or empirical evidence to support the family's version? Again, probably not.

Once, the oral histories and traditions of descendant groups were ignored by many archaeologists. This made no sense. The oral, traditional history of a group of people should not be dismissed and certainly can contain important and accurate information of value to archaeologists and historians. On the other hand, it also makes no sense to accept uncritically all oral traditions about the past as fact simply because the people telling the stories are the biological and cultural descendants of those who produced the archaeological sites being studied.

Roger Echo-Hawk, an archaeologist and a Native American, coordinates repatriation for the Denver Art Museum and the Colorado Historical Society. He has used tribal oral histories extensively in the process of connecting recovered skeletal remains with descendant tribal groups. Echo-Hawk (1997) clearly recognizes the great historical value of these oral histories, but he does not accept them unconditionally or uncritically, explicitly maintaining that the truth can be reached only by the combined use of oral history and archaeology. In fact, he labels the perspective that "Indian" knowledge based on oral history is superior to "white knowledge" based on archaeology a "racialist paradigm" (Echo-Hawk 1997:101).

FIGURE 2.10 Human bones may be viewed as valuable scientific specimens and stored in universities, museums, and laboratories, but they also may be the revered remains of living people's ancestors. The solemn ceremonies shown here depict the reconsecration and reburial of human remains excavated by archaeologists and returned to the descendants of the people represented by the bones: Eyak Indians (Cordova, Alaska, top; CORBIS/Natalie Forbes) and Euroamericans (the Walton Family Cemetery, Griswold, Connecticut; courtesy Nick Bellantoni).

For example, despite seemingly overwhelming archaeological evidence, some Native Americans reject the notion that their ancestors arrived in the New World from Asia sometime before 15,000 years ago, in part because their oral histories record no such migration (Deloria 1995). Merely because it is their history does not make them right in their interpretation, however, any more so than would be the assertion that Egyptians did not build the pyramids more than 4,000 years ago because the modern residents of Egypt have no collective memory preserved in their oral traditions of having done so. Oral traditions are great sources of hypotheses, possible explanations for elements of a people's past. Archaeology provides the physical evidence by which the historical veracity of such hypotheses can be tested.

If you are looking here for an authoritative, definitive answer to the questions "Who owns the past?" and "Who should own the past?" I am afraid that you are going to be disappointed. As the title of yet another book on this issue phrases it, Indians and archaeologists are still in the process of attempting to find "common ground" on the issue of who owns the past (Swindler et al. 1997). Perhaps it will be through recognizing a multiplicity of ownerships of the past and a diversity of interpretations by descendants, historians, and archaeologists that we may be able to more fully and objectively assess and understand the stories that the archaeological record can tell us.

Read More

To learn about the broad diversity of views on the issue of who "owns" the past—some written by archaeologists, some written by Native Americans, and some written by archaeologists who are Native Americans—check out any and all of the following sources:

Biolsi, T., and L. Zimmerman, eds. 1997. *Indians and Anthropologists: Vine Deloria, Jr., and the Critique of Anthropology.* University of Tucson Press, Tucson.

Deloria Jr., V. 1995. *Red Earth, White Lies: Native Americans and the Myth of Scientific Fact.* Scribner's, New York.

Echo-Hawk, R. 1997. Forging a New Ancient History for Native America. In *Native Americans and Archaeologists: Stepping Stones to Common Ground,* edited by N. Swindler, K. E. Dongoske, R. Anyon, and A. S. Downer, 88–102. AltaMira Press, Walnut Creek, California.

Feder, K. L. 1999a. Indians and Archaeologists: Conflicting Views of Myth and Science. *Skeptic* 5(3):74–80.

Jemison, G. P. 1997. Who Owns the Past? In *Native Americans and Archaeologists: Stepping Stones to Common Ground,* edited by N. Swindler, K. E. Dongoske, R. Anyon, and A. S. Downer, 57–63. AltaMira Press, Walnut Creek, California.

Messenger, P. M., ed. 1993. *The Ethics of Collecting Cultural Property: Whose Culture? Whose Property?* University of New Mexico Press, Albuquerque.

Swindler, N., K. E. Dongoske, R. Anyon, and A. S. Downer, eds. 1997. *Native Americans and Archaeologists: Stepping Stones to Common Ground.* AltaMira Press, Walnut Creek, California.

Thomas, D. H. 2000. *Skull Wars: Kennewick Man, Archaeology, and the Battle for Native American Identity.* Basic Books, New York.

Watkins, J. 2000. *Indigenous Archaeology.* AltaMira Press, Walnut Creek, California.

What Kinds of People Go into Archaeology?

Almost every generation comes up with a popular—and thoroughly misguided—impression of who archaeologists are and what they should look like. In American movies made in the 1930s and 1940s, for example, archaeologists were almost universally Egyptologists. Quite eccentric, these white-haired, bearded gentlemen ordinarily had beautiful daughters who, of course, accompanied their fathers on expeditions to godforsaken parts of the world, searching for secret or mystical knowledge possessed by ancient people. In revealing this occult information through their research, these archaeologists unleashed terrible calamities upon an unsuspecting world (Figure 2.11).

In another caricature, most clearly exemplified in the Indiana Jones movies and more recently in *The Mummy* and *The Mummy Returns*, archaeologists are dashing, rather romantic, madcap adventurers, swashbuckling a swath across the Middle East or Egypt, finding glorious treasure, and fighting Nazis while continuing their tendency to inadvertently unleash the demons of some ancient hell. Oh, and in this version of the caricature, the archaeologist always "gets the girl."

It should go without saying that Hollywood's primary goals rest in selling tickets and popcorn, not in verisimilitude. To begin with, archaeologists are not necessarily, or even most often, men. Though in the past often counseled against going into archaeology (Claassen 1994), women, in fact, have long made a significant contribution to the discipline, more than enough by more than twenty-five years ago, in fact, to base a book on their achievements and

FIGURE 2.11 Though it seems to happen all the time to archaeologists in Hollywood epics such as the 1932 black-and-white classic *The Mummy*, personally, I have been an archaeologist for more than twenty-five years, and I have yet to awaken a mummy in suspended animation. (© Bettman/CORBIS)

exploits in revealing the secrets of the ancient past (Williams 1981). In 1997 the Society for American Archaeology (SAA; http://www.saa.org) published a statistical analysis of its more than 5,000 members and about 1,000 non-member archaeologists written by Melinda Zeder (1997), herself a highly regarded archaeologist at the Smithsonian Institution and a member of the SAA. This census of American archaeologists was rather striking in showing that, while among older archaeologists—and, therefore, people who became archaeologists fifty, sixty, or even seventy years ago—the majority, indeed, were men, among successively younger generations of archaeologists, women represented an increasing fraction of the field (Figure 2.12). In the youngest cohort among those sampled, people in their twenties and probably still in graduate school when the survey was taken, women represented almost exactly half the field (Zeder 1997:11). Although Lara Croft is, by the labeling of her originators, a "tomb raider" and not an archaeologist, I suppose one could argue that her rise to prominence among video game and movie action heroes who get involved with antiquities parallels the rise of female archaeologists in the late twentieth and early twenty-first centuries. I do not know of any archaeologists, however, who view Lara Croft as a role model for young women interested in pursuing a career in archaeology.

Most stereotypes also represent archaeologists as white Europeans or Americans, studiously yet romantically revealing the ancient past, most often of non-European peoples. In a sense, unfortunately, this caricature resonates with not just a little truth. European and American archaeologists have long

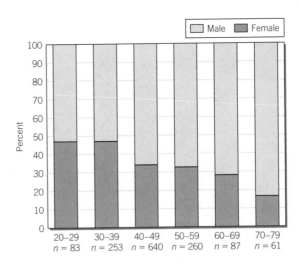

FIGURE 2.12 Graph showing the percentages of male and female archaeologists (vertical axis) within each age group by decade (horizontal axis). Note the steady increase as you move to the left along the graph in the percentages of female archaeologists in each age group until we find that, among archaeologists in their twenties, nearly half are women. (Melinda Zeder and AltaMira Press)

traveled to Egypt as well as Africa south of the Sahara, Mexico, Peru, Cambodia, India, and Pakistan and, like an invading colonial army, appropriated the prehistories and ancient histories of the native peoples, removing the artifacts recovered for display in European museums and monopolizing all conversation about their antiquity. In America archaeology has long tended to be a rather exclusive club with, once again, "foreigners" (that is, white folks of European descent) dominating the research and discussion of the ancient history of native peoples, in this case American Indians. In Zeder's (1997:13) analysis of SAA members, as of 1997, people of white European ancestry accounted for about 98% of the group. Members of the SAA who characterized their ethnicity as African American, Asian, or Native American could be counted on the fingers, if not of one hand, then of four: there were only two African Americans, four Asians, and ten Native Americans out of the 1,700 or so surveys returned for analysis. There were only fifteen Hispanics in the group, and five of them were from Latin American countries, conducting archaeology in their own nations.

Archaeology has much work to do in this regard, but the field is transforming in many ways. Today, though much of the paleoanthropology of Africa conducted in search of our earliest human ancestors continues to be carried out by European and American scholars (or African scholars of European descent), they now work in collaboration with native African archaeologists and paleontologists. It is almost impossible to see a television documentary about the latest discoveries regarding ancient Egypt that does not include the substantial participation of native Egyptian archaeologists led by the guiding hand of researcher Zahi Hawass (Figure 2.13), whose official Egyptian government title is undersecretary of the state for the Giza Monuments (these are the three large pyramid complexes—including the sphinx—located along the Nile at Giza; http://www.guardians.net/hawass/).

In essence, throughout the world people are reclaiming the archaeological study of their ancestors, and archaeologists come in all ethnicities and nationalities. In the United States, where archaeologists of European descent continue to statistically dominate the archaeological investigation of the Native American past, a small, dedicated, and growing cadre of Indian archaeologists are telling the story of their own ancient ancestors. (For example, see the book *Indigenous Archaeology* by Joe Watkins 2000, an archaeologist who works for the federal government; he is a Choctaw Indian.) The Navajo Nation in Arizona even has its own archaeology department (http://www.nau.edu/nnad) that conducts archaeology and trains Navajo and other native archaeology students in the study of their own past.

In a similar vein the historical context of the "peculiar institution" of slavery has become grist for the mill of historical archaeology (Ferguson 1992; McKee 1995). Because slaves were compelled in many states to remain illiterate as a matter of law, they could not tell their own stories through the written word. In fact, generally it was those who *owned* slaves and not those who *were* slaves who wrote about slavery in the American North and South. Certainly, the objectivity of these historical descriptions of the institution of slavery by slave owners cannot necessarily be trusted.

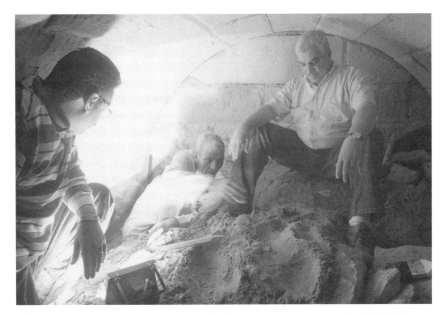

FIGURE 2.13 Undersecretary of state for the Giza monuments, archaeologist Zahi Hawass (right) is seen here supervising the excavation of a 2,500-year-old tomb found in 2001 during construction in a Cairo neighborhood. (Reuters NewMedia Inc./CORBIS)

As a result some archaeologists have focused their attentions on the institution of slavery. The archaeological record of plantations, including the remains of slave quarters, is in this sense a far more democratic and objective source of data than the written record, especially concerning such physical qualities of slave life as diet, housing, and material culture. Also, items of material culture that were intentionally hidden from slave masters by African captives, especially items related to the practice of forbidden non-Christian, native African religious behaviors, provide a unique perspective on the nature of the intellectual resistance to captivity practiced by slaves in a way the written record cannot.

Although the majority of archaeologists conducting this work have been of European descent simply because the vast majority of archaeologists in the United States are of European descent, this, too, is changing. A colleague and friend, Warren Perry (Central Connecticut State University), is one of a growing group of African American archaeologists. Perry has conducted research in Africa and the United States and is the director of the archaeological component of the African Burial Ground project, in which the graves of more than 400 African captives buried in the southern end of Manhattan island in New York are being examined (Perry and Blakey 1997). In a sense, in this project it is the children of slaves, not the children of slave masters, who are revealing the nature of captivity as reflected in the archaeological record.

The point is that neither of the sexes and no particular ethnic group has a monopoly on a passion for the past. A fascination for antiquity knows no gender, cultural, or political boundaries. As in all other fields of human intellectual endeavor, archaeology can only benefit from the multiplicity of perspectives that results, at least in part, from the diversity of the life histories of its practitioners (Feder 1999b).

Read More

For a hint at the diversity that characterizes the community of archaeologists, any of the following sources would be a good place to start.

Claasen, C. P., ed. 1994. *Women in Archaeology.* University of Pennsylvania Press, Philadelphia.

Feder, K. L., ed. 1999b. *Lessons from the Past.* Mayfield Publishing, Mountain View, California.

Ferguson, L. 1992. *Uncommon Ground: Archaeology and Early African America, 1650–1800.* Smithsonian Institution Press, Washington, D.C.

McKee, L. 1995. The Earth Is Their Witness. *The Sciences* 35(2):36–41.

Perry, W., and M. Blakey. 1997. Archaeology as Community Service: The African Burial Ground Project in New York City. *North American Dialogue* 2(1):1–5.

Watkins, J. 2000. *Indigenous Archaeology.* AltaMira Press, Walnut Creek, California.

Williams, B., ed. 1981. *Breakthrough: Women in Archaeology.* Walker & Company, New York.

Zeder, M. A. 1997. *The American Archaeologist: A Profile.* AltaMira Press, Walnut Creek, California.

Study Questions

1. What is archaeology? Define the term in a single sentence, and not a run-on sentence!

2. What kinds of data are the focus of archaeological analysis?

3. Do archaeologists study dinosaurs? (Here's a hint: No.) Why not?

4. Are archaeologists also geologists?

5. On what world areas do archaeologists focus their energies? Which areas are they not interested in studying?

6. On what time period(s) do archaeologists focus their energies? Which time periods are they not interested in studying?

7. How do anthropologists define culture?

8. What is adaptation? How do human beings adapt?

9. Is culture uniquely human? Do any other species exhibit behaviors that we can call cultural?

10. Contrast the adaptation of any wild animal species with which you are familiar and human beings who live in the same region as that species.

11. What is the scientific method? How does it work? Does archaeology qualify as a science?

12. How did the Renaissance contribute to the development of the science of archaeology?

13. How did people in Europe in the eighteenth and nineteenth centuries explain symmetrically shaped pieces of chipped stone (today called hand axes) found deep in the soil, often associated with the bones of extinct animals?

14. What was important about John Frere's discovery at Hoxne in the late eighteenth century?

15. The author Donald K. Grayson (1983) titled his book *The Establishment of Antiquity*. How did thinkers in the eighteenth and nineteenth centuries establish the great antiquity of the Earth, life, and the human presence on Earth?

16. How did the desire to solve the so-called mystery of the mounds contribute to the development of archaeology in the United States?

17. How did the desire to solve the perceived mystery of the origins of the native peoples of the New World contribute to the development of archaeology in the New World?

18. Odds are that the archaeology course you are taking in which this book is required reading is offered by your school's department of anthropology. Why is it generally the case that archaeology is positioned in a university or college's anthropology department?

19. What are the legal requirements for becoming an archaeologist?

20. What training and experience are required by the federal government for anyone applying to excavate an archaeological site on federal land?

21. Explain the concept of "cultural resources." How does this concept relate to archaeological site preservation?

22. In what fields are professional archaeologists ordinarily trained?

23. How does an archaeologist become a member of the Register of Professional Archaeologists?

24. What is meant by the question "Who owns the past?"

25. By law, who owns archaeological material found on private property? By law, who owns archaeological material found on public property?

26. Describe the demographic profile of archaeologists today. How has that demographic profile changed over the past several decades?

3 | What Archaeologists Want to Know

- **What Kinds of Research Goals Do Archaeologists Have?**

- **What Is It That Archaeologists Want to Find Out?**

  Is Garbage Really All That Informative on the Subject of Human Behavior?

The archaeological research we were conducting in Peoples State Forest, as discussed earlier, was goal oriented. We weren't just digging holes looking for interesting stuff merely to satisfy our archaeological curiosity. A common slur is reflected by the following sarcastic definition of the field: Archaeology is simply what archaeologists like to do. Well, OK, it is that, but it is far more. Archaeologists enter the field or the laboratory with an often quite specific set of goals in mind. This chapter focuses on a discussion of what it is that archeologists hope to accomplish by excavating and analyzing the archaeological record.

What Kinds of Research Goals Do Archaeologists Have?

As mentioned in earlier sections, archaeology is not a treasure hunt. Our purpose is not just to look for interesting or impressively ancient things, and our goal is not simply to fill displays with moldy objects that museum-goers will find captivating. As scientists, archaeologists seek to answer questions about the lives lived by past peoples, and we propose and then attempt to test hypotheses explaining those lives. In the broadest sense our ultimate research goal is knowledge, and we endeavor to attain that knowledge, as all scientists do, first by observing (in our case by observing the world of the human past by finding and analyzing the material remains left behind by human beings), then by proposing explanations for what those remains signify (these are our hypotheses, explanations we propose for why people lived as they did in the past), and finally by testing the validity of those proposed explanations with additional evidence (Shafer 1997).

CULTURE HISTORY

Though not our only concern, archaeologists in one way or another have always had as a research goal constructing, modifying, and fine-tuning the **culture history** of the regions in which they work. Culture history is the story of what happened and when, and, as mentioned in the previous chapter, reconstructing the sequential story of human antiquity was one of the field's most significant goals in the first half of the twentieth century. In other words, archaeologists focused on writing a "history" for a region and time, often where no written history, in the usual sense of that word, existed because the people left no written record behind. One of the classic works of archaeology, written by one of the icons of the profession, V. Gordon Childe (1942), said it as forcefully and as simply as possible; the book in question is titled and is about *What Happened in History.*

In some parts of the world the study of prehistory has a lengthy pedigree, and the framework of a local chronological sequence of what happened when is fairly well established. Revision is always possible, of course, and every archaeological project in an area can contribute to the goal of constructing culture history, sometimes by clarifying or refining an existing well-documented sequence and sometimes by overturning a chronology that had been accepted previously.

Sometimes chronological issues that one might have thought—or at least hoped would already have been resolved continue to vex researchers and continue to need basic research and data collection. For example, much to the chagrin of American archaeologists at least, the question of when human beings first entered into the New World remains unanswered, at least in any kind of definitive way. For a long time many archaeologists, though by no means all, believed the question had finally been laid to rest: The data seemed to indicate an initial migration sometime around 12,000 years ago from Asia across a land bridge in an area called **Beringia** (sometimes called the **Bering Land Bridge**) connecting northeast Asia (Siberia) and northwest North America (Alaska) that was exposed during the end of the Pleistocene, or Ice Age. However, a number of sites that may be far older than 12,000 years have been located and in some cases intensively excavated in the New World. Some of these sites are thousands of kilometers distant from the area of Beringia, indicating that even older sites necessarily remain to be found in that region if, in fact, that was the point of entry for ancient peoples into the New World. The chronology and nature of human movement into the Americas is a fundamental research question that remains unresolved. More than a little research time and money continues to be invested in attempting to settle this fundamental issue of the culture history of the New World (Dillehay 2000; Dixon 1999; Meltzer 1993, 1997).

Culture history, though signigicant and, one could argue, the major achievement of archaeology in the first half of the twentieth century, is not the only research issue that intrigues archaeology and not the only concern that guides our work today. Many modern anthropologists view culture as a means of adaptation, a complex series of strategies that enable the survival of the people who practice the culture. Whereas most other animal species rely almost entirely on their physical characteristics for survival, human beings also have strategies to invent, develop, and refine behaviors that enable their continued existence. Making tools, building houses, controlling fire, trading for valuable raw materials with neighbors, and making alliances are all behaviors that are made possible by our vast intelligence. These behaviors differ from group to group, are all elements of culture, and both directly and indirectly enable our survival. Humans think these things up and teach them to their children, who continue to develop and refine the ways of carrying them out. These behaviors leave material manifestations in the forms of artifacts, ecofacts, and features: Past peoples made spear points that were useful in hunting the animals on which they subsisted; they constructed domiciles that enabled them to withstand the long cold winters or blazing summers of their home territories; they built hearths to warm their houses and cook their food; and they traded with neighbors to obtain valuable raw materials for making the tools they needed to hunt, build houses, or start fires. The focus on how a people adapted to a particular set of environmental circumstances, that is, how they developed a behavioral strategy for survival given a particular set of natural resources under a particular climatic regime, is called **cultural ecology**. Understanding the nature of the cultural ecological adaptation—being able to describe an ancient way of life of a particular group of people at a particular place at a particular period of time within the environmental parameters established at that place and time—and being able to explain why they lived as they did is another of the goals of archaeological research.

DESCRIBING AND EXPLAINING CULTURAL DIVERSITY

Understanding the great diversity of human adaptation is an important goal of anthropology in general and of the anthropological archaeologist in particular. Cultural anthropologists conduct **ethnographic research** among a living people, observe and describe a lifeway, and then attempt to explain the nature of the adaptation of the people they study (Figure 3.1).

In the case of ethnographic research, however, the amount of time various human groups have been studied is only a tiny percentage of the time these groups have been around. The earliest ethnographers began living with cultures different from their own just a bit more than a hundred years ago, so, at best, ethnographic data has a time depth of only about that long. In contrast, the archaeological record of individual groups of people reflects a far greater

FIGURE 3.1 Cultural anthropologists Abigail Adams, seen in the rear of this photo, has over the course of her career lived for extended periods among the Maya in Central America. Her recent focus is on Maya spirituality. Here she poses among the family of a Maya "spirit medium." (Courtesy Abigail Adams)

amount of time. By excavating a series of sites from different time periods, archaeologists can follow the evolution of a group of people for hundreds or even thousands of years. Over such a long period of time, a group was likely to encounter great changes in its natural environment, its technology may have undergone enormous change, and it may have come into direct contact with a diverse array of other human groups. Only the archaeological record possesses a breadth of time sufficient to reveal how people adjust to changes in their natural and cultural environments over not just decades or centuries but millennia. Only the archaeological record provides the researcher with the totality of a people's chronology, a sufficiently large chunk of their story to assess the evolution of their technology, subsistence systems, social practices, religious tradtions—in fact, their entire culture—over not just one or two generations but along the length of their history. And only the archaeological record presents a thick enough slice of time to expose the lengthy story of the impacts of the movement of ideas across cultural boundaries.

Examining and explaining the diverse ways in which different cultures adapted to their environments, responded to changes in those environments, and reacted to contact with peoples of different cultures is a significant goal of archaeological research. Studying an ancient people across a lengthy expanse of time can illuminate how they responded to great changes and may even provide insights for facing such changes in the present (Binford 1962, 1968).

Giving Voice to the Voiceless

For the vast majority of the time human beings and our evolutionary ancestors have been around, there are no written documents. As mentioned previously, written history dates back to not much more than 6,000 years ago, but human beings and our ancestors have been around for, arguably, 1,000 times longer than this; our hominid family has now been traced back to more than 6 million years ago. Even once history begins with the development of writing in places such as Mesopotamia, Egypt, Pakistan, China, and Mesoamerica, what's written down is quite limited. For example, in Mesopotamia and Egypt much of the early writing is not about the lives of people but about commodoties, consisting of lists of goods and lands. In Mesoamerica early written records focus on the lineages of kings. The lives of most people in most places largely were neglected by the early scribes.

One can even argue that in the more recent historical past, the written record focuses on the rich and famous and ignores the lives of common people and slaves. As archaeologist James Deetz has phrased it, archaeology

> ... provides access to the ways all people, not just a small group of literate people, organized their physical lives. If only the written records, rich and detailed as they are, are studied, then the conclusions will reflect on the story of a small minority of deviant, wealthy, white males, and little else. I do not think we want that for our national history; therefore, we need archaeologists to find what was left behind by everybody. (1991:6).

Consider the fact that in the American South, the "peculiar institution" of slavery was written about, if at all, mostly by people who owned slaves. By and large, the people who were enslaved were denied the opportunity to provide their written perspectives; throughout the South it was even illegal to teach slaves to read and write. So how can we know about slavery in the American South in a way that is objective and inclusive and in a manner that materially reflects the horrors of capitvity? The classic research of archaeologist Charles Fairbanks (1976) at Cannon's Point plantation on St. Simons Island, Florida, addresses this issue precisely.

Fairbanks excavated slave cabins, an overseer's cabin, and the area around the plantation's main house, gaining insights into plantation life and showing in a very concrete way the differences among the lives of slave owners, overseers, and slaves. As Fairbanks states, "Many of these differences are barely hinted at in the numerous accounts of southern plantation life" (1976:172).

For example, you might have thought that while the institution of slavery is utterly morally indefensible, at least slaves must have been well fed by their owners to keep them healthy as workers. Fairbanks, however, found that, far from being well fed, slaves, after a full day of servitude, still had to supplement the food provided by the plantation owner. Among the food remains found around the slave cabins and the overseer's house, Fairbanks was able to identify great quantities of opossum and raccoon, small wild game the slaves probably trapped in the evenings after work was done. The excavation adjacent to the big house revealed no such faunal remains. Instead, here Fairbanks recovered the remains of beef, pork, deer, sea bass, and sea trout (1976:172).

More recently, archaeology is revealing the prevalence of slavery even in areas where traditional history downplays its significance. For example, though it is often assumed that slavery was confined to the southern states, archaeological research is now revealing the widespread exploitation of African captives in the North as well. In Connecticut alone, documentary records of the late eighteenth century indicate the presence of 6,000 individuals of African descent, and most of them were slaves (Sawyer 2005). Warren Perry's (2006) excavation and analysis of the remains of more than 400 individuals at the African Burial Ground in lower Manhattan should put to rest forever the notion that slavery was confined to the South. His joint work with Jerry Sawyer (2005) has revealed the importance of slavery to northern economies in their investigation of a plantation, not in Georgia, the Carolinas, or Mississippi, but in Connecticut. What history forgets and historians neglect, the archaeological record reveals.

Revealing the lives of the forgotten and neglected represents a vital task of the archaeologist. Archaeological research, whether it is focused on sites of great antiquity or time periods much closer to our own, has the capacity to provide a voice to the voiceless of the past.

Knowing the Past Provides a Vision of the Future

Archaeology also contributes to our ongoing discussion about the direction our species is taking toward its uncertain future. Consider one of the most important issues facing the modern world: climate change. Whether human beings are the root cause of what appears to be planetary warming—especially since the inception of the industrial revolution—is vigorously debated, but there seems to be little controversy among climatologists on the existence of global warming. What will be the long-term consequences of this warming? What economic dislocations will result over not just years or even decades but centuries, during which time the map of agricultural lands will constantly change and the soil in regions that once earned the deserved characterization "bread basket" will dry up and blow away?

Human beings in the past experienced vast changes in their climates, and the archaeological record provides us with models for how our ancestors responded to those changes. It is important to know that periods of vast, planetwide climate change have challenged human beings in the ancient past. For example, ancient peoples experienced the coming of the Ice Age, technically the geological epoch labeled the **Pleistocene**, when worldwide temperatures plunged and then recovered intermittently and much of Europe, the northern half of North America, and higher elevations elsewhere saw enormous, thick fields of ice spread out to cover large sections of those continents. Coastlines across the face of the planet were redrawn when the levels of the world's oceans declined as sea water evaporated, fell as snow in higher lattitudes, and fed the growth of the glaciers. Human beings faced powerful environmental discontinuities throughout the Pleistocene, which, contrary to the implications of its popular name (the Ice Age), was interspersed by numerous periods of temperature rises resulting in glacial meltoff and attendant sea level rises. The stories of human reactions and responses to such changes vary: Some groups expanded into previously unoccupied territory, some shifted their subsistence as previously reliable food sources became less reliable or disappeared completely, some developed new modes of subsistence in which human beings supplemented nature in the production of food resources, and some, inevitably, became extinct, unable to respond quickly enough to climate change. It should go without saying that modern people, faced with clear evidence of climate change—whether long term or short term, whether fueled by our own behavior or controlled by natural forces beyond our control—need to consider the impacts of these kinds of changes on past people. It is at least potentially important to understand how our ancestors responded to such changes in the past to provide insights into how we might respond—and how we might plan to respond—in the future (Butzer 1982).

Chapter 3: Interactive Exercise

Understanding the nature of human behavioral change and stability over long periods of time, during which the rules of the game may be altered dramatically, is a significant goal of archaeological research. Like most archaeological projects, our research goals in Peoples State Forest included culture history, culture description, and the nature of change over a lengthy period of time.

Read More

Archaeologists, perhaps none more then Lewis R. Binford, have thought long and hard about how the study of the ancient past can contribute to our understanding of humanity. Binford's seminal articles, first published in the 1960s, resonate in the discipline more than thirty years later and are more than worth a read. I have also included a few citations of popular publications focusing on one of the cultural historical goals of those interested in New World archaeology: figuring out when, how, and from where people first entered into the Americas.

Binford, L. 1962. Archaeology as Anthropology. *American Antiquity* 28:217-25.

Binford, L. R. 1968. Archaeological Perspectives. In *New Perspectives in Archaeology,* edited by S. R. Binford and L. R. Binford, 5–32. Aldine Publishing, Chicago.

Butzer, K. W. 1982. *Archaeology as Human Ecology.* Cambridge University Press, Cambridge.

Childe, V. G. 1942. *What Happened in History.* Pelican Books, Baltimore.

Dillehay, T. D. 2000. *The Settlement of the Americas: A New Prehistory.* Basic Books, New York.

Dixon, E. J. 1999. *Bones, Boats, and Bison: Archaeology and the First Colonization of Western North America.* University of New Mexico Press, Albuquerque.

Meltzer, D. J. 1993. Search for the First Americans. In *Smithsonian: Exploring the Ancient World*. Smithsonian Books, Washington, D.C.

———. 1997. Monte Verde and the Plesitocene Peopling of America. *Science* 276:754–55.

Shafer, H. 1997a. Goals of Archaeological Investigation. In *Field Methods in Archaeology*, edited by T. R. Hester, H. J. Shafer, and K. L. Feder, 5–20. Mayfield Publishing, Mountain View, California.

What Is It That Archaeologists Want to Find Out?

In a sense archaeologists serve in the manner of journalists reporting on the lives of past peoples. In the cliché journalists need to ask and answer the following questions when reporting a story: where? when? what? who? how? and why? In fact, at least a couple of archaeology textbooks have organized their discussions of the purposes of archaeology around these (or similar) journalistic questions (Feder and Park 2007; Renfrew and Bahn 2000). Archaeologists attempt to find out the answers to these same questions about peoples in the past. Where did past peoples live? (Where can we find the locations of their former villages, burial grounds, hunting camps, farmsteads, quarries, mills, battlefields, and sacred places?) When did a people live at a particular place? (When did they arrive? When did they adopt new behaviors? When did they leave?) Who were the people who lived at the sites we excavate? (Who were their ancestors? Who are their descendants?) What remains did they leave behind of their tools, weapons, jewelry, clothing, structures, icons, and even their own bodies? (What can we find of these things to use as evidence of their ways of life?) How did they live their lives? (How did they survive? How did they feed their children? How did they get along with their neighbors? How did they govern themselves? How did they obtain the raw materials needed to make their tools, construct and heat their houses, cook their food, and store their valuables? In essence, how did they respond to the challenges of their world?) Finally, why did they live as they did? (Why did they come to this spot? Why did they change, or why did they remain the same? Why did they leave and not return, or why did they die off?)

Every human society represents what amounts to an experiment in survival. By asking and attempting to answer the previous questions, archaeologists hope to illuminate and comprehend those experiments in survival. All groups of people develop their own strategies for dealing with the challenges that life presents. Finding sufficient clean water to drink and food to eat; collecting enough wood to provide fuel for fires or raw materials for homes; collecting the stone or metal to make the tools necessary to hunt or to prepare the soil for planting; extracting clay from the earth to make pots in which to store or cook food; harnessing the energy of a stream to power a sawmill or gristmill; organizing families and coordinating the labor of a group of people; governing themselves; raising children to become competent adults; responding to life's tragedies; and producing a safe, protective, and secure cultural environment into which people can be born and can develop as individuals—these are all things that culture must enable, and each culture finds its own way of accomplishing these tasks.

Archaeologists hope to illuminate the cultures of past peoples, to puzzle out their many and varied strategies for survival. It is probably naive to believe that from the lifeways of past peoples archaeology will reveal great insights about the human condition that will enable our own survival. I find it unlikely that our survival into the future will be facilitated in some way by the work of archaeologists. Nevertheless, humanity is characterized by its ability and, perhaps, need to reflect upon itself. The goal of understanding the lengthy and fascinating pathways we all have taken to reach our current state is an honorable one. There is great value in exposing the enormous diversity of the human approach to survival and in illuminating the story of how groups of people across the vast stretches of time represented by the archaeological record developed ways of life that enabled their survival. Essentially, then, archaeologists hope to find out how human groups developed ways of life by finding and analyzing the material objects—the garbage people discarded, the material they lost, the stuff they put away for safe keeping, and the objects they simply left behind—that were a part of that strategy for survival.

Read More

To see how various archaeologists perceive the fundamental questions we can pose about past cultures, take a look at any of these textbooks.

Ashmore, W., and R. J. Sharer. 1999. *Discovering Our Past: A Brief Introduction to Archaeology*. Mayfield Publishing, Mountain View, California.

Fagan, B. M. 2000. *In the Beginning: An Introduction to Archaeology*. 7th ed. Prentice Hall, Upper Saddle River, New Jersey.

———. 2002. *Archaeology: A Brief Introduction*. 4th ed. Prentice Hall, Upper Saddle River, New Jersey.

Feder, K. L., and M. A. Park. 2007. *Human Antiquity: An Introduction to Physical Anthropology and Archaeology*. Mayfield Publishing, Mountain View, California.

Renfrew, C., and P. Bahn. 2000. *Archaeology: Theories, Method, and Practice*. Thames & Hudson, New York.

Sharer, R. J., and W. Ashmore. 2003. *Archaeology: Discovering Our Past*. 2d ed. McGraw-Hill, New York.

Staeck, J. 2002. *Back to the Earth: An Introduction to Archaeology*. McGraw-Hill, New York.

Thomas, D. H. 1998a. *Archaeology*. 3d ed. Wadsworth, Belmont, California.

———. 1998b. *Archaeology: Down to Earth*. Wadsworth, Belmont, California.

IS GARBAGE REALLY ALL THAT INFORMATIVE ON THE SUBJECT OF HUMAN BEHAVIOR?

Calling A. J. Weberman a fan of songwriter, singer, poet, philosopher, and folk-rock icon Bob Dylan is not nearly an accurate enough representation of Weberman's obsession with the music and life of the composer of so many anthems of the 1960s and 1970s (Jacobson 2001). At some point in the 1960s, after careful and relentless—and, it has been suggested, chemically enhanced—listening to the then collected works of the master songwriter, Weberman decided that he—and maybe he alone—had cracked the cleverly obscure "code" that he—and, again, maybe he alone—believed lay at the heart of the often startlingly layered lyrics of Bob Dylan's compositions. During this period Weberman came to the realization that it should be his role in life to disseminate the true meaning behind Dylan's songs. As part of that task he established in his Greenwich Village, New York, apartment what amounted to a Bob Dylan "database" that incorporated a colossal amount of Dylan-related material, including tapes of unreleased recordings, newspaper and magazine articles, and, as it turns out, stuff he swiped from Bob Dylan's trash cans.

Apparently, while passing by Dylan's Greenwich Village apartment one day in late 1970, Weberman experienced an epiphany, a sudden and intuitive flash. Oh sure, Dylan had granted his share of interviews and had revealed aspects of his life to the press, but who could trust the veracity or utility of a secretive Bob Dylan providing obscure answers to the insipid and self-serving questions of reporters who didn't truly understand the meaning of Dylan's work? Dylan could control an interview, answering only those questions that he wished to and in ways that revealed little about his true self. However, in front of the apartment house were Dylan's garbage cans, containers of items of great power and value, housing items that had actually been used by Bob Dylan, material reflections of the true life lived inside the walls of his apartment. Dylan could lie and obfuscate when confronted with questions about his life and work, but garbage cannot lie, it cannot mislead. Garbage is pure data, revealing truths about the people who used the items before discarding them.

Weberman walked over to the trash cans that day in 1970, opened the lids, and stole (if that is the correct word for taking material out of the trash) some of Dylan's material culture. Weberman brought the stuff home and analyzed it the way an Egyptologist might pore over a hieroglyphic text. Thus he initiated a new front in the struggle to both understand and reveal the essence of Bob Dylan. Weberman made numerous subsequent field trips to "excavate" artifacts that had passed through Dylan's hands and house to the miniature and temporary archaeological "sites" of the great songwriter's trash cans. Weberman even offered classes in Dylan "garbology" and conducted expeditions to Dylan's house to train students in his brand of fieldwork. He published articles in a number of underground and not so underground 1970s publications wherein he presented his fantastic interpretations of the meaning of what Bob Dylan had thrown away in the trash.

Weberman's seemingly single-minded obsession with Bob Dylan expanded to include other celebrities whose garbage he collected, analyzed, and reported on. The trash of former vice presidents (Spiro Agnew, who had resigned in disgrace under President Nixon), the garbage of the wives of former presidents (Jackie Kennedy), and the refuse of writers (Norman Mailer) and actors (Dustin Hoffman) all became part of Weberman's garbology archive.

Weberman certainly was and, as nearly as I can tell, continues to be one strange dude. Until recently he produced a website discussing his life work in garbology; unfortunately, the URL has gone dead, apparently after Weberman was arrested for drug possession. I will leave it to you to assess the irony here: The evidence used to convict Weberman was obtained by federal agents when they trawled through, of course, his trash.

I will not pass judgment on any of his seemingly bizarre interpretations of Bob Dylan's lyrics, nor do I have much to say about the legality of mining living people's trash to obtain insights into their lives. I will say, however, that Weberman discovered, albeit in an odd and interesting way, an axiom at the core of archaeology: There is a comprehensible relationship between human behavior and the objects they made, used, and discarded. Weberman did not have access—at least not much—to Bob Dylan himself because Dylan elected not to talk to him after their one conversation, which ended rather disastrously, so Weberman collected Dylan's trash and allowed the discarded materials to "talk" to him instead.

Though Weberman's focus on Dylan may seem more than a bit obsessive, his approach to learning what Dylan was really like is sceintifically reasonable, and real archaeologists have applied the same general technique, though legally and with their subjects' consent. For more than thirty years, for example, archaeologist William Rathje and his students have been examining the rubbish folks throw out in their trash cans as part of the Garbage Project (Harrison, Rathje, and Hughes 1975; Rathje and Murphey 1992). These archaeologists of modern rubbish have been showing up at peoples' curbs and doorsteps before the regular trash pickup in a number of cities, taking the material collected to the archaeology lab for a detailed analysis. Their research shows one major advantage of trash over personal interviews with people: Garbage never lies. For example, Rathje's research has consistently shown that when you ask people how much beer they purchase and consume at home, most report very little or none. However, when you pick through the trash of those same, self-professed abstainers from alcohol consumption, you find large quantities of beer bottles and cans. Some households where interviewees asserted that beer was not purchased or consumed at home had trash bins where containers representing more than

FIGURE 3.2 Bill Rathje conducting dump archaeology. (© James A. Sugar/CORBIS)

200 ounces of beer were found each week of the study (Rathje and Murphey 1992:68).

More recently Rathje has been conducting actual archaeological excavations at modern landfills and trash dumps (Figure 3.2; Rathje and Murphy 1992). This research is making a contribution to the discussion of the very important issues of trash disposal and recycling. Rathje has found that materials commonly assumed to be environmentally neutral because, or so it was thought, they readily decompose in landfills are really not neutral after all. Decades-old paper and even some food products have been found in Rathje's landfill excavations, preserved all too well at the bottom of traditional dumps and causing planners to rethink landfill design. Though it doesn't match most common expectations about the romance of archaeology, the archaeology of modern society has made significant contributions to our understanding of the kinds of information that might be coded into garbage, regardless of its age, and has revealed important and practical insights about our own culture's trash, waste, and recycling habits.

Archaeologists do not often have access to people who lived in the past for the rather obvious reason that most of them are long dead. We have little choice but to fall back on the material remains of their behavior, much of it their garbage, to talk to us in the present about lives lived long ago. Weberman's term *garbology*, after all, is not all that inaccurate in describing what it is that archaeologists do.

Read More

To see just how insights about a culture, including our own, can be derived from the study of garbage, read the article that started it all or get the terrific book coauthored by "Mr. Garbologist," William Rathje.

Harrison, G. G., W. L. Rathje, and W. W. Hughes. 1975. Food Waste Behavior in an Urban Population. *Journal of Nutrition Education* 7(1):13–16.

Rathje, W., and C. Murphy. 1992. *Rubbish: The Archaeology of Garbage*. HarperCollins, New York.

Sullivan, R. 1998. *The Meadowlands*. Scribner's, New York.

Study Questions

1. What are the research goals of archaeology? What do archaeologists hope to learn about the human past through the study of the material remains of human behavior?

2. What is "culture history"? Why does it continue to be at least one of the goals of many archaeological research projects?

3. Describe how archaeological research contributes to our knowledge of the diversity of human cultural adaptations.

4. How does archaeology contribute to our understanding of culture in ways that the ethnography of living groups of people cannot?

5. List some challenges facing people in the modern world. How might archaeology uniquely contribute to our examination of these problems?

6. Consider the issue of global warming. How might the archaeological study of the ancient human past provide modern people with insights about the cultural impacts of climate change in the future.

7. List the one-word questions that journalists ostensibly ask and hope to answer when writing a news story. Phrase those questions in terms of the archaeological record, viewing the archaeologist as the journalist of humanity's past times.

8. Who is A. J. Weberman? What does Weberman's interesting methodology for studying the life of Bob Dylan have to do with archaeology?

9. What is garbology?

4 | Doing Archaeology

PRACTICAL CONSIDERATIONS

- **What Determines Where an Archaeologist Investigates in the First Place?**

- **How Is Archaeological Research Funded, and Why?**

- **What Laws Regulate Where Archaeologists Can Dig?**

  What Are the Ethical Obligations of Archaeologists?
  Who Gets to Dig at an Archaeological Site?

- **Is Archaeology Really a Dangerous Pursuit?**

All scientific endeavors, like our excavations at the Wood Lily site, are aimed at expanding our understanding of the way things were, are, or will be. Biologists focus on the evolution and ecology of living things. Geologists investigate the nature of the Earth. Physicists delve into the nature and behavior of the physical building blocks of the universe. Archaeologists literally and figuratively dig into human antiquity through the examination of the material left behind by past people. All sciences must address a host of practical issues at the same time they assess more fundamental questions about the origins of life, the evolution of the planet, the nature of matter, or the chronology of ancient human history. This chapter focuses on the practical concerns of the archaeologist.

What Determines Where an Archaeologist Investigates in the First Place?

There are many different reasons why an archaeologist may choose to conduct research at a given place. We chose to examine the land within the boundaries of Peoples State Forest for several reasons. We had a research goal in mind: We wanted to study the ways in which the ancient inhabitants of southern New England used upland tracts of land, and Peoples State Forest was well suited to our purpose. The land contained within Peoples represents a noncoastal, primarily nonriverine, inland and upland locale, which, when we started the project in 1986, was not the kind of habitat that had been extensively investigated by archaeologists in southern New England. It also is relatively undisturbed habitat and presented us with an opportunity to investigate a large chunk of real estate that had not been completely made over into roads, shopping plazas, and general suburban sprawl. Essentially, we elected to dig in Peoples State Forest because we believed we could learn new things about the pattern of land use by the aboriginal people of Connecticut. This is an important point to make. Archaeologists don't just go out and dig because they enjoy fieldwork or even just because they need to train students. We conduct research to answer specific questions and to test hypotheses about the lives of ancient peoples.

Because ours was a university project, supported by our institution and funded largely through the tuition paid by students obtaining six college credits and archaeological training through our program, we had the luxury of pursuing our interest in the settlement patterns of the aboriginal inhabitants of southern New England for no other reason than the fact that we were intensely interested in that issue (Figure 4.1). Many university-based archaeological research projects have a similar advantage: The educational institution recognizes the significance of such projects and supports its archaeological faculty in the pursuit of their research interests everywhere in the world.

Other archaeological research may be chosen for far more practical reasons. Much of the archaeology conducted in the United States today may be characterized as **compliance archaeology**, which is part of a broader approach to historic preservation called **cultural resource management (CRM)**. CRM represents a philosophy that views prehistoric and historic sites—the remnants of ancient communities, old battlefields, houses, forts, etc.—as "resources" that deserve preservation through various procedures of "management" that may include actual physical protection from looting, restoration, curation, and detailed investigation, including excavation. The "compliance" part of the equation concerns archaeology mandated in order to "comply" with laws passed to help preserve cultural resources.

The federal government of the United States has since at least 1906 (http://www.cr.nps.gov/local-law/ anti1906.htm) enacted extensive legislation protecting archaeological sites on public lands and, especially since the early 1960s, laws requiring the determination of possible impacts on archaeological "resources" that might result from federally funded, mandated, or permitted (in the sense that formal permits are required from the federal government

FIGURE 4.1 2005 archaeology field school in West Simsbury, Connecticut. (K. L. Feder)

before a project may commence) projects. (See Thomas King's 1998 book *Cultural Resource Laws and Practice* for an insightful discussion of historic preservation legislation, and visit http://www.cr.nps.gov/linklaws.htm for links to the actual text of the most important federal laws protecting archaeological sites.) This legislation acts to protect archaeological sites that may be affected by government activity by contracting with archaeologists to look for and conduct at least preliminary examinations of sites in a project area. Here, the research universe is determined not simply on the basis of an archaeologist's curiosity or desire to cover a particular area. Instead, it is defined by the practical concerns involved in answering a very specific question: Are there any sites in the specific area that may be affected by activity carried out by or enabled by (through funding or permitting) the federal government?

For example, when the federal government, in its application of the Clean Water Act, requires a local municipality to respond to a pollution problem through the construction of a sewage treatment facility, the government legally requires an assessment called an **Environmental Impact Statement** that provides a detailed analysis of the possible negative impacts of a project on historical resources within or adjacent to the project area. In this example, the government may sponsor an archaeological investigation restricted to the area to be directly affected by the construction of a water treatment facility and the placement of sewer pipes. Simply put, many archaeologists do not independently decide where they will dig on the basis of their own research interests or analytical goals; they are contracted to look in particular places because any sites that might be in those places may be threatened by a construction project—an interstate highway, an airport, a sewer system—funded, mandated, or permitted by the U.S. government.

Local governments, including those of states, counties, and even towns, may have their own diverse regulations requiring an assessment of the potential for damage or destruction of archaeological sites in an area where construction is planned. It is becoming increasingly common for town governments to include consideration of archaeological sites in the impact assessments required by conservation commissions or other town boards that must approve construction projects before they can proceed. Here, too, archaeologists may be hired to make such assessments, and the areas they are contracted to study are determined by the geographical scope of the construction project. The point here is that although you might think that most or even all archaeological work is inspired by the particular geographical or general research interests of archaeologists, this is not the case. A fair portion of the archaeology conducted in the United States is located according to the agendas of those who are paying the bills for the archaeological work, and those agendas are often dictated by laws that have been passed to protect archaeological sites endangered by federally or state mandated projects.

How Is Archaeological Research Funded, and Why?

What is arguably the most famous archaeological discovery of the twentieth century almost didn't happen because the money supporting the project was about to run out. Archaeologist Howard Carter's excavations in Egypt in the early decades of the twentieth century were funded, as were many archaeological projects during this period, by a wealthy benefactor, in this case the earl of Carnarvon (Figure 4.2), a member of the British nobility (Buckley 1976; Fagan 1994; Hoving 1978).

Carnarvon developed an interest in Egyptology literally by accident. After a terrible (and historically very early!) automobile wreck in 1901, Carnarvon's injuries left him weak and unable to abide the cold and damp winters of England. As a result he began to spend his winters in warmer climes, especially in Egypt, where boredom led him to request an **archaeological concession** from the government, essentially a legal permit to excavate in a small area near his hotel. Of course, Carnarvon didn't do any of the actual digging; he merely paid the bills and spent his time watching from a shaded, screened-off area while his hired workers excavated.

Though little of importance was found in Carnarvon's first season of digging—the biggest discovery made by his crew was a mummified cat—he found the process fascinating and decided to devote much of his time and resources to Egyptology. In his desire to contribute to the archaeology of Egypt, Carnarvon introduced himself to Howard Carter, an archaeologist who, though only 28, had been working in Egypt for ten years, and the two soon became a formidable team. Carnarvon possessed the political connections to obtain archaeological concessions from the government and the money to support the research; Carter possessed the archaeological skills to conduct the excavations, identify the artifacts, and analyze the material recovered.

FIGURE 4.2 Wealthy members of the British nobility such as earl of Carnarvon often funded archaeological expeditions. Carnarvon's interest in ancient Egypt brought him together with Egyptologist Howard Carter and led to the discovery of the fabulous and largely intact tomb of the pharaoh Tutankhamen.

Their partnership was quite successful, at least initially, and Carter, under Carnarvon's sponsorship, discovered and excavated a number of important tombs of private citizens of ancient Egypt. Of course, both Carter and Carnarvon had grander aspirations and hoped they would be able to find the unplundered tomb of not just an ancient citizen of Egypt but of a pharaoh.

With that goal in mind, the partners were delighted when, in 1917, Carnarvon obtained the coveted concession to dig in the Valley of the Kings, a pharaonic burial ground located on the west bank of the Nile, across from the modern city of Luxor, then called Thebes (Figure 4.3). This concession was exactly what Carnarvon and Carter were hoping for, but with this concession came a dramatic rise in the cost of the excavations. In fact, as expenses rose Carter and Carnarvon begin purchasing plundered Egyptian antiquities in the market in Cairo with the intent of selling them in Europe for a handsome profit. This plan, apparently, did not result in much of an income, as Carnarvon kept most of the purchased artifacts for his own private collection, but it is

FIGURE 4.3 After an intense period of construction of mortuary pyramids, ancient Egyptians began burying their pharaohs here in the Valley of the Kings, located on the west bank of the Nile, across from the modern city of Luxor. King Tut's tomb is located in Valley of the Kings. (M. H. Feder)

ironic that a reputable archaeological research project might have been funded by selling objects illegally obtained from ancient tombs.

Be that as it may, Carter's excavations in the Valley of the Kings were crushingly disappointing. It appeared that previous excavations, combined with looting, had already emptied the valley of any important finds. Finally, in 1922, after more than fifteen years of providing the financial backing for Carter's expeditions and after five years of an unsuccessful search for the unplundered tomb of a pharaoh in the Valley of the Kings, Carnarvon ran out of both patience and the will to keep funding the project. In fact, it was with Carnarvon's displeasure and increasing impatience in mind that Carter left Egypt and returned to England in the summer of 1922 to implore the earl to continue providing financial support for his work.

Carnarvon would hear none of it. The earl told Carter that he was finished funding excavations in Egypt. Carter begged him to continue, going so far as to offer to pay the excavation's expenses out of his own pocket if Carnarvon, who owned the archaeological concession, would simply allow the excavation to continue for one more season. Carnarvon was so moved by Carter's offer that he relented, agreeing to extend the concession and even to pay the bills, but only for one more season.

Carter returned to Egypt, and in a stroke of luck that sounds like it was written by a Hollywood scriptwriter desperate for a happy ending, in November of 1922, mere weeks after Carnarvon threatened to cut off all funding, one of

Carter's workers discovered the entryway to the spectacular and justifiably famous burial chamber of the Egyptian pharaoh Tutankhamen. At last, he and Carnarvon had their unspoiled tomb (Carter and Mace 1923; Figure 4.4).

Wealthy individuals such as Carnarvon funded archaeology for many and varied personal reasons. Though not trained in archaeology and often unwilling or unable to endure the rigors of full-time fieldwork, many benefactors simply were fascinated by antiquity and wished to contribute in the best way they could by paying for archaeological research. Certainly, many benefactors hoped to achieve notoriety and not just a little personal aggrandizement by providing such financial backing. Furthermore, wealthy patrons commonly signed contracts with their archaeologists, allowing the benefactors to personally donate recovered materials to museums (where their names would adorn the displays) and even to keep whatever they wished for their personal collections.

This pattern of funding necessarily colored archaeological research for a long time. Wealthy patrons funded projects that they found interesting. Commonly and not coincidentally, these were projects that illuminated the lives of wealthy people in antiquity. After all, the archaeological remains of the homes and burial chambers of the rich and famous of the ancient world were where the most spectacular artifacts could be found. Gold and lapis lazuli death masks, alabaster vases, and ebony chairs inlaid with ivory (all objects found in Tut's tomb and the kinds of things desperately sought after by museums) simply are not found in the houses or graves of common people, workers, and slaves.

As a result, the houses and graves of common people, workers, and slaves—in fact, the majority of the population in ancient societies—were not the focus

FIGURE 4.4 Archaeologists removing artifacts from the unspoiled tomb of the Egyptian pharaoh Tutankhamen. (© Underwood & Underwood/Corbis)

of most such archaeological work. Few wealthy patrons wanted to subsidize research that would illuminate the lives of the poor and downtrodden of antiquity, if only because the material culture of the lower classes was plain, simple, and not nearly as impressive as that of the nobility. Wealthy patrons were happy to see their names associated with museum displays of spectacular gold, silver, and alabaster objects found in a pharaoh's tomb. Few such patrons hoped to see their names associated with a similar display of plain pottery or wooden tools found in the house of a worker or farmer.

An additional consequence of this pattern of funding is that archaeological objects often were taken from their place of origin and deposited in museums located in the countries of the benefactor. Many archaeological **assemblages** (for example, the objects that together made up the grave furniture and goods of a pharaoh's burial chamber) became dispersed, scattered to various locations, removed from their association with all the other objects with which they were found, and torn from their contexts. Many important artifacts, housed in private collections, were not available for study or even public viewing and became isolated objets d'art (art objects) rather than scientific components of a unified package reflecting a particular set of behaviors at a single place and time. It was, in fact, concern that the Tutankhamen funerary assemblage would meet a similar fate that inspired the Egyptian government to require that it remain in Egypt, the property of the Egyptian people. The stipulations of the contract Carnarvon had signed with Carter were not carried out when the Egyptian government insisted that the objects found in Tut's tomb remain together in Egypt rather than be removed piecemeal to various museums in European capitals and the personal collections of the wealthy.

Although wealthy benefactors continue to subsidize archaeological research, the major financial support today is from universities, museums, private institutes and societies, and governments. Because their motives for supporting archaeology differ significantly from those of most of the wealthy patrons of the eighteenth, nineteenth, and early twentieth centuries, the kinds of archaeological investigations possible have changed and expanded. Private organizations such as the National Geographic Society (NGS; see http://www .nationalgeographic.com/ for the NGS homepage, and see http://www .nationalgeographic.com/research/grant/rg1.html for detailed information about the society's funding of research) and federal funding agencies such as the National Science Foundation (http://www.nsf.gov/) have as their fundamental goal the expansion of our scientific understanding of the world, including our understanding of the ancient world, and they fund projects accordingly. As mentioned earlier, universities also fund archaeology directly and indirectly as they would research conducted by any of their faculty, indirectly by supplying laboratory space, equipment, and supplies, as well as directly through money for salaries, graduate students, and support services.

In 1966 the U.S. congress passed and President Lyndon Johnson signed the **National Historic Preservation Act (NHPA)** (you can download a copy of the act as amended in 2000 at http://www.achp.gov/nhpa.html). That act, perhaps more than any other piece of federal legislation, established within the government a culture of concern for historical places in the U.S. Identification, recognition, protection, and preservation of places and sites significant to our national and local histories became the official policy of the federal government with the passage of NHPA.

NHPA assigned the **National Park Service (NPS)** (http://www.nps.gov/) the task of funding and coordinating historic resource preservation on a national level. The act also set up and partially funded the system in which each individual state established a position called the **State Historic Preservation Officer (SHPO)** to develop and maintain a state policy of historic preservation. Section 106 of NHPA established the requirement among federal agencies to assess and report on any of their activities (for example, if the NPS wished to build a new road through a national park or if the Army Corps of Engineers planned the construction of a new levee) to take into consideration any deleterious effects those activities might have on historic resources.

Again, much of the archaeology conducted in the United States today is categorized as "compliance archaeology," which is required of governmental agencies, states, local municipalities, and even private developers in order to comply with a broad array of historic preservation legislation on the federal, state, county, and town levels. Perhaps most significant of these laws is the **National Environmental Protection Act** (http://ceq.eh.doe.gov/nepa/regs/nepa/nepaeqia.htm). This law requires that when the federal government is funding a project (for example, a highway, a flood control project, or a community septic system), the potential impact on archaeological resources must be assessed, much in the way the act requires the assessment of a project's impact on natural resources such as air, water, vegetation, and animal life. Archaeologists are hired to examine particular tracts of land that will be affected by these projects to pinpoint sites that might be adversely impacted, to assess the severity of impact, to weigh that against the significance of the site, and to help mitigate any such impacts.

In the United States a growing number of Native American groups are supporting the archaeological investigation of their own histories. For example, the Navajo Nation, whose reservation is in Arizona and New Mexico, has its own archaeology department (http://www.nau.edu/nnad/) with a self-proclaimed goal to preserve and protect the cultural heritage of the Navajo people. The Mashantucket Pequot tribe of southeastern Connecticut has used some of the proceeds of its enormously successful gaming operation to build a state-of-the-art cultural heritage center whose focus is, in part, on the archaeological heritage of the tribe (http://www.pequotmuseum.org/). There is an archaeology research facility at the museum, and tribal archaeologists conduct research both on the current reservation and on land that once was part of the Mashantucket homeland. The Mashantucket, like many Native American tribes in the East, came close to extinction, and they view archaeology of their homeland as one way in which they can recapture a part of their ancient history that might otherwise have been lost (Figure 4.5).

The funding of archaeological projects becomes far more democratic when, rather than being obliged to fulfill the personal goals or motivations of an individual patron, the kind of work attempted is determined (1) by an anthropologically or historically trained archaeologist who is approaching particular

FIGURE 4.5 In some cases Native Americans have taken control of the archaeological research of their own ancestors, encouraging tribal members themselves to become archaeologists. The Mashantucket Pequot share the results of that work in their own museum. Archaeological excavations in the foreground; casino and hotel complex in the background. (Courtesy Kevin McBride, Pequot Tribal Nation)

research questions; (2) when private funding agencies simply wish to support the accumulation of knowledge about the past; (3) when government agencies fund research as part of a general policy of preservation, study, and dissemination of information about the past to an interested citizenry; and (4) when people hope to recapture their own lost history.

Our research in Peoples State Forest was supported by a combination of university and federal resources. Some summers, my university paid my salary as I taught the archaeology field school and students paid tuition for taking the course. My university also provided laboratory space, equipment, and supplies as well as a vehicle for transporting students. In addition the project was supported by money supplied by the National Park Service in the form of a preservation and planning grant wherein money was provided for archaeological research, in a sense before the fact, to determine the archaeological sensitivity of an area before any sites were threatened by development. There were no Tut tombs to be found in Peoples State Forest, and it is enormously unlikely that a wealthy patron of archaeology at the turn of the twenty-first century would have been enamored of the bits and pieces of stone tools and ceramic vessels we found in our research. Our work was made possible by the way such research is funded today, whereby the potential scientific contribution of a project—not the promise of finding pretty things—is the most significant variable in determining funding.

Read More

The search for and excavation of the tomb of Egyptian pharaoh Tutankhamen is emblematic of how major archaeological expeditions were funded in the early years of the discipline. The following sources, along with conveying the excitement of discovery, reflect the fact that archaeology was conducted in the first place because wealthy benefactors supported the work.

Buckley, T. 1976. The Discovery of Tutankhamun's Tomb. In *The Treasures of Tutankhamun*, edited by K. S. Gilbert, J. K. Holt, and S. Hudson, 9–18. Metropolitan Museum of Art, New York.

Fagan, B. 1994. *Quest for the Past: Great Discoveries in Archaeology.* Waveland Press, Prospect Heights, Illinois.

Hoving, T. 1978. *Tutankhamun, the Untold Story.* Simon & Schuster, New York.

 ## What Laws Regulate Where Archaeologists Can Dig?

I think many archaeologists would like to be awarded special badges upon conferral of our Ph.D.s that bestowed on us the unfettered right to conduct fieldwork wherever our research interests directed us. Instead, unfortunately (or maybe fortunately), archaeologists are like everybody else and must obey local property laws. In the United States the rights of private property owners are highly regarded, legally protected, and supercede our research interests and intellectual curiosity. Any archaeologist who ventures onto private land to conduct research without getting the permission of the property owner is guilty of trespassing and subject to the penalties for the commission of that crime as meted out by the municipality in which the trespassing took place.

It should be pointed out that in the United States, and in contrast to the laws of many other countries, holders of real estate own not just the surface of the land but virtually everything buried on their property, including oil, minerals, and archaeological material. The only exception to this relates to human burials that might turn up on private land. Though the particulars differ from state to state, most states have laws that protect human remains, and a landowner usually does not have the right to disturb or remove burials on his or her property without going through a legally mandated process. For example, when graves are located on private land in Connecticut, a formal process is initiated. The police and state medical examiner must be notified; they will determine if the remains are associated with a crime or those of a missing person (Figure 4.6).

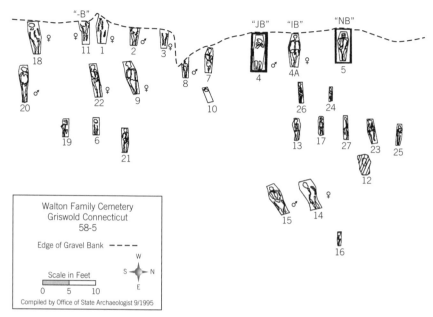

FIGURE 4.6 The first skeleton at what turned out to be the lost Walton family cemetery was found by a couple of kids riding their bikes down the embankment of a gravel quarry. Once the state medical examiner determined that the remains were not those of a missing person, a crew from the office of the state archaeologist commenced excavation and preservation of the more than two dozen graves shown on this map. After descendants were found and notified, the remains were studied and then reburied in a church graveyard nearby. (Courtesy Nick Bellantoni)

If the bones are not those of a murder victim or an accidental death, the state archaeologist is called in to help determine the affiliation of the deceased. If the remains are those of a Native American, a formal council made up of representatives from a number of tribes is convened to decide the disposition of the bones. If the bones are not Native American, the law requires that the descendants of the deceased, if they can be found, must be contacted. The landowner ordinarily cannot simply move human remains to a more convenient location to allow for development without first obtaining permission from the descendants of the deceased. As mentioned, a federal law—the **Native American Graves Protection and Repatriation Act**—specifically protects the physical remains of American Indians and Native Hawaiians located on federal lands.

The bottom line here is straightforward: An owner of a piece of property has the right to allow or deny access to his or her property to anyone (at least anyone without a warrant), including an archaeologist who might want to dig there, and, except for human remains, anything found on private property is considered to belong to the property owner. An archaeologist must obtain permission to conduct research on private property, always aware of the fact that any archaeological materials found on private land remain the property of the landowner unless some other legally binding arrangement has been made.

The rules concerning archaeological work on public lands are far different. The federal government owns a tremendous amount of property, especially in the form of national parks, forests, monuments, and military bases. Archaeological sites on federal lands are considered to be part of our national heritage and the property of all U.S. citizens as a group. As mandated by the National Historic Preservation Act discussed earlier in this chapter, the government, through the Department of Agriculture, the Defense Department, and especially the National Park Service (an agency of the Department of the Interior), protects sites on the land it administers and closely regulates archaeological access to these lands through the Archaeological Resources Protection Act of 1979 (http://www2.cr.nps.gov/laws/archprotect.htm). A regulation of that act, 43 CFR 7, titled The Protection of Archaeological Resources (http://www.cr.nps.gov/ local-law/43cfr7.htm), provides a detailed set of rules (Section 7.8a) about who can conduct archaeological research and how they need to go about justifying such research on federally administered land.

These regulations stipulate that an archaeologist must obtain formal permission to conduct archaeological research on public lands. Federal agencies charged with the duty of protecting sites have strict rules concerning to whom they will grant archaeological permits. Along with possessing the level of training and experience required by 43 CFR 7, he or she must submit a proposal for research on public land, which is evaluated by archaeologists who serve on the staff of the government agency in charge of the land in question. Perhaps of greatest importance, the regulation makes it clear that archaeological research on federally administered lands will be permitted only when that research has the potential to contribute to our understanding of the human past and only if the researcher agrees to share the results of the research with the true owners of the property, the citizens of the United States. As the regulation indicates:

> The proposed work is to be undertaken for the purpose of furthering archaeological knowledge in the public interest, which may include but need not be limited to, scientific or scholarly research, and preservation of archaeological data.

The **American Antiquities Act of 1906** (http://www.cr.nps.gov/local-law/anti1906.htm) initially established a fine of no more than $500 and a maximum of ninety days in jail for anyone convicted of excavating without official permission and thereby injuring or destroying an archaeological site on federal property. More recently, the penalties have become far more severe: Anyone found in violation of the Archaeological Resources Protection Act of 1979 is subject to an initial fine of up to $10,000 and one year in jail. If the monetary value of the artifacts taken from federal lands exceeds $500, the penalty may double. Penalties dramatically increase with any subsequent violations and convictions. In December 2006, for example, two Ohio men pled guilty to looting an archaeological site on federal land in Kentucky. Their sentencing is still more than two months away as I write this, but one is eligible for a fine of up to $250,000 and two years in prison for the offense. Obviously, the federal government takes very seriously its responsibility to protect archaeological resources on lands it administers.

There are many different rules that regulate archaeological access to lands owned by states or local municipalities. Almost always, formal permission must be obtained from those municipalities for archaeological investigation. To obtain permission to conduct our archaeological research in Peoples State Forest in 1986, we submitted a formal request to the Department of Environmental Protection (DEP) of the state of Connecticut, the agency that administers state forest land. Today, such a proposal would need to be assessed by both the DEP and the Office of the Connecticut State Archaeologist.

Chapter 4:
Interactive
Exercise

Read More

Because laws are in a constant state of flux, the best place to read about the current state of historic preservation legislation is on the homepage of the National Park Service, in particular, their list of historic preservation laws (http://www.cr.nps.gov/linklaws.htm). The following books provide good historical context for these laws.

King, T. F. 1998. *Cultural Resource Laws and Practice: An Introductory Guide.* Altamira Press, Walnut Creek, California.

King, T. F., P. P. Hickman, and G. Berg. 1977. *Anthropology in Historic Preservation: Caring for Culture's Clutter.* Academic Press, New York.

McGimsey III, C. R. 1972. *Public Archaeology.* Seminar Press, New York.

WHAT ARE THE ETHICAL OBLIGATIONS OF ARCHAEOLOGISTS?

Several years ago, after finishing an archaeology lecture to a boisterous group of fifth and sixth graders, one of the kids followed me out to my vehicle, ostensibly to help me lug my equipment. In actuality he had something on his mind, a question, the answer to which might help him decide whether he, too, would like to pursue a career in archaeology. As I was loading the slide projector and artifact replicas in my car, the kid queried me: "Can you get rich doing archaeology?" I gave him the usual response about how scientists follow their interests because they believe they can make a difference in people's lives, because they have an abiding interest in some element of the world around them, because they want to know about stuff. Scientists don't expect to become rich, and, in all likelihood, I wasn't ever going to be rich. But that's OK by me. The kid looked up at me, incredulously, and asked, "But I bet you could make a mint by selling the artifacts you find."

"Oh no! No! I would never sell artifacts. These things we spend all that time finding, recovering, and analyzing are far more valuable to us in terms of their scientific meaning, in terms of what they can tell us about the lives of people who lived in the past. Selling them would be unethical. I wouldn't, no archaeologist would, do that." The kid just responded with an expression of bemusement. He shook his head, walked away, and said "That's crazy. I bet you could get rich selling that stuff."

Archaeologists are faced with ethical issues all the time; whether or not we should sell artifacts isn't much of a challenge. We should not do that (Braden

2006), but we are faced with other, thornier ethical dilemmas that challenge the ways in which we conduct our research. For example, one of the primary ethical challenges faced by modern archaeologists rests in the fact that the archaeological record is the equivalent of a nonrenewable natural resource. Think oil or coal. Nonrenewable resources can be used up, leaving us with nothing to fuel our automobiles, heat our homes, or excavate and analyze. Sure, the archaeological record is always inherently being added to. Each time you lose a pen as you walk across campus, whenever your trash is hauled to the dump, every instance in which you dispose of organic waste in a compost heap, you contribute to that general record. However, in terms of its specific content, the archaeological record is limited and finite. There are a certain number of burials of Egyptian pharaohs, a bounded number of sites of the first Americans, a fixed quantity of Civil War battlefields, and a certain number of sites of the first farmers of western Asia. With each site destroyed by development, with each site vandalized by artifact hunters, and, it is sad to say, with each site excavated by an archaeologist, there is one fewer of each of these kinds of sites in the world, and no new ones reflecting these time periods, places, and peoples are being made. When the last Egyptian pharaoh is vandalized, when the final Paleo-Indian site is excavated, when the last Civil War battlefield has been turned into a parking lot, and when the final early agricultural site in western Asia has been carpet bombed, there will be no more of them left from which archaeologists can capture the story of the elements of the human past uniquely contained in those sites.

Because of this, even though most of us enjoy fieldwork immensely and have spent a good portion of our careers searching for sites that we hope someday to investigate, many archaeologists argue that it is unethical for archaeologists to add to the destruction and elimination of those sites that remain by excavating them without a vital reason, simply because of a vague interest in knowing what's there. Similarly, it is maintained by many archaeologists that it is unethical to excavate a site just because you would like to train the next generation of archaeologists; train enough archaeologists and there won't be any sites for subsequent archaeologists to excavate! In other words, at this point in the history of the discipline, many archaeologists practice a conservation ethic and think long and hard about the necessity of excavating an archaeological site. Sites should be excavated only if they are threatened by development or natural destruction (for example, if a site is being destroyed by a river eroding its banks) or as part of a research project with specific goals that can be achieved only through the excavation of those sites. Even then, a site should not be excavated in its entirety, with a portion set aside and left for future archaeologists, who almost certainly will possess data recovery techniques and methods of analysis we today can scarcely imagine.

Archaeologists excavate sites with the intention of revealing some previously unexamined element of the past. Without the publication of the results of this research, however, very little revealing goes on; neither the community of archaeologists nor the general public gains much from an excavation when the results are never reported. The fact that this happens far too often is called by archaeologist Brian Fagan (2006) "archaeology's dirty secret," maintaining that there should be a lot less digging and a lot more discussion about what's already been dug. So we can add to the ethical dilemmas faced by archaeologists the problem that it is ethical to conduct fieldwork only if the results of that work are shared.

Finally, consider the discussion earlier of "who owns the past?" Most archaeologists would agree that they are morally obligated to the living descendants of those people whose lives they are investigating through the excavation of the remnants of their communities, but what does "morally obligated" mean materially? Should all archaeologists obtain permission from descendant groups, for example, Native Americans, even if the site being excavated isn't on a reservation? If not permission, certainly an archaeologist might feel obliged at least to share his or her plans with a descendant group, to keep them informed of the work's progress, perhaps to encourage participation in the project by those descendants, and to provide accessible reports of the results of the work to these people. Of course, this raises several issues, including: How does the archaeologist determine whether there are any lineal descendants still around? Who are these descendants, and how can they be tracked down? What if there is broad disagreement among descendants concerning the appropriateness of the research? Worse, what if there is broad agreement among descendants that the excavations should not be undertaken or that archaeological excavation is never acceptable?

My colleague Warren Perry is an African American archaeologist and is firmly committed to involving descendant communities in his archaeological research. For example, when archaeological work was planned at the African Burial Ground in New York City (see chapter 13), the input of local residents was actively sought and their participation encouraged. Of course, the fact that many of the researchers in the project also were African Americans was important, but I think the success of this project and the cooperation and support of the descendant community transcended "race." Because they were included in discussions from the very beginning of the project, because their input and expertise in African cultural practices was sought out, because they were treated respectfully, and because they recognized that the work was illuminating a previously hidden part of their own history, the descendant community embraced the project, recognized its significance, and helped in whatever way it could. When the human remains were reinterred, local residents of the area participated in festivities honoring their ancestors (Figure 4.7).

As noted, Warren Perry is an African American, and the descendant community in lower Manhattan was largely African American. However, it is often the case, especially in North America, that archaeologists are not members of the same national or ethnic group as the people who produced the archaeological site they are excavating. This may raise even more vexing ethical considerations. Archaeologists may be considered by them to be untrustworthy outsiders who simply want to desecrate their ancestors' graves. It is seldom simple or easy. Unfortunately, archaeological research cannot be divorced from the broader historical context of the treatment of American Indians by American institutions (Thomas 2000). The burden must always be on the archaeologist to attempt to breach such barriers.

FIGURE 4.7 Local community involvement was crucial in the archaeological excavation and analysis of the African Burial Ground found during construction in lower Manhattan. When the research was completed, a festival was held to honor the lives of the African captives who had died and been buried in the cemetery and small wooden coffins (shown here) were crafted to hold the remains of the more than 400 African captives recovered from the burial ground. (Courtesy Warren Perry).

Who Gets to Dig at an Archaeological Site?

Most archaeology conducted in the United States today results from the application of historic preservation laws passed on the federal, state, and even town level (so-called compliance archaeology, as defined previously in this chapter in What Determines Where an Archaeologist Investigates in the First Place?). As noted in chapter 2 (How Do You Get to Be an Archaeologist?) these federal and state laws often stipulate the qualifications of an individual who wants to participate in an archaeological project on federal property or for a project mandated and paid for by the government. The question, "Who gets to dig at an archaeological site?" when the dig has been mandated and paid for by the government can be answered by reference to the laws that required the archaeology in the first place; the person must have formal archaeological training, almost always at a university, and sufficient experience to conduct the work.

Many digs in the United States and Canada, however, aren't madated by law but are conducted by university or college departments of anthropology, archaeology, or history. Most of the people who participate in these archaeological excavations are undergraduate students at those universities. Many of the students participate as part of their training for a career in archaeology.

Students from other academic departments (geology, biology, environmental sciences, or virtually any other area) participate for the unique experience—and credits—they gain. Students can sign up for a **field school** run by the appropriate department at their university or can apply to field programs offered at most other universities and receive academic credit at their home institution. Field schools are treated as academic courses by most universities and may involve classroom work, library research, laboratory work, and, especially, field experience. Field schools may run for several weeks or even a few months, during which time students receive an intensive introduction—often eight or more hours a day, five days a week—to the methods of archaeological fieldwork.

Beyond learning how to dig, field school participants make a significant contribution to archaeological research. As an undergraduate student majoring in anthropology, I trained at a field school at the University of Cincinnati, where I learned how to excavate a site by participating in the excavation of a 3,500-year-old site located in the Ohio River Valley. Like my fellow students in that field school, I was doing more than simply training for a career in archaeology. (In fact, the ethical precepts of the archaeological profession preclude the excavation of a site for the sole purpose of training students.) When I learned archaeological field techniques, my work was overseen by experienced graduate students and a professor (Kent Vickery). The grunt work we contributed to the project produced the data that allowed for a detailed study of the nature of an ancient habitation site on the Ohio River (Vickery 1976).

Most of the field research I have conducted over the past twenty-five years would have been impossible if not for the contributions of undergraduate students, who, in return for the work they did for me (and their tuition payment), received training in archaeological field research. Every year the Archaeological Institute of America (AIA) publishes *The Archaeological Fieldwork Opportunities Bulletin,* a comprehensive listing of field schools and projects seeking volunteers (Mozina 2003). If you are interested in participating in a dig, this book is the best place to find opportunities (you can locate information about the fieldwork bulletin by clicking the fieldwork link at that AIA's homepage: http://www.archaeological.org/).

Participation in a university- or museum-sponsored archaeological research project is not restricted to university students. Motivated high school students become involved in university-sponsored projects and obtain academic credit as well. Many projects also encourage the participation of nonstudent volunteers; I have found that lecturing to historical societies, libraries, and local business and civic groups often generates interest in volunteering from elementary school kids to retired seniors. Depending on volunteers' availability and skills, we encourage their participation. There even are organizations that specialize in providing a formal means by which nonscientists can participate in and contribute to research projects all over the country. The best-known of these is the EarthWatch Institute (http://www.earthwatch.org/). Each year EarthWatch brings together more than a hundred scientists in seven primary fields of study (endangered ecosystems, oceans, biodiversity, cultural diversity, global change, world health, and archaeology) and thousands of enthusiastic participants. It is the proverbial win-win situation, one in which scientists can accomplish an enormous amount of work (through what amounts to donated labor) and people are given the opportunity to help study African elephants, excavate a 2,000-year-old burial ground in Poland, or investigate the ecology of koala bears. In essence, the question posed at the start of this section (Who gets to dig at an archaeological site?) has a simple answer: anyone motivated and willing to devote a substantial chunk of time for the physically challenging but intellectually stimulating, satisfying, and rewarding work of excavation.

Read More

For a listing of current fieldwork opportunities, investigate the comprehensive annual guide by the Archaeological Institute of America.

Mozina, M. 2003. *Archaeology Fieldwork Bulletin.* Archaeological Institute of America, Boston.

 ## Is Archaeology Really a Dangerous Pursuit?

During the course of an archaeological field season, hundreds upon hundreds of field schools, museum and university research projects, and government-mandated archaeological surveys are conducted across the face of the globe. Thousands upon thousands of experienced, professional archaeology field-workers, serious archaeology students, and casual, one-shot volunteers participate in field projects and are paid, trained, or simply have a wonderful life experience. For the vast majority of these people, the worst that happens is a bad sunburn, some annoying insect bites, tired muscles, and the occasional sprained ankle. It is important to note, however, that there are serious dangers, both natural and artificial, facing anyone who spends a substantial amount of time outdoors, and archaeology fieldworkers need to be aware of issues that pose serious dangers to their health and the health of the people they teach or employ (Poirier and Feder 2001).

Many of the dangers posed by archaeological fieldwork sound prosaic and, truly, are not ordinarily life threatening. For example, the vast majority of fieldworkers have experienced the maddeningly itchy rash produced by contact with the urushiol oil present on the leaves of poison ivy, poison oak, and poison sumac (Figure 4.8). Urushiol is powerful and nasty stuff—according to one website (http://poisonivy.aesir.com/view/fastfacts.html), .25 ounce of the oil, equally distributed, is enough to produce a rash on every person in the world— but the rash it produces is usually not much more than an annoyance. To be sure, you have to be careful not to scratch the rash, especially not to the point that it can become infected. Still, it won't kill you and goes away after a bit, and there are many marginally useful products on the market that help alleviate the itch. More than 90% of people exhibit some reaction to urushiol, but the level of reaction varies greatly (even within a person's lifetime), and some cases

FIGURE 4.8 "Leaves of three, let it be." Wise words for the archaeologist. These three leaves belong to the poison ivy plant.

can be severe. I strongly recommend to my students, no matter how hot it may get, to wear shoes (no sandals) and long pants in the field to minimize the possiblity of exposure, but not everyone heeds that advice. One of my students, never having previously encountered poison ivy and thinking herself immune, ignored that counsel and pushed through a patch of waist-high ivy while wearing especially short shorts. After a visit to an emergency clinic and a prescription for an anti-inflamatory medication, she ended up missing several days of field school. As the old saying concerning poison ivy goes, "Leaves of three? Let it be." It's good advice.

Insect bites are almost an inevitable consequence of being outside in the spring, summer, or fall. The various benefits and drawbacks of bug spray with DEET (the official cologne-perfume of my field crew), vitamin B supplements, and products such as Skin-So-Soft are the subject of vigorous debates among field crews. Obviously, bee stings are dangerous for those who are severely allergic, but for most people stings and bites are little more than an irritation.

In some areas and in some years, however, encounters with local insects can have far more serious consequences. For example, 2002 was the year that West Nile virus became a significant public health issue. Unknown in the Western Hemisphere before 1999, the virus is spread by mosquitoes and can infect birds, horses, some other mammals, and human beings, some of whom get sick with flulike symptoms and a few of whom even die as a result. West Nile is so recent a danger that when a colleague and I edited a book on health and safety in archaeology (*Dangerous Places: Health, Safety, and Archaeology*, Poirier and Feder 2001), we didn't cover it at all as a threat to the health of archaeological fieldworkers. In 2006, the last year for which statistics are available as

I write this section of the book, there were 4,268 reported cases of West Nile in humans in forty-seven of the fifty United States (Figure 4.9; only Maine, New Hampshire, and Vermont, reported no human cases). Also in 2006, 177 of those who contracted West Nile died from the disease or its complications. It is a serious public health issue and one that is of particular concern to archaeologists who, by the nature of their field of study, must spend lots of time outside, where the risk of mosquito bites is high.

An entire chapter of the book I coedited was devoted to the debilitating bacterial disease *Borrelia burgdorferi*, which is carried by deer ticks (*Ixodes scapularis*, Bellatonni 2001). The bacteria that cause the disease enter your body while the tick is attached, collecting your blood. The disease can begin as a rash, develop into flulike symptoms, and, if untreated with a vigorous course of antibiotics, can lead to arthritislike symptoms, nerve damage, and worse. Lyme disease, named for the Connecticut town where it was first diagnosed, is primarily seen in the northeast, mid-Atlantic, and north-central states of the United States; according to the Centers for Disease Control, more than 23,000 cases were reported in 2005, four-fifths of which were in the states of Connecticut, Massachusetts, New York, New Jersey, Pennsylvania, and Maryland (http://www.cdc.gov/ncidod/dvbid/lyme/ld_rptdLymeCasesbyState.htm; Figure 4.10).

I find it somewhat amusing, in an admittedly dark sense, when local health officials recommend to people that for protection against Lyme disease and West Nile virus, it is best to stay out of the woods. We can't get very much archaeology done anywhere else, so complete avoidance simply isn't an option for archaeologists—we stoically perceive these dangers as occupational hazards. We slather ourselves in spray—whose side effects I choose not to think

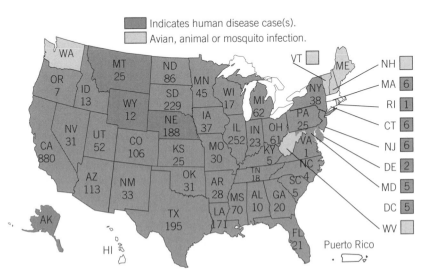

FIGURE 4.9 Distribution of human cases of the West Nile virus in 2006 as reported by the National Center for Infectious Diseases, a division of federal agency the Centers for Disease Control.

about—and do regular tick checks. We are careful, not panicked, about the dangers presented by insect-borne diseases.

Rabies is a disease that justifiably terrifies people: It is virtually 100% fatal if not treated (Morganti and Tartt 2001). In 2003 more than 7,000 cases of rabies were reported in animals in the United States (Figure 4.11); Krebs et al. 2004). Thankfully, cases in humans in the US are extremely rare; there were only three cases reported to the Centers for Disease Control in that same year. Worldwide, the disease is far more prevalent in humans; according to the National Center for Infections Diseases(http//www.cdc.gov/ncid/dvrd/rabies/) an estimated 55,000 people die of rabies each year.

According to the Centers for Disease Control, dogs are the primary carriers worldwide, responsible for about 90% of the human infections each year. Due to a vigorous program of vaccinating our canine and feline pets against rabies, dogs are not the primary carriers in the United States. Domesticated cats and dogs together represented only about 6% of reported cases of rabies in animals in the U.S. in 2003. In 2003 the primary rabies vectors in the United States were raccoons (36.7%), skunks (29.4%), bats (16.9%), and foxes (6.4%) (Krebs et al. 2004), though the significance of each of these species varies regionally. In terms of transmission to human beings, bats are the primary culprits in the United States.

Other animal-borne viruses also pose a hazard to archaeologists in the field. Carried by mice and deposited in their feces, for example, the hantavirus can lead to serious consequences when it is inhaled, leading to pulmonary distress and even death when not treated immediately.

Obviously, even healthy wild animals can present a danger to archaeologists. Terry del Bene, a good friend and esteemed colleague, tells of conducting archaeological survey work in Alaska and being given, as part of his

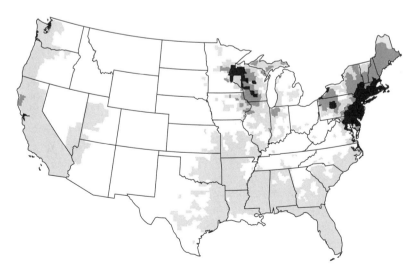

FIGURE 4.10 Distribution of human cases of Lyme disease in 2005 as reported by the National Center for Infectious Diseases. Darker zones represent more cases.

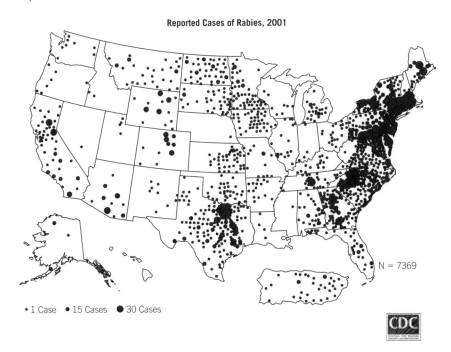

Reported Cases of Rabies, 2001

• 1 Case   • 15 Cases   ● 30 Cases

N = 7369

FIGURE 4.11 Distribution of cases in the United States of rabies in animals for the year 2001 as reported by the federal agency the Centers for Disease Control.

archaeological tool kit, a hand gun. He was told to keep the pistol loaded when in the field and when encountering an angry grizzly bear always to remember that only the first five bullets in the barrel were meant for the bear. Apparently, if those first five shots merely annoyed the rampaging beast, the final bullet was intended as the escape of last resort for the unlucky archaeologist. I assume they were pulling Terry's leg—or perhaps he was pulling mine. Poisonous snakes are another source of potential danger. There are four species of poisonous snakes in North America: rattlesnake, cottonmouth, copperhead, and coral snake. Numerous subspecies, such as the western rattler, can kill even a healthy adult not treated with antivenin. Other snakes don't pack enough punch to kill an adult but can make you feel pretty awful. In more than twenty-five years of archaeological fieldwork experience in New England, I have never encountered a venomous snake, at least not while actually in the field. I recently ran into a meter-long copperhead while weed-whacking in the front of my house, but never in the field.

Dangerous viral and bacterial infections and diseases can be carried by molds, spores, and fungi. Valley fever, for example, is a condition caused by inhaling the spores of a soil-dwelling fungus, *Coccidioides immitis*. Coccidioides has been reported primarily in the American Southwest (Fink and Komatsu 2001). For most, the resulting disease consists of little more than what passes for a bout with the flu. However, in some instances chronic disability can result and, though rare, even death. Histoplasmosis is another airborne fungal disease present in the soil, resulting, rather unpleasantly, from the accumulated excrement of bats and birds. It can result in the usual flulike symptoms, but in rare instances it spreads beyond the lungs and may require hospitalization.

Historical archaeologists, in particular those who work in abandoned mines, factories, workshops, and even cemeteries of societies that used potent, poisonous chemicals in their industrial processes, may be exposed to levels of contaminants far beyond what we would allow under modern regimes of workplace protection regulations. For example, embalmers historically used arsenic to preserve the remains of the deceased, and this poisonous chemical can lie hidden in cemetery soils archaeologists encounter (Konefes and McGee 2001). Lead used in paint manufacturing (Saunders and Chandler 2001) as well as mercury and lead used in ore processing (Reno, Bloyd, and Hardesty 2001) all pose dangers to those who disturb the soils in which these toxic elements repose. Archaeologist Michael Roberts (2001:160–64) has compiled an extensive list of chemicals that were used in various industries in Boston (including shipping, woodworking, metal, paint, leather, rubber, felt, textiles, printing, and plastics manufacturing, not to mention the chemical industry itself) long before there were regulations concerning their disposal. After perusing the list, it should come as no surprise that archaeologists in urban areas increasingly are trained in handling hazardous wastes and conduct archaeology in HAZ-MAT (hazardous materials) suits.

Battlefield historians and archaeologists need to be concerned about safety as well. Unexploded ordinance, labeled UXO (in other words, bullets and bombs that were fired but that did not detonate), often lie buried at battlefields. Enormously unpredictable, scraping with a trowel or striking with a shovel may be all that is needed to detonate them. As archaeologists Dana Linck and Joe W. Vann III (2001:169) put it, archaeologists of historical battlefields who do not contact experts in unexploded munitions to clear an area before they excavate "dig fast" and "die young." No archaeologist in the twenty-first century wants to be remembered by a footnote in history texts as the final casualty of the Civil War, so great care is advised for battlefield archaeologists.

Finally, it is not just elements of the natural environment or hazardous wastes left behind by past peoples that pose dangers to archaeologists. Archaeological field methods themselves may also endanger the lives of members of a field crew. Construction crews must obey OSHA (Occupational Safety and Health Administration) regulations concerning the digging of deep pits in which people will work. The danger of wall collapse is always present, and virtually every year workers are seriously injured and even killed when laboring at the bottom of an excavation—for a house foundation, a mine or quarry, or underground tunnel—when the walls collapse on top of them. Archaeologists may not usually dig as deeply or extensively as miners, quarry operators, or house builders, but our pits are sometimes more than deep enough to pose a danger to those who work within them if they are not carefully monitored and their walls adequately supported. For example, as recently as 2005 an Austrian archaeologist, Marcus Koller, was killed when the 2.5-meter-deep excavation trench in which he was working collapsed on him (The Digger 2005).

Finally, archaeologists often work outside and sometimes in areas where other people are conducting assorted illegal activities, including the looting of sites and drug-running. An archaeologist may be seen as a threatening annoyance to these criminals. For example, regretably but not surprisingly, Iraqi archaeologist Abdul Amir Hamadani reported being shot at by looters when he attempted to visit and assess the status of archaeological sites (Farchakh 2004).

The point of this discussion is merely this: Archaeological fieldwork presents dangers to the health and safety of people working in the field. Awareness of these dangers and a proactive approach should minimize the danger and ensure that the field is as safe a place as it is interesting.

Read More

If you would like to become scared out of your wits about the prospect of actually participating in archaeological fieldwork, read any of the following. The point is not to scare anybody away from archaeology but to alert archaeologists to the potential and too-often-ignored but very real dangers in the field.

Bellantoni, N. F. 2001. Ticked Off: Lyme Disease and Archaeologists. In *Dangerous Places: Health, Safety, and Archaeology*, edited by D. Poirier and K. L. Feder, 3–10. Bergin & Garvey, Westport, Connecticut.

Fink, T. M., and K. K. Komatsu. 2001. The Fungus Among Us: *Coccidioidomycosis* ("Valley Fever"). In *Dangerous Places: Health, Safety, and Archaeology*, edited by D. Poirier and K. L. Feder, 21–30. Bergin & Garvey, Westport, Connecticut.

Konefes, J. L., and M. K. McGee. 2001. Old Cemeteries, Arsenic, and Health Safety. In *Dangerous Places: Health, Safety, and Archaeology*, edited by D. Poirier and K. L. Feder, 79–106. Bergin & Garvey, Westport, Connecticut.

Linck, D., and J. W. Vann III. 2001. Dig Fast, Die Young: Unexploded Ordnance and Archaeology. In *Dangerous Places: Health, Safety, and Archaeology*, edited by D. Poirier and K. L. Feder, 169–88. Bergin & Garvey, Westport, Connecticut.

Morganti, T., and N. Tartt. 2001. Rabies: A Short Discourse. In *Dangerous Places: Health, Safety, and Archaeology*, edited by D. Poirier and K. L. Feder, 11–20. Bergin & Garvey, Westport, Connecticut.

Poirier, D., and K. L. Feder. 2001. *Dangerous Places: Health, Safety, and Archaeology*. Bergin & Garvey, Westport, Connecticut.

Reno, R. L., S. R. Boyd, and D. L. Hardesty. 2001. Chemical Soup: Archaeological Hazards at Western Ore-Processing Sites. In *Dangerous Places: Health, Safety, and Archaeology*, edited by D. Poirier and K. L. Feder, 205–20. Bergin & Garvey, Westport, Connecticut.

Roberts, M. 2001. Beneath City Streets: Brief Observations on the Urban Landscape. In *Dangerous Places: Health, Safety, and Archaeology*, edited by D. Poirier and K. L. Feder, 157–68. Bergin and Garvey, Westport, Connecticut.

Saunders, C., and S. R. Chandler. 2001. Get the Lead Out. In *Dangerous Places: Health, Safety, and Archaeology*, edited by D. Poirier and K. L. Feder, 189–204. Bergin & Garvey, Westport, Connecticut.

Study Questions

1. Why was my crew of archaeologists digging test pits in Peoples State Forest in Connecticut?

2. What are the most common reasons for conducting an archaeological survey in a given region?

3. Use the project that discovered the tomb of Egyptian pharaoh Tutankhamen as an example of how archaeological projects were supported in the past. What problems accompanied such funding?

4. What are the major funding sources for archaeological research today?

5. What is the rationale of the federal government of the United States for funding archaeological projects?

6. What is "compliance archaeology"? With what are archaeologists complying?

7. What is an Environmental Impact Statement?

8. What special rights do archaeologists have to gain access to private property to look for sites?

9. How does the law relate to the archaeological excavation of human remains?

10. What is the Native American Graves and Repatriation Act?

11. What does the Archaeological Resources Protection Act of 1979 require of archaeological work proposed on federal land?

12. What was the purpose of the American Antiquities Act of 1906?

13. In what ways did the Archaeological Resources Protection Act of 1979 expand upon or toughen the American Antiquities Act of 1906?

14. What are the most common—and rather mundane—health issues faced by field archaeologists?

15. Discuss the serious bacterial and chemical dangers faced by field scientists, especially those who dig up dirt.

16. What are the particular concerns of archaeologists who work at historical sites where the effluvia of past industries and manufacturing processes yet reside in the soil they excavate?

17. Researchers Dana Linck and J. W. Vann write "Dig fast, die young." What's that about?

5 | A Community's Shadow

THE ARCHAEOLOGICAL SITE

- **What Is an "Archaeological Site," and How Do You Know When You've Found One?**

- **What Kinds of Stuff Do Archaeologists Find at Sites?**

- **How Are Archaeological Sites Made?**
  Site Formation
  Why Do Archaeologists Need to Dig; Why Are Most Sites Buried?
  How Are Archaeological Sites Altered Once Buried?

The archaeological **site** is a fundamental concept in archaeology. It is the archaeological manifestation in the present of people performing tasks and living out their lives at some point in the past. I have already refered to the place that is the focus of the archaeological narrative in chapter 3 as the "Wood Lily site." What do we mean by that term? In this chapter you will find a detailed definition of the "site" as well as a discussion of how sites come into existence.

 What Is an "Archaeological Site," and How Do You Know When You've Found One?

An archaeological site is a place where people once lived or worked or where they carried out specific tasks such as hunting animals; collecting edible nuts;

catching fish; quarrying for metals, minerals, or clay; fighting a battle with their enemies; worshipping their gods; grinding meal; milling lumber; and burying their dead. Crucially, a site is a place where the material remnants of these activities and behaviors can be found. "Villages," "quarries," "cemeteries," "hunting camps," "mill towns," "sacred locations," "battlefields," and the like are the places where people carried out their tasks and where the events of their lives took place (Figure 5.1).

These terms—*cemeteries, hunting camps, battlefields,* and so on—represent human **behavioral contexts**, reflecting how ancient peoples perceived and used these places. Of course, people other than archaeologists don't think in terms of the behavioral contexts of the places they use, they just use them for the purposes intended: to bury the dead, camp, quarry stone or metal, fight battles, grind corn, worship, or simply carry out their daily tasks. The *site*, the thing archaeologists look for and investigate, represents what's left behind by people as a result of their having buried their dead, collected resources, planted crops, hunted game animals, disposed of their trash, and so on. The site, in other words, represents the physical remnants of these human activities, the spoor or trace of a community of people living their lives at a particular place and time. If the village, camp, or quarry represents the behavioral context of a group of people, the site reflects the **archaeological context** of these same folks.

These material manifestations of behavior occur accidentally: People do not set out to produce archaeological sites. People do not ordinarily leave things behind with the deliberate purpose of giving future archaeologists something to find and analyze. Today we may set aside time capsules with a selection of items that exemplify our time and place for future people who might be interested in what life was like "way back when." Change is so rapid these days, our cultural attention span is so short, and we seem so anxious to connect to the past that time capsules tend to be opened just a few decades after they were sealed up. The inhabitants of the dim mists of the 1990s seem quaint and foreign with their CRT computer monitors, MP3 players that could hold only a few dozen tunes, and Pokémon. Archaeological sites do not reflect the self-conscious attempts by past peoples to communicate through material objects the essence of their time on life's stage to an unimaginable future generation of scientists. Sites come into existence through largely unintentional cultural processes.

There are no archaeological "road signs" alerting the inquiring archaeologist to the presence of a site. Archaeologists know they are at a site when, in the course of survey, they encounter physical evidence in the form of **site constituents** (**artifacts, ecofacts**, and/or **features**). *Site constituents* is just a fancy way of describing the things and facilities that people made and used and then lost, discarded, or simply left behind and that have been preserved into the present (McManamon 1984). When an archaeologist finds flint flakes or pottery shards while screening the dirt from a test excavation, he or she knows that the location is an archaeological site. In the subsequent **excavation** the archaeologist hopes to determine the cultural meaning of the site, that is, its

Chapter 5:
Slide Show

FIGURE 5.1 Archaeological sites, such as the remnants of the Roman city of Pompeii (top), a stone lined burial chamber in Britanny, in northwest France (center), and the Giza plateau in Egypt, where resides the Great Sphinx (bottom), are places where people once lived, worked, or carried out a task and where physical evidence of those activities can be found, recovered, and analyzed. (Top and center photos by K. L. Feder, bottom by M. H. Feder).

function and significance to the people who left behind the material remains that today represent the archaeological record of their lives.

Read More

Although "archaeological site" might seem like a difficult concept to define, you certainly would know when you encountered one. Archaeologists have attempted to explain the "site" in formal ways. I have always employed an article by Frank McManamon, who, in his capacity as the director of the federal archaeology program of the National Park Service, ought to know.

McManamon, F. P. 1984. Discovering Sites Unseen. In *Advances in Archaeological Method and Theory*, edited by M. B. Schiffer, vol. 7, 223–92. Academic Press, New York.

 ## What Kinds of Stuff Do Archaeologists Find at Sites?

Archaeologists usually divide the materials we find into the following (or similar) categories: **artifacts, ecofacts**, and **features.** Archaeologist Frank McManamon (1984) has labeled these items the "constituents" of archaeological sites. During the survey phase of an archaeological project, when we are examining an area for the possible presence of sites, these constituents are essentially what we are looking for most directly, the first clues of a past human presence. The site represents the big picture. Artifacts, ecofacts, and features are the pieces of the puzzle, the bits we find and put together to reveal the big picture.

Artifacts are defined simply as the things people made and used and that have by various processes become part of the archaeological record. Artifacts usually are further distinguished by the fact that they are portable; people could pick them up and carry them from place to place. Before these objects actually became "artifacts," they were, among other things, hardware, tools, weapons, items of personal adornment (such as jewelry and religious symbols), storage containers, cooking apparatuses, and fasteners as well as broken bits and pieces all these items and any of the waste fragments produced in their manufacture. Archaeologist Michael Schiffer (1972, 1976) refers to the actual function of items in a society, what they were used for and what they meant to the people who made and used them, in essence, what they might have called these things, as their cultural or behavioral contexts. People make and use hardware, tools, weapons, and so on; they don't set out to produce artifacts any more than you would consider the pen in your pocket, the watch on your wrist, the clothes you are wearing, or the computer on which you may be reading this book an artifact. Those things, in fact, are not artifacts—at least, not yet. In fact, all of your tools, utensils, jewelry, keepsakes, toys, treasures, knickknacks, gear, junk—all of your possessions, all of your stuff—are "artifacts in waiting." *Artifact* is the general term archaeologists apply to these things once they have entered into the archaeological record (Figure 5.2). The term *artifact* reflects what Schiffer labels the archaeological context of these items in the present.

Ecofacts include any environmental elements that become part of the archaeological record as a result of human activity, generally reflecting their use

FIGURE 5.2 When the objects that people made and used become part of the archaeological record, we call them artifacts. The stone drill, clay sculpture, and pottery fragment shown here are all artifacts. (K. L. Feder)

without substantial or goal-oriented modification. It can sometimes be a subtle distinction, but it is an important one to recognize. Ecofacts are not, in the strict sense of the term, artifacts because they were not so modified by people that we would consider them to have been manufactured. These items weren't, in the strict sense of these words, tools or weapons or treasures made by people to serve a particular purpose. Instead, they were used and deposited by people in the conduct of their activities without being *made* into anything. A good example of an ecofact is a piece of wood burned in a hearth fire. Certainly, its presence in the hearth and its burning are the result of human activity—a person collected the wood and put it in a fireplace, using it as fuel—but one wouldn't call the burned wood a tool per se, as you would had the piece of wood instead been shaped and used as a spear. Ecofacts include unmodified (in the sense of not intentionally made into something) wood, nutshells and nutmeat fragments, seeds, pollen, and animal bones if their presence at a site is the result of human activity (Figure 5.3). If an unmodified animal bone is found in the trash heap at an archaeological site, perhaps exhibiting cut marks where a stone tool was used to remove meat, the bone itself is an ecofact. It is an element of the environment—part of an animal—whose presence and appearance are the result of human activity (in this case, hunting and butchering).

On the other hand, an animal bone found at a site bearing engravings of lunar phases, perhaps used as a calendar, clearly is an artifact, an item modified by people to serve a particular purpose. So the left foreleg of a deer killed, butchered, cooked, and eaten by a group of people and then disposed of in the kitchen trash is an ecofact; the right foreleg of the same animal if, for example, it was modified for use as a tent stake and then tossed in the trash after it cracked is an artifact.

A **feature** is an accumulation of material at a particular place and, therefore, represents a different level of analysis than an artifact or ecofact. Features often are a concentration of artifacts and/or ecofacts as well as structural remains (Figure 5.4). Features are nonportable and spatially bounded, often resulting from an activity or set of activities in which items used together or disposed of together were deposited. For example, the ground where a stone tool maker removed sharp flakes from a stone **core** by **percussion flaking** with a stone hammer and then shaped and sharpened some of those flakes into particular tool types will become littered with **debitage** (waste flakes of stone too small to be of use), battered chunks of **hammerstone**, nearly complete tools broken in the final stages of manufacture and then abandoned, and pieces of antler ground off in **pressure flaking.** Each of these items individually—waste flakes, snapped tools, hammerstone chunks, ground antler fragments—are artifacts. Together, they demarcate space that we might call an **activity area**, that is, its behavioral context, a place where people conducted an activity, whose archaeological manifestation is a feature. Hearths, burials, workshops, and house remains are all archaeological features.

Taken together, the presence of artifacts, ecofacts, and features define an archaeological site, which was, in life, a place where people may have lived, worked, carried out a particular task, and even died and were buried—and in some instances where they did all these things.

FIGURE 5.3 The term *ecofact* refers to elements of the environment that are found at archaeological sites and that reflect the activity of human beings; here are shown charcoal from an ancient fireplace (top) and the bones of bison killed in an ancient hunt (bottom; courtesy Kent Buchler).

FIGURE 5.4 An archaeological feature is the reflection of the activity that took place at a particular place and time and usually includes the artifacts and ecofacts used or produced by that activity. Examples include a 4,200-year-old meat roasting platform in Connecticut (top), a tiled floor in Pompeii (center), and a stone burial chamber in northwestern France (bottom). (K. L. Feder)

Read More

For more details on how archaeologists formally label the categories of materials that constitute the archaeological record, the following sources are most helpful.

McManamon, F. P. 1984. Discovering Sites Unseen. In *Advances in Archaeological Method and Theory*, edited by M. B. Schiffer, vol. 7, 223–92. Academic Press, New York.

Schiffer, M. B. 1972. Archaeological Context and Systemic Context. *American Antiquity* 37:156–65.

———. 1976. *Behavioral Archaeology*. Academic Press, New York.

 ## How Are Archaeological Sites Made?

In his book *Behavioral Archaeology* (1976), his book *Formation Processes of the Archaeological Record* (1987), and in a number of articles he authored in the 1970s and 1980s (Schiffer 1972, 1975, 1983), archaeologist Michael Schiffer formally laid out the processes by which archaeological sites come into existence. In the overwhelming majority of cases, these processes of **archaeological site formation** operate entirely unintentionally. People do not ordinarily set out to create archaeological sites; they do not consciously or intentionally contribute to the archaeological record, hoping that sometime in the future someone will excavate and analyze their leavings. An exception to this general rule in the modern era would be time capsules. For the most part, however, stuff ends up "archaeological" by accident through a number of often rather obvious, commonsense processes. Schiffer enumerated these **site formation processes** as (1) loss, (2) discard, (3) caching, and (4) abandonment.

SITE FORMATION

Obviously enough, people lose stuff, and if no one picks up these lost items, another set of processes works its magic and ensconces them in the archaeological record. Loss is a process by which even today's modern material culture is being transmitted into the archaeological record. Walk across your campus, for example, especially on dirt paths, keeping your gaze on the ground. See how many pens, pencils, and coins you can find, lost by your cohorts. Much of this stuff is dirty, broken from people stepping on it, and generally ignored. Over time the items may be covered by loose soil or mud after a rain and become part of the archaeological record of your campus. Consider also those folks who trawl popular beaches with metal detectors, looking for lost money, keys, class rings, and other jewelry that became covered in sand almost instantly upon being dropped. People have always dropped and lost things, a simple process that has long contributed to the archaeological record.

Here's an example. A few years ago a local landowner called me. The previous year the gentleman decided to resod his lawn and thought it would be a good idea to first remove the stones and pebbles from the soil. To accomplish this he constructed a screen, coincidentally similar to the kind of device archaeologists use to aid in the recovery of artifacts during test pitting and excavation. Apparently, early in the process the landowner found the tip of a chipped stone spear point. Naturally, he was fascinated by the discovery and hoped to find more evidence of ancient artifacts in his soil. He continued screening the soil for the better part of a year—not as an archaeological enterprise, but as preparation for new sod. He never found anything else. Nothing. He wondered how a single, broken object could end up on a large expanse of land (Figure 5.5).

Had the man's property been the location of an ancient village inhabited for a long period of time by a sizeable population of people, we would expect there to be plenty of physical evidence of that occupation: All the stuff the inhabitants lost, discarded, secreted away, or simply abandoned. It was pretty clear that though the man was not an archaeologist and might have missed some of the subtler clues of ancient activity, after screening all the soil on his property over the course of a year, he would have found a lot more than a single broken spear point if he were in the middle of an ancient village site. It seems to be an inviolable rule of human behavior: Wherever people live or work, they make and leave a mess behind. Archaeologists are grateful for that tendency, because such a "mess" of artifacts, ecofacts, and features together constitutes the archaeological record.

Though we cannot say for certain how the broken spear point ended up in soil that many years later became part of this man's suburban house lot, loss is

FIGURE 5.5 This broken spear point was an isolated find; no other archaeological artifacts were found in spatial association with it. (K. L. Feder)

a reasonable possibility. Maybe at some time in the past, at that spot a hunter threw a spear at an animal and missed. The spear struck the ground, perhaps hitting a rock, and the stone point snapped in two. The spear shaft was easy to find, with the base of the stone point still attached, and the hunter probably recovered it. But the tip, broken off and lost in the leaves or pine needles, wasn't worth searching for and might not have been worth the effort even if it could have been found. It was left where it fell, to be incorporated into the soil and to be found by sheer accident and coincidence many years later by someone curious enough about its meaning to contact the closest archaeologist: me.

Perhaps the most significant site formation process that contributes to the creation of archaeological sites is discard. For example, in the course of making stone tools, a certain amount of waste called **debitage** is produced. These stone waste chips, perhaps too small to be of any use or too awkwardly shaped to be salvaged by the tool maker, are simply left where they fall in the process of removing stone flakes from a core. Trash left like this, where it initially falls to earth, is called **primary refuse** (Figure 5.6).

Once made and part of a **tool kit**, tools may simply wear out or break. A dull stone edge can be resharpened for a while but eventually can become useless, and the tool will be discarded. Some stone tools may break in such a way as to make their reworking or mending impossible or more time consuming than simply starting from scratch and making a new one.

Ceramic fragments are often found in prodigious numbers at archaeological sites. At a recent excavation of a tiny site covering only about 50 square meters (a little more than 500 square feet, the area of a good-sized living room)

FIGURE 5.6 Lithic scatter. Note the scatter of pieces of chipped stone, particularly in the center of this photograph. These bits of stone, the largest of which is no more than 5 centimeters (about 2 inches) across, represent primary refuse, waste flakes left just where they fell to the ground during the process of stone tool production at, in this case, a nearly 5,000-year-old site. (K. L. Feder)

in the Farmington River Archaeological project, we found only a handful of stone tools but more than 200 broken pieces of pottery, probably all from one or two smashed pots. Pottery, though extremely useful as waterproof vessels, fireproof cooking containers, and generally durable serving dishes, is breakable and will shatter into sometimes hundreds of pieces when dropped on a hard enough surface.

I occasionally make pottery. It's a lot of work, and there are many steps in the production of even a simple utilitarian piece. I am certain, however, that throwing and trimming a new pot, bisque firing, glazing, and then glaze firing it are much easier and more sensible then trying to mend and make useful again an old pot that has been smashed into a hundred small fragments. What happens when a pot breaks? The broken fragments, or **sherds**, may be left where they fall or, more often, swept up and placed in a trash pit or pile. Left where they fell, the potsherds would be primary refuse as we just defined it. Discarded material that is gathered and deposited in a special trash pit or pile is said to be **secondary refuse.**

Some activities produce garbage as a matter of course, when people extract the useful part of a resource from the useless. People may find walnuts, chestnuts, or hickory nuts tasty, but the shells that enclose the nutmeats are not digestible and may simply be thrown away. Corn kernels are nutritious, but the cobs on which they grow are not edible and may be viewed as nothing more than rubbish. Deer meat may be packed with protein; the antlers may be useful as pressure flaking tools for sharpening the edges of stone knives, scrapers, or arrow points; some of the bones contain large amounts of nutritious marrow; but many of the bones, especially the smaller ones, may be of little use to people. Much of this stuff—nutshells, seed hulls, bone fragments, shells, and so on—though useful in certain technologies, may also be perceived by people as useless trash and may end up in a **kitchen midden** or dump. As soon as these materials end up in the pile, pit, dump, or midden, they enter into the archaeological site formation stream, and, if not dragged away by an animal or recovered and recycled for use by someone else centuries or millennia later, they may, as archaeological objects, contribute to our knowledge of the diet, technology, or other practices of a group of people (Figure 5.7).

Another behavior of human beings that can contribute to the formation of archaeological sites is the practice of stashing away stuff intended for later use. The French verb "to hide" is *cacher*, and in English the word "cache" is used both as a verb (meaning "to hide away for safekeeping") and as a noun (for the actual place—a "cache"—where something is hidden away). When we find a pit with a stash of projectile points, crystals, or some other material at an archaeological site, we often interpret it as just such a **cache**, a feature that reflects an accumulation of stuff that was put away or stored. In the case of a true cache, we often assume that the person who stored the material had every intention of returning to retrieve it when needed but for one reason or another—and lucky for the archaeologist—they never did, and neither did anyone else. When we find a discrete accumulation of artifacts, not broken bits that obviously made their way into the ground as refuse but material that the maker probably intended to retrieve, we call it a cache. This behavior is yet

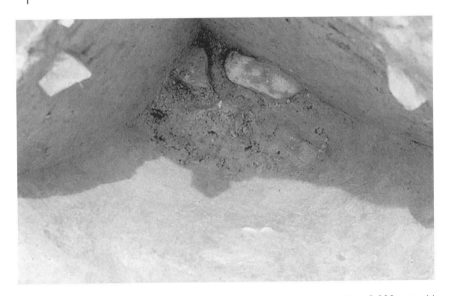

FIGURE 5.7 Looking down into an excavated trash pit found at a more than 3,000-year-old site in Ohio. Here, the pit matrix—the trash that was thrown into the pit by the inhabitants of the site—is in the process of being recovered and returned to the lab for analysis. Broken stones, white flecks of bone, and black fragments of burned wood can still be seen at the bottom and along the walls of the pit. (K. L. Feder)

another process by which objects move from the realm of a living culture to the world of the archaeological record.

A cache may also represent a desire to remove objects or remains from the above-ground secular world in which we all live to a sacred realm sometimes represented by the Earth itself. In a sense an intentional human or animal burial is an example of such a cache: the placement of the remains of a loved one in a way that serves a practical sanitary purpose by disposing of a corpse and that also produces a memorial to the deceased, consecrating and, perhaps, marking the place where their mortal remains are housed.

Even objects alone, without human remains, may be buried for ceremonial purposes, essentially put into the Earth as offerings to gods or spirits. It seems the only explanation for the Glazier Blade Cache (Figure 5.8), a neatly arranged, tight cluster of thirty large stone blades that we excavated in Granby, Connecticut, in 1993 (http://archnet.asu.edu/archives/lithic/blades/glazier.html). At a mean length of more than 13.5 centimeters (5.3 inches), with the largest measuring more than 18 centimeters (7 inches), it seems unlikely that these objects were ever intended for use, and, indeed, there is no evidence along their edges that they had ever been used. The Glazier blades were placed into an isolated pit in the ground about 1,600 years ago. The pit itself was not part of a site; no additional archaeological material was found anywhere nearby. It is at least plausible that these blades were placed into the ground as an offering, the details of which we will never know.

Finally, people sometimes abandon material for reasons we may never fully understand. Tools, food, and personal possessions may be left where they were

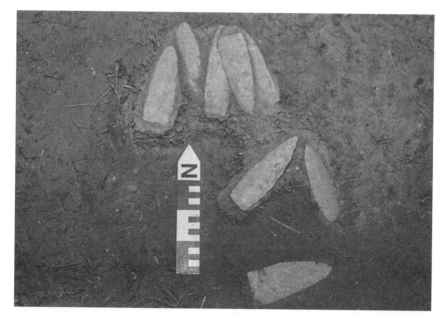

FIGURE 5.8 Eight stone blades of the total of thirty that were found in the Glazier Blade Cache located in the town of Granby, Connecticut. These blades were neatly stacked in a shallow pit approximately 1,600 years ago. (K. L. Feder)

being used or stored when people abandoned a place as the result of a catastrophe. A house may catch fire, and many of the items stored there may be abandoned or burned and become part of the archaeological record. A natural cataclysm (for example, a volcanic eruption) may inspire the inhabitants of a community to flee, leaving their possessions behind to be covered by ash or lava. An aggressive enemy might descend upon an unsuspecting village whose inhabitants abandon their homes and most of their possessions. The attackers may cart away many of the valuables and ignore everyday items, which then become part of the archaeological record through abandonment.

The site formation processes described contribute to the production of the archaeological record. It would seem that without tragedy, destruction, forgetfulness, carelessness, sloppiness, and catastrophe the archaeological record wouldn't amount to much.

Read More

To find out more about how archaeologists explain the ways in which human behavior becomes transformed into an archaeological record of that behavior, the following books and articles—most, but not all, by archaeologist Michael Schiffer—are an enormous help.

Dunnell, R. C. 1992. The Notion Site. In *Space, Time, and Archaeological Landscapes*, edited by J. Rossignol and L. Wandsnider, 21–41. Plenum Press, New York.

Ebert, J. I. 1992. *Distributional Archaeology*. University of New Mexico Press, Albuquerque.

Schiffer, M. B. 1972. Archaeological Context and Systemic Context. *American Antiquity* 37:156–65.

———. 1975. Archaeology as a Behavioral Science. *American Anthropologist* 77:836–48.

———. 1976. *Behavioral Archaeology*. Academic Press, New York.

———. 1983. Toward the Identification of Site Formation Processes. *American Antiquity* 48:673–706.

———. 1987. *Formation Processes of the Archaeological Record*. University of New Mexico Press, Albuquerque.

Why Do Archaeologists Need to Dig; Why Are Most Sites Buried?

Once tools become artifacts, food becomes organic refuse, and hearths, tool-making areas, and houses become features—in other words, once the material people made and used and then lost, cached, abandoned, or disposed of becomes part of the archaeological record—a number of other natural and cultural processes may be applied that either help preserve the remains in their original spatial contexts or may serve to alter the stuff physically, chemically, and in terms of its location. The application of these processes explains why in most cases archaeologists need to dig down into the ground in order to reveal and recover archaeological remains.

For example, rivers and streams regularly burst over their banks and deposit a layer of silt that covers everything over which the water flows. A single flood episode may leave only a fraction of a centimeter of deposit that may, in turn, blow away once it becomes dry, but large-scale floods have been known to deposit more than a meter of silt. Multiple floods over many years can build up thick deposits over archaeological material, producing a chronological sequence in the soil with a series of archaeological layers representing different episodes of occupation of a particular place separated by deposits laid down during flooding.

Outside the limits of a river or stream's **floodplain**, other natural processes can cover archaeological material. Leaves and pine needles build up on the surface of a forest floor and decay, ensconcing the stuff that people lost or discarded in a blanket of humus. Humus eventually becomes the soil in which archaeologists probe for those objects left behind by past peoples. Generally, this all happens rather slowly, so in most places recent and built-up features are often still visible on the surface, but ancient material dropped or deposited by people many hundreds or thousands of years ago becomes covered up. Those materials that are preserved while covered make up the subsurface archaeological record.

Other processes of waterborne deposition occur along the shores of lakes as well as in coastal regions. Like rivers, lakes are affected by fluctuations in precipitation and may expand and contract as a result. Sites that are located close to a lake shore may end up being inundated during periods of high water and may be covered entirely by the sand, gravel, and silt carried by the expanding lake waters. These are called **lacustrine** deposits.

Just as lake levels may fluctuate, resulting in the inundation of sites, the world's ocean levels change, in some cases quite dramatically. When sea level rises (as it has been doing for the last 12,000 years or so), sites located along coasts may become covered not only by rising water but by marine deposits of sand, gravel, silt, and rock moved around by tide and wave action. For example, we know that about 14,000 years ago, worldwide sea level was at least 100 meters (nearly 330 feet) lower than it is today because a much larger proportion of the world's ocean water was locked up in the ice sheets that covered much of northern North America and the higher elevations of South America, Europe, and Asia. As a result, continental coasts were located much farther out, in places that are miles out to sea today. Archaeological sites actually have been found by probing those areas now underwater but that in antiquity were coastal regions. Using submersible vehicles, researchers Daryl W. Fedje and Heiner Josenhans (2000), for example, have explored a section of ancient coast off Alaska and recovered a 10,000-year-old spear point at a site that today is 53 meters (about 175 feet) below the ocean's surface but that was, rather obviously, dry and very hospitable land in the distant past.

Nearly everything eventually goes downhill (certainly literally, and some might argue figuratively, as well). Gravity acts to move soil, gravel, and even rock downslope, and this material can blanket archaeological material, in some cases protecting the stuff left behind at abandoned habitations. A village located at the base of a hill or foot of a mountain may be slowly (and sometimes not so slowly) covered with soil and rock eroding off the high ground. Even very large rocks can move downhill as a result of gravity, covering archaeological materials at the base of the hill. These covering deposits pulled downslope by gravity are called **colluvium.**

Though wind cannot ordinarily move heavy rocks or boulders, it can push around enormous quantities of **unconsolidated** (loose) **material**, for example, sand, which can cover and protect archaeological sites. These **aeolian** deposits play a major role in covering sites, especially in such dry parts of the world as areas of the Middle East, where there is a shortage of plant life to hold the soil in place. Windblown sand can accumulate and cover an abandoned village, producing a natural time capsule of a community.

Catastrophic processes may act to cover archaeological material. An erupting volcano may eject tons of ash, which can cover a village almost instantaneously, killing thousands and creating and covering an archaeological site in the process. The eruption of Mt. Vesuvius in A.D. 79 obliterated the Roman city of Pompeii in a virtual heartbeat, destroying and forever freezing the moment of destruction of an ancient metropolis (Figure 5.9; Guzzo, D'Ambrosio, and Foglia 2000).

Sometime near A.D. 1491, a Native American village in what is today the state of Washington was blanketed by a landslide (Pascua 1991). Like a coating of slip smeared onto a pot, a slush of waterlogged earth rushed down the hillside above the village, plowing down everything above ground and enfolding

FIGURE 5.9 The agency of a community's destruction may also be the factor that preserves its remains as an archaeological site. Volcanic Mt. Vesuvius looms in the background. The city of Pompeii was destroyed, but its remains were preserved by the eruption of Vesuvius in A.D. 79.

everything on the surface in a thick slurry of mud. The village was destroyed by the mudslide, but the archaeological manifestation of that village produced by the catastrophe (now called the Ozette site) was remarkably well preserved by being packed in mud until its rediscovery 500 years later in A.D. 1991. Ozette, like Pompeii, represents a moment frozen in time, a village of people destroyed and an archaeological site created in the same instant.

Whichever natural process is at work to blanket the surface at a given place, archaeological material gets covered up, and archaeologists must adopt the motto of the utility provider in New York City, Consolidated Edison, which is forever apologizing for disrupting the flow of traffic in the city by repairing underground utilities: "Dig We Must." And dig we do, as well.

How Are Archaeological Sites Altered Once Buried?

Once buried, archaeological materials are not housed in a sterile, static environment, perfectly preserved until the timely arrival of the curious archaeologist. Unfortunately, as noted earlier, sites are not hermetically sealed time capsules but, instead, are often located in active depositional environments characterized by processes of decay and destruction. For example, most soils bloom with biological activity, filled with organisms whose diets consist of organic residues that end up in the soil. Unfortunately, those residues include the bones and plant remains that, if preserved, would enable us to reconstruct ancient diets and artifacts made of bone, wood, plant fibers, and animal hides. Preservation of these organic residues may depend on the level of biological activity of the soils in which they are deposited; in New England and in many other temperate and tropical forest zones, organic residues may be rare and difficult to find.

Soil chemistry also affects archaeological material buried in that soil. For example, low pH reflecting high soil acidity has an enormous impact on preservation, leaving few organic remains intact. Areas where coniferous trees are abundant and where their needles accumulate on the ground commonly have corrosively acidic soils where most remains other than ceramics or stone are destroyed after only a very few years. Bone may be preserved in high pH alkaline soils, but such an environment may be no better than acidic soil for the preservation of plant remains. Some chemical processes serve to preserve remains as well. For example, high quantities of copper in the soil may serve as a preservative for organic remains. Most soils do not have a sufficient natural quantity of copper to accomplish this, but organic objects near copper artifacts may be preserved where they come in contact with the metal.

Physical processes also serve to alter archaeological material. Flowing water across the surface of an abandoned village may move and even entirely remove site elements before the water subsides and before it has the opportunity to cover the site with silt. A coastal site may be so eroded by the powerful action of ocean waves that it may be washed away in its entirety.

Once deposited and covered by soil, alternate freezing and thawing with attendant expansion and contraction may serve to break up delicate remains subjected to this kind of rough physical weathering. Even the process by which the ground is moistened by rain and floodwater that percolates through the soil and then dries out may cause expansion and contraction, during which especially delicate archaeological material may be broken up.

You can see why many archaeologists focus on stone and ceramic objects. Stone is especially resilient and will remain intact under virtually all soil conditions. Ceramic objects may easily break, but the resulting sherds are pretty tough and will be perserved under most soil conditions.

Finally, the activities of subsequent human groups may serve to disturb, move, and even destroy the remains of previous inhabitants of an area. Certainly, our modern capacity to alter the landscape is greater than anything seen in the past—and as a result, our construction of highways, shopping malls, parking lots, and homes destroys sites at an acclerating rate. However, ancient peoples also dug holes, constructed foundations, plowed fields, buried their dead, and so on and in so doing disturbed the archaeological remains left behind by peoples even more ancient than them.

It must be admitted that with all of the barriers established by nature and history between the past and the present, it is remarkable that anything remains for the archaeologist to recover. But exist they do, and the search for those preserved traces is the focus of the following chapter.

Read More

To learn more about the processes that serve to bury archaeological sites, read virtually any geology textbook. For more information on the specific examples mentioned in this section, check out the following resources.

Fedje, D. W., and H. Josenhans. 2000. Drowned Forests and Archaeology on the Continental Shelf of British Columbia, Canada. *Geology* 28:99–102.

Guzzo, P. G., A. D'Ambrosio, and A. Foglia. 2000. *Pompeii*. Getty Trust Publication, Los Angeles.

Pascua, M. P. 1991. A Makah Village in 1491: Ozette. *National Geographic* 180(4):38–53.

Study Questions

1. What is an artifact?
2. What is an ecofact?
3. What is a feature?
4. What is the fundamental difference between an artifact and an ecofact?
5. Provide a general list of possible archaeological features.
6. How does an area where an activity was carried out (e.g., stone tool making) become transformed into the archaeological context of a feature?
7. The terms *artifact, ecofact,* and *feature* denote the archaeological contexts of things unearthed by archaeologists. Name some possible behavioral contexts of artifacts, ecofacts, and features.
8. What is a site formation process? What does it do?
9. What are the primary archaeological site formation processes enumerated by archaeologist Michael Schiffer?
10. After carefully screening all his topsoil to allow for a better lawn, a local landowner finds a single, isolated stone spear point. What are some possible ways in which that spear point became part of the archaeological record? What site formation processes may have been at work?
11. What is the difference between primary and secondary refuse? From the perspective of an archaeologist excavating a site, what are the advantages and disadvantages of these different elements of the archaeological record?
12. What is a cache? In what way is a cache a unique kind of archaeological feature?
13. Define the term *archaeological site.*

14. Provide a list of ten different entities for which the term *archaeological site* would be appropriate.

15. What is "behavioral context"? What is "archaeological context"?

16. Name the "constituents" of archaeological sites.

17. The site concept represents the archaeological context of what?

6

Searching for the Past

ARCHAEOLOGICAL SITE SURVEY

- **How Do Archaeologists Know Where to Look for Sites?**

  How GIS Help Identify Places Where Sites Are Likely to Be Found?

- **What Are the Mechanics of Looking for and Finding Sites?**

- **What Forms the Basis of an Archaeological "Sampling Strategy"?**

- **How Can You Find Archaeological Sites Just by Walking Around?**

- **How Deep Do You Have to Dig to Find Archaeological Material?**

  How Can Archaeologists Probe the Subsurface Without Digging Holes?

OK, so I get quite a bit of mileage out of the story presented in the narrative about how I predicted with astonishing precision the location where my field crew would find the archaeological site we called Wood Lily. I don't think I am giving away any trade secrets when I tell you that it took little more than common sense and a bit of archaeological expreience to accomplish this seemingly clairvoyant feat. This chapter lets you in on the ways in which the location of a site like Wood Lily can be accurately forecast.

How Do Archaeologists Know Where to Look for Sites?

In a regional archaeological survey like the one we conducted in Peoples State Forest, we were not simply looking for sites, we were attempting to understand more broadly an ancient pattern of land use. Sites are important, of course, but our perspective went beyond simply the site to encompass a broader investigation of the overall use of the landscape by the ancient residents of northwestern Connecticut. On this point archaeologist Robin Dunnell (1992) proposes that the archaeological record is not composed solely of separate and discrete locations where artifacts and features are found. He maintains that the archaeological record, instead, is essentially continuous across the landscape, reflecting the temporally lengthy and geographically unbroken use of that landscape by human groups. People may live in a particular place (and produce a site), but we must not lose sight of the fact that people may exploit a broad region for hunting; fishing; collecting plant foods; harvesting plants; gathering resources such as stone, clay, and metal; burying their dead; trading with friends; fighting enemies; and worshipping their gods. Many of these activities leave physical evidence behind, and we need to find and interpret those traces as they appear across an entire landscape to better understand an ancient culture. Using the analogy of a photograph on this same issue, Ebert (1992:245–46) proposes that focusing on the individual site is equivalent to viewing ancient life as a series of discrete snapshots, with each site viewed as a separate photograph in time. Ebert suggests that the archaeological record is actually more like a single, lengthy, time-exposure photograph of a natural and cultural landscape, a picture with images overlapping in space and time. Some parts of the photograph may be brighter—these would be places used more intensively and that we call sites—but the image is nonetheless nearly continuous. It is useful therefore to expand our focus from the use of individual places to that of the entire landscape used by ancient people. This focus is called, in fact, **landscape archaeology** and conforms to our approach in the Peoples State Forest survey.

This pattern of use of a landscape is called the **settlement pattern** of an ancient group of people and leaves behind what archaeologists William Marquardt and Carol Crumley have called a **landscape signature** (1987:7). That landscape signature consists of the geographical locations of cities, towns, villages and camps, quarries, mills and factories, sacred places, shrines, burial grounds, battlefields, and so on. These entities were established by past peoples in various places for myriad reasons (Dincauze 1978; Feder 1997b; Schiffer, Sullivan, and Klinger 1978). For example, a city may have developed along a river where transportation and trade would have been easiest. Quarries were placed, obviously enough, where the resources being quarried were located.

Sacred places may have been located far from a population center, in a cave or near an awe-inspiring view or impressive rock formation imbued with sacred meaning by the ancient people (Figure 6.1). A hidden overlook near an animal trail is an obvious place for a hunting camp. A secluded, hidden niche in a cliff may have been an appealing place to settle for a people with nasty neighbors. A fall-line where rapids create a situation conducive to fishing during the seasonal upstream migration of anadromous fish such as salmon provides an opportunity for the exploitation of a rich source of food. The area along a narrow section of a stream that can be easily impounded and controlled so that the water can be used to turn a waterwheel, whose energy can in turn be used to power a grist, saw, or carding mill, would have appealed to people who used the energy of flowing water to power their industry. A topographically flat area with organically rich soil was attractive to agricultural people. A spot near an ancient volcano with an abundant deposit of obsidian easily flaked into sharp-edged tools would draw people who relied on stone for their tools and weapons. A place with gentle topography, a reliable source of good drinking water (a spring or a permanent watercourse), and an abundant source of wood for construction and fuel, with natural protection (a surrounding wetland or adjacent mountain) was a sensible spot for a permanent village (Figure 6.2). Humans have even decided which places to avoid (for example, a no-man's land between hostile groups or locations believed to be inhabited by evil spirits).

Chapter 6:
Interactive
Exercise

Locales that afford useful natural characteristics—remembering that *useful*, in our application of the term, is culturally defined and differs among different groups of people—are logical places for people to have used and are logical places to examine in the search of the material evidence of past peoples. People use the landscape in ways that are both sensible and predictable, at least from their own perspective. No single type of landscape will have monopolized the attention of past peoples, and, therefore, no single type of landform will have a monopoly of sites.

Once we recognize the elements of an area that were attractive to people of a given culture in a particular period of time, we can both explain the locations of the archaeological sites we have found and accurately predict the most reasonable locations to look for sites that we have yet to find. Archaeologists employ a series of commonsense techniques in **site survey**, the process of searching for the locations where archaeological material can be found (Feder 1997b).

By examining detailed maps archaeologists can identify particular places where the confluence of a number of important features of the landscape makes it likely that sites will be found. Each human group develops its own practice of land use—a **settlement pattern**—that depends on a complex interplay of their subsistence focus (whether they are foragers or farmers, hunters or fisherfolk, generalists relying on a broad array of food sources or specialists focusing on a small number of highly productive foods), mode of technology (whether stone or metal is the predominant raw material for their tools; if they make ceramics; if they rely on wood for construction or on stone, clay, earth, or bone; if they power their industry with flowing water), and their yearly pattern of land use and seasonality (whether they are **sedentary**, living in one

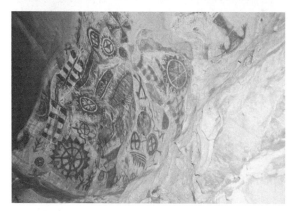

FIGURE 6.1 People distribute themselves across the landscape, often in ways that are consistent and comprehensible. Here, a modern Connecticut city, Hartford, developed along a natural route of communication and trade (top), residents of the Farmgton Valley collected lithic raw materials at a natural out-crop (center), and people painted ceremonial images in a cave in California. By understanding a group's pattern of land use, we can predict the locations where the archaeological traces can be found.

FIGURE 6.2 A hidden niche in a cliff face (where a small building can be ensconced—Montezuma's Castle in Arizona), a narrow stream bed where the flowing water can easily be diverted (for storing the potential energy of impounded water—a breached mill dam in Granby, Connecticut), and the broad swath cut by a meandering river (the Farmington River in central Connecticut) each presented a past people with an opportunity. The archaeological record reflects the exploitation of those opportunities. (K. L. Feder)

place all year relying on the resources offered there; **nomadic**, moving from place to place on a regular schedule following the availability of resources; or their settlement pattern falls somewhere between sedentary and nomadic).

In the search for sites, archaeologists need to be inclusive. Looking for sites in the kinds of places where we have always found sites while conducting previous research—for example, in the land adjacent to a major river—will ensure that we find sites in only those kinds of places. Our prophecy of finding sites in particular spots will be self-fulfilling, but our picture of a past people's land use will be incomplete. Even though we may be fairly certain where, for example, village sites with their rich artifact assemblages might be discovered because of a distinct pattern in the location of villages already found, we cannot restrict our search to only those kinds of areas. We need to investigate a broad diversity of landscapes in our hope to illuminate the concomitant diverse nature of an ancient human land use pattern.

I accurately predicted the location of the Wood Lily site in Peoples State Forest because three significant features of the surrounding landscape were readily apparent on the topographic map we were using in the field: (1) proximity to a freshwater stream; (2) the presence, within an area of rather rough and uneven topography, of a flat surface sufficiently large to allow for a number of structures; and (3) a terrace immediately to the west of the location high enough to provide a windbreak, adding an element of protection from the weather for anyone living east of the ridge (Figure 6.3). In other words, Wood Lily would have been a clever place to live, and one can almost always rely on the cleverness of ancient peoples whose lives depended on choosing wisely the locations of their villages, encampments, and locations for resource extraction.

Read More

To find out more about the process of successfully predicting locations of archaeological sites, any of the following resources are helpful.

Dincauze, D. F. 1978. Surveying for Cultural Resources: Don't Rush Out with a Shovel. In *Conservation Archaeology in the Northeast: Toward a Research Orientation*, edited by A. Speiss, vol. 3, 51–59. Peabody Museum of Archaeology and Ethnology, Cambridge, Massachusetts.

Feder, K. L. 1997b. Site Survey. In *Field Methods in Archaeology*, edited by T. R. Hester, H. J. Shafer, and K. L. Feder, 41–68. Mayfield Publishing, Mountain View, California.

Marquardt, W. H., and C. Crumley. 1987. Theoretical Issues in the Analysis of Spatial Patterning. In *Regional Dynamics: Burgundian Landscapes in Historical Perspective*, edited by C. L. Crumley and W. H. Marquardt, 1–18. Academic Press, San Diego.

Schiffer, M. B., A. P. Sullivan, and T. C. Klinger. 1978. The Design of Archaeological Surveys. *World Archaeology* 10:1–28.

FIGURE 6.3 People established a settlement for sensible reasons at the location we called the Wood Lily site. The community was located on a flat terrace broad enough to space out a number of small wooden structures, there was easy access to freshwater directly behind the location from which I took the photo, and ahead, to the west, was a slope big enough to serve as a wind break. (K. L. Feder)

How GIS Help Identify Places Where Sites Are Likely to Be Found?

Once we locate an archaeological site, our next step is to determine why an ancient people positioned themselves there. Why did they select this particular place to settle in a village, build a mill complex, quarry metal ore, or establish a hunting camp?

Our interest in accurately locating a site on a map can be traced, in part, to the applicability in archaeology of an old real estate cliché: "There are three important factors to consider when determining the value of a piece of real estate: location, location, location." Recognizing the factors that influenced a group's decision to use a specific location on their landscape allows us to explain their pattern of land use. Understanding that pattern allows us successfully to predict the location of other sites in places we have not yet looked. A given place provides people, both modern and ancient, a particular set of benefits. Human beings have always based their decisions to settle or exploit a particular place on their own set of complex calculations concerning the benefits of the location (Feder 1997b; Marquardt and Crumley 1987).

Our task, then, becomes one of assessing as many variables as possible in our attempt to reveal that set of calculations. Our ability to do this is greatly enhanced through the use of a mapping and analytical tool called **Geographic Information Systems (GIS).**

GIS refer to an analytical tool useful in the examination and interpretation of spatially distributed information through the production of maps that convey the nature of the relationships among sets of spatially distributed data (McPherron and Dibble 2002; Wheatley and Gillings 2002). Essentially, GIS consist of computer mapping software (commercially produced and distributed packages include *ArcView, ArcGIS,* and *Geomedia*) that allow archaeologists (or geographers, geologists, botanists, zoologists, etc.) to produce maps simultaneously depicting the distribution of an enormous number of variables across a given landscape. The scale of that landscape can range from that of a single archaeological feature to that of a site, a geographic region, a continent, or even the entire world. All combinations of spatially distributed variables can be depicated on the map. Overlaying the geographical distributions of each of those variables may reveal patterns and correlations in their spatial distributions that might not otherwise be apparent (Figure 6.4).

Imagine a grid superimposed over an entire region with a series of measurements (of **continuous variables**) and expressions (of **discontinuous** or **nominal variables**) recorded at each point on the grid: for example, elevation, slope and soil pH (measurable, continuous variables) and soil type and presence or absence of flowing water (discontinuous variables, for which the value at any given point is not a measurement but a name). Those measurements or records represent a database and may be stored in a spreadsheet where each column represents a spatially distributed variable and each row represents a location on the grid where each variable's expression at that spot is recorded. In other words, each cell in the spreadsheet has a value or name that represents the expression of a given variable (for example, elevation or soil type) at a given place (for example, the X,Y coordinate) on the gridded region being mapped.

GIS programs can combine the distributions of some or all of these variables into a single or multiple maps on which their spatial association may become apparent (for example, sites might always be near flowing water and a source of good stone, but never above a certain elevation). This provides us with a clue as to where to look for sites in subsequent testing and where sites might be unlikely.

Along with mapping points and places on a map (e.g., stone flakes at a place where tools were made within a site, sites located in the Mississippi River Valley, or pyramids in Egypt), non-spatial data can be linked to the mapped locations. For example, using GIS an archaeologist can map the locations of every excavated artifact, linking all the data associated with each mapped artifact. The resulting file is interactive; viewing a map of artifact locations on the computer, a researcher can click on each object and bring up a box that contains

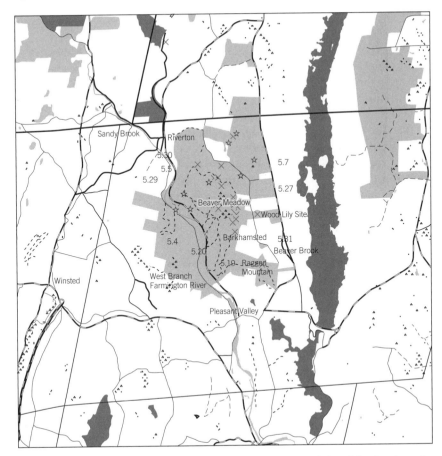

FIGURE 6.4 GIS map showing Peoples State Forest with the boundaries of the forest, roads, drainage streams, and archaeological site locations each making up a layer of the map. (Keegan Associates)

information about it, including all measurements, raw material, depth at which it was found, name of excavator, and anything else deemed significant.

GIS doesn't necessarily produce new data, but it allows us to examine data in new ways. Our imperfect and limited minds have a difficult time decrypting vast arrays of data stored in spreadsheets with tens of columns and hundreds of rows. The visual patterning that becomes apparent in the mapping of these data is far easier for our minds to absorb and is a valuable tool in providing insights into how these spatially distributed data might be patterned or correlated.

Read More

To find out more about the role of landscape in archaeological analysis, see the following resources; in particular, take a look at the book by Wheatley and Gillings on the use of GIS in archaeology.

Feder, K. L. 1997b. Site Survey. In *Field Methods in Archaeology*, edited by T. R. Hester, H. J. Shafer, and K. L. Feder, 41–68. Mayfield Publishing, Mountain View, California.

Marquardt, W. H., and C. Crumley. 1987. Theoretical Issues in the Analysis of Spatial Patterning. In *Regional Dynamics: Burgundian Landscapes in Historical Perspective*, edited by C. L. Crumley and W. H. Marquardt, 1–18. Academic Press, San Diego.

McPherron, S. P., and H. L. Dibble. 2002. *Using Computers in Archaeology*. McGraw-Hill, New York.

Wheatley, D., and M. Gillings. 2002. *Spatial Technology and Archaeology: The Archaeological Applications of GIS*. Taylor & Francis, London.

What Are the Mechanics of Looking for and Finding Sites?

The search for archaeological sites in any survey ordinarily progresses through a number of steps (Feder 1997b). Archaeologists often begin, perhaps rather obviously, with a **literature search.** Have other researchers—professional archaeologists or hobbyists—encountered archaeological material in an area and then published or in other ways shared the details of their discovery? Professional archaeologists often publish the results of their research in journals geared to other professional archaeologists. Some of these journals concentrate on broad issues in archaeology, but others are focused more narrowly on regional prehistory and are a great source for site-specific information. Many local archaeological societies that have among their members both professional and avocational archaeologists publish newsletters or bulletins and articles concerning the research conducted by members. Research reports unpublished in traditional outlets may be available in local libraries, museums, state historic preservation offices, state archaeologists' offices, or online (for example, there is a wealth of such material housed at the ArchNet website: http://archnet.asu.edu/).

When material concerning the location of sites has not been published or even recorded, artifact collectors may be approached directly for any information they are willing to supply. Many hobbyists do not actually dig to find sites but take advantage of already-disturbed soil layers. Probably most commonly, many collectors walk farmers' fields soon after plowing, looking for artifacts that had been buried but are now exposed in the furrows, brought up to the surface by the plow blade (Figure 6.5). Newspaper articles about ongoing research may encourage local collectors to identify themselves and share their knowledge about the location of sites.

Sometimes the discovery of important archaeological sites relies on serendipity. The Glazier Blade cache site mentioned earlier is a textbook example: The site itself was located by sheer luck, and only a string of coincidences led to my involvement. By chance, the small, ancient pit in which the stone blades had been so carefully stacked by the ancient inhabitants of the

FIGURE 6.5 A sharp eye, a tight focus, and a strong back are valuable assets for an archaeologist walking a recently plowed field, scanning the furrows for archaeological evidence of a previous occupation of the area. (K. L. Feder)

Farmington River Valley was located at the base of a slope, just below where a storm pipe exited the soil, directing storm runoff from the street down to the wetland behind the houses in a quiet neighborhood. A few years ago a torrential downpour had pushed quite a bit of water through that drain, and the swiftly flowing water washed away the soil that rested, coincidentally, on top of the pit where the blades had been cached. Had the drainpipe poked out of the slope a few inches farther north or south, the water would not have eroded and exposed the top of the pit, and the artifacts, in all probability, would not have been discovered.

Mr. Ron Glazier, the property owner, takes great pride in his landscaping and was concerned about property damage from the storm. He examined his yard after the downpour and found that the water that had funneled through the storm drainpipe, indeed, had caused erosion on the slope behind his house. Glazier clearly recognized that the large, symmetrical slice of stone exposed by the drainage pipe water was no ordinary rock but actually the finely flaked tip of a huge spear point. Glazier immediately cleared away the surrounding soil and exposed an enormous, **bifacially** flaked stone blade, which he then pulled from the ground.

In another useful coincidence, Glazier had recently purchased an automobile from a local dealer, Dick Wagner, who happens to have a great interest in archaeology. Aware of this interest, Glazier excitedly contacted Wagner about the stone blade and brought it to the dealership. Wagner is more specifically interested in Mesoamerican prehistory and, though he ooed and aahed about the size of the stone blade, he couldn't tell Glazier much about the artifact: He didn't know what the raw material was, couldn't guess its age, and wasn't sure about its cultural affiliation. And now another lucky happenstance: Because of his general interest in archaeology and history, Wagner is a member of the local historical society, which, on occasion, has invited me to give slide lectures on local archaeology. Wagner and I had spoken on a number of occasions about archaeology, and he advised Glazier to contact me as a local "expert."

While all this was going on, a few more storms struck the area, a few more deluges passed through the storm pipe, and, as luck would have it, a few more blades were exposed and recovered by Glazier. On Wagner's recommendation, Glazier called me and described his discovery; by then he had pulled no fewer than sixteen gargantuan stone blades from the base of the slope, and he invited me to come and take a look. It all sounded far too good to be true. Based on

Glazier's information, the artifacts were larger by far than anything we had found in the Farmington Valley, and I visited his home to examine what I fully expected to be a handful of large, naturally fractured rocks that just happened to "fit nicely in the hand." Much to my surprise, when I met with Glazier he brought me into his living room and showed me sixteen of the largest spear points I had ever seen. They were all neatly symmetrical, finely flaked, and huge, indeed more than four times the length of the spear points we had been finding in the Farmington

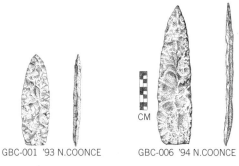

GBC-001 '93 N.COONCE   GBC-006 '94 N.COONCE

FIGURE 6.6 Examples of two of the thirty Glazier Blades, extraordinarily large, flaked stone tools recovered from a cache discovered in Granby, Connecticut. (Courtesy Noel Coonce-Ewing)

Valley. Needless to say, I was floored by the size of the artifacts, by the expertise reflected by the work of the tool maker or tool makers, and by the concentration of the spear points in one spot. Glazier invited us to conduct a formal excavation in the area where he had found the artifacts, and, by the time we were done, there were thirty blades in all (Figure 6.6). And it all happened due to a series of lucky breaks.

Certainly, as exciting as the Glazier Blades experience was, archaeologists cannot simply linger hopefully by the phone waiting for archaeological "lightning" to strike. We need to be proactive and seek out knowledge of other people. Questionnaires mailed to landowners in an area may generate valuable information about the discovery of artifacts by amateurs actively looking for artifacts or accidental discoveries by people digging into the soil for entirely mundane reasons such as putting in a swimming pool or planting a vegetable garden.

Of course, one needs to word the questionnaires carefully. A local farmer, the owner of a substantial tract of agricultural land in an area where others had found sites, did not initially return a survey I sent. When I ran into him later in the field season, I introduced myself and inquired about the survey, concerned that he may not have received it. He informed me that he had but didn't think it would help for him to return it because he had certainly never found any artifacts on his property. I expressed my surprise, explaining that a number of his neighbors had, indeed, found interesting artifacts on their land. The farmer was shocked, expressing his extreme skepticism about any such discoveries. "Well, I certainly haven't found any artifacts," he assured me. "Lots of arrowheads," he went on, "but never any artifacts." Whoops. I picked my jaw up from the floor and explained that the question about "artifacts" also included arrowheads (and pottery, stone drills, bone awls, soapstone bowls, and the like). The farmer rather reasonably chided me: "Well, why didn't you say so?" Of course, he was right, and I had been foolish to use a term not necessarily familiar to all people. It should go without saying that all subsequent versions of my questionnaire ask people about their discovery of arrowheads (and pottery, stone drills, and so on), and not artifacts.

Despite the poor wording of my initial questionnaire, I have experienced an extraordinary amount of interest and cooperation from local landowners. Often local people have found interesting artifacts (there's that word again) while plowing, planting, digging footings for an outbuilding, and so on and have stored them in old cigar boxes or coffee cans, always intending to ask someone about the relics but not knowing where to begin. Many of these people are more than happy to allow us to look at the material, and some even end up donating it to our university for research or teaching purposes. More than once, these "accidental archaeologists" have been able to identify the precise location where the archaeological remains in their possession were found, and further excavation by us has led to astonishing discoveries.

Historical records may also be useful in the search for sites. Property and tax records stored in county or town offices may pinpoint the locations of old houses, factories, mills, and cemeteries that have long ago been abandoned, fallen into disrepair, burned to the ground, or become overgrown and largely forgotten. Treaties may indicate the location of the villages of Native Americans that today, on the surface, appear to be little more than cornfields, woodlots, or suburban developments (Figure 6.7; Feder 1983). Historical documents may direct us to locations where hidden history can be revealed by archaeological excavation.

We employed all these information sources in our survey of Peoples State Forest, but, as in all archaeological surveys, we needed to go out into the field. In the analysis of aerial photographs, researchers talk about "ground truth," establishing the veracity and significance of features seen in aerial photographs by actually putting people down in those spots and seeing what they look like

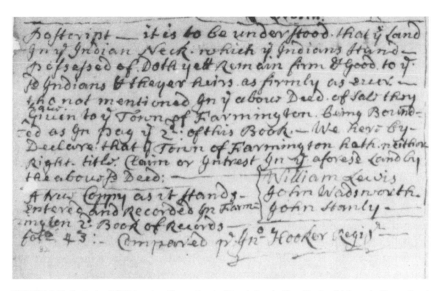

FIGURE 6.7 Part of a 1673 treaty citing a tract of land, "ye Indian Neck which ye Indians stand possessed of." Indian Neck was located, and a pedestrian survey confirmed the presence of a seventeenth-century Indian village.

on the ground. In the field an archaeological survey crew similarly attempts to assess the ground truth of the collected anecdotal, historical, and documentary evidence concerning the location of archaeological sites in a project area by putting people on the ground. Surface walkovers in areas suggested by background research can reveal the locations of foundations, old mill dams or raceways (the engineered, often stone-lined channels that directed water to the mill wheel), overgrown and abandoned cemeteries, trash dumps, middens, and so on.

In most places any sites except for the most recent are buried by a series of natural processes and we need to dig to find them. Archaeology in the twenty-first century may be a high-tech enterprise, with computers, laser transits, and GPS devices, but even so, the most common tool used in the search for buried sites is still the shovel. There is no universally applicable, efficient, or accurate way to see beneath the surface of the Earth in the search for the constituents of archaeological sites—we need to dig to find buried sites. **Shovel test pits** (sometimes simply referred to as **STPs**) are the decidedly low-tech method most archaeologists use to find buried archaeological remains (Krakker, Shott, and Welch 1983; Lightfoot 1986; Lovis 1976; Nance and Ball 1986).

There is no universal standard for the size and placement of shovel test pits or for how the soil brought up in these pits should be examined for the presence of artifacts or ecofacts. In the Farmington River Archaeological Project (FRAP) our test pits are square holes 50 centimeters on each side. Some researchers dig larger test pits, some dig smaller ones. Many dig test pits that are, more for the sake of convenience than anything else, shovel-sized and shovel-shaped, about the width (9 inches, or 22 centimeters) and shape of a standard shovel.

In FRAP all soil in a test pit is passed through one-eighth-inch mesh hardware cloth that has been attached to a small wooden frame. Many archaeologists screen with quarter-inch mesh. To cover a broad area, test pits are often placed along a straight line, or **transect** (Figure 6.8). Individual transects may be located entirely within subsections of a research area defined on the basis of similar characteristics (river floodplain, lakeside habitat, upland with steep slope, wetlands), or they may intentionally cut across several habitats. The goal is to extract a representative sample of sites to enable us to produce an accurate picture of whether and to what extent people in different time periods used these different environmental zones. Once a site is found, its precise location is measured and recorded.

Chapter 6:
Slide Show

Because we are testing only a fraction of the subsurface in a project area, we would like to find all the sites located within each of the transects along which we dig test pits. Certainly, if our test pits are extremely close together, we can find every site a transect actually intersects (Nance and Ball 1986). Such an intensive strategy, however, would represent what amounts to digging, not a sampling of holes in the ground but instead a continuous trench, sometimes across miles of territory. We can't really accomplish this in most circumstances, so we end up having to place test pits some distance apart, and there almost always are compromises to make between the desire to find all sites located along a transect and the need to accomplish a survey project before we reach

FIGURE 6.8 Field crew setting up a test pit transect. Once the line (in this case, north-south) is established, test excavations will be placed every 10 meters. All soil will be passed through one-eighth-inch mesh hardware cloth. (K. L. Feder)

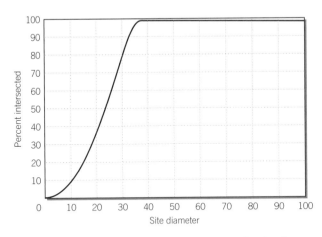

FIGURE 6.9 The graphic results of a simulation showing that the percentage of existing archaeological sites actually discovered, or "intersected," by a test pit in a test pit transect increases as the distance between the test pits approaches the diameter of the sites. (Courtesy Keith Kintigh)

retirement age and, ultimately, become archaeological specimens ourselves. There is no perfect, universally applicable figure for test pit interval that solves this dilemma. In an interesting mathematical simulation, archaeologist Keith Kintigh (1988) showed that as the distance between test pits approaches the actual linear extent of a site (the distance across which artifacts or ecofacts are found), site discovery approaches 100% (Figure 6.9). In other words, if the smallest sites in a region have archaeological material spread out across a length of about 20 meters, then you will find nearly all the sites a test pit transect cuts across if the distance between test pits is about 20 meters. We made every effort to adhere to that strategy in our survey of Peoples State Forest.

Read More

There is a vast archaeological literature concerned with site survey and the various methods archaeologists employ in the systematic search for sites. Read any and all of the following resources for a brief perspective on how archaeologists look for—and discover—archaeological sites:

Feder, K. L. 1983. "The Avaricious Humour of Designing Englishmen": The Ethnohistory of Land Transactions in the Farmington Valley. *Bulletin of the Archaeological Society of Connecticut* 45:29–40.

Feder, K. L. 1997b. Site Survey. In *Field Methods in Archaeology*, edited by T. R. Hester, H. J. Shafer, and K. L. Feder, 41–68. Mayfield Publishing, Mountain View, California.

Krakker, J. J., M. J. Shott, and P. D. Welch. 1983. Design and Evaluation of Shovel-Test Sampling in Regional Archaeology. *Journal of Field Archaeology* 10:469–80.

Lightfoot, K. G. 1986. Regional Surveys in the Eastern United States: The Strengths and Weaknesses of Implementing Subsurface Testing Programs. *American Antiquity* 51:484–504.

Lovis, W. A. 1976. Quarter Sections and Forests: An Example of Probability Sampling in the Northeastern Woodlands. *American Antiquity* 41:364–71.

Nance, J. D., and B. F. Ball. 1986. No Surprises? The Reliability and Validity of Test Pit Sampling. *American Antiquity* 51:457–83.

Shott, M. J. 1989. Shovel Test Sampling in Archaeological Survey: Comments on Nance and Ball and Lightfoot. *American Antiquity* 54:396–404.

 ## What Forms the Basis of an Archaeological "Sampling Strategy"?

Consider the 4,000 acres of Peoples State Forest. That is a large tract of land, densely covered with trees and with irregular and rough topography—by the standards of southern New England, anyway. The archaeological record representing past human use of the forest is, for the most part, obscured, having long ago been covered by soil. In order to reveal that record, we needed to peer under the leaf and needle litter, beneath the humus, and within the rich, rocky, and rooty soil.

Of course, we would have been very happy to have a high-tech method for imaging the subsurface of all those 4,000 acres without excavating, but, sadly, we have no such ability, at least not one that is effective and efficient in the literal neck of the woods where I do most of my fieldwork. To be sure, there are a number of procedures that collectively fall in to the category of **remote sensing** whereby, without digging, the subsurface is probed for the presence of artifacts and, more usually, buried features, but we do not yet have the ability to accurately and thoroughly image the soil beneath our feet.

Even if we could produce what amounted to an x-ray, CT scan, or MRI of the subsurface of our entire 4,000-acre study area down to bedrock, we would still be unable, in all likelihood, to distinguish cultural materials such as artifacts and ecofacts from the natural background noise of roots and rocks that populate the soil in incalculable numbers. Though I someday may be—and hope to be—proven wrong on this, the bottom line is that the time-consuming, back-breaking approach of **test pitting** is and will likely remain the most effective method for finding buried sites in rocky soil. Shovel test pits represent an incredibly laborious but successful strategy for peeking below the surface in our search for archaeological material. There really are no other alternatives that work so well.

In small projects and especially when an entire parcel of land is to be developed and all archaeological sites located there will probably be destroyed, we may excavate test pits across the entire area, distributing pits in a dense grid pattern. In many other situations we simply cannot test at this level of intensity. Certainly, we could not excavate all 4,000 acres of Peoples State Forest, and, equally certainly, archaeologists looking for sites almost everywhere else similarly cannot strip away all the soil down to bedrock, extracting a 100% sample of the subsurface in a project area to look for sites. This means that in our search for buried archaeological material, we almost always can examine only a small fraction, or "sample," of that subsurface. Because of the constraints of time, money, and a desire to cause as little ecological disruption to a place as possible, we usually rely on test pits dispersed across the expanse of a research area. The question then becomes: Where do we place those pits that we dig in the search for sites, and how densely do we distribute them? The answers to these questions are resolved by developing a **sampling strategy.**

Sampling strategies may differ depending on the research goals of the archaeologist (Orton 2000; Shafer 1997b; Whalen 1990). Sometimes the concentration may be on only a particular kind of landform in a region, or sites from only a single time period may be the focus. Usually, however, whether we are talking about the search for buried archaeological sites or the attempt to figure out who is ahead on election night, the goal of sampling is to produce a **sample** that is both **random** and **representative.**

Let's consider the example of sampling a small fraction of the electorate in order to get a statistical sense of how the entire **population** of voters is going to cast their ballots. Here, researchers design a sampling strategy that produces a sample that, though it represents only a small fraction of the population, in a statistical sense it "looks like" the population in miniature. Everyone has an equal chance of being included in the sample because individuals are chosen randomly. Further, it doesn't discriminate against any categories of people because it is representative. For example, if 50% of the entire electorate is female, then 50% of the sample should be, too. If 1% of the electorate is made up of millionaires, the sample should have about that same percentage of wealthy people. Men and women have been known to vote differently, and rich and poor people may vote differently as well. If you include proportionally more men or women, or more poor people or millionaires in the sample than there are in the entire population, your poll may not reflect accurately how the electorate as a whole will vote on election night. The sample will be skewed—it won't look like the population—and the results may be far different from those of the population.

We face a similar challenge in archaeological testing. When surveying a region, we hope to find a representative sample of the population of archaeological sites—a sample in which the relative percentages of sites of differing cultures, functions, and ages are very similar to those percentages in the entire population of all the sites in the region being investigated. Of course, we don't really know what the population of sites in a region looks like—we're conducting our archaeological research to figure this out. We can, however, increase the probability of obtaining a representative sample of sites by designing a strategy that tests different kinds of landforms and habitats in a region at the same level of intensity and by making sure that coverage is proportional to the percentage of land in a project area represented by each kind of land form and habitat. In other words, we randomly choose those specific areas within our sampling universe of property where test pits are excavated and proportions of the different kinds of land tested are represented in the sample in the same proportions in which they are found in the entire research area. For example, if only about 20% of a region can be characterized as floodplain and 50% as upland, then about those same percentages of test excavations should be located in the floodplain and the uplands (20% and 50%, respectively). If we skew our sample and excavate mainly on the floodplain (because its easier to access, the soil passes through the screening much more readily, and floodplain sites produce rich artifact assemblages), we may find great sites and lots of them, but our overall sample of sites will not be representative; our general impression of the pattern of ancient land use may be grossly distorted. You don't find sites where you don't look, and a host of special activity sites used by folks whose floodplain villages we do find, as well as the settlements of societies whose land use pattern was focused away from the floodplain, may remain unknown to us. So the key factor in assuring a useful and informative sample of the population of archaeological sites in a research area is to employ a strategy that produces an array of sites that are representative of the population as a whole. We do this by sampling land types in the research area that are measurably representative of the landforms in the area.

Read More

Sampling is a vast subject; most of the important works on sampling are not written by archaeologists but by statisticians. For sources directly related to how archaeologists deal with the fundamental problem that we can't dig up the entire world, but only bits and pieces of it, consult any of the following resources on sampling strategies in archaeology.

Mueller, J. 1975. *Sampling in Archaeology*. University of Arizona Press, Phoenix.

Orton, C. 2000. *Sampling in Archaeology*. Cambridge University Press, Cambridge.

Shafer, H. J. 1997b. Research Design and Sampling Techniques. In *Field Methods in Archaeology*, edited by T. R. Hester, H. Shafer, and K. L. Feder, 21–40. Mayfield, Mountain View, California.

Whalen, M. E. 1990. Sampling Versus Full-Coverage Survey: An Example from Western Texas. In *The Archaeology of Regions: A Case for Full-Coverage Survey*, edited by S. Fish and S. Kowalewski, 219–36. Smithsonian Institution Press, Washington, D.C.

How Can You Find Archaeological Sites Just by Walking Around?

The common conception of an archaeologist is that of a scientist dusted in dirt, searching for specimens at the bottom of a perilously deep pit, and oblivious to the imminent and obvious danger posed by the tons of loose soil precariously mounded up all around. In fact, although archaeological material may be found deeply buried in the soil, it is also quite common to find sometimes even extraordinarily ancient material right under our noses, resting on the exposed, modern surface.

This variation in the depth at which archaeological materials are discovered exists for two very different reasons. On the one hand, human beings, especially when they work together in large, organized groups, can dramatically and drastically alter the face of the Earth. They can produce features that are, using the term of Schiffer et al. (1978), archaeologically **obtrusive.** Whether through carving out deep gouges in the Earth's surface to make canals; altering the flow of a stream to divert its water to power a mill wheel; building up and shaping the soil to produce huge, three-dimensional images of animals to worship the gods; or constructing monuments, temples, pyramids, or houses, people leave behind sometimes massive, durable traces of their labors, too deep, too tall, or too extensive to be covered by natural processes of soil accumulation on any kind of human time scale (Figure 6.10). The Great Pyramid of the pharaoh Khufu, the Square Tower House at Mesa Verde National Park in Colorado, and the pyramids of the Maya, for example, are so large as to leave traces on the surface that archaeologists can readily identify (Lehner 1997).

The huge adobe structure called Pueblo Bonito at Chaco Culture National Historical Park in New Mexico was three stories tall, made of regularly sized, durable brick, and contained more than 800 rooms (Figure 6.11; Cordell 1994; Sebastian 1992). Though it is only an urban legend that the Great Wall of China is visible to the naked eye from the moon (or something like that), the structure really does epitomize the term *stupendous*: It is about 7,000 kilometers (4,500 miles) long, ranges from 4.5 to 9 meters (15 to 30 feet) high, and is as much as 7.5 meters (25 feet) wide. It simply doesn't take much digging—in truth, it doesn't take any digging—to find features like these. Walking around with open eyes is all that is required. The process of eyeballing the surface for exposed artifacts, ecofacts, or features (including structural remains) is called simply **pedestrian survey**.

Such archaeological remains can be found simply by walking around with your eyes open for another reason: The environments in which they were found are of high archaeological **visibility.** In some regions, processes that serve to cover things left on the surface very quickly remove archaeological remains from the visible landscape, enfolding them in leaf litter, pine needles, sand, silt, and rock. Clearly, in those places, if a sufficiently long time has passed to cover items, archaeologists must dig to find that stuff, and a pedestrian survey may not readily pinpoint the location of archaeological material (Chartkoff 1978; Chartkoff and Chartkoff 1980; McManamon 1984).

FIGURE 6.10 The cliff dwelling, Square Tower House, at Mesa Verde, Colorado (top), and the Pyramid of the Magician at the ancient Maya site of Uxmal in the Yucatán Peninsula, Mexico (bottom), are quintessentially "obtrusive" archaeological remains. They are large, above-ground structures made of durable material. Even centuries after their construction, use, and abandonment, they are clearly recognizable. Although archaeology has long been conducted in their proximity, no digging was necessary to find them. (K. L. Feder)

On the other hand, there are regions in which these natural processes that cover material on the surface act very slowly or not at all. Items left on the surface for hundreds or thousands of years—in some instances even longer—may continue to reside in full view, exposed at the spot where human beings left them.

FIGURE 6.11 Pueblo Bonito in Chaco Canyon, New Mexico, is another example of an obtrusive remain built in an environment where sites decay slowly. (K. L. Feder)

At the same time, even in regions where material left on the surface is fairly quickly buried, there may be broad areas with high archaeological visibility as a result of erosion and other geological processes. For example, where a river erodes its bank, even deeply buried archaeological material may be exposed, rendering previously hidden items highly visible. Ancient episodes of land movement due to tectonic activity such as earthquakes can also contribute to archaeological visibility, tearing apart a section of the Earth's surface and exposing ancient layers of soil. Many of the most ancient hominid sites at Olduvai Gorge in Tanzania, Africa, were found through pedestrian survey (M. Leakey 1971; M. Leakey and A. Walker 1997; R. Leakey and R. Lewin 1992). The deeply buried remains of ancient skeletons and stone tools, enclosed in ancient strata hundreds of thousands and even millions of years old, have been exposed at the surface when the land was ripped apart by earthquake activity. Where the ancient layers were torn open, their edges are exposed to the surface, and paleoanthropologists scan them for signs of ancient human ancestors (Figure 6.12).

We can see another example of the usefulness of a surface inspection for archaeological remains on the largest of the Orkney Islands of Scotland (Ritchie 1995). Local residents of the island in the mid-nineteenth century were familiar with what they presumed to be a natural feature of the

FIGURE 6.12 Olduvai Gorge in East Africa is a geological gash across the Earth, exposing ancient strata and their contents. Paleoanthropologists have found ancient sites containing the skeletal remains and tools of ancient human ancestors without digging deeply but by perusing the ancient soil layers exposed in the gorge. (© Ric Ergenbright/CORBIS)

landscape, a mound of earth they called Skerrabra located on the shore of a protected bay on the island's west coast. An enormous northern Atlantic storm pounded the Orkneys in the winter of 1850, and the combined effect of an especially high tide and the fierce winds that accompanied the storm managed to peel the turf from the top of the mound. When residents left the safety of their homes to assess the damage after the storm, they found exposed in the truncated mound a maze of stone walls demarcating the remnants of a warren of eight interconnected rooms (Figure 6.13; Clarke and Maguire 1995).

Since then, the ancient village so revealed has attracted the interest of archaeologists. Now called Skara Brae, the site has been excavated, revealing a village that was first occupied more than 5,000 years ago and that had been enclosed in a protective blanket of sand for about 4,000 years (http://www .orkneyjar.com/history/skarabrae/).

FIGURE 6.13 The walls of the 5,000-year-old village of Skara Brae lay buried beneath the beach sand near a bay on the main Orkney Island, Scotland, until the gales of a powerful North Atlantic storm revealed them in 1850. (K. L. Feder)

Vegetation growth can render the archaeological visibility of even large-scale, obtrusive remains quite low. For example, the Maya of Mesoamerica (Coe 1993; Schele and Freidel 1990; Schele and Mathews 1998) and the Khmer civilization of Southeast Asia (Higham 2001) both developed in tropical regions where vegetation grows quickly—and thickly (Figure 6.14). In both of these cultures, people carved communities out of the thick, humid forest, clearing trees for cities, temples, pyramids, and tombs. These remains are obviously highly obtrusive, built on a monumental scale. The Maya city of Tikal is estimated to have had a population of 50,000 in A.D. 650 and is marked by beautiful and massive pyramids and temples of stone (Sabloff 1989).

Built in the twelfth century A.D., the Khmer temple of Angkor Wat has been called the largest religious structure ever built, covering several acres and characterized by five massive towers more than 60 meters (200 feet) tall (Mannikka 1996). Obtrusive, indeed, but when in the ebb and flow of great civilizations these sites were abandoned, the tireless and relentless jungle claimed both the Khmer and the Maya sites, cloaking their massive statues and edifices in vines, roots, and lush greenery (Figure 6.15). Their archaeological obtrusiveness was trumped by the low visibility of their respective regions, and both civilizations were forgotten and unknown, at least to the world beyond their own regions, until the forest was entered by explorers and scientists with machetes and the forest was once again forced back to reveal hidden archaeological treasures.

The utility of a pedestrian survey, therefore, is a complex product of the interplay of the obtrusiveness of the archaeological remains to be found

FIGURE 6.14 Even obtrusive remains may be cloaked by vegetation in regions where archaeological visibility is low. Here at Chichén Itza in the Yucatán Peninsula of Mexico, vegetation has been cleared away from the Maya structures, the so-called House of Doves and the Observatory (so named because it looks like one and served a similar purpose in naked eye astronomical observations). (K. L. Feder)

FIGURE 6.15 Parts of the Maya site of Chichén Itza have been left as they were first seen by Spanish explorers of the Yucatán Peninsula in the sixteenth century. (K. L. Feder)

and the archaeological visibility presented by the local environment. Where obtrusiveness and archaeological visibility both are high, a pedestrian survey can be an effective strategy in the search for archaeological remains (Feder 1997b). Where both obtrusiveness and visibility are low, rather obviously a pedestrian survey may be of little use. The usefulness of a pedestrian survey must be assessed on a case-by-case basis when obtrusiveness is high but visibility is low, or when visibility is high and obtrusiveness is low.

Read More

To find out more about pedestrian survey and how it can contribute to the discovery of obtrusive and/or highly visible archaeological remains, check out any of the following books and articles.

Chartkoff, J. L. 1978. Transect Sampling in Forests. *American Antiquity* 43:46–52.

Chartkoff, J. L., and K. K. Chartkoff. 1980. *The Discovery of Archaeological Sites: A Review of Methods and Techniques.* U.S. Forest Service.

Clarke, D., and P. Maguire. 1995. *Skara Brae: Northern Europe's Best Preserved Prehistoric Village.* Historic Scotland, Edinburgh, Scotland.

Coe, M. D. 1993. *The Maya.* Thames & Hudson, New York.

Cordell, L. 1994. Ancient Pueblo Peoples. In *Exploring the Ancient World.* Smithsonian Books, Washington, D.C.

Feder, K. L. 1997b. Site Survey. In *Field Methods in Archaeology*, edited by T. R. Hester, H. J. Shafer, and K. L. Feder, 41–68. Mayfield Publishing, Mountain View, California.

Higham, C. 2001. *The Civilization of Angkor.* University of California Press, Berkeley.

Leakey, M. 1971. *Olduvai Gorge 3*. Cambridge University Press, Cambridge, Massachusetts.

Leakey, M., and A. Walker. 1997. Early Hominid Fossils from Africa. *Scientific American* 276(6):74–79.

Leakey, R., and R. Lewin. 1992. *Origins Reconsidered: In Search of What Makes Us Human*. Doubleday, New York.

Lehner, M. 1997. *The Complete Pyramids*. Thames & Hudson, New York.

Mannikka, E. 1996. *Angkor Wat: Time, Space, and Kingship*. University of Hawaii Press, Honolulu.

McManamon, F. P. 1984. Discovering Sites Unseen. In *Advances in Archaeological Method and Theory*, edited by M. B. Schiffer, vol. 7, 223–92. Academic Press, New York.

Ritchie, A. 1995. *Prehistoric Orkney*. B. T. Batsford, London.

Sabloff, J. A. 1989. *The Cities of Ancient Mexico: Reconstructing a Lost World*. Thames & Hudson, New York.

Schele, L., and D. Freidel. 1990. *A Forest of Kings*. Quill William Morrow, New York.

Schele, L., and P. Mathews. 1998. *The Code of Kings: The Language of Seven Sacred Maya Temples and Tombs*. Scribner's, New York.

Sebastian, L. 1992. *The Chaco Anasazi: Sociopolitical Evolution in the Prehistoric Southwest*. Cambridge University Press, Cambridge.

How Deep Do You Have to Dig to Find Archaeological Material?

I can remember one field season scraping back the soil at the bottom of an excavation unit that was just a little more than 75 centimeters (almost 2.5 feet) deep. An elderly man with a small dog walked by, peered down at me, and asked what I was doing. I told him that we were conducting an archaeological excavation and showed him some of the artifacts that had been left in place in the soil for mapping at the bottom of the excavation unit. The old man shook his head and said to me, "You know; I never would have thought the Indians would have buried their stuff so deep." Right.

Of course, ancient people did bury trash as well as the bodies of their deceased compatriots, but most of the archaeological material we find becomes buried by natural processes. This raises the question of how deeply archaeological material is buried and, in turn, how deeply we need to dig to find it.

There really is no single answer to this question, primarily because each of the various processes proceeds at a different rate, and even the same processes proceed at different rates depending on the particular set of circumstances that apply in each instance. In southern New England, for example, for two sites of equal age, one located within the **floodplain** of a large river such as the Connecticut ordinarily will be buried far more deeply than one situated in the uplands. Especially before the institution of flood control procedures by local municipalities and, especially, by the Army Corps of Engineers (a federal agency), rivers left behind substantial flood deposits called **alluvium**, consisting of very fine-grained soil called **silt**, on a yearly basis. Alluvium can build up in a hurry, and sites along rivers can be buried fairly quickly and fairly deeply. The formation of a layer of soil outside the floodplain of a river usually occurs far more slowly because the processes that bury material on the surface proceed much more slowly.

Human activity, too, creates layers of soil. Especially when people live in large numbers in settled communities and where they construct durable buildings, material tends to pile up. When these communities are abandoned and where, for example, wind-blown sand covers the ruins, a later group may settle on the top, not necessarily aware that the remnants of a previous village lie under their new settlement. Over many years a series of communities may be established at the same location, one superimposed on top of the other as people elect to build their communities on the artificially created high ground. They may choose to settle the high ground because it is drier than the surrounding area and because it provides a better outlook for the presence of attacking enemies. Called **tells** in the Middle East, there can be more than a dozen villages so positioned on these high mounds (Figure 6.16). Obviously,

FIGURE 6.16 The hill in the foreground of this photo of Tel Hazor, Israel, on top of which ruins can be seen, is not natural but is the result of the accumulation of debris from a sequence of occupations—twenty-one, to be precise—one on top of the other. (© Richard T. Nowitz/CORBIS)

archaeologists may have to dig very deep before they encounter the archaeological remains of the earlier settlements.

Make no mistake: None of these processes of soil formation or deposition are entirely consistent or regular. None of them functions like a clock. You cannot simply measure the depth of an **occupation layer** at a site and plug the result into a universally applicable formula to come up with an age (Figure 6.17). Along a floodplain, for example, a series of years with minimal winter snowfall and dry springs will result in small floods or none at all in individual years, and, as a consequence, there will be very little, if any, deposition of silt. You can have a situation in which over the course of decades only a fraction of a centimeter is deposited. On the other hand, though rare, a single, enormous rainstorm resulting, for instance, from a hurricane may cause a devastating flood that may deposit several feet of alluvium all at once.

Along with processes of deposition, there are processes that work to strip away soil and slice through soil layers. Rivers and streams cut into their banks, heavy rains can wash away soil, a storm surge can tear up a shoreline and expose a buried site, and, especially where there are no trees or heavily rooted vegetation, the wind can remove enormous quantities of soil. Deeply buried, sometimes quite ancient, sites can be exposed on the surface by these processes. As mentioned earlier, in 1850 an enormous storm surge that struck the Orkney Islands (just north of the north-Scottish coast) exposed remains of a previously completely unknown 5,000-year-old archaeological village site, a place called Skara Brae. Sites where the remains of human ancestral forms, dating back not thousands but millions of years, have been found not by digging deeply—at least not initially—but by walking over the surface in areas where ancient

FIGURE 6.17 Looking down into an excavation unit at a floodplain site, one can readily see the occupation layer marked by stones and dark soil in a discernible layer among other layers free of stones. The layer shown here is approximately 3,200 years old. The soil above it has accumulated over the course of that 3,200-year period, the result of yearly flooding and alluvium deposition by a nearby river. (K. L. Feder)

deposits 1 million, 2 million, and even more years old were exposed by various processes of erosion.

There is no hard and fast rule concerning how deep an archaeological site may be buried and, therefore, how deeply we need to dig in order to find it, except for this: An archaeologist needs to be knowledgeable about the geology of an area being surveyed or excavated in order to ensure that he or she is digging deeply enough. Knowing the soil layers in which other sites in a region have been found and being familiar with the geological or **stratigraphic** sequence in an area is crucial. Archaeologists need to excavate to a depth sufficient to ensure that nothing archaeological would be found any deeper. Even adhering to this rule, it must be admitted that most of us have experienced that twinge when, about to fill in a test pit or excavation unit, we wonder: "What if I dug down just another centimeter?" (Archaeologists obsess in metric units, of course.)

Test pits may be excavated until a recognizable glacial deposit is encountered in regions where human occupation postdated the last period of glaciation. In some places the deepest testings of a region's stratigraphic sequence may reach bedrock, and in other places test pits may be excavated to a depth that reaches the water table.

Ultimately, we do have to draw the line somewhere, and our approach should be realistic. If, based on the solid evidence of a substantial amount of earlier work in an area, we are pretty sure no humans lived there before a certain point in the geological history of a region, then when we excavate down to those geological deposits we need dig no more deeply.

How Can Archaeologists Probe the Subsurface Without Digging Holes?

The stereotype of the archaeologist, pick-ax in hand, smashing through the door of a tomb has long been abandoned and replaced by the equally stereotypical image of a digger at the bottom of an enormous shaft, slowly and carefully brushing away soil with a whisk broom, painstakingly removing thin slices of earth with a razor-sharp mason's trowel, and exposing the tiniest of clues about antiquity with a dental pick. There is more than just a little reality to this more recent stereotype, but these simple, time-worn methods for conducting archaeological excavation can be supplemented with several more technologically advanced procedures.

As complex as an excavation may be, all excavations are essentially about removing the soil from over and around the stuff left behind in the past for discovery in the present, analyzing the spatial organization of the items, and recovering the ancient material for detailed study back in the laboratory. Moving soil carefully is made possible by the application of fairly low-tech procedures and pretty primitive tools such as shovels, brushes, and trowels. On the other hand, there are a number of ways in which we can reveal artifacts, ecofacts, and features from a distance (even though we do not actually move the soil or produce images of what the subsurface looks like) by discovering anomalies in the physical structure and/or chemical makeup of the soil that may have resulted from past human activity in an area (Weymouth 1986).

For example, in an **electrical resistivity survey**, an electrical current is passed through the soil between two probes. The conductivity of the soil between the probes (the ability of the soil to sustain an electrical current passing through it) and its related resistance to that current (its inherent opposition to the passing of an electrical current that is then translated into heat or some other form of energy) is controlled by a host of variables, water content being key.

Even long after someone in the past dug a pit or a trench and then filled it in, the soil in the pit can display a different degree of compaction than the surrounding soil. In fact, an experienced field archaeologist is often able to feel that difference when excavating even a very ancient pit; a trowel scraped across undisturbed soil simply feels different than when scraped across soil that was dug up to create a pit that was then filled back in. The difference in compaction causes a difference in water content, which, in turn, alters the conductivity of the soil in the filled pit or trench. Similarly, the conductivity of, for example, a buried stone wall and the resistance it presents to an electrical current passing through it will also be quite different from the conductivity of the soil in which the wall is buried, as will be its resistance to an electrical current.

In an electrical resistivity survey, we put probes in the ground and pass a current between them, move them regularly, and repeatedly pass an electrical current for each positioning of the probes, producing a detailed map of the conductivity of the subsurface soil. Based on deviations in soil conductivity, areas of soil disturbance or the presence of a large buried structure may be recognized, all without digging any test pits but instead by sticking metal probes into the ground and passing an electrical current between them. Whereas electrical resistivity surveying measures the soil's ability to conduct an electrical current, in **ground penetrating radar** the soil's response to an electromagnetic pulse is analyzed. In above-ground applications of radar such a pulse is directed out into the air, where it encounters objects that are dense enough to bounce the pulse back to where a receiver can measure it to determine the distance and shape of whatever object the pulse bounced off of. In ground penetrating radar the electromagnetic pulse is directed into the ground, and, at least in theory, a receiver measures the depth and size of whatever the pulse encountered that was dense enough to reflect it back to a receiver (Figure 6.18; Conyers 1995; Conyers and Goodman 1997). If the object or objects encountered by the electromagnetic pulse possess a shape that appears to be artificial (that is, not a product of nature), the archaeologist may elect to dig at its location to determine whether it is, in fact, the result of human activity

FIGURE 6.18 Remote sensing capabilities are rapidly growing in archaeology. Here, researchers using ground penetrating radar look for eighteenth-century graves among the replica buildings at Fort Vancouver, Washington. (Courtesy Larry B. Conyers)

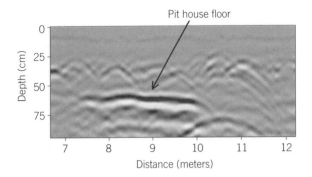

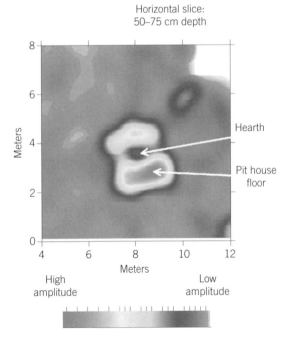

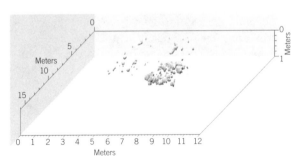

FIGURE 6.19 Three separate images of ground-penetrating radar readings taken on what turned out to be a buried prehistoric pithouse covered by windblown sand on the Oregon coast. The top image shows a strong reflection surface (alternating dark and light lines) in profile; the middle image shows this surface in map view; the bottom image converts many two-dimensional profiles into a 3-D representation of the feature by illustrating only the strongest reflections in the ground and making the sand matrix invisible. Remember, these images are of a buried feature that was not exposed; without any excavation, ground-penetrating rader revealed the presence of the remains of a buried pithouse (Courtesy Lawrence Conyers)

(Figure 6.19). Ground penetrating radar has been used successfully to locate and identify buried walls, foundations, and the compacted floors of houses (Weymouth 1986).

Instead of actively inserting energy into the ground in the form of an electrical current or an electromagnetic pulse, in **proton magnetometry** the Earth's own magnetic field is used in the search for buried archaeological material. In theory, when the magnetic field measuring device, called a magnetometer, is pulled along over a homogeneous soil body, the Earth's magnetic field is the same on the path along which the magnetometer is pulled. If, however, the soil is not homogeneous (for example, if there are burials, subterranean passageways, infilled canals, and so on), the Earth's magnetic field may deviate slightly, and this deviation turns up as an anomaly when the field is measured and mapped.

Although these approaches have had great successes, in many parts of the world the subsurface is quite complex, is not naturally homogeneous, and is loaded with rocks, roots, rodent burrows, and animal dens. Even without the presence of alterations wrought by past people, soil resistivity may vary greatly in different parts of a research area, radar may show the presence of dense buried objects, and magnetometers may reveal anomalies in the Earth's magnetic field. Such readings are called "anomalies" simply because they represent deviations from the expected reading (of a remote sensing device) *if* there were nothing of interest to the archaeologist buried in that spot. Detected anomalies, however, may turn out merely to reflect the presence of nonarchaeological material or be the result of recent disturbance. Detecting subsurface anomalies is merely an initial step, therefore, in an archaeological survey. Remote sensing methods are extremely useful in pointing out areas of great potential importance, but archaeologists still need to dig to determine what is called the ground truth of the reading, the true nature of whatever it is that is causing the machine to indicate the presence of something unexpected in the soil.

It can sometimes help when conducting an archaeological survey to get a remote "bird's eye" view of an area in order to recognize sometimes subtle, nonnatural irregularities in topography that resulted from past human activity. For example, Sheets and Sever (1988) were able to detect ancient footpaths in Costa Rica, too subtle to be recognized on the ground, by using a laser mounted in a plane. By bouncing a laser light off the ground surface, the researchers measured differences in elevation, detecting the very small and otherwise imperceptible topographic characteristics of the footpaths.

Along with small topographic anomalies, color and growth patterns in vegetation may result from the presence of buried archaeological remains. For example, some artifacts, ecofacts, and features may interfere with plant growth, stunting or even preventing development altogether. Other archaeological remains, especially organic deposits, may augment soil fertility and encourage growth, causing plants to grow faster, taller, denser, and even greener. These impacts may result in a spatial patterning of plant growth that reflects the spatial patterning of the archaeological remains on which the plants are growing.

FIGURE 6.20 Sometimes the presence of archaeological material has a noticeable impact on vegetation, either by encouraging or inhibiting its growth. As an example, note the ring of darker grass (shown by the arrows) visible from the top of Seip Mound in Ohio. The ring matches the location of decayed wooden posts that demarcated the walls of an ancient structure. (K. L. Feder)

The effect often is subtle and visible only from above (Figure 6.20). In some cases the visible light spectrum is not enough to reveal these patterns, and archaeologists have used infrared photography and even **thermography** to reveal patterns not visible to the naked eye.

Like other varieties of remote sensing, aerial reconnaissance can reveal patterns not immediately discernable to the archaeologist conducting a pedestrian survey. At the same time, as in other forms of remote sensing, the ground truth or ground significance needs to be tested through excavation.

Read More

For more information about remote sensing in archaeology, any of the following works would be a good place to start (especially Conyers and Goodman).

Conyers, L. B. 1995. The Use of Ground Penetrating Radar to Map the Buried Structures and Landscape of the Ceren Site, El Salvador. *Geoarchaeology* 10:275–99.

Conyers, L. B., and D. Goodman. 1997. *Ground-Penetrating Radar: An Introduction for Archaeologists.* Altamira Press, Walnut Creek, California.

Johnston, R. B. 1964. *Proton Magnetometry and Its Application to Archaeology: An Evaluation at Angel Site*. Research Series. Indiana Historical Society, Indianapolis.

Shapiro, G., and J. M. Williams. 1982. *A Search for the Eighteenth Century Village at Michilimackinac: A Soil Resistivity Survey*. Mackinac State Parks, Mackinaw City, Michigan.

Study Questions

1. How did I, with remarkable precision, predict the location of the Wood Lily site? Am I psychic, or what?

2. What were the environmental characteristics of the area in which Wood Lily was found that made predicting its location, if not a slam dunk, a pretty good bet?

3. What is a settlement pattern? How does an archaeologist study the settlement pattern of an ancient group of people?

4. What is a landscape signature? How is it related to a settlement pattern?

5. Within the context of an overall settlement pattern, a past people may have used different areas of their territory differently. How might an archaeologist figure out and explain these different uses?

6. How does an archaeologist distinguish the differing purposes of different sites within an overall landscape signature? How might an archaeologist distinguish a village, a hunting camp, a seed-gathering station, and a sacred place?

7. Discuss the concept of archaeological visibility. What world areas provide a high level of archaeological visibility? What world areas provide a low level of such visibility?

8. What does the term *obtrusive* mean in its archaeological use? What kinds of archaeological sites are obtrusive? What kinds of sites are not obtrusive?

9. Provide a listing of cultures that have produced an obtrusive archaeological record. Provide a listing of cultures that have produced nonobtrusive material.

10. What is "pedestrian" archaeology? What kinds of sites can be found in pedestrian archaeology? In what kinds of environments can pedestrian archaeology be found?

11. What natural processes might act to reveal archaeological remains even in environments that are otherwise characterized by low archaeological visibility?

12. The discovery of the village site of Skara Brae is an instance in which a natural phenomenon revealed an archaeological site in an environment

otherwise characterized by low archaeological visibility. Explain what that means and what happened in this case.

13. By what *general* natural processes are archaeological materials covered over?

14. How was the village of Pompeii transformed into an archaeological site? How was the village of Ozette transformed into an archaeological site?

15. As a general rule, how deep do archaeologists need to dig to find all the materials at an archaeological site?

16. What is the "occupation layer" of a site?

7

Revealing the Past

THE ARCHAEOLOGICAL EXCAVATION

- **How Is Archaeological Research Like Detective Work?**

- **How Do You Measure and Record the Precise Location of a Site?**

  How Are Archaeological Sites Named?

- **How Do Archaeologists Excavate Sites?**

  Why Are Archaeologists So Painstaking and Slow in Excavation?

- **What Tools Do Archaeologists Use to Expose and Recover Artifacts?**

- **What Is an Excavation Unit, and How Is It Labeled?**

  How Do Archaeologists Keep Track of Where Stuff Is Found at Sites?

- **Why Do Archaeologists Save All the Tiny Scraps of Stone, Bone, and Other Stuff?**

- **How Can You Determine the Size of an Ancient Habitation?**

- **What Preliminary Work Goes into an Archaeology Laboratory?**

Archaeologists spend an inordinate amount of time collecting data. The excavation we conducted at the Wood Lily site provided us with the data that allowed us to describe the activities conducted by its residents. This chapter presents a brief desctiption of the mechanics of archaeological data collection, focusing on the dig.

How Is Archaeological Research Like Detective Work?

Archaeological excavation has been likened to the work of a detective. Like all such analogies, it is imperfect, but we can make some useful comparisons between detective work and archaeology. A detective usually arrives at a scene after a crime has been committed. Based on physical evidence that remains at the scene—bullets from a gun, a knife blade, a jimmied lock, a broken window, blood spatters, footprints, fingerprints, even a dead body—a detective attempts to reconstruct the sequence of events that surrounded the commission of the crime. Determining the nature of the crime, when it occured, how it was carried out, "whodunnit," and the motive are all issues a detective attempts to resolve based, at least in part, on the physical evidence left behind and recovered at the scene. If our hypothetical detective were in the board game *Clue*, his or her goal might be to determine that Professor Plum committed the crime in the kitchen with the pipe wrench.

At the Wood Lily site we conducted our work not at the scene of a crime, but at the scene of a life. Our job was to reconstruct not necessarily a particular event (though there are many individual events we can reconstruct there), but a series of events that transpired during the time the place was occupied and used by human beings. Like detectives, archaeologists search for physical evidence to reconstruct what transpired at a particular place. In a general sense we ask and attempt to answer many of the same questions a detective might in solving a crime: What was the nature, not of the crime, but of the lives lived by the people at this place? When was this place occupied? How did the people conduct themselves here? Who were these people? Why did they live here, and why did they live as they did? Also like detectives, the raw data archaeologists use in our efforts to answer these questions consist of the physical evidence unintentionally left behind by the people whose lives we are hoping to understand.

Continuing the detective analogy: You may be familiar with the French detective Hercule Poirot, the literary invention of the famous mystery novelist Agatha Christie. He's not as famous as Sir Arthur Conan Doyle's Sherlock Holmes or even Christie's other crime solver, Miss Marple, but he's a terrific character nonetheless. Poirot's catchphrase when encountering a crime scene, spoken in his thickly accented English, is "Touch nothing." It is of the utmost importance at a crime scene not to disturb anything, not to contaminate any evidence, not to destroy or lose any of the often subtle clues that might enable the solution of a crime. The importance of "touching nothing" is similar when excavating an archaeological site. Crucial evidence at a site might consist of a barest whisper of pollen, the tiniest flecks of charcoal, the most delicate fragments of bone, or invisible residues of blood on a stone knife. It would be supremely ironic if in our attempt to find and recover the evidence of past lives at a site, we destroyed that same evidence through lack of care. As detectives of the past, archaeologists make every effort to salvage every scrap of evidence that might inform us of the lives lived at the sites we study.

How Do You Measure and Record the Precise Location of a Site?

I suppose it is rather ironic that as an archaeologist who spends quite a bit of time directing fieldwork deep in the forests of southern New England, I am pretty much hopeless when it comes to finding my way in the woods. With the proper equipment, even just a simple compass, I'm fine, but I have zero innate sense of direction. This became embarrassingly apparent a couple of years ago when I led a troop of dedicated archaeology students to begin work at a site located deep in the McLean Game Refuge in Granby, Connecticut. After walking for twenty minutes in what I thought was the direction of the site, I led the crew to the top of a rise, where I expected to find our datum stake demarcating the zero point of the site from which all other measurements were taken. Instead, we looked back down on our truck: I had managed to make a complete circle through the woods back to where we had started. I felt like a homing pigeon.

Of course, the ability to precisely determine a site's location is important if you hope to find it again (duh!). Equally important is the task of being able to record the precise location of a site on a map on which important environmental variables (slope, distance to freshwater, soil type, bedrock characteristics, and so on) have already been identified. By pinpointing the location of a place used by past peoples, we can accurately convey the positioning of a site in an environmental context, and that context includes the most likely factors on which a people in the past based their land use decisions.

Typically, archaeologists bring actual paper copies of U.S. Geological Survey (USGS) topographic quadrangle maps into the field, or they carry digital versions on laptop computers. In fact, however, these quite useful maps are of a scale that does not really allow for sufficient precision when attempting to pinpoint the location of an archaeological site, especially a small one. The quad sheets are produced from aerial photographs, and the scale is 1:24,000. Though quite good for conveying significant topographic and hydraulic features— these maps show all major elevation changes as well as rivers, streams, brooks, lakes, ponds, and wetlands—the scale at which they are drawn is a bit large for accurately and precisely mapping the location of small archaeological sites. At their scale 1 inch on the map is about 2,000 feet on the ground (1 centimeter on the map translates into 240 meters). Put another way, a straight line on the map about 2.625 inches in length represents a mile on the ground (1 centimeter on the map is the equivalent of about .24 kilometers on the ground). At this scale a site relatively large by New England standards, for example, one about 50 meters (164 feet) across would be proportionally only about 2 millimeters (about 0.08 of an inch) across on the map. The point of all this annoying math is simple: It is extremely difficult to eyeball the exact location of a site on a USGS topographic map, especially when the site itself may be no more than a few tens of feet across. At this scale many archaeological sites are barely pinpoints; when we mark such a site's location with a pencil, in some cases the mark itself is bigger than the site (Feder 2001).

Fortunately, we no longer need to "guesstimate" the location of a site. Our ability today to far place a site far more accurately on a broader landscape is made possible through the **Global Positioning System (GPS).** Initiated in 1973, the GPS currently consists of a web of twenty-four satellites orbiting Earth at an altitude of about 12,600 miles (20,000 kilometers; Figure 7.1). At any given time and from any location on the planet, the signals of between five and eight (and sometimes even more) of the satellites can be received. These satellites emit radio signals that can be processed by GPS receivers here on Earth, and from those readings GPS receivers can provide precise and accurate information concerning location in three dimensions (latitude, longitude, and elevation).

Generally, with handheld receivers locations can be measured accurately to within a range of about 20 meters. Additionally, the Federal Aviation Authority is developing the **Wide Area Augmentation System**, which uses ground stations in conjunction with the satellites to improve accuracy to within 7 and even 2 meters. With corrections available from known, fixed locations, even greater accuracy can be achieved, and locations can be pinpointed to within a remarkable 1 meter on our planet's 510,000,000,000,000 square meters!

One can readily see how useful the ability to pinpoint to within just a few meters the location of friendly and hostile troops would be in a battlefield situation. It should come as no surprise, therefore, that the GPS is funded, maintained, and controlled by the U.S. Department of Defense. Its original and still primary purpose is one of military support, and GPS signals originally were encrypted so that only the U.S. military and its allies could access the signals. Recognizing the great potential of the GPS system for civilian use, the signals were made available to everyone in the mid-1980s, but for a time only the U.S. military and its allies could access the *pure* signal from the satellites. Called "selective availability," the Department of Defense degraded the signal available to everyone else (remember, "everyone else" included Iraqi troops in the 1991 Persian Gulf War engaged in combat against American soldiers), allowing for less accuracy. Under selective availability, nonmilitary measurements were accurate to within only about 100 meters, still not bad on a rather large planet but of limited use to archaeologists who needed to locate their sites much more precisely.

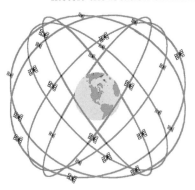

FIGURE 7.1 Schematic diagram showing satellite positioning in the Global Positioning System. A very accurate measurement of your location (and the location of an archaeological site you are standing on top of) can be determined by using a hand-held GPS device when it can "see" five or more of the satellites. (Courtesy Peter H. Dana, The Geographer's Craft Project, Department of Geography, University of Colorado at Boulder)

As a result of newly developed abilities to block the signals to an enemy during combat, degrading signal accuracy became unnecessary, and the selective availability program was ended in May 2000. Since that time pure satellite signals have been accessible to anyone with a GPS receiver. An experiment was conducted at a fixed point at a known location just before and immediately after selective availability was suspended. With the degraded signal, 95% of the measurements taken over a twenty-four-hour period at a known location fell within a circle whose radius was measured at 45 meters. After selective availability was turned off, measurements taken over the next twenty-four hours fell within a circle whose radius was only 6.3 meters around the actual location (http://www.colorado.edu/geography/gcraft/notes/gps/gps_f.html).

Basic handheld GPS receivers with monochrome displays are widely available and sell for about $100. Devices with mapping capabilities and color displays are more expensive but start at only about $250 (fancier devices with higher-resolution screens can be twice that). Even then, most feature-packed handhelds are only a little bigger in size and weight than the average cell phone. (Figure 7.2). Most of these truly remarkable and useful devices can be connected to a computer, and the locational information collected and stored in the handheld receiver can be uploaded and automatically indicated on digital maps that can be purchased in various software packages. These maps are at a far smaller scale than that provided by USGS topographical maps. A handheld GPS receiver can track and record the distance, average speed, duration, direction, and change in elevation walked by a hiker or archaeology survey crew; a mapping-capable GPS unit can display the route on a map. Along with the ability to accurately position areas walked in a pedestrian survey, the configuration of test-pit transects, and the precise locations of archaeological sites my group has surveyed, for me there is an added bonus to using a GPS handheld device: I no longer walk in circles attempting to find sites in the woods.

Read More

With a handheld GPS device and any of these comprehensive guides to GPS systems and approaches, you'll nearly always be able to locate an archaeological site with enormous precision—and you will hardly ever get lost in the woods:

El-Rabbany, A. 2002. *Introduction to GPS: The Global Positioning System*. Artech House, Boston.

Hotchkiss, N. J. 1999. *A Comprehensive Guide to Land Navigation with GPS*. Alexis Publishing, Leesburg, Virginia.

Letham, L. 2001. *GPS Made Easy*. Mountaineers Books, Seattle.

How Are Archaeological Sites Named?

Archaeological sites have long been named in a number of traditional and informal ways. When sites are located on private lands, it is common to name the site after the landowner. For example, the Glazier Blade Cache site mentioned earlier was named after Ron Glazier, on whose property the site was located. Sites are

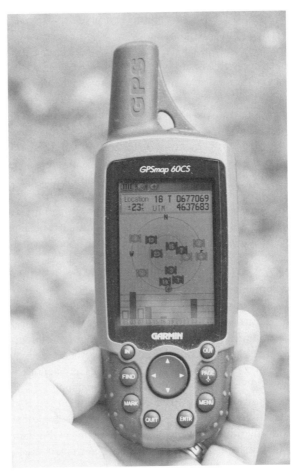

FIGURE 7.2 Photo of the screen of my Garmin GPSmap 60CS handheld device, showing the location and elevation of my house in the UTM system. (K. L. Feder)

often named after their discoverers or according to a local landmark. One example is the Vail Site in Maine, named after its discoverer, local hunting guide and amateur archaeologist Francis Vail. The Ragged Mountain Rockshelter site is descriptively named; it is located in a rock shelter (a long and narrow overhang of rock) on Ragged Mountain in Barkhamsted, Connecticut. Sites are sometimes given colorful, even whimsical, names that reflect their appearance: Cliff Palace in southern Colorado, indeed, looks like a palace secreted in a niche just under a cliff (Figure 7.3, top); Mound City in Ohio consists of about two dozen earth mounds (Figure 7.3, bottom), with the entire grouping surrounded by an earth wall, giving the place the appearance of a city of mounds. Site names can get fanciful and even reflect errors in historical attribution, but these names often stick anyway: Montezuma's Castle (see Figure 6.2, top) in Arizona doesn't look much like a castle, and Montezuma (now usually spelled Moctezuma), the Aztec king encountered by the Spanish in 1519, had nothing to do with it; the Toltecs,

FIGURE 7.3 Cliff Palace (top, in Mesa Verde National Park, Colorado) and Mound City (bottom, in Chilichothe, Ohio) are aptly descriptive names given to those two archaeological sites. (K. L. Feder)

a group who preceded the historical Aztecs in central Mexico, had nothing to do with Toltec Mounds in Arkansas; the Aztec Ruins in New Mexico were built by Pueblo Indians, not the Aztecs.

With no individual landowner and no particular discoverer, we named the Wood Lily site for the flowers that were in bloom near the road where we started the test pit transect, along which we found the site. The most important element in site naming is to assign a unique identifier to avoid confusion with any other site.

Although names are easier to remember than numbers, named sites are also given numerical identifiers. The common names we apply to sites are not as important as are their official designations assigned variously by a state archaeologist, historic preservation office, or other official government entity or museum. These official designations are not arbitrary: They provide in a coded format information about the site and its location. A national system of site designation includes a numerical prefix that locates the site by state, with states assigned numbers alphabetically. Using this system, the national designation for every site in Alabama, for example, begins with the numeral 1 because Alabama is the first state in an alphabetical listing of all the states. All archaeological sites listed in Connecticut begin with the numeral 6 because Connecticut was sixth in an alphabetical listing of the states before Alaska and Hawaii became states.

The next part of the national archaeological site designator is a two-letter abbreviation for the county in which the site is located. The final part of the designator is simply a number that reflects a tally of the archaeological sites in a given county in the order of their discovery or, often, the order in which they have been reported to the person in charge of maintaining the list for a given state. For example, 6LF21 is the twenty-first site listed in the county of Litchfield (LF), Connecticut (6). The site is known among Connecticut archaeologists as Templeton (for the property owner) and has the oldest radiocarbon date of any site in the state (10,190 B.P.).

Some states, such as my own, do not have many counties, and county boundaries may be geographically insignificant, historically unimportant, and politically meaningless. Counties in some states exhibit a tremendous amount of variation in terms of size, and certainly counties in some states are much larger than typical counties in other states; I imagine that counties in some states are bigger than some states in their entirety. As a result, some states have moved away from a county-based system of site naming. In Connecticut the state archaeologist provides official town-based designations for sites, in which each site designator begins with a numerical prefix that reflects the alphabetical position of the town where the site is located. For example, all sites found in the town of Barkhamsted, Connecticut, are assigned a designator prefix of 5 because that town is fifth in an alphabetical listing of Connecticut's 169 towns. After the town location prefix, a number appears that reflects, again, the order in which sites located in the town have been discovered and reported to the state archaeologist. However a site is named, the designator should be unique and provide information to anyone who reads its name, allowing a researcher to easily determine at least the general location of the site.

Read More

For a brief discussion of the conventions of site naming see the following book:

Stewart, R. M. 2002. *Archaeology: Basic Field Methods*. Kendall/Hunt Publishing, Dubuque, Iowa.

How Do Archaeologists Excavate Sites?

You know the old joke that asks the question "How should you react when encountering an angry grizzly bear?" "Very carefully" is the response spoken only half in jest. The same answer, again only half jokingly, applies to the question posed by the title of this segment: How do archaeologists excavate sites? Indeed, very carefully (Hester 1997a; Stewart 2002). It is one of the great ironies of archaeological research that we seek out places where the material remains of past human activity have nearly miraculously escaped destruction and dismemberment through natural processes and modern development, and, once found, we dig them up and, in so doing, destroy those preserved places.

It is important to understand that sites are not just accumulations of artifacts and ecofacts. Sites are the archaeological manifestations once-living communities of people. Sites consist of all the artifacts and ecofacts as well as all of the space between them. Remember our discussion of how archaeological sites are formed. Sites come into existence by people losing, discarding, caching, and abandoning material *at particular places* (within their village, hunting camp, farmstead, quarry, mill, cemetery, and so on). The particular places where those deposited objects can be found by the archaeologist often are the places where people carried out tasks: where they made spear points or pottery; where they hunted and butchered animals; where they cooked their food or conducted religious ceremonies; where they spilled their blood in pitched battles fought for reasons we can never know; where they ground grain between massive millwheels, prepared wool for spinning, or milled enormous trees into lumber; where they extracted clay for the manufacture of ceramics; where they played games; or simply where they threw stuff away. The fact that a particular object can be found at a particular place and in spatial association with other objects at an archaeological site informs us about what transpired at that place within what was a community of people.

Certainly, the last thing we want to do as archaeologists (who hope to figure out what went on in a community by examining the site produced by the behavior of the inhabitants) is to destroy this vital spatial component of the evidence. I have already likened archaeology to detective work. Detectives are not merely interested in collecting individual items. A collection of disconnected bits of evidence tells only part of the story of what transpired at a crime scene. Detectives need to know the precise location where each item (bullet casings, glass shards, footprints) was found and its **spatial associations** with other items (which bits of evidence were found together). A bag filled with bullets is only partially informative. A detailed map showing where each bullet was found—specifically in relation to each other bullet, shattered windows, footprints, and the dead body—along with the bullets themselves (which can be analyzed in a laboratory to determine if they all came from the same gun, if any show traces of blood, and so on) allows for a far more detailed, precise, and accurate reconstruction of the scene than do the bullets alone (Figure 7.4).

Chapter 7:
Slide Show

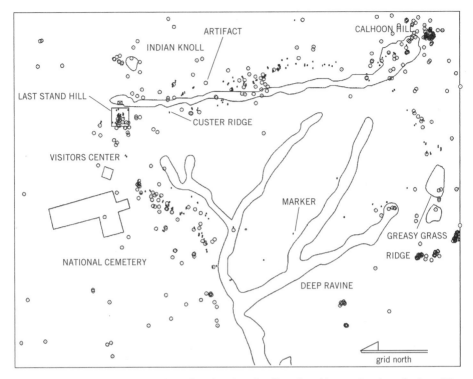

FIGURE 7.4 A detailed analysis of the location of artifacts found in a surface investigation of the place where the Battle of the Little Big Horn was fought has provided researchers with fresh insights into the flow of the battle between Custer and his Seventh Cavalry and the Sioux and associated tribes who defeated him. (Courtesy Doug Scott)

Consider an intact, carefully preserved crime scene where everything has been left in place. The mapped locations of the bullets can be used to determine the trajectory of the projectiles. Those trajectories can then be traced back to their source(s), and the detective can pinpoint the location(s) from which the shots were fired. That spot, once identified, can be investigated for additional clues that will contribute to the solution of the crime. Compare that intact and carefully examined crime scene to a bag of bullets collected at the site with no spatial data. If you were a detective, which scenario would you prefer?

Just as a detective must collect all the individual bits of evidence and return these items to a laboratory for detailed analysis, archaeologists must do the same. And just as detectives must preserve all of the spatial data encoded in those bits of evidence—what material was found where—to thoroughly reconstruct what happened at a crime scene, archaeologists must preserve the spatial data of a site—what artifacts and ecofacts were found where—by careful data recovery and record-keeping. By accurately and thoroughly mapping the locations of artifacts and ecofacts, we can, in a sense, preserve the three-dimensional (location and depth) data necessary to preserve the spatial organization of a site, even as we dismantle it to study its individual components.

Read More

Archaeologists spend a lot of time agonizing about excavation: how to preserve as much of the information presented at an archaeological site as possible, recognizing that excavation itself can be a destructive process. As a result, an enormous number of publications focus on the problems and challenges of the process of excavation. For three of the best broad and nearly inclusive summaries, see the following resources.

Dancey, W. S. 1981. *Archaeological Field Methods: An Introduction.* Burgess International Group, New York.

Hester, T. R. 1997a. Methods of Excavation. In *Field Methods in Archaeology*, edited by T. R. Hester, H. J. Shafer, and K. L. Feder, 69–112. Mayfield Publishing, Mountain View, California.

Stewart, R. M. 2002. *Archaeology: Basic Field Methods.* Kendall/Hunt Publishing, Dubuque, Iowa.

WHY ARE ARCHAEOLOGISTS SO PAINSTAKING AND SLOW IN EXCAVATION?

Most people find it terribly surprising how long the various components of archaeological fieldwork take. Visitors to my excavations often are amazed when they learn from two seemingly intelligent, industrious, and hardworking students, as they are troweling a level at the bottom of a 2-meter–by–2-meter excavation unit no more than a couple of feet deep, that they have been working in that one spot for two weeks. I can remember as a field school student our crew being called in to recover some woolly mammoth bones accidentally uncovered by a home builder. The archaeologists arrived with their trowels and dental picks, ready to excavate the often tiny and always delicate fragments of 10,000-year-old elephant bones and tusks. The construction people were appalled at the low-tech approach we were employing; a backhoe operator told us he could get the bones out in just a minute or two. He promised he would be "real careful." We turned down his generous offer and continued, using the time-honored tool kit of the archaeology fieldworker.

There are a number of commonsense reasons why archaeologists take so much time and are so careful in excavating sites. Like the 10,000-year-old woolly mammoth bones, much of the evidence that makes up the archaeological record is delicate and fragile, already largely broken up in the process of being transformed from its behavioral context to its archaeological context and then by natural processes in the soil. A backhoe may be quick, and the operator may be extremely efficient, careful, and perfectly good at removing an archaeologically sterile overburden of soil stratigraphically above a site, but even an expertly employed backhoe is simply incapable of safely recovering archaeological material.

Along with being fragile, a fair percentage of the archaeological record consists of tiny bits of evidence. As indicated a number of times in this book (it is an archaeological mantra of sorts), archaeological research is not a treasure hunt, and sometimes even the smallest, most unimpressive fragments of artifacts and ecofacts may be enormously informative and contribute to our understanding of some aspect of an ancient people's way of life. It is time consuming to expose and recover all these small objects, measure them in their locations, and then bag them to take for further analysis in the lab, but it is more than worthwhile in our effort to understand an ancient way of life, especially one that has left behind little more than the tiny fragments we recover.

Finally, the fundamental irony of archaeological fieldwork has already been discussed: When we excavate a site, we destroy it. Ordinarily, we get only one shot at discovery, recording objects in situ, and recovery. It is a professional obligation to accomplish these tasks responsibly, and that means carefully, which in turn almost always means slowly. Whatever the time period and whatever the culture, there are a finite number of archaeological sites, and each one that is lost through development, erosion, looting, or well-meaning but inadequate archaeological research diminishes the database proportionally. It is our duty, therefore, to excavate archaeological sites as carefully as possible and, furthermore, the reason we try to leave parts of unthreatened sites unexcavated, saving them for future archaeologists with more sophisticated methods for discovering and recovering the precious undisturbed evidence.

Read More

For more detailed discussions of the importance of careful archaeological excavation, any of the following sources will provide important additional information.

Baker, B. W., B. S. Shaffer, and D. G. Steele. 1997. Basic Approaches in Archaeological Faunal Analysis. In *Field Methods in Archaeology*, edited by T. R. Hester, H. J. Shafer, and K. L. Feder, 298–318. Mayfield Publishing, Mountain View, California.

Hester, T. R. 1997a. Methods of Excavation. In *Field Methods in Archaeology*, edited by T. R. Hester, H. J. Shafer, and K. L. Feder, 69–112. Mayfield Publishing, Mountain View, California.

———. 1997b. The Handling and Conservation of Artifacts in the Field. In *Field Methods in Archaeology*, edited by T. R. Hester, H. J. Shafer, and K. L. Feder, 143–58. Mayfield Publishing, Mountain View, California.

Holloway, R. G. 1997. Excavation and Recovery of Botanical Materials from Archaeological Sites. In *Field Methods in Archaeology*, edited by T. R. Hester, H. J. Shafer, and K. L. Feder, 283–97. Mayfield Publishing, Mountain View, California.

Stewart, R. M. 2002. *Archaeology: Basic Field Methods*. Kendall/Hunt Publishing, Dubuque, Iowa.

What Tools Do Archaeologists Use to Expose and Recover Artifacts?

Whenever you see archaeologists on a television drama or in a movie, they're forever using whisk brooms and dustpans to extract the dust of the ages from the precious artifacts that will enable them to solve the vexing mysteries of human antiquity. Something like that. Well, to be honest, I hardly ever use a whisk broom. Here in the forests of southern New England, the soil is mostly moist and rocky, and whisk brooms aren't very effective; they just get clogged up and heavily laden with mud. Some of my colleagues, however, swear by whisk brooms, but even they will admit that the most valuable tool in the arsenal of the archaeologist is the venerable mason's trowel: a pointed steel blade, roughly in the shape of a diamond, with a handle welded (never riveted, please) at one end along its long axis (Figure 7.5). Mason's trowels are made by companies such as Red Devil and Sears, but the Marshalltown trowel has attained the status of icon in the archaeological community. Marshalltown trowels can last for years, decreasing in size as they are continually resharpened (Flannery 1982). One of the annual awards bestowed by the Society for American Archaeology, in fact, is a plaque adorned with a gold-painted Marshalltown trowel.

Whenever I go to the hardware store to pick up some new trowels, I invariably run into a homeowner intent on doing a little masonry work but unfamiliar with the tools needed to build that brick wall around his or her patio or flowerbed. For some reason, I must appear to know my way around the toolshed, and I'm often asked about the best trowel to accomplish the task. I have given up trying to explain the rather idiosyncratic function of the trowels I purchase, so I just go ahead and recommend Marshalltowns. I guess they're as good at laying brick as they are at excavating an archaeological site. At least I've never had any complaints.

In all seriousness, the tools archaeologists use in the field have the primary purpose of removing the soil matrix surrounding archaeological material and then extracting those materials from that matrix. We use whatever works. Under certain soil conditions archaeologists may very carefully employ shovels and picks, for example, to get through a dense, resistant, culturally sterile layer in the soil in order to reach lower levels in which artifacts, ecofacts, and features are known (through previous testing or having been exposed by natrual erosion) to be concentrated. Responsible archaeologists have even been known to employ

FIGURE 7.5 Though not a Marshalltown, this trowel has lasted a good long time. (K. L. Feder)

heavy earth-moving equipment including backhoes, tractors, and plows in survey and excavation. Remember the discussion earlier (chapter 6) about archaeologists walking agricultural fields in their search for sites? Archaeologists have forgone the farmer and used tractors to plow fields, not in preparation for planting, but intentionally to expose artifacts in the top several inches of soil (Trubowitz 1981). Once shovel testing has revealed the existence of a thick layer of soil lacking any archaeological material lying above a deep layer with artifacts, earth-moving equipment may be called in to efficiently—and carefully—remove the sterile overburden. It's always a matter of what works at exposing while not damaging or disturbing the buried archaeological layer.

The trowel, with its blade kept razor-sharp, is an effective tool for scraping soil from the surface of an excavation unit in thin slices and also for smoothing and straightening the vertical walls of the unit. When artifacts or ecofacts are exposed by trowel work, they are left exactly where we found them: We use the Latin phrase **in situ** to characterize an object in its precise place of discovery. Archaeologists everywhere formally apologize to the Latinists among us when we admit that we often refer to objects removed from their place of discovery as being "out of situ," which, I have on good authority, is not proper Latin.

In any event, we leave items in place first just to see if they are in spatial association with other objects yet to be found in the square and second to allow for mapping the material and then for photography. A unit's vertical walls are scraped with the trowel to provide a smooth, clean profile of the soil at a site, allowing for a detailed examination of its stratigraphy and identifying the precise layer or layers in which archaeological material is found. The trowel is also used in collecting soil samples for analysis in the laboratory. Some archaeologists grind and sharpen a notch in one of the back edges of the trowel for use as a small root cutter, and, though I cannot personally recommend it, many of my students extol the virtues of a sharp Marshalltown as a back scratcher for those hard-to-reach mosquito bites or patches of poison ivy rash.

Plenty of other tools are helpful in carrying out the fundamental task of removing soil from around artifacts and ecofacts and in exposing features (Figure 7.6). Even trowels miniaturized by years of resharpening often are still too large to safely expose very small objects.

Dental picks work well to remove the soil surrounding small bits of charcoal, pottery shards, and tiny stone flakes. Fine tweezers— the kind you can purchase at science supply houses that are used in

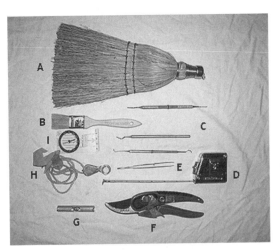

FIGURE 7.6 After the trowel, a typical archaeology tool kit includes these objects: (A) whisk broom, (B) small brush, (C) dental picks, (D) tape measure, (E) tweezers, (F) root cutters, (G) bubble level, (H) 10X loupe (magnifier), and (I) compass. (K. L. Feder)

biology labs, not the cheapies you can buy at a drugstore for removing splinters or attending to your cuticles—are useful for picking up very small and delicate remains. Metal-bladed trowels and dental picks can cause damage to soft material (bone, for instance), and many archaeologists make scraping tools out of bamboo, which generally is hard enough to excavate soil in small bits but soft enough to prevent damage to breakable objects. Toothbrushes, soft paint brushes, and airbrushes (small, soft brushes attached to a rubber or plastic bulb that, when squeezed, sends a puff of air down the bristles of the brush) can be extremely useful in gently prodding soil away from archaeological specimens, both those in situ as well as items newly extracted from the soil. And yes, it is to be admitted that under many conditions, particularly where the soil is dry and easily brushed away, whisk brooms can be extremely useful in removing the matrix above and around archaeological material.

Read More

For brief discussions of the archaeologist's tool kit (including Kent Flannery's parable about the revered and esteemed Marshalltown trowel), see the following resources.

Flannery, K. V. 1982. The Golden Marshalltown: A Parable for the Archaeology of the 1980s. *American Anthropologist* 84:265–78.

Hester, T. R. 1997a. Methods of Excavation. In *Field Methods in Archaeology*, edited by T. R. Hester, H. J. Shafer, and K. L. Feder, 69–112. Mayfield Publishing, Mountain View, California.

Stewart, R. M. 2002. *Archaeology: Basic Field Methods*. Kendall/Hunt Publishing, Dubuque, Iowa.

Winans, M. C., and R. C. Winans. 1993. Measuring Systems, Techniques, and Equipment for Taphonomic Studies. In *Practical Archaeology: Field and Laboratory Techniques and Archaeological Logistics*, edited by B. D. Dillon, 33–38. Institute of Archaeology, Los Angeles.

What Is an Excavation Unit, and How Is It Labeled?

Imagine an enormous piece of graph paper laid out across a landscape, and you have a pretty good idea of the way in which excavators divide an archaeological site into spatial entities called **excavation units**—but you needn't call them that in the field, where the term "squares" will suffice (Figure 7.7). Archaeological sites vary widely in size, from just a few square meters to several square kilometers. Very small sites can be excavated in their entirety, and a human mind—even that of a mosquito-bitten overworked archaeologist—can take them in all at once. Most sites are far too large for that and need to be excavated and analyzed in manageable bites. The excavation unit is the manageable bite, usually square in shape (that's why we call them "squares"). At one time the standard size of an excavation unit was the "6-foot square": a

S16E10

S10E16

S10E7

S8E2

S6E9

S6E5

S2E8

S1E4

S2E1

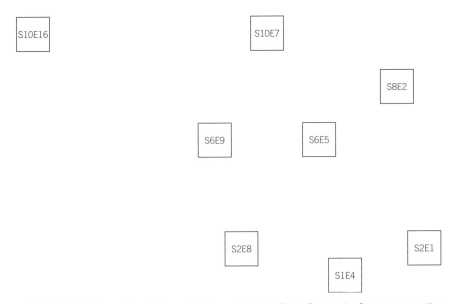

FIGURE 7.7 Archaeological site overlain by a site grid defining 2-meter-by-2-meter excavation units (top). Wooden stakes have been placed firmly in the ground at the corners of each unit of the grid, and the lines have been defined by sturdy string nailed into the tops of the stakes. Plan of excavation units at the Firetown Meadow site in Simsbury, Connecticut (bottom). Each of the nine excavation units is a one-meter square and bears its locational designation in meters south and east of datum. (K. L. Feder)

square 6 feet long on each of its sides (there even was an instructional film about archaeological excavation called, appropriately enough, *The Six-Foot Square*). Almost all archaeologists have shifted to the metric system, which, once mastered, truly is more sensible than the English system, with much more easily convertible units, and the standard size of an excavation unit has become 2 meters on a side (an area, rather obviously, of 4 square meters). Depending on site size and conditions, a unit may be smaller or larger and may not even be a square at all but a rectangular trench. Some historical archaeologists in the United States have argued for retention of the English system of inches, feet, and yards in excavating historical sites. These researchers have a point: The features they excavate (house foundations, mill races, iron foundries, and so on) were built to specifications of the English system, so it makes sense to excavate these features using the same measurements of the system that was used in their construction.

Whatever the shape or precise size of an excavation unit or the system of measurement employed, the motives for digging in regular, small-scale units are the same: The method divides the physical labor of excavating a site into manageable units and provides a framework by which the locations of all recovered materials, at least at the level of the excavation unit, can be expeditiously recorded. That framework is a site grid, the enormous, imaginary piece of graph paper mentioned at the beginning of this section.

The designator for each unit is its location on an orthogonal grid, a series of equally spaced parallel lines intersected by another set of equally spaced lines parallel to each other and perpendicular to the first set of lines (in other words, a grid with all right angles). The grid is commonly oriented north-south and east-west, although the actual orientation of the site or of the landscape to be excavated may cause this to vary. However the grid is oriented, one point on the grid where two of the perpendicular lines intersect is labeled the **datum;** on a standard graph this is called the origin and represents the 0,0 location. Ordinarily, the datum is placed at a margin of the site or even offsite. Every location—each grid point as well as the precise positioning of each artifact, ecofact, and feature found within the site—is keyed into the location of the origin of the grid in terms of its distance to the north or south and its distance to the east or west of the datum point.

This method keys everything within the site relative to an arbitrarily designated 0,0 point, and in so doing we can then place all site locations within an absolute spatial frame of reference. The precise geographic location of the datum can be calculated to great precision in terms of, for example, longitude and latitude, though more commonly exact location is measured in reference to the **Universal Transverse Mercator (UTM)**, a military grid system based on the metric system and used by cartographers. Especially in the past, the site datum might be referenced to a nearby physical benchmark, a permanent marker (often of concrete), whose location has been accurately measured and recorded and that appears on maps of an area. Today, the precise location of datum can often be determined by use of a Global Positioning System (GPS) unit.

Each excavation unit is designated by its location on the grid relative to the datum, or 0,0, point. By tradition an excavation unit may be labeled by the

FIGURE 7.8 A 1-meter-by-1-meter square archaeological excavation unit. (K. L. Feder)

coordinates of its southwest corner. For example, a 2-meter–by–2-meter square unit whose four corners are demarcated by the points on the grid 20 meters north-38 meters east, 22 meters north-38 meters east, 20 meters north-40 meters east, and 22 meters north-40 meters east (all measurements north or east of the datum) is most often designated: N20E38, that point being the southwest corner of the unit (Figure 7.8). When artifacts or ecofacts are found in a unit, they are bagged together when removed from the soil, and the bag is clearly marked with the unit designation along with the stratigraphic slice, or the depth from which the material in the bag was recovered. In this way, though the archaeologist has removed the specimens from their positions in situ, the location and depth of their recovery has been recorded and preserved.

Read More

The crucial task of recording where objects are found at a site can be time consuming and tedious. We begin the process of recording locations by dividing a site into excavation units. For a discussion of the process of laying out a site grid and labeling individual analytical units, see the following sources.

Dancey, W. S. 1981. *Archaeological Field Methods: An Introduction.* Burgess International Group, New York.

Feder, K. L. 1997a. Data Preservation: Recording and Collecting. In *Field Methods in Archaeology,* edited by T. R. Hester, H. J. Shafer, and K. L. Feder, 113–42. Mayfield Publishing, Mountain View, California.

Knapton, L. K. 1997. Archaeological Mapping, Site Grids, and Surveying. In *Field Methods in Archaeology,* edited by T. R. Hester, H. J. Shafer, and K. L. Feder, 177–234. Mayfield Publishing, Mountain View, California.

Stewart, R. M. 2002. *Archaeology: Basic Field Methods.* Kendall/Hunt Publishing, Dubuque, Iowa.

How Do Archaeologists Keep Track of Where Stuff Is Found at Sites?

We sometimes say in archaeology that through our work we hope to paint a picture of an ancient way of life. It's not a great metaphor, but it does convey a reasonably accurate impression of at least one of the things we hope to accomplish by excavating and analyzing archaeological sites.

My colleague Mike Park uses this analogy: Do you remember from art history the pointillism method of producing paintings by placing a series of very short brushstrokes or "points" of paint on a canvas? This interesting method has resulted in some terrific paintings. Georges Seurat is one of the best known pointillists, and when you stand back far enough to view his paintings (for example, *Sunday Afternoon on the Island of the Grande Jatte*), the individual points of color seamlessly blend together to convey uniquely beautiful images of Seurat's nineteenth-century France.

Suppose we wanted to study one of Seurat's paintings and further suppose that to do so we simply collected all the dots of paint from the canvas, removing them from the painting and analyzing them individually. We might learn a lot about the paint Seurat used, but we would never know what the painting looked like, what scene or people the painter depicted. In our desire to study the painting, we would have destroyed the story told by the painter.

Suppose now that we still were obliged to remove all the points of paint from a canvas to study the paint, the canvas, and the technology used to apply the paint to the canvas, but we also hoped to examine and understand the message conveyed by the painter. As we took it apart, piece by piece, paint point by paint point, we would need to keep an absolutely accurate and thorough record of where each and every paint point originated, map them precisely, and then re-create the image in order to study it.

We don't ordinarily need to do this to a painting, but we almost always need to do it for an archaeological site. We usually cannot just leave a site as is. We need to expose it and then remove its individual elements to study and preserve them. In order to preserve the story of a way of life told by the blending of the "brushstrokes" (the artifacts, ecofacts, and features), we must make accurate measurements of their locations. This enables us to put the image back together and tell the story of the life lived by a people at a particular place and time.

The exact location of an artifact, ecofact, or feature is called its **provenience.** When an artifact or ecofact is encountered in an excavation unit, it is left in place so that its location can be measured. Large artifacts, ecofacts, and especially features will have a series of locational points measured to provide an outline of their locations that can then be transferred to a map. These locations first may be measured relative to the southwest corner of the excavation unit in which the items were found (Figure 7.8).

A measurement relative to the southwest corner provides a measurement for everything found in every excavation unit at a site relative to the site datum. With all these locations mapped in, the archaeologist can produce a detailed and accurate map of the locations of artifacts, ecofacts, and features relative to the site datum and, importantly, relative to all other artifacts, ecofacts, and features found at the site. Often, as each layer is exposed and all items revealed have been mapped before removal to the lab, a photograph is taken to produce a permanent visual record of the in situ spatial locations and associations of all the material exposed in the soil level through excavation. Especially with digital photography, this is an easy, reliable, and inexpensive way of recording the artifacts, ecofacts, and features revealed in each excavated layer in a unit.

Remember that a site is not just a two-dimensional entity. On the one hand, a site occupied for a very short period of time may be represented by a thin layer of material all at the same approximate depth from the modern surface. On the other hand, a site occupied for an extended period—with material slowly accumulated underfoot over years, decades, and even centuries—may be found in a thick band of cultural material of varying depths from the surface. It is not enough, therefore, to take only a two-dimensional reading of the location of an artifact, ecofact, or feature. We also need to measure the depths from which material was recovered in order to place these items in their proper **stratigraphic** context.

One low-tech way of accomplishing this measurement involves the use of a carpenter's bubble level. The level is hung from a string attached to the stake marking the southwest corner of an excavation unit. When pulled taut over the unit and with the bubble centered, that string defines a fixed plane from which we can take depth measurements (Figure 7.9). A tape measure or carpenter's rule held vertically is used to measure the depth of an occupation level or the

FIGURE 7.9 Use of a decidedly low-tech piece of equipment, a carpenter's suspended bubble level, to measure the depth of an excavation unit and to maintain a flat excavation surface. (K. L. Feder)

surface on which an artifact or ecofact rests relative to the string. The height of all the strings in each of the excavation units can be determined relative to the elevation of the datum point, enabling the determination of a fixed depth of all archaeological material recovered at the site.

A "medium-tech" way of accomplishing depth measurement involves the use of one of a number of surveying devices, for example, an **alidade** (Figure 7.10). An alidade is essentially a telescope with crosshairs, mounted on a flat base that can be positioned on a **plane table.**

When the plane table is leveled on a tripod located, for example, directly over the datum, the precise height of the crosshairs in the center of the telescope site can be measured (how high the alidade sits over the surface at the site datum). A **stadia rod**, which is essentially a long, rigid ruler, is then placed at the spot where depth or elevation needs measuring. The line of sight of someone looking through the alidade to the gradation on the stadia rod represents a precise measurement of the depth of the surface on which the rod is resting relative to the height of the alidade's crosshairs. Subtracting the measured height of the alidade above the point where it is located from the

FIGURE 7.10 The plane table is leveled on top of a tripod, and the alidade is placed on the table. The precise height of the crosshairs in the alidade lens is measured, and the depth of artifacts can be measured relative to those crosshairs. (K. L. Feder)

measurement read on the stadia rod reveals the actual depth of the surface the rod is resting on from the surface under the alidade, which, in this case, is the site datum. The depth of everything so measured at a site can be determined relative to the datum. When the site is so large that the alidade must be moved away from the datum, as long as the elevation of the point it is being moved to is measured first, all subsequent elevation or depth measurements can be tied back in to the site datum. A higher-tech method involves the use of a more expensive piece of equipment called a **total station**, which includes as its heart a **laser transit**, a device you likely have seen highway engineers use. The laser transit sits on a tripod and looks a bit like those mounted binocular sighting devices you find at scenic overlooks (Figure 7.11).

As in work with the alidade, a fieldworker places a stadia rod on the spot whose depth is being measured. Unlike work with the alidade, instead of actually looking though the transit to obtain a measurement, the device itself sends out a beam of laser light that bounces off the rod and returns to the transit receiver, where the precise gradation intersected by the light can be recorded and the exact distance from the transit to the stadia rod can be calculated. These measurements can be automatically adjusted for the height of the transit, stored in the transit's memory, and downloaded to a computer, where any one of a number of mapping programs can produce a map showing the natural topography of a site, the positioning of the excavation units, and the locations and depths of every artifact, ecofact, and feature encountered in the excavation. It sounds cool, and it is.

In a recent application we needed to accurately record the locations of gravestones in the abandoned cemetery of a nineteenth-century community located in northwestern Connecticut (see Figure 7.11). Many of the stones were broken close to the base, and the tops had been moved elsewhere in the cemetery. We needed a precise map of the location of each gravestone base set in the ground to produce a map of the cemetery as a whole, and we wanted to locate the tops of those that had been broken off. The total station allowed for an exact and efficient mapping of each stone's location and the production of an accurate map of the graveyard (Figure 7.12). The same very accurate procedure can be used to produce directly a topographic map of a site, a site grid, and a precise distribution map of all items horizontally and vertical revealed through excavation.

Read More

Keeping track of where stuff is found at a site can be time consuming and tedious, but it is extremely important. We can begin the process of recording the location of discovery of archaeological materials by dividing a site into excavation units. For a discussion of mapping the precise locations of archaeological material within the established analytical units within the grid, refer to any of the following resources. See especially McPherron and Dibble for the use of laser transits.

Dancey, W. S. 1981. *Archaeological Field Methods: An Introduction.* Burgess International Group, New York.

FIGURE 7.11 A total station is the most accurate of the methods discussed here for mapping the locations and depths of archaeological materials. Here, surveyors map the precise locations of gravestones in an eighteenth- and nineteenth-century cemetery. (K. L. Feder)

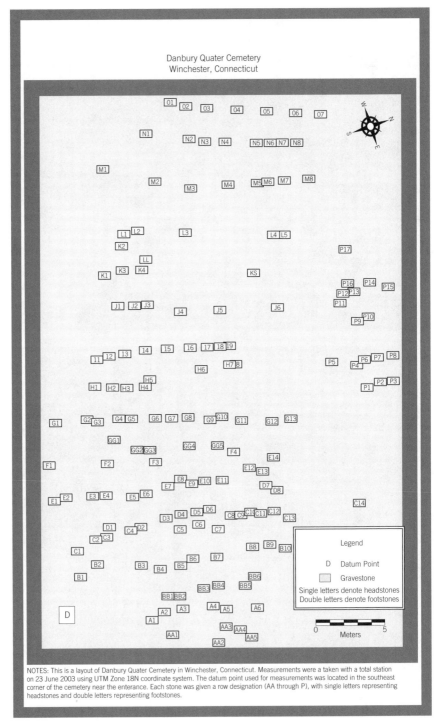

FIGURE 7.12 The map of gravestone locations produced using the total station in the project shown in Figure 7.11. (Cartography by Christine Pittsley)

Feder, K. L. 1997a. Data Preservation: Recording and Collecting. In *Field Methods in Archaeology*, edited by T. R. Hester, H. J. Shafer, and K. L. Feder, 113–42. Mayfield Publishing, Mountain View, California.

Knapton, L. K. 1997. Archaeological Mapping, Site Grids, and Surveying. In *Field Methods in Archaeology*, edited by T. R. Hester, H. Shafer, and K. L. Feder, 177–234. Mayfield Publishing, Mountain View, California.

McPherron, S. P., and H. L. Dibble. 2002. *Using Computers in Archaeology*. McGraw-Hill, New York.

Stewart, R. M. 2002. *Archaeology: Basic Field Methods*. Kendall/Hunt Publishing, Dubuque, Iowa.

Winans, M. C., and R. C. Winans. 1993. Measuring Systems, Techniques, and Equipment for Taphonomic Studies. In *Practical Archaeology: Field and Laboratory Techniques and Archaeological Logistics*, edited by B. D. Dillon, 33–38. Institute of Archaeology, Los Angeles.

Why Do Archaeologists Save All the Tiny Scraps of Stone, Bone, and Other Stuff?

Archaeologists can fairly be characterized as packrats. As a group we can be awfully obsessive about recovering, saving, and taking back to the lab every tiny scrap that might conceivably be the result of human activity in the past. I have on occasion wondered to myself when taking an inordinate amount of time to recover some tiny bits of animal bone, burned nut fragments, or stone flakes what the ancient people would think if they could see this grown person so zealously, almost fanatically, picking up tiny, seemingly insignificant pieces of what they would perceive as their garbage. It is important to remember that much of what archaeologists so laboriously and compulsively recover is, after all, stuff ancient people thought so little of that they threw it away.

Remember from our earlier discussion that archaeology is not a treasure hunt. Our goal is not to find beautiful objects reflecting a level of artistic skill that we can appreciate today, although it sometimes happens. Our ultimate goal is far broader than the illumination of the aesthetic sensibilities and artistic abilities of ancient human beings: We strive to find out as much as we can about a past way of life, and it turns out that the trash people discard provides us with an enormous amount of valuable information that can enable us to reach our goal. Small fragments of bone, little bits of charred seeds, and pieces of shell, corn cobs, and squash rind provide significant information about the diet of a group of people.

Even the tiniest flakes of stone removed from a tool to sharpen its edge, shattered bits of a hammerstone, and broken stone preforms resulting from mistakes in the tool making process can illuminate the technology employed by a people to produce the tools necessary for their subsistence. Pieces of pottery smaller than your thumbnail may allow us to reconstruct the type of kiln an ancient people used to fire their ceramics. Even the bodily wastes of people—yes, their feces—in those rare instances when they have been preserved, are a treasure trove of information about the diet, disease, and over-all health of the people who deposited these particular ecofacts.

Nearly thirty years after I learned field methods, I now pass along to my own field school students an object lesson I learned. Back in 1972 we students each spent at least one entire day in the lab along with a graduate student whose job it was to process the material brought to the facility on each previous day. The grad student first ran us through the procedures employed in the project related to cleaning and inventorying artifacts and ecofacts by laying out some material recovered at the site that had already been processed. When we came to some admittedly small flakes of quartz, one of the other students working in the lab that day—it wasn't me, I swear—said something like: "Oh, are those the things we should be keeping? I found lots but just threw them away.... " Ouch. To be sure, there was a large pile of stones dis-carded behind the lab building, objects that had been brought back from the site and that had turned out to be nothing more than rocks collected a bit overzealously by inexperienced diggers fearful of discarding anything that could be significant. But that's okay. Material collected during excavation that turns out to be noncultural, just rocks or modern seeds or fresh bone, can always be discarded. However, it is far more difficult to re-recover important data from the **backdirt**, the sifted soil piled in mounds adjacent to an excava-tion unit.

There is a remarkable story encoded into even the humblest of archaeologi-cal specimens. The collection of data, not pretty objects, is the goal of archaeo-logical fieldwork, and nothing should be overlooked in our desire to illuminate the lives of a past group of people.

Read More

For a discussion of the reasons for the archaeologist's obsession with recover-ing all available evidence at a site, see any of the following books or chapters about archaeological methodology.

Baker, B. W., B. S. Shaffer, and D. G. Steele. 1997. Basic Approaches in Archaeological Faunal Analysis. In *Field Methods in Archaeology*, edited by T. R. Hester, H. J. Shafer, and K. L. Feder, 298–318. Mayfield Publishing, Mountain View, California.

Dancey, W. S. 1981. *Archaeological Field Methods: An Introduction*. Burgess International Group, New York.

Hester, T. R. 1997b. The Handling and Conservation of Artifacts in the Field. In *Field Methods in Archaeology*, edited by T. R. Hester, H. J. Shafer, and K. L. Feder, 143–58. Mayfield Publishing, Mountain View, California.

Holloway, R. G. 1997. Excavation and Recovery of Botanical Materials from Archaeological Sites. In *Field Methods in Archaeology*, edited by T. R. Hester, H. J. Shafer, and K. L. Feder, 283–97. Mayfield Publishing, Mountain View, California.

Stewart, R. M. 2002. *Archaeology: Basic Field Methods*. Kendall/Hunt Publishing, Dubuque, Iowa.

How Can You Determine the Size of an Ancient Habitation?

Reflecting the spatial nature of the communities, encampments, quarries, industrial zones, and so on that produced them, archaeological sites are spatially bounded. The places that people used had centers, edges, and boundaries that marked the end of these places. In simplest terms this means that if you were to dig test pits at regular intervals in a series of lines radiating from the geographic midpoint of a site, in some of those test pits you would find an abundance of artifacts and ecofacts, in some test excavations you would find fewer archaeological materials, and at some point along each line you would start digging pits in which no archaeological materials would be found. When you reached a point where test pits began producing no artifacts or ecofacts, you would have moved past the edge of the place once used by people (at least you would have moved beyond the zone where they manufactured, used, or deposited elements of their material culture) and passed beyond the margins of the resulting archaeological site.

Think about driving through a large city filled with buildings and people. In the center of the city, the buildings are numerous and close together. As you approach the outskirts of the city, the buildings may be smaller and fewer in number. At the city's margins there may be less densely occupied suburbs with fewer structures and a less concentrated population. When you reach the edge of the suburbs surrounding the city you may encounter a stretch in which the environs are rural and you do not see any structures or people. Drive far enough and you may encounter the outskirts of the suburbs of yet another city.

Of course, this spatial pattern is not always so neat and simple. Even within the boundaries of a site, you may encounter test pits in which no materials are found. You certainly cannot, on the basis of one or even a few closely spaced pits (perhaps only a few meters apart) in which no archaeological material is found, conclude that you have passed beyond the margins of a site. Consider the analogy we used for determining the edges of a city. In New York City we certainly could not correctly assume that we had reached the end of the metropolis simply because there were no (or few) buildings when in our drive we encountered the 843 acres of Central Park. In very short order, as we drive through the park, we would reach the other side and encounter another dense array of enormous buildings, merely having passed from Central Park East to Central Park West.

Inside the boundaries of what any observer would recognize as part of a community, we may come across places where activities were carried out (storytelling or dancing, for example) that resulted in little or no physical evidence of their conduct because the activities themselves did not involve the use of items of material culture. Transform that community into an archaeological site, and test pits might provide no evidence for these practices. Remember, archaeologists are dependent to a large extent on people using and losing or discarding stuff. There is no hard and fast rule here—and it would certainly vary depending on the distance between test pits—but, generally, when testing across a site with test pits or borings or cores, when archaeological material runs out along a transect and doesn't pick up again, it is assumed that the line has passed beyond the margins of the site.

Another complication concerns the overlap of different occupations of the same place. We may be able accurately to outline the horizontal extent of a site, but that outline may not necessarily correspond to the spatial extent of an individual occupation of a particular place. The same general spot may have been occupied on more than one and even on numerous occasions; the same appealing features of a spot may have attracted repeated human settlement over a long span of time. Some of those temporally distinct settlements may overlap spatially but only partially. So we may have a series of sites of varying sizes and spatial patterns superimposed one on top of the other, with part of some of the temporally distinct occupations stratigraphically interdigitated. In such cases archaeologists must take into careful consideration the stratigraphic level in which artifacts or ecofacts are found. Only in this way can we distinguish the materials found in differing levels and dating to different occupations of the same place, assuring that the materials found in one test pit are from the same stratum and, therefore, belong to the same occupation as the materials found in another pit.

What Preliminary Work Goes into an Archaeology Laboratory?

Finding "stuff" (archaeological artifacts, ecofacts, and features) at places where people once lived, worked, or extracted resources (sites) represents the data collection phase of archaeological analysis, a fun phase, to be sure, but only one step in the process. Much of the work of extracting information from the raw data of archaeological site components—and enabling us to say something interesting and perhaps even important about the lives of a past people—occurs not in the field but in the laboratory (Sutton and Arkush 2002).

A commonly used metaphor in archaeological research maintains that with careful enough analysis, the artifacts and other materials we study can "speak" to us and tell us about the lives of the people who made, used, and left these things behind. It is important to realize, though, as the title of a popular archaeology book suggests (*Making Silent Stones Speak*, Schick and Toth 1993), the materials we recover at archaeological sites sometimes jealously guard their secrets. These objects are not always "forthcoming"; we have to "make them speak," and they speak not in any human tongue but in the alien language of material culture. Before we can translate that language and interrogate the archaeological materials we have recovered, we need to spend a bit of time doing some essential housekeeping (Figure 7.13). Traditionally, artifacts were cleaned as a first step upon arrival in the archaeology lab. Chipping patterns on a stone tool or finely etched designs on a potsherd may be obscured by dirt adhering to their surfaces. Rather obviously, this dirt needs to be removed to facilitate analysis of the objects. However, archaeologists have increasingly recognized that microscopic residues of plant material (for example, pollen and

FIGURE 7.13 Field crew members in the lab inventorying artifacts that have been brought in from the field. (K. L. Feder)

especially **phytoliths**) and even of animal remains (especially blood) may lie hidden in the pits and crevices of an artifact's surface. At least a sample of objects may remain uncleaned in order to extract possible residues for analysis.

Once artifacts and ecofacts arrive at the archaeology lab, the materials recovered at a site need to be logged in and inventoried (Feder 1997a). Every object may receive its own unique **accession** or inventory designation. That unique identifier may be written directly on the object itself.

The next time you visit a museum with archaeological specimens, look carefully at each of the displayed objects and you most likely will see a number, often written in India ink. On a broken pot that has been reassembled, you may even be able to find separate numbers on each of the pieces. Some coding systems employ a system of colored dots, and more recently some have employed machine readable barcodes. Whatever technique is used, the purpose is the same: to assign every object with a unique identifier that itself may be written in a readable code that conveys important information about the artifact, for example, the site, excavation unit, and stratigraphic unit in which it was found. For instance, a numerical prefix in an inventory number may identify the site from which an artifact was recovered, the next number may represent the excavation unit, the next the stratigraphic unit or level, and the next may simply be a running tally of artifacts recovered in a given unit.

Beyond this basic "geographic" information about an object, a tremendous amount of information can be recorded for even quite small archaeological specimens, far more than can be coded into an accession or inventory number (for example, the precisely measured location of its discovery, the exact depth at which it was recovered, the appearance of the soil in which it was found, other objects located nearby, its raw material, the name of the excavator, the date of its discovery, and so on). This information certainly cannot fit on the object itself, even in a coded form, but it can be recorded in a paper or digital inventory. A unique identifier, along with supplying basic information about the location where an object was recovered, also allows the archaeologist to permanently conjoin each object with the information recorded about that object in the inventory.

As we analyze, compare, synthesize, and place in context the material recovered from a site, which may include thousands of individual specimens with many attributes measured or recorded for each, the database of even a small site quickly attains great size and complexity. A site inventory allows us to manage that complexity and creates a format in which patterns and correlations among artifacts and their locations can be recognized.

The actual inventory for a site may take the form of a standard computer software spreadsheet (Microsoft Excel may be the most common commercial program) or database management software (for example, File Maker Pro) (McPherron and Dibble 2002). The first column in a spreadsheet may be reserved for the inventory number of each specimen, the unique designator for each object that has been written or printed on the object itself or on the bag, envelope, canister, box, or other container in which it is stored. The next column may represent the raw material of the object (stone, ceramic, wood), the next a descriptor (spear point, potsherd, burned wood), the next its weight, then a precise horizontal location or provenience, then its stratigraphic level, and so on. The resulting simple database allows us to perform statistical analyses on the raw data encoded in the materials recovered at the site. Use of a computer spreadsheet or database allows us, for example, to determine quite easily the percentages of different lithic raw materials used by the site's inhabitants to make spear points or to separate for analysis materials found in different stratigraphic layers. The preliminary work in the lab allows us to keep track of the materials we have laboriously recovered in the field and begins the process of extracting the information about an ancient lifeway encoded in those materials.

Read More

Some people find lab work to be the most fascinating part of archaeological research. Others find it tiresome and tedious. Everyone recognizes, however, that data collection in the field is only one part of the process by which we illuminate the past. For a far more detailed discussion of what goes on in the archaeology laboratory, check out any of the following resources (other than the Schick and Toth reference, which is an interesting read, but not about archaeological laboratory methods).

Dillon, B. D. 1993. *Practical Archaeology: Field and Laboratory Techniques and Archaeological Logistics.* Institute of Archaeology, Los Angeles, California.

Feder, K. L. 1997a. Data Preservation: Recording and Collecting. In *Field Methods in Archaeology,* edited by T. R. Hester, H. J. Shafer, and K. L. Feder, pp. 41–68. Mayfield Publishing, Mountain View, California.

McPherron, S. P., and H. L. Dibble. 2002. *Using Computers in Archaeology.* McGraw-Hill, New York.

Rice, P. C. 1998. *Doing Archaeology: A Hands-On Laboratory Manual.* Mayfield Publishing, Mountain View, California.

Schick, K. D., and N. Toth. 1993. *Making Silent Stones Speak: Human Evolution and the Dawn of Technology.* Simon & Schuster, New York.

Sutton, M. Q., and B. S. Arkush. 2002. *Archaeological Laboratory Methods: An Introduction.* Kendall/Hunt Publishing, Dubuque, Iowa.

Study Questions

1. I use the image of a detective working at the scene of a crime as an analogy for the archaeologist working "at the scene of a life." Explain that metaphor—how is archaeology like detective work?

2. How does a hand-held GPS unit allow for accurately locating an archaeological site on a map. How accurately can a site be located using a standard commercial GPS unit?

3. How are archaeological sites divided up into manageable bites? Discuss the site grid.

4. How are excavation units at archaeological sites designated and labeled?

5. Where and what is the site datum?

6. Why do archaeologists attempt to recover small, seemingly insignificant pieces of chipped stone, broken ceramics, nutshell, seeds, charcoal, and bone?

7. What are the primary tools that commonly make up the archaeologist's tool kit? What functions do each of these tools serve?

8. What do we mean by the Latin term "in situ"?

9. The standard archaeological tools—trowel, whisk broom, dental pick, toothbrush, airbrush—serve what fundamental purpose in fieldwork? Why not just dig up a site with a shovel and screen all the dirt?

10. What does an archaeologist mean by "spatial association"? What might the close spatial associations of objects at an archaeological site tell us about human behavior that produced such a spatial distribution?

11. I hand you a bag of ten stone artifacts. You analyze them. I present you with those same ten artifacts, this time laid out in the exact locations

where people left them a thousand years ago. What information is lacking in the first scenario that can be recovered in the second?

12. What is the provenience of an artifact?

13. What are the three dimensions of an in situ artifact?

14. How is the horizontal component of an artifact's provenience measured?

15. How is the vertical component of an artifact's provenience measured? What different tools are commonly used?

16. How can an archaeologist measure the spatial extent of a site?

17. How are archaeological materials inventoried in the lab?

8 Interpreting the Past

GAUGING THE AGE OF AN ARCHAEOLOGICAL SITE

- **How Old Does Something Have to Be in Order to Be Considered "Archaeological" in the First Place?**

- **How Do Archaeologists Know How Old Artifacts and Sites Are?**

- **What Are Relative Dating Techniques?**
  How Can You Date Sites by Stratigraphic Analysis?
  How Can You Determine a Relative Date for a Site by Reference to Artifact Style?

- **What Are Chronometric or Absolute Dating Methods?**
  How Does Dendrochronology Work?
  What Are the Most Commonly Used Radiometric Dating Methods Relied on by Archaeologists?
  How Can the Shifting Location of Magnetic North Be Used to Date Sites?
  How Can You Determine an Absolute Date for a Site by Reference to Style?

People are fascinated by antiquity; the older the better for most. It should come as no surprise, therefore, that one of the first questions I hear people ask when they show me an artifact that they have found or when I talk about a specimen discovered in my fieldwork is: "How old is it?" And, indeed, that question is one of the first that comes to the mind of the professional archaeologist as well when confronted with a newly discovered site or specimen. I told you in chapter 1 that the Wood Lily site is about 3,000 years old. How did I know that? This chapter focuses on the procedures we employ to determine the age of an archaeological specimen or habitation.

How Old Does Something Have to Be in Order to Be Considered "Archaeological" in the First Place?

A local business in central Connecticut is hoping to demolish an office building constructed not quite fifty years ago and designed by a well-known and respected architect. Many local residents and aficionados of architecture have objected, asserting that the building is historically significant, having won a prestigious architectural award upon its completion and been the focus of much discussion and emulation soon after construction. Debate about this issue even reached the state capital, where one skeptical, sixty-something state legislator said that for anything to be historically significant it must be older than him. Perhaps he has a valid point, perhaps not, but it is an interesting general question: How old does something have to be in order to be archaeological or historical?

I should remind you that archaeology does not focus just on ancient sites or sites of a particular time period or degree of antiquity. Prehistoric archaeology is only one of the subfields of the discipline. Historical archaeology, in which researchers excavate relatively recent sites (some that may be less than a century old and that have voluminous associated written documents), is a vibrant and growing part of the field. This subfield includes the archaeological investigation of presidents' homes (McKee 1995), African American cemeteries (Perry and Blakey 1997), battlefields (Scott et al. 1989), locations of historical tragedies (Hardesty 1997), the analysis of legends (Feder 1994), solving mysteries (King et al. 2001), revealing the lives lived by those whom history has ignored and reviled (Ferguson 1992; McGuire and Paynter 1991), and chronicling the history of a great modern metropolis (Cantwell and Wall 2001).

At least in a theoretical sense, therefore, there is no age restriction for archaeological material. Anything can be considered part of the archaeological record, from 2.5-million-year-old stone chopping tools to literally yesterday's trash. In fact, an entire subfield within archaeology focuses on modern garbage. For more than twenty-seven years archaeologist William Rathje and his students have been examining the rubbish folks throw out in their trash cans as part of the Garbage Project (Harrison, Rathje, and Hughes 1975; http://bara.arizona.edu/gs.htm). These archaeologists of modern rubbish have been showing up at peoples' curbs and doorsteps before the regular trash pickup in a number of cities, taking the material collected to the archaeology lab for detailed analysis.

More recently Rathje has been conducting actual archaeological excavations at modern landfills and trash dumps (Figure 3.2; Rathje and Murphy 1992). Though it doesn't match most common expectations about the romance of archaeology, the archaeology of modern society has made significant contributions to our understanding of the kinds of information that might be coded into garbage, regardless of its age, and has revealed important and practical insights about our own culture's trash, waste, and recycling habits.

Of course, while theoretically there is no required degree of antiquity for something to be considered archaeological, in practice we do apply some commonsense standards, though these generally are not absolute. Recall the Archaeological Resources Protection Act of 1979, the purpose of which is to protect archaeological material on federal property. If that law did not specify how old something had to be in order to qualify as archaeological, then— because essentially all material culture is potentially of archaeological importance—you would be in violation of the act if, for example, you picked up a dollar bill you saw lying on the ground in a national park. For that matter, even picking up trash that a thoughtless hiker left along a trail might be seen as a violation of the Archaeological Resources Protection Act; after all, today's litter is tomorrow's archaeological treasure! Avoiding any such problems, the act specifies that to qualify as archaeological, by statute, items must be a minimum of one hundred years old. Anything younger than that, at least according to the regulations, is, in fact, just trash.

The federal government, even within its own regulations, is not consistent regarding the age necessary for sites or artifacts of archaeological or historical significance. Another federal regulation stipulates that for a historical site to be technically eligible for inclusion on a national honor role called the **National Register of Historic Places** (http://www.nps.gov/history/nr/), established by the federal **National Historic Preservation Act of 1966** (http://www.achp.gov/nhpa.html), it must be a minimum of fifty years old, half the age of that required in the Archaeological Resources Protection Act. Even here there is some wiggle room, and the regulations allow that a site may be eligible for the register even if it is less than fifty years old if it can be established that it is of "exceptional significance" (Figure 8.1).

In fact, the structure I discussed at the start of this section—the Wilde Building on the campus of the CIGNA corporation in Bloomfield, Connecticut— was considered for inclusion on the National Register in 2004, even though it was built in 1957 (and, therefore, a few years shy of the fifty-year rule).

Please note that whatever fixed stipulation related to age is made concerning the archaeological status of an artifact or location, time moves ahead, as does the status. A forty-nine-year-old building that doesn't technically qualify for the National Register today becomes eligible in one year. A ninety-nine-and-a-half-year-old artifact that you can legally pick up in a national park becomes a protected object in a few months. If this book is successful and is used for several years as a required textbook in university archaeology courses,

FIGURE 8.1 The oldest continuously operated McDonald's with the original double-arch design turned fifty in 2003. Considering the impact McDonald's has had on American eating habits specifically and on culture in general, it should come as no surprise that this outlet, located in Downey, California, was eligible for inclusion on the National Register of Historic Places even before 2003. (© Reuters NewMedia Inc./CORBIS)

I will have to alter the discussion of the Wilde Building; any technical argument about its eligibility for the National Register became moot in 2007, when it turned fifty. The bottom line is that any determination of a minimum age for something to be considered archaeological is going to be arbitrary and rather subjective, and we need to apply a bit of common sense.

Read More

Any of the following sources are good examples of the study of sites that don't match the stereotype of archaeology's focus only on sites that are enormously old.

Cantwell, A.-M., and D. dizerega. Wall. 2001. *Unearthing Gotham*. Yale University Press, New Haven, Connecticut.

Feder, K. L. 1994. *A Village of Outcasts: Historical Archaeology and Documentary Research at the Lighthouse Site*. Mayfield Publishing, Mountain View, California.

Hardesty, D. L. 1997. *The Archaeology of the Donner Party*. University of Nevada Press, Reno.

Harrison, G. G., W. L. Rathje, and W. W. Hughes. 1975. Food Waste Behavior in an Urban Population. *Journal of Nutrition Education* 7(1): 13–16.

King, T. F., R. S. Jacobson, K. R. Burns, and K. Spading. 2001. *Amelia Earhart's Shoes: Is the Mystery Solved?* Altamira Press, Walnut Creek, California.

McKee, L. 1995. The Earth Is Their Witness. *The Sciences* 35(2):36–41.

Perry, W., and M. Blakey. 1997. Archaeology as Community Service: The African Burial Ground Project in New York City. *North American Dialogue* 2(1):1–5.

Rathje, W., and C. Murphy. 1992. *Rubbish: The Archaeology of Garbage.* HarperCollins, New York.

Scott, D., R. A. Fox Jr., M. Conner, and J. Harmon. 1989. *Archaeological Perspectives on the Battle of the Little Big Horn.* University of Oklahoma Press, Norman.

How Do Archaeologists Know How Old Artifacts and Sites Are?

Would that it were the case that like our modern coins, ancient peoples stamped the year of manufacture on all their objects. Archaeological dating would be quite simple, indeed, if all one needed to do upon recovery of a spear point or potsherd was to apply a little spit to the surface or wipe with a damp cloth to reveal an object's date, though we probably would be quite skeptical of the authenticity of an object that bore a date such as 2000 B.C.

Artifacts are generally not conveniently dated, so we need to assess age in other ways. For example, archaeologists have long employed procedures of artifact sequencing in their preliminary attempts to date sites. These sequencing procedures, called **relative dating**, whereby artifacts or sites are placed in chronological order or sequence without specific age assignment, often continue to be the first step in attempting to date archaeological material.

An arrangement of artifacts or sites into a chronological sequence is useful, but of course we hope to do more than simply put things in order; we also would like to be able to assign accurate and precise dates to the materials we recover. In fact, we archaeologists also have techniques at our disposal that enable the assignment of an actual year or range of years to an artifact or site. **Chronometric** or **absolute dating** methods have inspired a revolution in archaeological analysis, enabling our discussion of the prehistoric past to parallel the analysis by historians of the more recent past.

If you hope to figure out "what happened when?" as one of your research goals, you need to be able to solve for the "when" variable. Relative methods are a start, providing the archaeologist with an order to "what happened." Absolute methods take us a significant step beyond this, allowing us to position the events of antiquity onto a continuous and objective calendar.

Read More

For broad-based discussions of dating methods in archaeology, these books are good place to start.

Fleming, S. J. 1977. *Dating in Archaeology: A Guide to Scientific Techniques.* Palgrave Macmillan, New York.

Michels, J. W. 1973. *Dating Methods in Archaeology*. Seminar Press, New York.

Taylor, R. E., and M. J. Aitken, eds. 1997. *Chronometric Dating in Archaeology*. Plenum Publishing, New York.

 ## What Are Relative Dating Techniques?

For much of the long history of archaeology, determining the age of a site or artifact was extremely difficult and ordinarily a rather imprecise, indirect, and even subjective enterprise. Unless the site was from a culture and time period characterized by writing and a calendar, sites were often dated by reference to their geological context: how deeply the site materials were buried and in what stratigraphic layer they were found.

In other instances, sites were arranged in chronological order based on the invalid assumption of an inevitable increase in sophistication of technology through time. For example, the painted cave sites of Europe, with their fabulous tableaux of ancient animal life, were long sequenced on the basis of an assumed pattern of increasing artistic sophistication; more primitive art renderings were assumed to be older than those that modern viewers perceived to be more artistically advanced. The caves bearing this artwork were assigned to a hypothetical chronological sequence of stages on this basis.

You can imagine how inaccurate this turned out to be. Consider the subjective nature of the notion "level of artistic sophistication." Also consider the evolution of Western art over the last few centuries. Imagine attempting to place art since the Renaissance in a chronological sequence solely on the basis of personal perception of the degree of "sophistication" or complexity or technological skill reflected in the art. It is unlikely that we would get the chronological order right. It is likely, in fact, that we would often get it precisely backward. In all probability, for example, we would place the simple geometric forms of an artist such as Paul Klee of the late nineteenth and early twentieth centuries sequentially before the exquisite realism of Michelangelo, who actually painted 400 years before Klee was even born. As it turns out, in fact, some of the oldest ancient cave art discovered in Europe appears to be among the most technically and artistically sophisticated in terms of the realism of the depictions of Ice Age animals. Specifically, the stunningly splendid paintings of animals found in Chauvet Cave in France date to 32,000 years ago and are among the most sophisticated of the images found in the caves, far more realistic and beautifully rendered than most of the cave paintings that date to more recent times (Chauvet, Deschamps, and Hillaire 1996).

The moral is that you simply cannot safely arrange sites or artifacts in chronological sequence based solely on a presumed pattern of an increase in sophistication through time. You will derive incorrect chronologies as often as not. That doesn't mean that patterns of stylistic change cannot be used to help us figure out chronological patterns. In fact, there seem to be common blueprints for how styles replace one another, which we can use in developing at least relative chronological sequences. These blueprints are based not on any assumption of the inevitable evolution of greater technical or artistic abilities or expertise, but on more general patterns of change through time. Again, the result is a relative sequence of sites without any firmly associated calendar or year dates, providing us with a temporal framework for a region or ancient culture.

HOW CAN YOU DATE SITES BY STRATIGRAPHIC ANALYSIS?

Attempting to put archaeological materials in a chronological sequence has long been a goal of archaeological research. As long ago as 1799, British surveyor William Smith recognized that the rock and soil beneath our feet come in distinct layers and that these layers, laid down in sequence, were not just local phenomena but could be traced for miles (Grayson 1983). These layers, called **strata** (each one called a **stratum**), can be mapped and studied across an extensive region. Individual layers are distinguishable on the basis of color, texture (rocky, gravelly, sandy, silty, clayey), and chemical makeup. The sequential arrangement of strata is called their **stratigraphy.** Though no year date can be determined directly, where archaeological materials are found within distinct layers in a stratigraphic sequence, their age can be determined relative to other materials found in lower (older) layers, higher (younger) layers, or to objects found in the same layer (Harris 1979; Harris 1989; Harris, Brown, and Brown 1993).

Archaeologists still use the basic principles of stratigraphic sequencing that William Smith discovered more than 200 years ago. Essentially, when excavating a site, archaeologists are extremely careful about maintaining the stratigraphic integrity of all materials found, keeping track of the precise level from which each artifact and ecofact is recovered. If you have seen photographs of archaeological excavations or video documentaries about archaeological research, you may have wondered why the walls of excavation units are usually precisely vertical and why in large excavation units there may even be quadrilateral blocks of soil left unexcavated. Those excavators' obsession with flat, straight, cleanly scraped unit walls and intact soil blocks represent an attempt to maintain precise and accurate stratigraphic controls, intact soil layers that can serve as reference points of overall site stratigraphy (Figure 8.2).

When stratigraphic sequences are more or less intact and undisturbed, it should be fairly obvious that archaeological materials can be placed in a relative chronological sequence on the basis of their position in layers superimposed one on top of another. If, for example, the same location was occupied on several occasions, the chronological order of those occupations can be determined by the stratigraphic position of the archaeological material left behind in each occupation.

Remember, as we dig down archaeologists reveal the stratigraphic sequence in reverse order, encountering the most recent levels first and successively older layers as we dig deeper. Take, for example, a chronological sequence of human activity revealed in the soil layers of a small test excavation adjacent to the Farmington River in the town of Avon, Connecticut. The first artifact

FIGURE 8.2 Stratigraphic profile showing two distinctly colored soil layers at the Tulmeadow North Site in West Simsbury, Connecticut. Most of the artifacts were found below the junction of the upper, darker soil horizon with the lower lighter layer.

encountered in the test excavation (and, therefore, the most recent of the items we recovered) was very close to the surface, situated within the root mat of the vegetation growing there. This first artifact was a broken yellow plastic toy motorcycle, probably lost by a kid playing near the Farmington River. OK, so it wasn't a particularly ancient artifact, or one that might inspire someone to pursue a career in archaeology. The excavator, an archaeology student, was actually surprised that I instructed him to treat the object the way we would any archaeological specimen, measuring its precise depth and location, placing it in a small artifact bag, and carefully labeling the bag with site and excavation unit information.

If my student was amused by this first artifact encountered in the stratigraphic sequence revealed in our excavation, he was embarrassed by the next find, nestled in a distinct soil layer underling the root mat. In that somewhat older layer my student uncovered the fragmentary but unmistakable remains of an empty condom wrapper. Try as I might to convince the student that this was, in fact, an archaeological artifact—after all, archaeology is defined as the study of the material remains of human behavior, and the wrapper was, most certainly, a material remain of human behavior—I'm not sure he ever actually accepted my argument. He had no choice, however, and went about the process of measuring the location of the discovery and gingerly placing the condom wrapper into a specimen bag for return to the lab.

Beneath the layer of soil in which the wrapper was found, a cluster of more obviously artifactual material was recovered in the excavation. My digger found fragments of white-glazed ceramics, some window glass, and rusty, square-cut nails. Though not the kinds of material that generate National Geographic television documentaries, at least this was clearly old stuff, and its location in a soil level below the condom wrapper (which was, in turn, below the toy motorcycle) showed very nicely the sequence of activities that had transpired at this spot along the Farmington River.

Beneath the layer in which the ceramics, glass, and nails were found we encountered a number of layers, distinguishable by slight differences in soil color and texture in which no artifacts were encountered. Then, in our progression down through additional layers, back through time, yet another stratum was found

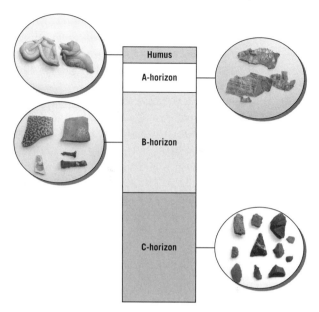

FIGURE 8.3 Drawing of the stratigraphic profile of a test pit located along the Farmington River in the town of Avon, Connecticut, with photos of the artifacts found in each level. Note that there is evidence of four temporally distinct episodes of activity at this spot.

bearing evidence of a past human presence. In this lower layer we found fragments of thick-walled pottery, this time without glaze, along with stone chips and a triangular object of chipped stone that looked like it had been used as the tip of an arrow, the business end of a hunting weapon (Figure 8.3).

Clearly, in this example we could enumerate four temporally distinct episodes of human activity at the place where we were digging. Moving forward through time, from the oldest stratum to the most recently deposited, it appeared that a person or persons dropped or intentionally left behind part of a hunting weapon and some pottery. Sometime later—we cannot tell how much later, we only know it happened later because we found the evidence in a soil layer that was superimposed on a number of other layers laid down in sequence—a person or persons bearing a different material culture that included glazed pottery, glass, and metal disposed of or dropped some of their stuff. Sometime after this, again we cannot be certain how long after, another activity took place (this one involving a condom, and I will leave it to your imagination exactly what happened). Finally, again at a later time, a child lost, left behind for safekeeping, hid, or simply threw away an object made of yellow plastic, a toy motorcycle reflecting the diagnostic material culture of yet another society.

To be sure, we might have looked for a date or company stamp on the toy, and this might have enabled a determination of an actual date for the toy. The same might be true for the condom wrapper. The glazed ceramics bore a particular design, and there could have been a maker's mark, which would have allowed for a year date for its manufacture. The arrowhead was of a particular shape and design whose age could be identified by comparison to other similar-looking artifacts. This tale shows how, based on the relative position of objects recovered in soil layers, a chronological sequence of events or occupations can be determined.

You may have noticed that in this discussion of stratigraphy I have labored mightily to avoid saying that, essentially, the deeper something is found, the older it is. Though this often is the case, it sometimes is not because of natural and cultural phenomena that disturb stratigraphic sequences. For example, ancient peoples could—and did—dig deep holes that cut through older deposits, and their artifacts may end up in the bottom of those pits at a sub-stantially greater depth than older artifacts whose layer was inadvertently and unknowingly cut through by the more recent hole diggers.

Animals can also add to the confusion. I can remember excavating a beer bottle at the same measured depth as the artifacts from a site dated to just shy of 2,000 years old. Though it might be fun to report the archaeological discovery of beer bottling and drinking during the ancient Woodland period of southern New England, alas there was a more mundane explanation. The beer bottle actually dated to a far more modern period and ended up at the same depth as the ancient artifacts because it was located at the bottom of a filled-in woodchuck burrow. I also cannot report that this provides new insights into the behavior of social drinking among woodchucks. More likely, the bottle fell or was dropped into the burrow by a human beer drinker. The burrow was later filled in with silt by river flooding.

Instead of saying that the deeper an object is found, the older it is, the **law of superposition** in stratigraphic analysis maintains that the relative position of an archaeological object in a sequence of layers determines its age (the same, younger, or older) relative to other objects found in the stratigraphic sequence. Objects are as old as the layers that were the living surface when they were deposited, and that is not always necessarily the layer in which they ended up.

Read More

You can find the particulars of stratigraphy, including the history of the concept as well as the methods by which it is exposed, analyzed, and interpreted, on the pages of the following sample of publications.

Adams, R. E. W., and Fred Valdez Jr. 1997. Stratigraphy. In *Field Methods in Archaeology*, edited by T. R. Hester, H. J. Shafer, and R. L. Feder, 235–52. Mayfield Publishing, Mountain View, California.

Grayson, D. K. 1983. *The Establishment of Human Antiquity*. Academic Press, New York.

Harris, E. C. 1979. The Laws of Archaeological Stratigraphy. *World Archaeology* 11:111–17.

———. 1989. *Principles of Archaeological Stratigraphy*. Academic Press, New York.

Harris, E. C., G. J. Brown, and M. R. Brown III, eds. 1993. *Practices of Archaeological Stratigraphy*. Academic Press, New York.

How Can You Determine a Relative Date for a Site by Reference to Artifact Style?

One relative method of dating relies on technological or stylistic change through time but avoids the overly simplistic assumption that objects that look more sophisticated or advanced to us are necessarily younger than objects that appear to reflect a perceived simpler technology or artistic ability. Rather than assuming a particular direction of change, the relative dating technique called **seriation** relies instead on a common statistical pattern of technological or stylistic change.

In many cases, when a new way of accomplishing a task is introduced into a culture, whether through invention or by adopting it from another group, it starts off small, with most folks skeptical and resistant to the new idea. Few people even attempt the innovative approach, whether it involves designs on gravestones, methods of illuminating buildings, making spear points, or burying the dead. However, if the new way of making tools, decorating pots, producing food, storing seeds, or designing gravestones is objectively recognized to be more efficient than the old method, or if the new style is subjectively perceived to be more attractive by the ancient people or more reflective of their changed thinking about a subject, the initial resistance is overcome, its degree of penetration in the community increases, and people may begin to abandon the old practice and embrace the new. Eventually, this new and revolutionary technology or style becomes widely accepted, reaches a peak in popularity, and attains the level of common practice; almost everybody does it that way, and it has become the norm. In the nearly inevitable process of change, however, an even newer way of achieving the same result may be introduced. This new practice again starts out small, is met with skepticism and resistance, and few people try it. If the new approach is recognized to be more efficient than the old, it begins to increase in use and replaces the old way, and the cycle continues.

Consider in our own history, for example, the ways in which we store and sell carbonated beverages (Figure 8.4). In the 1950s soda and beer could be purchased in cylindrical, 12-ounce cans that could be opened only with a separate tool, a can opener that punched a triangular hole in the top of the can (actually, two holes were punched, the second of which facilitated the pouring of the beverage through the first). Though the can was a convenient, lightweight, and durable container (it didn't break like a glass bottle does when dropped), needing a separate tool to open it was a drawback. Though I was just a kid in the 1950s, I can remember too many picnics and beach outings when the desperation was palpable upon the realization that our powerful summer thirst could not be slaked because we had forgotten the opener (called the "church key" for rather obvious reasons).

To address the inconvenience of a container that needed a separate tool to open it, in the early 1960s a new can type was introduced for which no discrete opening tool was needed. The top of the new cans contained an oddly curving outline incised into the metal. The incised shape was riveted at one end to a metal ring, which, when it worked properly, could be bent up from the can top.

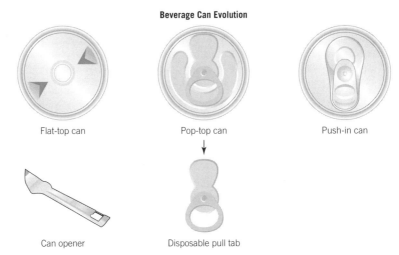

Beverage Can Evolution

Flat-top can   Pop-top can   Push-in can

Can opener   Disposable pull tab

FIGURE 8.4 Twelve-ounce beverage cans, seen from the top. From left to right, a can that needs a can opener to get to its contents, a pull-tab can, and the current push tab.

When the metal ring was pulled up and away from the can, the "pop top" ripped cleanly away from the can along the incised outline and voilà, the can was now open and ready to be poured. Well, in theory. Too often, when bent back and up to enable gripping, the ring simply broke off, making entry into the can problematic at best. The new can design did make can opening easier though, and over a period of just a few years the technology was tweaked and opening the can became a bit easier and more reliable. The old opener-dependent can design disappeared, having been replaced by the new type.

The new design, though an advance over the old, was far from perfect and created a new, initially unforeseen problem. Though the can could be opened easily, without the need for a separate tool, the design created a separate piece of metal that needed to be discarded: the so-called pop-top. Unfortunately, the metal pop-tops became ubiquitous pieces of litter, a significant new tributary to the waste stream of the 1960s, scattered across the beautiful beaches and parks where people brought their carbonated beverages. Of course, the ecologists among the soda and beer drinkers came up with a solution to the pop-top dilemma: Instead of littering the pop-tops on the ground, they merely dropped the pop-top back into the can immediately after opening and then proceeded to drink from the can. I have no data to back up my assertion that trips to emergency rooms for stomach x-rays took a sharp upturn after the inception of this practice, but I imagine that especially among heavy beer drinkers, this could have become a significant public health issue if drinkers found it difficult to remember when they found no loose pop-top jingling in the can of beer they had just drained whether they had thrown it away or swallowed it.

Perhaps in response to the problems created by tens of millions of sharp pieces of metal created by the pop-top can, in the early 1970s canning companies came up with yet another can design, a version of the one we are all familiar with today. Instead of a can that opened by removing a piece of the top, the new design caused part of a roughly circular section of the top to push down and in, remaining attached to the top of the can while opening a hole large enough to pour or drink from directly. This design was produced initially in small numbers, and as the technology was perfected and people got used to the new cans, it replaced the pop-top design, which over a period of just a few years disappeared almost entirely.

How does any of this apply to practice of archaeological dating? The pattern of introduction of a new design (first the pop-top can and then the push-in can), its initially small penetration in the marketplace, and its slow acceptance, growth, and eventual complete replacement of the old way is a pattern seen almost universally in stylistic change through time. The pattern exhibited in the changes in soda and beer cans is a model and even an archetype for changes in ancient artifact styles and technologies, and that pattern reflects not just change but change through time (Figure 8.5).

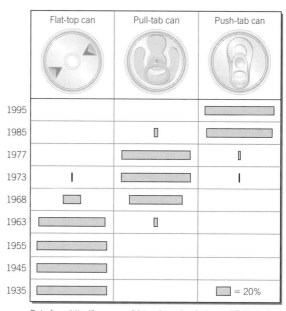

Data from http://bcca.com/history/overview4.php and T. V. Carley, personal communication

FIGURE 8.5 A seriation graph showing the slow replacement, in temporal sequence, of the initially ubiquitous opener-requiring can with the disposable pull-tab can, and then the inevitable replacement of that container type with the currently used push tab. (K. L. Feder)

Suppose you have a number of sites, each of which dates to a different, narrow slice of time in the history of a culture. Each site represents a point along a temporal continuum of technological and stylistic change, during which different ways of accomplishing the same task may overlap. At each site differing percentages of folks achieve the same results (how they open beverage cans, paint images on cave walls, manufacture spear points, decorate pottery, or mark their graves) in a number of different ways that at different times are "old fashioned," "modern," or "cutting edge." If you measure at each site the popularity of the various overlapping ways of achieving the same result (for example, the percentage of artifacts showing cans that need can openers, the percentage of disposable pop-top cans, and the percentage of push-in cans at each site, with each site representing a slice of time), you can consistently arrange the sites in order based on the pattern of new ideas starting small, growing in acceptance, reaching a peak, and then declining as they are replaced by a newer way. You can visualize this with a standard **seriation graph**, in which the prevalence of each style or technological method is represented in a column of the graph. Horizontal bars whose lengths are proportional to the percentages of each method (how many cans at a particular site are opened with a tool, how many are pop-tops, and how many are push-ins) within each narrow band of time are drawn in each column.

Gravestones

This same interpretation applies to other examples of artifact evolution. Consider the stones erected to mark the graves of New Englanders in the seventeenth through nineteenth centuries (Figure 8.6). A seriation graph representing the change in the designs carved on these gravestones (gravestone are, after all, artifacts) found in graveyards (these are, after all, sites) dating from the early 1600s through the early 1900s throughout New England shows a distinct pattern of seriation (Dethlefsen and Deetz 1966). The earliest stones tend to have an image of a defleshed skull carved (often incised, sometimes in bas-relief) on top. Later, by the early to mid-eighteenth century, the skull has transformed into a fully fleshed cherubic face, a fat little angel, often with wings. Nineteenth-century gravestones abandon the cherub, and New England gravestones often have an image of weeping willow trees hanging over an urn sculpted onto their surfaces.

FIGURE 8.6 Examples of the Death's head, cherub, and urn and willow design on gravestones found in northeastern North America. (K. L. Feder)

We are at a great advantage in conducting a seriation of New England gravestones because we have actual dates on the artifacts, but suppose we didn't. We could still arrange the individual gravestones into a sensible chronological order because the percentages represented by the lengths of the bars on the graphs for each style (skulls, cherubs, and urn-and-willow designs) change in a patterned way, reflecting a steady increase or decrease across time (Figure 8.7).

Examine the graph shown in Figure 8.7. There is really only one way to arrange the order of the bars to produce a pattern of steady increase and decrease (and the reverse is equally plausible). The death's heads show up first and are at a peak in their popularity when the cherub design is introduced. Slowly but surely, having an angelic face carved on the top of a tombstone increased in popularity at the expense of the death's head design. Over several decades an increasing segment of the graveyard population have a cherub carved on the top of their markers and a decreasing segment have a death's head. By the end of the 1700s the death's head designs are no longer being made, and nearly everybody is having a cherub carved on their gravestone. Just as surely as the cherub replaced the death's head, a new pattern takes hold at the end of the 1700s and beginning of the 1800s. Instead of a skeletal or angelic face, people began placing a willow tree on their gravestones, usually depicted bending over what looks like an urn. This urn-and-willow design takes hold and increases in popularity over the decades, eclipsing the cherub design and,

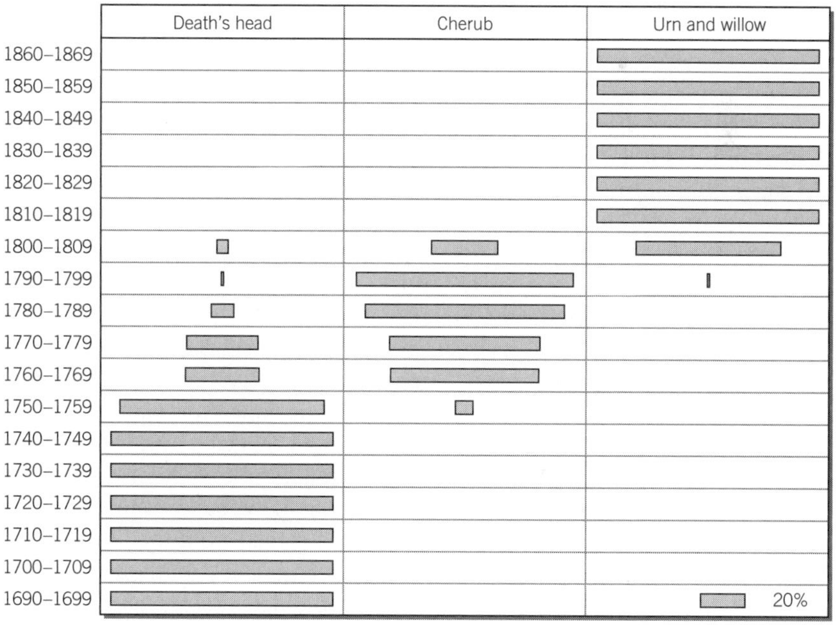

	Death's head	Cherub	Urn and willow
1860–1869			▭▭▭▭
1850–1859			▭▭▭▭
1840–1849			▭▭▭▭
1830–1839			▭▭▭▭
1820–1829			▭▭▭▭
1810–1819			▭▭▭▭
1800–1809	□	▭▭	▭▭▭
1790–1799	∣	▭▭▭▭▭	∣
1780–1789	▫	▭▭▭▭▭	
1770–1779	▭▭	▭▭▭	
1760–1769	▭▭	▭▭▭	
1750–1759	▭▭▭▭	□	
1740–1749	▭▭▭▭		
1730–1739	▭▭▭▭		
1720–1729	▭▭▭▭		
1710–1719	▭▭▭▭		
1700–1709	▭▭▭▭		
1690–1699	▭▭▭▭		▭▭ 20%

FIGURE 8.7 Seriation graph of a sample of seventeenth-, eighteenth-, and nineteenth-century New England gravestones. Just as surely as the beverage can evolved in terms of the technology of its opening, the designs carved onto gravestones also evolved, with themes being replaced to fit the fashion of their time. (K. L. Feder)

ultimately, replacing it altogether. This design is the norm on stones that mark the graves of people who died in the middle through the end of the nineteenth century. Following this common pattern, with a few sites representing slices of time and where a style or technology changed through time, the sites themselves can be placed in a chronological sequence based on the patterned change in the percentages of the styles through time.

Read More

You can find a nicely detailed discussion of seriation in the textbook by O'Brien and Lyman. The gravestone article is a fascinating example of the application of seriation.

Dethlefsen, E., and J. Deetz. 1966. Death's Heads, Cherubs, and Willow Trees: Experimental Archaeology in Colonial Cemeteries. *American Antiquity* 31:502–10.

O'Brien, M. J., and R. L. Lyman. 1999. *Seriation, Stratigraphy, and Index Fossils: The Backbone of Archaeological Dating.* Kluwer Academic Publishers, New York.

 ## What Are Chronometric or Absolute Dating Methods?

Absolute dating methods are those procedures that provide an actual age in years for an archaeological artifact, ecofact, or site. Labeling a date as "absolute" does not imply that it is precise (it can be a broad range of years) or even that it is necessarily accurate. To avoid confusion on this point, some archaeologists prefer the less-ambiguous term **chronometric dating** (literally, the "measurement of time") for dating methods that provide a year or range of years.

I sit in front of my computer and edit this on July 27 in the year A.D. 2006, an accurate (it is correct) and precise (exact) date. I was born nearly fifty-four years ago, another accurate and fairly precise date. I received a Ph.D. in anthropology in 1982 (accurate and fairly precise). I'm not exactly certain when my ancestors migrated to the United States from Europe, but I know it was more than one hundred years ago (accurate, but not so precise). The Wood Lily site was occupied approximately 3,000 years ago (I'm pretty sure that's accurate, and it is fairly precise). The first people to enter the New World arrived sometime between 12,000 and 30,000 years ago (I think that's accurate, but it isn't very precise). Our human ancestors began making stone tools sometime between 2.4 and 2.5 million years ago (probably accurate, but certainly not precise). The human (**hominid**) evolutionary line diverged from the line that led to the modern apes (**pongids**) sometime between 5 and 7 million years ago (probably accurate, but not at all precise). All the dates just listed, from the actual calendar date when I wrote these words to the broad 2-million-year range for the split between the hominids and the pongids, are absolute, or chronometric, because we can apply numbers, even an imprecisely broad range of numbers, to the events, artifacts, ecofacts, or sites.

By far the most accurate and precise absolute dating method is based on biology, specifically a highly regular, measurable, and dependable natural calendar built into trees. Called **dendrochronology**, this method relies on the addition of a distinct growth ring for each year of a tree's life. Our discussion of ancient trees in chapter 1 and my reference to the precise ages of some of the oldest trees in North America were based on data produced through dendrochronology.

Within absolute methods of dating, there is an entire category called **radiometric.** These methods are based on natural processes of radioactive decay and rely on the fact that in each case the decay itself (as well as the resulting impacts of the decay on archaeological specimens) occurs at a constant rate that can be accurately measured. The constant rate of radioactive decay as well as the rate at which the changes caused by the decay accumulate can be viewed as natural clocks (or at least natural calendars) that we can use to date archaeological specimens.

Additionally, we can determine an absolute date for an artifact with which we cannot directly associate a radiometric or dendrochronological date when the object reflects a style with a narrowly constrained period of popularity that has been so dated. In other words, artifacts of a given, easily recognized style may have been recovered at lots of archaeological sites where they have all been dated to the same period of time. When you are confronted with an artifact with precisely the same form or style, it is a good bet that it dates to the same period.

Individual artifacts, ecofacts, or features at a site can be dated using whatever techniques apply in particular circumstances, depending on the time period of the object being dated, the materials actually recovered and datable, and the budgetary constraints of a given project. That's an important point. Even the best-funded excavation can derive dates for only a very small fraction of the material actually recovered at a site. Based on careful stratigraphic analysis, however, we may be confident that the dates we obtain directly on a few objects (all, for example, recovered from a single stratigraphic level) can be associated with and applied to all the other objects recovered from the same stratum. Though we may state that a site is a particular age, we don't really date the site directly, only individual objects recovered at the site. When an archaeologist states, for example, that a site is 1,000 years old, that means that a small sample of individual artifacts or ecofacts have been absolutely dated, and the full extent of the occupation (all the other artifacts and ecofacts) occurred in a narrowly constrained stratigraphic level. Those few directly derived dates are then associated with everything else and are used to measure the date of the occupation of the site.

Association is the key here. An object, for example, a piece of burned wood, may be accurately dated directly through the application of a chronometric technique (see radiocarbon dating below), but if that object cannot be confidently linked to the timing of the occupation of the site, that date simply will not apply to the site. A recent forest fire, for instance, may deposit charcoal on top of an ancient site. Suppose a burrowing animal digs a hole down through the site and some of the recent charcoal descends to the same level as the ancient cultural material by falling into the burrow (remember the story told previously in this chapter of a modern beer bottle found at the same depth as the artifacts found at a nearly 2,000-year-old site; that bottle had fallen into a woodchuck burrow). The animal burrow may fill in with soil, and unless great care is taken in excavating and recording stratigraphy, the researcher may be confused when the charcoal he or she thought was produced when the site was occupied because it was found at the same depth produces a very recent date. This just points out the importance of being careful with the application of our dating methods and the necessity of making certain that the dated object is associated with the site for which you are attempting to determine an age.

Read More

For broad-based discussions of dating methods in archaeology, these books are good places to start.

Fleming, S. J. 1977. *Dating in Archaeology: A Guide to Scientific Techniques.* Palgrave Macmillan, New York.

Michels, J. W. 1973. *Dating Methods in Archaeology.* Seminar Press, New York.

Taylor, R. E., and M. J. Aitken, eds. 1997. *Chronometric Dating in Archaeology.* Plenum Publishing, New York.

HOW DOES DENDROCHRONOLOGY WORK?

In chapter 1 I used the study of an old tree through the examination of its annual growth rings as a metaphor for the study of past peoples by the examination of the material culture they left behind. As mentioned in that chapter, the actual study of tree rings to determine the nature of past climates and as a dating method is called **dendrochronology.**

Although it might be obvious that the age of a living or newly felled tree can be determined simply by counting its rings, it is not so obvious how a tree ring count can help date an ancient archaeological site, especially one that dates to long before any living tree. The key to accomplishing this rests in the creation of a regional **master sequence** of tree rings (Baillie 1990; Schweingruber 1988).

The width of individual tree rings in a region tends to vary on a yearly basis as a result of changes in climatic variables crucial to tree growth. In some areas the amount of precipitation in the spring is the most important determinant of tree ring width in any year. In other areas spring temperature is the determining factor. For example, in a year of substantial spring rainfall, most of the trees in the **Four Corners** region of the American Southwest (a wide area around the intersection of Arizona, New Mexico, Utah, and Colorado) add a proportionally wide ring. When the spring rains are sparse, most of those same trees will add a proportionally thinner ring. When timbers that include a portion or even all the diameter of the tree trunks from which they were cut were incorporated into ancient structures, and where those timbers have been preserved, archaeologists can extract cross-sections showing a sequence of the tree rings produced during part or even all of the tree's lifetime. Looking across a section of tree rings, you can see the ebb and flow of rain across the years.

Good enough, but that still doesn't explain the use of dendrochronology as a dating method. Luckily for archaeologists who rely on dendrochronology, there is no repeating pattern of rainfall variation and, therefore, no chronological sequence of ring width sizes that repeats across time. In other words, any sufficiently long period of years has a unique sequence of rainfall amounts that is never repeated. As a result, any sufficiently long sequence of tree ring widths also is unique and never repeated. That unique sequence is what makes dendrochronology a viable and highly accurate dating method. It all begins with a living or newly felled tree for which the tree ring sequence can be anchored in time; the most recent tree ring represents the current year (Figure 8.8).

Suppose a tree is one hundred years old. We can cross-section the tree, revealing a sequence of thin, intermediate, and thick rings. Our next task is to look at the tree rings of a number of dead trees. With a little bit of luck, we can find a tree with a pattern of tree ring widths toward the end of its life that matches the sequence of ring widths of the early years of the old living tree. Because we know that the matching part of the sequence of varying widths is unique in time and has never been repeated, we can safely conclude that the two trees were contemporaries for the period of time their rings show the same varied sequence of thin and thick rings. That knowledge enables us to tie in the dead tree with the sequence we have already anchored in time. So, for example, if the last ten rings of the dead tree show the same sequence of ring widths as the first ten rings of the live, one-hundred-year-old tree, we can determine when the dead tree died or was cut down. The final ring of the dead tree corresponds to the tenth ring of the live one. The live tree is one hundred years old, this year is 2007, so its first ring grew in 1907. The dead tree's final ring corresponds to the tenth ring of the live tree, the tenth ring of the live tree corresponds to 1917, so the dead tree's last ring

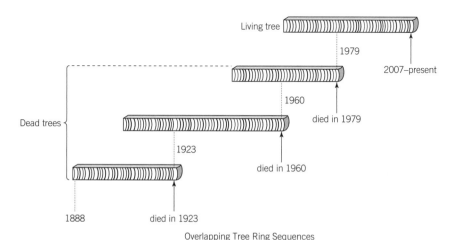

Overlapping Tree Ring Sequences

FIGURE 8.8 Tree ring sequence of four trees. The top sequence is that of a living tree; its most recent ring, on the far right, represents the current year. The other trees overlap successively with one another, allowing us the ability to place them all in a continuous master sequence of time.

grew in 1915. If that dead tree ended up as a log found in a structure (for example, the remains of a log cabin), we have a precise, absolute date for when the tree was cut down and, by inference, a date for when the cabin was built. At least we know it was built sometime after the tree was cut down, and we can gauge precisely when that occurred.

The same process of finding successively older trees whose ring sequences overlap at least a part of those exhibited by trees already incorporated into the regional sequence is applied to produce a master sequence. Though overlapping the tree ring sequences of hundreds of trees, both living and dead, is a painstaking process, master sequences for tree ring widths have been developed for various parts of the world.

Consider, for example, a relatively short tree ring master sequence developed in Massachusetts by the Oxford Dendrochronology Lab (Miles et al. 2002). Using a stand of living old-growth red oaks identified on Mt. Wachusett, along with red and white oak timbers sampled in a series of historical structures, a nearly 500-year master sequence was produced, covering the period A.D. 1513 to A.D. 1996. This master chronology of oak tree ring thickness enabled the precise and accurate dating of the felling of trees from which the sampled timbers were milled and then used in building construction in eastern Massachusetts beginning in the early seventeenth century. Specifically, 156 samples were extracted from 122 oak timbers found in ten historic structures, and the resulting sequences of tree ring thicknesses in those timbers were compared to the tree ring width sequence presented in the master chronology. In this way construction episodes (including original construction dates and subsequent additions) in seven houses and three churches were fixed in time.

Master sequences arching back to far earlier periods are available in a number of parts of the world. The Laboratory of Tree Ring Research (LTRR) at the University of Arizona is one of the best-known dendrochronology labs in the world and has worked out much of the master sequence for the American Southwest (http://www.ltrr.arizona.edu/). The master sequence derived by LTRR from bristlecone pines in the American West goes back twenty times further than the Massachusetts chronology, to more than 9,000 years ago. Sheffield University in Great Britain has produced a master sequence for England that spans the last 7,000 (http://www.shef.ac.uk/archaeology/research/dendrochronology/what-is-dendro.html). The master sequence derived from pine trees in Germany now extends to more than 10,000 years ago and, when linked to the oak series, allows for a sequence of tree rings that can be used to calibrate radiocarbon dates back to more than 11,800 years ago (Kromer and Spurk 1998).

In each application of dendrochronology, when a section of a timber is found in an archaeological or historical context (for example, in a hearth or in a standing structure), the sequence of tree ring widths is compared to that presented by the geographically closest master sequence. When the width sequence in the archaeological specimen matches a section of the master sequence, the years of that tree's life can be firmly placed in time. Its final year, represented by the last ring it grew, obviously is the first year the tree could have been incorporated into an archaeological structure or facility. Barring any great delay between the year of the tree's death and the year it was used by a past people, we can confidently assign a date to a site based on the year the tree died.

Read More

To learn more about dendrochronology, check out any of these sources.

Baillie, M. G. L. 1990. *Tree Ring Dating and Archaeology.* University of Chicago Press, Chicago.

Kromer, B., and M. Spurk. 1998. Revision and Tentative Extension of the Tree-Ring Based 14C Calibration, 9,200–11,855 cal BP. *Radiocarbon* 40(3):1117–26.

Schweingruber, F. H. 1988. *Tree Rings: Basics and Applications of Dendrochronology.* D. Reidel Publishing, Boston.

Steinitz, M. 2002. Tree-Ring Dates Offer Insight on Massachusetts Buildings. *Preservation Advocate,* 1, 6–7, 10.

WHAT ARE THE MOST COMMONLY USED RADIOMETRIC DATING METHODS RELIED ON BY ARCHAEOLOGISTS?

More than likely, you have heard of **carbon dating** (or **radiocarbon dating** or **C-14 dating**), which is probably the most widely used absolute dating method and certainly is the most commonly applied radiometric procedure in archaeology (http://www.c14dating.com). Radiometric dating techniques rely on the fixed rate of decay of an unstable (**radioactive**) variety (**isotope**) of an element into a stable variety of that same element or another element altogether. That fixed rate of decay, expressed as a **half-life** (the time it takes for half of the unstable portion of an element to change into a stable substance), provides a natural clock by which we can measure the age of some categories of artifacts and ecofacts (Bowman 1990; Libby 1952; Taylor 1987).

For example, carbon is found in the atmosphere (in the form of carbon dioxide, or CO_2, which makes up just .035% of the atmosphere, compared to 78% nitrogen and 21% oxygen). Along with oxygen, nitrogen, and phosphorus, carbon is one of the so-called building blocks of life and is found in all living things. As you probably remember from high school biology, plants respire; in a manner of speaking, they breathe. When we breathe, our lungs extract oxygen from the air and supply it to our blood, and our bodies ultimately combine that oxygen with carbon, which we exhale as carbon dioxide. In photosynthesis plants do the reverse, taking in carbon dioxide from the air, breaking the chemical bonds between the carbon and the two oxygen atoms in CO_2, and, together with water, producing carbohydrates that become stems, bark, fruits, seeds, roots, branches, and so on. Having extracted the carbon in CO_2 through photosynthesis, plants exhale the oxygen as a waste product.

Carbon comes in a few varieties, or isotopes. The most common isotope is C-12, the stable form of the element, with an atomic nucleus consisting of six positively charged particles called protons and six neutral particles called neutrons. Carbon also comes in unstable, or radioactive, varieties, including the isotopes C-13 and C-14. C-12, C-13, and C-14 all have six protons in their nuclei. That number is what makes them carbon; if their number of protons were different, they would be entirely different elements (for example, boron if they had five protons, nitrogen if they had seven, or oxygen if they had eight). What differentiates the nuclei of these different isotopes of carbon is their number of neutrons. The math here is easy: C-12 has six neutrons (6 protons + 6 neutrons = 12, C-12's atomic weight), C-13 has six protons and seven neutrons (6 protons + 7 neutrons = 13), and C-14 has six protons and eight neutrons (6 protons + 8 neutrons = its atomic weight of 14). (Figure 8.9)

Almost all the carbon on our planet is the stable variety, C-12, with an equal number of protons and neutrons in its nucleus. There is, however, some C-14 produced in the air when ..iftly moving cosmic rays that stream out of the Sun (a result of the nuclear reactions by which the sun radiates energy) collide with atoms in the upper atmosphere, freeing neutrons from their nuclei. Those free neutrons produced by these collisions go flying through the atmosphere, and some smash into nitrogen atoms (which, as was just pointed out, make up the bulk—78%—of the atmosphere). In some of these collisions the neutron displaces a proton in the nucleus of the nitrogen atom. In other words, the struck proton streams out of the nucleus, and the invading neutron stays put. (Think of the free neutron as a cue ball imparting all its forward momentum to the seven ball, a proton in the nitrogen nucleus; the seven ball zips off into the corner pocket, and the cue ball stays put at the point of impact.) Nitrogen atoms that experience this cease being nitrogen. Their nuclei no longer consist of seven protons and seven neutrons because they have lost a proton and gained a neutron in the collision. Their nuclei now have six protons (the original seven minus that one that got bumped out) and eight neutrons (the original seven plus the one that crashed into the nucleus and stayed put),

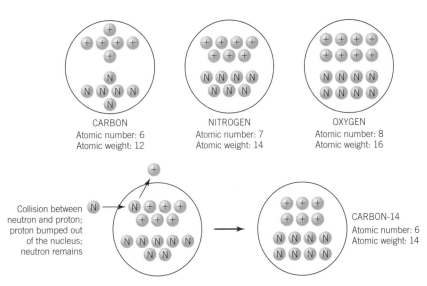

FIGURE 8.9 Schematic drawing of the atomic nuclei of a carbon, nitrogen, and oxygen atom, showing the number of protons in the nucleus of each of these elements, as well as the number of neutrons in their most common, stable isotopes. Not actual size (sorry for that lame joke).

making them carbon (six protons), not the common variety with six neutrons but a variety with eight. In the designation "C-12," the twelve represents the isotope's atomic mass (6 protons + 6 neutrons). The atomic mass of the transmuted nitrogen is fourteen (6 protons + 8 neutrons), making it C-14.

Chemically, C-14 is virtually identical to C-12. It combines with oxygen to form carbon dioxide, just like C-12. The isotope C-14 carbon dioxide is just like C-12 carbon dioxide and is used much the same as C-12 by plants in photosynthesis. When ingested in the form of seeds, roots, berries, fruits, nuts, and so on, C-14 carbon is digested and then used in the bodies of animals, just like C-12, to make bone, blood, muscle, nerves, and skin. All living things consist in part of the carbon atoms they obtained by respiring (if they are plants) or by eating plants or other animals (if they are animals), and all living things have the same ratio of C-12 to C-14, which, in turn, is in the same proportion in the atmosphere (for those dying to know, only about one in every trillion carbon atoms is of the C-14 variety; put more accurately, only about $1.3 \times 10^{-10}\%$ of all of the carbon on Earth is of the C-14 variety, and that same proportion is found in the atmosphere, in plants, in animals, and in you).

This proportion remains the same as long as an organism lives and continues to respire (if it's a plant) or eat (if it's an animal). But C-14 is unstable and, therefore, radioactive, decaying back to nitrogen over time. In fact, the decay rate has been carefully measured for C-14. It takes about 5,730 years for half of any quantity of C-14 to decay back into nitrogen. In another 5,730 years, half of what was left after the first 5,730 years then decays to nitrogen. Half of that decays after another half-life, and so on.

When an organism is no longer respiring or eating, it can no longer replace the C-14 that decays to nitrogen while it is alive. As a result, we have what amounts to a natural hourglass (Figure 8.10). We know the rate at which the sand pours out of the top (the decay rate measured as a half-life), we can figure out how much sand (C-14) must have been in the hour glass in the first place, we can measure how much of the sand on top (C-14) has poured (decayed) into the bottom (turned to nitrogen), and from that we can come up with a pretty accurate estimate for how long it has been since the hourglass was turned over (the length of time since the plant or animal that produced the sample being dated died and, therefore, stopped ingesting "fresh" carbon). For example, the mass of a fragment of burned wood recovered from an archaeological site can be precisely measured, and from this we can determine how much C-14 would be in the sample if it were part of a living plant today. We then can measure how much of the C-14 yet remains in the archaeological sample, and, based on the known rate of decay, we can figure out about how long ago the wood was cut off a living tree or how long ago the tree it was part of died and, therefore, about how long ago a human being used the wood to make a fire. When you ask "how old is the Wood Lily site" and I say, "Oh, 3,000 years," my succinct answer is really shorthand for "The wood that we found in the fireplace at Wood Lily comes from a branch of a tree whose C-14 content indicates that it was no longer taking in fresh C-14 (the branch was cut off or fell from the tree or the entire tree was cut down) about 3,000 years ago, and, therefore, we think that this is about the time a human being gathered that wood and made a fire to cook some food, so the site is about that old."

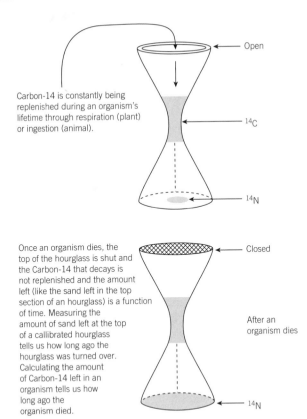

Carbon-14 is constantly being
replenished during an organism's
lifetime through respiration (plant)
or ingestion (animal).

Open

^{14}C

^{14}N

Once an organism dies, the
top of the hourglass is shut and
the Carbon-14 that decays is
not replenished and the amount
left (like the sand left in the top
section of an hourglass) is a function
of time. Measuring the
amount of sand left at the top
of a callibrated hourglass
tells us how long ago the
hourglass was turned over.
Calculating the amount
of Carbon-14 left in an
organism tells us how
long ago the
organism died.

Closed

After an
organism dies

^{14}N

FIGURE 8.10 The process of radioactive decay of ^{14}C can be
likened to the sands pouring out of the top of an hourglass. In an
hourglass, sand escapes the top chamber and accumulates on
the bottom at a fixed rate; the amount of sand left on top can be
used to calculate how long ago the hourglass was flipped over. In
an analogous manner, ^{14}C decays to nitrogen at a fixed rate; the
amount of radiocarbon left in the remains of an organism can be
used to determine how long ago it died.

Radiocarbon dating requires a sophisticated laboratory set-up, and labs
charge for the procedure. As of the summer of 2006, the going rate for standard
radiocarbon analysis with a large sample (at least three grams [.1 oz] of carbon)
was about $350. An accelerator mass spectromotry (AMS) date requires a far
smaller sample (as little as 500 micrograms; that's .5 milligrams, or an almost
imperceptible .0000176 oz), produces a more precise date, and costs about $600
per sample. You can learn more about the details of sample sizes, preparation,
and specific procedures on the website of Beta Analytic Corporation, the
world's most active C-14 lab, processing more than 12,000 samples each year
(http://www.radiocarbon.com). Beta Analytic is a firm we have long used to
provide our radiocarbon dates. They produced the dates for Wood Lily discussed in chapter 1: 3,010±110 B.P. (Beta-37776) and 2,960±70 (Beta-37093).

(Warning: A mathematical explanation of radiometric dates follows.) I'm sure you noticed the ±factor that follows the dates. Radiocarbon dating, like all forms of radiometric dating, is statistical in nature. In a sense, it's like tossing a coin. If you flip a coin ten times, you are most likely to obtain a result of five tails and five heads, but you can't be certain of that result. In any series of ten throws, you might get six heads and four tails, or seven heads and three tails, or ten heads and no tails, even with a perfectly legitimate coin. If you flip a coin ten times, how many heads do you predict you'll likely get? Five is a good guess, but it's better to predict 5 heads ± a certain factor to increase the likelihood that you'll be on the money (a bad pun, to be sure). There's a level of chance built into the system, and the same is true with radioactive decay; the half-life measurement for any radioactive substance is a statistical measure based on a normal distribution (bell curve) of measurements of the decay rate. By definition, in any normal distribution 66.67% (two-thirds) of all cases graphed will fall between one standard deviation above and one standard deviation below the mean; 95% will fall between two standard deviations (a mathematical measure of the "average" deviation from the mean in a given sample) above and below the mean. For the radiocarbon dates mentioned, the ± factor represents one standard deviation above and below the mean for the particular count done on the sample. For example, in the case of the first date, 3010 years is the mean date determined by measuring how much C-14 was still left and decaying in that sample recovered at Wood Lily. The standard deviation for that sample was given as 110 years. So, there is a 66.67% chance that the charcoal recovered at that spot at the Wood Lily site is between 3,120 and 2,900 years old (3,010 plus or minus one standard deviation), and there is a 95% chance that the charcoal dates to between 3,230 and 2,790 years ago (3,010 plus or minus two standard deviations). So, when we state that the Wood Lily site is around 3,000 years old, it's based on a summary number derived from a statistical measurement of the most likely age of the burned wood recovered in a particular sample.

There is one additional point to consider. In an earlier paragraph I expressed the Wood Lily radiocarbon dates as ages "B.P." B.P. stands for "before present." Many archaeologists prefer using B.P. because it avoids tying in the age of an archaeological site to the birth of Jesus, which you do when using B.C. The birth of Jesus is, of course, a key point in time for Christians but not necessarily for non-Christians. Beyond this, whenever you read a B.C. date, you need to do a little mathematical calculation (add 2,007 in the year 2007, add 2,008 in the year 2008, etc.) to determine the age of the site, which is, after all, what you really want to know, how many years ago the site in question was occupied by people. B.P. sounds like it also solves this issue, except for the fact that the present is always changing, it isn't a fixed point in time. The "present" as I write this in early 2007 won't be the present anymore by the time you are reading this in 2008, 2009, or 2010. To address the fact that the present isn't really a fixed point in time, archaeologists and chronologists decided to alter reality (not really, we've just altered the use of the word) and have agreed that for archaeological dating puroposes, the "present" is defined as 1950. The real present and the defined present were about the same in the 1950s and 1960s, but they are now separated by more than fifty years, adding to the confusion. When I told you that the first

Wood Lily carbon date was 3,010 B.P. that's 3,010 years before 1950, not today. That's confusing, I know. I attempt in my lecturing and writing to gloss over this unfortunate complexity and simply indicate about how many years ago a site was occupied or about how long ago something happened. The good news here is that despite all the confusion I may have just introduced, we're still good in stating that the Wood Lily site was occupied about 3,000 years ago.

Based on what you know, you should have figured out that radiocarbon dating works only on things that once were alive or part of living things (wood, bone, leather, hair, seeds, nuts, fruits, skin, antler, horn, teeth, shell). Its range of temporal applicability also is limited. Very recent items have not experienced enough C-14 decay to accurately determine their age. At the other end of the continuum, after too many half-lives virtually no C-14 is left to measure, and the age cannot be determined accurately. In practice, specimens younger than a few hundred years or older than about 40,000 years (about seven half-lives) fall outside of the range of radiocarbon dating.

Radiocarbon dates require a little interpretation before they can be converted to true calendar dates. It turns out that the proportion of C-14 to C-12 in the atmosphere has varied through time. As a result, specimens that date to periods when the C-14 proportion in the atmosphere, and, therefore, in everything that was alive during that period, was higher than it is today will produce carbon dates that are too young. Conversely, specimens that were alive during periods when the C-14 proportion was lower will appear to be older than they actually are.

A fix for this, at least for the last 11,000 years or so, has been calculated using tree rings (Bowman 1990). Individual tree rings, whose precise year age can be determined based on a master sequence, have been radiocarbon dated. For a large number of individual tree rings for which we can determine a precise age in years, dendrochronologists have also determined age by radiocarbon dating. Once a tree ring has been laid down, no new carbon is incorporated into it. This means that C-14 dates for interior rings—the earlier rings in a tree's life—will be older than those derived for exterior rings. This is most recognizable in very old trees and adds another possible error factor to radiocarbon dating, the so-called old wood effect. For example, if a person cut down a 200-year-old tree for firewood a 1,000 years ago and used the interior segment of the trunk, the radiocarbon date will probaly read 1,200 years of age, dating to when the portion of the tree used in the fire grew, not to when the tree was cut down. This is why archaeologists prefer using short-lived parts of plants in radiocarbon dating (for example, seeds or nuts) rather than trunks of old trees.

In any event, because individual tree rings stop taking in new carbon after the year in which they are laid down, dendrochronologists working with those who perform radiocarbon dates can produce two dates for a large sequence of tree rings: one based on dendrochronology (these are absolutely precise and accurate dates, so they serve as the control, or independent, variable) and one based on radiocarbon dating of those same rings for which they can determine tree ring dates (the carbon dates are the dependent variable). A graph can be drawn depicting the relationship between the tree ring true calendar dates and the C-14 dates for those same rings (Figure 8.11). The resulting graph, called a **calibration curve**, shows the degree of correspondence between tree ring and

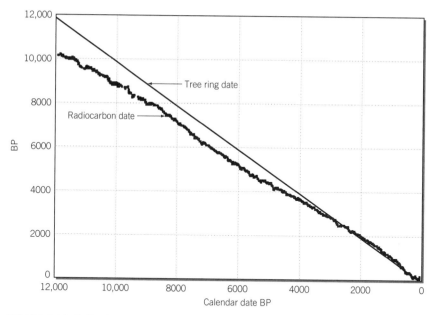

FIGURE 8.11 Calibration curve worked out for radiocarbon dates for the past 12,000 years based on dendrochronology. (University of Groningen, Center for Isotope Research)

C-14 dates across a long stretch of time. This allows us to apply a correction factor to the C-14 dates (http://www.cio.phys.rug.nl/HTML-docs/Verslag/97/CD-01.htm). As can be seen in Figure 8.11, from recent times until about 2,500 years ago, C-14 dates are a pretty good match for tree-ring calendar dates. Beyond that, it is apparent that C-14 dates undershoot the actual age of items by an increasing amount, up to several hundred years. Along with providing the results of a C-14 analysis, radiocarbon labs also provide the corrected dates based on the tree ring calibration curve. You can go online and use the standard calibration program to determine the most probable calendar dates for radio-carbon determinations (http://www.calib.qub.ac.uk/calib).

Chapter 8: Interactive Exercise

Radiocarbon calibrations are being worked out for the period before 11,000 years ago. For example, carbon dates have been calculated for organic remains extracted from **varves**, sediments laid down annually along lake and ocean shore-lines. Varves can be counted back through time in a manner analogous to tree rings. Each varve represents one year, so its actual year date can be precisely deter-mined by counting back to it from the varve deposited in the current year.

One of the most important of these varve sequences, stretching from 11,000 to about 45,000 years ago, has been worked out at Lake Suigetsu in Japan (Kitagawa and van der plicht 1998). Each of more than 250 carbon dates was compared to the calendar years determined for each of the varves from which the carbon dated material was recovered. A calibration curve based on varves was then produced in the same way as was the one derived from tree rings, the varve date is the independent variable, and the carbon date is the dependent variable in the equation. The Lake Suigetsu calibration shows that from 11,000 years ago to about 45,000 years ago, C-14 dates are consistently too young compared to the very accurate varve dates, on the order of a few thousand years, with the difference increasing for older dates (Kitagawa and van der Plicht 1998).

Calibration has also been extended well beyond 11,000 years ago by comparing C14 dates and those determined through an extremely precise and accurate dating procedure based on the radioactive decay of uranium to thorium. Researcher Richard G. Fairbanks and his colleagues produced an extensive series of pairs of dates—each pair included a radiocarbon date and a $^{230}Th/^{234}U/^{238}U$ date for material derived from the same source, coral from coral reefs (coral was part of a community of living organisms that took up carbon from the surrounding seawater), extending the calibration of radiocarbon dates back to about 50,000 years ago (Fairbanks et al. 2005). You can check out his calibration program on the website of the Lamont Doherty Earth Observatory at Columbia University (http://radiocarbon.ldeo.columbia.edu/research/radcarbcal.htm). Type in a radiocarbon date in the appropriate box on the left, include a standard deviation (try 100 years), and then just click "Compute." You can do this with the two radiocarbon dates we obtained for the Wood Lily site: 3,010±110 and 2,960±70. Calibration confirms that the Wood Lily site was occupied just a little more than 3,000 years ago: The two radiocarbon dates produce calibrated dates of, respectively, 3,196±153 and 3,128±113 years ago.

Other radiometric methods are used by archaeologists to determine the age of a site. For example, **potassium/argon (K/Ar)** dating is based on the known rate of decay of an unstable isotope of the element potassium into the gas argon (Deino, Renne, and Swisher 1998). Potassium is an abundant element in the Earth's crust and can be found in **igneous** rock. When lava comes out of a volcano, any argon that had previously accumulated in the rock is released into the atmosphere, essentially setting the natural clock in the lava to time zero. When the lava solidifies, argon begins accumulating as the unstable potassium atoms decay, getting trapped in the now-solid rock. The age of the rock itself can be determined by measuring the amount of argon that has built up and calculating the length of time it would have taken for that amount to accumulate based on the half-life of radioactive potassium, which has been measured at 1.25 billion years.

A chunk of volcanic rock such as basalt or rhyolite, or even an entire lava flow, can be dated in this way, but the K/Ar method ordinarily doesn't date an archaeological site, at least not directly. We might be able to date the rock itself from which a human crafted a tool, but that doesn't really date the artifact. Think about it: I can collect a sample of basalt today from the mountain that brackets the eastern margin of the Farmington River Valley in central Connecticut. The eruption that resulted in the lava flow that produced our local basalt occurred about 200 million years ago, and K/Ar produces dates of about that age for the Talcott Mountain basalt. Suppose I were to make a spear point out of a chunk of that basalt today. Then suppose I sent off the point to a lab that conducted K/Ar dating. The spear point sample would produce an age of about 200 million years, but that certainly isn't how old the tool itself is; I just made it!

So K/Ar dating is not usually used to date an artifact, but it can be applied to rock in an intact level. Here's where our understanding of stratigraphy comes in handy. When archaeological materials are found in a stratigraphic layer above one lava flow and below another, we can bracket the age of the site by reference to K/Ar dates derived for both layers (Figure 8.12). If, for example, the volcanic deposit that underlies the site dates to 2.15 million years ago, and if the overlying layer dates to 1.85 million years ago, we know that the archaeological site dates to sometime between those two dates.

In one spectacular instance, the K/Ar method actually dated a site directly. At the site of Laetoli, in Tanzania, Africa, a series of humanlike footprints were found in a hardened deposit of volcanic ash (Leakey and Hay 1979). Two, and possibly three, individuals had walked across a newly laid bed of ash in the distant past. The ash hardened to the consistency of concrete after a gentle rain and later was covered by additional deposits. When the footprint trail was discovered and excavated by paleoanthropologists Mary Leakey and Tim White, samples of the hardened ash were dated using the K/Ar method. The result: The ash was deposited 3.5 million years ago. The footprints are virtually indistinguishable from those made by modern human beings, showing that, though their brains were the size of chimpanzees', even at this early date our human ancestors walked much in the manner of modern people.

As a result of the extremely long half-life of radioactive potassium, this technique has no effective upper limit: Nothing on Earth is too old for the

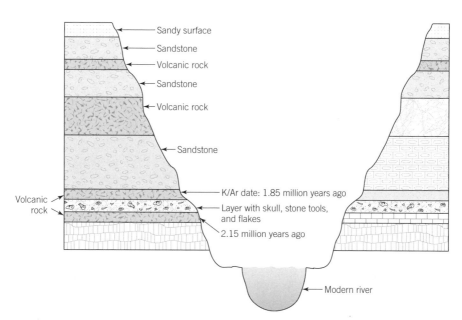

FIGURE 8.12 Combining stratigraphic analysis with potassium/argon dating has enabled scientists to bracket the ages of ancient hominid skeletons and artifacts. In this hypothetical example the remains of a human ancestor have been found in a layer overlying a lava flow dated through potassium/argon to 2.15 million years ago and underlying a subsequent flow dating to 1.85 million years. The hominid remains must date, therefore, to some time between 1.85 and 2.15 million years ago.

procedure. On the other hand, however, anything younger than a 100,000 years or thereabouts is too young for the technique to produce accurate results; not enough of the radioactive potassium has decayed to argon.

Carbon and potassium/argon dating techniques are based on measurement of the decreasing amount of an unstable isotope remaining in a substance (C-14) or in the increasing amount of what the unstable isotope decays to (K/AR). Another set of dating procedures relies instead on the measurement of the regularly occurring changes or damage that result during the process of radioactive decay. **Electron spin resonance (ESR)**, for example, calculates the accumulation of electrons (the negative particles that make up an atom) that become trapped at higher than normal, or "ground state," energy levels in crystalline material (including fossilized bones or teeth) as a result of radioactivity in the surrounding environment (Grün 1993). Based on measurements of the background radiation in the area immediately surrounding the artifact or ecofact, the rate at which the electron trapping occurs can be calculated. From that, the age of the material can be determined: We know the rate at which the trapping occurs and how much has occurred, thus enabling a calculation of age.

Thermoluminescence (TL) and **optically stimulated luminescence (OSL)** also are radiation damage dating techniques. Here, the background radiation in the soil surrounding, for example, a buried ceramic or stone object produces energy that becomes stored in the atomic structure of the object. When the archaeological object is recovered, the energy that has accumulated as a result of the background radiation can be released through the application of heat (thermoluminescence) or laser light (optically stimulated luminescence) and then measured. As was the case for ESR, knowing the rate of energy accumulation in an archaeological object once it ended up in the soil, and then knowing how much energy has actually accumulated, allows for a calculation of how long the object has been accumulating the energy, in other words, how old it is (for details about the procedures from a laboratory that conducts TL analysis, see http://www.users.globalnet.co.uk/~qtls).

Read More

There are an enormous numbers of publications on the general topic of radiometric dating methods in archaeology, with each technique generating its own literature. A very brief sample follows:

Bard, E. 2001. Extending the Calibrated Radiocarbon Record. *Science* 292:2443–44.

Beck, J. W., D. A. Richards, R. Lawrence, et al. 2001. Extremely Large Variations of Atmospheric 14C Concentration During the Last Glacial Period. *Science* 292:2453–58.

Bowman, S. 1990. *Radiocarbon Dating*. University of California Press, Berkeley.

Dalrymple, G. B., and M. A. Lanphere. 1969. *Potassium-Argon Dating*. W. H. Freeman, San Francisco.

Deino, A., P. R. Renne, and C. C. Swisher III. 1998. 40Ar/39Ar Dating in Paleoanthropology and Archaeology. *Evolutionary Anthropology* 6(2):63–75.

Grün, R. 1993. Electron Spin Resonance Dating in Paleoanthropology. *Evolutionary Anthropology* 2(5):172–81.

Kitagawa, H., and J. van der Plicht. 1998. Atmospheric Radiocarbon Calibration to 45,000 BP: Late Glacial Fluctuations and Cosmogenic Istope Production. *Science* 279: 1187–90.

Leakey, M. D., and R. L. Hay. 1979. Pliocene Footprints in the Laetolil Beds at Laetoli, Northern Tanzania. *Nature* 278:317–23.

Libby, W. F. 1952. *Radiocarbon Dating.* Chicago University Press, Chicago.

Stuiver, M., and J. van der Plicht, eds. 1998. Intcal 98: Calibration Issue. *Radiocarbon* 40(3): 1041–1164.

Taylor, R. E. 1987. *Radiocarbon Dating: An Archaeological Perspective.* Academic Press, London.

HOW CAN THE SHIFTING LOCATION OF MAGNETIC NORTH BE USED TO DATE SITES?

Most of us have used a compass at one time or another in our lives. Maybe we've hiked in the woods and used a field compass to get our bearings. Lots of cars now come with digital compass readouts on the instrument panel, so even when we're lost we know the direction in which we are getting increasing lost. Most of us also know that a compass needle is simply a little magnet that aligns along a north-south line conforming to the alignment of the magnetic field of our planet. Many of us don't know, however, that the magnetic field of the Earth is not fixed: It continuously shifts around a little, and in the past the field has even flipped entirely, with north and south actually shifting 180 degrees (this happened most recently about 780,000 years ago).

As the Earth's magnetic field shifts its alignment, the location of magnetic north shifts as well. The needle in a compass, since it points to magnetic north when it aligns with our planet's magnetic field, points in a slightly different direction as the field shifts.

This would be interesting but seemingly not relevant to our discussion of archaeological dating methods save for one fact: Naturally occurring magnetic minerals are abundant on the Earth's surface and, under the right circumstances, reflecting the phenomenon called **paleomagnetism**, will align with our planet's magnetic field at a particular time and maintain that alignment even after the precise alignment of the field shifts. For example, magnetic minerals in a flow of molten lava will, like tiny compass needles, align with the Earth's magnetic field. Once the lava solidifies, the magnetic minerals maintain that alignment because they are now in a solid, immovable substance and cannot shift even though the planet's field may shift. In essence, the magnetic minerals represent a fossil of the alignment of the Earth's magnetic field at the time they were part of a plastic, malleable lava flow.

Suppose we find such an ancient lava flow and measure the past alignment of the Earth's magnetic field by examining the alignment of the magnetic minerals in the flow. Then suppose that we apply a chronometric dating procedure—for example, potassium-argon—to the lava. This provides us with an absolute date for a particular magnetic field alignment, and whenever we find another rock flow exhibiting the same alignment, we can deduce that this new flow was deposited at about the same time.

Archaeologists can apply a similar analysis to more recent objects by taking advantage of the phenomenon called **archaeomagnetism**. Just as the orientation of magnetic particles in an ancient lava flow retains the alignment of the time when they were deposited, magnetic orientation can also be preserved in cultural features. For example, magnetic minerals in the clay from which the bricks of a kiln were made may all align with the Earth's magnetic field and point to the location of magnetic north during the time of their use in that kiln (Eighmy and Howard 1991). Examination of the alignment of such natural compasses and subsequent dating of these features by use of the chronometric techniques discussed in this chapter have allowed for the construction of a master curve of the location of magnetic north for the period between A.D. 600 and 1975 (Figure 8.13; Eighmy and Sternberg 1990; Lengyel and Eighmy 2002). The map shows the wandering of magnetic north and the shifting of the Earth's magnetic field for this period of nearly 1,400 years. When the orientation of the Earth's magnetic field has been preserved in features found at additional archaeological sites, an estimate of the site's age can be deduced based on where those natural compasses point to and when, with reference to the map shown in Figure 8.13, that direction was the location of true north in the past.

How Can You Determine an Absolute Date for a Site by Reference to Style?

The ways in which people decorate their pots, make their spears, build their houses, bury their dead, prepare their food, and so on change over time. Sometimes these changes represent genuine progress in the complexity or efficiency of a technology. Some changes reflect little more than the vicissitudes of fashion. Whatever the case, when we are familiar with a culture and aware of when these changes in style or ways of doing things took place, we can date objects or even entire sites on the basis of these styles.

For example, I am certain that your university keeps copies of their catalogs of years past. Suppose the year has been ripped from the cover of a couple of the catalogs so there is no written indication of the catalog's year date. Now suppose I describe the covers of a couple of the catalogs to you. One has a photograph on the cover of two students, one male and one female. The man has a short haircut with a big wave in the front, sticking up and obviously kept in place with some sort of gel. He is wearing a sweater with the university's initials sewn onto the pocket, white pants with a thin belt, and penny loafers on his feet. The woman has her hair in a ponytail, is wearing a skirt appliquéd with the image of a poodle, and on her feet wears two-toned, so-called saddle shoes. You will immediately know that the catalog dates to the 1950s, not because you lived through that period but because you are familiar with the styles of the period from photographs of your parents or endless, merciless high school productions of the musical *Grease*.

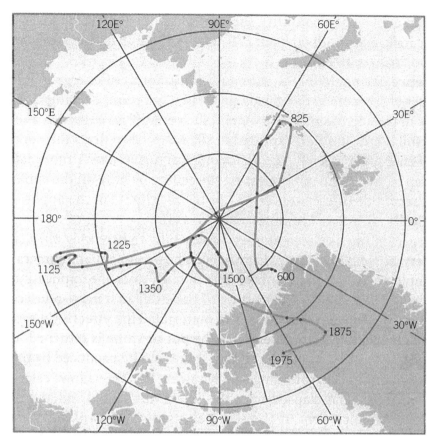

FIGURE 8.13 Master curve of the location of magnetic north for the period between A.D. 600 and 1975. The map shows the wandering of magnetic north and the shifting of the Earth's magnetic field for this period of nearly 1,400 years. (From Eighmy and Sternberg 1990; Lengyel and Eighmy 2002)

Suppose I next describe a copy of your university's annual catalog with a photograph, again, of two students, again a male and female. Now the man has wild, scraggly hair hanging down his back, a beard, a tie-dyed t-shirt, ripped jeans with an American flag sewn on the knee, and, well, there is no need to describe his shoes because he isn't wearing any. Except for the beard, the woman looks just like the man. Once again, though you might not be able to guess the exact year, you will likely correctly hypothesize that the catalog dates to the late 1960s or early 1970s. Love, peace, and music. It's all about paying attention to the changing of styles and having familiarity with the time frame when those styles changed.

How about this: I admit to being a little geeky. I tend to jump in and buy whatever new piece of technology is being offered at the local electronics store. I walk in, see something ultra-cool, think "Shiney!" (OK, only fans of *Firefly* will get that), and out comes the credit card. That's probably why I have every major version of the Apple iPod—as I write this, that's five generations of players—from the first, now looking pretty clunky edition, to the current video iPod (Minis and Nanos don't count here, and, OK gen 3 belongs to my older son and gen 5 belongs to my younger boy, but I bought them, so they are kind of mine). Look at Figure 8.14. Each generation of iPod looks a bit different

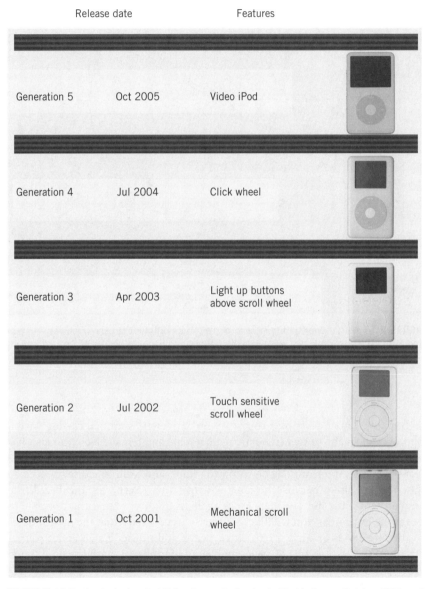

	Release date	Features
Generation 5	Oct 2005	Video iPod
Generation 4	Jul 2004	Click wheel
Generation 3	Apr 2003	Light up buttons above scroll wheel
Generation 2	Jul 2002	Touch sensitive scroll wheel
Generation 1	Oct 2001	Mechanical scroll wheel

FIGURE 8.14 Technological and stylistic change in the Apple iPod between October 2001 and October 2005. The iPod has gone through five officially recognized "generations," each of which appeared in a restricted period of time. If you know the pattern of change, you can determine the time period when a particular iPod was manufactured.

and reflects the evolution of digital music player technology and capabilities. Technology changes through time, whether that technology relates to stone tools, digital music players, pyramids, laptops, cave paintings, cell phones, or anything else you can think of. Once you know the timing of those changes, you can use the artifacts to gauge time.

Just as you recognize and can accurately, if not absolutely precisely, identify the period to which an object dates because of your familiarity with the recent history of your own culture, an archaeologist can do the same with ancient cultures with which he or she is familiar. When someone hands an afficianado of music players an iPod with light-up buttons above a touch-sensitive wheel, he or she knows that it dates to a period after April 2003 (see Figure 8.14). When someone hands an archaeologist in the New World a

FIGURE 8.15 Clovis points were manufactured during a relatively limited period of time—between about 13,000 and 10,000 years ago. Knowing that, the recovery of a similar, distinctive looking artifact at a site provides a good estimate of the age of the site.

relatively long, finely made stone spear point bearing a concave channel, or "flute" (as in a fluted column in a building), that begins as the base and reaches to about halfway up the weapon's length, he or she will instantly suggest that the spear point dates to sometime between 12,000 and 11,000 years ago (Figure 8.15). There's no magic, psychic power, or intuition here, only a familiarity with that style of artifact. Fluted points have been found throughout North America. Wherever they have been found in archaeological contexts, the dates derived from associated organic remains through radiocarbon dating indicate something in the neighborhood of about 11,800 to 11,200 years ago. When someone hands me a fluted point devoid of site context and lacking any association with directly datable material, I nevertheless am pretty confident when I suggest that the weapon probably dates to somewhere between 11,000 and 12,000 years ago.

Study Questions

1. What is the minimum age a site or artifact must be, from a theoretical perspective, for it technically to be "archaeological"?

2. What is the minimum age a site or artifact must be for it to be archaeological according to the Archaeological Resources Protection Act of 1979?

3. What is the minimum age a site must be in order to qualify for the National Register of Historic Places? Are there exceptions? If so, under what circumstances are they granted?

4. What is chronometric, or absolute, dating? What is relative dating?

5. What are the most common relative dating techniques in archaeology?

6. Discuss the use of degree of artistic sophistication as a dating method in archaeology.

7. Discuss stratigraphy. How does the concept of the law of superposition allow us to relatively date archaeological occupations?

8. Discuss the relative sequence revealed by the test pit excavated in Avon, Connecticut, as detailed in this book.

9. "The deeper something is, the older it is." Can we apply this simple rule in archaeological dating? Why or why not?

10. Can stylistic change through time be used to date archaeological sites?

11. You are a future archaeologist. You excavate a series of sites of slightly differing ages, but all from the early twenty-first century. How might a knowledge of the history of the iPod help you in dating those sites?

12. How does seriation work? What is the assumption at the core of seriation?

13. Discuss the application of seriation. Use the example provided for the seriation of beverage can containers in the second half of the twentieth century. Use the example of New England gravestone designs.

14. What are the most common methods of chronometric dating?

15. Tree rings are easy enough to understand when we're dealing with a living tree: Count the rings to see how old the tree is. But how does this help us date ancient archaeological sites?

16. What is the process behind establishing a master sequence of tree rings for a given region? How does a master sequence enable the dating of an old, now long-dead tree found incorporated into an ancient structure?

17. How did the establishment of a master chronology for the sixteenth through twentieth centuries assist in the dating of old houses in eastern Massachusetts?

18. List the most important radiometric dating techniques used in archaeology.

19. How does radiocarbon dating work? Where does C-14 come from? How does it get into living things? Why does C-14 decay? How does that decay provide a natural clock or calendar that can be used in dating archaeological material?

20. The accuracy of radiocarbon dating relies on what turns out to be a faulty assumption: There has always been a constant ratio of stable C-12 to unstable C-14 in the Earth's atmosphere. How do tree rings provide a work-around, at least for the last 11,000 years or so?

21. What is the tree ring calibration curve? How is it applied to radiocarbon dating?

22. What are varves? How has the analysis of varves contributed to improving the accuracy of carbon dating?

23. How has uranium series dating pushed back the calibration of radiocarbon dates to nearly the full extent of the method's chronological applicability?

24. Using the on-line calibration program produced by the Lamont Doherty Earth Observatory at Columbia University, determine the calendar dates for the following radiocarbon dates derived for sites in the Farmington River Valley in Connecticut: Glazier Site: 1,630±80; Beaver Brook: 1,310±60; Alsop Meadow: 4,920±250; Loomis II: 1,940±95.

24. How does potassium/argon dating work? What can actually be dated using this technique?

25. List some of the radiation damage dating techniques. How do those apply to archaeological specimens?

26. I have dated charcoal found in a fireplace at the Wood Lily site through radiocarbon dating to about 3,000 years ago. I have concluded from this that the site itself was occupied about 3,000 years ago. What was my reasoning?

27. How do you know the approximate age (perhaps to the correct decade) of an older automobile that has just driven by? How does your reasoning apply in archaeology?

28. How does archaeomagnetism work?

9 Interpreting the Past

THE ENVIRONMENTAL CONTEXTS OF ANTIQUITY

- **Why Do Archaeologists Want to Know About Ancient Environments?**

  Does the Environment Cause Certain Adaptations?

- **How Do Archaeologists Reconstruct the Environment?**

  How Can Little Creatures Called Foraminifera Tell Us About Climate Change?

  What's Pollen Good For, Besides Making Us Sneeze?

  What Is a Pollen Profile?

  How Can You Identify Tree Species from Bits of Burned Wood?

Human beings, no less than other living things in the present as well as in the past, depend absolutely on the environment for survival. Today most scientists and laypeople alike are deeply concerned about the human contribution to climate change. Hardly a day goes by without a news report concerning global warming and ongoing glacial melt-off in Antarctica, Greenland, the Arctic, and higher elevations around the world and the potentially devastating impacts, especially along the densely populated coasts of the world, of sea level rise. The availability of critical resources such as stone, clay, wood, and metals, agricultural productivity, seasonality, and so on all had enormous impacts on the lives of ancient human beings and their societies, and changes in those variables will certainly have an impact on us. It should come as no surprise, then, that archaeologists are interested in past climates and past environments in our attempt to understand the adaptational contexts for ancient peoples. This chapter addresses the strategies employed by archaeologists to reconstruct those adaptational contexts, those ancient environments.

Why Do Archaeologists Want to Know About Ancient Environments?

You've likely heard the old expression, generally attributed to Mark Twain, "Everybody talks about the weather, but nobody does anything about it." It seems to apply as well now early in the twenty-first century as it did when it was first written more than one hundred years ago. Here in my own Connecticut town, everybody is talking about an intense and highly localized thunderstorm that struck just two days ago as I write this. A cluster of aged sycamore trees lost large branches, a couple of cars were destroyed, an old building that is now part of a historical museum was clipped by a falling branch, and a few thousand people were without power for several hours. On a far more catastrophic scale, remember all the cable news talking heads covering hurricane Katrina and the devastation left in its wake along the Gulf Coast, killing more than 1,000 people and disrupting the lives of thousands more in Biloxi, Gulfport, and New Orleans. Everyone talks about the severe, incessant, triple-digit summer heat experienced by people in the American Southwest, the ridiculous snow accumulations (more than 1,100 inches—that's more than 96 feet) in a single winter in the Mt Rainier range in Washington State, the breathtaking wind gust speeds of greater than 200 miles an hour registered on Mt Washington, New Hampshire, and so on.

We talk about the weather—the extremes listed above and the everyday, normal vicissitudes of warm and cold, dry and humid, calm and wind, clear and cloudy, rainy and dry—because it provides the daily backdrop of our lives: What kind of clothes to wear, will you need an umbrella, should we put snow boots on the kids, shorts or long pants, do we need to put snow tires on the car, what's the heating bill going to be this winter, what's the cooling bill going to look like this summer, ad infinitum. The weather affects everything from the price of orange juice (an early frost will hike the price) and movie attendance (theaters are empty on beautiful weekends and filled when it's raining) to our moods (think of seasonal affective disorder, or SAD whereby some people may descend into a deep depression during the cold, dark winter months) and even our health (our bodies need sunshine to produce vitamin D; some diseases have distinct geographic distributions, for example, malaria, yellow fever, and sleeping sickness, which are all diseases of the Tropics, and refer back to Figure 4.10 and look at the map of the geographic distribution of Lyme disease in the United States).

The environment can be viewed as the stage upon which the drama of our lives plays out. The environment just as surely provided the many stages upon which the manifold dramas of the lives of past peoples played out. As scientists interested in those lives, we recognize the importance of understanding the nature of those ancient environments and how people adjusted and adapted to them.

Does the Environment Cause Certain Adaptations?

As important as the environment is in providing the backdrop for a society's way of life, it is important to understand that social scientists today do not view the environment as causing a particular cultural response. This perspective has not always held sway. There was a school of though, especially among geographers but also some anthropologists, in the mid-nineteenth century that proposed a more deterministic perspective. In fact, it was called **environmental determinism**. Environmental determinists essentially believed that some environments were so inherently easy to adapt to—the climate was equable, natural foods and other resources abundant and easy to collect—that people didn't need to work or think particularly hard in order to carve out a pleasant existence. Under these steady and abundant conditions, the environmental determinists maintained, a people wouldn't progress simply because they didn't need to and there was no overriding necessity to develop new ideas and strategies, no compelling reason to invent new ways of producing food or organizing their labor. In this view in certain environments most of the time people could, essentially, "chill". When they were hungry, they could simply reach over to the nearest bush or stream and collect enough food to eat, without even breaking a sweat, either literal or metaphorical. There was no need to work hard, no challenges to rise to, nothing to compel progress, and as a result in the view of the environmental determinists these cultures stagnated.

These determinists, believed at the same time, that some environments were far more challenging and forced people living in them to be inventive, creative, and think fast on their feet, and if they didn't, they died. In the environmental determinist view, these more challenging environments—especially continental climates with long, cold winters, warm, humid summers and, perhaps above all else, weather characterized by climatic instability, unpredictability, inconsistency, and heterogeneity (if you don't like the weather, wait until tomorrow because it's bound to be a whole lot different)—fostered greater inventiveness among the people living under these conditions and encouraged their technological progress. In the environmental determinist view cultural evolution occurred where conditions obliged cultural progress.

Not surprisingly, most environmental determinists interpreted the climates of northern Europe and North America to be the most challenging environments on the planet, thus explaining their view that the most advanced cultures on Earth were found in Europe and North America. You may have already guessed that the vast majority of these environmental determinists were Europeans and North Americans. One of my junior high school social studies teachers still taught from an environmental determinist perspective, asserting that European and Euroamerican civilization was dominant in the twentieth century because our climates were not only challenging but just precisely the right kind of challenging (not too little, not too much, but just right) to produce our highly evolved technologies.

A fundamental problem in environmental determinism was posed by the historical and archaeological records. Great civilizations, representing clear evidence of the inventiveness, great intellectual capacity, and enormous material achievements of their peoples had evolved under myriad environmental regimes, not just those characterized by continental climates. Ancient Egypt developed along a narrow floodplain surrounded by a harsh desert, the Maya built their great city-states in a tropical rainforest, the Shang civilization of China arose within a river valley located in an area with a continental climate, and the Inca of South America built a great empire in an area characterized by towering mountains. There was no environment or climate type that monopolized the history of civilization, no single environment type that determined cultural development.

Beyond this, although the climate that characterized the world of environmental determinists of the mid-nineteenth century hadn't changed substantially for thousands of years, as revealed by the archaeological record, cultures all over the world had undergone vast changes in that same period of time. Each of the civilizations just listed had evolved over great stretches of time, and each of them had fallen, all during periods of relative environmental stability; climate change had not caused them to evolve great civilizations, and climate change had not been responsible for their collapse. Each one of these civilizations, had developed, flourished, and then collapsed without their environments changing at all. It was asked rhetorically if the same Sun that had shone over the great civilizations of Greece and Rome did not still shine over their impoverished descendants. Environmental determinism was rejected because it simply didn't fit the historical facts.

Human beings are the active agents in producing a culture, and the environment is the passive element in the equation. The environment does not determine the adaptation, it merely provides the possibilities for a group of people to respond to. Of course, people living in the Arctic do not develop agriculture, people living in a desert don't develop a maritime culture, and so on. Most environments, however, are not so limited or limiting and provide people living in them a wealth of opportunities and choices. The environments do not, in fact they cannot, cause a particular choice to be made by a people. People choose to exploit certain resources and ignore others, they make choices about how they will use the landscape, they invent strategies for survival based on their own inventiveness, they are subject to historical accidents, they encounter other groups, and their cultural trajectory my be deflected by the different ideas and approaches they may take from those encounters.

Recognizing the complex and dynamic nature of the relationships among human beings, their cultures, and the environments in which they live, anthropologists developed an approach called **cultural ecology**. In the cultural ecological approach we don't ascribe causation to the environment. Instead, we investigate the many ways in which different peoples responded, reacted, adjusted, and adapted to the environments in which they lived and how those people responded, reacted, adjusted, and adapted to changes in those environments when they changed. This last analysis may be particularly useful to modern people as we attempt to face down the apparently vast environmental changes that appear to mark our own future.

 ## How Do Archaeologists Reconstruct the Environment?

Almost certainly, if I were to mention a particular environment type, each of us would be able to conjure up in our minds an image of that environment that included the stereotypical plants and animals that flourish there. If I were to mention, for example, the desert Southwest of the United States, most of you would imagine cactus (probably the iconic saguaro cactus that flourishes in parts of Arizona, Southwestern California, and Northern Mexico as well as all those Roadrunner cartoons); if I mentioned the Great Plains of North America, I bet most of us would picture a scene with tall grass and buffalo (technically, these American buffalo are not buffalo at all, they're bison). The prompt of "African jungle" might result in images of elephants and gorillas; "Arctic" might inspire thoughts of polar bears and maybe caribou. These stereotypical images come to mind because, indeed, these plants and animals live in those areas and not in the others (elephants don't live in Alaska, saguaro cactus doesn't grow in the African Tropics, there are no gorillas in the Great Plains). The plants and animals just mentioned live where they do because they are supremely well adapted to those areas and not to the others. Consider polar bear exhibits in the southern United States, where the conditions of the Arctic must be fabricated indoors; the bears wouldn't last long in the severely hot summers of the American South.

The point of this exercise is this: Different plants and animals thrive under different environmental conditions, and we know what those conditions are. As a result, plant and animal remains found at archaeological sites are diagnostic of the climatic conditions that prevailed in an area in the past. When we can date those remains and sites, we can deduce the environmental conditions that characterized that time period at the place where the remains were found.

Here's an example. The North American caribou (*Rangifer tarandus*) is adapted to live in the tundra and taiga biomes (look ahead at Figure 9.6). Caribou are adapted to life where the winters are long, the climate is cold, and trees are sparse. Unlike deer, caribou don't need shrubs, acorns, and hickory nuts to survive; they subsist on a diet made up largely of the moss and lichens that are prevalent throughout the Arctic.

The conditions for caribou survival are not those of downstate New York, which is characterized by thick deciduous forest and warm, humid summers. Nevertheless, caribou was found among the food remains recovered by archaeologists at the Dutchess Quarry Cave site. There, in an occupation level dated to more than 11,000 years ago, archaeologists found a spear point and an accumulation of caribou bones. The presence of caribou reflects one element of the subsistence focus of the people who lived in the cave, and it also indicates the nature of the surrounding environment when the cave was occupied. If there were caribou in the area, it is likely that a tundra or taiga environment characterized the region.

Other animals and plants are exquisitely adapted to a narrow set of environmental conditions. Their discovery in association with archaeological remains defines with great precision the prevalent conditions faced by the people who lived there during that time period.

Some snail species, for example, thrive under a very narrow range of temperature and moisture conditions. When they are found in association with archaeological remains, we can accurately infer the conditions faced by the people who lived in the area at the same time. For instance, Earth scientist Jennifer Smith and her colleagues at Washington University in St. Louis have collected ancient snails from the shores of a small lake in the Kharga Oasis located in the extremely arid region of western Egypt (Smith et al. 2004). Many artifacts have been found nearby, dating to 130,000 years ago during the period called the Middle Stone Age. The snail shells recovered (*Melanoides tuberculata*) imply the existence of moist conditions 130,000 years ago. The snails were able to survive because the small modern lake then was a more substantial and stable body of water. The stable lake could have existed 130,000 years ago only if conditions were considerably wetter than they are today. Chemical analysis of the shells themselves further supports the fact that their shells were growing during a period when water was consistently plentiful. Wetter conditions may explain the rich archaeological record for this period in western Egypt. Many paleoanthropologists believe that this period marks the time when anatomically modern *Homo sapiens*—people who were physically identical to modern human beings—expanded out of Africa for the first time into Europe and Asia. The wetter conditions implied by the snails at Kharga Oasis may explain, in part, what enabled and perhaps even encouraged the expansion of modern people from more tropical regions in the south to the north and into the rest of the Old World.

How Can Little Creatures Called Foraminifera Tell Us About Climate Change?

Long-term changes in worldwide climate are sometimes preserved in the shells of marine organisms called foraminifera, often just referred to as "forams." Here's how analysis of these tiny creatures—they are often only about 1mm (.04 inch) in length—can help us reconstruct global climate in antiquity.

You all know that water's chemical symbol is H_2O, reflecting the presence of two atoms of hydrogen and one atom of oxygen in each water molecule. Just as there are different isotopes of carbon (see chapter 8), there are a number of different isotopes of oxygen in nature. The most common, ^{16}O (with eight protons and eight neutrons in the nucleus, for an atomic weight of 16), constitutes about 99.765% of all of the oxygen on our planet. There also is ^{18}O (with eight protons and ten neutrons in its nucleus, for an atomic weight of 18). Only about .1995% of the world's oxygen supply is ^{18}O. That may seem like a small number—and proportionally, it is—but that still represents a lot of ^{18}O atoms in the planet's overall oxygen supply. The remainder of the oxygen on Earth, ^{17}O, is rarer still.

^{16}O and ^{18}O combine equally well with hydrogen to form water; neither form of oxygen is preferred or avoided by hydrogen atoms, so you would expect that the percentage of ^{16}O compared to ^{18}O would be the same in seawater as it is in the atmosphere (99.765% and .1995%, respectively). In fact, however, the concentration of water molecules in the oceans with the ^{16}O isotope compared to those with ^{18}O is not at those constant figures but varies as the climate changes.

These variations happen because of the difference in mass between the different isotopes of oxygen. Although a couple of neutrons might not seem like much, on an atomic level the difference in mass, between ^{16}O and ^{18}O is actually pretty substantial. Because it has two additional neutrons in its nucleus, ^{18}O is about 12.5% heavier than ^{16}O. Water molecules containing the heavier version of oxygen are heavier as well. As a result of their increased mass, a greater amount of energy is required to cause their evaporation. As a result, they don't evaporate as readily as water bearing the lighter form of oxygen. Because a higher proportion of ^{16}O water molecules evaporate compared to ^{18}O water, the ocean is, however briefly, proportionally depleted of ^{16}O or, viewing it from another perspective, has its ^{18}O water proportion equally briefly augmented through the process of evaporation.

Ordinarily, this has no effect on the concentration of oxygen isotopes in seawater, since the evaporated water falls as rain and quickly returns to the ocean, thus keeping the ^{16}O level, for the most part, constant. There have been times in our planet's history, however, when climate has cooled substantially and evaporating water has not rapidly returned to the oceans as rainfall. It has, instead, fallen as snow and ice and, where it has fallen on land, remained for lengthy periods of time, forming enormous ice fields called glaciers, especially in northern latitudes and higher elevations. During prolonged intervals of global cooling, for instance for long periods during the geological epoch known as the Pleistocene (from about 1.8 million to 10,000 years ago), the ocean was, for lengthy and measurable periods of time, proportionally depleted of its lighter ^{16}O water.

How do we know this, and how can we use this fact to reconstruct climate change on a worldwide scale? It goes back to foraminifera. Forams incorporate seawater into their shells. That, in a sense, fossilizes the ratio of ^{16}O to ^{18}O present in that seawater when those forams were alive. When forams have been recovered from soil layers in ocean cores and when those layers can be dated, researchers can tell if the planet's climate during that period was different from the modern condition. If the world was colder, for example, the recovered forams will have proportionally less ^{16}O than modern ones because when they were alive more of the lighter oxygen water molecules evaporated, fell as snow, and remained in frozen deposits on land. By the same reasoning, when ancient foram shells exhibit the same proportion of ^{16}O and ^{18}O as do modern ones, it implies a level of worldwide ice coverage similar to that of the modern world and, therefore, a worldwide temperature similar to today. Finally, if the recovered forams show a higher proportion of ^{16}O than modern shells show, it indicates a higher ^{16}O concentration in seawater than at present, suggesting a warmer period with less ice covering our planet. Perhaps, if human-induced

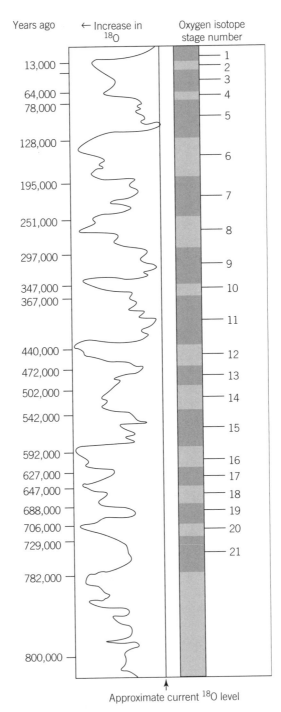

FIGURE 9.1 Shacketon/Opdyke oxygen isotope curve covering that last 800,000 years. The concentration of oxygen isotopes in the shells of foraminifera is used to calculate large-scale, world-wide temperature patterns; higher concentrations of ^{18}O are interpreted as resulting from increased areas of permanent ice fields on the planet and, therefore, lower temperatures. (From Shackleton and Opdyke, 1973).

global warming is not addressed sufficiently, future forams will have increasingly high levels of ^{16}O as the oceans become literally flooded by lighter oxygen as all of our planet's ice melts away. I am not sure that I find it all that comforting, but if global warming causes our extinction, the fact of that warming will be preserved in tiny marine organisms in the form of an increase in the ^{16}O concentration in their shells.

A graph depicting the changes in oxygen isotope proportions between 780,000 years ago and the present has been produced by researchers (Shackleton and Opdyke 1976). As you can see in Figure 9.1, modern human beings and our immediate ancestors have been faced with substantial and frequent changes in worldwide temperatures and attendant ice coverage and sea level changes when significant quantities of ocean water were locked up as ice on dry land. It is remarkable to consider that we know this because of the oxygen isotope content of tiny shells of marine organisms.

What's Pollen Good for, Besides Making Us Sneeze?

Everybody in my family sneezes. Lots. We all are afflicted by respiratory allergies; my wife and both of our children have asthma. I am just allergic. My allergies first emerged when I was a teenager. I was tested and reacted positively to animal dander, dust, grass, and all manner of tree pollen. Essentially, I am allergic to air. My wife began sneezing and wheezing when she was in her twenties, and at this point I think she has a closer relationship with her inhaler than she has with most people. Both of our kids are mucous factories and are on medication year-round to prevent the wheezing, sneezing, itchy eyes, and general misery that come with the territory of respiratory allergies. Though all four of us exhibit allergy symptoms year-round, we suffer the most in the spring. Around our house there's no need to check the local news for the pollen count; you can come up with a pretty accurate estimate just by looking at our red, sore eyes and by counting the sneezes.

Pollen grains serve a purpose beyond making us miserable; they are the male gametes in plant sexual reproduction. In other words, each pollen grain is the equivalent of a sperm cell, a tiny package with half the genetic instructions necessary to produce the next generation of a species of plant. There are two features of pollen grains that make them especially useful in **paleoenvironmental** reconstruction and, therefore, to archaeologists who hope to understand the environmental context within which a past people developed a way of life. First, under certain depositional conditions, pollen grains can survive for a very long time. Pollen grains have been recovered that are hundreds, thousands, and even tens of thousands of years old. Unlike bark, seeds, roots, fruits, wood, and leaves, which decay to dust in a short period of time under most circumstances, pollen is far more likely to survive. In fact, some of the pollen that was produced by trees, bushes, and grasses during the time when an archaeological site was a village of people and that rained down upon middens, trash dumps, and nearby wetlands (where pollen is preserved particularly well) can be recovered and analyzed by field scientists long after the trees, bushes, and grasses that produced the pollen have long since decayed away.

The other key feature of pollen is its species-specific appearance. The pollen grains produced by each plant species are distinguishable in appearance from those produced by every other plant species. For example, take a look at the four examples of pollen grains shown in Figure 9.2. Each of the three tree species (alder, pine, and oak) and the common woodland sedge (a grasslike plant) represented in the figure produces a morphologically distinct form of pollen. By familiarizing themselves with the morphology of pollen, scientists called **palynologists**—I know, it would be easier to remember if they were called pollenologists, but that's the way it goes—become adept at recognizing the pollen grains of a large array of plant species.

What this all means for environmental reconstruction is that when pollen has been preserved and recovered at or adjacent to an archaeological site from a soil layer that is contemporaneous with the site's occupation, we can begin to put together a list of the plants the site's former inhabitants encountered in

A. Alder pollen (*Alnus serrulata*)

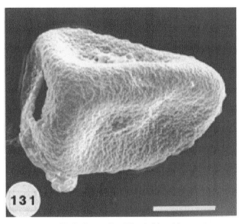

B. Sedge pollen (*Carex blanda*)

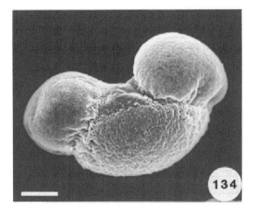

C. Pine pollen (*Pinus glabra*)

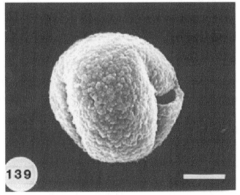

D. Oak pollen (*Quercus falcata*)

FIGURE 9.2 Examples of pollen grains: alder (Alnus serrulata), sedge (Carex blanda), pine (Pinus glabra), and oak (Quercus falcata). (Courtesy Gretchen D. Jones, USDA-ARS, APMRU)

their territory and had available for exploitation: to eat, make containers, weave mats, build houses, make rope, burn for fuel, and so on. Beyond simply putting together a list of plant resources in an area during a particular time period, such information may be a preliminary step in reconstructing the overall environment, especially the climate of an area when a site was occupied. Many plant species have a relatively narrow range of acceptable environmental conditions in which they can survive. The presence of a plant species in a place where it cannot now grow—because the current conditions are too hot or too cold, too dry or too wet—is a good indicator that the climate was different when the site was occupied.

WHAT IS A POLLEN PROFILE?

A far more detailed picture of an ancient climate can be constructed not by simply putting together a species list from pollen grains recovered in a cultural layer in a stratigraphic sequence but by producing a **pollen profile**, in which the actual percentages of recovered pollen grains are calculated for a succession of time periods. Of course, it would be great if these pollen percentages could be neatly and directly translated into species percentages—for example, if 30% of the pollen found falling on a site during a given period was that of pine trees, it would mean that 30% of the vegetation in the vicinity of a site was pine trees—but it doesn't work out that way. Some species produce proportionally larger amounts of pollen than do others (pine is one of them), and the pollen of some species is more aerodynamic and flies farther when airborne (pine again). In fact, pine pollen may show up in a given place, even though there are no pine trees in the immediate vicinity, simply because pine trees produce an overabundance of pollen that can travel great distances on the wind. The percentage of pollen at a given place, therefore, is not simply the result of the abundance of the species, but a complex interplay of factors. Species abundance (what we need to assess to reconstruct a local plant community and an ancient environment) is only one factor in the equation.

Brilliant solutions to scientific quandaries often rely on elegant workarounds. Palynologists, especially Margaret Davis of Yale, devised a brilliant, simple, and elegant solution to the pollen problem. Instead of attempting to come up with a complex and convoluted way to convert pollen percentages to actual tree or plant percentages directly, Davis (1969a, 1969b) simply took the pollen percentages recovered from ancient strata and compared those figures to the percentages of pollen raining in various locations *today*. Palynologists have calculated modern pollen percentages the same way they figure the pollen count announced on the evening news, using sticky tape to capture modern pollen floating through the air. Where the pollen percentages in the modern and ancient samples were similar, Davis concluded that the ancient and modern plant communities were similar, and, therefore, the ancient climate was similar to the modern location with a similar pollen profile.

For example, Davis collected a series of soil cores from the bottom of Roger's Lake in southeastern Connecticut. She recognized a number of natural strata in the cores and determined their ages by radiocarbon dating organic material

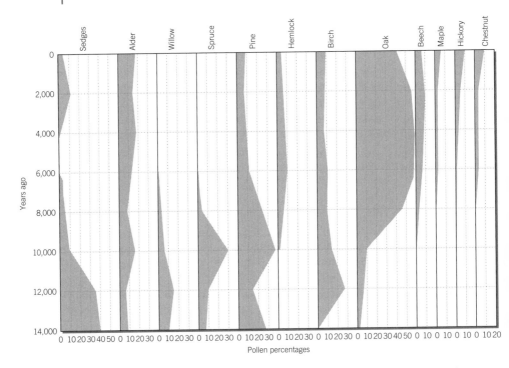

FIGURE 9.3 The pollen profile at Roger's Lake, southeastern Connecticut, showing a dramatic change in the local plant communities over the last 14,000 years. (K. L. Feder)

that had been preserved in the various layers of the soil column. Davis then recovered pollen from each of the column's strata and counted the grains, deriving the percentages of pollen for a bunch of different species in each of the strata in the core, which she then depicted in a graph (Figure 9.3). With these percentages in hand, Davis searched for areas in eastern North America (where Roger's Lake is located) where the modern pollen percentages appeared to be most similar to those she calculated for each of the ancient dated strata.

The **pollen rain** falling on Roger's Lake around 14,000 years ago doesn't match up at all with the modern rain falling at its location today. In fact, today one would have to go far to the north, about as far north as you can go in Arctic Canada, to find a plant community producing a mix of pollen percentages similar to what was falling on Roger's Lake and vicinity 14,000 years ago (Figure 9.4). In the 12,000-year-old stratum from the Roger's Lake core, a mix of pollen percentages was derived that closely matches the profile that today falls in the central region of the east shore of Hudson's Bay. From the 10,000-year level in the Roger's Lake core, a mix of pollen was falling that is similar to what today is found around Lake Ontario. It wasn't until the 8,000-year-old level that Davis found a mix of pollen similar to what was falling on Roger's Lake in modern times, if we define modern times as about A.D. 1600, before Europeans entered the region, cleared huge swaths of Connecticut's forests,

FIGURE 9.4 The pollen falling on Roger's Lake, in southeastern Connecticut between 14,000 and 12,000 years ago matches in its makeup and percentages, the pollen that currently falls in the northernmost regions of Canada, in, in fact, the Canadian tundra. The climate there today is a good match for what the climate must have been like in southeastern Connecticut in the period between 14,000 and 12,000 years ago.

and introduced new plants and crops to the area (Figure 9.5). Yes, humans, too, have an impact on the plant communities of a region, and the pollen profile is just one example.

Of course, there are complications in the process of reconstructing an ancient climate through the use of palynology. While our hope is to find a close match between an ancient pollen profile and the modern pollen rain of a particular place, researchers sometimes recover profiles with no modern analogues, because sometimes there is no place on Earth today with plant communities and climates that are a close match for a particular time and place in the past.

Beyond this, plant communities and their attendant pollen profiles may change through time without climate being the primary factor. For instance, the biological phenomenon of succession can also explain changes in plant communities through time. An area denuded of plant life by, for example, a massive flood, a volcanic eruption, or intentional clearing by people for agriculture or construction may ultimately see a "succession" of plant species colonize, thrive, and then ultimately be replaced by a series of other species until a stable population is established. So-called pioneer species are the first to begin growing but may become pushed out by secondary growth, which may be, in

FIGURE 9.5 The modern vegetation that blankets the Farmington Valley in central Connecticut is a result of a combination of climate and culture. (K. L. Feder)

turn, replaced by a more permanent mix of climax species. Palynologists are, of course, aware of this process and consider succession a possible explanation of the change in a pollen profile through time. Despite this complication, it is nevetheless the case that when modern analogues are available and when pollen implies relative stability of plant communities, palynolgy provides a firm basis for reconstructing those communities and the climates that supported them.

What would it have been like to live in southeastern Connecticut 14,000 years ago? What was the weather like? What kinds of plants were growing? How long were the various seasons? How much did it snow? What animals would have been attracted to the conditions that characterized the area? A visit to the Arctic coast of northeastern Canada provides the best model for southeast Connecticut 15 millennia ago. How about 12,000 years ago? According to pollen analysis, we can begin to answer this question by traveling north to the east shore of Hudson's Bay and examining current conditions there. And 10,000 years ago? The north shore of Lake Ontario provides the best analogue to answer our questions.

Look at Figure 9.6. It's a map showing the general boundaries of the major **biomes** that characterize North America. Biomes represent geographical regions in which live distinct communities of plants and animals adapted to a suite of particular environmental conditions. The biomes of North America

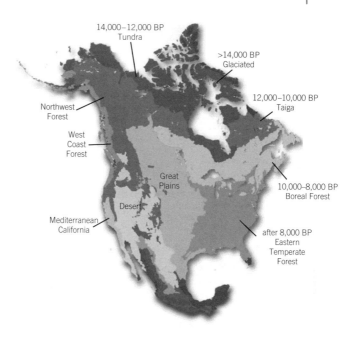

FIGURE 9.6 This map of the biomes of North America, combined with the Roger's Lake pollen profile, provides us with a series of environmental portraits of Connecticut through time.

14,000–12,000 BP
Tundra

>14,000 BP
Glaciated

12,000–10,000 BP
Taiga

Northwest Forest

West Coast Forest

Great Plains

10,000–8,000 BP
Boreal Forest

Desert

Mediterranean California

after 8,000 BP
Eastern Temperate Forest

include tundra, taiga, boreal forest, temperate deciduous forest, grassland and savanna, tropical forest, and desert and semidesert. Within each of the biomes that characterize northeastern North America, I have inserted a range of years. These ranges represent the period during which the conditions that characterize each of these modern biomes were prevalent in southeastern Connecticut; in other words, each time range represents the period when the pollen falling on Rogers Lake is a close match for the modern pollen produced by the plant communities in each of those biomes. Human beings living in southeastern Connecticut in particular and southern New England in general were faced with the environmental conditions similar to those in each of those biomes.

Chapter 9:
Slide Show

Remember, the environment, including the climate as well as the plant and animal communities that characterize a location, provide the context for human adaptation. The environment cannot cause people to behave in a certain way, but it certainly produces limits and possibilities. If we hope to understand the cultural adaptation of a past people, we need to illuminate the setting of that adaptation; we need to understand the conditions to which a past people adapted. So understanding an ancient environment is crucial to our understanding of an ancient culture.

Palynology is an important tool in this effort. Pollen analysis can provide archaeologists with a detailed picture of the plant community with which an ancient human community interacted, along with insights into the nature of the climate that defined the plant community and to which human groups developed cultural adaptations.

Read More

To find out more about the procedures of pollen recovery and analysis, and for examples of Margaret Davis's work in Connecticut, see the following sources.

Bryant, V. M. Jr., and R. G. Holloway. 1983. The Role of Palynology in Archaeology. In *Advances in Archaeological Method and Theory*, edited by M. B. Schiffer, 191–224. Academic Press, New York.

Davis, M. B. 1969a. Climatic Changes in Southern Connecticut Recorded by Pollen Deposition at Rogers Lake. *Ecology* 50:409–22.

———. 1969b. Palynology and Environmental History During the Quaternary Period. *American Scientist* 57:317–32.

Dimbleby, G. W. 1985. *The Palynology of Archaeological Sites*. Academic Press, London.

Holloway, R. G. 1997. Excavation and Recovery of Botanical Materials from Archaeological Sites. In *Field Methods in Archaeology*, edited by T. R. Hester, H. J. Shafer, and K. L. Feder, 283–97. Mayfield Publishing, Mountain View, California.

Pearsall, D. M. 2000. *Paleoethnobotany: A Handbook of Procedures*. Academic Press, San Diego.

How Can You Identify Tree Species from Bits of Burned Wood?

It can be hard enough to distinguish one tree from another when walking around in a living forest. I do OK, at least in the spring and summer, when the trees in the mixed deciduous forest of southern New England where I live and work are decked out in their leafy finery. Maple, oak, birch, and hickory all produce leaves that are distinct and easy to identify after a little practice. Among the conifers, hemlocks are easily differentiated from pine, which is easy to discriminate from spruce, which is nothing like larch.

Come fall, however, things get a lot more challenging for me. The conifers are still pretty easy, but once I get past white birch with its uniquely colored bark, I am pretty much clueless when it comes to separating out the deciduous trees. Without their leaves, I am lost. Good tree identification guides provide photographs of leaves, fruits or nuts, and the bark of each species, and that can be quite helpful (Little 1987), but imagine how incredibly more complicated this process of tree identification becomes when we have no leaves or bark, in fact, no living trees at all, but just little fragments of wood and, on top of this, these little pieces of wood have been preserved only because they have been burned.

In fact, however, the wood produced by individual genera and sometimes individual species of trees certainly is distinguishable, especially in terms of its microstructure. With the use of reference slides, specimen collections, and photomicrographs, analysts can identify tree species even from small burned fragments (McWeeney 2002).

For example, burned wood samples recovered from the occupation surfaces of two sites we excavated in the past few years were provided to our botanical specialist, Dr. Cindy McWeeney. McWeeney was able to identify the wood of chestnut, oak, and hickory from two sites dating to more than 1,000 years ago

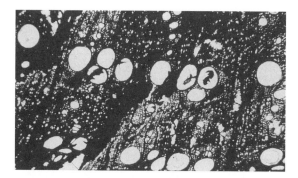

FIGURE 9.7 Cross-section of a sample of oak charcoal exhibiting morphological characteristics diagnostic of wood derived from the genus Quercus (oak). (Courtesy Cindy McWeeney)

(Figure 9.7). Because we know that these were not the only three tree species growing in southern New England at the time, we can suggest that the presence of just these three species in the charcoal assemblage resulted from a conscious decision on the part of the ancient inhabitants of the sites. They were selecting, in fact, three tree species that are known to produce a high, even, and steady output of heat. In fact, those of us who use wood to heat our houses know that hardwoods are much better for their steady heat output (and their lower production of creosote to gum up our chimneys).

Identifying the species of trees whose wood was used as fuel in a hearth, fireplace, or kiln provides us with a glimpse into the makeup of a forest in which a past people lived or to which they traveled for its resources. Knowing the tree species selected by a past people also provides insights into their behavior, offering a glimpse into their uses of the resources in their environment.

Read More

The following guide is a standard for identifying wood remains.

Hoadley, R. B. 1990. *Identifying Wood: Accurate Results with Simple Tools*. Taunton Press, Newtown, Connecticut.

Study Questions

1. What is the purpose of environmental reconstruction? Remembering that human beings adapt to their environments, why do archaeologists want to know about the environments of the past?

2. What is pollen? How can pollen be used to reconstruct the plant communities that flourished at a particular place in antiquity?

3. What is a pollen profile?

4. Can pollen percentages recovered at or near an ancient archaeological site be used to directly determine the percentages of various species of plants growing nearby? (I'll give you a hint: No.) Why not?

5. How did Margaret Davis use the pollen percentages she calculated for an ancient time period in the reconstruction of an ancient environment?

6. The pollen rain at Roger's Lake in southeastern Connecticut changed drastically after A.D. 1600, even though there is no evidence of a significant climate change at this time. What else might explain the change in the pollen rain at Roger's Lake at the cusp of the seventeenth century?

7. How can we know what tree species were used for fuel in an ancient fire? (I mean besides sending them to Cindy McWeeney.) Why might we want to know what kinds of wood were being used by ancient people?

10

Technology

HOW PEOPLE MADE THINGS

- **How Do Archaeologists Figure Out How Ancient People Made Things?**

  How Did Ancient People Make Stone Tools?
  What Are the Characteristics That Make a Rock Type Attractive to Stone Tool Makers?

- **Why Is Pottery of Such Great Importance to Archaeologists?**

  How Do You Make a Pot?

- **How Can You Determine the Source of a Raw Material Used by Ancient People?**

- **How Do Archaeologists Figure Out the Function of an Ancient Tool?**

- **How Do Archaeologists Examine Tools Made of Raw Materials Other Than Stone or Clay?**

- **How Do Archaeologists Investigate the Technology of Monumental Construction?**

An enormous chasm separates modern people, including people with higher degrees in anthropology, from the ancient folks whose lives we anthropologists hope to illuminate. We are separated from the people at Wood Lily and by all the other past peoples invesigated by archaeologists not by intellectual capacity (ancient, anatomically modern human beings were as intelligent as modern people and had our same potential to figure things out), but by vast stretches of time, unimaginably different environments, and at times seemingly irreconcilable cultural differences. Archaeologists attempt to bridge this chasm by recovering elements of the material cultures of the ancient peoples and by developing various strategies to unlock the secrets coded into those objects. We collect lots of direct evidence in the form of end products of the tool making technologies of ancient peoples (for example, we find their spear points and pots). How, though, do we figure out the often complex technological processes involved by studying the end results?

How Do Archaeologists Figure Out How Ancient People Made Things?

The term *back-engineering* is used to identify the sneaky strategy by which modern industries attempt to discover how their competitors manufacture their products—and then incorporate those methods into their own products. Essentially, back-engineering is figuring out how your competitor made a product by obtaining it and then taking it apart to figure out how your competitor put together the product in the first place.

FIGURE 10.1 Beautifully made spear point recovered at the 5,000-year-old Alsop Meadow site located in Avon, Connecticut.

Archaeologists employ a form of back-engineering to figure out how ancient peoples made their tools. We examine the end products of ancient technologies along with abandoned steps in the process (half-finished spear points, broken pieces of unfinished pottery, abandoned or incomplete construction projects), and then we try to put the technological process back together. For example, the process of making stone tools, specifically spear points, often proceeds in a series of steps beginning with the removal of a sizeable flake from a core by striking that core with a **hammerstone** in the process called **percussion flaking.** Once removed from the core, the large flake can be thinned by additional percussion, though this may be accomplished with a softer hammer, such as the blunt end of a piece of deer or elk antler. The soft hammer may be used for additional shaping as well, making the spear point symmetrical and assuring an aerodynamic quality to the projectile. Finally, the edge may be thinned to razor sharpness, and notches may be fashioned on the base to facilitate hafting onto a wooden shaft. The tool maker accomplishes these tasks not by percussion but by direct application of pressure with the pointed tip of a hard antler tine in the process called **pressure flaking.** Though each step in this process may obscure or eliminate many or even most of the scars left by earlier steps, a careful examination of the finished spear point (or knife, scraping tool, drill, saw, or engraving tool) often reveals some elements of the flaking patterns of those earlier steps (Figure 10.1).

Ethnography and **ethnohistory** may also provide information helpful in the reconstruction of an ancient technology. For example, although the manufacture of stone tools may be an alien technology to most of us, there are people— perhaps not in the present but in the not-so-distant past—for whom making stone tools was a crucial part of life. One of the most famous examples is a man by the name of Ishi. Ishi was a Yahi Indian living a traditional way of life until he was found near death in northern California in 1911 (Kroeber, Kroeber, and Gannett 2002). Ishi was a highly skilled stone tool maker, one of the few Native Americans in North America in the early twentieth century who still possessed this traditional skill. After being nursed back to health, Ishi spent the rest of his short life (he died in 1916) sharing his skills with interested scientists (Figure 10.2). It would not be an exaggeration to say that we owe to Ishi much of what we know about stone tool making in general among Native Americans (you can find photos of some of the tools Ishi made at http://hearstmuseum.berkeley.edu/exhibitions/ncc/4_2_2.html).

Finally, archaeologists also employ a hands-on approach to the analysis of tool making technologies in a process called **experimental archaeology.** Combining the information decrypted from ancient tools and provided by ethnography and ethnohistory, some researchers have attempted to recover ancient tool making

FIGURE 10.2 Ishi making stone tools using the pressure technique. Ishi's knowledge continues to contribute to our scientific understanding of stone tool making. (Phoebe Hearst Museum of Anthropology)

technologies through trial and error by actually trying to make the tools themselves (Coles 1997). Employing authentic raw materials, archaeologists have experimented with various methods and produced some stunningly accurate replicas of ancient tools. In Europe François Bordes spent much of his professional life decoding ancient stone tool technologies and then testing his conclusions by actually applying them through replication. In America Don Crabtree (1982) was responsible for solving many of the mysteries of stone tool making, again through the process of actually applying various methods and deducing which were the most likely to have been used by ancient peoples. Dozens of Bordes's and Crabtree's students—and dozens upon dozens of subsequent generations of archaeologists—continue to refine the knowledge base developed by these mentors. Today archaeologist and lithics expert Bruce Bradley, among many others, carries on in the tradition of Bordes and Crabtree, replicating stone tools and passing down this recaptured skill to the next generation of lithic replicators (http://www.primtech.net/; Figure 10.3).

I teach a course in experimental archaeology, focusing on stone tool replication. Through the course, students engage in an extremely valuable experience.

FIGURE 10.3 Ancient technology expert Bruce Bradley is shown using an antler hammer as a percussor to remove flakes from a nodule of stone in the process of stone tool making. (Courtesy Bruce Bradley)

Clearly, those who have actually spent time attempting to make stone tools have an enormous conceptual advantage in archaeological fieldwork. Students who have made stone tools have a much easier time recognizing lithic artifacts, particularly waste flakes, in the field than do those who haven't. When you spend an entire semester producing dozens of tools and thousands of fragments of debitage, you get a very good feel for what such flakes look like compared to stone broken by natural processes. Students also gain a unique perspective: They recognize the specific features of stone tools and their manufacturing waste products recovered at an ancient site because they have produced nearly identical stuff with their own hands. And, I have to admit, it is a real charge to

FIGURE 10.4 Replicating one of the trilithons at Stonehenge involved moving two 50-ton, 24-feet-tall slabs of concrete (top), erecting them (bottom), and then raising a 16-ton lintel to rest on top. All the twentieth-century workers on the project came away with an enormous amount of respect for the abilities of people who lived nearly 5,000 years ago. (Courtesy Horizon, BBC Science)

find instances in which ancient peoples experienced the same problems with a rock and sometimes made the same mistakes that you make on a regular basis.

Experimental archaeology is not just about stone tools. Experiments have been conducted in ancient pottery making, in house construction, in musical instrument making, in cooking, in fact, in every imaginable art, craft, and technology

FIGURE 10.5 A sample of the results of replicative experiments conducted by my students: Upper Paleolithic cave painting (upper left), Venus figurine (upper right), West African wooden mask (center), eighteenth-century New England Native American war club (bottom left), miniature pine needle mat (bottom right).

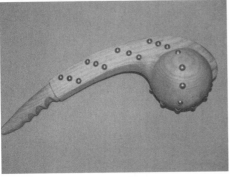

(Coles 1997). A series of large-scale experiments was conducted for public television and aired in Great Britain and the United States. The videos are great fun and include experiments in which a small replica of an Egyptian pyramid was built (Barnes 1997c), an Egyptian obelisk was erected (Barnes 1997b), Inca stone masonry was replicated (Barnes 1997a), the Roman Colosseum was assessed (Page and Cort 1997a), and one of the Stonehenge trilithons (two large upright slabs, each weighing 100,000 pounds, with a smaller cross piece balanced on top of the two uprights) was replicated (Page and Cort 1997b: Figure 10.4).

FIGURE 10.6 Archaeological experiments in which replicas are used to generate additional data about ancient technologies: grinding corn into meal in a stone metate (upper left), shooting a ballista (an ancient Greek weapon of mass destruction, upper right), starting a fire with a bow drill (center), launching a spear with an atlatl (lower left), shooting a bow and arrow (lower right).

The term project for each student in my experimental archaeology course requires them to go beyond replicating individual categories of stone tools and to carry out a more complex experiment. OK, they don't build six-meter-high replicas of Egyptian pyramids nor do they attempt to move 40,000 kilogram replicas of Stonehenge's trilithons, but they do some pretty amazing work, including the replication of Upper Paleolithic cave paintings, Venus figurines, fire-starting kits, and ancient Greece siege weapons (Figure 10.5). Archaeological experiments, however, are about far more than simply producing authentic-looking replicas. The goal of experimental archaeology is also to investigate and test ancient technologies. For example, among other things, my students have conducted time studies (how long does it take to produce a war club?); they have done efficiency studies (how finely can corn meal be ground using a stone mano and metate?); they have measured the light levels produced by replicas of Upper Paleolithic oil lamps based on lamps found in European painted caves; and they have compared the distance and accuracy of replicas of spear throwing devices (called atlatls by the Aztecs) and bows and arrows (Figure 10.6). Ultimately, it must be admitted that while it is a scientifically valuable approach, experimental archaeology also is great fun, providing both an intellectual and a visceral appreciation for the technological abilities of past peoples.

Chapter 10:
Slide Show

Read More

Experimental archaeology provides insights about ancient technologies in a way that no other analytical process can. To learn more about the ways in which archaeologists—and historians and engineers and musicians and so on—have employed experimental archaeology, read any of the following books and view the videos.

Barnes, M. 1997a. Inca. In *Secrets of Lost Empires. Nova*. WGBH, Boston.
————. 1997b. Obelisk. In *Secrets of Lost Empires. Nova*. WGBH, Boston.
————. 1997c. Pyramid. In *Secrets of Lost Empires. Nova*. WGBH, Boston.
Coles, J. M. 1997. *Experimental Archaeology*. Academic Press, London.
Crabtree, D. E. 1982. *An Introduction to Flint Working*. Idaho Museum of Natural History, Pocatello.
Kroeber, T., K. Kroeber, and L. Gannett. 2002. *Ishi in Two Worlds: A Biography of the Last Wild Indian in North America*. University of California Press, Berkeley.
Page, C., and J. Cort. 1997a. Colosseum. In *Secrets of Lost Empires. Nova*. WGBH, Boston.
————. 1997b. Stonehenge. In *Secrets of Lost Empires. Nova*. WGBH, Boston.

How Did Ancient People Make Stone Tools?

Archaeologists—most of us, anyway—love rocks. It's an occupational hazard. In many parts of the world (southern New England where I work is a good example) rocks are just about the only raw material that lasts well for long periods of time. Long after the wooden spears, splint baskets, hide clothing, bark containers, and woven mats have decayed to dust, the hornfels points that tipped those wooden spears, the flint knives used to cut the splints to make the baskets, the quartz scrapers used to prepare the animal hide for leggings, breechcloths, or tunics, and the microliths used to cut the reeds for weaving have been preserved, sometimes still sharp enough to apply to their intended tasks thousands of years after they were made. We like stone tools and expend an enormous part of our intellectual energy thinking about how such tools were made and used. This chapter focuses on the results of that intellectual labor. And as the t-shirt given me at the end of a field school a few years ago maintains, *Love Is Fleeting But Stone Tools Are Forever.*

Needless to say, as a result of the fact that most of what many archaeologists find are the durable stone tools people in the past made and used, we spend a lot of time attempting to figure out ways of coaxing information out of those tools. It is why I focus on stone tools in this chapter. As mentioned earlier, researchers approach this question of the manufacture of ancient stone tools in three ways: (1) by examining the tools for traces of their various manufacturing steps (the back-engineering approach), (2) by examining similar technologies practiced by people who lived in the not-too-distant past (ethnographic and ethnohistorical research), and (3) by experimental replication. More than a century of such research, particularly in terms of replication, has resulted in a vast body of knowledge related to the manufacture of stone tools in particular, resulting in a detailed vocabulary (Crabtree 1982) and a tremendous amount of experience in actually making stone tools. In a sense, twentieth- and twenty-first-century scholars have, by the careful examination of archaeological specimens, trial and error, and ethnohistorical research, reinvented and, it is hoped, authentically recaptured ancient stone working technologies.

Stone work begins with a nucleus of stone, a core of good, chippable rock. It helps if the core has facets (distinct sides or faces, such as in a cut gemstone) at least a couple of which meet at an angle of less than 90 degrees (a rounded, upside-down cone of rock with a flat top is ideal for many purposes). In the process of **percussion flaking**, the **knapper** applies force with a **percussor**, which can be a **hammerstone**, usually a spherical nodule of rock that comfortably fits in the dominant hand, or a propitiously shaped antler baton or hammer. The percussor does not need to be harder than the core because geometry, not just hardness, controls breakage. A rounded hammerstone, a rock without the facets or angles you look for in a core, can be extremely durable and nearly indestructible. Such a hammerstone can easily break flakes of stone from a harder rock that does have facets or angles.

With the hammerstone held in the dominant hand—right hand for righties, left hand for lefties—and holding the core or **object piece** in the other, the tool maker strikes the core at the margin of one of its flat surfaces, called a **striking platform**, near to where it forms a less-than-90-degree angle with another of its faces (Figure 10.7). The **angle of applied force** (determined as the angle between the striking platform and the trajectory of the hammerstone as it strikes the core) can vary and controls whether the flake is short and thin (an acute angle of applied force) or long and thicker (an angle of applied force closer to, but not exceeding, 90 degrees). When struck correctly, the force of the blow moves down through the interior of the core, close to the face of the rock. If strong enough, the force exceeds the **elastic limit** of the rock and literally

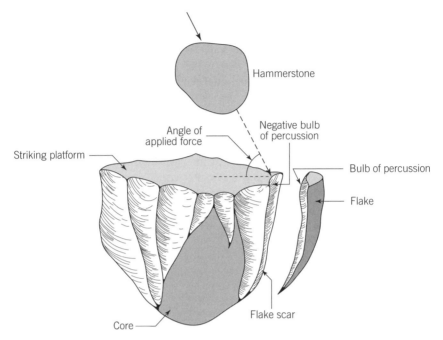

FIGURE 10.7 Removal of a stone flake from a core. The consistent application of a percussive strike with a hammerstone on the platform of the core can produce a large number of consistently sized and shaped sharp flakes that can be used as is or further worked into specific tools. (K. L. Feder)

peels a thin, sharp flake from the core. This process can be repeated many times, and a large number of similar flakes can be removed from the core.

These stone flakes may be extremely sharp and can even be used without further modification as cutting, piercing, or scraping tools (Figure 10.8). If, however, the desire is to craft a symmetrical, more complex tool (perhaps one that is aerodynamic and intended for use as a projectile tip or point of a spear, dart, or arrow), additional work needs to be accomplished. Some additional thinning and shaping may be necessary, and the knapper may shift to a smaller hammerstone or a softer percussor, such as the blunt end of an antler. Further edge straightening and thinning may be done by **pressure flaking**, whereby the pointy end of an antler, called the tine, is aligned against the edge, force is applied simply by pressing against the edge, and small flakes are literally pushed off the faces of the larger "parent" flake (Figure 10.9). The overall shape of the parent flake can be modified in this way, the edges can be straightened and thinned where needed, and a piece of work clearly recognizable as the result of human craft can be produced. Finally, if the tool maker desires, notches can be carved at the base of the tool in order to facilitate hafting onto a wooden or reed shaft. The notches can be produced by additional pressure flaking.

Stone tool making is anything but easy for a modern person to perfect. After all, unlike our ancient counterparts, we haven't been rehearsing the skill

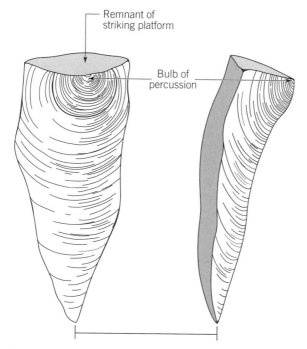

Remnant of
striking platform

Bulb of
percussion

FIGURE 10.8 Drawing of a long flake of stone removed from a rock that exhibits a pattern of conchoidal fracture. The force of the blow that detached the flake from the rock passed through like ripples on a pond, leaving remnants of those ripples on the surface of the flake. (K. L. Feder)

since childhood. In my experimental archaeology course, I first have the students attempt to replicate the oldest tools made by our hominid ancestors. The industry is called **Oldowan** after their place of discovery, Olduvai Gorge in eastern Africa. It takes my students some time to produce respectable, big, crude chopping tools and sharp slicing flakes that would be recognized as fairly legitimate by an actual member of the species *Homo habilis*, the makers of such tools as much as 2.5 million years ago. Students usually get pretty excited by their new skill until I remind them that *Homo habilis* had a brain size less than half that of a modern human being. That pretty much dissuades most of my students from taking their chopping tools home and putting them on their refrigerators. It is fair to say, however, that there are some lithic specialists in archaeology today who are masters of the craft and who can fabricate stone tools that are the technological and artistic equal of any produced in the ancient world. Bruce Bradley is one of those knappers, having attained a remarkable level of mastery of the art of stone tool making. Some of his handiwork is on display at his homepage (http://www.primtech.net/), where visitors also can purchase a videotape demonstrating, as words cannot possibly adequately convey, the fascinating process of making stone tools.

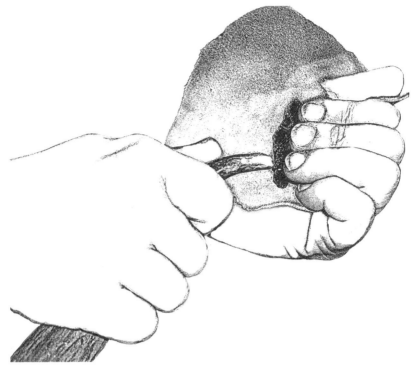

FIGURE 10.9 Pressure flaking involves the application of, rather obviously, pressure along the margins of a flake to thin (and, therefore, sharpen) the flake's edge or to alter the edge to a desired shape. (K. L. Feder)

Read More

Obviously, you cannot become a proficient replicator of stone tools by reading a couple of books or by viewing a videotape. But it's a start, and any of the following resources will provide you with some intellectual insights into the process:

Bradley, B. 1989. *Flintknapping.* Produced by INTERpark and Primitive Tech. Enterprises. Cortex, Colorado.

Crabtree, D. E. 1982. *An Introduction to Flint Working.* Idaho Museum of Natural History, Pocatello.

Kooyman, B. P. 2002. *Understanding Stone Tools and Archaeological Sites.* University of New Mexico Press, Albuquerque.

Whittaker, J. C. 1994. *Flintknapping: Making and Understanding Stone Tools.* University of Texas Press, Austin.

WHAT ARE THE CHARACTERISTICS THAT MAKE A ROCK TYPE ATTRACTIVE TO STONE TOOL MAKERS?

No later than about 2.5 million years ago, and probably substantially before this, our most ancient hominid ancestors had recognized that by manipulating objects in their environment they could make tools that were sharper, stronger, harder, and more durable than those that nature had provided them in the form of their teeth, fingernails, and muscles. Stone was among the first of the raw materials that these ancient ancestors relied on for the production of sharp and durable edges for cutting, piercing, scraping, sawing, pounding, and grinding.

It is clear from the archaeological record that these pioneers in stone tool technology learned that not all rock types were equal in how easily they could be made into useful tools, in how sharp an edge could be produced, and in how durable those sharp edges were. These most ancient ancestors became, in a sense, "experimental geologists" who figured out by trial and error, on the one hand, which rocks were too difficult to break or too soft or crumbly to make into useful tools and, on the other hand, which rocks broke in predictable and consistent ways, producing desirably thin, sharp, and durable working edges. By studying ancient artifacts and identifying the particular rock types used by peoples in different times and places to make chipped stone tools and by experimenting with those same rock types in an effort to replicate the stone tool making process, archaeologists have identified the key characteristics that made a lithic raw material attractive to tool makers (Crabtree 1982; Kooyman 2002; Luedtke 1992; Whittaker 1994).

The best rock types for making cutting, piercing, and scraping tools are **vitreous**, or glasslike. At some point during your childhood, you probably dropped a glass or a bottle on a hard surface, it shattered, and your mother or father was panicstricken, concerned that you might badly cut yourself on the sharp glass shards. Indeed, glass tends to break into very thin, extremely sharp fragments which, though dangerous to a barefoot kid who has just broken a drinking glass, is exactly the attribute someone making a spear point or butchering tool would find advantageous. In fact, making stone tools can be likened to controlled glass breakage.

Along with producing very thin, sharp edges when it breaks, glass also breaks consistently and predictably. It exhibits **conchoidal** fracture, in which an applied force literally flows through the homogeneous material like ripples across a pond (see Figure 10.8). The stone tool maker takes advantage of the consistent and predictable way that a force passes through materials that exhibit this fracture pattern to control the size and shape of the resulting flake.

If you consistently strike with a hard object a piece of glass or a glasslike rock (1) that has a less-than-90-degree angle between the surface you are striking (the striking platform) and the surface from which the flake is actually being removed and (2) with a consistent amount of force (3) at the same distance away from the intersection of the striking platform and the surface from which the flake is being removed, and (4) if you apply that force by striking or pressing the rock at a consistent angle (the angle of applied force), you will produce flakes of a consistent size and shape. After a lot of practice, a knapper can predict with a great degree of accuracy the size and shape of a flake before the core is struck and then can control the size and shape of the flake to be removed by altering the angle at which the force is applied and the precise point of impact between the hammer and the core. Bruce Bradley, an archaeologist and a lithic technology expert, has produced a terrific video that takes the viewer through the steps of making stone tools (Bradley 1989). At one point in the video, Bradley draws an outline on a sheet of paper of the tool he intends to make, a bifacially flaked spear point with side notches to aid in hafting the stone tip onto a wooden shaft. After completing the work, he superimposes the end product on the drawing he made before he began knapping. Like all great knappers, Bradley nitpicks his own work, but, in truth, the tool is a remarkably good, if not perfect, match. One point of this exercise is to show that stone tool manufacturing is not a random or informal process. An experienced stone tool maker doesn't simply smash two rocks together and hope for the best. Instead, tool making is a highly controlled and predictable process—well, for people with the skill of Bruce Bradley, anyway.

Nature produces a form of glass in volcanoes. Usually black and translucent along thin edges, **obsidian** is a remarkable and remarkably beautiful natural material. Obsidian was an important raw material for making stone tools wherever ancient peoples could find it, though its sharp edges can be very delicate and will break quite easily. Some other rock types are glasslike but to lesser degrees than obsidian. Flint, chalcedony, jasper, and chert are not natural glass but consist of tiny crystals cemented together. The crystals in these rock types are so small they are invisible to the naked eye and are described as **cryptocrystalline** (literally, "hidden crystals"). Because the crystals in cryptocrystalline rocks are so small, an applied force is not diverted along the intersections of the crystals as it passes through the stone, as is the case in rock types such as quartzite, in which the individual crystals that make up the rock are much larger (Luedtke 1992). As a result, the knapper—and not the rock—has a great deal of control over how the force he or she applies passes through the stone and, therefore, how the stone breaks. Cryptocrystalline rocks also exhibit conchoidal fracture. An applied force passes through them in a controllable fashion, enabling experienced knappers to peel consistently sized and shaped thin, sharp flakes off a struck core. These rocks also are useful raw materials for stone tool makers.

Read More

To find out more about the technical qualities that make a rock attractive to the stone tool maker, check out the following resources. Crabtree's venerable *An Introduction to Flint Working* is, essentially, a dictionary of terms and still the best place to start on this subject. Bradley's video will leave you in awe of his skill, and you will come away with a visceral appreciation for the intelligence it took for our ancestors to invent stone tool technology.

Bradley, B. 1989. *Flintknapping*, Produced by INTERpark and Primitive Tech. Enterprises. Cortez, Colorado.

Crabtree, D. E. 1982. *An Introduction to Flint Working*. Idaho Museum of Natural History, Pocatello.

Kooyman, B. P. 2002. *Understanding Stone Tools and Archaeological Sites*. University of New Mexico Press, Albuquerque.

Luedtke, B. E. 1992. *An Archaeologist's Guide to Chert and Flint*. Archaeological Research Tools 7. University of California Press, Los Angeles.

Whittaker, J. C. 1994. *Flintknapping: Making and Understanding Stone Tools*. University of Texas Press, Austin.

Why Is Pottery of Such Great Importance to Archaeologists?

I learned stone tool replication in graduate school where my lithic Yoda was Terry del Bene; be one with the rock and all that. That was more than thirty years ago, meaning that I have "knocked rocks" for about half my life. Though I make no claim at being particularly proficient at it, I enjoy it and spend much of the semester in my experimental archaeology course teaching lithic replication. Beyond my dabbling in Play-Doh in kindergarten and an ashtray I made in the third grade, however, until recently my knowledge about ceramics was indirect; I had never actually attempted to make anything out of clay. That changed in early 2002, when I enrolled in an adult beginner ceramics class at the Canton Clayworks, a local ceramics studio in Canton, Connecticut.

For the first month or so of my indoctrination to ceramics, I was convinced that I had reached my peak in ceramic ability back in kindergarten and with the ashtray I had made (and that my mother still has), but slowly my eyes, hands, and brain began to work together. I actually began to produce some bowls, plates, and mugs that, though artistically uninspired, actually looked more or less as I intended. There are a number of teachers at the studio, some of whom teach sculptural ceramics (where forms are built by hand), but most students learn wheel throwing from master potter and owner of the Clayworks, Tim Scull. The funny thing is, when you look around at the student projects at the studio and then you look at Tim's pots, you can tell he is our teacher. Tim likes delicate forms with thin walls. He emphasizes technical skill in his pots and insists that his students do the same. Each of our plates, bowls, and mugs have to be made with at least one "foot" and in the case of plates two feet. This means that the bottoms of our pots are never flat but have raised surfaces that diminish the possibility that the pot will stick to the kiln shelf when it is glaze fired. Tim likes traditional Asian ceramic forms and makes a lot of them; sure enough, many of Tim's students attempt ("attempt" is the operative word here) to emulate their teacher. Because the kilns represent a substantial financial investment, Tim insists on controlling the raw materials that he fires. Clay or glaze purchased elsewhere are unknown quantities, and to protect his investment, Tim is in charge of what gets fired in his kilns; everyone in the studio uses clays and glazes Tim provides.

Consider the variables in ceramic manufacture I just touched on: the manufacturing technique itself (hand building or wheel throwing); the source of the clay; the styles of the pots, including the forms made and designs applied; the finishing of the base; the firing in a particular kind of kiln; and the glazes used. Together, these variables reflect the conditions in one studio and probably will not match precisely the mix of variables at any other studio. In the modern setting, a ceramics expert examining the output of the studio and comparing it to the ceramics produced at other schools would notice such differences—and so would an archaeologist comparing the ceramics produced by ancient peoples.

In fact, Tim is creating an archaeological site. Canton Clayworks is located in a rural town and is surrounded by trees, with a little brook running down the hill at the back of the property. As I have come to learn through the unhappy lessons of a beginner potter, though they are durable containers, pots can break during or after their initial (bisque) firing, while being handled in the glazing process (I hate tongs), during the glaze firing, and when being handled by careless classmates (no names). Tim takes at least some of the broken fragments and tosses them down the hill. Instant archaeological site.

Read More

For basic guidebooks on the analysis and interpretation of ceramics for the archaeologist, four terrific sources follow.

Olin, J. S., and A. D. Franklin, eds. 1982. *Archaeological Ceramics*. Smithsonian Institution Press, Washington, D.C.

Orton, C., P. Tyers, and A. Vince. 1993. *Pottery in Archaeology*. Cambridge University Press, Cambridge.

Rye, O. S. 1981. *Pottery Technology: Principles and Reconstruction*. Taraxacum, Washington, D.C.

Shepard, A. 1982. *Ceramics for the Archaeologist*. Carnegie Institute of Washington, Washington, D.C.

HOW DO YOU MAKE A POT?

It may seem obvious that a stone can be struck to produce small, sharp, conveniently shaped, and useful tools. It may seem less evident that a substance that pretty much looks and feels like mud can be shaped, dried, and heated, and in so doing useful containers can be produced that may serve admirably for storage and cooking. Nevertheless, in a number of world areas, ancient peoples developed and perfected this technology beginning about 11,000 years ago in the Old World (specifically in Japan) and about 6,000 years ago in the New World (in northern South America).

Like stone tool makers, ceramicists pass through a series of steps, or a "production sequence" (Rye 1981). Of course, that process begins with the discovery and extraction of a raw material suitable for making fired vessels. The raw material is called **clay**, which is defined as any one of a number of minerals that are malleable when wet and, once shaped, will harden and retain that shape when dry. Further, when subjected to a high temperature—for example, in a fire or in a contained structure where heat is applied in a more controlled context, in other words, a **kiln**—clay undergoes both a chemical and a physical transformation resulting in a stiff, fairly durable, waterproof (or nearly so), and virtually fireproof material.

Once a clay source is located and the raw material collected, the clay is prepared for the manufacturing process. Impurities may be extracted, especially if they are irregularly sized and inconsistently spread throughout the **clay body**. Then, in order to add strength to the clay body, other ingredients may be added to the clay. Called **temper**, these ingredients may include sand, grit (ground up pieces of rock), ground up shell, and even small fragments of ground up ceramic material (Figure 10.10). Water may be removed or added to the clay in order to achieve homogeneity and the necessary consistency for effective shaping. The clay body cannot be so dry and hard that producing a form is

FIGURE 10.10 Ceramic sherd dating to about 2,500 years ago. The top shows the exterior surface of the sherd; the bottom shows the interior of the sherd along a break. The white chunks of material represent temper used to strengthen the clay body and to allow for more regular drying before firing.

impossible, and it cannot be so soft and wet that the form is unstable and the clay deforms after shaping. The clay is then kneaded sufficiently to thoroughly blend the temper and moisture within the clay, producing a consistent, homogeneous clay body.

The desired shape of the clay container is then produced in various ways: Pinching, coiling, molding, or shaping on a wheel are common methods of forming the soft clay. When the clay is still soft and moist, any one of a number of decorative processes may be applied. In eastern North America, for example, a paddle wrapped with twine was pressed into the still-soft clay to produce a pattern on the clay surface called **cord-marking** (Figure 10.11, top). Also, with the clay still soft,

FIGURE 10.11 Cord-marked ceramics (top). White arrows point to linear marks made in the moist, soft clay when a wooden paddle, wrapped with cord, was pushed against the surface. Sherds (bottom) decorated by impressing a toothed tool into the moist and soft clay.

an object may be impressed in the clay in an effort to produce an interesting look and texture on the pot's surface. The process may involve little more than the maker impressing a fingernail or the edge of a shell, but a more elaborately prepared stamp can be used to impart a design in the soft clay (Figure 10.11, bottom).

FIGURE 10.12 Sherds of vessels decorated by incising lines into dry but not yet fired clay (top). Painted and glazed ceramics (bottom).

Once the desired shape is produced and initial design elements added to the surface, the form is allowed to air dry. Much of the water evaporates until it becomes what modern potters call "leather hard." Additional decorative treatment may now be applied to the leather hard surface. For example, a sharp tool may be used to incise a crisply lined design on the pot's surface (Figure 10.12, top). Color may be added in the form of paint, or another colored clay may be applied, often as a liquid form called a **slip**. After the final designs have been added, the pot must next undergo the ultimate test, a literal trial by fire in a pit or kiln in which the malleable, moist clay is transformed into a hard, durable ceramic. Those pots that survive the thermal shock of firing were, in some parts of the world, further processed by the addition of a truly waterproof surface coating of **glaze** (Figure 10.12, bottom).

The ceramic production process presents the maker with a long list of choices, some of which are technological and some of which are artistically based. There is a great deal of flexibility built into the technology. In other words, there are lots of ways to make a functional pot, a pot that does the job of holding stuff, and there are lots of ways to decorate and design it and lots of ways to finish it. Those choices are made within a technological tradition—for example, native New World potters never used the pottery wheel, though many cultures in the Old World did—and within an artistic tradition. As Rye (1981) points out, the potters working within a particular culture probably all follow those traditions, obtaining their clay from the same sources, adding the same kinds of temper, making the same ceramic shapes, and applying the same kinds of decoration to pottery surfaces. And just as is the case for stone tool manufacture, physical evidence of ceramic production may be deposited at any point along that sequence, providing the archaeologist with direct evidence of the production process (Figure 10.13).

As is always the case in artifact analysis, when examining ceramics (from the tiniest of **potsherds** to complete, intact pots) the archaeologist attempts to decode the complex constellation of choices made by the ancient artisan. Once decoded, the analyst can reveal the existence of pottery traditions. Potters who grow up together learn and practice the current ceramic tradition together; share new ideas, designs and methods; and accept and incorporate some of these new patterns in their evolving tradition. This evolutionary development in a ceramic tradition can be seen in the archaeological record. For example, Figure 10.14 presents a chronological sequence of pottery styles for Connecticut, beginning with the earliest evidence of ceramics in the state (before 2,700 years ago up into the historic period). The names of each of many of the styles refer to places where they were first recognized (Windsor and Niantic, Connecticut, for example), as well as methods of surface treatment: dentate (a toothlike stamping in the clay before it was dried), cord-marked (impressing cord into the pot before it was dried), as well as brushed and stamped (again done before drying) and incised (done either before or after drying and before firing). The oldest pottery style in Connecticut, Vinette, can be found to the west in New York state at older sites. This suggests that the technology for making fired clay objects moved into southern New England from there.

Just like the ever-changing tradition of pottery making in ancient Connecticut, the pots produced at Canton Clayworks represent a "tradition," in which a group of people—a family, of sorts—have all learned from the same potter and

FIGURE 10.13 Remnants of burned clay at the Loomis II site in Windsor, Connecticut.

share a suite of pottery making behaviors recognizable in their finished products as well as in the broken pieces of those products. The same is true of a pottery making tradition in which a mother, who, along with her sisters, learned from their mother, teaches her daughter (just as this mother's sisters teach their daughters), and just as these daughters (all sisters or cousins) will teach their own daughters. The precise look of a pot results from a unique clustering of possibilities and decisions made by this family of women and will be discernibly different from those made by other families of women living upriver, on the other side of the mountain, or in an adjacent valley. Ceramic making is learned, and ceramics are made within the contexts of the social, political, and

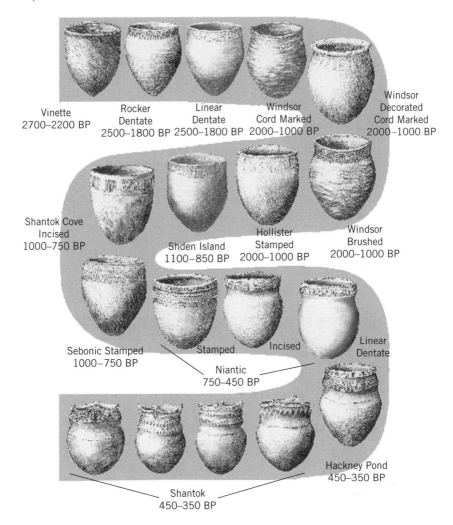

FIGURE 10.14 Chronological sequence of pottery forms in southern New England. (Courtesy Tara Prindle)

economic systems of the group. Those contexts, as intangible as they might be directly, are made tangible in the materials produced by people, and pottery is no exception. Ceramics are important to the archaeologist, therefore, because they were important to the people who made them, traded for them, cooked in them, stored stuff in them, and even buried their dead in them.

How Can You Determine the Source of a Raw Material Used by Ancient People?

There is a movement in law enforcement to include chemical tags in dangerous substances to allow for the precise tracing of those materials to their sources when they are used for nefarious purposes. For example, one strategy is to add a minute amount of a different nonreactive substance to the TNT sold by each of the legal suppliers of the explosive. Then, if a terrorist or more mundane criminal were to use some of that TNT in an illegal act, traces of the tagging substance would be found in the blast residue, and the explosives used in the crime could be traced to a particular supplier, who would be legally obliged to keep records of who purchased the material. In theory, this would allow for the identification of whoever purchased the explosives.

In a sense, nature has placed its own version of a unique chemical tag in many of the materials and substances used by ancient peoples. As in the forensic application, those natural tags are unique to each raw material source and can be used to trace a material from a site where an ancient people used it to make something back to the place where they directly or indirectly obtained it.

Obsidian from two different volcanic regions may look just the same to the naked eye and even under the microscope, but there very well may be slight differences in chemical makeup. The same holds true for the beautiful gemstone turquoise, in which each source may present a crazy quilt of colors and may, as well, exhibit a unique **chemical signature** distinguishable from every other turquoise source. Stone, clay, and metal sources may have unique profiles of trace contaminants that have little or no effect on the appearance, utility, or other qualities of the material. When those materials are found at archaeological sites made into spear points, pots, or knives, the trace element profile of the raw materials from which these artifacts were made can be determined and compared to the known profiles of the potential sources of those raw materials (Figure 10.15). When a match is made, an artifact at a site can be associated with the geographic source where the raw material from which it was made most likely originated.

There are several ways we can determine the chemical profiles of sources and artifacts and by which we may reveal minute traces of elements that might serve as unique markers. One such procedure is **neutron activation analysis (NAA)**, which can detect the presence of a wide range of substances down to extremely small amounts, measured in "parts per million" and even "parts per billion" (http://www.missouri.edu/~glascock/naa_over.htm). By bombarding a raw material sample with neutrons, NAA produces the chemical signature of a raw material—the presence and percentages of each element that makes up the material. Every chemical constituent of the bombarded material releases a unique signature of energy, providing a precise picture of the composition of a raw material down to the tiniest percentages of impurities. This aspect of NAA is useful to archaeologists because different sources for even the same raw materials have distinctly different chemical signatures. In other words, two samples of obsidian (or turquoise, clay, copper, etc.), each collected from a different source, may be indistinguishable to the naked eye, they just look like obsidian, but have recognizably different chemical compositions.

Consider the following mystery concerning the turquoise used by the ancient people of Mesoamerica in the production of beautifully rendered sculptures and masks (Figure 10.16). An estimated 1 million turquoise artifacts have been found throughout, mostly, central Mexico, but also in Guatemala, Belize, Honduras and Nicaragua (Powell 2005), but this presents a bit of a puzzle: There aren't any known extensive turquoise sources in that part of the world. There are,

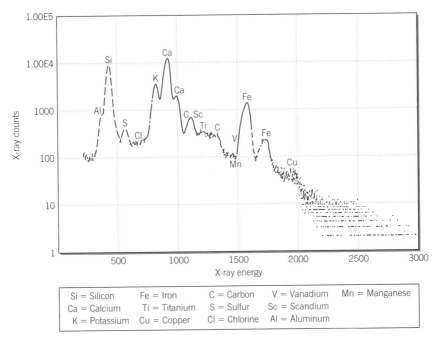

FIGURE 10.15 A reading of the chemical signature of the clay used to make a prehistoric pot as determined by PIXE (particle-induced x-ray emission). Although the raw materials from which an artifact was made (the stone used to make spear points, the clay used to manufacture pottery, or the gemstone carved into an effigy) may look similar on the outside, their chemical makeup may differ enough to indicate that they originated from different sources. That same trace element analysis may enable the archaeologist to trace the raw material to its geographic source. (Courtesy Harold Jull)

however substantial sources of exquisitely sky-blue turquoise in the American Southwest, which is, after all, not all that far away from central Mexico. Southwest turquoise, therefore, is a logical source for the raw material used by the artisans of ancient Mesoamerica. But how do we test the hypothesis that the raw material used by Mesoamerican artisans to produce turquoise sculptures, jewelry, and masks was obtained mostly in Arizona and New Mexico?

Archaeologist Phil Weigand has been investigating that turquoise for more than thirty years. Weigand has produced what amounts to a library of turquoise sources, extracting samples of the gemstone from forty-four sources in the American Southwest and California. As an undergraduate at the State University of New York at Stony Brook (now Stony Brook University) in the early 1970s, I was one of several students who helped in the preparation of samples from those turquoise sources for NAA. This process revealed the chemical signature of each source. At the same time, small samples of turquoise were extracted from finished artifacts found in Mesoamerica, which then underwent the same form of analysis, and their chemical signatures were revealed. Not surprisingly, many of the artifacts found in Mesoamerica revealed chemical signatures consistent with sources located in the American Southwest, supporting the hypothesis that, indeed, that is where the raw materials originated.

FIGURE 10.16 Finished turquoise artifacts found in ancient Mesoamerica were probably made from raw materials whose source can be traced to Arizona, New Mexico, and California.

Read More

The following sources offer interesting examples of the use of trace element chemistry to locate the sources of raw materials used by ancient peoples (clay and copper).

Juli, H., J. Trimble, and M. Monce. 2003. Trade and Tribal Boundaries in Late Prehistoric Southern New England: A Proton Induced X-Ray Emission (PIXE) Analysis of Connecticut Prehistoric Ceramics. *Northeast Anthropology* 65:31–52.

Powell, E. 2005. The Turquoise Trail. *Archaeology* 58(1):24–29.

Rapp, G., J. Allert, V. Vitali, et al. 2000. *Determining Archaeological Sources of Artifact Copper Source Characterization Using Trace Element Analysis.* University Press of America, Lanham, Maryland.

How Do Archaeologists Figure Out the Function of an Ancient Tool?

You might expect, or at least hope, that the function of an ancient tool would be self-evident, that you could determine the use of a tool just by looking at it. In some cases in which preservation is particularly good, residues of the material on which the tool was used—plant fibers, pollen, even blood—yet remain and can be recovered and identified, showing directly the tool's purpose (see chapter 11). Ordinarily, however, tool function is deduced by reference to tool appearance. This often poses problems, since, although it is true that form readily identifies function for some tools, this is not universally the case. Most of us would be hard pressed to figure out the use for many of the tools even in a modern toolbox based simply on what they look like. Suppose you had never seen a hammer and were confronted with one for the first time. A quick perusal of its form, feeling its heft and its balance in the hand, probably would give you an accurate estimation of the tool's function. But how about a screwdriver? Suppose you had never seen one before, and suppose additionally you had never seen any kind of screw. How easily could you figure out a screwdriver's use? Would you accurately deduce that it was a tool for installing or removing a particular type of metal fastener (the screw)? Maybe. You might just as likely decide that it was a weapon of some sort, intended for stabbing an enemy and inflicting great harm or even death. Now consider how much more difficult it is to identify the function of a tool when dealing with those made by members of a different, quite alien, and ancient culture.

Identification difficulty often forces archaeologists to rely on direct evidence of tool use rather than simply a tool's appearance. Direct evidence of use takes the form of wear traces that accumulate on tools during use. As you know, metal tools can become dull and scratched and can even sustain damage to their edges through vigorous use. That brand new Swiss army knife that can effortlessly slice through material will quickly dull by repeated use. The alteration through use to a metal knife's edge can be examined and recognized under magnification, and the same applies to stone tools. When stone tools are used to cut into or through raw materials such as wood, animal hide, bone, antler, or even other stone, the surface of the tool sustains varying kinds and degrees of unintentional alteration and damage.

For example, tiny stone blades were set in rows into bone or wooden handles by people in the Middle East more than 12,000 years ago, producing a kind of compound sickle useful in harvesting grains. As shown by archaeologist Ramona Unger-Hamilton (1989) in an experimental replication of these tools, repeated use of these sickles in a swinging motion against grain stalks results consistently in a dulling, smoothing, and unintentional polishing of the stone blade edges as they wear down as a result of that kind of use. The ancient sickle handles largely are gone, but thousands of the stone blades are found by archaeologists, showing a "sickle polish" identical to that seen in Unger-Hamilton's replication. In all likelihood, the archaeological artifacts exhibiting the same kind of wear had been used in a manner similar to the experimental examples.

So, the edge of a tool, whether it is a finely made utensil or a simple, unintentionally modified flake, bears evidence of use. The question then becomes: What kind of use? Again, we are faced with a challenge. Although the wear on the working edge of a stone tool is visible, at least under magnification, the function of the tool still is not intuitively obvious just by the appearance of the damage rendered by its use. Attempts to overcome this challenge resulted in a brilliantly clever piece of research initially conducted nearly thirty years ago. Archaeologist Lawrence Keeley was able through experiment to provide a series of prototypes of wear patterns for the various uses of stone tools ancient peoples may have employed (Keeley 1980).

Keeley began by making a large sample of stone tools with various kinds of edges. He then used each of these tools on a series of different raw materials, including wood, animal hide, bone, antler, and stone, performing a wide range of functions, including cutting, scraping, sawing, piercing, engraving, axing, wedging, and adzing (Figure 10.17). Through this work Keeley produced an extensive sample of models of wear patterns, covering as broad a range as possible of a combination of raw material of the tools, tool morphology, material used on, and mode of use—how the working edge of the tool was applied to the material it was used on.

Keeley found a number of unique results in terms of the appearance of **wear patterns** on the used tool edges, depending on how they were used and on what material. Those wear patterns manifested themselves as scratches called **striations**, as a smoothing of the surface called **polish**, as microflakes called **scalar scars** because they look like little fish scales peeled off of the surface of a tool, as **step scars** because the scars terminate abruptly at 90-degree-angle "steps," or as little nibbles taken off an edge called **half-moons** because of their shape (Keeley 1980; Figure 10.18). The patterns exhibited on any used tool edge were unique to the kind of activities for which the tool was used. In other words, the wear patterns were diagnostic of what the tool was used for. For example, an edge used to saw wood tended to exhibit striations running parallel to the edge on both faces, with narrow and shallow scalar scars also on both faces. On the other hand, drilling a hole in a piece of bone (say, to make a flute) resulted in a tool with a very different wear pattern, in this case a brightly polished surface on the high points of the tool, those edges directly in contact with the bone. Knowing the broad range of possible wear pattern outcomes from the experimental models, it is possible to accurately identify the function and use of an archaeological specimen. In essence, when an ancient tool exhibits wear patterns that look just like those seen on one of Keeley's models, it is reasonable to deduce that the artifact was used to perform a function similar to that of the experimental model.

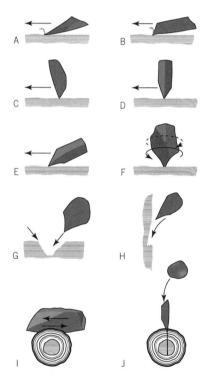

FIGURE 10.17 Models of stone tool use employed by Lawrence Keeley in his use-wear experiments: (A) whittling, (B) planing, (C) scraping, (D) graving, high angle, (E) graving, low angle, (F) boring, (G) chopping, (H) adzing, (I) sawing or cutting, and (J) wedging. (After Lawrence Keeley, 1980)

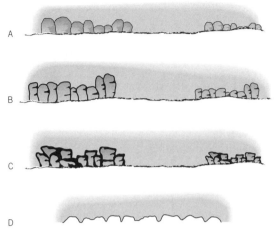

A

B

C

D

FIGURE 10.18 Patterns of edge damage resulting from tool use as defined experimentally by archaeologist Lawrence Keeley: (A) deep scalar scars (large, left; small, right), (B) shallow scalar scars (large, left; small, right), (C) step scars (large, left; small, right), and (D) half-moons. (After Lawrence Keeley, 1980)

Keeley went beyond assumption in his research and actually conducted a blind test. He made another set of tools, this time passing them along to a colleague, who used the tools in a variety of ways undisclosed to Keeley and maintained accurate records of how he used the tools. The colleague then returned the tools to Keeley, who compared them to his original tools (the set used in making models of wear patterns). Using those models, Keeley accurately identified the usage patterns for the second set of tools more than 85% of the time. In other words, in more than eight times out of ten, Keeley accurately deduced how a tool was used, and on what raw material, by compar-

Chapter 10:
Interactive
Exercise

ing its wear patterns to those he had produced in his tool use prototypes. Keeley's experiment in wear pattern production and subsequent refinements to the original research have allowed archaeologists to objectively assess the wear patterns on ancient tools and to confidently identify the ways in which they were used by ancient peoples.

Read More

The experimental program of Lawrence Keeley is a model for the interpretation of tool use through the application of replicative experiment. His book is the best place to start to expand your understanding of how archaeologists interpret use-wear patterns on stone tools by actually creating them:

Keeley, L. 1980. *Experimental Determination of Stone Tool Use: A Microwear Analysis.* University of Chicago Press, Chicago.

How Do Archaeologists Examine Tools Made of Raw Materials Other Than Stone or Clay?

As noted throughout this book, archaeologists in many parts of the world focus their attention on stone and ceramics simply because objects made from these materials are the most durable. We commonly find complete stone tools—entire spear points, axe heads, drills, knives, and so on—and substantial pieces of and even unbroken pots and fired clay sculptures, even in the most corrosive and biologically active depositional environments. Objects made of other raw materials including wood, plant fibers, wool, bone, antler, and metals are frequently found in some regions where the conditions for preservation are high but rare in many parts of the world where organic raw materials are dissolved by acid and eaten by microorganisms in the soil. New England, where I have conducted my fieldwork and where the Wood Lily site is located, is one of those places where, under most circumstances, organic material is less likely to be preserved for long periods in the soil. Sometimes even in these regions we get lucky, however. For example, long ago a basket may have been placed on the ground, the weight of its contents making an impression of the container's warp and weft, elements of the weaving process, in the soft soil. When that soil has a high clay content and is located near a fire, it may be unintentionally baked, and the impression of the basket may survive long after the basket has decayed to dust. As seen in our discussion of ceramics, people sometimes intentionally pressed fabric, cordage, shell, or a carved wooden tool into the clay before firing as part of the surface design. In these instances a negative impression of the weaving, the shell edge, or the design carved onto the wooden tool may be preserved in the ceramic.

Even in these regions where organic preservation is low, we can still conduct replicative experiments using less durable materials, basing our designs on ethnohistorical data. See Figure 10.5, where I have included photographs of the end products of a number of student replications, including an African mask, a New England Indian war club, and a southeastern U.S. native pine basket base.

Read More

There are excellent books detailing the history of and archaeological analysis of various raw materials. Check these out for the specifics on the archaeological analysis of each of these.

Adovasio, J. M. 1997. *Basketry Technology*. Aldine, Chicago.

Hurely, W. M. *Prehistoric Cordage: Identification on Pottery*. Taraxcum, Washington, D. C.

Luedtke, B. E. 1992. *An Archaeologist's Guide to Chert and Flint*. Archaeological Research Tools 7. University of California Press, Los Angeles.

Olin, J. S., and A. D. Franklin, eds. 1982. *Archaeological Ceramics*. Smithsonian Institution Press, Washington, D. C.

Orton, C., P. Tyers, and A. Vince. 1993. *Pottery in Archaeology*. Cambridge University Press, Cambridge.

Rye, O. S. 1981. *Pottery Technology: Principles and Reconstruction*. Taraxcum, Washington, D. C.

Turnbaugh, S. P., and W. A. Turnbaugh. 1986. *Indian Baskets*. Schiffer Publishing, West Chester, Pennsylvania.

Waldorf, D. C. 1984. *The Art of Flintknapping*. Moundbulider Books, Branson, Missouri.

Whittaker, J. C. 1994. *Flintnapping: Making and Understanding Stone Tools*. University of Texas Press, Austin.

How Do Archaeologists Investigate the Technology of Monumental Construction?

A culture is an ever-evolving, ever-changing phenomenon, a grand work in progress intended to provide a technological, economic, social, political, and ideological context for a people's lives. Every generation maintains traditions at the same time that its members develop refinements and elaborations of traditional ways of accomplishing tasks and behaving. In addition, every generation may invent entirely new ways of accomplishing the same tasks. Of course, as conditions change and as new discoveries are made or inventions developed, novel strategies to accomplish new tasks may arise as needed or even before the need is recognized in the first place, with the "need" defined by the invention rather than the other way around.

It is also certainly the case that human groups and their technologies do not develop in a vacuum. People who practice a particular way of life are not isolated and regularly come into contact with folks practicing similar, somewhat different, or even entirely alien ways of life. The possible results of contact between two different groups of people are many and diverse. One group may wipe out the members of another group or merely come to dominate them. The two groups may maintain a degree of separation, or one group may become incorporated into the other as peasants or slaves. Two groups may proceed as equals, trading with each other, forming alliances, or even ignoring each other altogether. However each group in this equation outwardly reacts to the other, ideas can transcend virtually any geographical or cultural barriers. Ordinarily, ideas are more mobile than people and sometimes can move easily between and among different groups—even enemies, and even people who don't speak the same language—and elements of the technology of one group of people are commonly adopted by other groups.

Archaeologists are specialists in the examination of cultural change, perhaps especially change in technology, over long periods of time. We often can construct chronological sequences for cultures that span decades, centuries, and even millennia. Using absolute dating or determining the stratigraphic arrangement of components of the same culture, we can assess the nature of change in a people's behavior as these changes are reflected in the material record. Refinements or elaborations in the end products of lithic, ceramic, or metallurgical technologies often are apparent in the archaeological record. Ways of crafting tools or ways of adding design elements to pottery—or even ways of building pyramids or temples—may change over time. By comparing artifacts found in different stratigraphic levels of the same site or artifacts found at different sites produced by the same culture but with different chronometric dates, archaeologists can illuminate and evaluate changes in technology through time.

The pattern exhibited by sequences of technological change in the archaeological record in a region may be useful in determining whether this change was internally driven or resulted from the movement or **diffusion** of ideas across cultural boundaries. The pattern of technological, artistic, or behavioral change assumed in seriation reflects internal change, and the general pattern in a seriation analysis applies in this case. In other words, when the archaeological record shows the first appearance of a technology as relatively rudimentary, evidencing lots of mistakes, and changing as a product of trial and error as a group gropes its way toward perfecting a new process, we conclude that the adoption and evolution of the new behavior was the result of internal patterns of cultural evolution. If, on the other hand, a new technology seems to have arrived full-blown and complete, with little evidence of the first halting steps in the development of a new way of doing things (to the people of the archaeological culture being examined), it may be hypothesized that the behavior was invented, developed, and perfected someplace else. In this case, rather than interpreting the culture in question as having developed the new technology independently, we conclude that they adopted it from a source outside their own culture (Clarke 1978).

Take, for example, a practice as complex as pyramid-building in ancient Egypt and Mesoamerica (Adams 1991; Lehner 1997). Archaeological evidence clearly shows that peoples on both sides of the Atlantic built monumental pyramidal structures. It certainly is valid to question whether these were independent developments or whether the art of pyramid-building developed first in only Egypt or Mesoamerica and whether the appearance of pyramids in the other location is the result of diffusion or borrowing.

In truth, Egyptian and Mesoamerican pyramids are quite different in appearance, in how they were constructed, and in how they were used (Arnold 1991; Sabloff 1989). Add to these differences the fact that the Egyptian pyramids are far older: The last of the Egyptian pyramids was built long before even the earliest of the Mesoamerican monuments, so it does not seem likely that one inspired the other. All of this argues for a separate and independent development of the pyramid in Egypt and Mesoamerica. But also consider the archaeological evidence for the development of the pyramid in both places. In both Egypt and Mesoamerica the archaeological record shows a long developmental sequence of pyramid-building lasting centuries and even millennia. For example, Egyptians didn't simply start the process by building enormous, perfectly constructed pyramids. They started small, with square-block structures called *mastabas* over the tombs of their rulers. In fact, the first large-scale burial monument for a pharaoh wasn't a pyramid at all but consisted of a series of mastabas of decreasing size placed one on top of the other (Figure 10.19, top).

After this "stepped pyramid" of the pharaoh Djoser, a later ruler, Sneferu, began the construction of a larger but similar structure that he decided to finish as a true pyramid, filling in the steps. This first attempt at a true pyramidal form failed, and the project was abandoned (Figure 10.19, bottom). All that remains today is the central core of the structure and the heaped-up remains of its surface; it is, in fact, usually called the "Collapsed Pyramid," though there probably was no catastrophic collapse, merely an abandonment and deterioration over an extended period of time.

Sneferu tried again but ran into similar problems about halfway through construction. When it became apparent that the surfaces of the second pyramid were too steep to sustain its own weight (cracks had formed toward the bottom, endangering the project), Sneferu's engineers changed the slope of the pyramid

FIGURE 10.19 The pharaoh Djoser's stepped pyramid represented an obvious next step in ancient Egypt in the evolution from older single-level mastabas (top). The "Collapsed Pyramid" was a construction project abandoned when cracks appeared at its base, probably the result of a too-steep angle of the pyramid's facing (bottom). (M. H. Feder)

toward the top, actually decreasing the angle of the pyramid faces (Figure 10.20, top). This strategy saved the project but resulted in an oddly shaped pyramid, bent inward at the top—not surprisingly, today the structure is called the "Bent Pyramid."

FIGURE 10.20 Called the "Bent Pyramid" for obvious reasons, the angle of the slope of this pyramid was altered midproject, probably as the result of problems with steep-angled pyramids attempted earlier (top). Sneferu's engineers and architects finally got it right with the Red Pyramid. The angle of the slope of this pyramid is found in all subsequent pyramids built by the ancient Egyptians, the clear result of trial and error (bottom). (M. H. Feder)

Sneferu's third attempt at pyramid-building succeeded (Figure 10.20, bottom), employing from the beginning the less severe angle used at the top of the "Bent Pyramid." This sequential pattern of improving technology, in this case over the course of the life of a single pharaoh, better conforms to a process of internal and independent development rather than to borrowing from elsewhere (Clayton 1994).

Archaeologists have found many of the tools ancient Egyptians used to quarry, shape, and move the literally millions of blocks of stone employed in their construction of pyramids and other monuments (Jackson and Stamp 2003). Metal chisels and wooden mallets, lengths of heavy-duty cordage, pulleys, rollers, and sledges have been recovered in excavations throughout Egypt (Arnold 1991). Some of the pyramid stones themselves possess "handling bosses"—bumps or knobs on otherwise smooth surfaces—that allowed for the attachment of rope. Other stones exhibit sockets for the placement of levers useful in lifting the stones up onto other stones.

Along with tools used in pyramid construction, we can also thank the Egyptians for directly clearing up some of our questions about how they did it. Consider, for example, a a 3,900-year-old wall painting showing workers transporting the enormous statue of a local ruler to his tomb (Figure 10.21). In the painting 176 men are tethered together as they pull the statue. One additional worker is depicted on the sled, pouring a liquid and almost certainly lubricating the ground in front of the statue. The monuments themselves, together with the remains of tools used in their construction, artistic depictions by the Egyptians, and even the experimental replication of the pyramid-building process by Egyptologist Mark Lehner and master stone mason Roger Hopkins (*This Old Pyramid 1993*) are revealing the secrets of monumental construction in the ancient world.

Mesoamerican pyramids show much the same processes, beginning with small, pyramidal platforms topped with temples, such as the Temple of the Magician at the site of Dzibichaltun, located in the north of the Yucatán Peninsula (Figure 10.22, top), and culminating with the enormous, awesome pyramids of Tikal, Palenque, and Chichen Itza (Figure 10.22, bottom). Relying on the same basic model, a similar analysis can be performed for everything from the development of agriculture to ceramic and lithic technology.

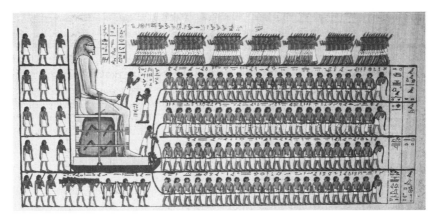

FIGURE 10.21 Ancient Egyptians themselves depicted the manner in which they quarried, transported, and erected large stone monuments. Here, from the tomb of a regional Egyptian functionary, artists showed the movement of an enormous statue, estimated to be about 6 m (20 ft) high, by 176 men pulling on ropes. One worker located just in front of the statue appears to be pouring a lubricant on the ground.

FIGURE 10.22 The small, stepped platforms built at the Maya site of Dzibichaltun in the northern Yucatán Peninsula, Mexico, (top) were pale harbingers of the magnificent pyramids that were built later in Maya history. The Temple of the Feathered Serpent (bottom) at the Maya site of Chichén Itza is one of the most beautiful of those constructed by the Maya, the culmination of a long history of monumental construction projects. This pyramid has been honored as one of the new Seven Wonders of the World (K. L. Feder)

Read More

For far more detailed discussions of the ancient civilizations of Egypt and Mexico, as well as discussions of the evidence for diffusion between them and of how archaeologists assess the possibility of ancient contacts between civilizations, take a look at these references.

Adams, R. E. W. 1991. *Prehistoric Mesoamerica*. University of Oklahoma Press, Norman.

Arnold, D. 1991. *Building in Egypt: Pharaonic Stone Masonry*. Oxford University Press, Oxford.

Clarke, D. L. 1978. *Analytical Archaeology*. Columbia University Press, New York.

Clayton, P. A. 1994. *Chronicle of the Pharaohs: The Reign-by-Reign Record of the Rulers and Dynasties of Ancient Egypt*. Thames & Hudson, London.

Feder, K. L. 2002. *Frauds, Myths, and Mysteries: Science and Pseudoscience in Archaeology*. McGraw-Hill/Mayfield Publishing, Mountain View, California.

Lehner, M. 1997. *The Complete Pyramids*. Thames & Hudson, New York.

Sabloff, J. A. 1989. *The Cities of Ancient Mexico: Reconstructing a Lost World*. Thames & Hudson, New York.

Study Questions

1. What does an archaeologist mean by the term *exotic material?*

2. What are the characteristics that make a lithic raw material desirable to a knapper?

3. What is "conchoidal fracture"?

4. Describe the "geography" and geometry of a stone core from which a knapper can produce stone flakes.

5. Describe the "geography" and geometry of a stone flake just removed from a core from which a knapper can produce a tool.

6. How can the analysis of trace element chemistry aid in attempting to track a raw material used by a past people to its geographic source?

7. Walk through the steps to remove a flake from a core by direct percussion.

8. Walk through the steps to thin a flake by pressure applied bifacially.

9. Describe the role played by Ishi in the ability of modern archaeologists to understand the manufacture of stone tools.

10. How does experimental reconstruction aid in our understanding of ancient stone tool technologies?

11. How does experimental archaeology aid in our understanding of how ancient tools were used?

12. Name and describe the kinds of wear or damage that occur on the edges of stone tools.

13. Describe how archaeologist Lawrence Keeley's experiment showed that wear patterns on stone tools were specific to particular kinds of tool use on specific raw materials.

14. How did archaeologist Lawrence Keeley determine how experimental replica tools he had made were used by a colleague? How did the results of his experiment apply to the analysis of archaeological artifacts?

15. How do craft objects (e.g., pottery) inform us about a past people's technology?

16. How do craft objects (e.g., pottery) inform us about aspects of a past people's culture, beyond just technology?

17. What is diffusion?

18. How can an archaeologist distinguish between the diffusion of an idea from one source to other groups and the independent invention of a similar idea by different groups?

19. There are pyramids in Egypt and pyramids in Mexico. Did the idea of the pyramid originate in one of those places and diffuse to the other, or was the pyramid invented and developed independently in both? How can you tell?

20. Suppose the pyramid in concept and execution was invented only in Egypt and spread to Mexico in ancient times. What would the archaeological investigation of the appearance and development of the pyramid in Mexico show? What does it really show?

11

Putting Food on the Table

RECONSTRUCTING ANCIENT DIETS

Later in this chapter, I cite the cliché "You are what you eat." A version of this phrase (in French) can be traced back as far as the early nineteenth century (the version most are familiar with dates to the 1920s and 1930s in, of all things, an advertisement for beef) and has long been intended as a medical warning; if you eat unhealthy foods, you, too, will be unhealthy. Eat foods that are healthy, and so will you be.

In the context of this chapter, the lives of a group of people are significantly affected by what they eat in many fundamental ways, not just in terms of their biological health. The species of animals they hunt, tend, or have domesticated; the plants they gather or plant; the seasonality of the resources they depend on for their subsistence; all these things have a tremendous amount of influence on a group's economic and social lives. In manifold ways we all are, and past peoples really were, at least to an extent, what they ate. This chapter summarizes the ways in which archaeologists collect and interpret the data needed to reconstruct the diets of ancient peoples.

Why Do Archaeologists Want to Know What Foods Were Eaten by Ancient People?

This chapter focuses on the strategies employed by archaeologists in our attempts to figure out the diets of past people, but our intent is broader than simply coming up with a list of foods eaten in antiquity. Identifying the seeds, fruits, nuts, stalks, or bones found at an archaeological site certainly allows us to develop a listing of the foods eaten by the people who lived there, and that is important in and of itself in attempting to paint a complete picture of the lives of a past people. Knowing which foods were eaten by an ancient group, however, provides greater insights into the nature of their societies than just what they ate. Importantly, the behavior and characteristics of different animal and plant species used as food played a role in shaping the behavior of the human groups that exploited them (Binford 1987).

In northeast North America, for example, white-tailed deer played an important role in the subsistence quest (Figure 11.1). Whitetails are, essentially, solitary animals. The males live by themselves, seeking out the company of females only during the breeding season in November. Sometimes in winter you will see a handful of females browsing together—we once counted nineteen whitetails walking along a trail behind our house—but for the most part, the largest social groupings consist of a female and one or two of her offspring; there are no vast herds of white-tailed deer communally traversing the eastern woodlands in a migratory cycle.

The generally solitary nature of whitetails had an obvious impact on the behavior of those human groups that depended on them for their meat and hides. Solitary animals are taken by hunters, rather obviously, one at a time, and it makes sense for hunters to go out singly or in small groups to stalk them. A small social group of hunter-gatherers made up of just a few families with a small handful of hunters can do quite nicely with whitetails. An older buck may provide close to 200 pounds of meat that, when preserved by drying

FIGURE 11.1 The white-tailed deer was an important resource for the inhabitants of the Wood Lily site and across its range in North America.

and combined with other foods (in stews, for example), is sufficient to feed a small group of people for quite some time. The point is, because groups in the northeast were heavily dependent on white-tailed deer for their subsistence, the nature of whitetail behavior molded their hunting behavior, and the requirements of these hunting strategies had a significant impact on the size and makeup of their social groupings.

Compare this to another North American species hunted for food, the American bison (*Bison bison*). Bison are gregarious, and individual bison herds number in the hundreds and even the thousands. A hunter will almost inevitably run into not a single animal but many tens of animals. Although a hunter might be able to isolate an individual animal for capture, because bison tend to act in unison to a threat this might be difficult—and why would a hunter feel constrained to kill only one animal when many could be killed simultaneously, providing a substantial amount of meat and a large number of hides?

A hunting strategy appropriate for the capture of a single deer might be inappropriate for a species that travels in large numbers, such as bison. And, in fact, unlike deer hunting, cooperative hunts involving many hunters in an organized effort to kill not just a single animal but tens of creatures and even hundreds in a single hunt (Figure 11.2) were common among Plains Indians in the historical period (Wheat 1972). Archaeological evidence shows that such large-scale, cooperative hunts were conducted more than 10,000 years ago. The skeletons of as many as 200 bison have been found in these mass killings. In some of these hunts, segments of herds were isolated and then herded into quagmires of sand, where they became trapped and were easy pickings for hunters with spears (Frison 1974). In other instances the bison were stampeded over cliffs where the fall would kill most of the animals, who then could be butchered in place. To accomplish this complex, organized, cooperative hunt, a large social group might be called on to participate. Some participants might have the job of isolating a segment of the bison population from the larger group. Some might start fires and make noises in an effort to panic the isolated animals. Others might be charged with the task of directing the panicked animals toward a cliff, while still others might position themselves at the base of the cliff to kill any animals that survived the fall and to begin the task of butchering the animals and drying the huge amounts of meat collected from a kill of that size. For more information about communal bison hunts, check

FIGURE 11.2 Part of an extensive bed of ancient bison bones found at the Certain Site in Oklahoma is shown here as it is being excavated by archaeologists. This level of bone concentration resulted from a mass killing of these large animals at this spot. (Courtesy Kent Buehler)

out the website of the Head-Smashed-In-Buffalo Jump archaeological site at: http://www.head-smashed-in.com/home.html.

Surely then, the nature of the animals hunted rendered differing hunting strategies appropriate, and human groups reacted accordingly. Knowing which animals were exploited by a past people goes far beyond just clarifying their food preferences; it provides an important perspective on how the subsistence base may have contributed to the contours of the rest of their way of life.

Of course, not all animals exploited by people were wild. In some parts of the world, beginning about 11,000 years ago, human beings began the process of plant and animal domestication. It probably began as a slow process of tending to and encouraging the growth of wild stands of plants and by the capture, corralling, and taming of wild animals, which led to actually changing them through selective breeding—weeding out plants that didn't produce large quantities of easily harvested food and killing off aggressive, nasty beasts and allowing only those with attractive characteristics to breed (thus passing down those traits to subsequent generations).

In selective breeding of plants, people have usually (but not always) chosen for larger seeds with thinner seed coats, and of animals smaller size, a less aggressive disposition (for safety), a woollier coat (for fiber production), higher milk production (for food), and amount of meat produced. Archaeological evidence of domestication of plants such as wheat and maize includes, in addition to larger seed or kernal size and thinner inedible seed coats, plants that were easier to harvest. In the wild most ancestral maize and wheat plants developed very brittle connections between seed and stalk once the seeds ripen. Such a seed-dispersal mechanism is useful in nature, providing a natural mechanism by which ripe seeds are scattered over the ground, a process of self-planting for next year's wild crop. A seed-dispersal mechanism that allows ripe seeds to readily fall off the plant is disadvantageous to human harvesting for the very reason that the seeds tend to fall off and scatter on the ground as soon as a human attempts to collect them. People tended to select for individual plants in ancestral maize and wheat fields that didn't develop this brittle "rachis," and this selective process can be seen in the archaeological record with the appearance and dominance of nonbrittle seed connections in archaeological specimens (Smith 1995).

Smaller overall size and smaller teeth and jaws than wild versions of an animal species are physical characteristics that are seen in the archaeological record and interpreted as evidence of selective breeding and domestication. In fact, it is a decrease in jaw size in particular that provides the basis for our recognition of the earliest separation of the domestic dog from the wild wolf (Olson 1985; Pennisi 2002).

A shift in the geographic distribution of wild plants and animals without any evidence of a natural climate change may also hint at a human agency at work. As we noted in chapter 9, plants and animals have natural ranges; they thrive in areas where nature provides them with the temperatures, moisture levels, and other resources to which they have adapted and on which they depend. Human beings long ago figured out that by intentionally modifying those conditions—by providing additional water, by protecting delicate shoots from frost, by building structures in which animals can be housed and buffered against the elements—the geographic range in which a plant or animal species might survive can be greatly extended.

In fact, the archaeological record is replete with examples of the appearance of plant and animal species exploited by people outside their naturally restricted range. For example, even where no seeds have been recovered archaeologically, pollen can provide us with an idea of the plant species available to ancient peoples in a given region. Pollen from the teosinte plant has been found at the 7,100-year-old occupation of the San Andrés site located in the wetlands along Mexico's eastern shoreline. Teosinte, the wild ancestor of the plant that was to become the staple crop in Native American agriculture, maize, is not native to the Gulf Coast location of San Andrés (Pope et al. 2001). The researchers propose that the presence of teosinte pollen at this site suggests that the inhabitants had taken an active role in extending the survival of this valuable food plant, tending and caring for it in a habitat to which it was not naturally well adapted.

Other evidence of domestication is a bit more subtle. For example, the population statistics of wild animals are distinguishable from domesticated stock. Among domestic herd animals, males are nearly always killed off when they are young: Very few bulls or rams are needed for breeding and, because they tend be larger and more aggressive, it may make sense to eliminate most of them from a captive population. Females, on the other hand, are kept around for a while: They can produce milk as well as multiple offspring over a long period of time. When Chinese scientists found a population profile in the assemblage of pig bones at Zengpiyan Cave in Guilan Province, it showed that 85 percent of the animals were males less than two years old, and they concluded that the population represented an early attempt at selective breeding (Chang 1986). Similarly, though they are not morphologically different from the bones of wild members of their species, the bones of goats found at the archaeological site Ganj Dareh in Iran show that the site's inhabitants habitually killed off males when they were still quite young. This elimination indicates a level of control over the breeding process, which implies the existence of a captive population of the animals (Zeder and Hesse 2000).

Read More

Zooarchaeology, the study of animals whose remains have been found at archaeological sites, has produced a vast literature. The following works serve as guides to identifying animals from their bones and then interpreting the human behaviors that resulted in the deposition of those bones at sites.

Baker, B. W., B. S. Shaffer, and D. G. Steele. 1997. Basic Approaches in Archaeological Faunal Analysis. In *Field Methods in Archaeology*, edited by T. R. Hester, H. J. Shafer, and K. L. Feder, 298–318. Mayfield Publishing, Mountain View, California.

Binford, L. 1987. *Bones: Ancient Men and Modern Myths*. Academic Press, New York.

Chang, K.-c. 1986. *The Archaeology of Ancient China*. 4th ed. Yale University Press, New Haven, Connecticut.

Chaplin, R. E. 1971. *The Study of Animal Bones from Archaeological Sites*. Seminar Press, London.

Frison, G., ed. 1974. *The Casper Site: A Hell Gap Bison Kill on the High Plains*. Academic Press, New York.

Gilbert, B. M. 1973. *Mammalian Osteo-Archaeology: North America*. Missouri Archaeological Society, Columbia.

Hesse, B., and P. Wapnish. 1985. *Animal Bone Archaeology*. Manuals on Archaeology 5. Taraxacum, Washington, D.C.

Klein, R. G., and K. Cruz-Uribe. 1984. *The Analysis of Animal Bones from Archaeological Sites*. University of Chicago Press, Chicago.

O'Connor, T. 2000. *The Archaeology of Animal Bones*. Texas A&M Press, College Station.

Olson, S. J. 1985. *Origins of the Domestic Dog: The Fossil Record*. University of Arizona Press, Tucson.

Reitz, E. J. 1999. *Zooarchaeology*. Cambridge University Press, Cambridge.

Wheat, J. B. 1972. *The Olsen-Chubbuck Site: A Paleo Indian Bison Kill*. Memoir of the Society for American Archaeology 26, Salt Lake City.

Zeder, M. A., and B. Hesse. 2000. The Initial Domestication of Goats (*Capra hircus*) in the Zagros Mountains 10,000 Years Ago. *Science* 287:2254–57.

How Do Archaeologists Know What Foods Ancient People Ate?

As you have read here earlier—and incessantly—archaeology is based in large part on scrutiny of the material remains of human behavior. Analysis of a past people's diet is no different. The subsistence pattern of a group of people can be revealed through examination of the tools they used in the gathering, storage, processing, and preparation of their foods as well as through the recovery and analysis of the physical remains of the foods they ate and that have fortuitously been preserved.

For example, hunting equipment is an indication of the role of hunting in an ancient people's diet; arrow or spear points used for killing animals along with knives for butchering them are an indication that hunting played a role in subsistence. Fish hooks, net weights, and the remnants of fish weirs or traps indicate that fishing played a role in the diet. Stone hoes, metal plow blades, and fire-hardened digging sticks indicate that horticulture or agriculture contributed to an ancient people's food base. Apparatuses for grinding nuts, seeds, and grain into flour, including manos and metates as well as mortars and pestles, may signify the production of flour as part of the food base of an ancient group. Clearly, the presence of the apparatuses used in hunting, fishing, shellfish collecting, plant gathering, and agricultural production indicates that these subsistence modes were employed by a past people (Figure 11.3).

Beyond examining the probable functions of artifacts, archaeological features may also indicate the nature of the foods that were processed at a site. Consider the "thermopolia," essentially a food stand discovered at Pompeii. Frozen at the instant of the Roman city's destruction by the volcanic eruption

FIGURE 11.3 The shape of some artifacts implies their function. Shown here are hunting weapons in the form of spear points (upper left), preparation tools in the form of sharp-edged stone knives (upper right), and a milling stone, probably used for grinding corn into meal (bottom). The morphology of these artifacts suggests their use.

of Vesuvius in August of A.D. 79, Figure 11.4 (top) shows the L-shaped counter with marble inlay and built-in food and beverage containers. In the background is a painting of gods including Dionysis and Mercury feasting on fruits and meats (Figure 11.4, bottom).

FIGURE 11.4 A food serving feature at Pompeii (top). In the background is a painting of an assortment of gods, including Dionysis and Mercury (bottom).

FIGURE 11.5 An archaeological feature, such as this 4,250-year-old platform of stones on which meat was roasted, represents a combination of artifacts and/or ecofacts (in this case, the stones themselves, charcoal, bone fragments, and a spear point) demarcating a place where people once carried out an activity. The white arrow (top) points to the location where a spearpoint (bottom) was discovered. (K. L. Feder)

Another example of a food preparation feature is a platform of stones on which cuts of meat were grilled at the 4,250-year-old Avon Old Farms Brook site in Avon, Connecticut (Figure 11.5, top). Think of a modern barbeque with a metal grill for holding meat over charcoal; in the roasting platform at Avon Old Farms Brook, large stones served as the grilling platform on top of a fire pit. Along with charcoal found under the stones and bits of deer bone scattered among the stones (see the discussion of osteological analysis that follows), immediately adjacent to and at the same level as the platform of burned stones we found the virtual "smoking gun," a nearly intact spear point missing only its tip that in all likelihood was used to dispatch at least one of the animals cooked on the platform (Figure 11.5, bottom).

More direct evidence of a diet in the form of actual food remains can be more difficult to find. Food is, by its very nature, organic, and therein lies a problem. Artifacts made of durable, inorganic raw materials, such as the food counter at Pompeii or the roasting platform stones and spear point in Connecticut, are preserved well under virtually all soil conditions. The same cannot be said for organic remains. Acidic soils, for example, dissolve organics. Biologically active soils are populated by creatures, both multi- and unicellular, whose entire existence is based on their ingestion and breakdown of organic materials deposited in the soil. These tiny recycling factories care not at all whether some of the materials they are happily munching on are just leaf litter and decomposing old wood or are, instead, valuable archaeological ecofacts. Unfortunately for the archaeologist, these remains all taste equally good to the worms and single-celled organisms that inhabit the soil. So, under conditions of high levels of soil acidity and biological activity, organic remains may not be preserved well, if at all.

Fortunately, some forms of preparation coincidentally aid in the preservation of food remains. For example, many foods eaten by people are processed in such a way as to extract the edible parts from more durable inedible parts such as bone and shell, which are then disposed of or used for nondietary purposes. For instance, meat may be removed from bone, which is then discarded. The meat may be gone, invisible to the archaeologist, but the more durable, discarded bones, with their evidence of cut and slice marks from butchering with stone or metal tools, become part of the archaeological record. Nut meats are removed from their shells, and the shells may be discarded. The shells and even some of the nut meat itself may rest preserved in trash pits and hearths. Kernels of corn are extracted from their cobs, cereal grains (such as wheat, barley, rye, and oats) are removed from their stalks, shellfish are scooped from their shells, and squash is scraped from its rind.

The act of grilling, roasting, or baking may serve to aid in the preservation of some organic remains. For example, in New England nutshells or nut meats deposited in the soil may not be preserved well or long under certain conditions, but burning (for example, roasting nuts in an open fire) renders the remains much less susceptible to decay and, apparently, not as tasty to the little critters that would otherwise eat them (Figure 11.6). The burned nutshells, corncobs, cereal plant stalks, and squash rinds, along with burned kernels and grains that were left behind on their stalks, may be discarded in a pile called a **kitchen midden**, relegated to a trash pit, heaped in a dump, broadcast on the

FIGURE 11.6 Charred nutshells (acorn and hickory) from a cooking feature excavated at a 2,000-year-old site located in Windsor, Connecticut. (K. L. Feder)

surface of a field, or simply left where they fell during processing, cooking, or eating. Archaeologists can find these middens, pits, piles, and scatters; excavate these features; and then identify the foods that made up the diet of the people who produced the archaeological site being investigated.

In a process called **flotation** archaeologists use the fact that these pieces of bone, seeds, nutshells, and rinds, all have a different specific gravity than that of water (a fixed volume of the archaeological material weighs either more or less than, but not the same as, the same fixed volume of water). This enables the separation of the organic archaeological materials from their surrounding soil matrix. Archaeologists commonly collect a 100 percent sample of a feature's soil. Either in the field or back in the lab, the soil is poured into a container filled with water. In the field this may involve placing a bucket in a stream, and in the lab, where there is access to running water and electricity, the water may be frothed with air from an electrical pump passed through a bubbler—the kind used to oxygenate the water in a fish tank—to aid in the separation

FIGURE 11.7 On-site flotation in the Ohio River. The bottom of the galvanized bucket has been removed, and a heavy hardware cloth mesh and fine screening have been fastened to the base. The bucket is partially submerged in the river water, then soil is poured in: Organic remains float to the top, and inorganic material is caught by the mesh. (K. L. Feder)

process. Whether using the natural movement of stream water or the artificial flow from a hose, any material that is lighter and has a lower specific gravity than water (for example, seeds and charcoal) will float to the surface, where it can be skimmed and then dried for identification. Next, the muddy slurry left behind can be poured through fine screening, whereby materials that are heavier than water and have a higher specific gravity than water (for example, bone) are trapped and can be recovered, dried, and then identified. The water and fine soil particles pass through the screen (Figure 11.7).

In a recent application of this procedure, we recovered organic material from two sites in the McLean Game Refuge in Granby, Connecticut. We then supplied the recovered material to Dr. Cindy McWeeney, an expert in botanical identification and analysis. She was able to identify pieces of charred hickory nutshell, indicating the use of hickory in the diet at a site occupied about 1,000 years ago. She was also able to identify the tree species whose wood fueled the fire in which the hickory nuts were roasted: oak, maple, chestnut, and pine.

HOW DO ARCHAEOLOGISTS IDENTIFY THE SOURCE OF FRAGMENTARY ORGANIC REMAINS FOUND AT ARCHAEOLOGICAL SITES?

Unfortunately, the process of preparing food for a meal may result in fragmentation of the durable parts: Seeds may be ground up for meal; nutshells are broken into; and bone is sliced, cut, and smashed (to get at the marrow). Many archaeology labs house **comparative collections** of the bones of animals and fish that live in an area, the shells of shellfish that might have been exploited in a region, and examples of edible seeds, nuts, and nutshells. Books provide encyclopedic coverage of animal bones, seeds, and nuts, and many contain photographs and drawings that can be used to identify archaeological specimens (for example, *Mammalian Osteo-Archaeology: North America* by B. Miles Gilbert 1973; also see Baker, Shaffer, and Steele 1997; Chaplin 1971; Gilbert 1973; Hesse and Wapnish 1985; Klein and Cruz-Uribe 1984). Recovered archaeological specimens, often broken into small fragments, may be extremely difficult to identify, and a good comparative collection can be a very useful tool in recognizing and identifying the sources for the ecofacts found at an archaeological site.

The faunal comparative collection in my lab was produced by a student as part of a year-long independent study course (Figure 11.8). The student (David Palmer, who is now a dentist; I have no idea if there is any connection between his putting together an osteological comparative collection and his chosen line of work) drove all over the state obtaining the carcasses of illegally hunted animals (out of season, lack of a hunting license, trespassing on private property, taking more than the legally allowed limit) that had been seized by the state Department of Environmental Protection (DEP). He also looked for and collected fresh roadkills. The collection was so inclusive that I accused Palmer of driving around looking for live animals to run over himself, but he denied it.

Palmer boiled the flesh off the animals and produced a rather thorough "bone library," storing each animal skeleton in its own container. Many students are startled when they open the box labeled "Hockey Uniform" to find the entire disarticulated (the bones are all separated) skeleton of an adult male deer instead of clothing. At least I tell them it's a deer and not a hockey player. Clearly the project deserved an A, but just to give the student a hard time (that's

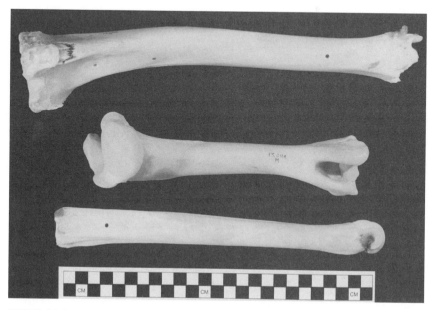

FIGURE 11.8 Major elements of a deer skeleton, (*Odocoileus virginianus*) from our osteological comparative collection, which is useful in identifying the species and skeletal elements recovered at an archaeological site. (K. L. Feder)

part of the job description for university professors), I told Palmer that I would give him an A only if, by using his comparative collection, he could identify a small, intact, triangular bone that we had recovered from a 2,000-year-old hearth at the Loomis II village site in Windsor, Connecticut (which we had excavated the previous summer). I was only kidding, of course, but Palmer immediately rose to the occasion, stating that he knew exactly which bone it was. He reached into the hockey uniform box containing the adult male deer skeleton, rummaged around for a bit, and then pulled out the precise, if a bit larger, match for the archaeological specimen: a phalange, or toe bone, of a white-tailed deer (*Odocoileus virginianus*; Figure 11.9). Certainly I gave Palmer an A for his

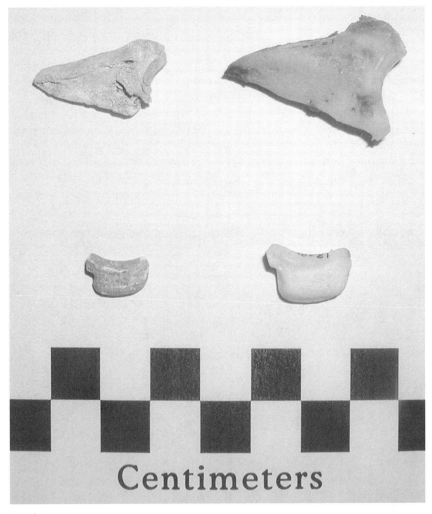

FIGURE 11.9 The small bone elements on the left are from an archaeological site located in Connecticut that has been radiocarbon dated to nearly 2,000 years ago. The two precisely matching bones (except for the fact that they are a little bigger) on the right are from our osteological comparative collection, specifically from a white-tailed deer. (K. L. Feder)

efforts, and we have employed the osteological comparative collection ever since to identify the animal species exploited by people in our archaeological research.

How Can You Tell What Kind of Animal Was Killed or Butchered with an Ancient Stone Tool?

Regardless of how you might feel about the death penalty (personally, I support capital punishment for telemarketers, but that's just me), one can't help but be given pause by the all-too-frequently aired stories on the evening news of some unfortunate—yet, ultimately, incredibly lucky—man or woman walking out of prison after languishing on death row for ten, fifteen, or twenty years. These innocent people often share the fact that after years of professing their innocence, they were finally freed, just before their scheduled execution, after being proven innocent through the application of residue analysis. Forensic investigators now recognize that even years after a crime was committed, a tiny splash of blood may remain concealed on the curve of a serrated blade, a minute clump of the murderer's skin cells may yet reside under the fingernails of the victim, and semen can still be recovered from the clothing of a rape victim. These residues can be recovered and analyzed for blood type and even DNA, enabling investigators to positively rule out innocent individuals—leading to dramatic releases from prison and, in some cases, enabling positive identification of the actual perpetrator of the crime.

The same capillary action by which a tiny droplet of blood may be pulled up along the mechanically polished striations of a stainless steel knife blade also acts on tiny droplets of blood to pull them along the interstices of tiny crystals of stone in a cryptocrystalline material, up and away from the cutting edge of a knife blade made of stone. Dried and hidden in tiny cavities and striations on the stone blade, the blood may remain hidden for thousands of years. In certain cases the blood can be recovered, and the animal species that produced the blood can be identified.

One of the most widely applied techniques for blood residue analysis used in modern law enforcement is **cross-over immunoelectrophoresis (CIEP).** Precisely the same procedure is used to determine the presence of blood on an ancient weapon and to identify the species that was the source of the blood. The process is based on immunological testing of any residue on a stone tool. The antisera of a number of potential animal sources (including human) are applied to the residue recovered from a tool. Each antiserum consists of antibodies that are species-specific and will, therefore, biologically react to antigens in the blood of only the same species. In other words, when blood residue is recovered from an ancient stone blade, that residue is divided into a number of samples, each of which is then exposed to the antiserum from a different animal species. If the ancient blood is not from the same species as the antiserum, there is no immunological reaction. If, however, the blood residue and the added antiserum come from the same species, the antiserum "recognizes" the antigens in the blood sample and reacts to them.

For example, Loy and Dixon (1998) examined a number of ancient stone tools in Alaska dating to as much as 10,000 years ago. They were able to recover blood residue from the tools, which they then identified as having come from woolly mammoths, bison, bears, sheep, caribou, and musk oxen. At the other side of the continent, in eastern Quebec, a series of tools from sites dating to about the same age in the La Martre River Valley were examined for blood residue (Chalifoux 1999). The researchers obtained positive reactions for rabbits, deer, bears, sea lions, trout, and rats from the blood residue recovered from the sample of ancient tools. At another series of 9,000-year-old sites excavated in what is today Yellowstone National Park, traces of blood from deer, elk, rabbits, dogs, and bears were identified on stone spear points, scrapers, and scraping tools (Cannon 1995).

Read More

Any of the examples cited here provide brief, fascinating discussions of the potential of residue analysis in archaeology.

Cannon, K. P. 1995. Blood Residue Analyses of Ancient Stone Tools Reveal Clues to Prehistoric Subsistence Patterns in Yellowstone. *CRM* 18(2):14–16.

Chalifoux, É. 1999. Paleoindian Occupations on the Gaspé Peninsula. *Northeast Anthropology* 57:69–79.

Loy, T. H., and E. J. Dixon. 1998. Blood Residues on Fluted Points from Eastern Beringia Indicate Mammoth Predation as Part of a Big-Game Hunting Tradition. *American Antiquity* 63:21–46.

How Can You Tell What Kinds of Plants Were Collected or Processed with an Ancient Stone Tool?

Much in the same way that the residues of animals killed and butchered by ancient peoples may linger in the nicked edges of the weapons used to kill them and the tools used to prepare them for dinner, plant remains also can adhere to the working edges of utensils for decades, centuries, and even millennia. Recovery and analysis of those remains provide the archaeologist with a database that can allow for the detailed reconstruction of an ancient people's diet.

As mentioned earlier, organic residues left by plants often are not particularly durable, and bits of wood fiber left on an axe blade, mano, or knife probably will disappear as a result of biological activity in the soil in which these artifacts are deposited. However, species-specific **starch grains** can be preserved for millennia on the surface of a tool used to grind seeds or kernels. For example, at the 20,000-year-old level of the Ohalo II site in Israel, a team led by paleobotanist Dolores Piperno (Piperno et al. 2004) recovered wild barley remains from the surface of a large basalt grinding stone found at the site. Knowing that people in the Middle East were using barely more than 10,000 years before they domesticated and farmed it provides insights into the process of plant domestication; although we may call the shift to farming the "Agricultural Revolution," that shift was a slow process that took thousands of years.

As mentioned earlier, plants produce **phytoliths**, a nonorganic residue made up of microscopic mineral particles, more precisely defined as opal silica bodies. Because they are not organic, phytoliths are not eaten or recycled by bacteria or other small organisms, and because they are minerals, phytoliths can be extremely durable, persisting in the soil or adhering to tools for a very long time. Beyond their durability is the fact that different plant genera and species produce a suite of morphologically distinct phytoliths (Figure 11.10). When a researcher trained and experienced in phytolith identification is presented with a sample recovered from the soils at an archaeological site or extracted from the cracks and crevices of ancient tools, he or she can diagnose the species of the plants that grew in the vicinity of the settlement, that were brought back to the community from elsewhere, or that were processed with the tools found at the site.

Dolores Piperno, Anthony Ranere, Irene Holst, and Patricia Hansell (2000) were able to recover phytoliths adhering to a variety of milling stones excavated at the Aguadulce Shelter site in Panama that dated from between 7,000 and 5,000 years ago. Archaeological tools do not come with little tags clearing up questions we have concerning their use, but the shape and heft of the "milling stones" suggested both their name and the fact that they might have

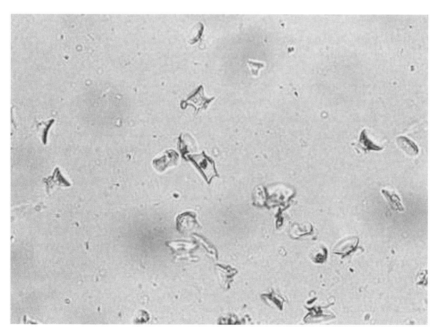

FIGURE 11.10 Phytoliths, much like pollen, exhibit two characteristics that make them useful to the archaeologist: They are durable, and each species produces distinct forms. When phytoliths are recovered from the surfaces of tools, the species of the plants on which the tools were used can be identified. Phytoliths produced by maize are shown here. (Pearsall, Deborah M. Phytoliths in the Flora of Ecuador: The University of Missouri Online Phytolith Database, http://www.missouri.edu/~phyto/)

been used to grind seeds or roots. In this case the phytoliths secreted in cracks on the tool surfaces not only showed that the tools had been used to grind plant material, the phytoliths also showed which plants had been processed with the tools. The researchers found phytoliths diagnostic of a number of starchy tropical plants, especially manioc, arrowroot, and yams. Along with milling roots and yams, the people of the Aguadulce Shelter were also processing maize with their grinding stones.

Evidence of maize in the form of **phytoliths** has also been found adhering to the surfaces of pottery sherds recovered at sites dating to 4,200 years ago in coastal Ecuador (Brown 2001). Along with not thoroughly fastidiously cleaning their dinner dishes, the inhabitants of these Ecuadoran sites weren't all that fussy about cleaning their teeth; maize remains have been found in the tartar of the teeth of two human skeletons excavated there. Remember that the next time you forget to floss.

In these cases by recovering the microscopic remnants of plants processed by ancient tools and by finding durable food remains attached to teeth, analysis of plant residues is allowing archaeologists to directly address questions related to the origins of agriculture in the New World. More generally, phytolith research is providing a unique avenue of inquiry into the use of plants by past peoples, often by producing the raw data being used to illuminate the story of the origins of agriculture (Piperno and Flannery 2001 for maize; Piperno and Pearsall 1998 for root crops of South America; Piperno and Stothert 2003 for squash).

Researchers have also looked for food remains on the interior surfaces of the ceramic vessels in which various foods were cooked, served, or stored. It's a lucky thing, for example, that the people of the ancient Maya civilization of Central America weren't too fastidious about washing out their spouted "teapot" vessels. Researchers have applied a procedure called **high-performance liquid chromatography (HPLC)** to the dry residues recovered from the insides of fourteen of these pouring vessels manufactured by the Maya as long ago as 600 b.c. at the site of Colha, Belize (Hurst et al. 2002). Residues bearing the chemical signature of chocolate were recovered from the insides of three of these vessels. The cacao plant was domesticated by people in the New World, and the residues on the Colha vessels predate the previous oldest evidence of the brewing of a chocolate beverage by the Maya by a thousand years. Chocolate-based beverages were a favorite of the Maya, and, as the residue analysis shows, they have a long history in Central America. Some argue that maize represents the most significant domesticated crop contributed by the native peoples of America to the rest of the world; I think that many of us—certainly any of us who have tasted chocolate—would beg to differ.

When I participated as a student in my first archaeology field school, we made certain to clean every stone tool to make it easier to analyze the edges for use wear. Thirty years later archaeologists are rethinking the desirability of cleaning those edges before investigating the possibility that biological residues remain that can directly inform us about the animals killed as well as the plant foods processed and eaten by the tool users.

Read More

In each of the following publications, you can read informative accounts of the successful recovery of plant remnants from the surfaces of archaeological artifacts that were used to prepare foods such as squash, chocolate, and maize.

Hurst W. J., et al. 2002. Cacao Usage by the Earliest Maya Civilization. *Nature* 418:289–90.

Piperno, D., and K. Flannery. 2001. The Earliest Archaeological Maize (*Zea mays* L.). *Proceedings of the National Academy of Sciences* 98:2101–03.

Piperno, D., and K. A. Stothert. 2003. Phytolith Evidence for Early Holocene *Cucurbita* Domestication in Southwest Ecuador. *Science* 299:1054–57.

Piperno, D. R., and D. M. Pearsall. 1998. *The Origins of Agriculture in the Lowland Neotropics*. Academic Press, Orlando, Florida.

Piperno, D. R., et al. 2000. Starch Grains Reveal Early Root Crop Horticulture in the Panamanian Tropical Forest. *Nature* 407:894–97.

How Can You Determine the Importance of an Animal Species in a People's Diet?

Perhaps the simplest gauge of the abundance and inferred importance of a particular animal species in the diet of an ancient people is a raw count of the numbers of bones of each species recovered at an archaeological excavation. This statistic is called, simply enough, the **Number of Identified Specimens**, or **NISP**, and it can provide a useful first impression of the relative significance of each species to an ancient diet (Klein and Cruz-Uribe 1984). Pretty clearly, animals represented by lots of bones probably were more important in the diet than were those with few bones recovered in hearths and trash pits.

NISP, along with being simple, can also be misleading by ignoring the fact that some animals have more bones than others. Of greater concern is the fact that NISP does not distinguish whole bones from fragments. That poses a real problem, as you can well imagine. Suppose, for example, that when preparing meat for consumption, deer bones were broken into small fragments to get at their nutritious marrow, but other mammal bones were not. That would greatly inflate the seeming importance of deer in the diet; a single animal might produce hundreds and hundreds of counts in the NISP, while the significance of other species might be grossly underestimated because their less-broken-up bones contribute far less to the NISP than their importance in the diet might actually have been.

Another, more complex and, in a sense, conservative statistic addresses this problem of over- and under-representation. It works not by counting individual bones but by calculating the minimum number of animals represented by those bones.

Let's use an analogy to figure out how this process works. Suppose I dropped you off in the middle of a junkyard and gave you the task of estimating the number of automobiles that had been disposed of there. The problem is that there are no complete cars in the junkyard, only some of their constituent parts. How would you go about the task?

You might begin by looking for major, important components of cars, pieces that are found one per car. The engine block would be one such component. Every car has an engine—and no car has more than one—so you might count the number of engine blocks and suggest that number as a guess for the number of autos abandoned at the junkyard.

BONE ELEMENT	DEPOSIT A	B	C	TOTAL
Cranium	3	3	1	7
Mandible	9	24	4	37
Scapula	5	19	2	26
Humerus	4	15	6	25
Radius	9	21	8	38
Ulna	3	6	2	11
Metacarpal	5	26	6	37
Pelvis	10	0	0	10
Femur	2	4	1	7
Tibia	7	17	8	32
Calcaneum	0	0	2	2
Astragalus	0	0	0	0
Metatarsal	10	20	9	39

Calculation of the minimum number of sheep recovered from three deposits (A, B, and C) excavated at the Treasury Site, a Saxon farm excavated in London (data from Chaplin 1971). There are 271 individual bones listed here, and each one could have come from a different animal. There could have been, therefore, as many as 271 animals whose remains were represented at the site. But there could have been far fewer; in calculating the number of animals represented at an archaeological deposit, the Minimum Number approach is conservative, assuming that if multiple bone elements could have come from the same individual animal, they did. For example, the 39 metatarsals (foot bones) could have come from fewer than 39 individual animals since each sheep has more than one metatarsal. The 7 crania could have come from no fewer than 7 individuals and the 10 pelvises could have come from no fewer than 10 animals, but some of the crania and some of the pelvises may have come from the same individual animals; in calculating the MNI, it is assumed that the 7 crania and 7 of the 10 pelvises all did come from the same 7 individuals. By the same reasoning, the 37 mandibles could have come from no fewer than 37 animals (some or all of which could have also been represented by the crania and pelvises just enumerated). Based on the above chart, there are the remains of a minimum of 37 animals at the old farm site, though there could have been many more.

FIGURE 11.11 To determine the minimum number of individuals of an animal species represented at an archaeological site, you need to count all the different skeletal elements recovered. (Based on data from Chaplin, 1971)

Now, suppose I tell you that you can't just rely on engines because some of them had been removed from the junkyard entirely. Luckily, however, other parts of those cars (for example, gas tanks) had been left behind. Every car has a gas tank, and you might count those. You couldn't assume that the gas tanks you have counted belonged to different cars from those already counted based on their engine blocks. You almost certainly would be counting some cars twice, once for their engine blocks and once for their gas tanks. Being conservative and not wanting to overestimate the number of cars, you might assume that because each car must have had both an engine block and a gas tank, an engine and tank together still represent only one car. That assumption might underestimate the number of cars—a gas tank and engine block might not belong to the same car, even though you are counting them together as belonging to the same auto—but that's OK; it is more reasonable to come up with a baseline reflecting the minimum possible number rather than a maximum.

If you counted twenty engine blocks and thirty gas tanks in the junkyard, there still must have been a minimum of thirty cars in the junkyard; you would assume that the first twenty gas tanks came from the same cars as represented by the twenty engine blocks (that's twenty cars), but the next ten gas tanks must reflect the presence of ten additional cars whose engine blocks are missing. If you continued this counting of major car components, always assuming that if parts could have belonged to the same automobile, they did, you would come up with a minimum number of cars; there could be more, though you couldn't prove it, but there could be no fewer.

Archaeologists use the same reasoning to come up with a statistic called the **MNI**, or **Minimum Number of Individuals**, in a faunal assemblage. Although a cooking or trash feature may present the archaeologist with a jumble of bone fragments, a conservative, minimum estimate of the number of animals killed, butchered, and cooked can be determined in much the same way as is shown in the junkyard car example. We assume that skeletal elements that are "redundant" (meaning that they could have come from the same animal) did come from the same creature. You may, for example, find the fragmentary, butchered crania of ten white-tailed deer at a site. From this you can conclude with certainty that there must have been at least ten deer killed by the ancient inhabitants. Now suppose that we also recovered thirty right shoulder blades of the same species of deer. Though we couldn't prove it, we assume that ten of those belonged to the deer already represented by the ten crania. The twenty right shoulder blades with no corresponding crania would have to belong to twenty additional deer (we'll assume there were no mutant deer with supernumerary right shoulder blades). So the MNI for deer at the site would be thirty (Figure 11.11 shows a similar analysis for sheep).

We are aided in our MNI calculations by the ability to distinguish the bones of males from females as well as animals who died at different stages of their lives. A right and left lower leg might come from the same deer, but not if one came from a male and the other a female, or if one came from an animal that died young and the other from a much older one.

As useful as the MNI statistic may be, you might have identified an inadequacy. Although it might be very valuable in providing an estimate of the number of animals represented in the faunal assemblage, our goal as archaeologists is not to perform an animal census but to reconstruct an ancient diet. To accomplish this we must remember that, rather obviously, merely knowing the numbers of animals represented in an assemblage isn't enough. We need to be able to figure out how much food those animals contributed to the diet, and not all animals are equal as sources of meat (and hides). For example, a single, large adult white-tailed deer produces a lot more meat (nearly 20 kg [44 lbs]) of meat in an experiment to test whitetail meat productivity (Madrigal and Holt 2002) than does a smaller animal such as, for example, a raccoon. A head count of animals of each species isn't enough; to reconstruct an ancient diet we need to calculate how much meat each of those individuals probably provided.

To derive a useful indication of the biomass of a given animal species represented at an archaeological site, the MNI statistic may be multiplied by the amount of meat probably provided by each individual animal to get a better idea of the significance of each species in an ancient diet. Such an estimate provides a pretty good relative measure of the importance of each meat producing animal in an ancient diet

Read More

Any of the zooarchaeology guides cited in the section "Why Do Archaeologists Want to Know the Animal Species Exploited by Ancient People?" will walk you through the process of determining the minimum numbers of a particular species represented by the bones recovered at an archaeological site.

Chaplin, R. E. 1971. *The Study of Animal Bones from Archaeological Sites*. Seminar Press, London.

Hesse, B., and P. Wapnish. 1985. *Animal Bone Archaeology*. Taraxacum, Washington, D.C. Klein, R. G., and K. Cruz-Uribe. 1984. *The Analysis of Animal Bones from Archaeological Sites*. University of Chicago Press, Chicago.

O'Connor, T. 2000. *The Archaeology of Animal Bones*. Texas A&M Press, College Station.

Reitz, E. J. 1999. *Zooarchaeology*. Cambridge University Press, Cambridge.

CAN HUMAN WASTE BE USED TO HELP
RECONSTRUCT DIET?

Though it certainly is not the most romantic weapon in the archaeologist's analytical arsenal, food remains that have actually been ingested by, passed through the digestive systems of, and then been excreted by ancient peoples provide direct if unpleasant evidence of diet. The remains of prehistoric feces, called **paleofeces** or **coprolites**, are sometimes preserved, though this is quite rare (Bryant and Williams-Dean 1978). Because our human digestive tract is not entirely efficient, some of the material we ingest fails to be entirely digested and is excreted, sometimes with so little alteration that it is recognizable. Our bodies are not very good, for instance, at breaking down some forms of cellulose in plant foods, and this material passes through our systems sometimes more or less intact. When human feces have been deposited in a stable, dry environment (where the deposit is not rained on, temperature does not vary widely, and there are no animals who might like to recyle some of the undigested food), they may be preserved for long periods of time. Bones, whole and fragmentary, seeds and seed casings, shells, and even meat cells can be extracted from coprolites. These data are about as direct as we can get in the analysis of an ancient diet. In fact, much of our understanding of the earliest agriculture in the New World is based on undigested food remains found in coprolites excavated in caves in the highlands of Mexico (MacNeish 1967).

Read More

Here are references for the material in this section.

Gilbert, B. M. 1973. *Mammalian Osteo-Archaeology: North America*. Missouri Archaeological Society, Columbia.

MacNeish, R. S. 1967. An Interdisciplinary Approach to an Archaeological Problem. In *Prehistory of the Tehuacan Valley: Volume One—Environment and Subsistence*, edited by D. Beyers, 14–23. University of Texas Press, Austin.

Pearsall, D. M. 2000. *Paleoethnobotany: A Handbook of Procedures*. Academic Press, San Diego.

Piperno, D. R., and D. M. Pearsall. 1998. *The Origins of Agriculture in the Lowland Neotropics*. Academic Press, Orlando, Florida.

How Does Skeletal Chemistry Help Us Reconstruct an Ancient Diet?

I began this chapter by mentioning the cliché "You are what you eat." It turns out that there is more than just a "grain" of truth in that statement (sorry for the bad pun). I know a lot of people who swear that you can actually see every candy bar they have ever eaten right there on their hips, but that has yet to be tested archaeologically. In fact, however, the chemistry of certain foods does have a measurable effect on the human skeleton. A careful chemical analysis of human bones can reveal at least some general information about a person's diet. We can't count candy bars, but we can reveal some details about the significance of meat in a diet and even the kinds of grains that contributed to subsistence.

For example, the ratio of stable **isotopes** of carbon and nitrogen have been determined for herbivores and carnivores. As you move up the food chain, one of the stable isotopes of nitrogen (^{15}N) becomes increasingly concentrated. Herbivores have a higher concentration than do the plants they eat, and carnivores, in turn, have a concentration higher than that of the herbivores they eat. Because humans are omnivores whose diets may vary greatly, from strict vegetarianism to nearly exclusive meat-eating, the concentration of ^{15}N in certain groups and individuals may vary greatly depending on the proportion of plant food to animal flesh in their diets. Essentially, vegetarians have low concentrations of ^{15}N, while heavy meat-eaters have higher concentrations. Using this as a guide, researchers have calculated the ^{15}N concentration in the bones of an extinct hominid, an individual member of the well-known Neandertals found in a cave in Croatia (Richards et al. 2000). The result resembled the concentration measured for a control group consisting of the bones of an animal whose dietary preference was well known, specifically, a carnivore (the saber-toothed cat). The cats and the Neandertals both had a higher proportion of ^{15}N than that seen among known herbivores. This has been interpreted as meaning that the Neandertals relied heavily on meat in their diet.

Compare these results to those derived for the 5,300-year-old remains of the "Ice Man," a nearly intact human body found in the Alps in 1991 (for more on the Ice Man, see chapter 13). In his case researchers measured the ^{15}N concentration in preserved hair (Macko et al. 1999). The Ice Man's ^{15}N levels were lower than those seen in modern human beings, who ingest a mixed diet of meat, grains, and vegetables and much closer to modern people who practice vegetarianism, a good indication that plant foods made up the bulk of the Ice Man's diet.

Remember from our discussion of carbon dating that there are three isotopes of carbon: ^{12}C, ^{13}C, and ^{14}C. There are three metabolically different photosynthesis processes, or pathways, by which plants use solar energy to produce food, labeled C-3, C-4, and CAM, and all three pathways use ^{12}C and ^{14}C in the same proportion as that in the atmosphere—they don't prefer one of the isotopes over the other. However, C-4 pathway plants more readily use carbon dioxide containing the ^{13}C isotope than do those plants that use the C-3 or CAM pathways. What this means is that C-4 pathway plants have a higher concentration of ^{13}C than do C-3 or CAM plants. When animals, including human beings, ingest plant food, they incorporate carbon into their bodies, including their skeletons. A preference for or limited availability of plants following one of these pathways will result in a ^{13}C proportion in their bones that reflects the bias in the plants they eat. Simply, if you eat a lot of C-4 plants, your bones will reflect their higher ^{13}C concentration, and if you eat less of the C-4 pathway plants, the ^{13}C concentration in your bones will be lower.

Researchers in Great Britain have used this fact in their analysis of 183 human skeletons, 19 dating to the period before the adoption of agriculture there—between 9,000 and 5,200 years ago—and the rest (164 people) to the period immediately following the adoption of an agricultural way of life—between 5,200 and 4,500 years ago, looking specifically at the ratio of the two stable isotopes of carbon in their bones (Richards et al. 2003). It turns out that fish and marine mammals have relatively high levels of ^{13}C, and, not surprisingly, the bones of people who eat lots of fish and marine mammals do as well. The preagricultural inhabitants of Great Britain, at least the people whose bones were analyzed in this research, had a high concentration of ^{13}C relative to ^{12}C. Seafood probably contributed significantly to their diets.

The skeletal remains in the sample dating to after 5,200 years ago and, therefore, after the adoption of an agricultural way of life show a sharp drop in their concentration of ^{13}C. We know that wheat and oats were important domesticated crops in northern European agriculture, and these are C-3 pathway plants with a low concentration of the ^{13}C isotope compared to fish and marine mammals. The authors of the study conclude that C-3 pathway plants, probably wheat and oats, abruptly replaced marine resources in the diet of Britons beginning 5,200 years ago, marking the beginning of food production as the primary mode of subsistence there. It is interesting to point out that when the Ice Man's ^{13}C concentrations were measured in the study mentioned earlier (Macko et al. 2000), those results also showed low levels of ^{13}C, indicating a similar heavy reliance on local C-3 pathway cereal crops.

Most of the indigenous wild plant foods eaten by ancient Native Americans north of Mexico were C-3 plants, with their lower concentration of ^{13}C (Smith 1995). Not surprisingly, the bones of Native Americans dating to before about A.D. 1000 (when indigenous plant foods formed the core of subsistence in the Midwest) show a proportionally low concentration of ^{13}C as well, reflecting the nature of their diet.

The stereotypical American Indian crop is maize, but maize (or corn) is not native to North America. It is a tropical plant native to Mesoamerica, was domesticated there more than 7,000 years ago, and shows up in small amounts at archaeological sites in North America about 3,000 years later as a result of **diffusion**. Maize does not follow the photosynthetic pathway of most of the wild plants eaten by the native peoples of North America. Maize is a C-4 plant, with a proportionally higher concentration of ^{13}C. In a remarkable turn, after about A.D. 1000 the skeletons of Native Americans found in the Midwest show a marked jump in ^{13}C proportion compared to their ancestors (Figure 11.12). This seems to be strong evidence that, although maize had already been introduced into North America no later than 2,800 years earlier, it wasn't until after A.D. 1000 that it became a significant and perhaps dominant part of the aboriginal diet, whose impact shows up in the chemistry of the bones of native peoples.

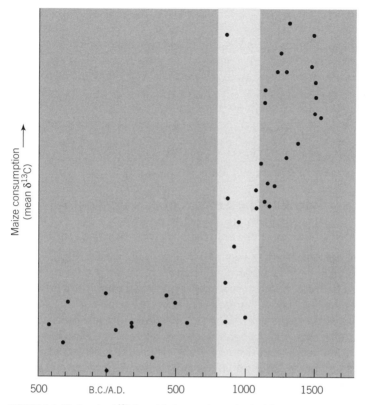

FIGURE 11.12 Levels of ¹³C found in human bones in the Mississippi Valley dating from 500 B.C. through A.D. 1600. The marked increase in ¹³C seen around A.D. 1000 is interpreted as resulting from an equally marked increase in the importance of maize in the diet.(Bruce Smith)

As noted, the ratio of stable isotopes of carbon and nitrogen can be used to reconstruct the diet of an ancient group of people. The carbon-to-nitrogen ratios detected in the bones of Neanderthals at the Marillac site in France are similar to those seen in wolves and hyenas that lived in Europe during the same period, sometime between 45,000 and 40,000 years ago (Richards et al. 2000). This suggests to the researchers that like the big canids of the time period, the Neanderthals at Marillac were largely meat eaters and, therefore, successful and accomplished hunters. Indeed, you *are* what you eat, and the chemistry of human bones is beginning to reveal dietary preferences in remarkable ways.

Read More

To learn more about reconstructing the diets of ancient peoples through the chemical analysis of their bones, have a look at the references that follow.

Price, T. D., ed. 1989. *The Chemistry of Prehistoric Bone.* Cambridge University Press, Cambridge.

Price, T. D., M. J. Schoeninger, and G. J. Armelagos. 1985. Bone Chemistry and Past Behavior: An Overview. *Journal of Human Evolution* 14:419–47.

Richards, M. P., P. P. Pettitt, E. Trinkaus, et al. 2000. Neanderthal Diet at Vindija and Neanderthal Predation: The Evidence from Stable Isotopes. *Proceedings of the National Academy of Sciences* 97:7663–66.

Sandford, M. K. 1992. A Reconsideration of Trace Element Analysis. In *Skeletal Biology of Past Peoples: Research Methods,* edited by S. R. Saunders and A. M. Katzenberg, 153–74. Wiley-Liss, New York.

Smith, B. D. 1995. *The Emergence of Agriculture.* Scientific American Library, New York.

How Can the Season of a Settlement's Occupation Be Determined?

As you will remember, in instances in which archaeologists rely on chronometric dating methods other than dendrochronology for determining the age of a site, the error factor is usually in the tens and even the hundreds of years. It may seem paradoxical then for me to say that even though most chronometric dating methods are not precise and the plus-or-minus error factor in years can be substantial, I still might be able to tell you the month or at least the seasons a site was occupied. But there is no contradiction, because assigning a month or season of occupation relies on a different set of data than do chronometric dating techniques.

Essentially, human beings depend to one degree or another on resources, especially food resources, that are available on a sometimes fairly restricted seasonal basis. Knowing the season or even the month of availability of resources whose remains are found at an archaeological site provides a way to determine the season or month of site occupation. Because some foods can be stored for an extended period of time, seasonal availability does not necessarily restrict the time of occupation to the season or month when the resource was collected. So this form of analysis indicates the month or season when a group must have been present, but it cannot be used to prove when it was not present.

For example, during fall in the eastern woodlands of North America, oaks produce acorns, and chestnut, walnut, and hickory trees produce their respective nuts (Bernstein 1999). Finding the remains of the shells and nut meats of acorns, chestnuts, walnuts, and hickory nuts at an archaeological site is a good indicator that the site was occupied in the fall of the year, but not necessarily only in the fall. People can collect nuts only when they are available, which is soon after they ripen and before animals collect them all or they get covered up by leaves and needles. Certainly, nuts left in their shells can be stored for a substantial length of time, so the recovery of nutshells or charred nut meats is strong evidence that a site was occupied in the fall, but not necessarily exclusively: The site's inhabitants may have harvested large quantities of nuts in the fall, stored a portion of them, and continued to subsist on nuts well into the winter and beyond.

As a result of migratory patterns, some fish species are available in significant numbers over a relatively narrow window of time during the year. Every fall, for example, Pacific salmon make an epic migration, traveling sometimes hundreds of miles from the ocean back upriver and ultimately (and remarkably) home to the streams in which they hatched, where they proceed to mate and the females lay eggs. Swimming in great numbers and fighting the river's flow, these fish were easily caught in enormous quantities by peoples who organized their seasonal schedules around the upstream journey of the salmon each fall. Atlantic salmon conduct their spawning runs in the spring, and many sites located along streams with significant fall lines in the East, such as the 8,000-year-old Neville site, located in New Hampshire along the Amoskeag River, were most likely occupied in the spring to take advatage of the abundance of food during the spawning run (Dincauze 1976). Here too, preservation and storage are possible—dried salmon can remain edible for a long time. So the presence of salmon at a site doesn't mean that the site was inhabited only during a single season, but it must have been inhabited at least during the spawning run to allow for capture of the fish.

In some cases the ages of juvenile animals hunted by a people can indicate the season of harvest. Unlike human beings, who are sexually receptive virtually all the time (well, nearly), most animal species have a relatively brief rutting season, when females are sexually receptive and fertile and during which they can become pregnant. Also, because the females of most species have a rather regular period of gestation, the births of offspring in a population of animals occur in a rather narrow range of time during the year (again, unlike humans, whose births are distributed fairly evenly across the year).

Once born, the young of any animal species go through a series of developmental processes that are obvious on the outside—they get larger, their muscles increase in strength, they may grow horns or antlers—and that are also apparent on the inside, including the animal's bones. Changes to skeletons that reflect growth and increasing maturity usually occur at a regular and consistent rate and at relatively fixed times during development. These changes can be used to gauge the age of a subadult animal—we will see the same analytical process applied to human skeletons as well.

We can figure out the season or even the month that an animal was hunted—and, therefore, the season or month a site was occupied—because we know when animals of the hunted species are born, and we can determine the approximate age of death from the morphology of the animal's bones. Let me give you an example: The breeding season of the American bison (commonly called the buffalo and technically *Bison bison*) extends from middle to late summer, July through September. The length of gestation for a bison varies from 270 to 300 days, so most bison are born in the three-month period of March, April, and May. Bison do not achieve sexual maturity until about the age of two, and between birth and that time their bones grow, develop, and achieve adult form following a rather firmly timed schedule. In other words, as a bison matures, its bones progress through a series of somewhat consistently

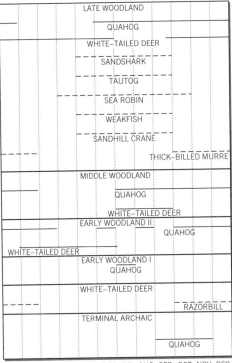

FIGURE 11.13 Diagram showing food resources recovered by excavators at the Greenwich Cove site located on Narragansett Bay in Rhode Island. The horizontal line associated with each of the species reflects the months during which that species would have been available to the site's residents and, therefore, the months during which the site was probably occupied, broken down by five periods of southern New England prehistory (Terminal Archaic, Early Woodland I and II, Middle Woodland, Late Woodland). (Courtesy David Bernstein)

measured changes in appearance, so their appearance, in turn, can be used to accurately estimate a developing bison's age.

Now, suppose we excavate an archaeological site where bison meat was a major component of subsistence. Further, suppose that where juvenile bison were hunted, they all can be determined to have been about eighteen months old based on the morphology of their maturing bones. Count forward eighteen months from their births in March, April, and May and you get to August, September, and October (of the following year). Therefore, those eighteen-month-old bison whose butchered bones were found at this site were most likely hunted sometime during those three months, the late summer and early fall. Using just such an approach, archaeologist R. J. Carter (1997) examined the mandibles of roe deer recovered at the 10,700-year-old Star Carr site in England. Carter determined that the ages of the roe deer suggested that they had been killed by the inhabitants sometime during March and April, so the site must have been occupied at least during the early spring.

We don't have any bison in Connecticut, but we do have lots of white-tailed deer. The whitetail rutting season in Connecticut is quite short, beginning in early November. Individual females are sexually receptive for only a few days, but not all at exactly the same time. Overall, the deer population rut usually lasts less than a month. Therefore, most does get pregnant in November. The gestation period for a deer lasts about 200 days, or a bit less than seven months, so most fawns are born in May or June. The size of the phalange of the white-tailed deer

Chapter 11:
Interactive
Exercise

recovered at the 2,000-year-old Loomis II site in Windsor, Connecticut, indicated an age of about nine months. A nine-month-old deer born in May or June would have been killed in February or March, indicating that whatever other time of year it may have been inhabited, the Loomis II site almost certainly was occupied in the late winter or very early spring.

Looking at all the seasonally available foods recovered at a site allows the creation of a seasonality chart (Figure 11.13). The overlapping patterns of seasonal availability allow for a determination of the periods during the year that a site was occupied.

Read More

Determining the seasons during which a particular archaeological site was occupied relies to a great degree on the analysis of faunal and botanical remains. For detailed discussions of the task of determining seasonality and examples of the process, have a look at any of the following sources.

Baker, B. W., B. S. Shaffer, and D. G. Steele. 1997. Basic Approaches in Archaeological Faunal Analysis. In *Field Methods in Archaeology*, edited by T. R. Hester, H. J. Shafer, and K. L. Feder, 298–318. Mayfield Publishing, Mountain View, California.

Bernstein, D. J. 1999. Prehistoric Use of Plant Foods on Long Island and Block Island Sounds. In *Current Northeast Paleoethnobotany*, edited by J. P. Hart, 101–19. New York State Musuem, Albany.

Carter, R. J. 1997. Age Estimation of the Roe Deer (*Capreolus capreolus*) Mandibles from the Mesolithic Site of Star Carr, Yorkshire, Based on Radiographs of Mandibular Tooth Development. *Journal of the Zoological Society of London* 241:495–502.

Chaplin, R. E. 1971. *The Study of Animal Bones from Archaeological Sites*. Seminar Press, London.

Davis, S. J. M. 1995. *The Archaeology of Animals*. Yale University Press, New Haven, Connecticut.

Dincauze, D. F. 1976. *The Neville Site: Eight Thousand Years at Amoskeag*. Peabody Museum of Archaeology and Ethnology, Cambridge, Massachusetts.

Klein, R. G., and K. Cruz-Uribe. 1984. *The Analysis of Animal Bones from Archaeological Sites*. University of Chicago Press, Chicago.

Reitz, E. J. 1999. *Zooarchaeology*. Cambridge University Press, Cambridge.

Wheat, J. B. 1972. *The Olsen-Chubbuck Site: A Paleo Indian Bison Kill*. Memoir of the Society for American Archaeology 26, Salt Lake City.

Study Questions

1. What kinds of evidence support the hypothesis that hunting contributed to the subsistence of the inhabitants of the Wood Lily site?

2. What foods do foragers rely on?

3. What is the purpose of "flotation"? Describe the process.

4. What is the purpose of a faunal and floral comparative collection?

5. How might an artifact assemblage suggest, at least qualitatively, the subsistence base of an archaeological group?

6. What are paleofeces, or coprolites? How does their analysis assist in reconstructing the diet of a past people?

7. Why is it important to know not just that an ancient people hunted, but what animals they hunted?

8. How do the strategies for hunting deer differ from those for hunting bison? How might a reliance on deer versus a reliance on bison affect other elements of a culture?

9. How do archaeologists identify the use of domesticated animals by a past people?

10. Why may it not be a good idea to wash archaeological stone tools when they are returned to the lab for analysis?

11. How does blood residue analysis work? Provide a couple of examples whereby the recovery of blood residues on even very ancient tools has resulted in a precise identification of the animal species killed and butchered by the ancient people who used the tools.

12. What are phytoliths? How does analysis of phytoliths contribute to our understanding of an ancient diet?

13. Describe the process of determining the minimum number of individuals (MNI) of a particular animal species recovered at an archaeological site. Why do we want to know the MNI?

14. How does an analysis of human skeletal chemistry contribute to our understanding of an ancient diet?

15. How do archaeologists determine the season of a village's occupation?

16. The bones of primarily eighteen-month-old individuals of an animal species with a rutting season in mid-May and a two-month gestation period are found at an archaeological site. In which month was the site probably occupied?

12

Families, Neighbors, and Strangers

RECONSTRUCTING ANCIENT SOCIAL SYSTEMS

- **Can Archaeologists Figure Out the Social Relationships of Past People?**

- **Can Archaeologists Figure Out the Roles of Males and Females in Ancient Societies?**

- **How Does an Archaeologist Approach Issues of Economic, Social, and Political Inequality in an Ancient Society?**

- **How Is Ethnicity Reflected in the Archaeological Record?**

- **Can Archaeologists Reconstruct Ancient Religious Practices?**

  How Are Rituals Preserved in the Archaeological Record?

- **How Do Archaeologists Trace the Movement of People and Ideas Across a Social Landscape?**

- **How Can Archaeologists Reveal Ways of Life of People Whose Reality Was So Different from Our Own?**

I began the previous chapter with a cliché: "You are what you eat." I'll begin this one with another one: "Man does not live by bread alone." The primary source of this phrase is the Old Testament of the Bible (Deuteronomy), and it's repeated a couple of times in the New Testament. It is intended to convey the fact that along with the human need for physical sustanence, people also have spiritual needs. I'm using the phrase here to impart something a bit more than this. To be sure, the people at Wood Lily had to fulfill basic biological requirements, that is, they had to gather or produce sufficient food to feed the men, women, and children who lived at the site. But human beings gather or produce those foods as members of a social group. We are social animals, and most of us rely on and even occasionally enjoy the company of others. The social lives of the residents of Wood Lily or of any other ancient community might seem a rather more difficult aspect of their lives to reconstruct than tool-making or diet. After all, archaeology is the study of the material remains of human behavior. In what ways do family, friendship, alliances, and so on. leave behind material remains? This chapter is about how archaeologists, sometimes in rather clever, less-than-obvious ways, are able to get at this rather nonmaterial element of people's lives.

 ## Can Archaeologists Figure Out the Social Relationships of Past People?

The Broadway musical *Fiddler on the Roof* concerns a community of Jews trying to maintain their unique identity as a small minority in rural, late nineteenth-century Russia. One of the highlights of the show occurs when Tevye, the patriarch of the family that is the focus of the story, sings the song "Tradition" in an attempt to explain how, even under trying circumstances as a beleaguered and oppressed minority, a people can and, in fact, must remain true to their history, their religion, and their culture. In Tevye's spoken dialogue within the song, he enumerates some of the cultural traditions of his people, and regarding any one of these traditions, says: "You may ask, 'How did this tradition get started?' I'll tell you: I don't know. But it's a tradition!" Tevye makes an interesting point here. Traditions are important not because they necessarily have any particular meaning or rationale today and not because they are utilitarian or provide anything of immediate practical value. Traditions are important, nonetheless, because they serve to bind a people together as a community over the long haul.

Human beings carry out their tasks, raise and educate their children, worship their gods, fight their battles, and organize the social fabric of their societies, at least in part, on the basis of tradition, the sources of which most people, like Tevye, cannot identify or specify. As children, all human beings become **enculturated;** we become practitioners of a particular culture and members of a cultural group. Every day of our lives we are taught how to be a member of our group, both explicitly through training by adults, teachers, and mentors and implicitly by watching those around us and emulating their behavior. We all, to one extent or another, from the most conservative "traditionalists" among us to those who fancy themselves freethinkers and radicals, follow Tevye in embracing many of the traditions and traditional behaviors of our culture. As an adult and as a parent, I must admit that many of the social rules I balked at as a kid I now impose on my own children. It's "tradition." Most of us yearn to be accepted as a member of a group, and one way to accomplish this is to behave in a way that tradition demands. Simply by watching our parents go about their daily routines, we are trained in the appropriate behavior of men and women; we acquire food preferences and patterns of food preparation; we worship their gods; we learn how to knit or sew, to take care of an automobile, to balance a checkbook, to build a house, and so on. Now think about how many of those behaviors coincidentally involve material objects: food, utensils, tools, construction materials. We make material things, use them, consume them, and discard them all within the context of our cultural traditions. How these material objects look, how they wear out, and how they end up in the ground as archaeological artifacts and ecofacts all reflect, to one extent or another, our traditional behaviors. Traditions, therefore, are encoded into those objects and in this way are conveyed to archaeologists through the archaeological record.

Take, for example, a simple stone spear point made by a member of a particular ancient society. Certainly, part of the morphology of a usable spear point is dictated by functional necessity. A stone intended to be the tip of a hunting spear must have a sharp point to penetrate an animal's skin. Its form should allow it to fly straight and true toward its intended target. Its edges should be thin and sharp enough to cut deep into the prey yet strong enough to sustain the force of impact with the sometimes tough hide of an animal. The butt end of a stone point should be of a shape and form that allow for its hafting onto a wooden shaft so it will not fall off as soon as it strikes its intended victim.

Taken together, however, these functional prerequisites still leave an enormous amount of freedom for the stone tool maker in terms of the shape to make the point and still have it be an effective weapon (Figure 12.1). Its sharp edges can be straight or serrated, and those edges can be linear or curved. With two straight sides and a base, the point will be triangular, but there is still a choice of equilateral or isosceles. Curved sides work equally well, and an effective spear point may look like a willow leaf. The necessity of shaping the base of a point to facilitate hafting still allows for a wide variety of channels or notches, single or multiple, deep or shallow, located along the point's sides, at the corners, or along the base. In many cases these individual variations do not affect in the least the essential functional characteristics of the weapon. Now imagine all the combinations and permutations of these variables in considering the possibilities of the appearances of perfectly serviceable stone spear points, and you see that on the basis of form alone, there is a huge range of acceptable outcomes for a stone spear point maker. It is unlikely in the extreme that there were "laws" concerning what your spear point had to look like in any given society. Especially if they came into contact with other groups of people with different traditions of tool making, the knappers within a given group certainly realized that there were other shapes that worked just as well as their own. Individual spear makers were perfectly capable of expressing

FIGURE 12.1 All these spear points are functionally equivalent; they could all be used to perform the same task. Nevertheless, each is different from the other. Those differences may very well reflect not functional necessities but social aspects of the teaching of tool making.

their individuality, but overall, artisans tended not to drastically alter their own practice because, well, there were traditions that needed to be followed.

When we excavate archaeological sites, it is pretty common to find that during a single period of time, nearly all the stone spear points look pretty much alike, just variations on a theme. Take, for example, the fluted points of Paleo-Indians, dating to more than 10,000 years ago (see Figure 8.15). The Clovis variety is found all over the United States and Canada, and, wherever they are found, they look much the same: They are more than twice as long as they are wide; their edges begin in parallel at the base and then curve in toward the top; and they exhibit channels, or "flutes," on both of their faces, which begin at the base and reach up to somewhat less than halfway toward the top. All Clovis points share another common feature: They are concave along their bases. On this characteristic, however, there is some easily recognizable geographic variation. Clovis points in the East tend to have a greatly exaggerated concavity at the base compared to those found in the West. The depth of this concavity reaches its maximum at the Vail site in Maine (Gramly 1982) and Debert in Nova Scotia (MacDonald 1985). We cannot say why this deeply concave base developed, but we certainly can recognize it and wonder about what it signifies.

A particular way of crafting a stone spear point—or ceramic vessel, necklace, house, or burial—is determined by a cultural tradition, passed from the artisan to the apprentice, which may mean, simply, from mother to daughter, father to son, or either parent to a daughter or son. In the way things are accomplished in any individual culture (shape of their spear points, shape and designs pressed into their pottery vessels, appearance of items of adornment, configuration of their dwellings, form of burial chambers) we may ask, like Tevye, "How did this tradition [of stone point making, pot making, jewelry manufacturing, house construction, or burying of the dead] get started?" Like Tevye, we will be forced to answer, "I don't know," and like Tevye, we understand that these different cultural practices, these ways of doing things within each culture, are all part of and the result of "tradition." Therein lies our archaeological application of the concept of tradition. Traditions are passed down within a social system of enculturation. If men make spear points and are taught as boys how to make stone tools by their fathers, then their points will share many of the features of the men from whom they learned the craft. If most of the spear points found at a site share many morphological similarities, it may mean that members of each generation of stone tool makers learned their trade from their fathers, who learned from their fathers, and so on. All these men may have shared in a tool making tradition because they were related, descendants of a tool maker who started a particular stone tool making tradition many generations earlier.

Chapter 12: Interactive Exercise

An archaeologist will recognize the great similarities—or the great differences—in spear points, pots, jewelry, houses, and burials at an archaeological site and may draw conclusions about the nature of the social system of enculturation of the society. For example, if men made the spear points and if all, or nearly all, the points recovered at a site share the same basic template, it might be the case that all the men were related to one another and that the tool making tradition reflected in the appearance of their spear points had been passed down in the same family.

In a small social group where the evidence indicates that related men stayed put, they might have had to marry a woman from outside the group because all the women born into the group would be related to all the men. When men stayed in the group upon marriage and their wives left their village of birth to move in with their husband's group, the postmarital residence pattern is called **patrilocality.**

Suppose the spear points found at a site exhibit a great deal of variation and follow no similar template or model. This might signify that the men in the group learned their tool making from different families following different traditions and then brought these differing traditions with them to their new place of residence. In other words, these men came together because of marriage. They left the villages where they were born to live with their wives, who stayed in their own birth-village, a postmarital residence pattern called **matrilocality.** Here, if women made pottery, we might expect them to have followed a common family tradition within which pottery making was taught and passed down.

Though traditions serve to bind a people together, they are neither universally adhered to within a society nor necessarily fixed or constant. Within any group of people, there may be what amounts to a normal distribution of traditional behavior, a pattern in which most people fall out at about the mean or average. Some cultural conservatives may be more comfortable adhering to older patterns, decrying any alteration to the traditions they learned as children. Others may be ahead of the behavioral curve—or maybe on another curve altogether—following traditions not yet accepted and, perhaps, never to become the norm of society. For example, you won't find many seventy- or eighty-year-old people in America with lots of body and facial piercings, but it is increasingly common among teenagers and twenty-somethings. The practice of body and facial piercings represents a tradition, perhaps one that will never represent the "norm," but it is a tradition, nonetheless, the practice of which would be noticed by and of interest to the archaeologist.

Traditions may be fluid, that is, they may evolve and develop as a people do as they encounter and interact with groups other than their own and as old beliefs or practices shift to accommodate changes in the natural and cultural environment. For example, we have already talked a bit about the traditional designs carved into the gravestones of New England's colonial inhabitants (chapter 8). We noticed how the common seventeenth-century New England practice of carving a skull on a gravestone gave way first to the cherub face and later the urn and willow design, as the Puritan belief in predestination was replaced with a growing acceptance by other Protestant groups of the possibility that heaven was attainable through good works on Earth.

While the norm changed from death's head, to cherub, to urn and willow, some, especially older people, refused to change their practice of the tradition.

FIGURE 12.2 The urn and willow design had been extremely popular on New England gravestones in the early through late nineteenth century. It was no longer the norm by the times of George and Maria Crocker's deaths in 1912 and 1925, repectively. Nevertheless, exhibiting a degree of cultural conservatism, these now passé designs were carved on their tombstones in the second and third decades of the twentieth century.

Though urn and willow designs tend to disappear in New England cemeteries toward the end of the nineteenth century, they are sometimes found on gravestones that date well into the twentieth century. Upon his death in 1912, for example, ninety-year-old George Crocker and his family, probably including his wife, elected to have the by-then out-of-fashion urn and willow carved on his tombstone (Figure 12.2, left). Thirteen years later this same design was craved on his wife Maria Crocker's stone when she died in 1925 at the age of seventy-five (Figure 12.2, right).

Traditions may be maintained for generations, or they may quickly shift through time. These traditions may be rigorously adhered to by virtually everyone in a group, or their practice may be pretty flexible. Whatever the case, the remarkable point of all this is simple: Even nonmaterial elements of culture such as social systems affect and, therefore, become encoded in things as basic as spear points and pottery. Who we are—the families into which we were born and into which we may marry, our position in life, our social standing, our economic position, our political power, and a host of our traditional behaviors—all may be encoded in the objects we own, in the artifacts that are deposited in and around our homes, and even in the graves that ultimately receive us. It is the job of the archaeologists to be clever enough to crack that code.

Read More

To find out more about the basis for the assertion that social patterns are encoded in the material archaeological record of tools, pots, burials, and so on, and for some examples, see any of the following sources.

Binford, L. 1962. Archaeology as Anthropology. *American Antiquity* 28:217–25.

Deetz, J. 1965. *The Dynamics of Stylistic Change in Arikara Ceramics.* University of Illinois Series in Anthropology 4. University of Illinois, Urbana.

Gramly, R. M. 1982. *The Vail Site: A Paleo-Indian Encampment in Maine.* Buffalo Society of Natural Sciences, Buffalo, New York.

MacDonald, G. F. 1985. *Debert: A Paleo-Indian Site in Central Nova Scotia.* Persimmon Press, Buffalo, New York.

 ## Can Archaeologists Figure Out the Roles of Males and Females in Ancient Societies?

Reading any one of a number of books or articles about human prehistory written fifty years ago might lead one to believe that women evolved rather later than men in the development of our species and then, once they arrived on the scene, did little more than bear and look after children. That might be a bit of an exaggeration, but there's more than just a little truth to it. In the stories archaeologists told of the human past, it would seem that men were responsible for nearly every important development, every great leap forward in technology. Men were responsible for all the important and meaningful tasks needed for the survival of the group: They made stone tools and then wrenched the people's subsistence out of the chaos of nature, hunting ferocious beasts and bringing meat back to camp to supply the group; they traveled on heroic journeys to obtain desperately needed raw materials; and they fought pitched battles against their enemies. And then, when they were done, the men retired to the mysterious depths of spectacular caverns and in their spare time, of course, invented the painterly arts as part of mystical ceremonies of renewal of nature and redemption of themselves.

Though I may have exaggerated these images of what a feminist might call an androcentric view of prehistory, I have not done so to the point of distortion. Especially in popular imaginings of the human past, men are presented as active, and women, if they exist at all in these reconstructions, are passive elements, observers of the activities of men, part of the audience, even part of the scenery. In her analysis of more than 300 artistic recreations depicting scenes of human antiquity, Diane Gifford-Gonzalez (1993) calculated that 100% of the individuals shown hunting, carrying game, or conducting a ritual were men. Nine out of ten of those shown painting an image on a cave wall were men. In the same artwork surveyed, 100% of the adults shown attending to, just holding or, even coming in contact with a child were women. The only activity other than child rearing that women were depicted as engaging in was making hide clothing. Gifford-Gonzalez even jokes about this, calling the typical woman depicted in artistic representations of ancient societies "the drudge on the hide." I had to laugh at that description when, fairly recently, I visited a relatively new series of dioramas devoted to the topic of human evolution at the American Museum of Natural History in New York City. The dioramas are fabulously well made, showing upright locomotion, hunting, and Paleolithic artistry. And there, in the diorama showing three human ancestors engaged in what the diorama designer surely perceived to be typical tasks, is a man, standing strong and tall, sharpening his wooden spear point, preparing for the fierce, daily battle to provide subsistence for his family. At his feet is a woman sewing—as you may have guessed—an animal hide.

Is this really the way it was or, at least, the only way it was? The truth is that archaeologists who focus on prehistoric societies can determine the sex of a tool maker or of a tool user only in rare circumstances. In a few cases fingerprints impressed on clay when it was soft (for example, on a piece of ceramic kiln furniture or on the inside of a vessel situated in a position where the surface can no longer be reached for smoothing when the top has been constricted) have been preserved when the clay was fired (Figure 12.3). The individual ridges that make up a woman's fingerprint tend to be smaller than those of a man and, therefore, on average, there are more ridges across 1 cm of a woman's finger than on a man's. With this in mind, when a fingerprint has been preserved, you can determine with a fair degree of accuracy whether the print belonged to a man or woman and, by inference, the sex of the person who made the ceramic object (Figure 12.4).

It must be admitted that at least some of the sex role stereotyping archaeologists are sometimes guilty of results not from careful consideration of archaeological cultures but from imposing, probably unconsciously, the biases and assumptions of our own culture. Consider this: My colleague Lucianne Lavin

FIGURE 12.3 Fingerprints preserved on ceramic fragment made by African captives in New York City in the eighteenth century. (Courtesy Warren Perry)

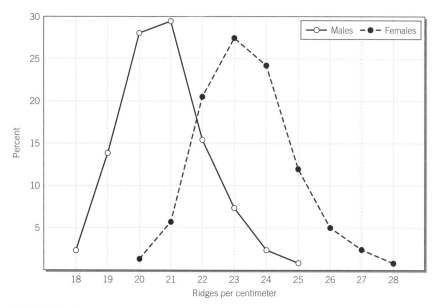

FIGURE 12.4 Graph showing the bimodal nature of the distribution of the number of individual fingerprint ridges per centimeter. Women, because the individual ridges in fingerprints tend to be narrower, tend to have a greater number of these ridges than do men. This tendency can be used to identify the sex of an individual who left fingerprints behind—at a crime scene or on the clay of an ancient pottery vessel. (From Cummins and Midlo, 1961)

knows more about ancient pottery, especially the kind made by the inhabitants of prehistoric New England, than anybody I know (Lavin 1997, 1998; Lavin and Kra 1994). A few years ago, Lavin organized a symposium on ancient ceramics, inviting a number of researchers to present papers specifically on the work they were doing on pottery here in the Northeast. Because Lavin and I are friends and because she knew I had recently excavated a site that produced a large number of **potsherds**, she invited me to present a paper on my preliminary analysis of the clay the potters had used to produce their wares. The symposium was an all-day affair, with both a morning and an afternoon session. Although I had received a program several weeks earlier and, as a result, knew the identities of all of the participants, I hadn't fully realized one curious fact about the symposium until I carefully scanned the names in the program while waiting for the morning session to start. Of the dozen or so paper presenters, I was, in a fundamental way, unique. All of the other symposium presenters that day were female; I was the only male. A peculiar coincidence, I thought, but one that I have seen repeated since in multiple contexts.

So what's the deal? Is biology destiny, after all, at least when it comes to the investigation of ancient technology and material culture? Does the apparent correlation, imperfect as it is, between sex and research among modern archaeologists essentially repeat the cultural patterns of ancient societies? In other words, are male archaeologists today, through some deep, genetic bond, reflecting a subconscious "brotherhood" with the ancient stone tool makers they study? Are female archaeologists drawn to the investigation of ceramic artifacts because their "sisters" of long ago manufactured these things, and can it all be traced to the fact that both groups—ancient and modern women—have two X chromosomes? Or is it simply the fact that sex role stereotyping (not in ancient "primitive" societies, but in our modern society of archaeologists) is at the root of this pattern? Are male archaeologists attracted to the study of ancient stone tools because, as males, they are more interested in the things they believe males made? Are female archaeologists attracted to the study of ceramics because, as females, they are interested in the things they believe females made? And do we assume males made stone tools (for use in hunting and warfare) and women made pottery (for use in domestic activities such as food preparation and storage) not because of any genetic predisposition but because those are the stereotypes that match the expectations of our own society? Is this just another version of the question, do boys play with toy soldiers and girls play with dolls as a result of the different wiring in the male and female brain or as the result of socialization? And, finally, it occurs to me to ask, who should be the subject of our analysis anyway: ancient people or modern archaeologists?

This brings me to the work of archaeologist Joan Gero (1997), who doubly upsets the applecart I have just neatly set up by being a woman interested in stone tools who also maintains that stone tools almost certainly were made by ancient women. In Gero's discourse on what she identifies as "genderlithics," she makes a number of key points. She points out that with the exception of certain stone procurement activities that require a significant amount of upper body strength, women are physically just as capable of making stone tools as are men. From my experience in my experimental archaeology course, I must concur.

By and large, although strength is needed to flake stone, knowing where to hit a stone core is much more important than brute force. Just as important, Gero cites a number of ethnographic cases on record in which women were observed making stone tools, including first-hand accounts of Australian Aborigine women manufacturing stone axes and of Native American women making arrow points by pressure flaking. The fact that women are physically capable of making stone tools, combined with the ethnographic evidence of women making stone tools in some cultures, forces us to reassess assumptions about sex roles that are based on the stereotyping done by our own culture.

In our own society we are blurring the distinctions between traditional tasks that were perceived as "women's work" and "men's work," but wasn't there a valid reason for the sexual division of labor in the past? Certainly, men tend to be larger and more heavily muscled than women, and this often, though not always, translates into greater physical strength, so it might be advantageous to have men do the work that requires this greater strength. Sexual dimorphism need not be destiny, but it probably is the case that in some societies men and women had vastly different responsibilities based on men tending to be larger and stronger. Nevertheless, we shouldn't presume to apply recent stereotypes about modern men and women to people of the past. The overall strength of an individual is a flexible characteristic and depends on diet and conditioning. Remember, I have never encountered a woman in my experimental archaeology course who could not make stone tools due to a lack of strength. Check out the incredible archery skills of female Olympic athletes if you are skeptical about the ability of women to master the bow and arrow.

I think we make a mistake if, by default, we assume that if a task required skill, training, strength, guile, cunning, and intelligence, it must have been the purview of males. We should admit that we really don't know. In the end, it is most reasonable to suggest that ancient societies required contributions from everyone, whatever their abilities. Sex is only one factor in a host of characteristics that determine what a person is most capable of contributing to the survival of the group. See all the chapters in the book *Engendering Archaeology: Women and Prehistory* (Gero and Conkey 1997) as well as works by Roberta Gilchrist (1999), Bettina Arnold and Nancy Wicker (2001), and Diana diZerega Wall (1994) for a diversity of approaches to figuring out the roles of women and men in ancient societies.

Read More

For a detailed discussion of the ways in which archaeologists can assess the roles of men and women in past societies, start with any of the following sources.

Arnold, B. and N. L. Wicker, eds. 2001. *Gender and the Archaeology of Death*. Rowman & Littlefield, Lanham, Maryland.

Gero, J. M. 1997. Genderlithics: Woman's Roles in Stone Tool Production. In *Engendering Archaeology: Women and Prehistory*, edited by J. M. Gero and M. W. Conkey, 163–93. Blackwell, Oxford.

Gero, J. M., and M. W. Conkey, eds. 1997. *Engendering Archaeology: Women and Prehistory.* Blackwell, Oxford.

Gifford-Gonzalez, D. 1993. You Can Hide, but You Can't Run: Representation of Women's Work in Illustrations of Paleolithic Life. *Visual Anthropology Review* 9(1):23–41.

Gilchrist, R. 1999. *Gender and Archaeology: Contesting the Past.* Routledge, London.

Wall, D. diZerega. 1994. *The Archaeology of Gender: Separating the Spheres in Urban America.* Plenum, New York.

How Does an Archaeologist Approach Issues of Economic, Social, and Political Inequality in an Ancient Society?

The people who lived at the Wood Lily site were mobile hunter-gatherers. Most such groups are essentially **egalitarian.** Though the common usage of that word might imply that everyone is equal in an egalitarian society, this is not actually true. Even within such a society, there almost certainly will be inequality among different categories of people defined and recognized by the group. Only within the age and sex categories recognized by the egalitarian group is everyone more or less equal. For example, an egalitarian people may distinguish the following categories of individuals as having different statuses, responsibilities, and attendant expectations concerning how others should treat them: young children, older kids, adolescents, adult males, adult females, elderly males, elderly females. The individuals will not necessarily be "equal" across group boundaries, but within each of these hypothetical subdivisions almost everyone has about the same wealth, status, and authority.

Where this occurs, we may characterize at least some of the differences across these categories as "achieved." You achieve greater status, for example, simply by the achievement of getting older and more experienced and, therefore, worthy of greater respect and, at least in some things, deserving of a few more material benefits.

As a result of the existence of achieved statuses, there may be differences in the numbers and kinds of possessions individuals may accumulate—and that archaeologists might find—across these subdivisions. For example, people within a social category of "people deserving of respect because of their great age" may have more stuff than individuals in other social categories. Nobody within one of these categories, however, accumulates a disproportionate amount of wealth, no one's social standing is any higher than anyone else's, and, with the possible exception of the leader of a community, no one within the recognized age and sex category has any say or authority over anyone else in the same category.

Egalitarian societies are not beset by anarchy. Especially in small social groups, these age and sex categories and, especially, the family may provide a more than adequate framework on which interpersonal behavior is based.

In most such societies parents command the respect of their children and control their behavior. Adults in middle age may have more authority and receive more respect than young adults. Elderly adults may be revered, and their advice may be heeded more than that of younger adults. In some cases men may dominate the decision-making process, and in other instances women may control the important decisions made by the group.

Most of us have an expectation of having our work rewarded by decent pay that allows us to provide food, shelter, and clothing for ourselves and our families. At the same time, in our society there also is the expectation that, along with the necessities of life, we will be able to accumulate wealth in the form of a bunch of other stuff including nice clothes, a good car, and assorted gadgets and gizmos. Some of us, it is understood, will be able to accumulate more than others because the work we do is more highly regarded and the pay is better—because it takes a substantial amount of training, involves life and death situations, is more physically dangerous, and so on. What we accumulate we get to keep and even pass down to our children.

It is interesting to point out that in many egalitarian societies the very notion of the accumulation of wealth that is personally monopolized is alien. In fact, social traditions exist in many egalitarian societies that prevent such personal accumulation. For example, among the Zhun/twasi people of the Kalahari (sometimes called the !Kung San or just the San), the hunter who successfully kills an animal does not own the meat that he returns to the village; that meat is owned by whoever made the arrow that was used to kill the animal (Lee 1979). The owner of the meat does not hoard it, nor can he or she sell it. In fact, for the Zhun/twasi the benefit of owning the meat is that the owner is the one who gets to give it away, to distribute it to the rest of the members of the group.

Certainly, not all societies are egalitarian. Family structure may provide a framework sufficient for organizing a hunting party, digging a well, building a house, or moving a settlement. As a society grows in population, however, it may outgrow the ability of family structure to efficiently organize labor and make decisions. The scale of the projects undertaken by large populations may exceed the organizational capacity of a single family, with its kin-based level of control. Building an extensive network of canals to irrigate a valley, constructing an impregnable defensive wall around a settlement, or conscripting an army to defend a region against an aggressive enemy may require the cooperation and coordination of many families, and a social and political structure that transcends the individual family may become necessary.

Societies in which the organization of labor and the coordination of activity are controlled by a structure beyond the family are said to be complex. In contrast to egalitarian societies, **rank societies** confer higher levels of status and authority on certain individuals or groups (arranged in a hierarchy of "ranks") who direct and to some extent control people's labor on a large scale, ostensibly for the good of the group. It often ends up, as well, that the group's labor is controlled for the good of those individuals with higher status and authority. Increased wealth may flow into their hands because they can command it and, it must be admitted, because the rest of the people, not so privileged, may view the greater wealth of those higher in the pecking order as deserved, the legitimate result of higher status.

Though in rank societies this higher status may start off as achieved—people obtain higher status for the services they provide to the society—in **complex societies** the achieved higher status within a particular rank may become solidified and made permanent, to be passed down to subsequent generations within the rank. The people within such ranks have a higher social and economic status not because of what they have accomplished but simply because they were born into it; their status is said not to have been achieved but "ascribed."

In some complex societies disproportionate amounts of status, authority, and wealth become concentrated in what are no longer flexible ranks but permanent and fixed classes of people. These societies become socially (and economically and politically) **stratified.** Just as we talked about sequential strata in soil, in the social application of the term society may be composed of a pyramid of strata or layers. A tiny fraction of the population (for example, families of the king, emperor, or pharaoh) resides in the top layer. A larger layer beneath the top represents the nobility. A still larger layer sits beneath the noble class and may be composed of craftspeople, merchants, and military officers. Finally, at the bottom rests the largest layer of all, consisting of the farmers, workers, peasants, and slaves whose labors allow for the existence of the economic, social, and politically bounded layers above them.

Differential wealth develops to reflect a society's stratification of status. That differential wealth is reflected in material objects: crowns, jewels, finely worked knickknacks made of rare and precious (therefore expensive) raw materials, larger and more elaborate residences, and so on. Material objects are the raw material of archaeological analysis, so it should come as no surprise that archaeologists find evidence of economic and attendant social and political inequality manifested in the archaeological record in terms of the material inequality of the objects found in domiciles and, especially, graves.

We found no burials of the egalitarian residents of the Wood Lily site. In the site as a whole, there was no evidence at all of the concentration of wealth in the hands of any individual. There were no hoards of precious raw materials in certain site locations, no concentrations of valuables monopolized by any individuals. In fact, the physical distribution of stuff at the site, more or less equally dispersed across the habitation, is probably an accurate reflection of the society of those who lived there: No place or person was more important than any other.

Compare this to what is demonstrated by the burial of Tutankhamen, the ruler of ancient Egypt between 1333 and 1323 B.C. Remember the discussion of how archaeological projects are funded. When archaeologist Howard Carter, funded by the wealthy nobleman the earl of Carnarvon, discovered the tomb in 1922, the mortal remains of the "boy-king" were located in the innermost of three nested coffins. Made of solid gold, the innermost sarcophagus actually contained the young pharaoh's body. It rested in another coffin constructed of wood and covered with a layer of hammered gold. The outermost coffin was fabricated in the same way: a framework of wood covered in gold. Surrounding the remains of the king, in a series of interconnected rooms, was a virtual warehouse of spectacular treasures. The inventory of the grave goods in Tut's tomb includes an overwhelming array of fabulous treasures: sculptures in gold and alabaster, painted wooden carvings of the gods of ancient Egypt, leopard-skin capes, ebony furniture, gilded storage chests, necklaces and bracelets (some inlaid with lapis lazuli and chalcedony), and gold rings. All the gifts presented to the dead king are remarkably well crafted and are exquisite examples of the stunning abilities and creativity of ancient Egypt's artisans. A king's treasure, literally, had been crammed into Tut's small death chamber in the Valley of the Kings. The death mask itself is stunning, a breathtaking object of gold and lapis so perfectly executed that to many people it represents the embodiment of the artistic achievement of ancient Egypt (Figure 12.5).

Tut's burial may be an extreme case, but it is an instructive example for us. Economic, social, and political inequality in life are reflected in the stuff to which individuals in complex societies have access and can accumulate. That stuff, whether it ends up in the archaeological record of someone's abandoned house or in their grave, provides

FIGURE 12.5 The deservedly renowned death mask of the Egyptian pharaoh Tutankhamen is emblematic of the artistic capabilities of ancient Egypt's artisans and is a clear material manifestation of the extreme level of economic, social, and political inequality that can characterize complex societies. Suffice it to say that while pharaohs were buried in this sort of splendor, those whose labors provided for the privileged lives—and deaths—of the noble class of ancient complex societies were not afforded the same in life or in death. (© Roger Wood/CORBIS)

us with a snapshot of that inequality, a material representation of a society with rich and poor, leaders and followers, a noble class and peasants and slaves. It is a picture that archaeologists are often successful at recognizing and interpreting.

How Is Ethnicity Reflected in the Archaeological Record?

As human beings, we adorn ourselves with all manner of jewelry, tattoos, clothing, and hairstyles, and we often festoon our cherished material objecs such as our houses, cars, and even our gravesites as part of a practice of announcing our ethnic allegiances to the rest of the world. Putting a "Kiss Me I'm Irish" bumpersticker on your car, hanging the flag of Puerto Rico on your house, wearing a traditional African dashiki (a shirt), braiding your hair in dreadlocks, and so on are all part of a pattern of showing pride in one's ethnic identity. These are all material manifestations of ethnic identity and, as such, are the kinds of things archaeologists look for when seeking out ethnicity in the archaeological record. However, ethnic markers such as these are not always obvious unless one is familiar with the culture being investigated.

Archaeologists Jerry Sawyer and Warren Perry, for example, were at first mystified by the accumulation of seemingly disconnected artifacts found during excavation of soil that had filled the crawl space of the mid-eighteenth-century Treadway home in Salem, Connecticut. From top to bottom, in a stratigraphic sequence of just a few centimeters, the researchers found a wheel hub overlaying a cluster of iron nails, pottery sherds, and glass fragments that, in turn, covered a horseshoe (with its open side pointing west). At the bottom of the artifact accumulation, the excavators found a large, multifaceted quartz crystal (Sawyer 2005). It was an odd mix of stuff, and it seemed even stranger that someone had gone to the trouble to secrete these items in the hard-to-get-to crawl space of a house.

Sawyer and Perry have subsequently found other examples of these seemingly inexplicable, intentionally deposited, apparently random clusters of artifacts, many of them including quartz crystals, in out-of-the-way places such as in crawl spaces, in cellar corners, and even under doorsills of eighteenth-century houses in southeastern Connecticut. Who may have been caching these crystals and other stuff in hideaways, places where others would probably not find them, and why were they doing it? Sawyer and Perry think they know.

The Treadway house where the described feature was found was the hub of a 1,000-acre farm located just north of the New Salem Plantation, where documentary evidence of slavery has been revealed (see chapter 3). We know there were African captives in Connecticut in the eighteenth century, when the house was occupied, and we know that this part of Connecticut was home to a large plantation that relied on the slave labor of a substantial number of African captives. We know something else: Back in Africa a common cultural tradition involved the production of sacred ritual bundles called *minkisi*. There were specific meanings to each of the items included, and, almost certainly not coincidentally, *minkisi* often included quartz crystals.

Sawyer and Perry have found other examples of what appear to be material reflections in the archaeological record of practices of African origin dating to eighteenth-century Connecticut. For example, they found stone cairns located in the cemetery associated with the New Salem Plantation. Stone cairns are not found in the cemeteries where the remains of people of European descent were buried but were used to mark burials in parts of West Africa.

The survival of African burial practices was seen clearly in the excavation of the African Burial Ground in lower Manhattan (Perry, Howson, and Bianco 2006). For example, among the more than 400 burials excavated researchers found a woman buried with a string of beads around her waist. In another case a man was buried in a wooden coffin, the lid of which was decorated with a series of iron tacks in the form of a *Sankofa* (Figure 12.6), a heart-shaped design used by the Akan people of Ghana and the Ivory Coast (Perry, Howson, and Holl 2006:222). These and other elements of the burials of African captives in lower Manhattan lead the researchers to conclude that treatment of the dead was one area in which slaves possessed some degree of autonomy; they may not have been able to control most aspects of their lives, but in death they were free.

FIGURE 12.6 The *sankofa* design was an important ritual symbol in West Africa. Its discovery on a coffin lid in the African Burial Ground in lower Manhattan (here, in brass tacks, you can see the subtle outline of a heart) is an example of how a material object reflects the ritual behavior of a particular group of people. (Courtesy Warren Perry)

Perry and Blakey (1997) view the maintenance of African traditions, especially in the context of private and hidden rituals such as the *minkisi*, as a form of resistance to captivity. African captives whose lives had been stolen from them and whose language and culture were being systematically purged as their families were being torn apart, tribal members separated, and traditional religious practices banned may have, in secret and without the knowledge of their captors and masters, preserved the practices of their cultures. Their insistence on maintaining their traditions was not recorded historically, but by making things and hiding them away, this element of ethnicity, as reflected by cultural preservation and perseverance, is revealed in the material record.

Can Archaeologists Reconstruct Ancient Religious Practices?

To the best of our knowledge, human beings are the only species with the ability to recognize the uncertainty of our own fates. As sentient creatures, we are intensely aware of the role played by serendipity (luck, both good and bad) in determining the length and the quality of our lives and the lives of those we love. Also, though other animals may react to the remains of their deceased companions in a manner that we recognize as mournful (elephants and chimpanzees, for example, have been observed behaving in ways that are eerily reminiscent of human mourning), humans are the only species who are cognizant of the essential fact that our lives are finite, that each of us dies. This is one reason why I sometimes envy my cats, but that's another story.

To one extent or another, humans also know how to behave to increase the likelihood of achieving well-being as well as success in the tasks they undertake. You may have heard the term *survival instinct*, a characteristic pretty clearly evident in human beings: For the most part, we tend to act in ways that materially increase the likelihood of our day-to-day survival. We know how to increase the odds in our favor to be successful in the hunt, grow food, raise our children, and stay healthy and safe. But we humans also know a dirty little secret: Life isn't fair. We know that no matter how careful we are, no matter how hard we try, no matter how much we study or practice, there is no guarantee of success. Sometimes, through no apparent fault of their own, people who try hard, work hard, and are sensible and careful, fail anyway, live miserable lives, and die far too young. They didn't deserve their fates, they didn't "have it coming," and they are not paying for their mistakes. They simply got the shaft; no reason, just bad luck. And we all know that it can happen to any of us.

Religion, at least in part, results from recognizing the insecure nature of our fates. There always is a gap between what we can do materially to ensure our success and health and that over which we have no material control. Humans often bridge that gap with the belief that there is a force—a god or gods, spirits, or other supernatural entities—that dictates serendipity, that actually controls that which to us is uncontrollable. That force can mitigate our bad breaks or have reasons for visiting tragedy upon us, reasons that we may someday learn.

With that faith, human beings gain at least a measure of a sense of control over the uncertainty that rules life. The uncertainty and volatility that characterize our existence and fuel our fears become less uncertain, less volatile, and less frightening when we believe in a force "bigger" than ourselves, a force with intelligence, a force that can be reasoned with and bargained with and that ultimately acts in our best interests.

Like every other behavior practiced by people, religion does not fossilize *directly*, leaving a physical impression in the ground that archaeologists need only expose to reveal a behavior. Like most other human behaviors, however, the conduct of religion results in the use of material objects and material consequences that are preserved and encoded elements of the behaviors. For example, some people may avoid certain serviceable rock types for stone tool making and use because the rock is considered to be imbued with a malevolent force. The reliance on a more distant and difficult-to-obtain rock type without demonstrable advantages may suggest the presence of an ideology that affects the selection of lithic raw materials. In another example, the presence of non-naturalistic, perhaps even supernaturalistic, images etched into or drawn on the rock surfaces of a cliff wall difficult to access and distant from any ancient

FIGURE 12.7 Petroglyphs such as those at Bellows Falls in Vermont (top), Newspaper Rock in Utah (center) and pictographs like those at the Honanki Site in Sedona, Arizona (bottom), are probably a reflection of the religious practices of ancient peoples. (K. L. Feder)

habitation—**petroglyphs** and **pictographs**—may indicate that the artwork was intended to mark a place sacred to a group of people (Figure 12.7).

Although resource avoidance and the marking of a place with nonnaturalistic images are difficult to interpret—and our hypotheses regarding religious connotations are even more challenging to test—there is a category of archaeological features that seems to be a more direct window into the religious practices, thoughts, and beliefs of an ancient people: burials. The treatment of the dead reflects a people's reaction to the fact of mortality and often manifests key aspects of their religious beliefs.

For example, as much as 80,000 years ago a variety of archaic or premodern human beings, the Neandertals, placed the remains of deceased comrades into trenches or pits, occasionally including tools and other objects before covering them with soil (Solecki 1971). More than 25,000 years ago, the people of Sungir', located about 150 km (100 miles) northeast of Moscow, Russia, buried five of their compatriots in what must have amounted to Paleolithic splendor (White 1993). An adolescent boy was buried with a cache of nearly 5,000 beads crafted from the ivory tusks of woolly mammoths. On his chest was a pendant carved from the same ivory. Around his waist was a belt from which its maker had suspended 250 polar fox teeth. Near the boy a young girl had been buried. In her grave were ivory disks carved with an intricate latticework, an ivory pin, and more than 5,000 ivory beads (Figure 12.8). Nearly 3,330 years ago, a young king who died suddenly was interred in a tomb intended for another. The tomb became a virtual storehouse for splendid objects whose spirits would be needed in the next life. Alabaster chalices, chests made of ebony and cedar, golden shrines, and a spectacular death mask crafted in solid gold and lapis lazuli are only a handful of the jumble of riches found in the tomb of the Egyptian pharaoh Tutankhamen (see Figure 12.5; Buckley 1976).

As broadly as the grave goods range in the burials of the Neandertal, the children of the Paleolithic, and the boy king of Egypt, they share the love, reverence, or perhaps fear with which the living responded to the deaths of a friend, a child, or a leader. Items of great value (made of rare and precious materials, works of great artistry that had taken enormous effort and time to craft) and items that perhaps were believed to be imbued with great spiritual power were placed in these graves. The people left behind may have believed that the spirit of the deceased needed the objects placed in the tomb for use in the afterlife. We know that this belief was the case for ancient Egyptians, because they left behind a written record describing their belief in the need for the spirit to have the trappings that surrounded it in life, but we cannot know with any certainty that this was the case for Neandertals or the people of Sungir'. Perhaps their practice of placing cherished items in a grave was more an act of grieving, something intended to comfort the living rather than provide for the dead. Whatever the case, together these artifacts tell a story of the lives of the dead and of how the people they left behind commemorated their lives and viewed the passage between life and death—probably the most significant and resonant issue upon which religious belief and practice focuses.

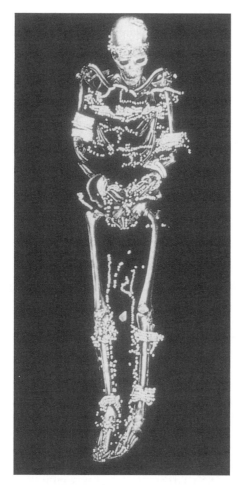

FIGURE 12.8 Burials are, almost by definition, material representations of ritual. Here, a burial ritual conducted near the modern Russian city of Moscow more than 25,000 years ago is preserved in the material objects placed in the grave along with the physical remains of the deceased. (© O. Bader/Musée de l'Homme)

HOW ARE RITUALS PRESERVED IN THE ARCHAEOLOGICAL RECORD?

Just about everyone I know, religious or not, performs rituals—mostly just innocuous, irrational little bits of behavior—on a regular basis. Think about the rituals practiced by modern athletes, for example: A baseball player makes the sign of the cross before batting; at the end of an inning, a fielder makes sure to avoid stepping on the foul line on his way to the dugout; a basketball player might always bounce the ball twice before attempting a free throw; a runner kisses her cross just before the starter's gun signifies the beginning of a race; a football team kneels in prayer in the locker room before running out onto the field. These all are intangible, fleeting behaviors with very little, if anything, in the way of material consequences and so would probably be invisible to a future archaeologist.

Some rituals, however, are more than this and may produce something material for an archaeologist to find and ponder. The *mankisi* bundle—a collection of sacred objects buried together to mark a place—mentioned earlier in this chapter is an example. Archaeologists in Mesoamerica often find ritual caches with pieces of flint, jade, obsidian, and maize at the bases of Maya stelae, upright pillars on which the Maya commonly left important messages about the foundation of a community, a king's accession to the throne, or victory in battle.

Ritual behavior can produce features larger and more enduring than artifact caches. The ancient people of the American Midwest, for example, ritually marked the landscape in sometimes monumental fashion (Lepper 1995, 1996, 2004). The so-called Adena and Hopewell people who dominated Ohio, Illinois, and Indiana between 2,800 and 1,500 years ago were adept at moving and piling up large quantities of earth (see chapter 2). Some of these piles were conical tombs up to nearly 25 meters (80 feet) high (see Figure 2.9, top); the deceased was interred, often in a log-lined tomb, at the base of the burial mound. More than simply marking the location of the tombs of important people, the Adena and Hopewell people also used earthen piles, ridges, and berms to enclose apparently sacred places, often the high, flat tops of topographic ridges. In other instances they produced enormous mounds in the forms of birds and animals. Among the most impressive of these **effigy mounds** is Serpent Mound in Ohio, a 411-meter (1,348-feet) long, sinuously coiled monument of earth (see Figure 2.9, center).

Though the meaning of some of this ritual marking of the landscape is lost to us, an argument can be made in some cases that the alignment of the monuments reflects the recognition and memorializing by ancient peoples of natural, astronomical alignments. An entire subfield of archaeology, called **archaeoastronomy**, in part consists of the search for such alignments.

Ancient peoples recognized, for instance, that the positions on the horizon of the rising and setting Sun change just a little each day during the course of a year. In the Northern Hemisphere during the course of a year, the Sun's location on the horizon at sunrise is a little farther north each day until about June 21. Today we call that day the summer solstice, and it is shown on our calendar as the first day of summer and the longest day of the year (in terms of the number of hours of daylight). Instead of continuing north along the horizon, after June 21 the position of the rising Sun shifts direction, appearing at sunrise a little farther south each day. By about September 21, the autumnal equinox—the first day of fall, a day with an equal number of hours of daylight and night—the Sun rises due east. After that the Sun continues its shift toward the south until about December 21. That day, the winter solstice, marks the first day of winter, the shortest day of the year (in terms of the number of hours of daylight) and the point in the year when the Sun halts its shift southward on the horizon and alters its direction yet again, this time appearing just a little farther north each day at sunrise. The location of the Sun at sunrise reaches due east again on March 21 or 22, the first day of spring—called the vernal equinox and, like the autumnal equinox, a day with an equal number of hours of daylight and night—and comes back to its farthest position north exactly one year after the cycle commenced, on June 21 or 22.

Ancient peoples recognized these significant points along the Sun's yearly journey, a journey that corresponded to seasonal changes in air temperature, food availability, and planting and harvesting schedules. In other words, the location of the Sun at sunrise represented, from a practical standpoint, a calendar and reflected, from a ritual standpoint, the mysteriously patterned movement of the source of light and heat upon which life itself depended. Not surprisingly, ancient peoples whose livelihoods and lives depended absolutely on the predictable patterning presented by the seasons, which were, in turn, tied into the location of the Sun in the sky, sometimes ritually marked those patterns on a monumental scale.

Some of the great megalithic monuments such as Stonehenge and Long Meg and Her Daughters reflect just such a ritual marking of sunrise on the summer solstice (Figure 12.9). Outside of the main part of Stonehenge stands the so-called heelstone (the stone called Long Meg is the analogous stone), a virtual gunsight aligned with the summer solstice sunrise. Standing in the center of the stone circle of Stonehenge and looking out directly over the so-called heelstone, the rising Sun flashes at its apex on the summer solstice, marking the first day of summer.

It is important to consider just how remarkable this is. An ancient people thought deeply about the location of the Sun. They observed the location of the Sun at first light, probably for years, recognized the pattern inherent in its daily location, and realized that it predictably performed this dance across the horizon every year. Then, to mark that location, to memorialize it, to ritualize it, and maybe even to feel, in some way, that they were helping assure that the pattern would always be repeated, over the course of several centuries

FIGURE 12.9 Human beings sometimes mark their rituals through the production of large-scale monuments of earth and stone. Here, the megalithic site Long Meg and Her Daughters memorialized rituals conducted more than 4,000 years ago in Great Britain by marking the location of the rising sun on the horizon at the summer solstice.

they invested a tremendous amount of energy in constructing a monument in stone to capture that pattern. Archaeologists and astronomers today are able to recognize the meaning and intent of those ancient thinkers and builders in the alignment of their monuments.

Read More

Have a look at any of the following references for a wide variety of ways in which the analysis of human burials has provided insights into the ceremonies and religious practices of past peoples.

Arnold, B., and N. L. Wicker, eds. 2001. *Gender and the Archaeology of Death*. Rowman & Littlefield, Lanham, Maryland.

Buckley, T. 1976. The Discovery of Tutankhamun's Tomb. In *The Treasures of Tutankhamun*, edited by K. S. Gilbert, J. K. Holt, and S. Hudson, 9–18. Metropolitan Museum of Art, New York.

Pearson, M. P. 2001. *The Archaeology of Death and Burial*. Texas A&M University Press, Austin.

Solecki, R. 1971. *Shanidar: The First Flower People*. Knopf, New York.

White, R. 1993. Technological and Social Dimensions of "Aurignacian-age" Body Ornaments across Europe. In *Before Lascaux: The Complex Record of the Early Upper Paleolithic*, edited by H. Knecht, A. Pike-Tay, and R. White, 277–99. CRC Press, Boca Raton, Florida.

Williams, H., ed. 2003. *Archaeologies of Remembrance: Death and Memory in Past Societies*. Plenum, New York.

 ## How Do Archaeologists Trace the Movement of People and Ideas Across a Social Landscape?

A recurring theme in this chapter has been that human beings, largely unintentionally, encode elements of their economic, social, political, and religious realities into the objects they make and use and that archaeologists dig up as artifacts. Following this, to answer the question posed by the title of this section, archaeologists rely on the axiom that artifacts represent the durable, interpretable manifestation of those ideas.

I have already used colonial grave markers as model artifacts in my discussion of seriation (chapter 8), and I am going to exploit them here again as an example of how an idea held by people of British ancestry about the appropriate design to place on a nineteenth-century gravestone can be traced archaeologically—that is, by looking at artifacts—across an ocean and over thousands of miles of land.

The vast majority of the early settlers of New England were from England, Scotland, Ireland, and Wales, people who, like the Jews of Anatevka in *Fiddler on the Roof*, shared a number of traditions. Among those traditions was one that involved gravestone design. Certainly, like how the hunters in a society manufacture spear points, how people make pottery, and how they prepare their meals, there is a pretty wide range of acceptable styles for how you mark the grave of a loved one. People within particular groups tend to follow rules that reflect the traditional ways of doing things, and those traditions may change, often only slowly, through time as new ideas become incorporated into their traditions.

I have already discussed the changes seen in colonial grave markers in New England and how the earliest popular design, dating to the seventeenth and early eighteenth centuries, the death's head, by the mid-eighteenth century had evolved into an angel or cherub's face, which was, in turn, supplanted by the urn and willow design beginning in the late eighteenth and culminating in the early nineteenth centuries. It shouldn't be surprising that as traditions evolve, as they shift through time, these changes ripple across a population, even one widely dispersed and separated by thousands of miles. Look at the images provided in Figure 12.10. On the top left is a photograph of a gravestone located on the largest of the Orkney Islands, north of the Scottish coast. On the top right is an image of a gravestone photogaphed in the cemetery in Simsbury, Connecticut's, town center. On the bottom is another image of a gravestone, this one taken in a cemetery in New Orleans, Louisiana. In each case, the design carved into the top of the stone is of a weeping willow tree arched over an urn.

Remember, there is an almost infinite number of different possible designs a person could have carved into the top of a grave marker for themselves or for a loved one. In the the three instances shown in Figure 12.10, the images are similar because those making the decisions about what they wanted carved onto the grave maker came from the same (or a very similar, historically related) culture in which the tradition in the nineteenth century was to have the image of a weeping willow tree on a gravestone. The gravestone is a physical manifestation of an idea about the appropriate desgin of a gravestone, a physical manifestation of a tradition.

In this case people moved to the Americas bringing their traditions of grave marking with them. However, ideas also can pass from group to group without human migration, just by people coming into contact with one another. For example, maize agriculture spread into and throughout North America, having originated in Mesoamerica where teosinte, the wild ancestor of maize, grows (see chapter 11). There is no evidence of widespread migration of Mesoamericans to the north, just the maize. Of course, the maize could not migrate by itself, but people can be pretty peripatetic—they walk around a lot. It is likely that through trade and travel, when groups without maize came into contact with those who planted the crop, its many advantages became apparent. They obtained some and went home with the new food source and new ideas concerning subsistence. The archaeological record clearly shows this south-to-north process beginning after 4,000 years ago (Smith 1995).

In the instance of historical gravestone design in the northeast, we have the historical record to help us understand the movement of both ideas and people from Great Britain to New England and then the spread of those people throughout North America as they continued to maintain a common tradition. Even if we didn't have the historical record to tell us that settlers from Great Britain came to America, the archaeological record of gravestones reflecting the practice of a shared tradition would have allowed us to make that connection.

FIGURE 12.10 The similarities among the designs placed on these three nineteenth-century gravestones reflect a common cultural heritage linking three different places in the world: Scotland (top), Connecticut (bottom left), and New Orleans (bottom right).

How Can Archaeologists Reveal Ways of Life of People Whose Reality Was So Different from Our Own?

Even though archaeologists represent a diversity of cultures, backgrounds, and life experiences, we are, in one important sense, a homogeneous group: We are all residents of the current period of time. I know that sounds odd and obvious. We are alive in the here and now. Of course. But it actually is a significant point. We may speak different languages, reside in different kinds of societies, engage in various traditions, and have dissimilar values, but trained archaeologists are all residents of the modern world. Most of us have attended school, read books, and received degrees in anthropology, history, or archaeology. We drive motor vehicles, buy our food at the grocery and our tools at the hardware store, communicate with cell phones, use computers, and so on. In other words, wherever we are from and whatever our backgrounds, the majority of us are wrapped up in the trappings of the modern world. The people we study, the people who left behind the arrowheads and pots, the temples and pyramids, the mundane trash pits and the amazing monuments—the people whose lives we hope to illuminate and comprehend—lived in times that were far different from ours. How can we denizens of the twenty-first century, even those of us with advanced degrees in anthropology and years of training and experience in archaeology, ever hope to comprehend the lives of people whose time and reality were so different from our own?

One set of strategies long employed by archaeologists in our attempt to bridge the gap between our own lives and those of ancient peoples—to relate to ways of life and periods of time fundamentally alien to our own—is called **ethnographic analogy.** *Ethnographic* refers to the lives and descriptions of living groups of people. *Analogy* is the comparison of two things that are assumed to be similar in fundamental ways such that knowledge and understanding of one allow for a more complete understanding of the other. Essentially, ethnographic analogy uses the detailed descriptions of living groups of people, or people who lived in a historically recent period, as models for illuminating the lives of ancient peoples. Ethnographic analogy relies on the assumption that information that can be gleaned from the extensively documented lives of people living in recent periods, folks whose lifeways were witnessed and recorded (by explorers, colonists, missionaries, soldiers, doctors, adventurers, traders, anthropologists, and the people themselves), can be used to help elucidate the lives of people who lived in antiquity. The descriptions of these living or recent people make sense when it can be shown that the cultures of the two groups—one ancient and the other more recent—are probably similar, or, more precisely, analogous.

For example, an archaeologist whose life experience is that of a modern, Western, middle-class individual might excavate a site left behind by ancient hunter-gatherers who lived during a period of extreme cold during the last ice age. The realities of the archaeologist and the people who produced the site could hardly be more different. The ancient people needed, on a daily basis, to extract from a capricious natural world everything on which they relied for survival. Hunting large game animals played a major role in their subsistence. They needed to make with their own hands every tool, weapon, and piece of equipment necessary for their continued existence. They were nomadic. Their lives were, on average, short; twenty-five was literally middle-aged, and it was rare to live past fifty. Infant mortality was high; during her lifetime a woman might give birth four, five, or more times, yet she might see only one or two of those children survive to adulthood. I do not wish to overstate the case here, but hunger, cold, disease, pain, and early death were a much larger part of their reality than the same factors are of our own, at least for those of us living the relatively privileged lives of college students and professors.

But there are people living today, or at least who lived in the last few hundred years, whose cultures and experiences have been recorded and whose reality was or is a reasonably close match to the Ice Age population just described. There are recent people who were hunters of wild animals and gatherers of wild plants. They made their own tools and weapons. They were nomadic. Life expectancy was short, and infant mortality was high. We cannot expect a perfect cultural concordance because the ancient people in the earlier example were inhabitants of Ice Age Europe of 125,000 years ago, and the recent group was the native people of Alaska. It seems reasonable, however, to attempt to extract insights into the lives of an ancient people by studying recent groups when the material conditions of their existence appear to be fundamentally similar.

Ethnographic analogy takes on many guises. In its traditional application archaeologists may scour ethnographies written about people with economies and technologies generally similar to those of the ancient people whose sites they excavate and whose lives they hope to illuminate. In the **direct historical approach** in ethnographic analogy, a closer connection is sought between the ancient and modern groups being compared. Ethnographic information about the actual biological and cultural descendants of the ancient people being investigated is used to explain what is found at the archaeological site. For example, in northeastern North America one group of missionaries, the Jesuits, lived among the Iroquois of New York state. At the same time the Jesuits were attempting to convert the Iroquois to Catholicism, they kept a detailed account of Iroquois lifeways. The resulting multivolume publication, called the *Jesuit Relations* (Greer 2000), provides a wealth of information, albeit not entirely objective, about the lifeways of the Iroquois. The Iroquois and their ancestors have lived in New York state for more than 1,000 years, and the information recorded by the Jesuits in the seventeenth century can be of enormous value to archaeologist hoping to understand the lives of the ancestors of the people whom the Jesuits so meticulously documented.

Even soldiers and explorers can provide important information in the direct historical approach to ethnographic analogy. For example, French explorer Samuel de Champlain visited the New World several times and traveled among the native peoples of Canada and New York state. Champlain also traveled along the coast of New England and encountered and recorded in some detail the native cultures that he found. Among his memoirs were artistic depictions of Indian villages he saw as he sailed along the coast (Figure 12.11). Champlain was not simply a passive observer of the Native Americans, he traded with

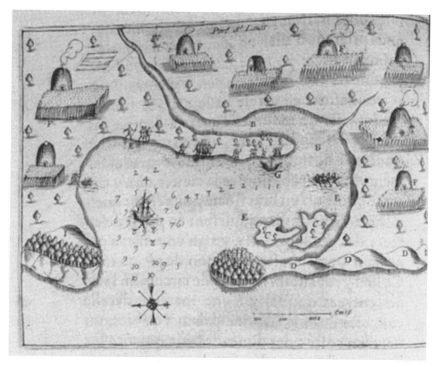

FIGURE 12.11 Especially in the New World, ethnohistory provides a rich source of information to the archaeologist. Here, a map provided by the expedition of French explorer Samuel de Champlain along the southern coast of New England provides an artistic depiction of a series of Indian houses and fields.

them and even fought alongside groups with which he was friendly against their traditional enemies.

Champlain's voyages and explorations are richly documented in his memoirs, and scattered throughout is fascinating information about the native people. Such information is of value to archaeologists investigating the archaeological sites of the Iroquois and their ancestors that date to before Champlain's visit and written account (Champlain 1966). Here's a brief example: In a pitched battle in which Champlain and his men were assisting one native group against another, Champlain was struck in the neck by an arrow. You might think this would have slowed down Champlain in his study of native culture, but he was one tough guy. In his memoirs Champlain recounts pulling the arrow from his neck, whereupon he immediately provided a detailed description of the raw materials from which the arrow was made!

Archaeologists recognize the many drawbacks of ethnographic analogy when the ethnographic information comes from an individual or group with a particular agenda, for example, missionaries or explorers. Even ethnographic information provided by cultural anthropologists may be of limited value to archaeologist because ethnographers may not focus on what so interests archaeologists: material culture. These drawbacks to the ethnographic database have inspired some archaeologists to take the situation into their own hands and conduct ethnography themselves. In **ethnoarchaeology**, or **living archaeology**, the archaeologist becomes the ethnographer, with a particular focus on the archaeological implications of his or her observations (David and Kramer 2001; Longacre 1991; Longacre and Skibo 1994).

Archaeologist Lewis Binford did precisely this in his ethnographic study of the Nunamiut people of the North American Arctic (1978). Binford examined Nunamiut methods of hunting, butchering, preparing, and cooking meat as well as how they discarded carcasses once they were done extracting everything edible. Binford used the behavior of these living people of the Arctic to provide a model that he then used to interpret archaeological remains at the prehistoric cave site of Combe Grenal in France that was occupied as much as 125,000 years ago (Binford 1987).

Binford used the Nunamiut as a model of the culture of the residents of Combe Grenal, even though the cave is located thousands of miles away from the Nunamiut home territory in Alaska, even though the two peoples are separated by 125,000 years, and even though the Nunamiut are biologically modern human beings and the residents of Combe Grenal were an ancient and archaic variety called the Neandertals. Despite their differences, Binford recognized similarities in the material parameters of the subsistence behaviors of the two peoples. For example, Binford saw stone tool cut marks on the animal bones recovered at Combe Grenal that were similar to those he had seen in the fresh kills of the Nunamiut. Specifically, Binford recognized that butchering cut marks on the lower jaws of wild cattle, reindeer, and horses at Combe Grenal were a close match in terms of location and orientation to those made by the Nunamiut on caribou jaws. The Nunamiut left those cut marks as a result of their effort to extract the caribou tongue, which they considered a delicacy. Binford concluded from this that the 125,000-year-old Neandertal residents of Combe Grenal extracted tongue meat in a manner similar to the modern Nunamiut of Alaska.

It is difficult, indeed, to bridge the temporal and cultural gaps between archaeologists and the people we study. Ethnographic analogy provides us with one way of attempting to do so.

Read More

To find out more about the archaeologist's use of the ethnohistorical record and the applications of ethnoarchaeology, consult any of the following sources.

Binford, L. 1978. *Nunamiut Ethnoarchaeology.* Academic Press, New York.

———. 1987. *Bones: Ancient Men and Modern Myths.* Academic Press, New York.

Champlain, S. D. 1966. *Voyages of Samuel de Champlain.* Burt Franklin, New York.

David, N., and C. Kramer. 2001. *Ethnoarchaeology in Action.* Cambridge University Press, Cambridge.

Greer, A., ed. 2000. *The Jesuit Relations: Natives and Missionaries in Seventeenth-Century North America.* Bedford/St. Martin's Press, New York.

Longacre, W. A., ed. 1991. *Ceramic Ethnoarchaeology.* University of Arizona Press, Tucson.

Longacre, W. A., and J. M. Skibo, eds. 1994. *Kalinga Ethnoarchaeology: Expanding Archaeological Method and Theory.* Smithsonian Institution Press, Washington, D.C.

Study Questions

1. What does it mean to say that a culture is the adaptation of a particular group of people?

2. What was the point of the reference to the song "Tradition" from the Broadway musical *Fiddler on the Roof* in my discussion of the archaeological reconstruction of an ancient social system?

3. How might the nature of the social system of a past group of people be encoded in the appearance and styles of the objects they manufactured for everyday use?

4. Explain how the appearance of ceramics made by the women living in the same village might reflect the fact that their people practiced a matrilocal postmarital residence pattern.

5. How might an archaeologist determine the nature of the postmarital residence pattern of a people by examining their material culture?

6. How do traditions of making stone tools or pottery, of burial of the dead, or of crafting baskets reflect the social systems within which such traditions developed?

7. In the division of labor in ancient societies, was biology destiny?

8. What does the work of archaeologist Diane Gifford-Gonzalez show about the stereotyping of sex roles by artists who have depicted ancient peoples and their lifeways? How are ancient men often depicted? How are ancient women often depicted?

9. Can archaeologists distinguish the labors of men from those of women through the analysis of an ancient material culture?

10. How does the work of Joan Gero call into question the sex role stereotyping often applied to the making of stone tools by ancient peoples?

11. What is meant by the term *economic inequality*? How about *social inequality* and *political inequality*?

12. What does it mean when we label an ancient society "egalitarian"?

13. What does it mean when we label an ancient society "complex"?

14. How are equality and inequality reflected in the archaeological record of an ancient group of people?

15. Why are burials so important when it comes to issues of the archaeological reconstruction of social, economic, and political systems?

16. Why are burials so important when it comes to the analysis of equality and inequality in an ancient society?

17. How does such an apparently immaterial part of the human condition, religion, end up encoded in the archaeological record?

18. What do Neandertal burials, a tomb like that of Tutankhamen, and the gravesites at Sungir' tell us about the social, political, and economic lives of the people responsible for them?

19. What is "ethnographic analogy"? Why do archaeologists employ this procedure?

20. What is the "direct historical approach" in ethnographic analogy?

21. What is ethnoarchaeology? Why do archaeologists sometimes get involved in ethnographic research?

13 Conversing with the Dead

BIOARCHAEOLOGY

- **Why Are Archaeologists Interested in Human Bones?**

  Why Is the Excavation of Human Skeletons a Contentious Issue?
  How Can You Determine the Sex of a Person from His or Her Skeleton?
  How Can You Determine the Age of a Person from His or Her Skeleton?
  How Can You Determine the Health of a Person from His or Her Skeleton?
  How Can You Determine the Ethnic Identity of a Person from His or Her Skeleton?
  How Can You Determine the Geographic Location of Where Someone Was Born and Grew Up?

Any one of a number of television crime shows incorporate the work of forensic scientists. Whether it's the medical examiner in any of the *Law and Order* shows, the scientists in the *CSI* franchise, or especially the characters in the show *Bones* (based on the work of an actual forensic anthropologist), it is clear that television drama writers and, one must assume, their audiences are fascinated by the stories told by dead bodies. Perhaps the gross-out factor contributes to this fascination (I understand that actors consider it a point of pride to have played a dead body on one of these shows; at least there aren't any lines to learn). More than this, however, it is remarkable how detailed a medical examiner's or forensic anthropologist's report can be—a virtual biography in bone. Though we recovered no human remains at Wood Lily, this chapter presents in detail the kinds of analysis we might have done had we found human remains at the site and the kinds of analysis that are done when such remains are recovered.

Why Are Archaeologists Interested in Human Bones?

The skeletal remains of human beings present archaeologists with an enormous reservoir of information about the life histories of past people, both individually and as groups. The human skeleton, essentially, is a slate onto which the person's significant biological and behavioral patterns and events have been recorded. For the archaeologist whose goal is to reconstruct these life histories, to expose these biological and behavioral group patterns, and to illuminate events experienced by people in the past, the bones of human beings—their "mortal remains"—are vital scientific specimens. The problem, of course, is that these "specimens" are also the often treasured and venerated remains of mothers and fathers, sisters and brothers, grandparents and great-grandparents stretching back across countless generations. This has become a major and contentious issue that plagues the relationship between archaeologists and the descendants of the people whose bones they excavate and analyze.

Why are archaeologists interested in human bones in the first place? This fascination is not the result of some ghoulish fixation on the remains of the dead. In fact, archaeologists are intrigued by humans bones precisely because skeletons can tell us about who an ancient person was in a broad and sometimes remarkably detailed sense when they can no longer tell us in their own words.

Consider the **demographic** background information that census takers or pollsters might collect to categorize you in the most fundamental ways possible. Certainly, they would want to know whether you are male or female. Obviously, they would want to know your age. Further, they might ask your "race," nationality, or ethnicity. They might even ask about health issues or nutritional patterns. These variables describe an individual; they describe you. Compiled for an entire population, producing frequencies, proportions, or mean values, these would provide **descriptive statistics**, the numbers that describe and summarize the key characteristics of the population in which you live.

With these descriptive statistics in hand, any other questions that might be posed or factors that might be addressed in a detailed numerical compilation of information about a community, state, or nation—how many years of schooling people tend to complete, the income levels of citizens, the number of children people have, their religion, their political affiliation, the chronic diseases that commonly afflict individuals, problems of malnutrition, and so on—can be examined for patterns of correlation and causality. Is there a relationship between sex and years of education, between race and income level, between age and political beliefs, between income level and disease? Through the various procedures of **inductive statistics**, the correlations between and among the variables that characterize a population can be assessed, allowing us to paint a picture of what it was like for an individual to live in a given society. **Biological archaeologists, forensic anthropologists**, and **biological** or **physical anthropologists** can assemble the descriptive statistics for the demography of a community by determining the sex, age, health, and even the ethnic affiliations of individuals through careful analysis of those individuals' skeletons.

Consider, for example, some demographic questions. What was the mean lifespan of people in ancient Egypt 4,000 years ago? Were the lifespans—as represented by mean age at death—of the pharaohs and noble classes different from those of farmers and workers (Romer 1984)? What was the actual ethnic background of the more than 400 people buried in what was labeled the "Negro Burial Ground" (now called the African Burial Ground) in lower Manhattan (Perry et al. 2006)? What was the **population profile** of these African captives? Is there evidence on their skeletons of repetitive stress injury typical for people who endure lives of hard physical labor? Is there physical evidence on their bones of physical abuse (beatings, overworking, torture) often inflicted upon slaves? What was the proportion of men to women in Mound 72, the mass grave of the great leader of Cahokia, an enormous Native American population center located on the Mississippi River in Illinois (Iseminger 1996)? Are nutritional differences exhibited between individuals (probably noblemen and noblewomen) buried in elaborate tombs containing finely made ceramics and jewelry and those people (probably peasants) interred in simple graves with few or no grave offerings at the Maya site of Altar de Sacrificios (Saul 1972; Smith 1972)? These are but a tiny fraction of the interesting questions that can be posed and answered through the analysis of human remains—and, certainly, the answers to these questions allow the archaeologist to develop a more complete understanding of the lives of ancient people.

WHY IS THE EXCAVATION OF HUMAN SKELETONS A CONTENTIOUS ISSUE?

Skeletal analysis raises a vexing ethical issue that should not be ignored by any archaeologist. In some parts of the world, the descendant communities stand in opposition to the archaeological study of the bones of their ancestors. This issue is nowhere more vigorously debated than in the United States.

The national organization of professional archaeologists, the Society for American Archaeology (http://www.saa.org), hosted a symposium on this issue at its annual meeting in 1996. Archaeologists, including Native American archaeologists, and Native Americans who were not involved in archaeology participated. That symposium resulted in a book (*Native Americans and Archaeologists: Stepping Stones to Common Ground*, 1997), in which many and varying opinions were expressed about the role and validity of archaeology within the native community. Consider the perspective of Rebecca Tsosie

(1997), a professor of law and a member of the Pascua Yaqui Indian tribe. She contends that it is a basic human right for a people, any people, to be able to pursue their own mode of religious and spiritual fulfillment and that such fulfillment necessarily requires control over the disposition of the remains of their deceased ancestors. Tsosie goes on to reject the notion that Native Americans and their culture are the equivalent of "resources" that are the communal property of all of the citizens of the United States in general and of archaeologists in particular. The remains of Native American ancestors, asserts Tsosie, should belong to their descendants, who alone should determine how those remains are treated on the basis of their own tribal traditions and customs. More than a few Native Americans, including some at the symposium, view archaeology in general and the excavation, analysis, and "warehousing" of the bones of their ancestors in particular as just one of a variety of types of colonialism, in this case carried out by scientists instead of the army or cattle ranchers (White Deer 1997).

Gary White Deer (1997:38), a world-renowned artist and member of the Choctaw tribe, has extensive experience in historic preservation on his reservation. He may be right when he points out that archaeologists might be a bit resentful, now that they are obliged by federal statute, in particular the **Native American Graves Protection and Repatriation Act** (http://www.usbr.gov/ nagpra/), to negotiate with "potential specimens." But as the subtitle of the symposium book suggests, archaeologists and Native Americans need to negotiate "stepping stones to common ground," and that is happening, particularly in those instances in which Indians themselves are in control of the archaeological work focusing on their ancestors. As earlier indicated, the Navajo Nation, the largest tribe in the United States, has its own archaeology program. The Mashantucket Pequot tribe in southeastern Connecticut has supported a vigorous archaeological program on its reservation, using some of the money generated by a hugely successful gambling and resort operation to build a cultural center where the archaeological material recovered on the reservation is analyzed, curated, and displayed.

A specific example of archaeologists and Indians working together on the thorny issue of human remains was seen in the analysis of the frozen vestiges of a Native American who died in his early twenties about 550 years ago and was found melting out of a glacier in British Columbia in 1999. His coat, crafted of squirrel fur, his bone and metal tools, and a meal of dried fish carried in a leather pouch had been encased in ice along with the young man himself. Together, the young man and his meager possessions had lain in the ice for more than five centuries.

Canadian law affords control of ancient archaeological remains to the descendants of the people who left those remains behind. In the case of the "Canadian Ice Man," members of the Champagne and Aishihik "First Nations," whose assent was required, strongly supported a scientific analysis of the remains of the person they called Kwaday Dan Ts'inchi—(Long Ago Person Found). "We want to know as much about him as we can. That's what science is for, right?" (Krajick 2002). This may sound like the kind of justification for analysis an archaeologist might offer, but the words were spoken by

Diane Strand, heritage officer of the Champagne-Aishihik in an interview in the magazine *Science*. Of course, I should also point out that after extracting sufficient samples for DNA tests still being conducted, the remains of Long Ago Person Found were cremated and his ashes returned to the place were he was found. Obviously, no further analysis applying yet-to-be-developed procedures will be possible in this case.

My colleague and good friend archaeologist Warren Perry has just participated in a multidisciplinary study involving the search for the remains of Broteer Smith, a study that had the complete blessing and support of the descendant family. Broteer Smith, also called Venture Smith, was born in Africa, but no one is certain exactly where. He became a captive there and was brought to America, where he became a slave, not on a southern plantation but in a northern household. By all accounts Broteer Smith was a remarkable person, intellilgent, physically imposing, ambitious, and focused on obtaining his freedom. We know that Smith convinced his owner to hire him out to other families (Smith's owner kept part of the proceeds) and in this way was able to make enough money to purchase his own freedom in 1765 and the freedom of his wife and children soon thereafter. Smith moved to Connecticut, where he became a very successful land owner and businessman. He died in 1805 and was buried in a graveyard in East Haddam, Connecticut.

Who was Broteer Smith? He told part of his story to a schoolteacher who wrote it all down. The saga was published (Smith 2004), but researchers want to know more, as does the descendant family. Where was he from? Was he the desendant of an African king? How was he able to overcome the insult of enslavement and lead a successful life? With the approval of the family, a team of forensic anthropologists, geneticists, and archaeologists excavated Venture Smith's gravesite in the summer of 2006, hoping to allow Smith to add to his autobiography, this time by sharing the secrets encoded in his bones. Scientists and family alike were hoping that enough intact DNA might be found in his bones to allow for a more precise tracing of Smith to a specific tribe or group of people in Africa. They also hoped that a carbon isotope analysis of his bones might produce a signature traceable to a particular place in Africa.

The disinterment was done in a respectful way under the watchful eyes of family members, who were there for every day of the excavation. Unfortunately, Smith's bones, it was determined, had decayed away utterly, and no DNA was recoverable. Equally unfortunately, although fragments of Smith's wife femurs were found in the grave, there was no intact DNA in those bones. The Broteer Smith project didn't result in the recovery of DNA, but it did show how the goals of archaeologists, forensic anthropologists, and descendant families can converge in the desire of everyone involved to learn more about past people.

Involvement of the descendant community is crucial in projects such as the Broteer Smith disinterment. Perry's work provides another wonderful example of the successful inclusion of the descendants of those being excavated. Perry was one of the directors of the challenging and enormously scaled excavation of the African Burial Ground in lower Manhattan, where the graves of more than 400 African captives were excavated when they were disturbed during construction of a federal building (Perry, Howson, and Bianco 2006a). Project participants involved the descendant community in every step of the project, and those descendants contributed significantly to determining the focus of the research. Descendants wanted to know the geographical origins of the people in the cemetery (from where in Africa had they originated). The descendants felt it crucial that researchers investigate the nature of the lives of the captives, that evidence of their resistence to captivity be highlighted, and that the ways in which these African captives "transformed" into African Americans be illuminated (Perry, Howson, and Bianco 2006:445b). Instead of a feeling of powerlessness as the remains of their ancestors were being excavated, the descendant community became empowered as the scientific analysis of those ancestors contributed to an understanding of their own history.

Dorothy Lippert, a Choctaw Indian and professional anthropologist, has been an eloquent and uniquely qualified commentator on the debate about the treatment of human remains, specifically those of Native Americans, but I think her commentary applies equally to all instances of the treatment and interpretation of human remains. As indicated, most scientists view human remains as valuable specimens that can tell us about the life histories of ancient people. As a scientist *and* a Native American, Lippert views the skeletal remains of human beings not as specimens but as the vehicles by which the ancestors of Native Americans can communicate with their descendants: "For many of our ancestors, skeletal analysis is the only way they are able to tell us their stories" (Lippert 1997:126). Lippert goes on to explain skeletal analysis as the process by which ancestors in the past can speak to their descendants in the present in their "voice made of bone." I would add to this stunning phrasing only that ancient peoples all over the world can speak to us in the present not only in their "voice made of bone," but of stone, wood, clay, and metal as well. The archaeological record, in its totality, allows for all our silent ancestors to speak to us and tell us of their lives. Finding those "stepping stones to common ground" between descendant communities and archaeologists is vital for those ancestors to be afforded the opportunity to tell all of us their stories.

How Can You Determine the Sex of a Person from His or Her Skeleton?

Among mammalian species, human beings exhibit a rather modest degree of **sexual dimorphism.** Human men and women certainly look different on the outside. Some of our body parts—those reflecting our primary and secondary sexual characteristics—clearly are not interchangeable, and men tend to possess a larger overall body size than do women. However, in many features the sexes are not as distinct among humans as they are, for example, among one of our nearest biological relatives, gorillas, whose males commonly are about twice as large as their female counterparts. On the other hand, the human sexes are far more readily distinguishable than those of hyenas, whose males and females are so similar in size, body form, and even in terms of the appearance of their external genitalia that, for the most part, only other hyenas can readily tell the difference.

Sexual dimorphism in mammals is exhibited on the inside as well, where, rather obviously, male and female internal sex organs differentiate the sexes absolutely. The size and general appearance of their skeletons and soft organs also differentiate males from females among mammals. Among our closest relatives, the apes, even with just the bones, the degree of dimorphism is sufficient to insure a nearly perfect identification of and distinction between the skeletons of males and females: Their skeletons are absolutely different, or nearly so, and with complete specimens they can always be accurately distinguished.

Sexual dimorphism is less obvious, however, in the human skeleton. Unlike many other species and rather inconveniently for those attempting to identify and differentiate the skeletons of male and female human beings, the skeletons of human males do not possess an absolutely distinguishing element, called a baculum, or "penis bone." The differences between human male and female skeletons instead are reflected in the measured differences of continuously distributed variables; in other words, the distinctions between the skeletons of men and women are differences not of kind, but of size.

Human males, for example, tend to be larger than human females. They usually are taller, heavier, and more robustly muscled, and these differences generally are reflected in the bones of their skeletons. So, though there are no bones unique to either sex, the bones of men within a given human population tend to be bigger, heavier, rougher, and denser than those of the women in the same population as a partial result of genetic predisposition. In other words, a zoologist can *always* distinguish the skeleton of a male sea lion from a female because the male has a penis bone, and, not surprisingly, the female does not. On the other hand, a forensic anthropologist can *usually* distinguish the skeleton of a human male from a human female because the individual bones of the male tend to fall on one end of a normal distribution, while those of a female tend to fall on the other. There is nearly always substantial overlap, however. For example, there are individual men whose bones are smaller and less robust than those of individual women in any group and that, therefore, cannot be accurately "sexed" by a forensic anthropologist, biological archaeologist, or biological anthropologist on the basis of size or robusticity alone.

Beyond those bones that contribute to stature, for example, the long bones of the leg (**femur, tibia**, and **fibula**), there are a number of measurements that, individually, help to distinguish human males from females in a population. Taken together, these skeletal elements and features help make the identification of the sex of an individual based on the skeleton extremely accurate. For example, most human males have a discernable ridge of bone over each of their eye orbits (or sockets), located near the eyebrows. Not all human males have a substantial **supraorbital torus**, but within any population men tend to have them, and women do not. When a **cranium** (technically, the **skull** consists of the cranium and the **mandible**, or lower jaw) is found with a substantial torus, the archaeologist or forensic anthropologist will suggest that it most likely belonged to a man, but there is no certainty based on this feature alone. Another cranial element that tends to distinguish men from women in terms of size and shape is the **mastoid process**, a bump of bone you can feel on your own cranium just behind and toward the bottom of each ear. Several muscles attach to the mastoid process that control extension and rotation of the head. Because the human male head tends to be larger and heavier than that of the female, these muscles need to be bigger, and, in turn, the male mastoid process tends to be larger (and rougher for firmer muscle attachment) than that of females. Also, the female mastoid process tends to be rather pointy, while the male version is flatter. Again, it is not a perfectly distinguishing feature, but it points in a particular direction.

It is in the bones of the pelvis that we find the clearest markers distinguishing human males from females. Although the bones of the rest of the body may be larger and more robust in men than in women, essentially they are functionally the same. In the pelvis, however, we encounter skeletal elements that don't perform the same functions in men and women. The bones of the pelvis provide the attachment points for the leg muscles in both men and women and thus determine our unique method of **bipedal locomotion** (walking on two feet), but in women the pelvis also serves the purpose of providing the walls of the birth canal, through which babies can be born. Proportional to other mammals, at birth human babies have enormous heads, and, rather unfortunately, as a result of the configuration of the human pelvis that enables us to walk on two feet, the human birth canal is proportionally small. This is one of the features of human anatomy that physical anthropologist Wilton Marion Krogman (1951) referred to as one of the "scars of human evolution."

Nature has dealt with this problem in a number of ways. Compared to other mammals, human babies are born at a proportionally earlier, more immature stage of development to enable them to pass through the constricted birth canal yet still be developed enough to survive outside the womb. Nature also seems to have tweaked the configuration of the geometry of the human female pelvis by widening an angled notch on the bone, called the **sciatic notch** after the nerve that passes down the pelvis from the back to the leg. A wider notch opens up the birth canal by a bit, ordinarily just enough to allow for safe passage by the baby during the birth process (Figure 13.1). Though there is quite a bit of variation in a large sample of human beings, the mean sciatic notch angle for women was calculated to be 74.4 degrees; for men in the same sample, the mean angle was only about two-thirds of this, at 50.4 degrees (Krogman 1973).

Even with this seemingly diagnostic anatomical feature, there was a bit of overlap: The smallest sciatic notch angle for a woman in the sample was about 61 degrees, and the largest angle for a man was more than this, about 65 degrees. Though an imperfect yardstick, it is one of the best single measurements by which the sex of an individual can be assessed. If you don't like measuring angles, there is even a literal "rule of thumb": If you can place your thumb straight into the notch and it fits snugly, the pelvis is that of a man; if your thumb can wiggle, it is of a woman. I suppose,

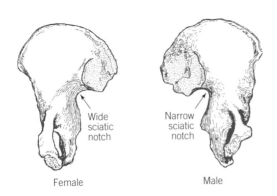

FIGURE 13.1 View of the human male and female pelvis showing the sciatic notch, which is diagnostically larger in women than in men.

rather ironically, that the accuracy of this rule of thumb, depends on the size of your thumb, which, in turn, depends to an extent on whether you are male or female.

In assessing the accuracy of the process of identifying the sex of an individual whose bones we are examining, it is clear that the more skeletal elements of an individual available, the more confident we can be in our conclusion. Having only a long bone to measure or just a cranial fragment inspires less confidence in our identification than if we have long bones, a cranium, and, especially, the pelvis of an individual. Even then, we cannot be 100% accurate, but we do get pretty close to perfection: Most forensic anthropologists claim a greater than 95% accuracy rate for the identification of the sex of an individual when the entire skeleton is available for analysis.

Read More

There are many fine guides to the subjects of forensic anthropology in general and human osteology in particular that discuss how an archaeologist can identify the sex of an individual based on his or her bones. The following list includes an old standard (Krogman 1973) and a host of newer, terrific textbooks, manuals, atlases, and guidebooks.

Bass, W. 1987. *Human Osteology: A Laboratory and Field Manual of the Human Skeleton*. Missouri Archaeological Society, Columbia.

Brothwell, D. R. 1972. *Digging Up Bones: The Excavation, Treatment, and Study of Human Skeletal Remains*. British Museum, London.

Burns, K. R. 1999. *The Forensic Anthropology Training Manual*. Prentice Hall, Upper Saddle River, New Jersey.

Byers, S. N. 2001. *Introduction to Forensic Anthropology: A Textbook*. Allyn & Bacon, Boston.

Hillson, S. 1996. *Dental Anthropology*. Cambridge University Press, Cambridge.

Krogman, W. M. 1951. The Scars of Human Evolution. *Scientific American* 185:54–57.

———. 1973. *The Human Skeleton in Forensic Medicine*. Charles C. Thomas, Springfield, Illinois.

Rhine, S. 1998. *Bone Voyage*. University of New Mexico Press, Santa Fe.

Scott, G. R., and C. G. Turner II. 2000. *The Anthropology of Modern Human Teeth: Dental Morphology and Its Variation in Recent Human Populations*. Cambridge University Press, Cambridge.

Ubelaker, D. H. 1978. *Human Skeletal Remains: Excavation, Analysis, Interpretation*. Aldine Manuals on Archaeology. Aldine, Chicago.

White, T. D., and P. A. Folkens. 1991. *Human Osteology*. Academic Press, New York.

HOW CAN YOU DETERMINE THE AGE OF A PERSON FROM HIS OR HER SKELETON?

How old are you? This book is read, primarily, by university students. Although an increasing number of older adults are registering for college courses—in the last few years I have seen a growing number of full-fledged adults in my classes, including parents taking courses at my university alongside their children—by and large university students are in their late teens and early twenties. That's probably your age range. At that age in our culture, few of you are all that interested in confronting the certainty of mortality, and so it is not surprising, when I assign the "gravestone project" in my introductory archaeology course, that the response is a nearly unanimous "Yuck!" Except in tragic and mercifully rare circumstances, most college-aged people don't spend a lot of time in graveyards, and the prospect of having to collect data from the gravestones in a graveyard, even ones as old as those the project requires (stones erected before 1880) is not often met with a great deal of enthusiasm, at least not initially.

I don't send my students to graveyards because of a morbid fascination on my part. Burying grounds actually are fascinating places and, no matter what their age, are archaeological sites. All gravestones, again no matter how long ago they were carved and erected, are artifacts of a particular culture and period of time, reflecting the religious beliefs and attitudes of a past people.

Gravestones

This assignment does not involve any digging but instead requires data collection and analysis. Students collect data from gravestones—the artifacts of the graveyard—including overall size, raw material, shape, and design as well as the written information on the stones, including name, sex (which often is inferred from the name or an assigned status such as "wife of" or "son of"), year of birth, and date of death. Knowing these two dates allows us to determine the age at death of the person buried beneath the gravestone and then, with a large sample of stones from a graveyard, the mean age at death for the people who lived and died in a given town.

Among the various analyses students conduct in the graveyard are a number that can be called **demographic. Demography** is the statistical analysis of a population, including, among a large number of variables, its size, age distribution, longevity, sex ratio, and ethnic makeup. Knowing the demography of a community allows archaeologists to paint a statistical picture of the communities represented in graveyards. The demographic study of a seventeenth-, eighteenth-, or nineteenth-century Connecticut town might not seem all that engaging to you. I know it doesn't, at least not at first, to the students in my classes. But something remarkable happens to many young people of college age when they enter an old graveyard and see the overwhelming number of people there who died in their youth, who, in fact, died when they were about the same age as the students collecting the presumed dry demographic data required in the assignment.

Most of us grew up in a time and in a society in which teenagers and even people well into their twenties are, demographically at least, children. Life expectancy in North America is among the highest in the world. By the reckoning of the U.S. Centers for Disease Control, as of 2003 (the latest year for which these statistics are available as of this writing), at birth the life expectancy of a man is 74.8 and of a woman is 80.1 (http://www.cdc.gov/nchs/data/hestat/finaldeaths03_tables.pdf).

You probably haven't thought long and hard about how these numbers, in many ways, have an overwhelming impact on how you live your life. But think about it: male or female, at age eighteen you still have more than 75% of your life to live. You have the luxury of enough time to go to college, make your parents crazy by trying out a wide variety of majors (none of which will get you a well-paying job when you graduate), go to graduate school, "find yourself," and experiment with lots of different elements of life all before you settle down, choose a pathway, and maybe raise a family. Now imagine how entirely different your life, your perspective, your fate would be if you were a member of a society in which the mean age at death were half the American average, a reasonable estimate of longevity for many past societies as well as for many modern ones in the undeveloped world. Imagine how different your life experience might be if you grew up in a society in which death in childhood was not a thankfully infrequent tragedy, but a common occurrence, a misfortune that touched virtually everyone, at least indirectly (Figure 13.2). In such a society, at eighteen you would be about half finished with life, and suddenly the issue of time would loom large. You would know too many people your age and younger who had died. In such a society, at eighteen there would no longer seem to be all the time in the world to grow up, choose a life path, and take on the responsibilities of adulthood. At eighteen, time is already running out in some societies: When you are eighteen years old in a society in which the mean age at death is thirty-six, you are already, literally, "middle aged" (Figure 13.3)

Chapter 13:
Interactive
Exercise

At some level, many of my students who prowl an old cemetery, at first merely to fulfill a requirement of the project and then, at least for some, out of curiosity about the lives of the people buried there, make that connection and consider how different everything about their lives would be if they had been born 300, 200, or even one hundred years earlier. Knowing something as simple as the mean age of death in a society (ancient or modern) provides us with a fundamental insight about the nature of the lives of the people who lived in those societies. The analysis of human skeletons allows us to make this determination.

Skeletons

Upon meeting a child for the first time, you probably guess his or her age on the basis of stature. It's obvious enough: Kids start off small, get bigger as they get older, and reach maximum height as adults. Until a person reaches his or her full size, stature is a good first indicator of age, and the same is true for skeletal remains. The overall height of an individual, based on the length of the bones of his or her skeleton, indicates the approximate age of the person at death, at least in an ordinal sense: infant, toddler, child, teenager, or adult.

A person's stature in life can be estimated by skeletal measurement, especially of the long bones of the legs. A number of formulas allow for an approximation of an individual's height based on the length of one of those bones, usually the **femur**, the longest of the leg bones. These formulas are different for the two sexes and also vary by ethnicity because bodily proportions differ among geographic groups of people. The following list shows formulas derived for stature estimation for men and women of European and African descent (Bass 1987).

Female European: Stature (± 3.72 cm) = 2.47 × femur length in cm + 54.10
Female African: Stature (± 3.41 cm) = 2.28 × femur length in cm + 59.76
Male European: Stature (± 3.94 cm) = 2.32 × femur length in cm + 65.53
Male African: Stature (± 3.91 cm) = 2.10 × femur length in cm + 72.22

FIGURE 13.2 New England gravestones marking the all-too-common deaths of young siblings: top, the three Glover sisters who died separately in the period 1776–1784; bottom, the Hart brothers, dead at five and seven years in 1776.

FIGURE 13.3 Colonial gravestones marking the interments of people who, today, would be considered young and middle-aged adults.

Along with a sequence of increasing height, dental development also provides a valuable gauge of the level of physical maturity and age. Ordinarily, human children arrive in the world toothless—much to the relief of nursing mothers—and a first set of teeth (the lower central incisors) doesn't begin to emerge until about six-and-a-half months. From there the timing of the appearance of the rest of the baby teeth, called **deciduous teeth**, is fairly consistent across our species until the second upper molars erupt at about two years (when there are twenty teeth in all, Figure 13.4). A child's teeth achieve a certain degree of stasis at two-and-a-half until, at about age six, the first permanent teeth erupt, molars in the lower jaw. Their appearance at about this age is so consistent that they are, in fact, called the six-year molars. At about the same age, the deciduous teeth (so named because they are shed like the leaves of deciduous, leaf-bearing trees) become fodder for the tooth fairy at a similarly consistent, relatively regular rate and are replaced by the adult, or permanent, teeth. From age six to about eighteen, the baby teeth all fall out according to a fairly regular timed schedule, adult teeth replace them, and additional permanent teeth erupt toward the back of an enlarging mouth until there are thirty-two permanent teeth.

The point here is not to prepare you for a career in dentistry, but to get across a methodology of age determination. Because of the regularity in timing of the eruption of each of the baby teeth, their shedding, and their replacement by adult dentition until the thirty-two adult teeth have produced the adult mouth, the mix of deciduous and permanent teeth charts the age of an individual. By reference to a simple table (http://www.dshs.state.tx.us/dental/healthy_mouths.shtm#primary), the approximate age of a living child or the age at which a deceased child died can be fairly easily and accurately determined based on which teeth are present, the stage of growth of these teeth, and which teeth have yet to erupt into the mouth.

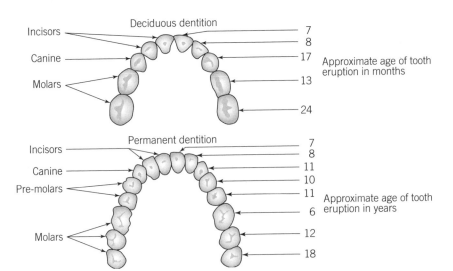

FIGURE 13.4 Schematic diagram showing the average age at which the deciduous (baby) and permanent (adult) teeth erupt in the human mouth. Reference to this pattern of tooth appearance allows the archaeologist to determine the probable age at death of an individual whose remains have been found at an archaeological site.

Beyond this the skeletons of human children are not just smaller versions of those of adults. Their individual bones are readily distinguishable from those of their parents not just in terms of size, but also in terms of form and configuration. In fact, while the adult human skeleton consists of 206 separate bones, a newborn child's skeleton has well over twice as many, about 450. Children don't have extra bones that are lost in development, but many of the individual bones of an adult begin as separate bone segments and join fully only when maturity and adult size are achieved.

In the **postcranial skeleton** the long bones also exhibit a developmental sequence of change that is regular enough to provide a sort of osteological calendar of an individual's lifespan. Just as the cranium of a newborn consists of seven separate bones, each of the bones of their arms, legs, hands, and feet consists of three distinct components at birth and during development. Each of these bones (as well as the clavicle, or collarbone) consists of a shaft called a **diaphysis** and two end caps, each called an **epiphysis.** The end caps are flexibly attached to their shafts by a strong band of cartilage. Much of the lengthening of these long bones during development occurs at these flexible junctions, and upon approaching adult size these cartilage connections ossify, become solid, and produce a single, continuous bone where initially there had been three separate boney elements connected by cartilage. Like the development of dentition, this process of ossification during physical development follows a schedule that is pretty consistent among all human children who are not suffering from severe malnutrition (Figure 13.5).

This consistency provides a timetable for estimating the age of a child whose development sadly was halted by death. For example, the **proximal epiphysis** (the upper end) fuses to the diaphysis of the femur at about age seventeen, while the **distal epiphysis** (lower end) of the same bone fuses to the shaft at about age nineteen. The distal epiphysis of the **humerus** (upper arm bone) fuses at sixteen or seventeen, while the proximal end doesn't fuse until twenty. If you are about that age or younger, x-rays or CT scans of your bones would enable a medical researcher to accurately estimate your age. Therefore, an examination of the progression of the fusion of epiphyses to their respective diaphyses provides an accurate estimate of how old a person was at death.

Changes in the human cranium also reflect a consistent pattern of development. Though we think of the cranium as a hollow, spherical vessel—a single-bone bowl that contains the human brain—in reality we begin life with a cranium of seven separate bones held together by bands of cartilage. Consider the reasons for this. The brain of a newborn human is only about 25% of its ultimate adult size. Compare this to chimpanzees, whose newborn brains are about 40% of their adult size. Even at this very early stage of development, the human baby has a very large head relative to the birth canal it must negotiate and whose size is restricted because of its primary function in the architecture of bipedal locomotion by the mother. To allow for the rather tight fit during birth, the cranium of the fetus is quite flexible. If it were a solid, inflexible sphere of bone, given its size it probably could not pass safely through the birth canal. Instead, the newborn cranial configuration of seven bone plates connected by flexible cartilage affords the head the malleability needed to safely pass through the birth

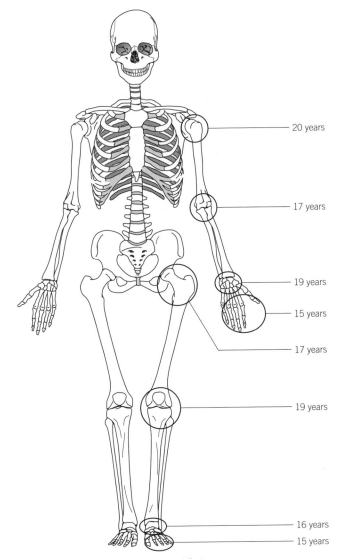

Approximate Ages of Epiphyseal Fusion

FIGURE 13.5 Diagram of the human skeleton showing the average age at which the end caps of the major long bones fuse to their shafts during development.

canal. There are substantial gaps between some of the bone plates, producing two **fontanelles**—the so-called soft spots on a baby's head—that contribute to the ability of the cranium to safely deform during birth. Along with its very small size, therefore, the cranium of a stillborn infant or very young child is quite recognizable because, unlike the skulls of older children and adults, once the cartilage connecting the cranial plates in newborn or infant remains decays, these plates are no longer connected and often are found as separate pieces.

Unlike all other mammalian species, in which growth rate slows substantially after birth, brain growth and, therefore, cranial growth in human newborns continues for the first year of life at about the same rate that characterized its prebirth growth. As a result the crania of newborn humans continue to exhibit relatively soft connections between the cranial plates, facilitating development as they grow in order to contain rapidly expanding brains during the first year of life. Although the cranial plates don't usually separate in a deceased toddler or older child, the boundaries between the cranial plates are clearly demarcated as rather thick junctions called **cranial sutures.** These sutures continue to fuse slowly during an individual's lifetime and provide a general impression of the age even of an adult based on how thoroughly the sutures have fused (Figure 13.6). As a result some forensic anthropologists maintain that suture closure provides a viable estimate of age at death to within about a decade. These sutures can become virtually obliterated in the crania of people of advanced age; a cranium with no remaining signs of sutures generally belongs to an individual who died in at least their seventies or eighties.

Physical development, therefore, is marked by fairly consistently timed changes in the human skeleton that can be used to determine age at death for a subadult. Once all the adult teeth are in and epiphyses are fused to their respective shafts, however, accurately aging a skeleton becomes more of a challenge, and our precision (technically meaning how narrow a range of years we

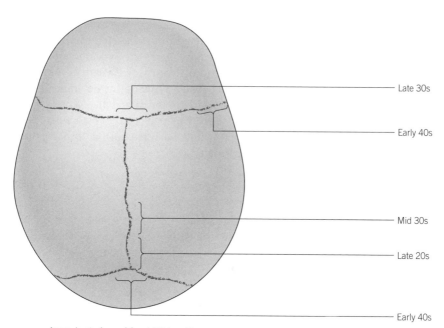

Approximate Ages of Cranial Suture Closure

FIGURE 13.6 Schematic diagram of the timing of cranial suture fusion during a human lifespan. Unfortunately, because the rate at which cranial sutures fade varies greatly from person to person, reference to degree of suture fusion is not viewed as a very accurate or precise method of determining an individual's age at death.

can accurately estimate) declines. As just mentioned, cranial suture closure occurs as we age, and, therefore, the degree of fusion or closure marked by the slow disappearance of the suture lines where the cranial plates came together can be used to provide a broad estimate for the age of an individual. Otherwise, with the exception of the clavicle, whose end caps don't fuse until well into the twenties, once an individual passes out of the teens skeletal changes are not precisely timed steps in physical development but instead reflect the slow, inevitable, and less precisely timed results of bones and joints slowly wearing out during the life of an individual. These degenerative processes do not provide a very accurate skeletal clock because the rate at which they operate varies among individuals depending on work history, which determines the degree of stress and abuse repetitive use inflicts on various bones and joints. When a sports announcer comments that a physician has determined that a thirty-year-old football player has the knees of a sixty-year-old, he or she is expressing this same notion.

Probably the most useful skeletal gauge of adult age occurs at the point in the skeleton where the left and right halves of the pelvis meet in the front. Called the **pubic symphysis**, the two faces of the pelvic bones preserve a record of wear and tear that occurs at a vaguely regular rate during our lives. Through examination of a large sample of human skeletons, some rough models of the appearance of the pubic bones of men and women throughout their lifetimes have been produced. By comparing the pubic symphysis of an archaeological skeleton to models of known age, a rough estimate, perhaps at a decadal level of precision, can be obtained.

In summary, careful analysis of a complete human skeleton can provide an accurate and rather precise estimate of an individual's age at death, but usually only if the person died in the first twenty or twenty-five years of life. After that our estimates become less precise, usually allowing for not much better than an estimate of the decade of life in which an individual died. Knowing the mean age of death in a population provides a vital perspective about what it was like to live in a past culture in which childhood was short, adulthood came quickly, and death was never a distant tragedy.

Chapter 13:
Interactive
Exercise

Read More

There are many fine guides to the subjects of forensic anthropology in general and human osteology in particular that discuss how an archaeologist can identify the age at death of an individual based on his or her bones. The following list includes an old standard (Krogman 1973) and a host of newer, terrific textbooks, manuals, atlases, and guidebooks.

Bass, W. 1987. *Human Osteology: A Laboratory and Field Manual of the Human Skeleton*. Missouri Archaeological Society, Columbia.

Brothwell, D. R. 1972. *Digging Up Bones: The Excavation, Treatment, and Study of Human Skeletal Remains*. British Museum, London.

Burns, K. R. 1999. *The Forensic Anthropology Training Manual*. Prentice Hall, Upper Saddle River, New Jersey.

Byers, S. N. 2001. *Introduction to Forensic Anthropology: A Textbook.* Allyn & Bacon, Boston.

Hillson, S. 1996. *Dental Anthropology.* Cambridge University Press, Cambridge.

Krogman, W. M. 1973. *The Human Skeleton in Forensic Medicine.* Charles C. Thomas, Springfield, Illinois.

Rhine, S. 1998. *Bone Voyage.* University of New Mexico Press, Santa Fe.

Scott, G. R., and C. G. Turner II. 2000. *The Anthropology of Modern Human Teeth: Dental Morphology and Its Variation in Recent Human Populations.* Cambridge University Press, Cambridge.

Ubelaker, D. H. 1978. *Human Skeletal Remains: Excavation, Analysis, Interpretation.* Aldine Manuals on Archaeology. Aldine, Chicago.

White, T. D., and P. A. Folkens. 1991. *Human Osteology.* Academic Press, New York.

How Can You Determine the Health of a Person from His or Her Skeleton?

I am quite certain that from anybody's perspective other than my own it must have been quite hilarious: It was the first day of field school, and I was leading a team of intrepid neophytes out for their first archaeological experience. My intention that day was to walk them along the river where many of our sites were located and out into a farmer's plowed field, where we would walk the furrows scanning for artifacts that had been exposed by the plow blade (as discussed in chapter 6) . It was supposed to be simple and uneventful, and it was, until it came time to instruct the crew on the safest way to cross over a rather innocuous little brook in our hike to the plowed field.

In truth, it would have been perfectly fine to walk through the brook. It was only a few inches deep, a few feet across, and rather still, but an old oak that had once grown on the bank of the brook had long ago fallen over, its curved trunk forming an arched, natural crossing. I had passed over the old trunk on numerous occasions without incident and simply wanted to make certain that everyone on the field crew would be able to make the crossing safely. I went over first, warning them that a bit of sand on top of the oak arch made the footing a little slippery. As I hit the patch of sand, naturally enough, I slipped and began sliding along the curved trunk, but conveniently enough toward the other side of the brook. "OK," I thought, "I'll simply surf down the tree trunk. My students will be impressed." The only problem with this plan was the fact that waiting for me at the other side were the spiky remnants of the tree's roots, on which I caught my left foot. This, in turn, tumbled me down like a stone, and I landed hard on the outside of my right foot on a rather sharply pointed rock embedded in the soil near the base of the dead oak. I had the presence of mind to get out one final joke—"Well, that's how *not* to get across the brook"—before the first wave of pain hit. I had sprained an ankle or two before and recognize that it can be uncomfortable, but nothing compared to this. I had no choice but to pretend I was perfectly OK, both for the sake of my dignity—did I forgot to mention how hilarious my students thought my little performance had been?—and for the fact that we were about a mile-and-a-half from our vehicle and only a couple of hours into our field day.

I'll spare you the details of how I managed to walk over plowed fields and eventually back to the truck, how I was able to drive it back to campus (using my left foot on the brake and gas; lucky for me it wasn't a standard transmission), and then how I managed to make it home. I'll also forego any discussion of the expression on the face of the emergency room doctor when I explained to him how I managed to mangle my foot, which the x-ray rather clearly indicated I had broken (fractured the fifth metatarsal, to be precise). For about ten years after I broke the bone, I could accurately predict rain (my right foot would begin to throb just before a storm), and now, more than twenty years later, the break can still be seen on x-rays of my right foot. My fifth metatarsal, in fact, bears eternal witness to my clumsy inability to cross a stream only about 3 feet across and 3 inches deep. And there's the lesson of my less-than-excellent adventure: Our skeletons bear eternal witness to the physical traumas that have afflicted us. Broken bones, fractures, knife wounds, and bullet holes become permanent records of acts of accident and violence written on our skeletons.

Consider, for example, the remarkably preserved, 5,200-year-old body found by hikers in the Alps in 1991, just on the Italian side of that nation's border with Austria (Spindler 1994). Although for ten years it was thought that the so-called Ice Man had frozen to death while attempting to cross the mountains in winter, recent CT scans have shown the presence of a stone blade deeply embedded in his shattered shoulder blade. The location of the arrow point indicates that it probably killed the Ice Man within a few hours of penetrating his body.

Although skeletons such as the Ice Man's bear witness to a quick, violent end, many human skeletons exhibit the results of a much slower kind of violence that inflicts not obvious trauma, but degeneration over a lengthy period of time. For example, the skeletal remains of thirty-six African slaves examined by Ted Rathburn (1987) bore witness to their lives of toil and exploitation. The degenerative bone disease exhibited in their shoulders, elbows, hips, and lower vertebrae in people far too young to have such a degree of damage through normal use indicates hard lives of stoop-and-bend labor in the field. It is one thing to read of the physical exploitation endured by slaves; it is another to see the agonizing results of that exploitation on their mortal remains.

Along with trauma and wearing out of bones and joints as a result of overuse, the human skeleton also can exhibit evidence of a number of diseases. **Paleopathology**, the study of ancient trauma and illness, can in some cases even help solve historical mysteries. For example, Nick Bellantoni, the state archaeologist of Connecticut, was called on to excavate an unmarked eighteenth-century cemetery in Griswold. It was clear during excavation that one of the crypts had been opened about a decade after burial and that the body within the crypt had been perversely violated (Figure 13.7). The ribs and vertebrae were in disarray, the skull had been moved onto the chest, and the bones of the upper legs had been removed from their correct anatomical positions and placed crosswise in front of the skull. Needless to say, this was not the standard form of burial in eighteenth- and nineteenth-century New England, and Bellantoni and colleagues searched for an answer to this rather disturbing puzzle (1997).

FIGURE 13.7 This photo shows a direct view into the grave of one of the individuals interred at the Walton family cemetery in Griswold, Connecticut. The skeleton was found as you see it, with (see black arrow) both femurs (the thigh bones) removed from their correct anatomical position and placed crosswise across the person's chest. (Courtesy Nick Bellantoni)

He found that answer, in part, in local nineteenth-century newspaper accounts that recorded, of all things, a vampire frenzy in southern New England during this period. Apparently, a handful of people were accused of vampirism in southeastern Connecticut and Rhode Island. From a modern, informed perspective the evidence was flimsy: The accused individuals had suffered long, debilitating illnesses and then, upon their deaths, many of those people close to them slowly deteriorated as well, becoming weak, pale, and listless, as if the life force were being "drained" (get it?) from their bodies. Then they, too, died. The cause was diagnosed as vampirism, and it was believed that those who died initially were rising from their graves and draining the blood of their loved ones, dragging them into the unholy world of the vampires. The only cure, it was thought, was the desecration of the presumed vampires' graves, the removal of their hearts (removing the need for blood), and the disruption of their bones, especially those of the legs to prevent them from rising from the graves and walking the night. The grave Bellantoni excavated fit the pattern, with the disturbed ribs indicating that the chest had been broken into and with the leg bones moved from their correct anatomical position.

The symptoms of vampirism described in the news accounts sounded quite a bit like those of tuberculosis, an infectious and deadly, not to mention entirely natural, bacterial disease that still affects millions of people each year by attacking their lungs. The extended period of listlessness, exhaustion, and pallor attributed to vampirism all match the symptoms of tuberculosis. The fact that after a family member died others in the family began exhibiting the same symptoms was not the result of the undead slowly draining the blood of their victims but probably of the infectious nature of the disease and its lengthy incubation period. The person infected with the tuberculosis bacilli coughs and sneezes, spreading the bacilli through the air, which may then be inhaled by others, especially people living in close quarters with the infected person, in other words, close members of the family.

Tuberculosis is easily diagnosed in a living person by examining the infected lungs, but it is far more difficult among those dead long enough to have had their lungs turn to dust. However, there is a diagnostic pathology that appears on the ribs of people suffering from tuberculosis. Sure enough, the whitish-gray, pitted lesions that are skeletal indicators of tuberculosis were found on a number of the ribs of the disturbed grave. It seems certain that Bellantoni solved the mystery of the disturbed grave through analysis of the skeleton of the man buried there.

Nutrition also has an effect on the human skeleton. For example, prolonged bouts of severe malnutrition can have a severe impact on development during childhood. The longitudinal (lengthwise) growth of our long bones can actually be interrupted if the deficiency is severe enough, leaving marks on the bones called **growth arrest lines** or, more commonly, **Harris Lines** (named for the researcher who was among the first to ascribe the lines to malnutrition). The appearance of these defects in the bones of adults indicates that their growth had actually halted temporarily during childhood as a result of malnutrition. Their growth resumed only after the bout of malnutrition ended (Figure 13.8).

Malnutrition during childhood may also manifest itself as a cracking or pitting of tooth enamel called **enamel hypoplasia.** Interestingly, hypoplasia occurs in permanent dentition, even though the malnutrition occurs during childhood. The germs of the adult teeth are already in a child's jaw under the baby teeth. A few years ago my then-eight-year-old had an x-ray as part of his regular dental checkup. Sure enough, just below the negative images of the teeth he already has in his mouth, there were bright little smudges. Those were the buds of his permanent teeth that have by now almost all erupted, replacing his baby teeth. It is the growth of the enamel of these forming adult teeth that is interrupted during childhood bouts of malnutrition, and the pathology shows up in the adult mouth.

Consider the cemetery, for example, at the Altar de Sacrificios site of the Maya civilization (Saul 1972; Smith 1972). The Maya represent an extraordinary native New World civilization, replete with great temples, pyramids, a

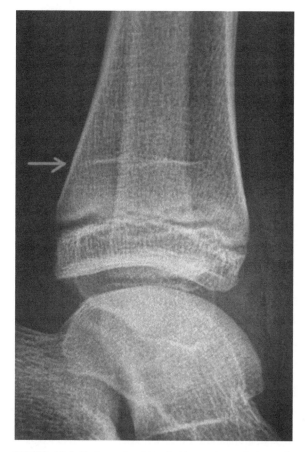

FIGURE 13.8 Radiograph of Harris Lines, also called growth arrest lines, which are skeletal evidence of malnutrition during childhood. (Courtesy Brian Tidey, www.radiographersreporting.com)

written language, and a sophisticated calendar. The Maya also produced a stratified society with great rulers, a noble class, specialist craftsmen and -women, and a vast peasantry. Researchers excavated 136 burials at the Altar de Sacrificios site. The grave goods interred with the Maya at the site reflect a range of wealth and status, probably representative of the different classes of Maya society. It should come as no surprise to learn that in a stratified society of rulers and peasants, wealth differences in life are represented in death as well. The graves at Altar de Sacrificios show this, with a few burials resplendent with finely made necklaces and ceramics, while most burials are far plainer, reflecting the lower economic status of the person buried.

It is common in class societies that the wealthy nobility eats well, even when food is scarce, and peasants starve, which is reflected at Altar de Sacrificios. Frank Saul (1972) identified the presence of enamel hypoplasia in the teeth of most of those buried at the site. He categorized the degree of hypoplasia in each of the skeletons along an ordinal scale (absent, slight, medium, pronounced). Researchers made the same kind of breakdown for the graves based on burial wealth (tombs of the wealthy, tombs of the middle class, and graves of the poor). Finally, a table was produced showing the relationship between the two variables, grave wealth and degree of hypoplasia in the same individuals. The results should shock no one: Individuals buried in the more elaborate tombs tended to exhibit either no or low levels of hypoplasia, while those buried with no indication of great wealth or status tended to have higher levels of the condition that is caused by malnutrition in childhood. Childhood malnutrition was uncommon among the Maya nobility at Altar de Sacrificios, but the same cannot be said for Maya peasants, whose teeth betrayed a fundamental element of class society.

Certainly, our skeletons are the products of genetics, but equally certainly their final appearance is a product of our life history: the traumas inflicted, the diseases endured, the toil that accompanied our activities in life, and the foods we were able to obtain. A careful examination of an ancient skeleton illuminates a life history; a careful examination of a community of skeletons illuminates the life of the community.

Read More

There are many fine guides to the subjects of forensic anthropology, in general, and human osteology, in particular, that discuss how an archaeologist can identify the health and nutritional status of an individual based on his or her bones. The following list includes an old standard (Krogman 1973) and a host of newer, terrific textbooks, manuals, atlases, and guidebooks. Also in this list are the specific sources cited in this segment as examples of the application of human osteology in archaeological analysis.

Bass, W. 1987. *Human Osteology: A Laboratory and Field Manual of the Human Skeleton*. Missouri Archaeological Society, Columbia.

Bellantoni, N. F., P. Sledzik, and D. A. Poirier. 1997. Rescue, Research, and Reburial: Walton Family Cemetery. In *In Remembrance: Archaeology and Death*, edited by D. Poirier and N. F. Bellantoni, 131–54. Bergin & Garvey, Westport, Connecticut.

Brothwell, D. R. 1972. *Digging Up Bones: The Excavation, Treatment, and Study of Human Skeletal Remains*. British Museum, London.

Burns, K. R. 1999. *The Forensic Anthropology Training Manual*. Prentice Hall, Upper Saddle River, New Jersey.

Byers, S. N. 2001. *Introduction to Forensic Anthropology: A Textbook*. Allyn & Bacon, Boston.

Krogman, W. M. 1973. *The Human Skeleton in Forensic Medicine*. Charles C. Thomas, Springfield, Illinois.

Rathbun, T. 1987. Health and Disease at a South Carolina Plantation. *American Journal of Physical Anthropology* 74:239–53.

Rhine, S. 1998. *Bone Voyage*. University of New Mexico Press, Santa Fe.

Saul, F. P. 1972. *The Human Skeletal Remains of Altar de Sacrificios*. Papers of the Peabody Museum of Archaeology and Ethnology 63, Cambridge, Massachusetts.

Smith, A. L. 1972. *Excavations at Altar de Sacrificios*. Papers of the Peabody Museum of Archaeology and Ethnology 62, Cambridge, Massachusetts.

Spindler, K. 1994. *The Man in the Ice.* Harmony Books, New York.

Ubelaker, D. H. 1978. *Human Skeletal Remains: Excavation, Analysis, Interpretation.* Aldine Manuals on Archaeology. Aldine, Chicago.

White, T. D., and P. A. Folkens. 1991. *Human Osteology.* Academic Press, New York.

How Can You Determine the Ethnic Identity of a Person from His or Her Skeleton?

Human beings come in a dizzying variety of shapes, sizes, colors, and configurations, and these different looks appear to vary geographically. In fact, if you were to ask the average American, I would guess that he or she might enumerate three distinct geographic **races** of humanity, labeling them variously as white, black, and yellow; or Caucasian, Negro, and Mongoloid; or European, African, and Asian; or any one of a number of other designations based on appearance or presumed continent of origin. Examined more closely, however, the usual tripartite division of humanity perceived by many Europeans and Americans masks a far greater degree of diversity within our species and makes separate categories seem more distinct than is really the case. In fact, there is at least as much variation within what are commonly called races as there is between them (Park 2005). There are no significant biological boundaries between people, no real genetic barriers, no distinct walls separating us. Human beings do not come in distinct and separate groupings but instead appear in a broad continuum reflected by a diversity of traits. Yes, there are very light-skinned folks and very dark-skinned folks, but there also are people with every conceivable skin shade in between. The same broad spectrum of expression applies to other human characteristics, such as hair color and texture, bodily sizes and proportions, and facial features. As a result, most biological scientists do not consider the common concept of human races particularly useful in describing human variation.

Of course, it cannot be ignored that people do vary in their outward physical appearance, and this variation is, to an extent, geographically linked. There are, indeed, patterns of location that relate to the particular expression of external human physical characteristics—darker skin tones are concentrated toward the equator, and people with squat bodies and relatively short arms and legs are concentrated in cold regions—and some of this may be the result of natural selection, with some physical characteristics conferring an advantage under certain environmental conditions. Beyond this, once we delve beneath the features of skin tone, hair texture and color, nose shape, and lip size, there are variations in the human skeleton that also statistically distinguish people from different parts of the world. Accurately determining the ethnic identity of a person from his or her skeleton, however, is a far more difficult task than determining age or sex. Forget what you may have heard about people of African ancestry having extra bones in their feet that provide them with an athletic advantage or other such nonsense. In truth, there are very few clear indicators of ethnicity in the human skeleton, although there are tendencies that may be used at least in attempting to approximate the ethnic-geographic origins of an individual.

For example, viewed from the front, the top of the crania of native people of Africa and Europe tends to be rounded, while that of those from Asia tends to come to a ridge or keel on top. Viewed in profile, the faces of European and Asian natives are quite flat, while those of Africans tend to be thrust forward (**prognathous**), especially at the jaw. The chin profile of Africans tends to be rounded, while that of Europeans is pointy and Asians are in between. Remember, these all are tendencies and not absolutely distinguishing features, and, as a result, their utility and accuracy in identifying the ethnic or geographic origins of an individual are not especially high.

A few skeletal features can be used to distinguish ethnicity a bit more clearly, though still only in a statistical sense. For example, the inside surfaces of the central incisors of Europeans and Africans tend to be shaped like flat blades, while those of Asians tend to be shaped more like shovels, scooped in the middle and with ridges on their lateral margins (Figure 13.9). However, not all Asians possess so-called **shovel-shaped incisors**, and the proportion of this tooth form varies within Asian populations. Generally, more than 50% of Asians within a given region exhibit some degree of shoveling, and in some populations it is found in more than 90% of individuals. Shovel-shaped incisors are not entirely absent among Africans or Europeans—in fact, for reasons that are in no way clear, shovel-shaped incisors are not all that rare in Sweden—but shoveling tends to be far less common among them. In addition, the very high level of incisor shoveling among Native Americans is interpreted as strong evidence of their Asian origins because that tooth feature is most common in Asia (Scott and Turner 2000).

Certainly, we should not simply throw up our hands and deny that determining the ethnic-geographic identity of an individual from his or her skeleton can be accomplished. On the other hand, we need to recognize that the degree of variation seen in human bones can make this a very difficult endeavor.

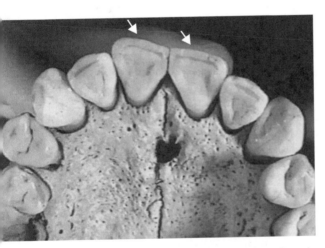

FIGURE 13.9 Shovel-shaped incisors, such as those in this jaw, are quite common among Native Americans and Asians and are rare in native Europeans, Africans, and Australians. (Courtesy John Seidel)

Scientists now have the ability under certain circumstances to extract DNA from bones, in particular, **mitochondrial DNA** (DNA located outside the nucleus of cells, in the cellular mitochondria). Modern human groups that originated in various parts of the world are characterized by their own unique clusters of particular mitochondrial DNA codes. These clusters are called **haplogroups** or **haplotypes**. In some cases these same haplogroups have been identified in the mitochondrial DNA recovered from ancient bones found by archaeologists. In these cases the ethnicity of the ancient person can be determined with a level of accuracy not possible by an analysis of gross morphological characteristics. For example, the five haplogroups designated A, B, C, D, and X are quite rare or entirely absent among Europeans, Africans, and native Australians but are widely seen among living Native Americans and Asians, lending further support for a genetic connection between the native peoples of Asia and the New World. These same haplogroups have been identified in the skeletal remains of Native Americans (Derenko et al. 2001), further supporting the idea that living Native Americans are the genetic descendants of Asians who entered the New World in antiquity. When gross skeletal morphology cannot provide an accurate assessment of the ethnic identity or geographic source of an individual or community, genetic analysis can help answer the question far more precisely.

Read More

There are many fine guides to the subjects of forensic anthropology in general and human osteology in particular that discuss how an archaeologist can identify the ethnic or geographic origin of an individual based on his or her bones. The following list includes an old standard (Krogman 1973) and a host of newer, terrific textbooks, manuals, atlases, and guidebooks.

Bass, W. 1987. *Human Osteology: A Laboratory and Field Manual of the Human Skeleton.* Missouri Archaeological Society, Columbia.

Brothwell, D. R. 1972. *Digging Up Bones: The Excavation, Treatment, and Study of Human Skeletal Remains.* British Museum, London.

Burns, K. R. 1999. *The Forensic Anthropology Training Manual.* Prentice Hall, Upper Saddle River, New Jersey.

Byers, S. N. 2001. *Introduction to Forensic Anthropology: A Textbook.* Allyn & Bacon, Boston.

Derenko, M. V., T. Grzybowski, B. A. Malyarchuk, et al. 2001. The Presence of Mitochondiral Haplogroup X in Altatians from South Siberia. *American Journal of Human Genetics* 69:237–41.

Hillson, S. 1996. *Dental Anthropology.* Cambridge University Press, Cambridge.

Krogman, W. M. 1973. *The Human Skeleton in Forensic Medicine.* Charles C. Thomas, Springfield, Illinois.

Park, M. A. 2002. *Biological Anthropology.* McGraw-Hill, New York.

Rhine, S. 1998. *Bone Voyage.* University of New Mexico Press, Santa Fe.

Scott, G. R., and C. G. Turner II. 2000. *The Anthropology of Modern Human Teeth: Dental Morphology and Its Variation in Recent Human Populations.* Cambridge University Press, Cambridge.

Ubelaker, D. H. 1978. *Human Skeletal Remains: Excavation, Analysis, Interpretation.* Aldine Manuals on Archaeology. Aldine, Chicago.

White, T. D., and P. A. Folkens. 1991. *Human Osteology.* Academic Press, New York.

How Can You Determine the Geographic Location of Where Someone Was Born and Grew Up?

The medical examiner (ME) on a recent crime show I was watching was faced with identifying the highly fragmented remains of a small child whose bones were all that remained to tell a story of life and death. Using the same procedures discussed in this chapter, the ME determined that the remains were those of a boy who was little more than five or six years old when he died. Beyond this, the ME's report concluded that the child appeared to be African in origin—the anatomical features of the remaining bones suggested this—and, even more precisely, that he had been born and had grown up in West Africa. The medical examiner in this fictional account based these last details on an isotopic analysis of several elements in the boy's bones and teeth, the concentrations of which are known to reflect and preserve the conditions that were prevalent when those bones and teeth were produced in the body. In other words, these bone and teeth isotope concentrations reflect environmental levels during an individual's development and continue to do so even after the person leaves the region of his or her birth.

One form of isotope analysis relies on differences in the proportions of the same isotopes (^{16}O and ^{18}O) discussed in chapter 9. Most of the oxygen present in your bones comes from the water you drink. That water originates in the rainfall in the region in which you live. The precise concentration of the heavier variety of oxygen in atmospheric moisture varies regionally, especially as a factor of elevation. The same reason given in chapter 9 for why ^{18}O-bearing water takes more energy that ^{16}O water to evaporate also explains why it condenses more readily as it rises: it's heavier. As water vapor rises to form clouds, the heavier water with ^{18}O disproportionately condenses (compared to ^{16}O water) and falls as rain. By the time those clouds reach higher elevations and their water falls as rain, it has already become relatively depleted of ^{18}O. As a result of this, people who live in low-lying areas tend to have a higher concentration of ^{18}O in their drinking water and, therefore, in their bones, and people who live at higher elevations have a lower concentration of the heavier oxygen. If you are born in a low-lying area and move to a higher elevation after childhood, the enamel of your teeth, because it forms when you are a child, will continue to reflect the relatively higher levels of ^{18}O of your place of birth.

Returning to the Ice Man for a moment, his remains were found at an elevation of about 3,300 meters (close to 11,000 feet), high enough to expect a relatively low level of ^{18}O in his bones and teeth. Nevertheless, analysis of the Ice Man's tooth enamel produced a much higher-than-expected figure for ^{18}O, a concentration far more in keeping with a childhood lived at a lower elevation (Müller et al. 2003).

Having determined that the Ice Man was born and raised at a lower elevation than where his remains were found, further isotope analysis allowed researchers to specify even more precisely where the Ice Man was born and where he spent his childhood. Along with oxygen isotopes in water, concentrations of various elements in the soil are absorbed by the plants that grow on those soils. Matching levels become established in the bones and teeth of the animals and people who eat them. The Ice Man's tooth enamel, reflecting the isotopic soil conditions of the area in which he developed physically, exhibits a particular composition of isotopes of the elements strontium (Sr) and lead (Pb) consistent with that measured in the soils of and plants growing in the Eisack River Valley located about 60 km (37 miles) southeast of the location where the

Ice Man was found (Müller et al. 2003). Researchers have concluded on this basis that the Ice Man may have died high in the Alps but probably spent his childhood in this nearby valley.

Study Questions

1. What is archaeological demography?

2. What are the descriptive statistics an archaeological demographer might be able to determine?

3. How does a demographic profile of a past society provide insights about the kinds of lives lived by its people?

4. What primary factors are at the core of the controversy between Native Americans and American archaeologists regarding the excavation, analysis, curation, and display of the skeletal remains of the ancestors of those Native Americans?

5. There's a bit of a false dichotomy presented in question 4; there are some individuals who are both Native Americans and American archaeologists. Summarize the opinions of the Native American archaeologists mentioned in this book about the issue of human remains.

6. What protections do the Native American Graves Protection and Repatriation Act afford to the graves and remains of Native Americans?

7. Can Native Americans and archaeologists reach a common ground on the issue of human remains?

8. Which features or characteristics of the human skeleton allow us to identity, with a fair degree of certainty, the sex of the individual whose bones are being examined?

9. What is sexual dimorphism?

10. Why are the bones of the human pelvis the best to examine when attempting to identify the sex of the person represented by the bones?

11. Which features or characteristics of the human skeleton allow us to identity, with a fair degree of certainty, the age of the individual whose bones are being examined?

12. What features of the human skeleton allow us to approximate the age of individuals through their teens and early twenties?

13. What features of the human skeleton allow us to approximate the age of individuals after they have passed their mid-twenties?

14. Which features or characteristics of the human skeleton allow us to assess the overall health of individuals whose bones are being examined? (Well, of course, they are dead, so their health isn't too good, but I mean the history of their health while they were alive.)

15. How does physical trauma manifest itself on human bones?

16. How do nutritional deficiencies manifest themselves on human bones?

17. How does disease manifest itself on human bones?

18. How did paleopathology contribute to a solution to the mystery of the violated grave found at the Walton family cemetery in Griswold, Connecticut?

19. How did an analysis of the burials at Altar de Sacrificios contribute to our understanding of Maya society?

20. How does ethnicity manifest itself on human bones?

21. How can isotope concentrations in bones and teeth suggest the geographic location in which a person was born and raised?

14 Wood Lily

ARCHAEOLOGICAL PORTRAIT OF A LIFE

- **The Environment of Wood Lily**

- **The Wood Lily Larder: Food for Thought**

- **Making Tools at Wood Lily**

- **Wood Lily Lives**

This book has focused on the methods employed by archaeologists to reconstruct the past lives and past cultures of human antiquity. The approaches described on these pages present us with the only methods available in the present by which we can, in a sense, travel back through time. Using these procedures, we can visit, however briefly, the world inhabited by the people of the site we found in 1986 in Peoples State Forest, Barkhamsted, Connecticut.

 The Environment of Wood Lily

The world in which the residents of Wood Lily lived, at least the physical environment in which they found themselves, would be readily recognized by any of us alive today in the eastern woodlands of North America. Pollen analysis and identification of wood in the fireplaces built by the inhabitants of the village that became the Wood Lily archaeological site show us that the trees growing there some 3,000 years ago reflect generally the same mix of species that currently characterizes the forests of southern New England, including

FIGURE 14.1 Typical eastern woodland landscape. A rich and diverse mixture of trees, plants, and animals made the eastern woodlands an attractive place to settle for both Native Americans and European colonists. (K. L. Feder)

especially oak, maple, hickory, pine, and birch (Figure 14.1). That's a good indication that the overall climate at Wood Lily 3,000 years ago—long, cold, snowy winters; rainy springs; long, humid, hot summers; and breathtaking, chilly autumns—was much the same as it is now in southern New England.

Although economically important species such as chestnut and elm are largely gone due to relatively recent historical fungal infestations (chestnut blight, which began its devastation in the early 1900s, and Dutch elm disease, first identified in the United States in 1930), many of the other tree species of the modern eastern woodlands are the same as those a resident of Wood Lily would have regularly encountered and have had available for use in building a home, crafting a spear, carving a bowl, making a bark container, producing a canoe, and fueling a fire. Even though wooden tools were not found at Wood Lily and no structural remains endured for our recovery, carbonized fragments of wood, burned in the villagers' fire hearths, were recovered and analyzed. Not surprisingly, we were able to determine that their fuel consisted mainly of oak and hickory.

 ## The Wood Lily Larder: Food for Thought

Fruit- and nut-bearing trees common in our contemporary woodlands, such as hickory, chestnut, and oak (acorns), would have provided food for the inhabitants of Wood Lily and, at the same time, would have attracted animals that would have been of great use to the people who lived there. The charred remains of acorn and hickory nutshells recovered in cooking features at the Wood Lily site provide direct evidence of the preparation of nut meats for use in the diet of the site's inhabitants.

The eastern woodlands of North America were—and, in many cases, continue to be—densely inhabited by a host of economically useful animals. A beautiful representation of this was produced by the artist Alan J. Rummler in the 1930s for the Norwalk High School cafeteria. His painting entitled *The Mammals of Connecticut* was a product of the Works Project Administration (WPA), a federally sponsored program to help put people, including artists, to work during the Great Depression. The mural, which is more than 10 feet wide and 6 feet tall, presents a pretty and pristine eastern woodland scene, though in all likelihood you wouldn't be able to get the depicted menagerie together in one place at the same time (Figure 14.2)

Clearly visible in Rummler's conception of an unspoiled Connecticut forest habitat are a family of deer, two raccoons, a couple of skunks, a woodchuck, a red fox, eastern cottontail rabbits, grey squirrels, red squirrels, an opossum, and a mother black bear and her cub. Many of the same species of animals depicted by Rummler in his 1930s forest tableau thrived in the wooded world inhabited by the residents of Wood Lily 3,000 years before the artist put brush to canvas. In fact, if you could travel through time and bring the residents of the village that became the Wood Lily archaeological site into our present, they would instantly recognize all the animals in the painting except the opossum, a relatively recent migrant into New England from the southern states. Other fur-bearing

FIGURE 14.2 This placid scene of Connecticut mammals was painted by the artist Alan J. Rummler as part of a WPA project to put people to work during the Great Depression. The mural was originally intended for Norwalk High School, and the cutout to the right is not a printing error: The mural was intended to bracket a doorway, and the missing part of the mural represents the location of a doorway in the school cafeteria.

animals common to the modern eastern woodlands (not depicted by Rummler but historically well known in our region and whose remains have been recovered at other archaeological sites in the East) are the beaver, northern river otter, porcupine, weasel, fisher, bobcat, and coyote. Also probably inhabiting the world of Wood Lily's residents were the eastern timber wolf and cougar, both of which are extinct in southern New England today but are historically well known in the region (before their habitat was dramatically altered and before they were intentionally eliminated because of the dangers they presented, primarily to livestock).

Bone fragments recovered at the Wood Lily site show directly that deer contributed significantly to the diet of the site's inhabitants. It is likely as well that deer hide, bones, and antlers were important raw materials used by the site's residents: the hide was used for clothing, blankets, and assorted coverings; pieces of the bones might have been shaped into awls, needles, fasteners, and other tools; and the antlers were probably used for **pressure flaking** implements.

We found no direct evidence in the form of faunal remains for the use of small mammals at the Wood Lily site. This probably is due to the high acidity of the soils in New England, a high level of biological activity (lots of bugs, worms, and microbes eating and recycling everything organic they can find), and intensive physical weathering due in part to significant and often rapid temperature changes in the soil and resulting episodes of alternate freezing and thawing. Smaller bones, especially ones not carbonized in a fire during cooking, usually don't stand a chance of being preserved in such soils. Nevertheless, it is likely that some of the smaller fur-bearing animals seen in Rummler's painting, along with the other mammals listed, would have been exploited by the residents of Wood Lily for their meat or for the warmth their fur could provide.

Along with this mammalian bestiary, southern New England is home to more than forty-five reptile and amphibian species, some of which, especially turtles and frogs, are edible and are known to have been used for food by native peoples in the seventeenth century. Another of Rummler's paintings, also intended for the Norwalk High School cafeteria, depicts the birds of Connecticut (Figure 14.3). Among the many different species he showed are those whose feathers were used by the native peoples whose lifeways were described by sixteenth-, seventeenth-, and eighteenth-century European explorers and colonists of Connecticut. Birds' feathers were used to fletch arrow shafts, and their meat was used as food. Turkeys and ducks especially were used by native peoples, and may have been on the menu at Wood Lily.

In the background of Rummler's mammal painting lies a body of water, a generic lake representative of those scattered throughout the woodlands of southern New England specifically and the eastern woodlands of North America in general. There is no lake in proximity to Wood Lily, but the community was adjacent to a permanent source of flowing freshwater in the form of a brook, unnamed on modern maps. The brook flows into a larger stream, Beaver Brook, which would likely have provided an abundance of freshwater fish for the site's inhabitants (Whitworth, Berrien, and Keller 1976). **Anadromous** species such as the Atlantic salmon, shortnose sturgeon, and American shad live a part of their lives in the salty waters of Long Island Sound and the Atlantic Ocean but

FIGURE 14.3 Artist Alan J. Rummler's companion painting to the *Mammals of Connecticut* depicting an assortment of the birds of the state and produced for the Norwalk High School cafeteria during the Great Depression. The blank corner indicates the location of a doorway in the school cafeteria.

FIGURE 14.4 Historical illustration of native fishing along the coast of Virginia by Theodore de Bry in 1590. Fresh- and saltwater fish have made significant contributions to the diets of many past and present peoples.

then migrate en masse into freshwater rivers and ultimately into stream nurseries, where they produce and deposit eggs before they die. Enormous "fish runs" reported by seventeenth- and eighteenth-century colonists represent eyewitness accounts of these seasonal migrations that would have provided an opportunity for the people living at sites such as Wood Lily to collect a tremendous amount of food in the form of fish in a very short period of time, food that they could have preserved by drying (Figure 14.4).

Along with anadromous fish, the brooks, streams, and rivers of the eastern woodlands teem with native fish that spend their entire lives locally in these watercourses. The local fish in Connecticut include a number of varieties of trout, pickerel, shad, perch, sunfish, and a nonanadromous landlocked salmon. Though no fish bones, teeth, or scales were found at Wood Lily—once again, the acidic and biologically active soil is hostile to the preservation of fish remains—the semilunar knives that dominated their stone tool kit (to be discussed in more detail later in this chapter) would have been efficient implements for slicing open the fish to separate the meat from the bones in order to prepare the edible part of the fish for drying.

 ## Making Tools at Wood Lily

For a people reliant on stone for a significant part of their tool kit, keeping a ready supply of projectile tips and cutting, sawing, scraping, piercing, and

FIGURE 14.5 A small sample of the most abundant artifact recovered at the Wood Lily site: small, discarded waste flakes of stone—in other words, debitage.

pounding tools on hand—and maintaining the sharpness of their edges—must have been an ongoing process. This explains in large measure the nature of much of the archaeological record at Wood Lily and other prehistoric sites in New England and, in fact, just about everywhere before the development of ceramic technology. In a chipped stone tool technology culture, tools and their edges are not simply ground into shape, they are flaked. This flaking produces a tremendous amount of **debitage**, or waste flakes, which can end up discarded on the ground where it fell in a workshop area or anywhere on a site where tools were made or maintained. It is not surprising, therefore, to find waste flakes at any archaeological site where a people who made chipped stone tools lived or carried out a task. In fact, these flakes often are the dominant element in an archaeological assemblage. Wood Lily is a perfect example of this. More than 5,400 waste flakes were recovered in nineteen 2-meter-by-2-meter excavation units at the site (Figure 14.5). Compare this to the total number of complete or broken chipped stone tools recovered in those same nineteen excavation units: fifty-three, including projectile points, drills, scrapers, knives, and other bifacially flaked tools (Figure 14.6).

The ratio of waste flakes to tools is often interpreted as an indication of the amount of tool making that was carried out at a site. It should be intuitively obvious that at a site with a small number of waste flakes relative to the number of finished tools, not much tool making was done. In the case of Wood Lily, the ratio

FIGURE 14.6 A sample of functional tool types recovered at the Wood Lily site, including spear points, knives, scraping tools, and a drill.

of waste flakes to tools was substantial, at 102.7:1. In other words, statistically, for every finished tool we found at Wood Lily, we recovered more than one hundred waste flakes. This high ratio of waste flakes to finished tools is a clear indicator that stone tool making was an important activity at the site.

We recovered only a single **hammerstone** at the site, which might seem surprising given the argument just presented that stone tool making was an ongoing process at Wood Lily (Figure 14.7). In fact, I wasn't all that surprised by this, based on my own experience as a knapper. A good hammerstone with just the right heft and shape is not something that tool makers would have left behind at the site. I maintained the same hammerstone for use in my stone tool replication demonstrations for several years. In truth, I got pretty attached to that rock. An almost perfect sphere of quartzite, I will admit that it got pretty battered after a while, but it worked extremely well in peeling flakes from flint and obsidian cores until its sadly lamented recent demise, when I foolishly attempted to use it to flake a very hard nodule of local basalt, a tough, volcanic rock. Before I killed it, I took that hammerstone with me to all my demonstrations and always brought it back to the lab, so it does not surprise me that the resident knappers at Wood Lily seem to have taken nearly all their hammerstones with them when they left the site for the last time.

FIGURE 14.7 One of the few intact hammerstones left behind by the tool makers at Wood Lily. (K. L. Feder)

FIGURE 14.8 A flint core. The shallow depressions located above and below the ridge that runs diagonally across the surface are places where flakes were removed. Those flakes were probably treated as blanks from which specific tools were made.

The fifty-three chipped stone tools recovered at Wood Lily were all made on large flakes removed from cores, primarily flint and quartz (Figure 14.8). Stone tool makers become adept at extracting as many large flakes from a core as they possibly can, but eventually all stone cores get used up and become too small, too battered, or too irregularly shaped to successfully and efficiently remove more flakes. At that point the core may be discarded, and, in fact, we found the remnants of seven such **exhausted cores** at Wood Lily (Figure 14.9).

Another category of stone artifacts is called **preform.** Preforms reflect a step in the manufacture of stone tools. A knapper can efficiently remove a large number of flakes from a core as a preliminary step in stone tool making. Next, the knapper may do a preliminary

FIGURE 14.9 After a number of large flakes have been removed to serve as blanks for specific tools, the remnant of the core, such as this one from Wood Lily, may simply be abandoned. The irregular surface seen here was produced by the removal of flakes prior to abandonment of this nucleus of stone (K. L. Feder)

FIGURE 14.10 A sample of large quartz (far right) and quartzite (left and center) preforms. These objects had been worked on both sides and both faces into general forms from which, with subsequent and more detailed percussion and pressure, final, finished tool forms would have been made.

thinning and shaping of the flakes, producing an assortment of partially made **blanks** that can at a moment's notice be retrieved from storage and rather quickly made into whatever tools are needed at that time: a spear point, knife, drill, scraper, and so on (Figure 14.10). It is a rather more efficient production strategy than one that requires beginning from scratch each time there is a need for a particular kind of tool. We found three preforms at Wood Lily, flakes that had clearly sustained additional work after their removal from cores, were chipped on both faces, but had been only very generally fashioned.

The fifty-three finished tools recovered in our excavation of Wood Lily reflect the diversity of activities conducted at the site. Altogether, we recovered the following finished tools (both intact and fragmented): twenty-five projectile points, five drills, seventeen knives, three scrapers, and three piercing tools. With such a tool kit the residents of the site could have hunted and killed animals, butchered them, removed the hides, prepared the hides for the manufacture of leather cloth, and prepared clothing from those hides.

Along with the chipped stone tools recovered at Wood Lily, we also excavated a single **ground stone** artifact, a tool whose working end was produced not by chipping off flakes but by grinding the edge down into a useable shape (Figure 14.11). The tool in question has a sharpened, curved edge and appears to be a gouge, a tool probably used to shape wood. I'm calling it a gouge because that's exactly what it looks like and also because of the wear patterns apparent on its working surface. Even with the naked eye, and certainly with a little magnification, a series of scratch marks can be seen on both faces, beginning at the working edge and then running back, perpendicular to that working edge of the tool, just as you might expect in a tool used to gouge into or hollow out a block of wood to make, for example, a bowl or a canoe.

FIGURE 14.11 A gouge recovered at the Wool Lily site (top). The slightly concave surface on the left is the working edge of the tool. The edge damage that accumulated on the working edge of this tool is visible in the bottom image. (K. L. Feder)

The categories of chipped tools—projectile points, drills, knives, scrapers, and piercing tools—are defined at least initially on the basis of morphology (what they look like). Stone spear or arrow points look like their modern metal counterparts. Stone drill bits also look essentially like modern metal ones, but in each case, and for each specific artifact so categorized, we have also carefully examined its edge with a stereoscopic microscope, using between ten- and eighty-power magnification. Tool use leaves diagnostic damage on the working surfaces of the tools, and we looked for these traces on each of our finished tools and fragments. We also looked at a 25% sample of the apparent waste flakes to determine if any of these had been used as ad hoc tools simply because they presented the stone tool worker with fortuitously shaped or sharp edges.

It turned out that many of the flint finished tools (quartz is notoriously difficult for detecting wear pattern), whose functions we hypothesized on the basis of form, exhibited wear patterns that were in keeping with those functions. What we labeled as drills or drill bits showed the kind of polish we expected in a tool used to bore a hole in a hard material (Figure 14.12).

The tools we labeled knives exhibited striations on both faces parallel to the working edge and little nibbles taken off their edges as a result of the pressure applied during the cutting process. The presence of small, shallow "scalar scars" (that look like little fish scales; Figure 14.13) again conforms to their use as knives, probably used in the cutting of bone (based on the results of the use-wear experiments conducted by Lawrence Keeley (1980) and highlighted in chapter 10). Scrapers exhibited striations and other evidence of damage on their working edges, but this time perpendicular to those edges, matching our expectations.

0   1   2 mm

FIGURE 14.12 Magnified image of the tip of an intact drill recovered at Wood Lily. Arrows point to areas where the twisting pattern of drill use produced polish on high spots and removed nibbles (half-moon scars; see Figure 10.18) from the edge. (K. L. Feder)

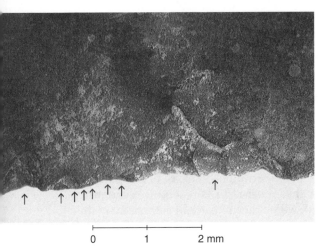

FIGURE 14.13 Magnified image of the edge of a cutting tool. The arrows point to several examples of scalar scars (see Figure 10.18) along the tool's edge, evidence of damage from rough use in cutting or slicing. (K. L. Feder)

0   1   2 mm

The piercing tools, perhaps used to make holes in leather to allow for a threaded bone or antler needle to pass through in sewing, exhibited a bit of polish exactly as might be expected from constant pressure while twisting through a tough animal hide. Only five of the more than 1,560 flakes (0.3%) we examined showed evidence of use, a good indicator that the vast majority of artifacts we initially labeled as waste flakes indeed were just that, not tools used by the village residents but merely the by-products of the tool-making process.

The spear points showed little actual wear. The job of these tools tends to be quick and nonrepetitive, so there is little opportunity for traces of damage to accumulate on a working edge. Many of these points, however, were found snapped just above the spot where they would have been hafted onto a wooden spear shaft, perhaps indicating that they had broken when thrown at an animal, missed the prey, and struck the ground or a tree or when they had slammed into the bone inside the animal.

The overall use of lithic raw materials at Wood Lily showed a nearly equal reliance on stone available locally and stone that needed to be traded or involved travel to obtain. About 52.3% of all the debitage and tools found at the site was of local quartz, and 46.3% was of flint available in the Hudson River Valley of New York state. The rest of the lithic assemblage was made up of fractional percentages of local hornfels (0.6%) and basalt (0.4%) as well as a number of other not clearly identifiable materials (0.4%).

Wood Lily Lives

These statistics and descriptions of what was found at the Wood Lily archaeological site do not represent the destination of archaeological travelers but a passport that provides us access to an ancient place and time. A community of people, not spear points, gouges, hammerstones, nut fragments, and deer bones, once lived on the banks of a small brook in a thick woodland in eastern North America. The physical evidence that constitutes the archaeological record at what we have called the Wood Lily site exposes us to shadowy glimpses of a community in which people lived more than 3,000 years ago. People lived at this place: They made tools from the raw materials they had at their disposal in order to wrest a living from their environment; they hunted and gathered food for subsistence using those tools; they traded for raw materials or traveled great distances for them; and they thrived in a time and a place by developing a way of life, a culture, different from our own but nevertheless familiar and recognizable. The people at Wood Lily represent one small example of the genius of our species for inhabiting an environment, exploiting what that environment has to offer, and developing a way of life in which a people can flourish. Their ancient story is merely a variation of our modern story. It is a story that we can recover by the processes described in this book, a story revealed by the science of archaeology.

Imagine a frothy stream skittering among the rocks as it meanders through a dense woodland. A low haze of mosquitoes clouds the air above the wet patches left in the brook's wake. At the bubbling stream's edge a lone deer stops for a drink, scattering the brook trout swimming in the water. The doe's eyes and ears are alert to any possible hint of danger, her white flag of a tail twitching at the anticipation of flight. Always busy, hyperkinetic gray squirrels sprint across tree branches overhead. The humid air is pierced by the call of a jay and the honk of geese as they overfly the terrace where the inhabitants of a place live their lives in the pleasant beauty of a woodland summer morning. In all likelihood these people could never have imagined that 3,000 years after their part was played on life's stage, strangers would contemplate their woodland, their stream, and their lives and attempt to capture its essence by examining little more than their lost spear points, broken knife blades, worn-out stone scrapers, forgotten axes, fragmented stone flakes, and detritus of their meals.

Study Questions

1. What was the environment like when the Wood Lily site was occupied?
2. What plant and animal resources were available for the inhabitants of the Wood Lily site?
3. Describe the stone tool assemblage at Wood Lily.
4. Based on the analysis of its stone tool assemblage, what activities can we conclude were conducted at the Wood Lily village?

Epilogue

CAN WE RECONSTRUCT THE PAST?

Walk through any major natural history or science museum, and you are apt to see life-sized dioramas depicting scenes of our contemporary natural world alongside conceptualizations of ordinary moments in human antiquity. I can remember, as a kid, being mesmerized by the animals displayed in these three-dimensional snapshots of nature at the American Museum of Natural History in New York City. The dioramas there were and are amazing, with scores of animals in lifelike poses, brightly illuminated in spectacularly naturalistic settings. Each scene depicted in the dioramas presents animals seemingly playing out a little drama of life and death in nature. These dioramas were to me like magical windows into a host of other worlds and other times. It is truly remarkable still; in the dark, cool, and cavernous great hall of a sprawling building in the heart of a gray, modern metropolis are brightly shimmering portals through which we can see the parched plains of southern Africa, the piercing intersection of snow and sky in the Arctic, and the color-speckled beauty of the autumn woodlands of eastern North America. (See Stephen Christopher Quinn's [2006] wonderful book detailing the history of the American Museum of Natural History dioramas, with historical photographs that chronicle their production.)

Well-done dioramas such as the ones at the American Museum of Natural History are splendidly realistic, achingly beautiful, luminous tableaux that appear to be actual natural moments frozen in time and space. It would seem that little more were needed than the snap of some omnipotent genie's fingers to instantaneously set in motion the two adult bull moose, forever frozen in their struggle for dominance in a thickly wooded world; for the lion pride to burst from the tall grass and rain death upon the zebras and gazelles nervously browsing alongside the waterhole; for the Gemsbok, locked in their eternal stare, to suddenly come alive and calmly walk out into the grand gallery; or for the two people, looking familiar yet foreign, set against the backdrop of an alien landscape sculpted by a volcano visible in the distance, to resume their arm-in-arm walk, leaving behind two sets of footprints demarcating their immortal stroll (Figure E.1).

Certainly, the animal displays produced today at respected museums are highly accurate and realistic depictions of events, behaviors, and processes that truly occur in the natural world, but what about dioramas that focus on the human past, those that depict human ancestors making tools, hunting, burying their dead, creating art, or worshipping their gods? Certainly they are intriguing, dramatic, and even moving, but do these dioramas provide clear glimpses

FIGURE E.1 A volcano erupts in the background of this African landscape as two ancient human ancestors stride over a blanket of ash in this diorama at the American Museum of Natural History in New York City. The artist responsible for this scene has presented a 3.6-million-year-old drama that resulted in the preserved footprints—seen here in the diorama as they were being made—discovered by paleoanthropologists Mary Leakey and Tim White in 1974–1975. (Photo by D. Finnin/ C. Chesek)

of our human world as it once existed, or are they really only clouded and darkened portals into a world that never was? We might ask the same of archaeologists concerning their ability to accurately craft images of the lives of people in the distant—and not so distant—past.

The dioramas at the American Museum of Natural History that depict our human ancestors present moments from our species' past both ordinary and extraordinary. In a sense, archaeologists attempt to accomplish something quite similar to the diorama makers, presenting word pictures of all the past places and past times that we study. Like the creators of these dioramas with their paints, papier-mâché trees, silk leaves, and, of course, stuffed and mounted animals, we hope to be able to produce, in the words we craft, the articles and books we publish, the lectures we present, and the websites we design, visions of moments in time. It is our hope, to be sure, that our creations are not just reflections of how we might presume or hope past people lived, not just-so stories that we find comfortable or useful or that affirm our own beliefs or preconceptions, but accurate narratives that expose the lives actually lived by our ancestors, faithful representations of their cultures and their worlds.

Producing dioramas and illuminating the human past alike are difficult and challenging undertakings. The purpose of this book certainly has not been to describe in every detail precisely how archaeologists go about the tasks of discovering places where evidence of the human past exists, recovering that evidence, and then analyzing and interpreting it. Instead, this work has been designed to give you an outline of these processes, a brief taste of how archaeologists attempt to recapture the complexity of human existence, often dating to periods of time that were far different from our own.

As noted earlier in this work, the title of a book by Kathy Schick and Nicholas Toth (1993) about archaeology (*Making Silent Stones Speak*) aptly presents the challenge all archaeologists face in the attempt to describe and learn from the past; the stones (and pots, and bones, and temples, and monuments) we excavate, uncover, and reveal do not speak for themselves. We have to make them speak. This book has been about the techniques archaeologists employ to make the things that have endured in the archaeological record speak to us about the lives of past human beings.

I especially like the phrasing used by well-known paleoanthropologist Pat Shipman in an interview for a documentary about human evolution. In describing some of her highly specialized research that looked at the tiny marks left behind on ancient bones by the stone tools wielded by our human ancestors, Shipman talked about having to "coax" information out of the objects in order to reveal the secrets they might possess and share about the ancient people who left those cut marks on the bones. In the end, much of archaeology is focused on doing just that: coaxing from the silent stones, bones, pots, seeds, pits, burials, temples, and monuments the secrets they may reveal about the lives lived by the peoples who preceded us on life's stage. If we do it well and if we are lucky, the images we resurrect of past peoples can intrigue, inform, inspire, and even excite us about human antiquity, enabling us, like the diorama makers, to construct, if only in our minds, shimmering windows through which the human past is made visible again.

Study Questions

1. How is a museum diorama a metaphor for the archaeological reconstruction of an ancient way of life?

2. What is the point, after all, of archaeological research?

Glossary

absolute dating: Dating techniques that provide an actual age in years or a range of years for archaeological artifacts, ecofacts, features, and sites. The precision offered by different absolute dating methods when applied to archaeological sites can range widely. In dendrochronology, for example, the precise year in which a tree was cut down can be determined, and, in another example, the maker's mark on a ceramic vessel can be traced to the precise year in which the maker produced a particular style of pottery. At the other extreme, some absolute dating techniques in their archaeological application may provide only a very broad possible range of thousands, tens of thousands, hundreds of thousands, and even millions of years. For example, the potassium/argon dating method may date a volcanic layer overlying archaeological material to 1 million years ago, and another layer underlying the site may date to 1.5 million years ago. In this case, we may conclude that the site is between 1 and 1.5 million years old (dating to sometime after the older volcanic flow and before the later deposit). Although the precision is not very high here (the range is a half-million years), this is still an absolute date. *Chronometric* dating is another term for absolute dating.

accession: A unique designator assigned to each artifact in an archaeological assemblage. An inventory number. With a unique accession number (or some other designator) assigned to each item found at a site, detailed information about each item (its precise location of discovery, depth and date of discovery, and so on) can be recorded in a paper inventory or computer database under its accession designator, allowing the information to be correctly associated with each item.

activity area: A general term for a spatially bounded area within a place inhabited or used by people where a particular task or tasks were carried out. Stuff may accumulate where activities were carried out as people lose or simply dispose of material they no longer need or that is of no further use. The discarded objects become artifacts and ecofacts; together they constitute an archaeological feature.

adaptation: An adaptation is a "strategy," in the broad sense of that term, for survival. The adaptations of nonhuman animals are primarily biological, the physical characteristics they possess that make survival possible. The primary adaptations of the human animal are literally strategies for survival— behaviors invented and refined by human groups to enable their survival.

aeolian: Fine particles of clay, silt, and sand deposited by the wind. In some parts of the world, archaeological sites commonly are covered entirely and preserved by aeolian deposits. In some cases, once a community is covered with sand, producing a hill, a subsequent group may settle the top of the hill, and the remnants of their community may be covered in aeolian deposits as well when is it abandoned. This process can be repeated several times at the same place, producing an enormous hill called a tell that encloses a sequence of the remains of several communities superimposed one on top of the other.

alidade: A surveying instrument that consists of a sighting scope mounted on a flat base. Resting on a leveled plane table, the alidade can be used to sight on a stadia rod to determine the precise depth of the surface on which the rod is resting.

alluvium: Material deposited by a flooding river; the soil that blankets the flood-plain of a river valley. Technically, alluvium consists of unconsolidated material: sand, gravel, and fine particles of rock. As a result of its fine fabric and rich organic content, alluvium produces soil that is attractive to farmers both ancient and modern. The regular deposition of alluvium, sometimes in a yearly cycle, can produce a substantial stratigraphic record with deeply buried archaeological material.

American Antiquities Act of 1906: The law that truly set the stage for federal preservation and protection of archaeological sites. This law was short and simple: It explicitly made illegal the destruction or defacement of archaeological sites on federal property and established a fine of up to $500 and a penalty of up to ninety days in jail for its violation. Further, it made digging sites on federal land illegal without a permit; such permits were limited to qualified individuals and issued only when the excavation benefited a recognized university or museum. The law further stipulated that archaeological excavation on public lands was for the public benefit and that material excavated needed to be made available to the public, in, for example, a public museum. (http://www.cr.nps.gov/local-law/anti1906.htm)

anadromous: Fish such as salmon and shad that live part of their lives in the sea but return each year to the freshwater stream where they hatched for females to lay their eggs, males to fertilize them, and then for them both to die. Their offspring hatch and mature in the freshwater, where they live for between one and three years and then migrate into the ocean. Large fish runs mark the point in the year when the fish swim upstream to reproduce, providing an ample food source for humans poised to exploit it.

angle of applied force: In percussion flaking, the angle between the striking platform and the trajectory of the hammerstone as you bring it down on the core or flake. In pressure flaking, the angle between the surface of the flake and the direction of the applied pressure. The angle of applied force should be less than 90 degrees in most circumstances. An angle approaching 90 degrees will tend to produce long flakes extending down the length of the core; an acute angle of applied force ordinarily will result in shorter but very thin sharp-edged flakes.

anthropologist: Scientists who focus on the broad analysis of human behavior within the discipline of anthropology.

anthropology: The holistic study of humanity. Whereas other social and behavioral sciences tend to specialize in and focus on individual elements of human behavior, such as, economics, political patterns, or social systems, anthropology looks broadly at how human beings behave and how that behavior has evolved. The examination of human physical evolution, cultural evolution, adaptation, and language.

archaeoastronomy: The archaeological examination of astronomically based knowledge and related practices of ancient people. Carved images of lunar phases, monuments constructed to keep track of the location of the rising sun along the horizon, and the alignment of buildings and roads toward the rising and setting of particular stars or constellations are all part of the archaeoastronomical database.

archaeological concession: The functional equivalent of a mining permit at an archaeological site. Archaeological concessions were common in the nineteenth and early twentieth centuries, granted by foreign governments providing formal and legal permission for archaeologists, most of whom were European or American, to excavate in these foreign countries.

archaeological context: Archaeologists can't travel back in time to observe directly the use and meaning of the elements of material culture found through excavation. When these objects are recovered, they are, by definition, in their archaeological contexts: artifacts or ecofacts in the ground, in particular soil levels, and in association with other artifacts and ecofacts. Careful analysis of these objects allows for a determination of how these objects were used—their behavioral contexts—by past peoples.

archaeological excavation: The exacting process of revealing the remains left behind by a past people, preserving the physical integrity of the objects revealed as well as their spatial contexts. By segmenting a site into manageable excavation units; by slowly peeling back the soil in each of those units in small increments by the use of hand tools; by leaving material, at least initially, precisely where it was found and, by inference, where a past people left the material through processes like discard, loss, and caching; by carefully measuring and mapping in three dimensions the exact locations where objects were found; and by taking these discovered objects and samples back to the lab for analysis, the information contained within a site is preserved in the process of archaeological excavation.

archaeological fieldwork: That portion of archaeological research that is conducted in the field. Examining soil surfaces through walkovers, or pedestrian surveys, as well as probing the subsurface through test excavations in the search for sites (survey) and, once found, the intensive investigation of individual sites by excavation.

Archaeological Resources Protection Act of 1979 (ARPA): This federal law expanded and clarified the American Antiquities Act of 1906, protecting archaeological materials located on federal land. Specifically, ARPA prohibits "unauthorized excavation, removal, damage, alteration, or defacement of archaeological resources." ARPA provides stiff penalties for its violation: a fine of up to $10,000 and one year in jail for a first offense and even more severe punishment for subsequent convictions. By passing this law and imposing substantial penalties on those convicted of violating it, the federal government was making an important statement: It takes seriously its responsibility to protect and preserve archaeological resources on federal land; these resources belong to all American citizens as a group, not to any individual, and those who violate the law will be punished. (http://www.cr.nps.gov/local-law/FHPL_ArchRsrcsProt.pdf)

archaeological site formation: Archaeological sites come into existence as the result of human behavior. Sites form by a series of site formation processes that include loss, discard, abandonment, and caching (storing for future use or as a ceremonial deposit).

archaeology: The study of the material remains of human behavior. Archaeology is the subdiscipline of anthropology (the study of people) that focuses on the lives of past peoples through the analysis of the things that they made, used, and then lost or discarded and that have fortuitously been preserved.

archaeomagnetism: Orientation of the Earth's magnetic field can become fixed in relatively recent cultural deposits such as the sediments in a canal or in the clay bricks lining a kiln. The date of a site can be determined when that orientation points to a location of magnetic north already fixed in space and time along a master curve.

artifact: Any portable object made by human beings. For an archaeological specimen to be an artifact, it must have been intentionally made, not merely the accidental result of human activity. Arrow points, pottery, bone needles, bricks, a mill wheel, and a plow blade are artifacts. Wood found in an ancient fireplace and the unintentionally modified bones of an animal hunted by a human being are not artifacts. Though they bear witness to human activity (burning, butchering), the wood and bones in this example were not made into anything. They are, instead, categorized as ecofacts.

assemblage: The entirety or individual subsets of the material culture recovered at an archaeological site or sites. All the artifacts or individual categories of artifacts. One can speak of the artifact assemblage for a particular site and by that mean all the artifacts. Or, for example, one can refer to the stone tool assemblage or ceramic assemblage, that is, the array of stone tools or ceramic objects found at a site, in a region, or dating to a particular time period.

backdirt: The excavated and screened soil that piles up around an excavation unit or test pit. Ostensibly—and hopefully—backdirt is devoid of cultural material, having already been carefully examined by the archaeologist.

behavioral context: Term given to describe the behavioral meaning of objects in the culture that produced and used them. If an ancient people produced a hunting weapon, for example, a spear point, its behavioral context, obviously enough, is that of a tool used in killing an animal in the hunt. Though archaeologists hope to discover the behavioral contexts of the objects found at archaeological sites, it isn't always obvious or immediately evident. Archaeologists first encounter an object's archaeological context.

Beringia: The area of northeastern Asia, northwestern North America, together with the Bering Sea that currently separates the two regions, that was a continuous landmass during periods of lowered sea level. The lowered sea level resulted from expanded ice fields in higher elevations and latitudes during the Pleistocene, commonly known as the Ice Age. Beringia was inhabited by cold-adapted plant and animal species and provided a route of migration between the Old and New Worlds. It is thought by most archaeologists that human beings in Asia expanded into Beringia from the west and south, eventually migrating into North America. Native Americans encountered by European explorers in the late tenth century A.D. (the Norse) and late fifteenth century (Columbus and those who followed) were the descendants of these Asian migrants.

Bering Land Bridge: The land, currently under the Bering Sea, that was exposed during periods of lowered sea level and that served as a metaphorical bridge between the Old and New Worlds. At its greatest extent this "bridge" was, from north to south, probably more than 1,500 km (close to 1,000 miles) wide, providing a broad and diverse route through its interior and along its southern coast for the movement of people into the New World.

bifacially: This refers to how a stone flake has been shaped and sharpened. A stone tool may have two edges, or margins, and two faces. The distance from margin to margin is the width of a flake, and the distance between its faces is its thickness. When a flake is shaped and sharpened by percussion and/or pressure on both faces, it is bifacially flaked. When sharpening or shaping flakes have been struck or pressed from only one of the flake's faces, it is said to be unifacially flaked.

biological anthropology: A branch of anthropology, the study of human beings, that focuses on the biological aspects of our species. Among the topics investigated by biological anthropologists are the biological evolution of human beings, the biological variations exhibited by modern human beings, forensic anthropology, and primatology (humans are primates, and primatologists also study the nonhuman primates, including monkeys and apes). Synonymous with physical anthropology.

biological archaeologist: Archaeologist who focuses on the biological environment in which past peoples lived and to which they adapted. Biological archaeologists usually focus on the physical remains of animals and plants found at archaeological sites in an attempt to reveal the nature of a past environment and the ways in which the people used that environment.

biome: A spatially extensive community of plants and animals living in a significantly large, recognizable habitat. North American biomes include tundra, taiga, mountain forest, temperate deciduous forest, tropical rain forest, grassland, and desert.

bipedal locomotion: The pattern of walking about on two feet. Among the primates (monkeys, apes, and human beings along with our evolutionary antecedents), only those in the human line exhibit a pattern of habitual or full-time bipedalism. We know this to be the case both by observing living creatures (of course) and by reconstructing the locomotive habits of deceased or extinct creatures by examination of their skeletal morphology. The bones reveal how the muscles must have worked, which, in turn, reveals how the creature got around.

blanks: Preforms. In the making of stone tools, after removing a flake from a core, the flake may be roughly shaped by percussion into a general form that later can be refined into a finished shape depending on the tool's intended function. The roughed-out piece, before final shaping, is called a blank.

C-14 dating: Carbon-14 dating. Carbon-14 (^{14}C) is a radioactive isotope (an unstable variety) of the element carbon. Most carbon is carbon-12. The "12" reflects the atomic weight of the most common configuration of the nucleus of the carbon atom, with six positively charged particles (protons) and six neutral particles (neutrons). Carbon-14 possesses two additional neutrons and is unstable, decaying at a known rate to the element nitrogen. Knowing its rate of decay (its half-life) and by measuring the amount of carbon-14 remaining in a substance, we can determine its age. When found at an archaeological site, the age of the site can be associated with the dated item or items.

cache: From the French verb *cacher*, to hide. A cache is, essentially, a stash of stuff placed away for safekeeping, such as a cluster of spear points or a hoard of coins, that is not retrieved (perhaps intentionally if the items were intended as a ceremonial offering, perhaps unintentionally when the person who deposited the cache died before retrieving the stored material).

calibration curve: One of the assumptions underpinning radiocarbon dating is that the ratio of stable carbon-12 to unstable carbon-14 has always been the same. It turns out that this is not the case and that a number of natural processes have served to alter that ratio by increasing or decreasing the rate at which carbon-14 was produced in the atmosphere. Things that were living when there was an overproduction (from a contemporary perspective) of C-14 will now appear to be younger, and things that were living when there was an underproduction of C-14 will now appear to be older, than they actually are. This problem has been addressed, at least in part, by determining the radiocarbon dates of individual tree rings. Once a tree ring is added in a living tree, no additional atmospheric carbon is added to it; in other words, if you were to carbon date the first ring in a living, 500-year-old tree, you should get a result in the vicinity of 500 years old. A comparison of tree ring dates and radiocarbon dates has been carried out, resulting in a calibration curve, which, in turn, is used to correct carbon dates to tree ring dates, which are absolutely accurate in terms of calendar dates.

carbon dating: Shorthand for radiocarbon dating.

ceramic: Objects made of fired clay. Pottery, which usually implies a vessel or plate for cooking, storing, or serving food, is a common end product of ceramic technology.

chemical signature: The chemical makeup of a particular raw material (flint, obsidian, copper ore, clay, and so on) at its geographic source (quarry, flow, deposit, mine) as well the chemical constituents of the raw materials of artifacts excavated at archaeological sites. The chemical signature often exhibits a complex array of elements in miniscule, or "trace," amounts and may be unique to a particular geographic source. The chemical signatures of artifacts can be revealed and then compared to possible source areas, enabling archaeologists to trace, sometimes quite precisely, the place from which past peoples obtained the materials, revealing past patterns of resource extraction, movement, and trade.

chronometric dating: Dating techniques that provide an actual age in years or a range of years for archaeological artifacts, ecofacts, features, or sites. The precision offered by different chronometric dating methods when applied to archaeological sites can range widely. In dendrochronology, for example, the precise year in which a tree was cut down can be determined and, in another example, the maker's mark on a ceramic vessel can be traced to the precise year in which the maker produced a particular style of pottery. At the other extreme, some chronometric dating techniques in their archaeological applications may provide only a broad possible range of thousands, tens of thousands, hundreds of thousands, or even millions of years. For example, the potassium/argon dating method may date a volcanic layer overlying archaeological material to 1 million years ago and another layer underlying the site may date to 1.5 million years ago. In this case we may conclude that the site is between 1 and 1.5 million years old (dating to sometime after the older volcanic flow and before the later deposit). Although the precision is not very high (the range is a half-million years), this is still a chronometric date. *Absolute dating* is another term for chronometric dating.

CIEP: See crossover immunoelectrophoresis.

colluvium: Imagine a very slow-acting avalanche, and you have a picture of colluviation and the production of colluvium. The rock, gravel, sand, silt, and clay that move downhill along a slope, covering material along the slope and especially at the bottom of the hill, is called colluvium.

clay: Sticky, fine-grained earth consisting of silicate minerals with a particle size typically less than 2 micrometers (.00016 inch) in diameter. When wet, clay can be shaped, and, when dried, it retains the shape it has been molded into. After baking at a high temperature, clay becomes ceramic, a durable, stiff, waterproof (or nearly so) material.

clay body: A particular kind of clay with specific characteristics including texture, color, absorbency, and plasticity.

comparative collection: Grouping of samples of animal bones, seeds, nuts, lithic raw materials, and so on that can aid in the identification of materials recovered at archaeological sites. A comparative collection is, essentially, a library of prototypes that serve as the models by which archaeological samples can be judged and identified. Comparative collections are particularly valuable when the archaeological specimens are highly fragmented.

complex society: Society in which authority, coordination of activity, and control of behavior are organized at a level beyond that of the family. Complex societies may have ranks or classes peopled by individuals with greater or lesser wealth, authority, or social standing than those in other ranks or classes.

compliance archaeology: Archaeological research conducted to fulfill legal mandates. Federal, state, and local governments in the United States have enacted a wide variety of laws aimed at preserving and protecting archaeological sites. The value of archaeological sites as cultural resources whose study can benefit all citizens has been formally recognized, and, especially when these cultural resources are endangered by construction or development, such laws compel developers to have archaeological work conducted to locate endangered cultural resources and, in some cases, to mitigate or diminish the deleterious impacts of development projects on archaeological sites. The archaeological research, in such cases, is conducted to comply with these laws, thus the term *compliance archaeology.*

conchoidal: A variety of fracture exhibited by some rock types. Literally meaning shell-like, with a smooth surface showing concavities and convexities. Rock types such as obsidian, flint, jasper, and chalcedony that exhibit conchoidal fracture break predictably and controllably. By a process of trial and error and by a long period of experimentation and repetition, knappers learn how conchoidal fracture is expressed by a rock type and develop an ability to predict and control the fracture to produce stone tools of regular and consistent sizes and shapes.

conjoin: To join together. In archaeology, broken fragments of artifacts that can be joined together. The top and bottom halves of a broken spear point and two fragments of a ceramic vessel are examples.

context: Shorthand for spatial context. The in situ location of an artifact, ecofact, or feature and the materials with which it was found.

continuous variable: Any variable whose expression is a measurement along a continuous scale. The length of a projectile point, the cranial capacities of ancient human ancestors, the volume of Egyptian pyramids, and the distance from an archaeological site to the geological source of a raw material used by the inhabitants of the site are all continuous variables because they can be measured.

coprolite: Fossilized feces. Because the digestive systems of animals, including human beings, are not 100 percent efficient, some ingested food is excreted in feces. As a result, the coprolites contain food remains and, therefore, provide data for dietary reconstruction.

cord marking: A technique for decorating a ceramic vessel. After the vessel has been shaped and while the clay is still soft and wet, a length of twine, sometimes wrapped around a wooden paddle, is pressed into the surface, adding an interesting texture while at the same time pressing together and more firmly joining the clay where individual coils meet.

core: A nodule of stone from which a tool maker detaches flakes by the application of a force, usually percussive, with a hammerstone. In some approaches the core is essentially sculpted into a tool; in others the core is merely the source for flakes, the flakes serving as blanks from which tools are then made.

cranial suture: The boundary lines between the cranial plates. When a human is born his or her cranium consists of seven more or less separate bony plates enclosing the brain. These plates are strongly connected with cartilage, and the squiggly lines seen where contiguous plates join are called cranial sutures. The cranial sutures ossify when the skull attains full growth, but the lines do not disappear right away. Bone growth that fuses adjoining plates continues during adulthood, eventually obscuring the sutures altogether. The degree of suture closure and disappearance can be used to gauge an individual's age at death, but this is neither terribly accurate nor precise, allowing for an estimation of age sometimes accurate to within about a decade.

cranium: The bony enclosure of the brain. Technically, the cranium is that part of the skull that includes the head, face, and upper jaw but not the mandible (lower jaw).

crew chief: The individual archaeological fieldworker in charge of a group of diggers. Especially in a large survey project covering a substantial amount of territory, a field crew may have to break up into a number of groups, each of which may cover a separate area. A crew chief directs the work of a group of test pit diggers or surface investigators, following the directions of the field director.

crossover immunoelectrophoresis (CIEP): Forensic analysis in which, in its archaeological application, blood residues are recovered from the edge of a stone or metal tool. These residues are then exposed to a series of different antisera derived from a number of known animal species. The antibodies present in each antiserum will react biologically to the antigen in the blood residue only when the antiserum and the blood come from the same animal species. A positive reaction when the antiserum and blood are mixed therefore indicates the presence of blood from the same species as that from which the antiserum was derived, allowing for an identification of the species of animal whose blood is on the tool.

cryptocrystalline: Literally meaning "hidden crystals," this refers to the fabric of a rock consisting of individual crystals cemented together whose crystals are too small to be visible even with a petrological microscope. When the individual crystals of a rock are relatively large, an applied force (percussion or pressure) tends to shatter the rock along the intersections of the crystals. An applied force to a rock with very small "hidden" crystals moves through the rock in a manner similar to how that force moves through glass—predictably, controllably, and producing thin, sharp edges. Cryptocrystalline rock is usually preferred for making stone tools by percussion and/or pressure.

cultural ecology: The study of the interrelationships between human groups and their environments. The cultural ecological approach views culture as an adaptive system.

cultural resource: A term that reflects the philosophy of the historic preservation movement. Just as we can identify the resources of our natural environment that make life possible—air, water, plants, and animals—we can also identify elements of the artificial, or human-made, environment that make life interesting, providing things that we can study and ponder and from which we can attain knowledge. Ancient archaeological sites, seventeenth-century mill remains, Civil War battlefields, nineteenth-century bridges, and the remnants of early twentieth-century factories are all defined as cultural resources, valuable elements of the human-made environment.

cultural resource management (CRM): The study, preservation, and protection of archaeological sites. Within the approach of CRM, the archaeological record is viewed as a non-renewable "cultural" or historical resource that is worthy of our consideration. Much of the archaeology currently conducted in the U.S. is done under the auspices of federally mandated CRM.

culture: The "extrasomatic" means of adaptation. In its broadest sense, culture is a strategy for survival based on ideas as opposed to the physical characteristics of our bodies provided by nature. We can hold a tool in a number of ways because of the inborn, physical characteristics of our hands. We also have the ability to invent a nearly infinite variety of tools that can be used by our hands. Culture is "extrasomatic," or beyond the body, beyond the biological and physical characteristics given us by nature. Culture is neverthless biologically based in that our capacity for culture is based on our enormous intelligence, made possible by a large and complex brain. Culture is constituted by all the behaviors that human beings have invented and passed down to subsequent generations. In a more specific sense a culture is the particular strategy for survival of an individual group of people.

culture history: Essentially, *what* happened *when* in a given region. An outline of the major cultural developments—adaptations, subsistence and settlement patterns, technological innovations, culture contacts, and so on—over time. In most world areas archaeologists have a good handle on the outline of local culture history, and simple charts are nearly ubiquitous, showing a column of culture names and developments from bottom (most ancient) to top (most recent).

datum: The origin, or 0, 0, location of a site grid. A site grid is analogous to a giant piece of graph paper superimposed over a site. Datum is the origin of this imaginary piece of graph paper, and excavation units—and, ultimately, everything recovered at a site—are defined and located in reference to this point.

debitage: The wastage produced in stone tool making. Stone tool making is a reductive technology; the maker starts with a piece of stone and sculpts a tool from this core of rock by removing what can be defined as excess. Some of these excess flakes removed in tool making can themselves be used as tools, but because of size or form, many of the flakes removed in tool making cannot be used and are waste. The waste is called debitage.

deciduous teeth: Human baby teeth. These are the teeth that become visible in the mouth during infancy and early childhood and are shed, like the leaves of deciduous trees in the fall, to be replaced by the permanent, or adult, teeth. The various deciduous teeth—the flat-faced incisors in the front, the pointed canine teeth adjacent to the incisors, and the larger grinding molars to the rear of a child's mouth—erupt through the gum line at a fairly consistent age and are then lost and replaced by the permanent teeth at a similarly consistent point during development. The presence or absence (because they haven't erupted yet or because they have already been shed to make room for the adult teeth) of deciduous teeth is a good gauge of the degree of development of the individual and, therefore, a pretty good indicator of how old the person is—or how old the person was when he or she died in the case of forensic or archaeological examples.

demographic: Anything referring to the "demography," or vital statistics, of a population. The basic population data collected and published in the census is demographic: overall population size, longevity, male-to-female ratio, ethnicity, and so on. Archaeologists approach demography in a number of ways. Those who study cultures with written records may have formal census data available for analysis. When examining the population statistics of prehistoric societies, demographic data is often collected from skeletal remains, whose study may allow for a statistical picture of a group of people if a sufficiently large, representative sample of the ancient population is available.

demography: The basic population data collected and published in the census is demographic: overall population size, longevity, male-to-female ratio, ethnicity, and so on. Archaeologists approach demography in a number of ways. Those who study cultures with written records may have formal census data available for analysis. When examining the population statistics of prehistoric societies, demographic data is often collected from skeletal remains, whose study may allow for a statistical picture of a group of people if a sufficiently large, representative sample of the ancient population is available.

dendrochronology: Tree ring dating. The actual year a tree was cut down and used, for example, by a past people to build a structure, can be determined by comparing the succession of rings in the ancient tree to those of a broad master sequence whose final ring represents the current year. The master sequence for a given region is constructed by examining a number of trees of overlapping ages. The master sequence consists of a series of rings of various thicknesses stretching back, in some areas, for more than 10,000 years. Tree ring thickness varies from year to year consistently across a region as a result of varying temperatures and amounts of rainfall. Ring thicknesses for even a short series of years are not repeated, so any ancient tree found in a region can be placed within the master sequence, and the year of its final ring can be determined, thus dating when the tree died or was cut down.

descriptive statistics: The numerical data that summarize the nature of a population. Descriptive statistics can exhibit the central tendency of a data set, for example, the mean, median, or mode of a variable. Your "average" for a semester, or, more formally, the mean score of all your individual grades, is a descriptive statistic. The mean length of spear points in a cache, the mean volume of the individual blocks making up the Great Pyramids in Egypt, and the mean cranial capacity (skull volume) of representatives of an ancient hominid species are all descriptive statistics. The standard deviation—a measure of how closely individuals in a sample cluster about the mean—is another descriptive statistic. Where descriptive statistics merely describe a population, inductive statistics provide a way to assess patterns, correlations, and cause-and-effect relationships between and among variables.

diaphysis: The shaft of each of the long bones; the individual bones of the legs, arms, hands, and feet; that portion of a long bone between the end caps (epiphyses).

diffusion: The movement of ideas across geographic distance and cultural boundaries. When new technologies or styles are reflected in the archaeological record at a particular archaeological site or within a particular region, it may be the result of local and independent invention or development of the new technology or idea, or it may be the result of the borrowing of the new behaviors as a result of diffusion.

direct historical approach: An approach in ethnographic analogy in which the culture of a group that represents the descendants of the people whose archaeological remains are being investigated is used as a source for models or analogies to explain the lifeways lived by the ancient group.

discontinuous variable: Variable whose possible expressions are not measurements but names. For example, eye color is a discontinuous variable whose most common possible expressions are brown, blue, and green. Lithic raw materials (for example, flint, obsidian, quartzite, quartz, and basalt), temper added to clay (for example, none, quartz grit, sand, shell, and ground up pieces of fired clay), and feature type (for example, burial, hearth, lithic cache, foundation, and midden) are examples of discontinuous variables. Also called nominal variables.

distal epiphysis: Each long bone in your body consists of a shaft—the diaphysis—and two end caps—the epiphyses. In the geography of the body, the distal epiphysis of each of those long bones is the end cap farther away from the trunk ("distant" means far from). The end cap closer, to or in "proximity to," the trunk is the proximal epiphysis.

ecofact: You won't find this term in the dictionary; it was invented by archaeologists who needed a way to differentiate archaeological specimens that were actually made by people (artifacts) from those that are present at an archaeological site because of human behavior, that may even show direct evidence of human manipulation, but that were not intentionally made into something by people. *Ecofact* is the term archaeologist Lewis Binford came up with. Ecofacts are elements from the environment (bone, stone, wood, seeds, nuts, shell) that were collected by people for their use (to eat or to warm themselves) but are not themselves tools or manufactured objects.

effigy mound: Earthen structure made in the shape of animals, both real and mythical, and people. The ancient people of the American Midwest, in particular, produced effigy mounds.

egalitarian: A society in which all the members within the group's recognized age and sex categories (for example, young children, adolescents, young adult men, young adult women, elderly people) have an equivalent amount of wealth, authority, and social standing. All members of an egalitarian society are not necessarily "equal," and there may be differences in wealth, authority, and social standing among the different groups.

elastic limit: Although rock may seem to be hard and brittle, many rock forms actually are flexible, at least at a microscopic level. They are, in fact, "elastic" and deform, if only very slightly, when a force—either percussion or pressure—is applied. Up to a certain level of applied force, the rock will rebound when the force is removed. Once a certain level is reached, a level that varies with each type of rock and even among different geographic sources of the same rock type, the rock cannot sustain the force and rebound and, instead, breaks. The maximum force a rock can sustain before breaking is its "elastic limit." In stone tool making the craftsperson exceeds the elastic limit of the rock to remove flakes.

electrical resistivity survey: A noninvasive procedure used in archaeological survey in which an electrical current is passed through the ground. Variations in soil resistance to the current are used to pinpoint the locations of archaeological artifacts and features.

electron spin resonance (ESR): Dating method based on the accumulation of energy in the form of electrons in atoms pushed into and then "trapped" at higher energy levels as a result of background radiation. In a given environment and for a given material, the electrons become trapped at a regular rate. The amount so trapped can be measured, and the amount of time it would have taken for all that trapping to have occurred once an object was buried can be determined.

enamel hypoplasia: Pits and other imperfections in the enamel of the permanent teeth, resulting from bouts of malnutrition during early childhood before those adult teeth appeared in the mouth. The nascent buds of the permanent teeth are present in the upper and lower jaws of newborns, below the buds of the deciduous dentition. Nutritional and other dietary problems (for example, an excess of fluoride) as well as childhood diseases, therefore, can have an impact on the adult teeth long before they erupt. Enamel hypoplasia is one example. Dietary and nutritional deficiencies in individuals, in entire populations, or in only certain segments of a population can be revealed by the discovery of enamel hypoplasia.

enculturated: To become a member of a culture, to learn the rules by which a society operates, and to follow them is to become enculturated. Children are born into a culture that is, after all, a set of learned behaviors. As they mature they grow into their culture—become enculturated—learning every day how to act, how to behave, and how to believe by being surrounded by people who are members of the culture who are acting, behaving, and believing in ways appropriate to the culture.

environmental determinism: The now-discredited view that the degree of "challenge" presented by a particular environment determines the level of technological complexity achieved by the people living there. Not surprisingly, Western European thinkers in the nineteenth century viewed the environments of Western Europe and North America as presenting exactly the right level of challenge to produce the world's most developed societies.

Environmental Impact Statement (EIS): Literally, a formal statement concerning the potential and real effects a given proposed development or construction project may have on the environment. Mandated by the federal government in the National Environmental Protection Act, an Environmental Impact Statement is often a detailed report prepared by experts in water, air, botanical, zoological, and cultural resources that assesses the possible damage to the environment, in the broadest sense of the word, of a federally funded or mandated project (for example, road construction, pipeline placement, or river dredging). Archaeological sites are defined as cultural resources, of value to all citizens, and worthy of federal concern and protection. Information provided in an EIS may result in an alteration of a proposed project in order to protect archaeological resources or may lead to the excavation of a site in order to salvage the information it contains before the project proceeds and the site's location is destroyed.

epiphysis (pl. epiphyses): Each end cap of each long bone in the body. When you are born each of your long bones consists of three segments: a shaft called the diaphysis and two end caps called epiphyses. The epiphyses are each joined to their diaphysis by a band of cartilage. The proximal epiphysis and distal epiphysis of each long bone permanently fuse to the contiguous diaphysis during a narrowly circumscribed period of an individual's development. As a result the age of a subadult individual can be estimated by examining his or her skeleton (by noninvasive imaging of a living person or by directly examining the bones of a deceased individual) and determining which of the epiphyses have already fused to their shafts and which have yet to solidly connect. The long bone epiphyses have all fused by the late teens or very early twenties. Once this has occurred, examining them can reveal only that the individual is at least that old.

ESR: See electron spin resonance.

ethnoarchaeology: A strategy employed by archaeologists to attempt to better understand the ways in which the archaeological record reflects the lives of a group of people. In ethnoarchaeology the archaeologist lives among a group of people in the manner of an ethnographer, focusing on how the behavior of the living group of people becomes transformed into an archaeological record of that behavior. Investigating how behavior becomes translated into an archaeological entity (a site) provides the archaeologist with insights into the question of how an archaeological entity (a site) reflects the behavior that produced it.

ethnographic analogy: Using the description of a living group of people—or a people who lived in the not-too-distant past and whose lifeways have been documented—as a model for understanding the lifeways of an archaeological group. A recent group whose way of life has been described is considered an appropriate source for comparisons and analogies when the two peoples— those whose archaeological remains we are trying to understand and the more recent group whose way of life has been described by eyewitnesses—appear to have lived under similar conditions in generally similar cultural settings.

ethnographic research: Ethnography is the observation and analysis of a living group of people. Archaeologists are interested in the study of a living group of people for at least two fundamental reasons: (1) the study of the living descendants of the people who left behind archaeological materials may provide insights into the meaning and significance of the material, and (2) even when no living descendants of the archaeological group can be identified, the analysis of living people, especially those living a way of life similar or analogous to that reflected in the archaeological record, may similarly provide insights in our analysis of the archaeological record.

ethnography: The study of a living group of people by living among them, observing their behavior, and participating in their daily activities. The published work describing the research of an ethnographer is also called an ethnography.

ethnohistory: Written descriptions of foreign or alien cultures produced not by trained ethnographers whose purpose was to describe such cultures but by explorers, adventurers, colonists, traders, missionaries, and others who encountered alien peoples accidentally while exploring, adventuring, colonizing, trading, or proselytizing. The advantage of ethnohistorical works rests in the fact that they are among the earliest descriptions of many of the world's non-European societies and, therefore, reflect the cultures of non-European peoples before they were significantly altered by such contact. The disadvantage rests in the fact that those who wrote ethnohistorical descriptions of alien cultures were generally not trained scientists, were not unbiased reporters, and had particular agendas and purposes that often detracted from the objectivity of their observations.

excavation: The careful and methodical exposure of subsurface archaeological material. Excavation is usually conducted with hand tools such as trowels, small brushes, and dental picks in an attempt to expose the materials left behind by a past people exactly where these past people left them. See archaeological excavation.

excavation unit: The individual analytical field unit at an archaeological site. Excavation units are often called "squares" because that is their form; often 2 meters on a side, but they can be 1-meter squares, 6-foot squares, or any other size, and they don't even have to be squares. Excavating in regularly sized and spaced units allows for site excavation in manageable "bites" and makes it easier for the principal investigator—and everyone else—to keep track of where items were found.

exhausted core: A stone nucleus that has had a series of flakes removed from it and now is either too small, too battered, or too oddly shaped to allow for the efficient removal of additional flakes.

exotic material: Any raw material used by a past people that is not native to their local area. Any raw material that had to be obtained through long-distance trade or by travel to a source outside the area in which a group commonly moved.

experimental archaeology: Answering questions about the cultures of past peoples by attempting to replicate particular elements of their behavior. Usually applied to material culture, experimental archaeologists attempt to figure out how tools were made and used by actually going through the trial-and-error process of making and using them. Experimental archaeology certainly contributes to our scientific understanding of specific processes of the technologies of past peoples, but it also does something more: It provides us with a visceral appreciation for past technologies through the humbling experience of actually trying to make and use things similar to objects made by past people.

faunal analysis: Examination of the animal bones recovered at an archaeological site. This analysis should provide information about the subsistence base of a group by identifying the animal species used. Other aspects of a group's subsistence strategy may also be revealed. Did they hunt wild animals, or are the remains those of domesticated species? Were they capable of capturing only very old and very young animals, or did they successfully hunt animals in their prime? Did they avoid killing females in their prime—females, after all, were important in producing the next generation of animals? Were they thorough or wasteful in their use of an animal's carcass?

feature: A combination of artifacts and/or ecofacts that together represents a location where an activity took place that resulted in the combined presence of artifacts and ecofacts. When people carry out tasks in activity areas, they often use material objects and, during the course of the activity, they may intentionally or accidentally leave some of those material objects behind. The remnants of a fireplace characterized by a concentration of charcoal and rocks; a work area where stone tools were once made and where now battered fragments of hammerstones, waste flakes, and tools broken during the tool making process litter the ground; a human burial with bones and grave goods (the treasured belongings of the deceased provided for use in the afterlife); a platform on which deer meat was once roasted and where now only a bed of burned stones, bits of charred wood, and flecks of bone remain; all of these are archaeological features.

femur: The bone of the upper leg; the thigh bone. The femur is the longest of the so-called long bones, which are, exactly as advertised, the long bones of the legs, arms, hands, and feet.

fibula: The smaller of the two bones of the lower leg. The larger lower leg bone is the tibia. Feel your shin; that large, flat bone just below the surface of your skin is your tibia. The fibula is behind the tibia, enclosed in muscle.

field director: Archaeological field worker in charge of the entire field crew while out in the field. Taking direction from the principal investigator, the field director gives instructions to the crew chiefs concerning the work on any given day.

field school: Intensive training, often offered as a course at a university, in archaeological fieldwork and laboratory work. Students may be trained in a diverse array of archaeological methods through a process of learning by doing. In most field schools students perform much of the grunt labor as they learn common procedures of archaeological survey, gridding, troweling, screening, mapping, recording, photographing, as well as procedures of cleaning, inventorying, and preliminary analysis in the lab. Field schools are conducted all over the world, and most offer college credit; many field school opportunities are listed in the *Archaeological Fieldwork Opportunities Bulletin* published by the Archaeological Institute of America (http://www.archaeological.org/webinfo .php?page = 10015).

floodplain: A flat expanse of land adjacent to a river or stream. A floodplain is commonly flooded on a yearly basis, particularly in spring as the result of heavy rainfalls and, in the north, meltoff of the winter snowpack. This flooding brings with it a heavy burden of silt—fine-grained material—that is deposited on the floodplain. Called alluvium, this silt consists of fine particles easily moved and deposited by flowing water and very few larger rocks. This can be extremely attractive to farming people, particularly those without machines to help turn over the soil in preparation for planting. This flooding also explains why archaeological material is often found deeply buried, the result of many years of flooding and attendant deposition.

flotation: A procedure used in archaeology to separate artifacts and ecofacts from excavated soil, either the soil matrix recovered from a feature or soil samples taken from ancient living surfaces, by the use of water. Flotation is based on the fact that in the vast majority of instances, the archaeological material you are trying to isolate and recover from the surrounding soil has a different specific gravity than water (the fixed volume of the archaeological material weighs more or less than but not the same as the same fixed volume of water). This means that when dumped into a pool of standing water (for example, in a basin or bucket) most archaeological remains will separate from the water either by floating to the top or sinking to the bottom. Materials that float (many organics) can be collected by skimming the water's surface. Materials that sink (lithics) can be extracted by draining the water through a fine mesh screen that will allow the water and most of the very fine soil particles, but not the artifacts or ecofacts, to pass through.

fontanelles: These are the so-called soft spots on a newborn baby's cranium. There are two fontanelles, one on top toward the front and one farther back where the bony cranial plates do not yet meet in the newborn skull. The presence of these gaps, where the brain is covered not in bone but in a thick layer of cartilage, allows for the flexibility needed in the relatively large newborn human skull in order to pass through the narrow human birth canal. The fontanelles close up during development: The smaller fontanelle at the rear of the skull fuses over at about three months of age, and the one toward the front closes at about a year-and-a-half.

forager: Term used to describe a subsistence strategy in which food is provided by any combination of hunting wild animals, fishing, shellfish collecting, and gathering the seeds, roots, nuts, fruits, and leaves of wild plants. All human groups were foragers until the development of food production technologies, whereby plants and animals were domesticated through a process called artificial selection. The earliest evidence of a shift away from foraging toward food production and, ultimately, full-blown agriculture occurred in the Middle East sometime soon after 12,000 years ago and then, independently, in a number of places in the Old and New Worlds sometime later.

forensic anthropologist: The word *forensic* refers specifically to the law, and forensic scientists apply scientific procedures to the investigation of a crime. Forensic anthropologists focus on human remains and contribute to our understanding of a past society's demography, including individual longevity, ethnicity, nutrition, disease, and trauma. And, in fact, just like forensic scientists who attempt to solve modern crimes, forensic anthropologists may reveal ancient ones. For example, in the case of the 9,400-year-old Kennewick Man in Oregon as well as the 5,000-year-old Ice Man found in the Italian Alps, forensic specialists found stone spear points embedded in their bodies. In the case of Kennewick Man the individual survived to live a long life after being impaled; in the case of the Ice Man, the spear wound probably contributed directly to his death.

Four Corners: The only place in the United States where four separate states meet at right angles. The four states are Arizona, New Mexico, Colorado, and Utah. The region is well known and even world renowned for its extraordinary archaeological heritage exemplified by the great houses of Chaco Canyon in New Mexico and the cliff dwellings of Mesa Verde in Colorado.

Geographic Information Systems (GIS): Computer mapping programs in which each variable is treated as a map layer. By superimposing layers that might include information about watercourses, topography, soil type, and so on as well as the locations of archaeological sites, patterns of site location in reference to those environmental variables may become apparent.

GIS: See Geographic Information Systems.

glaze: A glassy substance fused through the application of heat onto the surface of a ceramic form in order to produce a smooth, often glossy, waterproof surface.

Global Positioning System (GPS): System of precisely locating any point on Earth, originally developed exclusively for military use through the use of twenty-four satellites orbiting our planet. Less-precise, degraded satellite signals were first made available to anyone with a receiver, and as of May 2000, the nondegraded signal became available. With a handheld GPS unit costing just a few hundred dollars, the location of an archaeological site to within just a few meters can be determined, and its location in relation to surrounding resources—resources that may have played a role in a past people's use of the location in the first place—can be assessed.

GPS: See Global Positioning System.

ground penetrating radar: A noninvasive technique used in archaeology whereby an electromagnetic pulse is passed through the soil. This pulse encounters objects in the soil and is reflected back to a receiver. The radar operator may then be able to interpret the nature of objects that reflected the radar pulse, some of which may represent cultural remains, for example, buried walls or foundations.

ground stone: Stone tools made not by striking them with a rock or antler hammer to remove flakes nor by applying pressure to the edge to push off flakes, but by grinding the stone, often against the surface of another stone, to produce a shape and often a sharp and durable edge.

ground truth: The actual explanation for a feature identified through remote sensing. For example, after recognizing a pattern of plant growth from an aerial photograph, the archaeologist may test the significance, or "truth," of the pattern through a close-up examination on the "ground."

growth arrest lines: Horizontal cracks at the end of the diaphysis of a long bone that persist through adulthood, resulting from a bout of malnutrition during the developing years. Before the fusion of the epiphyses to their diaphysis, the long bone shaft grows out from its ends. If an individual experiences a period of severe malnutrition, growth may stop or at least slow down substantially. If the individual survives and resumes growth when nutrition is restored, a line or lines may appear, sometimes visible on the surface of the bone and sometimes recognizable only in x-ray. The presence of growth arrest lines, therefore, is an indication of nutritional deficiencies in an individual, an entire population, or only in certain segments of the population. Also called Harris Lines after the researcher who first recognized their cause.

half-life: The fixed, regular, and measurable amount of time it takes for half of the radioactive isotope in a substance to decay into its stable end product or to a step on the path to its stable form. Some radioactive isotopes of elements exhibit half-lives of no more than a fraction of a second, while some half-lives are measured in billions of years. The half-life is, in essence, a natural clock that can be used to date a substance whose age, when found at an archaeological site, can be associated with the site.

half-moon: A category of wear traces on stone tools. Unlike scalar scars, which are gouged out on the surface of a tool near the edge, these little crescent-shaped scars along a tool's working edges result when actual bites are taken from those edges during use. A tool that began with a straight edge may appear serrated after use that produced half-moon scarring. For example, a thin, sharp-edged stone tool used to incise a design on a piece of wood may result in a rapid and significant deterioration of the edge in the form of half-moon scars.

The tiny flakes removed in the process may become embedded in the material being worked on and produce striations on the tool as it rubs against them.

hammerstone: Tool used in the production of stone tools. The hammerstone is the percussor, the tool used to strike a stone core to remove flakes or to strike a flake in order to thin, sharpen, and shape a tool. The hammerstone needn't be harder than the core; often spherical and, therefore, without facets or angles of less than 90 degrees, a hammerstone's geometry provides it with much of its strength and durability.

haplogroup: Co-occurring genetic markers that are inherited together as a unit. The presence of certain recognized mitochondrial haplogroups may distinguish populations of human beings from one another and enable the tracing of historical connections among living peoples.

haplotype: A cluster of co-occurring genetic markers within particular haplogroups that are inherited together as a unit. The presence of certain recognized mitochondrial haplotypes may distinguish populations of human beings from one another and enable the tracing of historical connections among living peoples. For example, the fact that all five of the mitochondrial haplotypes found among Native Americans are also found in Asia and not in Africa, Europe, or Australia is interpreted to support the hypothesis of a historical connection between the native peoples of Asia and the Americas.

Harris Lines: Horizontal cracks at the end of the diaphysis of a long bone that persist through adulthood, resulting from a bout of malnutrition during the developing years. Before the fusion of the epiphyses to their diaphysis, the long bone shaft grows out from its ends. If an individual experiences a period of severe malnutrition, growth may stop or at least slow down substantially. If the individual survives and resumes growth when nutrition is restored, a line or lines may appear, sometimes visible on the surface of the bone and sometimes recognizable only in x-ray. The presence of growth arrest lines, therefore, is an indication of nutritional deficiencies in an individual, an entire population, or only in certain segments of the population. Named for the researcher who first recognized their cause. Also called by the accurately descriptive name growth arrest lines.

high-performance liquid chromatography (HPLC): A laboratory procedure for separating molecules in a sample by the application of high pressure. Once separated, the molecules can be identified. HPLC has been used to analyze ancient food residues adhering to the interiors of clay vessels.

hominid: The taxonomic family that includes human beings and species directly ancestral to humans. The first hominids are characterized by chimp-sized brains and exhibit a skeletal anatomy that enabled upright walking more than 6 million years ago, during the Pliocene epoch. Stone tool making dated to about 2.5 million years ago in the hominids, about the same time the hominid brain exhibited a dramatic increase in size beyond that of any ape species.

HPLC: See high-performance liquid chromatography.

humerus: The upper arm bone. It is entirely coincidental that at the far end (distal epiphysis) of the humerus is the "funny bone."

hunter-gatherer: A human group that feeds itself by hunting wild animals and collecting wild plants. In most such societies, though hunting provides the bulk of the protein, most of the caloric intake is supplied by plant food, and some suggest the term should be more appropriately *gatherer-hunters*. The term *forager* is preferred by many because it does not implicitly prioritize the importance of any one food source, and it is more inclusive, recognizing the possible significance of fish, shellfish, and egg collecting in the subsistence quest.

igneous: Volcanic rock formed when enormously hot, molten material in the Earth's interior cools and solidifies; granite, basalt, obsidian, pumice, and so on.

inductive statistics: Numerical analysis of patterns, correlations, and cause-and-effect relationships between and among variables. In descriptive statistics researchers can calculate numbers that summarize how a population (of people, spear points, archaeological sites, and so on) scores on a given variable. In inductive statistics researchers can calculate numbers or formulas that reveal any patterns of how a population scores on a number of variables. For example, inductive statistics may reveal that the measurement for one variable (for example, the thickness of the wall of a ceramic vessel) correlates with another (for example, its age). Knowing, in this example, that older pots have thicker walls may provide insights into the evolution of ceramic technology in a given society.

in situ: A Latin phrase meaning "in place." Archaeologists use the term specifically to characterize an exposed artifact that has been left, at least temporarily, in its original location of discovery. In some cases an in situ specimen is exactly where it was left behind (lost, discarded, cached, or abandoned) by a person at some time in the past.

isotope: In physics an isotope is a variety of the atomic structure of an element. All atoms of a given element have the same number of protons in their nuclei, but the number of neutrons may vary; different isotopes of an individual element have different numbers of neutrons in their nuclei. Some isotopes of an element are atomically stable, never changing. Others are unstable, or radioactive, changing at a regular rate by a process of decay into a stable end product. The fixed rate of decay of a radioactive isotope forms the basis of radiometric dating.

K/Ar: See potassium/argon dating.

kitchen midden: An aboveground accumulation or pile of residue from food preparation. Inedible material, spoilage, and excess is thrown on the pile and left to decay. The stuff that does not disappear—depending on the local soil condition this will often be bones, shells, and carbonized remains such as seed husks, nutshells, cobs, and rinds—becomes a kitchen midden.

knapper: A person who knaps, that is, to strike stone in an effort to shape the stone into a tool or produce flakes that can be used as is or be further shaped into tools. A flint knapper refers specifically to a stone tool maker who knaps flint. Knappers are also occasionally referred to as "rock-knockers."

knapping: The act of making stone tools.

lacustrine: Relating to lakes. Gravel, sand, silt, and clay that accumulate along the shoreline of a lake produce lacustrine deposits that may cover and preserve archaeological sites resulting from human activity along lake margins.

landscape archaeology: An archaeological approach and perspective that focuses on the distribution of archaeological material across a broad landscape rather than on a series of individual sites. In landscape archaeology the archaeological record is viewed not as a series of discrete loci of material, but as a spatially and temporally continuous record of human occupation and use.

landscape signature: Term suggested by archaeologists William Marquardt and Carole Crumley (1987) for the archaeological manifestation of a settlement pattern. A human group uses its territory and locates its villages, camps, burial grounds, sacred places, and so on in ways that are culturally determined. The spatial distribution of archaeological sites left behind, reflecting their pattern of land use, is the landscape signature of the group.

laser transit: Device used in surveying. Whereas old-style transits were visual sighting devices used to measure elevations (depths) and locations, laser transits emit a beam of laser light that bounces off a special stadia rod. The signal is captured by a receiver on the transit, where the precise distance and elevation of the point being measured are recorded and stored.

law of superposition: The commonsensical rule stating that the relative age of a soil layer (stratum) is determined by its position in an undisturbed vertical sequence of a number of layers (strata). In other words, more recent soil layers are superimposed over older layers. Under most circumstances this means that deeper layers in a sequence are older than layers higher in the same sequence, but natural and cultural processes can disturb these sequences, so it is best to examine a sequence of layers rather than simply to measure depth to determine the relative age of a stratum. The relative age of archaeological materials can be determined by reference to the soil layers in which they are found.

literature search: Primary stage in an archaeological research project in which publications are examined that might discuss earlier archaeological research in the proposed project area. In the past this was fairly straightforward, as most regions had a rather limited list of publications in which relevant material might appear. When we started the Farmington River Archaeological Project in which the Wood Lily site was discovered, about the only significant publication in which earlier archaeological research in the Farmington River Valley might be discussed was the *Bulletin of the Archaeological Society of Connecticut*. Today there is a substantial and growing body of "gray literature," including unpublished reports produced in compliance archaeology projects and nontraditionally published material sometimes available online. In Connecticut compliance archaeology reports are gathered by the Office of the State Archaeologist and made available to researchers in the Archives and Special Collections of the Thomas J. Dodd Research Center at the University of Connecticut (http://archnet.asu.edu/ archives/crm/conn/cttowns/introct.html). Other states and municipalities may handle such materials differently.

lithic: Adjective for stone. Any material composed of stone is lithic.

living archaeology: A strategy employed by archaeologists attempting to better understand the ways in which the archaeological record reflects the lives of a group of people. In ethnoarchaeology the archaeologist lives among a group of people in the manner of an ethnographer, focusing on how the behavior of the living group of people becomes transformed into an archaeological record of that behavior. Investigating how behavior becomes translated into an archaeological entity (a site) provides the archaeologist with insights into the question of how an archaeological entity (a site) reflects the behavior that produced it.

mandible: The lower jaw. The upper jaw is called the maxilla.

master sequence: In dendrochronology, tree ring sequence, extending in some cases for a period of more than 10,000 years, produced by overlapping the rings of a living tree with a series of successively older trees. Over the course of the time period covered in a regional master sequence, no section of the sequence of ring widths repeats itself. As a result, once a master sequence is established, the ring sequences of newly discovered, long-dead trees, including those cut down and used by ancient peoples, can be positioned precisely in the master sequence. The exact year of each ring in the master sequence is known because the end of the sequence is rooted in the present. Thus, the year in which any tree alive during any time represented in the sequence was cut down can be determined. If people cut it down and used it in a structure, the age of the tree can be applied to the age of the ancient dwelling and archaeological site.

mastoid process: In the geography of the skeleton, a process is a bump of bone. Each cranium has two mastoid processes, located at the base on the left and right sides. Feel directly behind your ears, at the level of the earlobes; those are your mastoid processes. The mastoid processes of men and women are a bit different in size and shape (men tend to have larger, rounded processes, while those of women are smaller and more pointy). This fact is used to help identify the sex of a deceased individual based on his or her skeleton.

material culture: That portion of the human strategy for survival that involves making and using objects: tools, weapons, containers, clothing, houses, items of adornment, art and craftwork, and so on.

matrilocal: A postmarital residence pattern in which, upon marriage, a man leaves the community (compound, neighborhood, or village) into which he was born and within which he was raised and moves into the compound, neighborhood, or village in which his wife and her family reside.

matrilocality: Refers to a pattern of postmarital residence in which a newly married couple lives in the village, compound, or house of the wife's parents. See matrilocal.

minimum number of individuals (MNI): This statistic represents a conservative estimate of the number of individual animals represented in the faunal assemblage at an archaeological site. In the MNI calculation it is assumed that "redundant" skeletal elements, different parts of an animal's body that could have belonged to the same individual—a right front leg and a left rear leg from an animal of the same sex and age, but not two right front legs or two heads—did belong to the same animal. The MNI reflects the minimum number of animals that we can state with certainty are represented in an assemblage.

mitochondrial DNA: A type of DNA, separate and distinct from the nuclear DNA, present in the mitochondria of an organism's cells. Unlike nuclear DNA, mitochondrial DNA (mtDNA) of the male and female is not combined in sexual reproduction. The mtDNA of only the female is transmitted to subsequent generations. The simplicity of mtDNA inheritance renders it a valuable tool in examining the relationships between modern populations and, when recovered from ancient bone, the relationships among ancient populations and between modern people and them.

MNI: See minimum number of individuals.

morphology: We use this term when referring to the form of anything. Biologists use it in reference to the form and structure of organisms, and anthropologists use it in the same way, usually applying it to the form of the skeletal remains of human beings and human ancestors. Archaeologists use the term as well, more often referring to the form or shape of tools.

NAGPRA: See Native American Graves Protection and Repatriation Act.

National Environmental Protection Act (NEPA): Federal law passed in 1969 whose stated purpose was to protect the environment, to minimize negative impacts on the environment by federally funded projects, and to encourage study of the natural world. NEPA is important for archaeologists because the nation's cultural and historical heritage were explicitly included in those elements of the environment that deserved protection and study. (http://ceq.eh.doe.gov/nepa/regs/nepa/nepaeqia.htm)

National Historic Preservation Act of 1966: This legislation formally established historic preservation as an official policy supported by the federal government of the United States. The spirit of this law is reflected in the wording of its preface, in which the authors expressed the belief that the history of the American people, reflected in part by cultural resources, should be preserved as a reflection of national heritage. This act also established the National Register of Historic Places.

National Museum of the American Indian Act of 1989: Federal law that established a national museum of American Indians to be included as part of the Smithsonian Institution. The museum is in Washington, D.C. (http://www.nmai.si.edu)

National Park Service (NPS): The government agency given the task of overseeing the nation's national parks. Recognizing that the national parks, with their vast acreage, contain many significant archaeological sites, the NPS includes a large cohort of archaeologists who oversee the protection, preservation, study, and public display of those sites on federal land.

National Register of Historic Places: Established and authorized in 1966 through the National Historic Preservation Act, the register amounts to an honor role of structures, places (including historic battlefields), and sites that meaningfully reflect significant episodes, events, people, or practices in American history (http://www.cr.nps.gov/nr/about.htm). Sites nominated to and accepted onto the register are deemed worthy of preservation because of their significance to national and local history.

Native American Graves Protection and Repatriation Act (NAGPRA) of 1990: Federal law that confers "ownership" of the biological remains of Native Americans (including Indians and Hawaiians) excavated in federally funded archaeology projects and/or stored in federal or federally funded facilities to the biological descendents of the people whose remains have been recovered and stored. NAGPRA also requires the return to descendents of those objects that have been kept in federal or federally supported museums, libraries, laboratories, and so on that are deemed sacred by the native peoples whose ancestors made the objects. (http://www.cr.nps.gov/nagpra/)

NEPA: See National Environmental Protection Act.

neutron activation analysis: Procedure for revealing the chemical signature of a raw material. In neutron activation analysis samples of a specific raw material (for example, turquoise, obsidian, copper, or iron ore) from a series of geographically distinct sources are irradiated with neutrons. Different elemental constituents in each sample then emit radiation at levels unique to each element. The identity of about sixty different elements can be detected and their concentrations measured (down to trace amounts measured in parts per billion) by the application of this method.

nomadic: A way of life in which a group of people regularly move their habitation. A nomadic way of life is not a random existence. Many nomadic groups follow a regular pattern of migration on a yearly basis, consistently moving each season to the same separate location when resources are most abundant there during the course of a year. These nomads essentially follow the geographically shifting abundance of natural resources, moving their residence according to the local availability of wild plant and animal foods.

nominal variable: Variable whose possible expressions are not measurements but names. For example, eye color is a nominal variable whose most common possible expressions are brown, blue, and green. Lithic raw material (for example, flint, obsidian, quartzite, quartz, and basalt), temper added to clay (for example, none, quartz grit, sand, shell, and ground up pieces of fired clay), and feature type (for example, burial, hearth, lithic cache, foundation, and midden) are examples of nominal variables. Also called discontinuous variables.

number of identified specimens (NISP): A statistic in faunal analysis that reflects the number of bones of each animal species represented in a faunal assemblage.

obsidian: Naturally produced volcanic glass, usually black and translucent at thin edges. Obsidian without impurities breaks very predictably and controllably, producing exceptionally sharp, thin edges. Though these thin edges can be rather delicate and brittle, many ancient peoples used obsidian to make cutting, piercing, slicing, and scraping tools.

object piece: In stone tool making, the stone that you are striking with a hammerstone or antler hammer or the stone to which you are applying pressure with a pressure flaking tool. It's simple enough: It's the "piece" of stone (core or flake) that is the "object" of your percussion or pressure.

obtrusive: Where past cultures produced large-scale modifications of the landscape and/or constructed buildings of durable material, the archaeological remains of these landscape features and structures are said to be obtrusive, that is, under the right conditions readily obvious to practically anyone simply walking about these remains. The archaeological visibility of even obtrusive remains, however, may sometimes be obscured by a heavy growth of vegetation. The Maya of Mesoamerica are a good example of this, having produced enormous, impressive, durable, and therefore highly obtrusive monuments, but in a tropical rain forest environment that has hidden much of their remains in thick vegetation, rendering the archaeological visibility of these features and sites sometimes quite low.

occupation layer: The actual layer that was the surface when an archaeological site was occupied. At sites that were not buried, the modern surface also was the occupation layer. At sites covered by alluvium or lake (lacustrine), shoreline (marine), slope (colluvium), or wind-blown (aeolian) deposits, the occupation layer is buried and recognizable stratigraphically as the surface upon which the vast majority of artifacts and ecofacts are found and the level where features dug into the soil (trash pits and hearths, for example) begin.

Oldowan: The name given to the earliest stone tool industry. First found in Olduvai Gorge in eastern Africa, Oldowan tools were manufactured of stone, often quartz or quartzite, pebbles. Using direct percussion, the tool maker struck the stone core, removing a large flake. The flake scar left on the core then became a striking platform for another flake, removed from a facet opposite from the first. The core was then turned around again, using the scar left by the second flake as another striking platform, and another flake was removed. This process was repeated several times, producing a large chopping tool and several sharp, thin cutting flakes. These tools have been dated to as much as 2.5 million years ago, and most were probably made by a human ancestor, *Homo habilis*.

optically stimulated luminescence (OSL): A variety of luminescence dating; see also thermoluminescence. Buried objects are subject to naturally occurring radiation in the soil. The energy released by radioactive decay may accumulate in rock and clay. If rock or clay is heated to a high temperature by people (rock in a fireplace or clay when fired to make a pot), the energy previously accumulated is released. In other words, the human activity sets the energy accumulation clock to zero. When then buried, energy released by background radiation begins to accumulate again in the rock and fired clay at a regular rate. In optically stimulated luminescence, laser light is used to release the energy so accumulated. The amount of time since the "clock" was set to zero by people can be determined, thus dating the human activity and, therefore, the archaeological site.

OSL: See optically stimulated luminescence.

osteology: The study of bones. Osteology can focus on the skeletal remains of animals (for example, to determine ancient human use of animals) or of human beings (for example, to analyze the population statistics, dietary features, and disease histories of an ancient people).

paleoenvironmental: Relating to the ancient environment of an area. Archaeologists seek to understand the nature of the paleoenvironment to which a human group adapted.

paleofeces: Ancient, preserved feces. Because the digestive systems of animals, including human beings, are not 100% efficient, some ingested food is excreted in feces. As a result the paleofeces contain food remains and, therefore, provide data for dietary reconstruction. The term *coprolite* is more commonly used, but, technically, coprolites are fossilized. Most human deposits are not.

paleomagnetism: A dating method based on movement of the Earth's magnetic poles. Magnetic minerals present in plastic material—for example, a hot lava flow—may preserve the alignment of the ever-shifting planetary magnetic field at the time the material solidified.

paleontologist: Scientist who studies ancient animals, ordinarily through the recovery and analysis of their bones.

paleopathology: The study of ancient trauma, infectious disease, and nutritional deficiencies. Such pathologies often leave permanent and recognizable marks on human skeletons. Decades, centuries, and even millennia after death, these pathologies often can be accurately diagnosed, providing insights into the conditions that afflicted individuals as well as entire communities.

palynologist: Scientist who studies pollen. Palynologists become expert in recovering pollen and identifying the species of plants that produced it. Palynologists can reconstruct ancient plant communities and, by inference, ancient climates by comparing the pollen profiles derived from ancient pollen assemblages to the pollen rain falling in modern locations with their known climates.

patrilocal: A postmarital residence pattern in which, upon marriage, a woman leaves the community (compound, neighborhood, or village) into which she was born and within which she was raised and moves into the compound, neighborhood, or village in which her husband and his family reside.

patrilocality: Refers to a pattern of postmarital residence in which a newly married couple lives in the village, compound, or house of the groom's parents. See patrilocal.

pedestrian survey: The phase of an archaeological survey in which the ground surface is scanned for the presence of archaeological remains. In those parts of the world where soil forms fairly rapidly and covers most small-scale remains, only large-scale, built features—things such as stone walls, house foundations, canals, stone-marked graves, monuments—will be visible on the surface and locatable in a pedestrian survey. In those places where soil formation is very slow, artifact clusters, hearth remains, and other small-scale remains may be visible on the surface and can be found in a pedestrian survey. In addition, even in those places where archaeological materials get covered up as a matter of course, other natural processes (for example, erosion along a river or by something a bit more catastrophic such as an earthquake) may serve to expose buried material that can be found in a pedestrian survey.

percussion flaking: A method of stone tool making in which a nucleus of stone is struck with a hammerstone or antler percussor in order to remove stone flakes. Percussion flaking may be used in a primary step in stone tool production in which large flakes that will be worked further into tools are removed from cores or in intermediate and final steps in which a tool is thinned, sharpened, and shaped into its final form.

percussor: The tool used in percussion flaking to remove flakes from a core. Ordinarily, the percussor may be of stone (a hammerstone) or of antler. In either case, the percussor does not need to be harder than the rock that makes up the core, it merely must be harder to break. The geometry of a percussor contributes to its durability.

petroglyph: Literally "rock writing." By incising or pounding, people produce images and designs on rock surfaces, often by exposing the lighter rock beneath a dark rock surface.

physical anthropologist: Practitioner of a branch of anthropology (the study of human beings) that focuses on the biological aspects of our species. Among the topics investigated by physical anthropologists are the biological evolution of human beings, the biological variation exhibited by modern human beings, forensic anthropology, primatology (humans are primates, and primatologists study the nonhuman primates, including monkeys and apes). Synonymous with biological anthropology.

phytolith: Microscopic, inorganic mineral particles produced by plants. Phytoliths are extremely durable and species-specific. Enormous databases are being compiled that allow researchers to examine phytoliths recovered in the soils or adhering to artifacts recovered at archaeological sites and to identify the species from which the phytoliths originated. (http://www.missouri.edu/~phyto).

pictograph: Design painted onto a rock surface.

plane table: A flat table mounted onto a tripod. A plane table can be leveled to serve as the base for an alidade.

Pleistocene: The geological epoch beginning 1.8 million years ago punctuated by periods of worldwide cooling, an increase in the area of land surfaces covered by snow and ice year-round, the expansion of often massively thick glaciers, and sea level decline. The Pleistocene is defined as having ended 10,000 years ago, replaced by the Holocene, but there is no hand evidence that the pattern of periodically much colder climates that characterized the Pleistocene has actually ended.

polish: A category of wear traces on stone tools. Polish appears on the face or faces of a stone tool in applications in which the surface(s) continually rubs against the smooth face of the material being worked on. For example, a long, thin stone drill may exhibit smoothing and polishing on high points as a result of rubbing against the material being drilled into. Even without the aid of a microscope, polish can be seen as a smoothed surface on a tool, sometimes dull, sometimes brightly reflecting light.

pollen: The male gamete in plant sexual reproduction. The pollen grains produced by different species are morphologically distinct from one another and, under the right conditions, can be preserved for millennia. Palynologists can recover pollen grains from the occupation layers at archaeological sites or in areas adjacent to sites where preservation is higher. They can then identify the species that produced the pollen, calculate the percentages of the pollen of the species represented, and then deduce the makeup of the plant communities that lived in the area of an ancient human habitation.

pollen analysis: Figuring out the makeup of a plant community at a particular time and place by the recovery and examination of the pollen deposited then and there. By using modern pollen profiles as models, an ancient pollen profile can be interpreted in reference to modern plant communities. Finally, the climatic conditions that characterize the modern plant community can be suggested as being similar to those that applied when the ancient similar pollen profile was produced.

pollen profile: The percentages, usually depicted in a graph, of the pollen of each of the species of plants contributed to an overall pollen assemblage at a given place and at a given time period compared over time. The increase or decrease in the percentage of individual plant species over time may be a product of a change in climate, either to the benefit or detriment of those species. A change in percentage through time may also result from cultural activity, including forest clearing, the introduction of new species, and farming. Pollen percentages also change through time as a result of the natural process of evolution of plant communities, called succession.

pollen rain: The pollen that actually falls on a region. Today the pollen rain may be collected with sticky tape. This sample of the pollen rain is then examined through a microscope in order to determine the percentages of the various plant species contributing to the pollen rain. An ancient pollen rain may be determined by palynologists, who recover preserved pollen in soil samples.

pongid: The taxonomic family that includes all ape species, both living and extinct. The first pongids date to sometime after 15 million years ago in the Miocene epoch, and they flourished thereafter. Today there are several pongid species, including, in Africa, gorillas, chimpanzees, and bonobos (formerly called pygmy chimpanzees), and, in Asia, orangutans, gibbons, and siamangs.

population: A term used in statistics. The population is the entire group in any data set. The population of sites in a project area means all the sites, known as well as those not yet (and perhaps never to be) discovered. We rarely have access to an entire population (of sites, particular kinds of artifacts, or the skeletons of all the members of an extinct hominid species). We are able to accurately describe, reveal patterns in, and investigate correlations within a population by analyzing a representative sample of that population.

population profile: In demography, a graphic representation of the breakdown of a population of people by sex and age. This graph, also called a population pyramid, depicts the percentage of a population in each decade of life, broken down by sex.

postcranial skeleton: The skeleton below and excluding the cranium.

potassium/argon (K/Ar): Dating method based on the decay of an unstable isotope of the element potassium into a stable and inert argon gas. The half-life of radioactive potassium, common in the Earth's crust, is 1.25 billion years, during which time its end product, argon gas, builds up at a regular rate in rock. By measuring how much argon has accumulated in a lava flow, the amount of time since the lava solidified can be determined.

potsherd: Fragment of pottery from a broken pot. Entire, intact pots are rare in archaeology. Most ceramic artifacts recovered are, in fact, potsherds, sometimes simply called sherds.

preceramic: Term usually applied regionally to refer to the period of time before the development or adoption of ceramic technology, especially the manufacture and use of pottery. People certainly can store items or cook food without ceramic vessels. In some parts of the world, the presence of soapstone or steatite provided a soft stone that could be carved into fireproof, watertight containers suitable for storing liquids and for use in cooking. Elsewhere, bark and woven containers were made that could hold liquids and that could be heated, not directly over a fire but by placing heated stones into their contents. Ceramics, however, allowed for the mass production of relatively durable containers, and people the world over recognized their utility. The earliest examples of pottery vessels date to a little more than 10,000 years ago in Japan and between 5,000 and 6,000 years ago in South America.

preform: A product of the process of making a stone tool. A perform represents a flake taken off a core and then worked in a preliminary, general way into a shape that can be further modified into a number of possible different final tool forms, depending on the particular need of the moment. The production of preforms in anticipation of the need to make tools at some point in the future is more efficient and convenient than to have to begin from scratch each time a new stone tool is needed.

prehistoric: Adjective modifying any site, culture, artifact, ecofact, feature, and so on that dates to the period before the development of writing. Because writing was not developed or adopted at the same time in all world areas, there can be no universally applied prehistoric time period. Prehistoric refers to a local sequence. In some areas, for example, Southwest Asia, *prehistoric* refers to the time before 6,000 years ago, when writing was first invented. In other parts of the world, for example, Mesoamerica, *prehistoric* refers to the time before about 2,000 years ago, when writing was developed there. In yet other parts of the world, for example, America north of Mexico, writing didn't develop independently but arrived with explorers and colonizers in the fifteenth century. In North America, therefore, *prehistoric* refers to the period before the arrival of Europeans.

prehistory: Literally, the period before the development of true writing or a written system of record keeping. The first written language dates to no more than 6,000 years ago, and the earliest hints of the use of symbols as a form of record keeping are about 10,000 years old, so everywhere in the world archaeological sites that are more than 6,000 years old are, by definition, prehistoric. It should be added that not all regions became historic at the same time, so the boundary between prehistory and history is not everywhere the same. The native people of Australia and North America, for example, did not independently develop writing systems, so their story is part of prehistory up until their contact with Europeans just a few hundred years ago. Because upright walking, tool making human ancestors date to 2.5 million years ago, human prehistory, therefore, constitutes well over 99% of the time human beings and our hominid ancestors have walked the planet.

pressure flaking: A method of stone tool making in which relatively small flakes are removed from larger flakes by the application of pressure. Pressure flaking tools are ordinarily made of antler or metal; bone and wood generally are too soft. Because the pressure flaking tool can be positioned precisely at the point where the knapper hopes to remove a flake, pressure flaking is used for the finer work in stone tool making, including precise edge sharpening, flake thinning, final shaping, and notching (to provide a firmer attachment of the stone point to a wooden or reed shaft).

primary refuse: Luckily for archaeologists, people tend not to be particularly fastidious about their discard habits. Human beings, including those in the distant past, have always consumed enormous amounts of resources to produce the material objects they needed or wanted and to provide their subsistence. Commonly, a portion of the raw materials from which material objects were made or from which food was extracted were perceived as trash and left just where the objects were made or the food was consumed. At the same time, most tools have a limited useful life and eventually either break or simply wear out and are then discarded. Tools (artifacts) or inedible materials produced in food preparation (ecofacts) discarded at their place of manufacture, use, or consumption are called primary refuse.

principal investigator: The director of any scientific endeavor, including archaeological research. The researcher who plans the project, obtains funding, directs the conduct of the study, and is responsible for the report or publication describing the results of the research.

prognathous: A jaw that protrudes from the rest of the face. Some human populations are relatively flat faced; viewed in profile, their faces are flat from their foreheads down to their chins. Other human groups are relatively prognathous, with their jaws protruding from the plane of the rest of their faces.

projectile point: A sharp piece of (usually) stone that is firmly attached to a wooden or reed shaft and is used as a weapon by throwing or shooting. *Projectile* is the generic term that includes spear points, darts, and arrowheads. Because the shape and size of a point does not necessarily clarify whether it was used to tip a spear, dart, or arrow shaft, archaeologists generally prefer the term *projectile point* unless they are certain of precisely which kind of projectile was attached to the tip.

proton magnetometry: A noninvasive technique used in archaeology in the search for buried remains. The proton magnetometer measures the strength of the Earth's magnetic field at the surface. The magnetometer may detect variations in that field above the locations of buried remains such as walls and foundations.

provenience: The precisely measured, three-dimensional, in situ location of an artifact, ecofact, or feature at an archaeological site. The provenience may be recorded as a single point for a very small object or as a series of points for larger artifacts and ecofacts and, especially, for the outline of features. Proveniences may be measured initially by reference to the southwest stake of an excavation unit (centimeters north and east of that stake) and depth below a fixed point (the top of the southwest stake or the ground surface at that stake's location). Proveniences are then converted to their location relative to the site datum.

proximal epiphysis: Each long bone in your body consists of a shaft (the diaphysis) and two end caps (the epiphyses). In the geography of the body, the proximal epiphysis of each of those long bones is the end cap closer to the trunk ("in proximity to" means "near" or "close to"). The end cap farther, or more distant, from the trunk is the distal epiphysis.

pubic symphysis: The point of connection, or "articulation", between the two halves of the pelvis. Connected by a band of cartilage, the two adjoining faces of the pubic symphysis go through a fairly regular process of change and deterioration during an individual's life. The appearance of the pubic symphysis, therefore, is pretty much time dependent and time consistent, allowing for a fairly accurate estimate of the age at death of an individual.

race: A term used to denote different "varieties" of humanity. There is no objective definition for what constitutes a particular race, no set of characteristics that represents precisely one group of people to the exclusion of all other groups. As a result, *race* is not used as a scientific term, and biological anthropologists usually refer to a multiplicity of varieties of human beings, often distributed geographically, but not to a small number (three? four?) of distinct human races.

radioactive: A substance that is unstable on the atomic level and that emits energy (radiation) as it decays into a more stable substance. That decay occurs at a fixed, regular, and measurable rate. That rate, once known, provides a natural clock or calendar that can be used to date an object through the measurement of how much of the radioactive substance remains or how much of the stable end product of the decay has accumulated.

radiocarbon dating: Radiometric dating procedure that measures the amount of carbon-14 (^{14}C) remaining in an item found at an archaeological site to determine its age. Carbon-14 is an unstable isotope of carbon. Its decay rate, expressed as a half-life, is known; therefore, when the amount of carbon-14 remaining in an item is measured, the age of the item can be determined.

radiometric: Dating techniques that are based on the regular rate of decay of an unstable (radioactive) variety (isotope) of an element. Because decay rates are known (through measurement), an estimate of how old an object is can be derived from the amount of the radioactive variety of an element remaining, or the amount of the stable end product the radioactive variety decays to. When the life history of the material being dated can be related to past people (for example, when humans cut down a tree containing radioactive carbon and used it to build a structure or when lava containing radioactive argon flowed directly over an ancient village), the date derived from the object being dated can be applied to the cultural material.

random: Refers to the nature of a sample. A sample is random if there is no bias and every member of a population has the same probability of being selected for inclusion. In the example of a site survey, every location in the project area would have an equal likelihood of being selected for testing.

rank society: A society in which there are a number of sociopolitical levels, or "ranks." These ranks do not confer economic power but do provide different levels of status or prestige.

relative dating: Refers to dating methods that place individual artifacts, ecofacts, features, or sites in a chronological sequence but without a determination of actual age. Applying a relative dating technique allows a researcher to conclude that one site is older than another, or that one artifact is younger than another, but does not provide an age in years for sites, artifacts, or any other archaeological materials.

remote sensing: Noninvasive process used in probing for archaeological sites without disturbing the soil. Remote sensing includes those procedures that employ instrumentation that is truly remote, such as satellite- and plane-based cameras. Remote sensing also includes approaches that use devices that can image or probe the characteristics of the subsurface, searching for anomalies that indicate the presence of artifacts or, more usually, patterns of soil disturbance that probably resulted from human activity (for example, burials, trenches, walls).

representative: Refers to the nature of a sample. A sample is representative if the various subcategories in the sample are included in the same or very nearly the same percentages as their percentages in the population. A sample of people in an electoral poll is representative if it reflects the same percentages of men and women; rich, middle class, and poor; Democrats and Republicans; and so on as the population from which the sample was drawn contains. A sample of tested locations in an archaeological survey is representative if the number of pits in each habitat contained in a project area is proportional to the area each of the habitats constitutes of the total project area (if 10% of the project area consists of floodplain, then 10% of the test pits should be located in the floodplain). In a perfect world an entirely random sample should also be representative. But the world is rarely perfect, and samples may be skewed accidentally. A sample can be made representative by making certain it reflects the characteristics of the population. In the example above, if, by chance only 7% of the test pits ended up in the floodplain, more test pits could be placed there to increase the percentage to the representative 10%.

representative sample: Ordinarily, in attempting to understand a given population (the population can be all voters in the state of Nebraska, all redwood trees in California, all archaeological sites in the lower Ohio Valley, and so on), only a fraction of a population—a sample—is examined. In most cases the entire population of any data set is simply too large and, therefore, too expensive and time consuming to examine, so only a part of it, a sample, is actually looked at. To ensure that the conclusions we reach about the subset of the population we investigate directly also apply to the population as a whole, we make every effort to examine a sample that "looks like" the population.

If a sample exhibits the same or very nearly the same characteristics of the population—the same percentages of men and women; Democrats and Republicans; young trees, middle-aged trees, and old trees; village sites, hunting camps, fishing loci, and quarries; and so on—the sample is said to be representative, and conclusions reached about the sample are likely to apply equally well to the larger population as a whole.

research strategy: Archaeological research is not random. It is not conducted merely to amuse archaeologists or provide opportunities for students to broaden their experience. At least it shouldn't be. Archaeological research is informed by research goals. Surveys are conducted and sites excavated in an attempt to answer questions about life in the past. The research goal may be designed to answer a very simple, practical question: Are there significant archaeological resources that may be destroyed by a planned development project? On the other hand, the research goal may focus on a better understanding of fundamental and very complex issues of human cultural evolution, for example, the nature and causes of the origins of the first complex state societies, commonly called "civilizations." The research strategy of a project consists of the methods by which archaeologists go about the process of reaching these research goals.

sample: A term used in statistics to signify that subset or portion of an entire population that the researcher has access to and is analyzing in an attempt to draw accurate and meaningful conclusions about the population as a whole. In most sciences, including archaeology, we cannot recover or it is far too inefficient to study an entire population, but instead we rely on a sample taken from that population. We increase the likelihood that our conclusions about the population based on a sample will be valid by making sure that we have extracted a representative sample of the population.

sampling strategy: The approach in an archaeological survey or excavation of selecting a fraction of an area or a site to search for the constituents of archaeological sites. The goals of sampling strategies differ on the basis of the research goal of the project as a whole. If an area is to be completely altered in a development project, the strategy may be to intensively sample the entire project area. In other cases the strategy may be to examine a representative sample, a portion of the project area that closely represents, on a smaller scale, the characteristics of the project area as a whole.

scalar scar: A category of wear traces on stone tools. Scalar scars are tiny flake scars, shaped like fish scales, representing the damage caused along a stone tool edge when the pressure applied in use results in the removal of small flakes of stone. Scalar scars usually appear on the face of a tool along the edge without deterioration to the edge itself. The same qualities of stone that allow a tool maker intentionally to remove flakes through pressure flaking may result in the accidental removal of flakes through the pressure applied in tool use. For example, the pressure applied when using a steep-edged scraping tool to smooth a wooden shaft in the production of a spear may remove small flakes from the tool's working edge, resulting in scalar scars along that edge.

sciatic notch: A deep indentation in the back of each half of the pelvis through which the sciatic nerve travels. The size of the notch affects the overall width of the pelvis. Females tend to have a substantially more widely angled notch, which allows for a wider birth canal. Of all the metrical characteristics of the human skeleton, there probably is the least overlap between the notch measurements taken for men and women. Because of this, the size of the sciatic notch can be used to accurately (but not perfectly) distinguish the skeleton of a woman from that of a man.

secondary refuse: People generally are slobs and have a tendency to leave their trash where it first falls to earth (primary refuse). In many instances, however, for reasons of safety (when the discarded material is dangerous: very sharp or even poisonous) or simply for sanitary reasons (the remains attract insects, attract dangerous animals, are a health risk, or just plain smell bad), people will pick up after themselves and place the trash in a separate trash deposit located a safe and reasonable distance away from where people are actually living or the trash may be buried in the ground. This trash, removed from its initial place of deposit, is called secondary refuse.

sedentary: A way of life in which a human group tends to inhabit a single location during the course of a year. Though active, healthy adults may be quite mobile, leaving home and staying for short periods at locations where resources are collected, they invariably return to their fixed home base inhabited by less mobile members of society, including the very old, the very young, and pregnant women close to giving birth. A sedentary way of life is made possible by an extremely rich local environment that provides sufficient wild foods for the group year-round and/or by an artificial increase in food resources through food production, in other words, agriculture.

semilunar knife: Stone or metal knife in the shape of a half-moon. The straight part of the half-moon is held or has a handle attached. The curved portion of the tool is the cutting edge. Called an *ulu* among the Inuit people of the Arctic, the semilunar knife was used in butchery, especially fish gutting.

seriation: A relative dating technique based on a common pattern of change in material culture. In many cases when a new way of accomplishing a task is invented or introduced in a society, it is initially adopted by a small fraction of the population and through time slowly increases in popularity until it reaches a peak in its acceptance. At some point yet another way of accomplishing the same task is invented or introduced, and this new way slowly grows in popularity, replacing the previously accepted method, which slowly decreases in use. Individual sites can be dated by measuring the proportions of use of different styles or methods and from this figuring out where they fit in a general continuum of technological or stylistic change through time.

seriation graph: A graphic representation of the level of popularity of a style or method of accomplishing a given task in a society as it changes through time, compared to the level of use of competing styles or methods. A seriation graph is sometimes called a "battleship curve" because of its appearance. Horizontal bars represent the popularity of styles or methods and are stacked in a commonsensical sequence reflecting a pattern of slow acceptance, increasing popularity, maximum use, and subsequent, almost inevitable, decrease as they are replaced by a new approach.

settlement pattern: The nature of land use and the resulting distribution across a landscape of habitations, work areas, burial grounds, encampments, sacred places, resource extraction areas, and so on by a human group. The settlement pattern of a group of people produces a unique archaeological landscape signature reflecting how those people used their territory.

sexual dimorphism: The nature and degree of difference between the sexes in a species. In some species there is an extreme level of sexual dimorphism, with one sex, usually but not always males, being much larger than females. In other species there is a very low degree of dimorphism, and males and females may be virtually indistinguishable, at least to the naked human eye. Undressed, living human males and females are fairly easy to distinguish, and the same can be said for male and female skeletons. Nevertheless, our overall degree of dimorphism falls somewhere between the extremes.

sherd: Broken piece of a ceramic object, usually a broken piece of pottery.

shovel-shaped incisors: A form of the incisors, the four flat teeth in the front and center of both the upper and lower jaws. The shovel shape refers to the interior surface of the incisors, where there are ridges along the margins giving the teeth the appearance, appropriately enough, of a shovel or spade. Shovel-shaped incisors are very common in Asian populations and in the teeth of Native Americans and are much less common in other populations. The presence of shovel-shaped incisors among human skeletal remains, modern or ancient, is a strong though imperfect indicator of an Asian source for the population. It is no coincidence that Native Americans exhibit very high levels of shoveling in their incisors if Asia is the source of the population.

shovel test pit: Test pit, sometimes called STP. Because test pits are usually but not always excavated with shovels, archaeologists tend to refer to them as test pits, often preceded by a common expletive.

silt: A deposit consisting of very fine mineral particles, technically between 1/16 and 1/256 mm in size—bigger than sand and smaller than clay particles. Silt is produced by the decomposition of preexisting rock and often makes up a substantial component of alluvium.

site: The archaeological term *site* is shorthand for *archaeological site*. An archaeological site is a place that people used in the past—they may have lived there or simply used the place to conduct a specific task or tasks (hunted, buried their dead, engaged in war, conducted a religious ceremony)—and where physical evidence of their use of the place remains in the form of artifacts and/or ecofacts.

site constituents: The things that make up the archaeological record and that, therefore, alert the archaeologist conducting a survey that he or she has found a site. Artifacts, ecofacts, and features are among archaeological site constituents.

site formation processes: The processes by which the material objects used, manipulated, altered, and manufactured by people become part of the archaeological record. Simply, people lose objects, throw them away, leave them behind, or abandon them when they are used up or of no use. These objects become deposited on the ground and in the ground (through intentional burial or placement in pits). By these processes archaeological sites are formed.

site survey: The search for archaeological sites. Site survey often includes a historical analysis of a study area, an examination of aerial photographs, a methodical surface inspection, and test excavations all aimed at discovering the location where people lived in the past and left behind evidence of their presence.

skull: The bones of the head, face, and upper and lower jaw. In other words, the skull consists of the cranium and the mandible. The skull exhibits differences between the sexes, it changes in a regular and patterned way from birth through old age, and it shows geographic variation in its morphology.

slip: A watery, thin mixture of clay brushed or poured over a clay vessel before firing, providing a smooth, consistent clay coating on its surface.

soapstone: A metamorphic rock consisting primarily of the mineral talc that is highly resistant to and retentive of heat. It is quite soft, can be fairly readily carved with stone or metal tools and, where available, was often used by ancient peoples to make cooking vessels. In more recent times soapstone's heat retention capacity rendered it suitable for colonial bed warmers. Called soapstone because of its slippery, soapy feel, its formal name is steatite.

spatial associations: The spatial linkages of material at an archaeological site. Items that are found in close proximity to one another and were probably deposited together as a result of their linkage in a behavioral context (as a hammer is linked to a nail) are said to be in spatial association with one another. A key rationale for initially leaving items in place (in situ) upon their discovery during excavation of an archaeological site, as well as providing a reason for the detailed and accurate recording of their exact place of discovery (their provenience), is to ensure that spatial associations are preserved, if only on paper, and that the behavioral meaning of those associations can be deduced.

spatial context: The location where an archaeological object is found and its spatial associations. Consider three different possible spatial contexts for the same artifact, a chipped stone spear point: (1) embedded in the butchered bone of a deer found in a fireplace, (2) one among several spear points found together as apparent offerings in a human burial, and (3) in a cluster of stone tools on the floor of the remains of a house. In each case the spear point's spatial context implies its use and significance in the culture that produced it , a use that cannot be determined simply by its morphology.

stadia rod: Essentially a large-format, rigid ruler, usually with metric gradations. The rod is usually collapsible, extending to more than 3 meters in length. The rod is placed on a surface whose precise location and depth are to be measured. The actual measuring may be accomplished with an alidade, old-style transit, or laser transit.

starch grains: Small pieces of starch produced by plants. The shapes of stach grains are species-specific. As a result, when starch grains are preserved on tools used to process plants, they can be recovered, and the plant species that produced the grains and on which the tool was used can be identified.

state historic preservation officer (SHPO): A federally mandated state administrator whose responsibilities include coordinating federal requirements for the protection, preservation, and study of cultural resources contained within that administrator's state.

steatite: A metamorphic rock that consists primarily of the mineral talc, and is highly resistant to and retentive of heat. It is quite soft, can be fairly readily carved with stone or metal tools, and, where available, was often used by ancient peoples to make cooking vessels. In more recent times steatite's heat retention capacity rendered it suitable for colonial bed warmers. Steatite is often known by its common name, "soapstone," for its slippery, soapy feel.

step scar: A category of wear traces on stone tools. Step scars are tiny flake scars that terminate abruptly at a right angle into the face of the rock, giving the appearance of tiny stair steps. Step scars are caused along a stone tool edge when the pressure applied during use results in the removal of small flakes of stone. Step scars usually appear on the face of a tool along the edge without deterioration to the edge itself. The same qualities of stone that allow a tool maker intentionally to remove flakes through pressure flaking may result in the accidental removal of flakes through the pressure applied in tool use. For example, the pressure applied to the edge of a stone tool while scraping the meat off a bone may remove small flakes from the tool's working edge, resulting in step scars along that edge.

STP: See shovel test pit.

strata: Naturally formed and often quite distinct superimposed layers of soil composed of differing percentages of rock, gravel, sand, silt, clay, and decayed and decaying organic material as well as cultural material left behind by past peoples. Different strata may exhibit different colors, textures, and chemical makeup, and the boundaries between them may be sharply defined. These differences in strata can be explained by the characteristics of the "parent material" from which the soil layer formed, the agency that laid down the layer (flowing water, wind, vulcanism, slope movement, and so on), the particular environmental conditions present when the layer formed, and the chemical and physical processes to which the soil has been subjected. The relative positions of cultural materials in a sequence of strata are often used to determine the relative ages of those materials.

stratified (societies): These are societies characterized by social- economic- political classes, or castes, into which people are born and, ordinarily, within which they and their descendants remain. These layered societies, with noble classes, merchant classes, workers, and peasants, characterize complex societies.

stratigraphic: Refers to the sequence of soil layers superimposed one on top of the other. Stratigraphic levels may result from natural processes of deposition (flooding, blowing wind, soil movement down and across a slope), chemical processes in the soil, and also human activity through movement of soil as well as the accumulation of trash.

stratigraphy: Analysis of the sequenced layering of rock and soil. The relative ages of archaeological materials can be determined by the position of the soil levels, or strata, in which the materials are found by reference to the law of superposition.

stratum: The singular of strata; a single or individual soil layer.

striations: Scratch marks found on tool surfaces and edges, usually parallel to each other and to the direction of use of a stone tool. Striations are a category of wear traces, a form of damage to or deterioration of a stone tool with use. For example, a durable, sharp-edged stone knife used to cut through bone usually exhibits striations on both faces parallel to its working edge.

striking platform: The surface of a core or flake—usually flat or platformlike—that the percussor (hammerstone or antler hammer) strikes in an attempt to remove a flake from a contiguous core or flake surface that intersects with the striking platform at an angle of less than 90 degrees.

supraorbital torus: A lump or protrusion of bone above the eye orbits, about where your eyebrows are located. Ancient and extinct varieties of hominids had a substantial and, in some cases, continuous ridge of bone over both eyes. In modern humans the torus is less pronounced and usually not continuous.

Within particular groups men tend to have larger ridges than women, and this feature is examined when attempting to determine the sex of an individual from his or her cranium.

survey: The search for archaeological sites. Site survey often includes historical analysis of a study area, an examination of aerial photographs, a methodical surface inspection, and test excavations, all aimed at discovering locations where people lived in the past and left behind evidence of their presence.

tell: Artificial hill that develops, primarily in the Middle East when sand accumulates around and over abandoned villages. In some instances subsequent inhabitants of a region elect to construct their villages on the tops of tells. When this happens the process can repeat itself, and the tell grows in size when these subsequent habitations are abandoned and sand accumulates around and over them. In this way some tells grow to a substantial height, enclosing a succession of villages one on top of the other and providing a stratigraphic sequence of habitations.

temper: Material added to clay to improve its drying characteristics and its strength. Temper commonly consists of sand, ground up bits of shell, quartz grit, and small pieces of previously fired clay (called grog).

test pit: Preliminary excavation carried out in the search for subsurface archaeological evidence. Test pits are excavated in the initial surveying for sites yet to be discovered and also in the preliminary examination of sites in an attempt to ascertain site size and function.

test pit form: Standardized form for consistently recording information concerning the test pits excavated in an archaeological survey. Test pit forms include at least the name and location of the project, a unique identifier for the pit (a number in a sequence along a transect, for example), a drawing of soil levels encountered with their recorded depths, a listing of any artifacts or ecofacts encountered in the soil levels of the pit and their precise recorded depths, a location of the test unit, the name of the excavator(s), and the date. Using a standardized form ensures that every crew member records the same information about each pit, which makes life infinitely easier for the person who analyzes the results of a survey transect.

test pitting: The process of excavating pits in an attempt to examine a sample of the soil below the ground surface of an area in the search for the archaeological components of sites.

thermography: A kind of thermal imaging involving the infrared spectrum. Buried objects including archaeological artifacts and features can affect vegetation growth which, though not visible to the naked eye, may be detectable by analysis of an area's infrared radiation.

thermoluminescence (TL): A variety of luminescence dating; see also optically stimulated luminescence. Buried objects are subject to naturally occurring radiation in the soil. The energy released by radioactive decay may accumulate in rock and clay. If rock or clay is heated to a high temperature by people (rock in a fireplace or clay when fired to make a pot), the energy previously accumulated is released. In other words, the human activity sets the energy accumulation "clock" to zero. When then buried, energy released by background radiation begins to accumulate again in the rock or fired clay at a regular rate. In thermoluminescence, heat is used to release the energy so accumulated. The amount of time since the "clock" was set to zero by people can be determined, thus dating the human activity and, therefore, the archaeological site.

tibia: The larger of the two bones of the lower leg. The smaller lower leg bone is the fibula. Feel your shin; the large, flat bone just below the surface of your skin is your tibia.

TL: See thermoluminescence.

tool kit: A tool kit is the entire assemblage of tools a past people made and used in an activity or set of activities. Look at the set of tools in your basement used in woodworking—hammers, saws, straightedges, and fasteners such as nails and screws—that is a woodworking tool kit. Look at the pots and pans, spatulas, knives, bowls, and even the oven and stove in your kitchen—that is your food preparation tool kit. In the same way, stone spear points and spear shafts, stone knives, and scraping tools represent the hunting tool kit of a past people.

topographic map: Map depicting the terrain of an area, including elevations. Archaeologists commonly use topographic maps published by the United States Geological Survey with a scale of 1:24,000. One inch on a map of this scale represents about 2,000 feet. Topographic maps, obviously, are of practical importance in locating archaeological sites. Also, in our attempt to understand how a past people used the landscape, we need to become familiar with that landscape; topographic maps are a useful tool in this effort.

total station: Surveying device that uses a laser transit to determine the precise distance and elevation of a point in space. A stadia rod is positioned at a location, and the transit emits a beam of light that hits the rod and bounces back to a receiver in the total station. The distance and elevation of the locations being measured are then calculated and stored in the total station, from which the information can be downloaded to a computer.

transect: Line through a project area along which test pits are excavated or surfaces are examined. Based on the sampling strategy developed for a particular project, transects may be located randomly or situated so as to cut across all the various habitats found in a research area. The surface is scanned for surface remains, and/or test pits are excavated along these transects at regular intervals and the subsurface examined for evidence of archaeological remains.

unconsolidated material: Geological deposit in which individual elements are separate and not cemented together. Sand and gravel, for instance, are representative of unconsolidated deposits.

United States Geological Survey (USGS): A branch of the U.S. Department of the Interior. Established in 1879, the USGS has the job of monitoring natural resources in the United States. As part of its mandate, the USGS produces topographic maps of the United States of numerous sizes and scales. The USGS maps most commonly used by archaeologists are the topographic quad sheets at 1:24,000 scale. Made from aerial photographs, these maps show major and minor drainages (rivers, streams, brooks), lakes, ponds, wetlands, and cultural features (roads, buildings) and provide detailed topographic information. USGS quad sheets serve as good base maps for archaeological survey projects.

Universal Transverse Mercator (UTM): A metric mapping and measurement system. The Earth is divided into sixty numbered north-south zones, each zone representing 6 degrees of the 360-degree, circular Earth when viewed from above the North Pole. Measurements of the precise location of any point within a zone are expressed in metric units. The boundaries of an archaeological site are often expressed using this system.

USGS: See United States Geological Survey.

UTM: See Universal Transverse Mercator.

varve: Sediments deposited annually in distinct and distinquishable layers along lake and ocean shorelines. Like tree rings in dendrochronology, by counting varves back from the most recently deposited layer (the current year), the precise calendar year date for each varve in a sequence can be determined. A carbon date derived from organic material extracted from a varve can be compared to the year date determined for that varve. When a sequence of such comparisons can be made, any pattern in the possible inaccuracy of the carbon dating technique through time can be assessed; in other words, it can be determined if carbon dates are consistently too old or too young for given stretches of time. Radiocarbon dates can then be calibrated or corrected by reference to the varve chronology.

visibility: Archaeological visibility is a relative measure of the ease with which archaeological remains can be spotted in a given area. Areas with high archaeological visibility may be characterized by slow natural processes that tend to cover material left on the surface, so even ancient materials may be exposed on the modern landscape. Vegetation growth also contributes to the degree of archaeological visibility; areas with rapid growth of thick vegetation present low levels of visibility, while areas that are sparsely vegetated have higher levels of archaeological visibility.

vitreous: Glasslike. Vitreous rock tends to break predictably and controllably, producing sharp edges suitable for making cutting, piercing, and scraping tools. In many world areas past peoples made tools from vitreous rock where it was locally available and traded for it in locations where it was not.

wear pattern: The damage that accumulates on the working edge of a stone tool. When a stone edge is used to cut, slice, scrape, or pierce a material (wood, animal flesh, bone, antler, stone, and so on), the edge of the stone tool deteriorates through abrasion and breakage. This deterioration or wear is reflected in striations, polish, and microchippage. Each manner of use, combined with the raw material of the tool and the nature of the material on which the tool is used, produces a unique pattern of wear on the tool itself. Examining the wear traces on an ancient stone tool, therefore, enables archaeologists to deduce the tool's function: how it was used and on what material.

Wide Area Augmentation System: A process added to the standard Global Positioning System that provides for even greater locational accuracy, down to about 2 meters.

Bibliography

2005. Archaeologist Killed in Trench Collapse. In *The Digger*. vol. 36 April. http://www.bajr.org/diggermagazine/Digger36/index.html

Adams, R. E. W. 1991. *Prehistoric Mesoamerica*. University of Oklahoma Press, Norman.

Adams, R. E. W. and F. Valdez, Jr. 1997. Stratigraphy. In *Field Methods in Archaeology*, edited by T. R. Hester, H. J. Shafer, and K. L. Feder, 235–52. Mayfield Publishing, Mountain View, California.

Adovasio, J. M. 1977. *Baskerty Techonology*. Aldine, Chicago.

Ames, K. M., and H. D. G. Maschner. 1999. *Peoples of the Northwest Coast*. Thames & Hudson, London.

Arnold, B., and N. L. Wicker, eds. 2001. *Gender and the Archaeology of Death*. Rowman & Littlefield, Lanham, Maryland.

Arnold, D. 1991. *Building in Egypt: Pharaonic Stone Masonry*. Oxford University Press, Oxford.

Ashmore, W., and R. J. Sharer. 1999. *Discovering Our Past: A Brief Introduction to Archaeology*. Mayfield Publishing, Mountain View, California.

Baillie, M. G. L. 1990. *Tree Ring Dating and Archaeology*. University of Chicago Press, Chicago.

Baker, B. W., B. S. Shaffer, and D. G. Steele. 1997. Basic Approaches in Archaeological Faunal Analysis. In *Field Methods in Archaeology*, edited by T. R. Hester, H. J. Shafer, and K. L. Feder, 298–318. Mayfield Publishing, Mountain View, California.

Bard, E. 2001. Extending the Calibrated Radiocarbon Record. *Science* 292:2443–44.

Barnes, M. 1997a. Pyramid. In *Secrets of Lost Empires*. Nova. WGBH, Boston.

———. 1997b. Obelisk. In *Secrets of Lost Empires*. Nova. WGBH, Boston.

———. 1997c. Inca. In *Secrets of Lost Empires*. Nova. WGBH, Boston.

Bass, W. 1987. *Human Osteology: A Laboratory and Field Manual of the Human Skeleton*. Missouri Archaeological Society, Columbia.

Beck, J. W., D. A. Richards, R. Lawrence, et al. 2001. Extremely Large Variations of Atmospheric 14C Concentration During the Last Glacial Period. *Science* 292:2453–58.

Bellantoni, N. F. 2001. Ticked Off: Lyme Disease and Archaeologists. In *Dangerous Places: Health, Safety, and Archaeology*, edited by D. Poirier and K. L. Feder, 3–10. Bergin & Garvey, Westport, Connecticut.

Bellantoni, N. F., P. Sledzik, and D. A. Poirier. 1997. Rescue, Research, and Reburial: Walton Family Cemetery. In *In Remembrance: Archaeology and Death*, edited by D. Poirier and N. F. Bellantoni. Bergin & Garvey, Westport, Connecticut.

Bernstein, D. J. 1999. Prehistoric Use of Plant Foods on Long Island and Block Island Sounds. In *Current Northeast Paleoethnobotany*, edited by J. P. Hart, 101–19. New York State Musuem, Albany.

Binford, L. 1962. Archaeology as Anthropology. *American Antiquity* 28:217–25.

———. 1978. *Nunamiut Ethnoarchaeology*. Academic Press, New York.

———. 1987. *Bones: Ancient Men and Modern Myths*. Academic Press, New York.

Binford, L. R. 1968. Archaeological Perspectives. In *New Perspectives in Archaeology*, edited by S. R. Binford and L. R. Binford, 5–32. Aldine Publishing, Chicago.

Biolsi, T., and L. Zimmerman, eds. 1997. *Indians and Anthropologists: Vine Deloria, Jr., and the Critique of Anthropology*. University of Arizona Press, Tucson.

Bowman, S. 1990. *Radiocarbon Dating*. University of California Press, Berkeley.

Braden, M. 2006. Trafficking in Treasures. In *Archaeological Ethics*, edited by K. D. Vitelli and C. Colwell-Chanthaphonh, 27–33. AltaMira Press, Lanham, Maryland.

Bradley, B. 1989. *Flintknapping*, (video). Produced by INTER park and Primitive Tech. Enterprises. Cortez, Colorado.

Brothwell, D. R. 1972. *Digging Up Bones: The Excavation, Treatment, and Study of Human Skeletal Remains*. British Museum, London.

Brown, K. 2001. New Trips Through the Back Alleys of Agriculture. *Science* 292:631–33.

Bryant Jr., V. M., and R. G. Holloway. 1983. The Role of Palynology in Archaeology. In *Advances in Archaeological Method and Theory*, edited by M. B. Schiffer, 191–224. Academic Press, New York.

Bryant, V., and G. Williams-Dean. 1978. The Coprolites of Man. *Scientific American* 238:100–09.

Buckley, T. 1976. The Discovery of Tutankhamun's Tomb. In *The Treasures of Tutankhamun*, edited by K. S. Gilbert, J. K. Holt, and S. Hudson, 9–18. Metropolitan Museum of Art, New York.

Burns, K. R. 1999. *The Forensic Anthropology Training Manual*. Prentice Hall, Upper Saddle River, New Jersey.

Butzer, K. W. 1982. *Archaeology as Human Ecology*. Cambridge University Press, Cambridge.

Byers, S. N. 2001. *Introduction to Forensic Anthropology: A Textbook*. Allyn & Bacon, Boston.

Cannon, K. P. 1995. Blood Residue Analyses of Ancient Stone Tools Reveal Clues to Prehistoric Subsistence Patterns in Yellowstone. *CRM* 18(2):14–16.

Cantwell, A.-M., and D.D. Wall. 2001. *Unearthing Gotham*. Yale University Press, New Haven, Connecticut.

Carter, H., and A. C. Mace. 1923. *The Discovery of the Tomb of Tutankhamen*. Cassell & Company, London.

Carter, R. J. 1997. Age Estimation of the Roe Deer (Capreolus capreolus) Mandibles from the Mesolithic Site of Star Carr, Yorkshire, Based on Radiographs of Mandibular tooth Development. *Journal of the Zoological Society of London* 241:495–502.

Chalifoux, É. 1999. Paleoindian Occupations on the Gaspé Peninsula. *Northeast Anthropology* 57:69–79.

Champlain, S.D. 1966. *Voyages of Samuel de Champlain*. Burt Franklin, New York.

Chang, K.-C. 1986. *The Archaeology of Ancient China*. 4th ed. Yale University Press, New Haven, Connecticut.

Chaplin, R. E. 1971. *The Study of Animal Bones from Archaeological Sites*. Seminar Press, London.

Chartkoff, J. L. 1978. Transect Sampling in Forests. *American Antiquity* 43:46–52.

Chartkoff, J. L., and K. K. Chartkoff. 1980. *The Discovery of Archaeological Sites: A Review of Methods and Techniques*. U.S. Forest Service.

Chauvet, J.-M., É. Deschamps, and C. Hillaire. 1996. *Dawn of Art: The Chauvet Cave*. Harry N. Abrams, New York.

Childe, V. G. 1942. *What Happened in History*. Pelican Books, Baltimore.

Claasen, C. P., ed. 1994. *Women in Archaeology*. University of Pennsylvania Press, Philadelphia.

Clarke, D., and P. Maguire. 1995. *Skara Brae: Northern Europe's Best Preserved Prehistoric Village*. Historic Scotland, Edin Burgh.

Clarke, D. L. 1978. *Analytical Archaeology*. Columbia University Press, New York.

Clayton, P. A. 1994. *Chronicle of the Pharaohs: The Reign-by-Reign Record of the Rulers and Dynasties of Ancient Egypt*. Thames & Hudson, London.

Coe, M. D. 1993. *The Maya*. Thames & Hudson, New York.

Coles, J. M. 1997. *Experimental Archaeology*. Academic Press, London.

Conyers, L. B. 1995. The Use of Ground Penetrating Radar to Map the Buried Structures and Landscape of the Ceren Site, El Salvador. *Geoarchaeology* 10:275–99.

Conyers, L. B., and D. Goodman. 1997. *Ground-Penetrating Radar: An Introduction for Archaeologists*. Altamira Press, Walnut Creek, California.

Cordell, L. 1994. *Ancient Pueblo Peoples*. Exploring the Ancient World. Smithsonian Books, Washington, D.C.

Crabtree, D. E. 1982. *An Introduction to Flint Working*. Idaho Museum of Natural History, Pocatello.

Cummins, H., and C. Midlo 1961. *Fingerprints, Palms, and Soles: An Inroduction to Dermatoglyphics*. Dover, New York.

Dalrymple, G. B., and M. A. Lanphere. 1969. *Potassium-Argon Dating*. W.H. Freeman, San Francisco.

Dancey, W. S. 1981. *Archaeological Field Methods: An Introduction*. Burgess International Group, New York.

David, N., and C. Kramer. 2001. *Ethnoarchaeology in Action*. Cambrideg University Press, Cambridge.

Davis, M. B. 1969a. Climatic Changes in Southern Connecticut Recorded by Pollen Deposition at Rogers Lake. *Ecology* 50:409–22.

———. 1969b. Palynology and Environmental History During the Quaternary Period. *American Scientist* 57:317–32.

Davis, S. J. M. 1995. *The Archaeology of Animals*. Yale University Press, New Haven, Connecticut.

Deetz, J. 1965. *The Dynamics of Stylistic Change in Arikara Ceramics*. University of Illinois Series in Anthropology 4. University of Illinois, Urbana.

———. 1991. Introduction. In *Historical Archaeology in Global Perspective*, edited by L. Falk, 1–9. Smithsonian Institution, Washington, D.C.

Deino, A., P. R. Renne, and C. C. Swisher III. 1998. Ar/39Ar Dating in Paleoanthropology and Archaeology. *Evolutionary Antrhopology* 6(2):63–75.

Deloria Jr., V. 1995. *Red Earth, White Lies: Native Americans and the Myth of Scientific Fact*. Scribners, New York.

Derenko, M. V., T. Grzybowski, B. A. Malyarchuk, et al. 2001. The Presence of Mitochondiral Haplogroup X in Altaians from South Siberia. *American Journal of Human Genetics* 69:237–41.

Dethlefsen, E., and J. Deetz. 1966. Death's Heads, Cherubs, and Willow Trees: Experimental Archaeology in Colonial Cemeteries. *American Antiquity* 31:502–10.

Dible, H., S. P. McPherron, and B. J. Roth. 2003. *Virtual Dig: A Simulated Archaeological Excavation of a Middle Paleolithic Site in France*. McGraw-Hill/Mayfield, New York.

Dillehay, T. D. 2000. *The Settlement of the Americas: A New Prehistory*. Basic Books, New York.

Dillon, B. D. 1993. *Practical Archaeology: Field and Laboratory Techniques and Archaeological Logistics*. Institute of Archaeology, Los Angeles.

Dimbleby, G. W. 1985. *The Palynology of Archaeological Sites*. Academic Press, London.

Dincauze, D. F. 1976. *The Neville Site: Eight-Thousand Years at Amoskeag*. Peabody Museum of Archaeology and Ethnology, Cambridge, Massachusetts.

———. 1978. Surveying for Cultural Resources: Don't Rush Out with a Shovel. In *Conservation Archaeology in the Northeast: Toward a Research Orientation*, edited by A. Speiss, 51–59. Vol. 3. Peabody Museum of Archaeology and Ethnology, Cambridge, Massachusetts.

Dixon, E.J. 1999. *Bones, Boats, and Bison: Archaeology and the First Colonization of Western North America*. University of New Mexico Press, Albuquerque.

Dunnell, R. C. 1992. The Notion Site. In *Space, Time, and Archaeological Landscapes*, edited by J. Rossignol and L. Wandsnider, 21–41. Plenum Press, New York.

Ebert, J. I. 1992. *Distributional Archaeology*. University of New Mexico Press, Albuquerque.

Echo-Hawk, R. 1997. Forging a New Ancient History for Native America. In *Native Americans and Archaeologists: Stepping Stones to Common Ground*, edited by N. Swindler, K. E. Dongoske, R. Anyon, et al., 88–102. Altamira Press, Walnut Creek, California.

Eighmy, J. L., and J. B. Howard 1991. Direct Dating of Prehistoric Canal Sediments Using Archaeomagnetism. *American Antiquity* 56:88–102.

Eighmy, J. L., and R. S. Sternberg, eds. 1990. *Archaeomagnetic Dating*. University of Arizona Press, Tucson.

El-Rabbany, A. 2002. *Introduction to GPS: The Global Positioning System*. Artech House, Boston.

Fagan, B. 1994. *Quest for the Past: Great Discoveries in Archaeology*. Waveland Press, Prospect Heights, Illinois.

———. 2006. Archaeology's Dirty Secret. In *Archaeological Ethics*, edited by K. D. Vitelli and C. Colwell-Chanthaphonh, 201–05. AltaMira Press, Lanham, Maryland.

Fagan, B. M., ed. 1996. *Eyewitness to Discovery: First-Person Accounts of More Than Fifty of the World's Greatest Archaeological Discoveries*. Oxford University Press, Oxford.

———. 2000. *In The Beginning: An Introduction to Archaeology*. 7th ed. Prentice Hall, New York.

———. 2002. *Archaeology: A Brief Introduction*. 4th ed. Prentice Hall, New York.

Fairbanks, C. 1976. Spaniards, Planters, Ships, and Slaves. *Archaeology* 29:164–72.

Fairbanks, R. G., M. A. Mortlock, T.-C. Chiu, et al. 2005. Marine Radiocarbon Calibration Curve Spanning 0 to 50,000 Years BP Based On Paired 230Th/234U/238U and 14C Dates on Pristine Corals. *Quaternary Science Reviews* 24:1781–96.

Farchakh, J. 2004. The Massacre of Mesopotamian Archaeology: Looting in Iraq Is out of Control. In *Conservation News*. Global Heritage Fund. http://www.globalheritagefund.org/news/conservation_news/massacre_mesopotamian_archaeology_sept21–2004.asp

Feder, K. L 1982. *The Spatial Dynamics of Activity at Anangula, Aleutians*. University of Connecticut.

———. 1983. "The Avaricious Humour of Designing Englishmen": The Ethnohistory of Land Transactions in the Farmington Valley. *Bulletin of the Archaeological Society of Connecticut* 45:29–40.

———. 1994 *A Village of Outcasts: Historical Archaeology and Documentary Research at the Lighthouse Site*. Mayfield Publishing, Mountain View, California.

———. 1997a. Data Preservation: Recording and Collecting. In *Field Methods in Archaeology*, edited by T. R. Hester, H. J. Shafer, and K. L. Feder, 113–42. Mayfield Publishing, Mountain View, California.

———. 1997b. Site Survey. In *Field Methods in Archaeology*, edited by T. R. Hester, H. J. Shafer, and K. L. Feder, 41–68. Mayfield Publishing, Mountain View, California.

———. 1999a. Indians and Archaeologists: Conflicting Views of Myth and Science. *Skeptic* 5(3):74–80.

———. 1999b. *Lessons from the Past*. Mayfield Publishing, Mountain View, California.

———. 2001. Prehistoric Land-Use Patterns in North-Central Connecticut: A Matter of Scale. In *Arcaheology of the Appalachian Highlands*, edited by L. P. Sullivan and S. C. Prezzano, 19–30. Univeristy of Tennessee Press, Knoxville.

———. 2006. *Frauds, Myths, and Mysteries: Science and Pseudoscience in Archaeology*. McGraw-Hill/Mayfield Publishing, Mountain View, California.

Feder, K. L., and M. A. Park. 2007. *Human Antiquity: An Introduction to Physical Anthropology and Archaeology*. Mayfield Publishing, Mountain View, California.

Fedje, D. W., and H. Josenhans. 2000. Drowned Forests and Archaeology on the Continental Shelf of British Columbia, Canada. *Geology* 28:99–102.

Ferguson, L. 1992. *Uncommon Ground: Archaeology and Early African America, 1650–1800*. Smithsonian Institution Press, Washington, D.C.

Fink, T. M., and K. K. Komatsu. 2001. The Fungus Among Us: Coccidioidomycosis ("Valley Fever"). In *Dangerous Places: Health, Safety, and Archaeology*, edited by D. Poirier and K. L. Feder, 21–30. Bergin & Garvey, Westport, Connecticut.

Flannery, K. V. 1982. The Golden Marshalltown: A Parable for the Archaeology of the 1980s. *American Anthropologist* 84:265–78.

Fleming, S. J. 1977. *Dating in Archaeology: A Guide to Scientific Techniques*. Palgrave Macmillan, New York.

Frere, J. 1800. Account of Flint Weapons Discovered in Hoxne in Suffolk. *Archaeologia* 13:204–05.

Frison, G., ed. 1974. *The Casper Site: A Hell Gap Bison Kill on the High Plains*. Academic Press, New York.

Garen, M. 2006. The War Within the War. In *Archaeological Ethics*, edited by K. D. Vitelli and C. Colwell-Chanthaphonh, 91–95. AltaMira Press, Lanham, Maryland.

Gero, J. M. 1997. Genderlithics: Women's Roles in Stone Tool Production. In *Engendering Archaeology: Women and Prehistory*, edited by J. M. Gero and M. W. Conkey, 163–93. Blackwell, Oxford.

Gero, J. M., and M. W. Conkey, eds. 1997. *Engendering Archaeology: Women and Prehistory*. Blackwell, Oxford.

Gifford-Gonzalez, D. 1993. You Can Hide, But You Can't Run: Representation of Women's Work in Illustrations of Paleolithic Life. *Visual Anthropology Review* 9(1):23–41.

Gilbert, B. M. 1973. *Mammalian Osteo-Archaeology: North America*. Missouri Archaeological Society, Columbia.

Gilchrist, R. 1999. *Gender and Archaeology: Contesting the Past*. Routledge, London.

Gramly, R. M. 1982. *The Vail Site: A Palaeo-Indian Encampment in Maine*. Bulletin of the Buffalo Society of Natural Sciences 30. Buffalo Society of Natural Sciences, Buffalo, New York.

Grayson, D. K. 1983. *The Establishment of Human Antiquity*. Academic Press, New York.

Greer, A., ed. 2000. *The Jesuit Relations: Natives and Missionaries in Seventeenth-Century North America*. Bedford/St. Martin's Press, New York.

Grün, R. 1993. Electron Spin Resonance Dating in Paleoanthropology. *Evolutionary Anthropology* 2(5):172–81.

Guzzo, P. G., A. D'Ambrosio, and A. Foglia. 2000. *Pompeii*. Getty Trust Publications, Los Angeles.

Harbottle, G., and P. Weigand. 1992. Turquoise in Precolumbian America. *Scientific American* 266(2):78–85.

Hardesty, D. L. 1997. *The Archaeology of the Donner Party*. University of Nevada Press, Reno.

Harris, E. C. 1979. The Laws of Archaeological Stratigraphy. *World Archaeology* 11:111–17.

———. 1997 *Principles of Archaeological Stratigraphy*. Academic Press, San Diego.

Harris, E. C., G. J. Brown, and M. R. B. III M.R. Brown III eds. 1993. *Practices of Archaeological Stratigraphy*. Academic Press, San Diego.

Harrison, G. G., W. L. Rathje, and W. W. Hughes. 1975. Food Waste Behavior in an Urban Population. *Journal of Nutrition Education* 7(1):13–16.

Haviland, W. 2001. *Cultural Anthropology*. Wadsworth, Chicago.

Hesse, B., and P. Wapnish. 1985. *Animal Bone Archaeology*. Manuals on Archaeology 5. Taraxacum, Washington, D.C.

Hester, T. R. 1997a. Methods of Excavation. In *Field Methods in Archaeology*, edited by T. R. Hester, H. J. Shafer, and K. L. Feder, 69–112. Mayfield Publishing, Mountain View, California.

———. 1997b. The Handling and Conervation of Artifacts in the Field. In *Field Methods in Archaeology*, edited by T. R. Hester, H. J. Shafer, and K. L. Feder, 143–58. Mayfield Publishing, Mountain View, California.

Higham, C. 2001. *The Civilization of Angkor*. University of California Press, Berkeley.

Hillson, S. 1996. *Dental Anthropology*. Cambridge University Press, Cambridge.

Hoadley, R. B. 1990. *Identifying Wood: Accurate Results with Simple Tools*. Taunton Press, Newtown, Connecticut.

Holloway, R. G. 1997. Excavation and Recovery of Botanical Materials from Archaeological Sites. In *Field Methods in Archaeology*, edited by T. R. Hester, H. J. Shafer, and K. L. Feder, 283–97. Mayfield Publishing, Mountain View, California.

Hotchkiss, N. J. 1999. *A Comprehensive Guide to Land Navigation with GPS*. Alexis Publishing, Leesburg, Virginia.

Hoving, T. 1978. *Tunankhamun, the Untold Story*. Simon & Schuster, New York.

Hurely, W. M. 1979. *Prehistoric Cordage: Identification On Pottery*. Taraxcum, Washington, D. C.

Hurst, W. J., S. M. T. Jr, T. G. Powis, et al. 2002. Cacao Usage by the Earliest Maya Civilization. *Nature* 418:289–90.

Iseminger, W. R. 1996. Mighty Cahokia. *Archaeology* 49(3):30–37.

Jackson, K., and J. Stamp. 2003. *Building the Great Pyramid*. Firefly Books, Buffalo, New York.

Jacobson, M. 2001. Tangled Up in Bob http://www.rollingstone .com/news/story/5932153/tangled_up_in_bob.

Jemison, G. P. 1997. Who Owns the Past? In *Native Americans and Archaeologists: Stepping Stones to Common Ground*, edited by N. Swindler, K. E. Dongoske, R. Anyon, et al., 57–63. Altamira, Walnut Creek, California.

Johnston, R. B. 1964. *Proton Magnetometry and Its Application to Archaeology: An Evaluation at Angel Site*. Research Series. Indiana Historical Society, Indianapolis.

Juli, H., J. Trimble, and M. Monce 2003. Trade and Tribal Boundaries in Late Prehistoric Southern New England: A Proton Induced X-Ray Emission (PIXE) Analysis of Connecticut Prehistoric Ceramics. *Northeast Anthropology* 65:31–52.

Keeley, L. 1980. *Experimental Determination of Stone Tool Use: A Microwear Analysis*. University of Chicago Press, Chicago.

King, T. F. 1998. *Cultural Resource Laws and Practice: An Introductory Guide*. Altamira Press, Walnut Creek, California.

King, T. F., P. P. Hickman, and G. Berg 1977. *Anthropology in Historic Preservation: Caring for Culture's Clutter*. Academic Press, New York.

King, T. F., R. S. Jacobson, K. R. Burns, et al. 2001. *Amelia Earhart's Shoes: Is the Mystery Solved*. Altamira Press, Walnut Creek, California.

Kintigh, K. W. 1988. The Effectiveness of Subsurface Testing: A Simulation Approach. *American Antiquity* 53:686–707.

Kitagawa, H., and J. v. d. Plicht 1998. Atmospheric Radiocarbon Calibration to 45,000 BP: Late Glacial Fluctuations and Cosmogenic Istope Production. *Science* 279:1187–90.

Klein, R. G., and K. Cruz-Uribe 1984. *The Analysis of Animal Bones from Archaeological Sites*. University of Chicago Press, Chicago.

Knapton, L. K. 1997. Archaeological Mapping, Site Grids, and Surveying. In *Field Methods in Archaeology*, edited by T. R. Hester, H. Shafer, and K. L. Feder, 177–234. Mayfield Publishing, Mountain View, California.

Konefes, J. L., and M. K. McGee 2001. Old Cemeteries, Arsenic, and Health Safety. In *Dangerous Places: Health, Safety, and Archaeology*, edited by D. Poirier and K. L. Feder, 79–106. Bergin & Garvey, Westport, Connecticut.

Kooyman, B. P. 2002. *Understanding Stone Tools and Archaeological Sites*. University of New Mexico Press, Albuquerque.

Kottak, C. 2004. *Anthropology: The Exploration of Human Diversity*. McGraw-Hill, New York.

Krajick, K. 2002. Melting Glaciers Release Ancient Relics. *Science* 296:454–56.

Krakker, J. J., M. J. Shott, and P. D. Welch. 1983. Design and Evaluation of Shovel-Test Sampling in Regional Archaeology. *Journal of Field Archaeology* 10:469–80.

Krebs, J. W., E. J. Mandel, D. L. Swerdlow, et al. 2004. Rabies Surveillance in the United States During 2003. *Journal of the American Veterinary Medicine Association* 225(12):1837–49.

Kroeber, T., K. Kroeber, and L. Gannett. 2002. *Ishi in Two Worlds: A Biography of the Last Wild Indian in North America*. University of California Press, Berkeley.

Krogman, W. M. 1951. The Scars of Human Evolution. *Scientific American* 185:54–57.

———. 1973. *The Human Skeleton in Forensic Medicine*. Charles C. Thomas, Springfield, Illinois.

Kromer, B., and M. Spurk. 1998. Revision and Tentative Extension of the Tree-Ring Based ^{14}C calibration, 9,200–11,855 cal BP. *Radiocarbon* 40(3):1117–26.

Lavin, L. 1980. Analysis of Ceramic Vessels from the Ben Hollister Site. *Bulletin of the Archaeological Society of Connecticut* 43:3–42.

———. 1997. Diversity in Southern New England Ceramics: Three Case Studies. *Bulletin of the Archaeological Society of Connecticut* 60:83–96.

———. 1998. The Windsor Tradition: Pottery Production and Popular Identity in Southern New England. *Northeast Anthropology* 56:1–17.

Lavin, L., and R. Kra 1994. Prehistoric Pottery Assemblages from Southern Connecticut: A Fresh Look at Ceramic Classification in Southern New England. *Bulletin of the Archaeological Society of Connecticut* 57:35–51.

Leakey, M. 1971. *Olduvai Gorge* 3. Cambridge University Press, Cambridge, Massachusetts.

Leakey, M., and A. Walker. 1997. Early Hominid Fossils from Africa. *Scientific American* 276(6):74–79.

Leakey, M. D., and R. L. Hay. 1979. Pliocene Footprints in the Laetolil Beds at Laetoli, Northern Tanzania. *Nature* 278:317–23.

Leakey, R., and R. Lewin. 1992. *Origins Reconsidered: In Search of What Makes Us Human*. Doubleday, New York.

Lee, R. B. 1979. *The !Kung San: Men, Women, and Work in a Foraging Society*. Cambridge University Press, New York.

Lehner, M. 1997. *The Complete Pyramids*. Thames & Hudson, New York.

Lengyel, S. N., and J. L. Eighmy. 2002. A Revision to the U.S. Southwest Archaeomagnetic Master Curve. *Journal of Archaeological Science* 29:1423–33.

Leonard, J. A., R. K. Wayne, J. Wheeler, et al. 2002. Ancient DNA Evidence for Old World Origin of New World Dogs. *Science* 298:1613–16.

Lepper, B. T. 1995. *People of the Mounds: Ohio's Hopewell Culture*. Hopewell Culture National Historical Park, Hopewell, Ohio.

———. 1996. The Newark Earthworks and the Geometric Enclosures of the Scioto Valley: Connections and Conjectures. In *A View from the Core: A Synthesis of Ohio Hopewell Archaeology*, edited by P. Pacheco, 226–41. Ohio Archaeological Council, Columbus.

———. 2004. *Ohio Archaeology: An Illustrated Chronicle of Ohio's Ancient American Indian*. Orange Frazer Press, Wilmington, Ohio.

Lepper, B. T., and J. Gill. 2000. The Newark Holy Stones. *Timeline* 17(3):16–25.

Letham, L. 2001. *GPS Made Easy*. Mountaineers Books, Seattle.

Libby, W. F. 1952. *Radiocarbon Dating*. Chicago University Press, Chicago.

Lightfoot, K. G. 1986. Regional Surveys in the Eastern United States: The Strengths and Weaknesses of Implementing Subsurface Testing Programs. *American Antiquity* 51:484–504.

Linck, D., and J. W. V. III. 2001. Dig Fast, Die Young: Unexploded Ordnance and Archaeology. In *Dangerous Places: Health, Safety, and Archaeology*, edited by D. Poirier and K. L. Feder, 169–88. Bergin & Garvey, Westport, Connecticut.

Lippert, D. 1997. In Front of the Mirror: Native Americans and Academic Archaeology. In *Native Americans and Archaeologists: Stepping Stones to Common Ground*, edited by N. Swindler, K. E. Dongoske, R. Anyon, et al., 120–27. Altamira, Walnut Creek, California.

Little, E. L. 1987. *The Audubon Society Field Guide to North American Trees: Eastern Region*. Borzoi Books, New York.

Longacre, W. A., ed. 1991. *Ceramic Ethnoarchaeology*. University of Arizona Press, Tucson.

Longacre, W. A., and J. M. Skibo, eds. 1994. *Kalinga Ethnoarchaeology: Expanding Archaeological Method and Theory*. Smithsonian Institution Press, Washington, D.C.

Lovis, W. A. 1976. Quarter Sections and Forests: An Example of Probability Sampling in the Northeastern Woodlands. *American Antiquity* 41:364–71.

Loy, T. H., and E. J. Dixon. 1998. Blood Residues on Fluted Points from Eastern Beringia Indicate Mammoth Predation as Part of a Big-Game Hunting Tradition. *American Antiquity* 63:21–46.

Luedtke, B. E. 1992. *An Archaeologist's Guide to Chert and Flint*. Archaeological Research Tools 7. Univeristy of California Press, Los Angeles.

MacDonald, G. F. 1985. *Debert: A Paleo-Indian Site in Central Nova Scotia*. Persimmon Press, Buffalo, New York.

Macko, S. S., G. Lubec, M. Teschler-Nicola, et al. 1999. The Ice Man's Diet as Reflected by the Stable Nitrogen and Carbon Isotopic Composition of His Hair. *FASAB Journal* 13:559–62.

MacNeish, R. S. 1967. An Interdisciplinary Approach to an Archaeological Problem. In *Prehistory of the Tehuacan Valley: Volume One—Environment and Subsistence*, edited by D. Beyers, 14–23. University of Texas Press, Austin.

Madrigal, T. C., and J. Z. Holt. 2002. White-Tailed Deer Meat and Marrow Return Rates and Their Application to Eastern Woodlands Archaeology. *American Antiquity* 67:745–59.

Mannikka, E. 1996. *Angkor Wat: Time, Space, and Kingship*. University of Hawai'i Press, Honolulu.

Marquardt, W. H., and C. Crumley. 1987. Theoretical Issues in the Analysis of Spatial Patterning. In *Regional Dynamics: Burgundian Landscapes in Historical Perspective*, edited by C. L. Crumley and W. H. Marquardt, 1–18. Academic Press, San Diego.

McGimsey III, C. R. 1972. *Public Archaeology*. Seminar Press, New York.

McGuire, R. H., and R. Paynter, eds. 1991. *The Archaeology of Inequality*. Blackwell, Cambridge, Massachusetts.

McIntosh, R. J., S. K. McIntosh, and T. Togola. 2006. People Without History. In *Archaeological Ethics*, edited by K. D. Vitelli and C. Colwell-Chanthaphonh, 125–34. AltaMira Press, Lanham, Maryland.

McKee, L. 1995. The Earth Is Their Witness. *The Sciences* 35(2):36–41.

McManamon, F. P. 1984. Discovering Sites Unseen. In *Advances in Archaeological Method and Theory*, edited by M. B. Schiffer, 223–92. Vol. 7. Academic Press, New York.

McPherron, S. P., and H. L. Dibble. 2002. *Using Computers in Archaeology*. McGraw-Hill, New York.

McWeeney, L. 2002. *The Charcoal Evidence from the Firetown North and Paine Sites, Granby, Connecticut*.

Meighan, C. W., and L. J. Zimmerman. 2006. Burying American Archaeology or Sharing Control of the Past. In *Archaeological Ethics*, edited by K. D. Vitelli and C. Colwell-Chanthaphonh, 167–75. AltaMira Press, Lanham, Maryland.

Meltzer, D. J. 1993. *Search for the first American*. Smithsonian: Exploring the Ancient World. Smithsonian Books, Washington, D. C.

———. 1997. Monte Verde and the Pleistocene Peopling of America. Science 276:754–755

Mercader, J., M. Panger, and C. Boesch. 2002. Excavation of a Chimpanzee Stone Tool Site in the African Rainforest. *Science* 296:1452–55.

Messenger, P. M., ed. 1993. *The Ethics of Collecting Cultural Property: Whose Culture? Whose Property*. University of New Mexico Press, Albuquerque.

Michels, J. W. 1973. *Dating Methods in Archaeology*. Seminar Press, New York.

Miles, D. H., M. J. Worthington, and A. A. Grady. 2002. Development of Standard Tree-Ring Chronologies for Dating Historic Structures in Eastern Massachusetts. Oxford Dendrochronological Lab, Oxford.

Miller, B. 2001. *Cultural Anthropology*. Allyn & Bacon, Boston.

Morganti, T., and N. Tartt. 2001. Rabies: A Short Discourse. In *Dangerous Places: Health, Safety, and Archaeology*, edited by D. Poirier and K. L. Feder, 11–20. Bergin & Garvey, Westport, Connecticut.

Mozina, M. 2003. *Archaeology Fieldwork Bulletin*. Archaeological Institute of America, Boston.

Mueller, J. 1975. *Sampling in Archaeology*. University of Arizona Press, Phoenix.

Müller, W., H. Fricke, A. N. Halliday, et al. 2003. Origin and Migration of the Apline Iceman. *Science* 302:862–66.

Nance, J. D., and B. F. Ball. 1986. No Surprises? The Reliability and Validity of Test Pit Sampling. *American Antiquity* 51:457–83.

O'Brien, M.J., and R. L. Lyman. 1999. *Seriation, Stratigraphy, and Index Fossils: The Backbone of Archaeological Dating*. Kluwer Academic Publishers, New York.

O'Connor, T. 2000. *The Archaeology of Animal Bones*. Texas A&M Press, College Station.

Olin, J. S., and A. D. Franklin, eds. 1982. *Archaeological Ceramics*. Smithsonian Institution Press, Washington, D.C.

Olson, S. J. 1985. *Origins of the Domestic Dog: The Fossil Record*. University of Arizona Press, Tucson.

Orton, C. 2000. *Sampling in Archaeology*. Cambridge University Press, Cambridge.

Orton, C., P. Tyers, and A. Vince. 1993. *Pottery in Archaeology*. Cambridge University Press, Cambridge.

Page, C., and J. Cort. 1997a. Stonehenge. In *Secrets of Lost Empires. Nova*. WGBH, Boston.

———. 1997b. Colosseum. In *Secrets of Lost Empires. Nova*. WGBH, Boston.

Park, M. A. 2005. *Biological Anthropology*. McGraw-Hill, New York.

———. 2003. *Introducing Anthropology: An Integrated Approach*. McGraw-Hill, New York.

Pascua, M. P. 1991. A Makah Village in 1491: Ozette. *National Geographic* 180(4):38–53.

Pearsall, D. M. 2000. *Paleoethnobotany: A Handbook of Procedures*. Academic Press, San Diego.

Pearson, M. P. 2001. *The Archaeology of Death and Burial*. Texas A&M University Press, Austin.

Pennisi, E. 2002. A Shaggy Dog History. *Science* 298:1540–42.

Perry, W., and M. Blakey. 1997. Archaeology as Community Service: The African Burial Ground Porject in New York City. *North American Dialogue* 2(1):1–5.

Perry, W. R., J. Howson and B. A. Bianco, eds. 2006a. *New York African Burial Ground Archaeology Final Report*. Vol. 1. United States General Services Administration, Washington, D.C.

Perry, W., J. Howson, and B. A. Bianco. 2006b. Summary and Conclusions. In *New York African Burial Ground Archaeology Final Report*, edited by W. R. Perry, J. Howson, and B. A. Bianco, 444–57. Vol. 1. United States General Services Administration, Washington, D.C.

Perry, W., J. Howson, and A. F. C. Holl. 2006. The Late-Middle Group. In *New York African Burial Ground Archaeology Final Report*, edited by W. R. Perry, J. Howson, and B. A. Bianco, 206–49. Vol. 1. United States General Services Administration, Washington, D.C.

Piperno, D., and K. Flannery. 2001. The Earliest Archaeological Maize (*Zea mays* L.). *Proceedings of the National Academy of Sciences* 98:2101–03.

Piperno, D., and K. A. Stothert. 2003. Phytolith Evidence for Early Holocene *Cucurbita* Domestication in Southwest Ecuador. *Science* 299:1054–57.

Piperno, D. R., and D. M. Pearsall. 1998. *The Origins of Agriculture in the Lowland Neotropics*. Academic Press, Orlando.

Piperno, D. R., A. J. Ranere, I. Holst, et al. 2000. Starch Grains Reveal Early Root Crop Horticulture in the Panamanian Tropical Forest. *Nature* 407:894–97.

Piperno, D. R., E. Weiss, I. Holst, et al. 2004. Processing of Wild Cereal Grains in the Upper Paleolithic Revealed by Starch Grain Analysis. *Nature* 430:670–73.

Poirier, D., and K. L. Feder. 2001. *Dangerous Places: Health, Safety, and Archaeology*. Bergin & Garvey, Westport, Connecticut.

Pope, K. O., M.E.D.Pohl, J. G. Jones, et al. 2001. Origin and Environmental Setting of Ancient Agriculture in the Lowlands of Mesoamerica. *Science* 292:1370–73.

Powell, E. 2005. The Turquoise Trail. *Archaeology* 58(1):24–29.

Price, T. D., ed. 1989. *The Chemisry of Prehistoric Bone*. Cambridge University Press, Cambridge.

Price, T. D., M. J. Schoeninger, and G. J. Armelagos. 1985. Bone Chemistry and Past Behavior: An Overview. *Journal of Human Evolution* 14:419–47.

Quinn, S. C. 2006. *Windows on Nature: The Great Habitat Dioramas of the American Museum of Natural History*. Harry N. Abrams, New York.

Rapp, G., J. Allert, V. Vitali, Z. Jing, et al. 2000. *Determining Archaeological Sources of Artifact Copper Source Characterization Using Trace Element Analysis*. University Press of America, Lanham, Maryland.

Rathburn, T. 1987. Health and Disease at a South Carolina Plantation. *American Journal of Physical Anthropology* 74:239–53.

Rathje, W., and C. Murphy. 1992. *Rubbish: The Archaeology of Garbage*. Harper Collins, New York.

Reitz, E. J. 1999. *Zooarchaeology*. Cambridge University Press, Cambridge.

Renfrew, C., and P. Bahn. 1996. *Archaeology: Theories, Methods, & Practice*. Thames & Hudson, New York.

———. 2000. *Archaeology: Theories, Method, and Practice*. Thames & Hudson, New York.

Reno, R. L., S. R. Boyd, and D. L. hardesty 2001. Chemical Soup: Archaeological Hazards at Western Ore-Processing Sites. In *Dangerous Places: Health, Safety, and Archaeology*, edited by D. Poirier and K. L. Feder, 205–20. Bergin & Garvey, Westport, Connecticut.

Rhine, S. 1998. *Bone Voyage*. University of New Mexico Press, Sante Fe.

Rice, P. C. 1998. *Doing Archaeology: A Hands-On Laboratory Manual*. Mayfield Publishing, Mountain View, California.

Richards, M. P., P. P. Pettitt, E. Trinkaus, et al. 2000. Neanderthal Diet at Vindija and Neanderthal Predation: The Evidence from Stable Isotopes. *Proceedings of the National Academy of Sciences* 97:7663–66.

Richards, M. P., R. J. Schulting, and R. E. M. Hedges. 2003. Sharp Shift in Diet at Onset of Neolithic. *Nature* 425:366.

Ritchie, A. 1995. *Prehistoric Orkney*. B.T. Batsford, London.

Roberts, M. 2001. Beneath City Streets: Brief Observations on the Urban Landscape. In *Dangerous Places: Health, Safety, and Archaeology*, edited by D. Poirier and K. L. Feder, 157–68. Bergin & Garvey, Westport, Connecticut.

Romer, J. 1984. *Ancient Lives: Daily Life in Egypt of the Pharaohs*. Holt, Rinehart & Winston, New York.

Rossignol, J., and L. Wandsnider 1992. *Space, Time, and Archaeological Landscapes*. Plenum Press, New York.

Rye, O. S. 1981. *Pottery Technology: Principles and Reconstruction*. Taraxacum, Washington, D.C.

Sabloff, J. A. 1989. *The Cities of Ancient Mexico: Reconstructing a Lost World*. Thames & Hudson, New York.

Sandford, M. K. 1992. A Reconsideration of Trace Element Analysis. In *Skeletal Biology of Past Peoples: Research Methods*, edited by S. R. Saunders and A. M. Katzenberg, 153–74. Wiley-Liss, New York.

Saul, F. P. 1972. *The Human Skeletal Remains of Altar de Sacrificios*. Papers of the Peabody Museum of Archaeology and Ethnology 63. Cambridge, Massachusetts.

Saunders, C., and S. R. Chandler. 2001. Get the Lead Out. In *Dangerous Places: Health, Safety, and Archaeology*, edited by D. Poirier and K. L. Feder, 189–204. Bergin & Garvey, Westport, Connecticut.

Sawyer, J. 2005. Plantations, Captive Africans, and African-Indians: Archaeological Investigations Into an Alternate View of 18th-century Connecticut. Paper presented at the Archaeological Society of Connecticut, Storrs, Connecticut.

Schele, L., and D. Freidel. 1990. *A Forest of Kings*. Quill William Morrow, New York.

Schele, L., and P. Mathews. 1998. *The Code of Kings: The Language of Seven Sacred Maya Temples and Tombs*. Scribner, New York.

Schick, K. D., and N. Toth. 1993. *Making Silent Stones Speak: Human Evolution and the Dawn of Technology*. Simon and Schuster, New York.

Schiffer, M. B. 1972. Archaeological Context and Systemic Context. *American Antiquity* 37:156–65.

———. 1975. Archaeology as a Behavioral Science. *American Anthropologist* 77:836–48.

———. 1976. *Behavioral Archaeology*. Academic Press, New York.

———. 1983. Toward the Identification of Site Formation Processes. *American Antiquity* 48:673–706.

———. 1987. *Formation Processes of the Archaeological Record*. University of New Mexico Press, Albuquerque.

Schiffer, M. B., A. P. Sullivan, and T. C. Klinger. 1978. The Design of Archaeological Surveys. *World Archaeology* 10:1–28.

Schnapp, A. 1996. *The Discovery of the Past: The Origins of Archaeology*. British Museum Press, London.

Schultz, E. A., and R. H. Lavenda. 2000. *Anthropology: A Perspective on the Human Condition*. McGraw-Hill, New York.

Schweingruber, F. H. 1988. *Tree Rings: Basics and Applications of Dendrochronology*. D. Reidel Publishing, Norwell, Massachusetts.

Scott, D., R. A. Fox. Jr., M. Conner, et al. 1989. *Archaeological Perspectives on the Battle of the Little Big Horn*. Univeristy of Oklahoma Press, Norman.

Scott, G. R., and C. G. T. II. 2000. *The Anthropology of Modern Human Teeth: Dental Morphology and Its Variation in Recent Human Populations*. Cambridge University Press, Cambridge.

Sebastian, L. 1992. *The Chaco Anasazi: Sociopolitical Evolution in the Prehistoric Southwest*. Cambridge University Press, Cambridge, Massachusetts.

Shackelton, N., and N. Opdyke. 1997. Oxygen Isotope and Paleomagnetic Stratigraphy of Equatorial Pacific Core V28–238: Oxygen Isotope Temperatures and Ice Volumes on A 10^5 And 10^6 Year Scale. Quaternary Research 3:39–55.

———. 1976 Oxygen-Isotope and Paleomagnetic Stratigraphy of Pacific Core V28–239 Late Pliocene and Latest Pleistocene. In Investigation of Late Quaternary Paleocenaography and Paleoclimatology, edited by R. M. Cline and J. Hays, 449–464. Vol. 145. Geological Society of America.

Shafer, H.J. 1997a. Goals of Archaeological Investigation. In *Field Methods in Archaeology*, edited by T. R. Hester, H. J. Shafer, and K. L. Feder, 5–20. Mayfield Publishing, Mountain View, California.

———. 1997b. Research Design and Sampling Technique. In *Field Methods in Archaeology*, edited by T. R. Hester, H. Shafer, and K. L. Feder, 21–40. Mayfield Publishing, Mountain View, California.

Shapiro, G., and J. M. Williams. 1982. *A Search for the Eightneeth Century Village at Michilimackinac: A Soil Resistivity Survey*. Mackinac State Parks.

Sharer, R. J., and W. Ashmore. 2003. *Archaeology: Discovering Our Past*. 2d ed. McGraw-Hill, New York.

Sheets, P., and T. Sever. 1988. High-Tech Wizardry. *Archaeology* (Nov–Dec):28–35.

Shepard, A. 1982. *Ceramics for the Archaeologist*. Carnegie Institute of Washington, Washington, D.C.

Shott, M. J. 1989. Shovel Test Sampling in Archaeological Survey: Comments on Nance and Ball and Lightfoot. *American Antiquity* 54:396–404.

Smith, A. L. 1972. *Excavations at Altar de Sacrificios*. Papers of the Peabody Museum of Archaeology and Ethnology 62. Cambridge, Massachusetts.

Smith, B. D. 1995. *The Emergence of Agriculture*. Scientific American Library, New York.

Smith, J. R., R. Giegengack, and H. Schwarcz 2004. Constraints on Pleistocene Pluvial Climates Through Stable-Isotope Analysis of Fossil-Spring Tufas and Associated

Gastropods, Kharga Oasis, Egypt. *Palaeogeography, Palaeoclimatology, Palaeoecology* 206(1–2):159–77.

Smith, V. 2004. *A Narrative of the Life and Adventures of Venture, A Native of Africa But Resident Above Sixty Years In the United States of America.* Kessinger Publishing, Whitefish, Montana.

Solecki, R. 1971. *Shanidar: The First Flower People.* Knopf, New York.

Spindler, K. 1994. *The Man in the Ice.* Harmony Books, New York.

Staeck, J. 2002. *Back to the Earth: An Introduction to Archaeology.* McGraw-Hill, New York.

Steinitz, M. 2002. Tree-Ring Dates Offer Insight on Massachusetts Buildings. In *Preservation Advocate,* 1, 6–7, 10.

Stewart, R. M. 2002. *Archaeology: Basic Field Methods.* Kendall/Hunt Publishing, Dubuque, Iowa.

Stiebing Jr, W. H. 1993. *Uncovering the Past: A History of Archaeology.* Oxford University Press, New York.

Stuiver, M., and v. d. Plicht. 1998. Intcal 98: Calibration Issue. *Radiocarbon* 40(3):1041–1164

Sullivan, R. 1998. *The Meadowlands.* Scribner, New York.

Sutton, M. Q., and B. S. Arkush. 2002. *Archaeological Laboratory Methods: An Introduction.* Kendall/Hunt Publishing, Dubuque, Iowa.

Swindler, N., K. E. Dongoske, R. Anyon, et al., eds. 1997. *Native Americans and Archaeologists: Stepping Stones to Common Ground.* Altamira Press, Walnut Creek, California.

Taylor, R. E. 1987. *Radiocarbon Dating: An Archaeological Perspective.* Academic Press, London.

Taylor, R. E., and M. J. Aitken, eds. 1997. *Chronometric Dating in Archaeology.* Plenum Publishing, New York.

Thomas, D. H. 1998. *Archaeology.* 3d ed. Wadsworth, Chicago.

———. 1999. *Archaeology: Down to Earth.* Wadsworth, New York.

———. 2000. *Skull Wars: Kennewick Man, Archaeology, and the Battle for Native American Identity.* Basic Books, New York.

Tringham, R., G. Cooper, G. Odell, et al. 1974. Experimentation in the Formation of Edge Damage: A New Approach to Lithic Analysis. *Journal of Field Archaeology* 1:171–96.

Trubowitz, N. 1981. The Use of the Plow in Archaeological Site Survey: An Experimental Example from Western New York. *American Center for Conservation Archaeology Reports* 8(5–6):16–21.

Tsosie, R. 1997. Indigenous Rights and Archaeology. In *Native Americans and Archaeologists: Stepping Stones to Common Ground,* edited by N. Swindler, K. E. Dongoske, R. Anyon, et al., 64–76. Altamira, Walnut Creek, California.

Turnbaugh, S. P., and W. A. Turnbaugh. 1986. *Indian Baskets.* Schiffer Publising, West Chester, Pennsylvania.

Ubelaker, D. H. 1978. *Human Skeletal Remains: Excavation, Analysis, Interpretation.* Aldine Manuals on Archaeology. Aldine, Chicago.

Unger-Hamilton, R. 1989. The Epi-Paleolithic Southern Levant and the Origins of Cultivation. *Current Anthropology* 30:88–103.

Van Riper, A. B. 1993. *Men Among the Mammoths: Victorian Science and the Discovery of Human Prehistory.* University of Chicago Press, Chicago.

Vickey, K. D. 1976. *An Approach to Inferring Archaeological Site Variability,* Indiana University.

Waldorf, D. C., 1984. *The Art of Flintnapping.* Moundbulider Books, Branson, Moissouri.

Wall, D. d. 1994. *The Archaeology of Gender: Separating the Spheres in Urban America.* Plenum, New York.

Watkins, J. 2000. *Indigenous Archaeology.* Altamira Press, Walnut Creek, California.

Weymouth, J. W. 1986. Geophysical Methods of Archaeological Site Surveying. In *Advances in Archaeological Method and Theory,* edited by M. B. Schiffer, 311–95. Vol. 9. Academic Press, Orlando.

Whalen, M. E. 1990. Sampling Versus Full-Coverage Survey: An Example from Western Texas. In *The Archaeology of Regions: A Case for Full-Coverage Survey,* edited by S. Fish and S. Kowalewski, 219–36. Smithsonian Institution Press, Washington, D.C.

Wheat, J. B. 1972. *The Olsen-Chubbuck Site: A Paleo Indian Bison Kill.* Memoir of the Society for American Archaeology 26. Salt Lake City.

Wheatley, D., and M. Gillings. 2002. *Spatial Technology and Archaeology: The Archaeological Applications of GIS.* Taylor & Francis, London.

White, R. 1993. Technological and Social Dimensions of "Aurignacian-age" Body Ornaments Across Europe. In *Before Lascaux: The Complex Record of the Early Upper Paleolithic,* edited by H. Knecht, A. Pike-Tay, and R. White, 277–99. CRC Press, Boca Raton.

White Deer, G. 1997. Return of the Sacred: Spirituality and the Scientific Imperative. In *Native Americans and Archaeologists: Stepping Stones to Common Ground,* edited by N. Swindler, K. E. Dongoske, R. Anyon, et al., 37–43. Altamira, Walnut Creek, California.

White, T. D., and P. A. Folkens. 1991. *Human Osteology.* Academic Press, New York.

Whittaker, J. C. 1994. *Flintknapping: Making and Understanding Stone Tools.* University of Texas Press, Austin.

Whitworth, W. R., P. L. Berrien, and W. T. Keller. 1976. *Freshwater Fishes of Connecticut.* Department of Environmental Protection, Hartford, Connecticut.

Willey, G. R., and J. A. Sabloff. 1993. *A History of American Archaeology.* W.H. Freeman, New York.

Williams, B., ed. 1981. *Breakthrough: Women in Archaeology.* Walker & Co., New York.

Williams, H., ed. 2003. *Archaeologies of Remembrance: Death and Memory in Past Societies.* Plenum, New York.

Winans, M. C., and R. C. Winans. 1993. Measuring Systems, Techniques, and Equipment for Taphonomic Studies. In *Practical Archaeology: Field and Laboratory Techniques and Archaeological Logistics,* edited by B. D. Dillon, 33–38. Institute of Archaeology, Los Angeles.

Yokoyama, Y., K. Lambeck, P. D. Deckker, et al. 2000. Timing of the Last Glacial Maximum from Observed Sea-Level Minima. *Nature* 406:713–16.

Zeder, M. A. 1997. *The American Archaeologist: A Profile.* Altamira Press, Walnut Creek, California.

Zeder, M. A., and B. Hesse. 2000. The Initial Domestication of Goats (Capra hircus) in the Zagros Mountains 10,000 Years Ago. *Science* 287:2254–57.

Index